Optimizing Compilers for Modern Architectures

A Dependence-Based Approach

About the Authors

Randy Allen received his A.B. summa cum laude in chemistry from Harvard University and his M.A. and Ph.D. in mathematical sciences from Rice University. After serving a research fellowship at Rice, Dr. Allen entered the practical world of industrial compiler construction. His career has spanned research, advanced development, and management at Ardent Computers, Sun Microsystems, Chronologic Simulation, Synopsys, and CynApps. He has authored or coauthored 15 conference and journal papers on computer optimization, restructuring compilers, and hardware simulation, and has served on program committees for Supercomputing and the Conference on Programming Language and Design Implementation. He has served as a consultant on optimizing compilers to a number of companies, including IBM, Intermetrics, Microtec Research, Apple, and Mentor Graphics. Dr. Allen is Founder and CEO of Catalytic, Inc., a startup exploiting advanced compiler technology.

Ken Kennedy is the John and Ann Doerr University Professor of Computational Engineering and Director of the *Center for High Performance Software Research* (HiPerSoft) at Rice University. He is a fellow of the Institute of Electrical and Electronics Engineers, the Association for Computing Machinery, and the American Association for the Advancement of Science and has been a member of the National Academy of Engineering since 1990. From 1997 to 1999, he served as cochair of the President's Information Technology Advisory Committee (PITAC). For his leadership in producing the PITAC report on funding of information technology research, he received the Computing Research Association Distinguished Service Award (1999) and the RCI Seymour Cray HPCC Industry Recognition Award (1999).

Professor Kennedy has published over 200 technical articles and supervised 36 Ph.D. dissertations on programming support software for high-performance computer systems. In recognition of his contributions to software for high-performance computation, he received the 1995 W. Wallace McDowell Award, the highest research award of the IEEE Computer Society. In 1999, he was named the third recipient of the ACM SIGPLAN Programming Languages Achievement Award.

Optimizing Compilers for Modern Architectures

A Dependence-Based Approach

Randy Allen
Consultant

Ken Kennedy
Rice University

MORGAN KAUFMANN PUBLISHERS

An Imprint of Elsevier

SAN FRANCISCO SAN DIEGO NEW YORK BOSTON
LONDON SYDNEY TOKYO

Senior Editor	Denise E. M. Penrose
Publishing Services Manager	Scott Norton
Assistant Publishing Services Manager	Edward Wade
Editorial Coordinator	Emilia Thiuri
Cover Design	Ross Carron Design
Text Design	Rebecca Evans & Associates
Technical Illustration	Dartmouth Publishing, Inc.
Composition	Nancy Logan
Copyeditor	Ken DellaPenta
Proofreader	Jennifer McClain
Indexer	Ty Koontz

Designations used by companies to distinguish their products are often claimed as trademarks or registered trademarks. In all instances in which Morgan Kaufmann Publishers is aware of a claim, the product names appear in initial capital or all capital letters. Readers, however, should contact the appropriate companies for more complete information regarding trademarks and registration.

Morgan Kaufmann Publishers
An Imprint of Elsevier
340 Pine Street, Sixth Floor, San Francisco, CA 94104-3205, USA
http://www.mkp.com

ACADEMIC PRESS
An Imprint of Elsevier
525 B Street, Suite 1900, San Diego, CA 92101-4495, USA
http://www.academicpress.com

Academic Press
Harcourt Place, 32 Jamestown Road, London, NW1 7BY, United Kingdom
http://www.academicpress.com

Printed and bound by CPI Group (UK) Ltd, Croydon, CR0 4YY

Transferred to Digital Print 2011

Library of Congress Control Number: 2001092381

ISBN-13: 978-1-55860-286-1
ISBN-10: 1-55860-286-0

To Horace Flatt, whose steadfast support and encouragement
made this work possible

Praise for Optimizing Compilers for Modern Architectures:
A Dependence-based Approach

"Dependence analysis is at the core of a huge class of program transformations and optimizations, including cache management, exploiting parallelism, and many others. The authors have provided information that is essential to practicing professionals in the area of high-performance computer architecture. An indispensable reference."

—Rohit Chandra, NARUS Inc.

"This book is the only place where the details of compiler analysis have been collected and described in a way that is critical for computational scientists. Allen and Kennedy provide the overview, detailed analysis, and programming examples in a form common to all scientific programmers, offering the implementor a better understanding of how to express software for modern architectures."

—Jack Dongarra, University of Tennessee and Oak Ridge National Laboratory

"This book is a comprehensive treatment of optimization for cache management, vectorization, parallelization, and more. The title refers to Modern Architectures, and indeed the subject matter is applicable from desktop systems to the world's fastest supercomputers."

—David Kuck, Intel

"Kennedy and Allen take a unique approach in this book. They focus on how compilation techniques work together to make practical program analysis and optimization algorithms for achieving good performance on parallel machines, whereas previous texts focus on the specific techniques. Every compiler writer should have a copy of this insightful and lively book in their library!"

—Kathryn S. McKinley, University of Texas at Austin

"The much awaited book by Randy Allen, a leading practitioner, and Ken Kennedy, a pioneer in compiler research, provides a skillful encapsulation of the results of more than 30 years of research and development in restructuring compilers—a significant part of which was done by the authors. The combination of staged introduction of each topic with the aid of examples and the detailed algorithmic layout of each optimization make this text an outstanding reference for the expert as well as for new students of the topic. This book constitutes yet the most complete and rich text of compiler optimization fundamentals and algorithms, an invaluable resource for researchers, educators and compiler developer."

—Constantine Polychronopoulos, University of Illinois Urbana-Champaign

"This book makes an extremely valuable contribution to the field of compilation, presenting the fundamentals of compiling technology for high performance computing systems. The authors provide careful and thorough descriptions of the analyses, including data and control dependences and interprocedural analysis, and the code transformations that can be applied as a result of the analyses. The book's organization and structure as well as the clear writing style make it an excellent text book, a highly valuable reference book, and a useful guide for implementing the techniques."

—Mary Lou Soffa, University of Pittsburgh

"*Optimizing Compilers* is unique in its description of a general framework for a reasoned approach to loop restructuring. We've struggled to make reasonable decisions regarding the ordering and profitability of loop transformations, and this book has solved that, proving to be very influential in our current compiler and CPU design work. This is a great reference book to have on hand."

—Reid Tatge, Fellow, Texas Instruments, Inc.

Contents

Preface

Compiler Design for Modern Architectures

One of the major influences on our understanding of the world is the way we describe it. Humans tend to frame their perceptions in terms of the concepts within the language used to convey those perceptions. Nowhere is this more evident than in the use of computer languages. The language used by a computer scientist influences everything from problem description to algorithmic approach to final implementation. A LISP programmer approaches a problem very differently from an IBM 370 assembly programmer.

Given this strong influence of language in the design of applications, along with the productivity advantages inherent in the use of higher-level languages, a major goal of research has been the development of computer languages that better support human understanding. While this research has resulted in languages that are easier to use, none has been widely adopted for use in the development of production applications. The principal reason is simple: efficiency—the executable programs generated from codes written in these languages are simply too slow for production use. The farther a problem description moves away from a computer's native instructions, the more difficult it becomes to map that description into those instructions.

If we are ever to make such languages practical, advanced compiler technology will be an essential tool for overcoming their inherent performance disadvantages. In other words, compiler optimization is an essential enabling technology for the use of higher-level languages. *Data dependence* is a fundamental compiler analysis tool for optimizing programs on modern machine architectures because it permits the compiler to reason about whether different code fragments access the same or different memory locations. Thus it can be used to determine whether a given program can be parallelized or when it can be made to reuse data in registers and cache more frequently. Yet data dependence is rarely taught in an introductory compiler course. As a result, most undergraduate computer science majors are never exposed to it.

A major goal of this book is to bring together in one volume a broad introduction to data dependence that can be used by practitioners and students alike to learn about data dependence and its application to important optimization problems, such as parallelization and compiler memory hierarchy management. Although data dependence has been explored by researchers since the early days of compilers in the 1960s, the most potent applications of dependence arise in contexts where loops and arrays are used. These constructs are essential for repeated computation, and repeated computation provides the most fertile ground for optimization. Extensions to dependence to support arrays and loops are the key focus of this book.

This work presents the theoretical fundamentals underlying loop-based dependence. It includes arguments for the correctness of dependence-based transformations and detailed procedures for dependence testing. It shows how to extend dependence to deal with control flow in loop nests and across the procedures of an entire program. This book also discusses how dependence can be used to address a number of important problems in compiling for modern computer systems, including parallelization to support different kinds of architectures (e.g., vector, multiprocessor, superscalar), compiler management of memory hierarchy, and scheduling for machines with instruction-level parallelism. Finally, it introduces some applications that are less well known, including hardware design, implementation of array languages, and compilation for message-passing systems.

However, the book goes well beyond basic theory to deal with the practical issues of applying dependence to optimization problems in real compilers. It achieves this goal by presenting efficient implementation algorithms, along with the insights from our combined experience in both research and commercial implementations. These insights are conveyed, wherever possible, through the use of examples, often with graphical depictions of dependence relations to convey the intuition underlying the issues under discussion. Most of the algorithms presented in the book are based on the implementations that we have constructed during our careers. These algorithms have been designed to achieve a high degree of precision without requiring running times that would make them impractical for use in compilers. Finally, we have included material in each chapter that discusses the relationship between what is presented and what actually gets implemented, including both strengths and weaknesses, from our own experience.

As a result of its blend of theory and practice, this book is suitable for use both as a text for academic instruction and as a reference for industrial practitioners. It assumes only that the reader is familiar with compilers at the level of a first undergraduate course and with the principles of machine design at the level of Hennessy and Patterson's *Computer Organization and Design: The Hardware/ Software Interface*. For the past several years, we have taught a one-semester graduate course at Rice University covering all of the material in the book. However, we believe that the material is also suitable for inclusion in an advanced undergraduate course. The writing is tutorial in style so that the reader can gain enough insight to become facile with the concepts presented. Furthermore, we have included discussion and exercises designed to help the student think more clearly about the underlying issues.

In order to meet the needs of the writer of commercial compilers, the book includes detailed presentations of the algorithms for dependence testing and transformation. A major reason for this is to make it possible for the practical compiler developer to avoid some of the pitfalls that we encountered in our own implementations over the past 20 years. For example, the details of the dependence tests in Chapter 3 are often difficult to get exactly right if derived from first principles. Thus we have endeavored to present complete algorithms whenever possible. Using the material included in this book, we have helped a number of companies implement dependence testing, vectorization, and parallelization in commercial products. We are confident that these strategies can be effective in practice.

This book is the product of a 20-year research project at Rice University to develop fundamental compiler technologies for vector and parallel computer systems. When we initiated this research project in 1979, we believed that source-to-source translators, rather than dependence-based compilers, would be needed to support vector machines. This reasoning was based on experience: implementations of dependence at the time required compile times that were too long to be practical, and their output could usually be improved by simple examination. We believed that the compile-time requirements would not be tolerated in a production compiler, but would be fine for a one-time source-to-source translator. Moreover, the output of a source-to-source translator could be tuned by a sophisticated programmer to achieve even better performance. One of the most satisfying outcomes of our research has been the discovery of how wrong our initial assumptions were—not only is dependence practical for production compilers, it is a far more powerful and applicable theory than we initially suspected. Any modern optimizing compiler has dependence as an essential component, and the optimizations that result apply not just to vector machines (where they do extremely well) but also to scalar machines or even hardware design.

Because of the continuing evolution of machine design, even the topics that might have seemed obsolete a few years ago (e.g., vectorization) are finding renewed importance. Vectorization methods are also useful for improving the performance of VLIW and superscalar machines by providing extra instruction-level parallelism in the innermost loop. However, this book is timely for a more fundamental reason. Because of the increasing gap between processor and memory performance, most optimizations that must be performed on modern architectures are related to memory access. Dependence provides a framework for reasoning about memory accesses that will continue to increase in usefulness.

Although we attempt to cover important work by many researchers, we have naturally focused on the work that was done at Rice University over the past two decades by the authors and their colleagues. We make no apology for this, as our goal is to put into print the combined store of knowledge from our experience in this field. Thus this work should not be viewed as an exhaustive survey of the literature but rather as a pragmatic guide to developing compilers based on dependence. As such it attempts to be tutorial in style, sometimes sacrificing technical details for clarity of presentation. Our overall goal is to give the reader a sufficient intuition that he or she could work effectively in this exciting branch of compilation.

Overview of the Content

The book is organized into 14 chapters whose content is summarized in the following paragraphs. The heart of the material is contained in the first 9 chapters; the remainder focuses on extensions of the basic material and on applications to different problem domains.

Chapter 1, *Compiler Challenges for High-Performance Architectures*, surveys and classifies modern computer architectures and discusses the fundamental compilation challenges presented by each class. Important topics include pipeline parallelism, vector instructions, asynchronous processor parallelism, superscalar and VLIW instructions, and memory hierarchy management. The concept of *dependence* is introduced as a mechanism for ensuring the safe use of parallelism.

Chapter 2, *Dependence Theory and Practice*, discusses the basic concept of dependence, along with a number of its properties, including direction and distance vectors. A principal goal is to prove the fundamental theorems that establish the correctness of transformations that preserve dependence, particularly in loop nests. The chapter concludes with a sample vectorization algorithm that illustrates the usefulness of dependence and that serves as a model for later material on vectorization and parallelization.

Chapter 3, *Dependence Testing*, presents a systematic introduction to testing dependence between pairs of references. Included are discussions of subscript classification, single-subscript tests, and tests for dependence in groups of coupled subscripts. The material emphasizes eliminating a dependence entirely where possible and getting the best possible approximation to the dependence properties such as direction vectors.

Chapter 4, *Preliminary Transformations*, covers essential transformations for accurate dependence analysis, including loop normalization, scalar data flow analysis, expression propagation and substitution, induction-variable substitution, and scalar renaming.

Chapter 5, *Enhancing Fine-Grained Parallelism*, focuses on inner loop parallelism of the kind needed to support vector instructions and VLIW or superscalar processors. The chapter explores variations on and extensions to the layered parallel code generation procedure introduced in Chapter 2. Particular attention is focused on loop interchange, scalar expansion, node splitting, array renaming, and loop skewing in the process of vectorization.

Chapter 6, *Creating Coarse-Grained Parallelism*, explores code generation strategies for symmetric multiprocessors, utilizing asynchronous parallelism in a uniform shared-memory system. The principal issue for such machines is finding parallelism of sufficient granularity to compensate for the higher cost of task start-up and synchronization. This cost necessitates interchanging a parallel loop to the outermost legal position rather than the innermost position required for vectorization. The chapter explores the use of loop interchange, array privatization, loop alignment and code replication, loop skewing, and various index-set splitting strategies to achieve the goal of finding usable parallelism in ordinary programs.

Chapter 7, *Handling Control Flow*, explores the complications introduced by branches in the analysis and transformation of programs. It treats two important strategies in depth. The first strategy is *if-conversion*, a mechanism for eliminating control flow by converting all statements under control flow branches to conditional assignment statements. If-conversion was introduced to support vectorization and is required to rewrite conditional statements as vector statements. The second strategy is to use *control dependence* edges from conditional statements to statements whose execution depends on them. This chapter shows that the meaning of a program is preserved if both data and control dependences are honored. Finally, the chapter demonstrates how control dependence fits into the standard transformation algorithms, including parallel code generation.

Chapter 8, *Improving Register Usage*, demonstrates how dependence, properly extended to include input dependences, can be an effective way to explore the potential for data reuse in processor registers. This chapter introduces *scalar replacement*, which essentially assigns a subscripted variable reference to a register. It also treats transformations that improve the overall level of reuse, including unroll-and-jam, loop interchange, loop alignment and loop fusion.

Chapter 9, *Managing Cache*, moves beyond simple data reuse to explore transformations that improve the performance of machines with cache memory hierarchies. Although most of the transformations that improve register reuse increase cache reuse as well, cache memories are more complicated because they are much larger than the typical register set and deal with data in blocks of several words. These differences create opportunities for transformations such as blocking loop nests to iterate over data sets that fit in cache and loop interchange to effect stride-one access in the inner loop. The chapter also explores *software prefetching*—the explicit use of instructions that move data blocks from memory to cache prior to the time that the data is needed.

Chapter 10, *Scheduling*, treats dependence-based methods to improve performance of superscalar and VLIW machines through compile-time instruction placement. Topics include list scheduling, trace scheduling, software pipelining, and vector operation chaining.

Chapter 11, *Interprocedural Analysis and Optimization*, discusses strategies for extending compiler analysis, including dependence analysis, to whole programs. The chapter presents algorithms for analyzing several important interprocedural problems, including side effects, aliases, and constant propagation. It then shows how to extend side effect analysis to array subsections. Other topics include interprocedural optimizations, such as inline substitution and procedure cloning, and management of interprocedural analysis and optimization.

Chapter 12, *Dependence in C and Hardware Design*, applies the analysis strategies presented in this book to two new problem areas. The first area is dependence testing and program transformation to optimize C programs. The second is application of dependence to hardware design, including methods for speeding up the simulation of designs and methods for synthesizing low-level hardware from high-level abstract specifications.

The material in Chapter 13, *Compiling Array Assignments*, covers methods for implementing the array assignment statement in Fortran 90 on scalar machines and machines with fixed-length vector registers. A major topic is the conversion of array assignment statements to scalar loops without requiring unbounded temporary storage.

The final chapter, *Compiling High Performance Fortran*, applies dependence to the generation of efficient message-passing code from High Performance Fortran, a variant of Fortran 90 that includes facilities for specifying how data arrays are to be laid out in the memories of a scalable parallel computer. Topics include computation partitioning according to the owner-computes rule and communication generation and optimization.

The material in these chapters can be organized into courses in several different ways. For an advanced undergraduate course, Chapters 2 through 7 provide a reasonably complete treatment of the issues in parallelization. For a course focused on uniprocessor optimization, some of the material in Chapter 5 (all but Sections 5.1, 5.2, and 5.7 through 5.9, which cover important transformations) and Chapter 6 (all but Sections 6.2 and 6.3) could be skipped in favor of including Chapters 8 and 9. On the other hand, a reader familiar with parallelization might wish to focus on the other applications, including memory hierarchy management, which are found in Chapters 8 through 10 and 12 through 14. As stated previously, we have succeeded in teaching all of the material in the book as a single one-semester graduate course at Rice University.

We have tried to make the book self-contained, assuming only that the reader is familiar with the basics of compiler and machine design. This desire necessitated the inclusion in Chapter 4 of some material on data flow analysis (Section 4.4) that would probably be covered in a basic compiler course. We felt that it was important to include this material in the book so you could view it in the context of the theory of dependence and transformation. We hope that we have succeeded in making this work readable and topical for both advanced students of compilation and practical compiler writers.

Chapter Structure and Features

We attempted to provide a consistent chapter structure throughout this book. Each chapter includes an introduction to provide an overview of the topic before the detailed technical treatment begins. The introduction typically uses examples to illustrate the problem addressed by the chapter.

Technical material is presented in a tutorial style that includes numerous examples illustrated by dependence graphs. Transformations are described using "before and after" code sequences. We include complete algorithms for the program transformations presented in order to make it straightforward for a practitioner to develop an implementation from the material. In most cases these algorithms are direct variants of ones that we have implemented in our own research and commercial systems. We have consistently striven in these implementations to ensure that the algorithms have acceptable asymptotic complexity for handling large programs efficiently. Algorithms are presented in an intuitive Algol-like notation that is useful for specification. However, we have added some special constructs for iterating over sets of elements (e.g., the **for each** loop) that help us avoid specifying the details of set implementations.

At the end of each chapter is a summary that reviews the main points that the chapter covers. This is followed by case studies, which present material on our real implementations, along with experimental evidence on the effectiveness of the strategies. Here you will find material on the design compromises required by production compilers. The final section, Historical Comments and References, reviews the related literature and discusses the origins and development of the ideas presented in the chapter, with citations of specific references that can be found at the end of the book.

At the end of each chapter are a small number of exercises that have been developed for our graduate course on this material. These exercises range from simple drills on the material to implementation assignments and research problems.

Supplementary Online Material

The Web pages associated with this book at *www.mkp.com/ocma/* contain numerous supplementary materials. In addition to updates and corrections discovered after the publication date, you will find Microsoft PowerPoint presentations used in our classes based on the book. In addition, we will add new exercises as they become available. The pages will also contain links to software that implements many of the concepts developed in this book from universities such as Rice as well as other publicly available sources.

Solutions to the exercises are available to instructors through the Morgan Kaufmann password-protected FTP site. Instructors can obtain the password from their MKP sales representative.

Acknowledgments

This book is the product of 20 years of research at Rice University that in turn relied upon countless years of related research at other institutions. The book itself has been 10 years and 6 different word processing systems in development. Any work of such breadth necessarily builds on the work of more than just two authors, and we want to acknowledge some of the many people whose efforts and ideas contributed to this book.

At the head of this list are the former Rice Ph.D. students whose research has defined most of the book's contents. Students whose thesis material is covered directly in various chapters include Vasanth Bala, David Callahan, Steve Carr, Keith Cooper, Ervan Darnell, Chen Ding, Gina Goff, Mary Hall, Paul Havlak, Kathryn McKinley, Allan Porterfield, Carl Rosene, Jerry Roth, Linda Torczon, Ajay Sethi, and Chau-Wen Tseng. Particular thanks go to those who contributed exercises: Chen Ding, Kathryn McKinley, and Jerry Roth. Equally important are the numerous graduate students, undergraduate students, and research and technical staff members, who have contributed to the development of PFC, ParaScope, the D System, and the Ardent Titan compiler. Among these, we especially acknowledge the technical staff members who helped lead these development projects: Vikram Adve, David Callahan, Keith Cooper, Mary Hall, Seema Hiranandani, Steve Johnson, Kathryn McKinley, John Mellor-Crummey, and Linda Torczon.

In addition, we have benefited from close interactions with outstanding colleagues during the development of this material. Randy Scarborough of IBM spent a great deal of time with us during the development of PFC and provided us with many insights and the perspective of a seasoned industrial compiler developer. Ben Wegbreit provided many stimulating discussions during the development of the Ardent Titan compiler, and Steve Wallach's interactions with us during his development of the Convex vectorizing compiler led to many improvements in our approach, including our attention to C.

Others who deserve specific mention are those researchers who contributed to the theoretical and practical foundations of optimization and dependence. These researchers, whose work we have liberally drawn upon, include Leslie Lamport, David Kuck, Utpal Banerjee, Michael Wolfe, Ron Cytron, John Cocke, Jack Schwartz, Frances Allen, Susan Graham, Monica Lam, and many more.

This book and research would not have come to fruition without the financial support of IBM, the National Science Foundation, the Defense Advanced Research Projects Agency, and the Department of Energy through the Los Alamos Computer Science Institute. We have been fortunate to have had a strong set of program managers who not only helped guide this research but also provided strong moral support. These managers include Horace Flatt, Fred Ris, Bill Harris, Kamal Abdali, Rick Adrion, Gil Weigand, Bob Lucas, Frederica Darema, and John Reynders.

An important part of the development of this book was its use in graduate-level courses. We are extremely grateful to those students and instructors who suffered through our initial versions and provided feedback on the many mistakes we had made. This book is a significantly better work because of the improvements you suggested.

The editorial staff of Morgan Kaufmann has been incredibly helpful in the production of this book. Emilia Thiuri provided consistent and able support in getting the book ready for production, and Edward Wade's patient and persistent attention to detail has been critical to the excellence of this book's content and appearance. The copyeditor, Ken DellaPenta, did an outstanding job of correcting our mistakes while ensuring consistency of the book's presentation. And the rest of the production staff—compositor Nancy Logan, proofreader Jennifer McClain, and indexer Ty Koontz—contributed greatly to the quality of the end result. We are also grateful for the excellent designs by Rebecca Evans & Associates (interior) and Ross Carron Design (cover), and for the faithful figure rendering by Dartmouth Publishing.

The reviewers, Tarek Abdelrahman, Benjamin Goldberg, Kathryn McKinley, Steven Carr, Allan Porterfield, Andrew Chien, Monica Enand, Rohit Chandra, and Bill Appelbe, provided many helpful suggestions for the improvement of the structure and content of the volume. Corrections for the second printing were provided by Agustin Arruabarrena, David Bartley, Adam Bordelon, Remko van Beusekom, John Callan, Arun Chauhan, Cristian Coarfa, Anshuman Dasgupta, Yuri Dotsenko, Jason Eckhardt, John Elliott, John Garvin, Jeroen Gordijn, Jacques-Olivier Haenni, Guohua Jin, Mike Johnson, Chris Kuhlman, Anton Lokhmotov, Anirban Mandal, Henry McNair, Alexander Motzkau, David Niedzielski, Tim O'Neill and his students, Jonas Skeppstedt, David Wohlford, Feng Xiaobing and his colleagues at the Chinese Academy of Sciences (who translated the book into Chinese), Edward Yang, Hongbo Yang, Fengmei Zhao, Yuan Zhao, and Lei Zhou. We are deeply grateful to our editor, Denise Penrose, without whose patient but firm guidance and positive attitude of support the book would not have been completed.

Finally, and most importantly, we would like to thank our families for their patience and encouragement and for the balance they have brought to our lives. Our wives, Vicki Allen and Carol Quillen, were incredibly supportive even when it meant that our attention was directed elsewhere for long periods of time, and they kept us centered when we were under the most stress. While the arrival of Jennifer and Caitlin slowed the writing process at times, they made life much more enjoyable and satisfying.

CHAPTER 1

Compiler Challenges for High-Performance Architectures

1.1 Overview and Goals

The past two decades have been exciting ones for high-performance computing. Desktop personal computers today feature computing power equivalent to the most powerful supercomputers of the late 1970s. Meanwhile, through the use of parallelism and innovations in the memory hierarchy, supercomputers have exceeded a sustained teraflop on real applications and are now setting their sights on 10 to 100 teraflops. High-end supercomputing systems can be seen as laboratories for software research and development because innovations developed on such systems eventually find their way to the desktop computer systems.

The phenomenal improvements in computer speeds have been the result of two effects. First, the underlying technology from which machines are constructed has seen remarkable advances on a pace predicted by Moore's Law. Figure 1.1 plots the peak performance of the fastest supercomputer by year from 1950 to 2000. The regression fit, which follows Moore's Law quite well, indicates that supercomputer performance has increased by two orders of magnitude every decade. However, technology by itself has not been enough. The four outlined regions show that differences in computer architecture—from scalar through superscalar and vector to parallel—have been necessary to keep performance on track. Clearly, parallelism of one form or another is essential to supercomputing performance.

But parallelism is not just for supercomputers anymore. Even though today's uniprocessors achieve phenomenal performance levels, they still cannot satisfy the thirst of image-processing applications and multimedia on the desktop. Meeting this demand has required uniprocessor designs to include many parallel features, such as multiple functional units, multiple-issue instruction processing, and

1

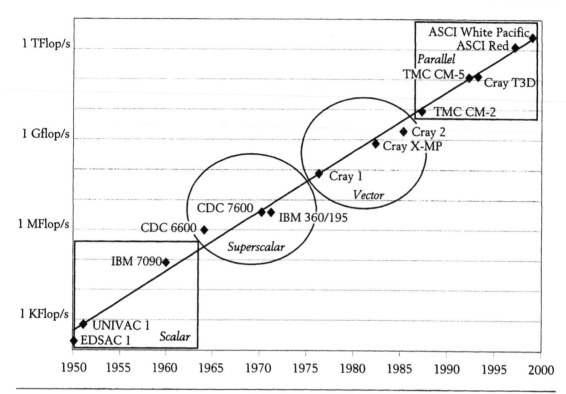

Figure 1.1 Performance of the fastest supercomputers over 50 years.

attached vector units. Even these strategies are not enough to satisfy the requirements for computation servers, which generally employ modest numbers (4 to 32) of processors. Clearly, parallelism has become a significant factor in the marketplace.

High-performance computers are not distinguished solely by parallelism. Because of the rapidly growing processor speed and the relatively slow pace of improvement of memory technology, most processors today have two or three levels of cache memory. These caches are designed to hide the long latencies inherent in the mismatch between processor speed and memory access time. They also improve effective memory bandwidth for data that is reused from cache.

Advances in computing power have not come without problems, however. As architectures have grown more complex to keep apace of Moore's Law, they have become more difficult to program. Most high-end application developers are painfully aware of the tricks needed to explicitly manage memory hierarchies and communication in today's scalable parallel systems. In an effort to squeeze more performance out of individual processors, programmers have even learned how to transform their codes by hand to improve instruction scheduling on multiple-issue uniprocessors.

Our view is that most of these hand transformations for high-performance computers should really be performed by compilers, libraries, and run-time systems. The compiler must play a special role because of its traditional responsibility for translating programs from a language suitable for use by human application developers to the native language of the target machine. While it is tempting to believe that the compiler's responsibility ends with the production of a *correct* machine-language translation of the source program, that by itself is not enough. The compiler must produce a suitably *efficient* program as well. If it fails to do so, application developers will abandon attempts to use the language.

The importance of efficiency in compiled code is not a recent observation. It has been implicit in the development of every successful computer language, beginning with the first version of Fortran. In the words of John Backus, reflecting in 1978 on the Fortran I effort [30]:

> It was our belief that if Fortran, during its first months, were to translate any reasonable "scientific" source program into an object program only half as fast as its hand-coded counterpart, then acceptance of our system would be in serious danger. . . . To this day I believe that our emphasis on object program efficiency rather than on language design was basically correct. I believe that had we failed to produce efficient programs, the widespread use of languages like Fortran would have been seriously delayed.
>
> In fact, I believe that we are in a similar, but unrecognized, situation today: in spite of all the fuss that has been made over myriad language details, current conventional languages are still very weak programming aids, and far more powerful languages would be in use today if anyone had found a way to make them run with adequate efficiency.

These words are as true today as they were four decades ago when Fortran was first developed. In fact, compiler technology has become even more important as machines have become more complex. The success of each innovation in computer architecture has been contingent on the ability of compiler technology to provide efficient language implementations for that innovation; in other words, the trend in modern machine architecture has been to shift the burden of achieving high performance from the hardware to the software. Compiler technology has been only partially successful in this task. Excellent techniques have been developed for vectorization, instruction scheduling, and management of multi-level memory hierarchies. Automatic parallelization, on the other hand, has been successful only for shared-memory parallel systems with a few processors; compiler parallelization for scalable machines remains an unsolved problem.

Fortunately, the underlying analysis structure needed to compile for the diverse collection of high-performance computer architectures available today exhibits substantial commonality. Most critical compilation tasks can be handled by transformations that reorder the instances of statements in the original program. The safety of these transformations (that is, whether they preserve the meaning of the program) is determined by the concept of *dependence*. Dependence has turned out to be an amazingly durable and broadly applicable concept.

In fact, this book might well be titled *Dependence-Based Compilation: Theory and Practice* because dependence is the unifying theme for the entire volume.

The principal goal of this book is to provide an introduction to dependence and the many transformation strategies that it supports. These compiler technologies have been developed over the past two decades to support machine complexity at the high end. Our aim is to provide a useful resource for the student of advanced compilation and the practicing compiler developer alike. The remainder of this chapter consists of a brief introduction to high-performance computer architectures and the compiler strategies needed to deal with them. The trade-offs among these strategies are illustrated by an extended example in which the same program is shown optimized for different machine organizations. Finally, we introduce the concept of dependence, which will form the basis for most of this book.

1.2   Pipelining

One of the earliest applications of parallelism in computer architectures was the use of *pipelining*—subdividing a complex operation into a sequence of independent segments so that, if the different segments use different resources, operations can be overlapped by starting an operation as soon as its predecessor has completed the first segment.

1.2.1   Pipelined Instruction Units

Consider as an example one of the earliest pipelines, the *instruction execution pipeline*. On the IBM 7094, a high-end scientific computer from the mid-1960s, each instruction was executed in two phases: the *instruction fetch* phase and the *execute* phase. Since the phases could be arranged to fetch from different data banks, the instruction fetch for the next instruction could often be overlapped with the execute phase of the current one. The notion of an instruction execution pipeline was further refined in the 1970s by the introduction, on the IBM 370 series, of a four-stage pipelined execute phase.

Instruction pipelines have become significantly more sophisticated over the years. Figure 1.2 gives the instruction pipeline for the DLX machine, used by Hennessy and Patterson to illustrate the principles of reduced instruction set computer (RISC) architectures [145]. DLX resembles many modern RISC machines, including the MIPS architecture found in machines manufactured by SGI.

On a modern RISC machine, typical instructions occur in one of three forms:

- *Register-to-register ALU operations:* These include all arithmetic operations such as integer and floating-point addition, subtraction, and so on.

- *Memory operations:* These instructions require a memory access. Load from memory into registers and store from registers into memory are prototypical examples.

IF	ID	EX	MEM	WB		
	IF	ID	EX	MEM	WB	
		IF	ID	EX	MEM	WB

| 1 | 2 | 3 | 4 | 5 | 6 | 7 |

Cycles

Figure 1.2 DLX instruction pipeline [145].

■ *Branch instructions:* These instructions change the location in memory from which the next instruction is to be executed, depending on the value of a condition. If the condition is true, the program counter is incremented by the immediate value in the instruction; otherwise the PC is left pointing to the next instruction in memory.

The DLX pipeline is designed to handle all three kinds of instructions. The pipeline includes the following stages:

1. Instruction fetch (IF)
2. Instruction decode (ID)
3. Execute (EX)
4. Memory access (MEM)
5. Writeback (WB)

Instruction fetch and decode are self-explanatory. For the purposes of execution, the EX and MEM stages are grouped. If the instruction is a register-to-register operation that can be performed in the arithmetic-logical unit (ALU), the instruction is completed in the EX stage. If it is a memory access, address calculation is performed in the EX stage and the memory access actually takes place in the MEM stage. Note that if the required memory location is not in cache, a miss occurs and the instruction will stall until the required block is brought into cache. If the instruction is a branch, the specified register is compared to zero in the execution phase, and the PC is set to the correct value in the MEM stage. The WB stage is used to write data back to registers; it is not used in a branch instruction.

If each pipeline stage uses different resources, the different stages of successive instructions can be overlapped. Figure 1.2 illustrates a schedule that is able to issue an instruction on every machine cycle. In other words, the average number of cycles per instruction in this ideal schedule will be 1, not counting the time required to start the pipeline. This ideal schedule is not always achievable, however, because a number of conditions, called *hazards*, can interfere. These will be discussed in Section 1.2.4.

1.2.2 Pipelined Execution Units

Unfortunately, many operations will take much longer than a single one of these shortened cycles. Most notable are the floating-point operations, which may take four or more cycles to complete. Consider, for example, the steps in a typical floating-point adder. Once both operands have been fetched from memory, they must be normalized to have the same exponent. Next, the two mantissas must be added together. Finally, the resulting addition may have to be renormalized before being stored into its destination. Figure 1.3 illustrates this process.

Since each segment in the addition unit is independent of the others, there is no reason why each segment cannot be simultaneously operating on different operands. Thus, if it is necessary to compute the sum of several pairs of numbers, the computation can be accelerated by overlapping the phases of the addition unit, as illustrated in Figure 1.4.

If the time required by each segment to work on one pair of operands is one cycle, then the time required to perform n additions without pipelining is $4n$ cycles. If the segments are overlapped so that the computation is pipelined, the n additions require $n + 3$ cycles, because once the pipe has been filled, the adder produces a result every cycle. Thus, for an infinite number of computations, the time to perform one addition is effectively reduced from 4 cycles to 1 cycle by pipelining.

A pipelined functional unit is effective only when the pipe is kept full; that is, only when there are operands available for operation on each segment clock cycle. Unfortunately, user computations rarely satisfy this requirement. As a result,

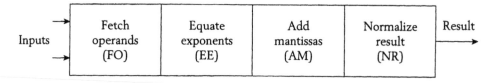

Figure 1.3 Typical floating-point adder.

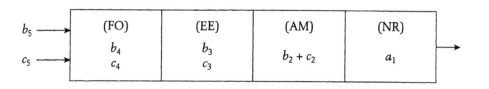

Figure 1.4 Snapshot of a pipelined execution unit computing $a_i = b_i + c_i$.

effectively utilizing a pipelined functional unit requires that something (usually the compiler) reorder the user computation so that the necessary operands are delivered fast enough to keep the pipe full.

1.2.3   **Parallel Functional Units**

When functional units are replicated, each unit can work on an independent instruction, as depicted in Figure 1.5. When the execution unit issues an instruction, it sends that instruction to a free functional unit if one exists. Otherwise it waits for a functional unit to become free. If there are n functional units, each of which takes m cycles to complete its operation, the machine is capable of issuing n/m operations per cycle on average. This type of parallelism, also known as *fine-grained parallelism*, may appear more attractive than pipelining at first glance, since it permits a wider range of operational freedom. However, there are associated costs. First, a pipelined unit costs only slightly more than a nonpipelined unit,[1] whereas multiple functional units obviously cost several times more than single functional units. Second, coordinating the functional units requires significantly more sophisticated execution logic than pipelined parallelism. Of course, it is possible to replicate pipelined functional units, thereby using both pipelining and multiple-unit parallelism.

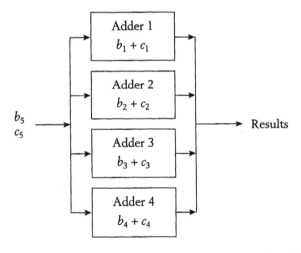

Figure 1.5 Multiple functional units.

---

1. Seymour Cray discovered this in the 1960s between the design for the Control Data 6600 (circa 1965), which used multiple units, and the Control Data 7600 (circa 1969), which used pipelining.

1.2.4   **Compiling for Scalar Pipelines**

The key performance barrier in pipelined architectures has been the existence of *pipeline stalls*. A stall occurs when a new set of inputs cannot be injected into the pipeline because of a condition called a *hazard*. Hennessy and Patterson [145] classify hazards into three categories:

1. *Structural hazards*, which occur because the machine resources do not support all possible combinations of instruction overlap that might occur.

2. *Data hazards*, which occur when the result produced by one instruction is needed by a subsequent instruction.

3. *Control hazards*, which occur because of the processing of branches

We will illustrate these three types of hazards with examples for the various pipelines discussed earlier in this chapter.

A structural hazard can occur whenever the implementation of a particular architecture does not have sufficient resources to support overlap of certain kinds. For example, if a machine has only one port to memory, it cannot overlap the fetch of instructions with the fetch of data. Such a restriction would essentially serialize the IBM 7094, reducing it to the performance of its predecessors. On a DLX with only one memory port, a stall would occur on the third instruction after every load because the data and instruction fetches would conflict (see Figure 1.6). A structural hazard of this kind cannot be avoided through compiler strategies on the DLX.

A data hazard can occur on any multistage pipeline such as the DLX. On modern machines most stalls are avoided by forwarding results from the ALU to the ALU for the next pipeline stage. Thus a sequence of instructions like

```
ADD    R1,R2,R3
SUB    R4,R1,R5
```

can be executed without delay because the result of the add is forwarded immediately to the execution stage of the subtract, without waiting for a writeback to registers. However, this is not possible in the following sequence:

```
LW     R1,0(R2)
ADD    R3,R1,R4
```

because the result of the load is not available until after the memory cycle. Thus we see a one-cycle stall, as depicted in Figure 1.7.

Compiler scheduling can eliminate this problem by inserting an instruction that does not use the register being loaded between the load and the add instructions above.

Pipelined functional units present a similar challenge for compiler scheduling because one instruction might need to wait for an input, computed by a previous

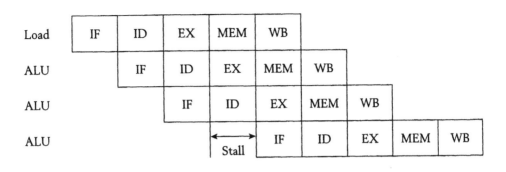

Figure 1.6 Structural hazard on the DLX with one memory port.

LW	R1,0(R2)	IF	ID	EX	MEM	WB			
ADD	R3,R1,R4		IF	ID	Stall	EX	MEM	WB	

Figure 1.7 DLX data hazard requiring a stall due to memory latency.

ADDF R3,R1,R2	IF	ID	EX1	EX2	MEM	WB		
ADDF R3,R3,R4		IF	ID	Stall	EX1	EX2	MEM	WB

Figure 1.8 DLX data hazard requiring a stall due to instruction latency.

instruction, that is still in the execution unit pipeline. On the DLX, multicycle operations have several execute stages, depending on the number of pipeline stages required to execute the operation. Suppose we wish to execute the following Fortran expression:

    A + B + C

on a machine where the pipeline for floating-point addition requires two stages. If the expression is evaluated in left-to-right order, the second addition will have to wait for one cycle before executing, as depicted in Figure 1.8.

Once again, compiler scheduling can help avoid these stalls. For example, suppose the expression to be evaluated is

    A + B + C + D

Each addition after the first will have to wait two cycles for the preceding addition to complete, requiring two stalls. On the other hand, if the compiler is able to regroup the additions as

```
(A+B) + (C+D)
```

the second addition can proceed one cycle after the first. There would still be a stall in the third addition, but the total number of stalls has been reduced by 1.

Control hazards occur because of branch instructions. On the DLX, a control hazard can cause a stall of three cycles, as shown in Figure 1.9. The processor begins fetching the instruction after the branch on the assumption that the branch will not be taken. If this assumption proves correct, then the pipeline will proceed without interruption. Whether the branch is to be taken will not be known until after the MEM phase of the branch instruction. If it is to be taken, then the instruction processing must restart at the new location and intermediate results from the instruction after the branch must be thrown away before any store to memory or writeback to registers. Thus when the branch is taken, we get an effective three-cycle stall.

Since three cycles is a huge penalty, machine designers go to great lengths to reduce this cost. One way to do this is by adding hardware to make it possible to determine the output of the condition and the branch target during the instruction decode (ID) stage. If the condition is simple, such as a test for equality to zero, both of these can be done with only one additional ALU. Thus for these simple branches the branch-taken pipeline stall can be reduced to a single cycle as shown in Figure 1.10. Note that there is no stall if the branch is not taken.

On the DLX with this implementation, there is no way to avoid a one-cycle stall on a branch taken through programming or compiler optimization. However,

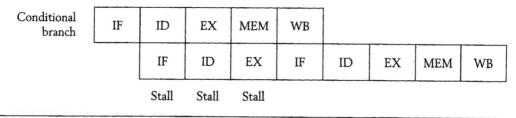

Figure 1.9 DLX control hazard on branch taken using naive implementation.

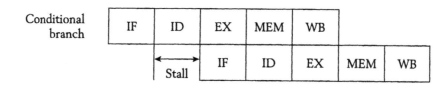

Figure 1.10 Reduced pipeline stalls through early recognition of branch target.

some RISC architectures provide a "branch-and-execute" instruction, which always executes the next instruction in sequence before performing the branch. This permits the compiler to rearrange instructions so that the last operation in the loop body, often a data store, is performed "under the branch."

As we have seen through these examples, the principal compiler strategy for overcoming the performance problems due to hazards is to rearrange instructions so that the stalls—particularly those due to data hazards—never occur. The discussion of this strategy, referred to as *instruction scheduling*, will be postponed until Section 1.4.2, which covers superscalar and VLIW architectures.

1.3 Vector Instructions

By the 1970s, the task of keeping the pipeline full from a standard instruction stream had become cumbersome. High-end supercomputers were using hardware strategies to look ahead in the instruction stream for operations that could be initiated without waiting for another operation to complete. These strategies made the instruction fetch and issue logic extremely complicated.

In an effort to simplify instruction processing, machine designers turned in the mid-1970s to an alternative approach in which certain instructions, called *vector instructions*, could fill floating pipelines all by themselves. This section discusses vector instructions and the issues involved in using them.

1.3.1 Vector Hardware Overview

A typical vector instruction initiates an elementwise operation on two vector quantities in memory or in fixed-length *vector registers*, which could be loaded from memory in a single operation. On the Cray 1, released in 1975, there were seven vector registers of 64 elements each. Each vector operation, including the load, could produce a result per cycle after a start-up delay equal to the length of the pipeline.

To avoid excessive start-up delays for linked vector instructions, many processors supported *chaining* of vector operations. Chaining entailed initiation of a vector operation waiting for an operand computed by a previous vector operation as soon as the first result was available. Thus the instruction sequence

```
VLOAD    VR1,M
VADD     VR3,VR2,VR1
```

would begin delivering results to VR3 after a delay equal to the sum of the start-up delays of vector load and vector add. Without chaining, the vector instruction would need to wait until the vector load completed before initiating the vector add.

Vector instructions dramatically simplified the process of issuing enough operations to keep the pipeline full. However, including these instructions had several drawbacks. First, they required significantly increased processor state for the vector registers. This increased the cost of processors and made context switching more complicated. Second, they expanded the total number of instructions in a machine by a significant amount, complicating instruction decode. Finally, vector instructions complicated the memory hierarchy design because they interfered with the operation of caches. To avoid the problem of excessive cache evictions and to keep bandwidth high, most vector machines bypassed the cache on vector loads and stores. This introduced the problem of maintaining coherency between memory and cache after vector operations. One company, Cray Research, avoided this problem by not using cache at all, substituting a collection of explicitly managed scalar temporary registers.

1.3.2   Compiling for Vector Pipelines

Although vector instructions simplify the task of filling instruction pipelines, they create new problems for the compiler and programmer. Principal among these is ensuring that the vector instructions exactly implement the loops that they are used to encode. The following sequence of vector operations adds two 64-element vectors[2] from A and B and stores the result into C.

```
VLOAD    V1,A
VLOAD    V2,B
VADD     V3,V1,V2
VSTORE   C,V3
```

Note that most vector operations interlock on load-store conflicts at registers, but not at memory (unlike uniprocessors such as the DLX).

In order to illustrate the primary compiler problem for vector machines, we introduce Fortran 90 vector notation. Vector operations in Fortran 90 have semantics that reflect those of most vector instruction sets. As such, they provide an easier way of presenting compiler issues for vector machines. The previous vector add operation would be written in Fortran 90 as

```
C(1:64) = A(1:64) + B(1:64)
```

Under the standard semantics for Fortran 90, an array assignment statement must be implemented to behave as if every input on the right-hand side of the assignment is loaded from memory before any element of the result is stored. In

---

2. Throughout this book, when no specific hardware vector length is stated, 64 is assumed, as that is the most common vector length.

other words, all inputs mentioned on the right-hand side refer to their values *before* the statement is executed.

Although Fortran 90 supports explicit vector operations, for historical reasons most programs are written in the Fortran 77 subdialect of Fortran 90 and hence use loops to specify operations that could be accelerated by vector hardware. The challenge for the compiler is to extract vector parallelism from these programs, which will be written using simple loops like the following:

```
DO I = 1, 64
   C(I) = A(I) + B(I)
ENDDO
```

Before it can schedule this loop on vector hardware, the compiler must determine whether the loop is semantically equivalent to the Fortran 90 array assignment above. If so, the assignment inside the loop can be vectorized by transliterating the references to the loop induction variable into corresponding triplet notation. However, this issue is not simple because the loop performs all the loads and stores corresponding to one iteration before beginning the next, while the array statement performs all loads before any stores. In the case above, either execution order produces the same final results, so that the meaning is precisely the same—hence the loop is referred to as *vectorizable*. However, a slightly different case demonstrates a potential problem:

```
DO I = 1, 64
   A(I+1) = A(I) + B(I)
ENDDO
```

Here each iteration of the Fortran 77 loop uses a result from the previous iteration, unlike the transliterated Fortran 90 array statement:

```
A(2:65) = A(1:64) + B(1:64)
```

In this Fortran 90 array statement, all inputs on the right reference old values. Hence, this second Fortran 77 loop is not vectorizable. Distinguishing between these two cases is the fundamental problem of vectorization and motivated the development of the theory of data dependence.

Given that the primary compiler problem for vector machines is uncovering vector operations, it may appear that using a language that contains explicit array operations (such as Fortran 90) solves the problem of vectorization. Unfortunately (or fortunately, if you make your livelihood as a compiler writer!), explicit array operations have an analogous set of compiling problems, as we shall see in Chapter 13.

1.4   Superscalar and VLIW Processors

A major disadvantage of vector operations is that they complicate instruction set design. In addition to a full complement of scalar instructions—hundreds on most modern machines—a vector processor must support a correspondingly large set of vector instructions, including not only instructions to perform computations, but also instructions to set up vector operations and conditional instructions that operate under bit-vector masks.

This complexity can be avoided. If we could issue one or more pipelined instructions on each cycle, it might be possible to fill the execution unit pipelines and produce results at a rate comparable to that of a vector processor. This is the basic idea behind superscalar and very long instruction word (VLIW)architectures.

1.4.1   Multiple-Issue Instruction Units

In both the superscalar and VLIW schemes, processors are designed to issue instructions as fast as possible, assuming all the inputs are ready. These machines are typically able to issue more than one instruction per cycle, up to some upper bound determined by the hardware.

Superscalar machines accomplish this by having hardware that looks ahead in the instruction stream for operations that are ready to execute. Thus, a superscalar processor can continue to issue instructions so long as each instruction it encounters is "ready." Some machines are even capable of issuing instructions out of order.

A VLIW processor, on the other hand, issues multiple instructions by executing a single "wide instruction" on each cycle. A wide instruction holds several normal instructions, all of which are to be issued at the same time. Typically, each of these instructions corresponds to an operation on a different functional unit. Thus, if a VLIW machine has two pipelined floating multiply units, it can issue two floating multiplications per cycle. On a VLIW system, the programmer or the compiler is expected to manage the execution schedule and pack the wide instruction words correctly—that is, so that no instruction is issued until all its inputs are ready. Thus, there is no need for special lookahead hardware on such machines.

Although superscalar and VLIW architectures can achieve the speed of vector execution, they have some disadvantages. First, they require significantly more bandwidth for fetching instructions from memory, making it imperative to have instruction caches large enough to hold all instructions in a typical loop. In addition, data fetches typically use the same memory hierarchy as simple processors, with all operands passing through the cache, which creates problems when the cache size is limited and operands are used only once. This was the reason that vector loads were designed to bypass the scalar cache on most vector machines.

An additional problem caused by passing values through cache is that stride-one data access becomes critical to good performance. If the access pattern in a loop is not consecutive, much of the available bandwidth between memory and cache will be wasted on operands that are not immediately used. Given that bandwidth limitations are a major problem on such machines, the issue is a serious one.

In the abstract, superscalar and VLIW machines can be thought of as vector processors because they can effectively exploit the parallelism exposed by vectorization. Indeed, many modern microprocessors, such as the PowerPC G4 used in Apple Macintoshes, include "vector units" that are really VLIW coprocessors.

1.4.2   Compiling for Multiple-Issue Processors

To achieve their full potential, superscalar and VLIW machines require careful planning of operations so that the machine resources are used to the fullest extent possible. Because most application developers do not program in machine language, it is the task of the compiler to carry out this planning process. This involves two challenges:

1. The compiler must recognize when operations are not related by dependence. Independent operations may be executed in any order relative to one another; dependent operations cannot.

2. The compiler must schedule instructions in the computation so that it requires as few total cycles as possible.

The first challenge can be addressed by vectorization because vectorization exposes many operations that can be executed in parallel. The second challenge, on the other hand, requires a compiler strategy called *instruction scheduling*, a major topic of Chapter 10. In its simplest form, instruction scheduling amounts to executing instructions as early as possible within the limits of processor resources and program dependence.

An often-repeated myth is that modern superscalar processors do not need scheduling because of the aggressive and powerful lookahead strategies they employ. Indeed, it is true that scheduling is less essential on superscalar architectures than it is on VLIW processors. Nevertheless, superscalar systems all have bounded-size windows for lookahead in the instruction stream and, as the amount of hardware parallelism increases, the search for parallel operations will need to widen to well beyond the limits of instruction stream lookahead. Compilers can help by rearranging the instruction stream to ensure that as much parallelism as possible fits within the lookahead window.

In this section, we concentrate on VLIW processors because they must be explicitly scheduled, thereby making the issues crystal clear. Furthermore, a good schedule for a VLIW processor also provides a good schedule for a superscalar with the same resources—listing the instructions in each cycle from the first to the last cycle should yield a superscalar program that does at least as well as the VLIW program from which it is generated.

To schedule straight-line code, the compiler must understand which instructions depend on other instructions and, for each dependence relation, how long a delay is required between the first and second instruction. To illustrate this, consider scheduling the following instruction sequence for a machine capable of issuing one instruction per cycle:

```
LF      R1,A
LF      R2,B
ADDF    R3,R1,R2
STF     X,R3
LF      R4,C
ADDF    R5,R3,R4
STF     Y,R5
```

If there is a two-cycle delay for loads from cache—that is, any instruction using the results of a load cannot issue until two cycles after the load is issued—and there is also a two-cycle delay for floating addition, then the scheduling of the sequence above can be improved by positioning the load of C earlier and the store of X later in the sequence:

```
LF      R1,A
LF      R2,B
LF      R4,C
ADDF    R3,R1,R2
ADDF    R5,R3,R4
STF     X,R3
STF     Y,R5
```

The first schedule takes 11 cycles to issue all instructions, because four 1-cycle delays must be inserted between instructions—one before each addition and each store. On the other hand, the second schedule takes only 8 cycles to issue all instructions because the only required delay is between the two additions.

The fragment above cannot be improved on a machine that can issue more than one instruction per cycle because there are too many dependences between instructions. However, consider the following sequence, which performs two independent additions:

```
LF      R1,A
LF      R2,B
ADDF    R3,R1,R2
STF     X,R3
LF      R4,C
LF      R5,D
ADDF    R6,R4,R5
STF     Y,R6
```

On a VLIW machine that can issue two loads and two adds per cycle, we could completely overlap the computation of the second expression with the computation of the first. On the other hand, if the machine can issue two loads but only one addition per cycle, we require an extra cycle, as the following schedule demonstrates:

LF R1,A	LF R4,C
LF R2,B	LF R5,D
Delay	Delay
ADDF R3,R1,R2	Delay
STF X,R3	ADDF R6,R4,R5
empty	STF Y,R6

Scheduling becomes more complicated in a loop, where the goal is to construct an equivalent loop of minimum length by overlapping computations from different iterations of the original loop. This type of scheduling, also known as "software pipelining," is discussed in Chapter 10.

1.5 **Processor Parallelism**

While pipelining is an effective way to speed up the execution of a single processor or functional unit, processor parallelism reduces the running time of an application by carrying out different tasks, or the same task on different data sets, simultaneously using multiple processors.

1.5.1 **Overview of Processor Parallelism**

There are two commonly used forms of processor parallelism, distinguished by their granularity of synchronization.

- *Synchronous processor parallelism:* This strategy replicates whole processors, with each processor executing the same program on different portions of the data space. Examples of this type of parallel system are the Thinking Machines CM-2, the MasPar MP-2, and the AMT DAP, all introduced in the late 1980s or the early 1990s. The main advantage of a synchronous system is that synchronization operations are cheap because the instructions are executed in lockstep, so these machines are capable of exploiting a much finer granularity of parallelism. On the other hand, synchronous machines are not very efficient on code with branches because they must execute the two sides of a branch in sequence, with different processors disabled on each side.

■ *Asynchronous processor parallelism:* This second form of parallelism replicates whole processors, but allows each processor to execute different programs or different parts of the same program with coarse-grained, explicit
synchronization. Figure 1.11 shows the organization of a typical asynchronous parallel machine with shared global memory. Processors using this
design are called *symmetric multiprocessors* (SMPs) and are available from a
variety of vendors including Compaq, Hewlett-Packard, IBM, Intel,
Sequent, Silicon Graphics, and Sun Microsystems. On these machines, any
required interprocessor synchronization must be explicitly specified
because the processors execute independently between synchronization
points. The problem with asynchronous parallelism is the relatively high
cost of starting up parallel tasks—a process must be spawned for each processor and processors must be synchronized before accessing any shared
data. Because of this high overhead, it is essential that parallel execution be
used only if there is enough work to compensate for the overhead.

In spite of its advantages, parallelism presents many problems for hardware
and software designers. When a machine contains multiple processors, some
mechanism is necessary to share the resources among the different processors. The
processors must also be able to communicate with each other in order to pass data
and coordinate computations, which involves sophisticated hardware mechanisms. Finally, the software for parallel machines is generally much more complicated than software for scalar and vector computers. For these reasons, parallel
processing took much longer than vector processing to achieve widespread acceptance. Nevertheless, as of the publication of this book, shared-memory parallel
computers with a modest number of processors have become the standard for science and engineering workstations.

Although parallel processing in its various forms can achieve impressive
speeds, fast hardware is only one prerequisite for fast programs. Unless software is
able to take effective advantage of the parallelism present within a processor, the

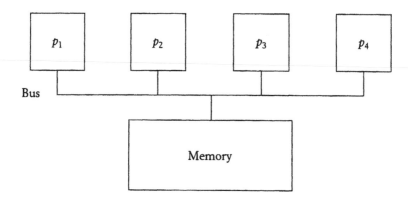

Figure 1.11 An asynchronous shared-memory multiprocessor.

hardware simply becomes a wasted, expensive resource. Accordingly, increasing the effective computation rate for applications requires developing mechanisms for exploiting parallelism at the language level.

1.5.2 Compiling for Asynchronous Parallelism

Although it might at first seem that compiling for asynchronous parallelism should present roughly the same challenges as vectorization, there are some additional complexities. First, execution schedules on parallel machines permit much more flexibility. To support our discussion of this topic, we introduce a Fortran notation for parallel loops.

The PARALLEL DO statement, which is similar to constructs in use in a number of dialects of Fortran, guarantees that there are no scheduling constraints among its iterations. As a result, the different iterations may be executed in parallel according to any schedule. In other words, the statement is an *assurance* from the programmer to the system that it should feel free to execute these iterations in parallel. In a 1966 paper, Bernstein [40] established that two iterations I_1 and I_2 can be safely executed in parallel if

1. iteration I_1 does not write into a location that is read by iteration I_2
2. iteration I_2 does not write into a location that is read by iteration I_1
3. iteration I_1 does not write into a location that is also written into by iteration I_2

As an illustration, consider the following example, which violates Bernstein's conditions:

```
PARALLEL DO I = 1, N
   A(I+1) = A(I) + B(I)
ENDDO
```

This simple case is analogous to the example used in vectorization. Here, the store into A(I+1) on one iteration modifies the same location that is loaded from A(I) on the next iteration. Because the schedule is unspecified, the result from the second of these iterations will differ, depending on whether the store on iteration 1 takes place first, in which case it will produce the same value as the sequential loop, or the load on iteration 2 occurs before the store on iteration 1, in which case the result will be different. Note that the answer may vary from execution to execution.

The following loop represents a more subtle case:

```
PARALLEL DO I = 1, N
   A(I-1) = A(I) + B(I)
ENDDO
```

Here, the store is into a location used on the *previous* iteration. On most vector architectures, this loop could be safely vectorized, but a parallelizing compiler must be more careful. Consider, for instance, the specific iterations I = 2 and I = 3. In the sequential analog, the fetch of A(2) that occurs on iteration 2 always precedes the store to A(2) on iteration 3. In the parallel version, this fetch may come before or after the store, causing the loop to compute different values for A.

Finally, consider a loop that violates the third Bernstein condition:

```
PARALLEL DO I = 1, N
    S = A(I) + B(I)
ENDDO
```

In the sequential analog, after execution of the loop, S always contains the same value—the one assigned on iteration N. In the parallel version, *any* iteration may be the last to execute, giving S a value that is highly nondeterministic.

To ensure correctness, a modern parallelizing compiler converts a sequential loop to a parallel one only when it is able to verify that all of Bernstein's conditions hold.

The second new problem introduced by asynchronous parallel machines is that of *granularity*. Because asynchronous parallel processes have large start-up and synchronization overhead, a parallel loop should not be initiated unless there is enough work to compensate for this added cost. By contrast, the synchronization overhead on vector units is small enough to permit profitable vectorization of even single-statement loops. Thus, because of the high cost of synchronizing processors, a programmer should attempt to minimize the frequency of synchronization generated by a parallel loop, which is equivalent to increasing the granularity of the parallel iterations.

For the compiler, the implication is that outer loops must be parallelized rather than the inner loops (which is the choice in vectorization), so as to minimize the number of times processors must be synchronized. Similarly, a compiler must be able to parallelize loops with subroutine and function calls because subroutine invocations are good sources of computation and almost any loop with a lot of computation will contain some calls. These considerations make the job of a parallelizing compiler much harder than the job of a vectorizing compiler because they obligate it to analyze much larger regions, including regions that span multiple procedures.

The final challenge faced by compilers for asynchronous parallel machines arises from the need to access large global memories. Some of the most historically important parallel systems (e.g., the Intel iPSC 860) did not have globally shared memory. Instead, each processor could access only the memory that was packaged with it. Such machines are sometimes called *multicomputers*, to distinguish them from *multiprocessors* (which typically share memory). Today's *SMP clusters* (e.g., the IBM SP) share memory among a small number of processors on a single node but cannot directly access the memory on a different node. Parallelizing compilers for multicomputers and SMP clusters must decide issues such as which memories hold which variables and when communication primitives are required to move data to a compute node that doesn't own it. These issues are difficult to address; they will be treated in Chapter 14.

1.6   Memory Hierarchy

One complicating aspect of every modern architecture is the memory hierarchy. As processor speeds continue to improve faster than memory speeds, the distance between main memory and processors (as measured in cycles for a register load) becomes greater. Two decades ago, loads from memory rarely took more than 4 cycles; today, load times in excess of 50 cycles are common. This trend is especially obvious on parallel machines, where complex interconnections are required to allow every processor access to all of memory. On parallel processors, load times may be as high as several hundred machine cycles. As a result, most machines include features that can be used to ameliorate the performance problems caused by long access times. Unfortunately, the ratio of processor speed to memory speed is unlikely to improve soon because total memory sizes are increasing as well, making a technology shift too expensive to consider seriously.

1.6.1   Overview of Memory Systems

There are two common measures of the performance of a memory system:

- *Latency* is the number of processor cycles required to deliver any single data element from memory.
- *Bandwidth* is the number of data elements that can be delivered to the processor from the memory system on each cycle.

For the purpose of analyzing performance, both measures are important. Latency determines the time that the processor must wait for a value requested from main memory. Many processors stall until a load from main memory completes; on these processors, it is important to minimize the number of requests to memory. Other processors will continue work with an outstanding request to memory, but must stall when the results are required by another operation; on those processors, it is important to try to schedule enough operations between a load and the use of its results to keep the processor busy. Bandwidth determines how many memory operations can be supported each cycle; the higher the bandwidth, the more memory values that can be fetched at one time.

There are two ways to deal with processor latency: avoidance and tolerance. *Latency avoidance* refers to strategies that reduce the typical latencies experienced in a computation. Memory hierarchies are the most common mechanisms for latency avoidance. If values that are referenced multiple times are stored in a fast intermediate memory, such as processor registers or cache, then references after the first will be much cheaper. Latency avoidance techniques also improve the effective utilization of memory bandwidth.

Latency tolerance means doing something else while data are being fetched. The use of explicit prefetching or nonblocking loads are two ways to tolerate latency. Another interesting latency tolerance mechanism, called *synchronous multithreading*, is employed on Cray/Tera MTA. This machine provides a fast context switch that makes it possible to change to a new execution stream every cycle. If enough streams are active and control is continually switched from one stream to another in a round-robin fashion, latencies will appear small to each stream.

In this book, we concentrate on latency avoidance through memory hierarchies and latency tolerance through cache line *prefetching* because they are more common in current practice. Although the intent of memory hierarchies is to transparently provide the performance of the fastest level of the hierarchy at roughly the cost of the slowest level, the extent to which that goal is achieved depends on how effectively programs reuse memory values in cache or registers. Restructuring programs to provide more opportunity for reuse can often lead to dramatic improvements in processor performance.

1.6.2   Compiling for Memory Hierarchy

Although memory hierarchies are intended to overcome the poor relative performance of system memory, they do not always succeed. When they fail, the result is very poor performance because the processor is always waiting for data. It is common for machines with cache memory to achieve high performance on small test problems (those most commonly used to benchmark machines before purchase), but perform poorly when the problem is increased to a realistic size. This usually means that the entire data set for the smaller problem could fit into cache, but the larger problem could not. As a result, a cache miss might occur on every data access for the large problem, but only once per array element on the smaller one.

A simple example will serve to illustrate the problem:

```
DO I = 1, N
   DO J = 1, M
      A(I) = A(I) + B(J)
   ENDDO
ENDDO
```

Assume that this loop nest is executed on a machine with one-word cache blocks and a cache that always replaces the least recently used (LRU) block when space is needed. Although the example code efficiently accesses the elements of array A, incurring only one miss per element, it will always miss on the access to B(J) if M is large enough. The crossover from good to bad performance occurs when M grows larger than the size of the cache in words. Because an element of B is not reused until all of the M - 1 other elements of B are used, when M is large enough, an LRU cache will evict each element of B before it has a chance to be reused on the next iteration of the I loop.

One way to alleviate this problem is to strip-mine the inner loop to a size that will fit in cache and interchange the "by-strip" loop to the outermost position:

```
DO JJ = 1, M, L
    DO I = 1, N
        DO J = JJ, JJ+L-1
            A(I) = A(I) + B(J)
        ENDDO
    ENDDO
ENDDO
```

Here, L must be smaller than the number of words in the cache. This second example misses only once for each element of B, since an element of B stays in the cache until all its uses are finished. The cost is an increase in the number of misses on references to A. However, the total number of misses on references to A is approximately $(NM)/L$ as opposed to NM misses on references to B in the original code.

While programmers can make changes like this to their source programs, doing so leads to machine-specific code that must be retargeted by hand to each new machine. We believe this kind of machine-specific optimization should be the job of the optimizing compiler. Later chapters will show how compiler technology developed for vectorizing and parallelizing compilers can be adapted to optimizing use of memory hierarchy.

1.7 A Case Study: Matrix Multiplication

To illustrate how machine architecture affects the way a particular computation should be programmed for highest efficiency, we now show some different arrangements of the code for matrix multiplication, a computation that is at the heart of many important scientific applications. A typical Fortran loop nest to compute the product of two matrices A and B is shown below:

```
DO I = 1, N
    DO J = 1, N
        C(J,I) = 0.0
        DO K = 1, N
            C(J,I) = C(J,I) + A(J,K) * B(K,I)
        ENDDO
    ENDDO
ENDDO
```

This code fragment employs a simple strategy to compute the product matrix C: the two outer loops select a specific element of the product matrix to compute, and the inner loop computes that element by taking the inner product of the appropriate row of the first input and column of the second. On a scalar machine (one supporting no parallel processing or vector operations), this code makes excellent use of the hardware. Since the inner loop accumulates products into C(J,I), there is no need to access memory (either fetches or stores) for C during that loop. Instead, the intermediate results can be kept in a scalar register until the loop has completed, and then stored to memory. When presented with this fragment, a good optimizing compiler should generate code that comes close to the optimal performance possible on a scalar machine, although this requires recognizing that the address of the array quantity C(J,I) is invariant in the inner loop and can be allocated to a register.

On a scalar machine with a pipelined floating-point unit, the same code is not likely to fare as well. The code runs efficiently on a nonpipelined scalar machine because the result of one iteration of the innermost loop is immediately used on the next, making it possible to reuse the result from a register. On a pipelined machine, each iteration must wait until the final addition on the previous iteration is available before it can begin its own final addition (see Figure 1.12). One way to overcome this problem is to work on four different iterations of an outer loop at the same time, thus filling the four pipe stages with four independent computations, as shown in Figure 1.13. The Fortran code to accomplish this is given below (here N is assumed to be a multiple of four):

```
DO I = 1, N
   DO J = 1, N, 4
      C(J,I) = 0.0
      C(J+1,I) = 0.0
      C(J+2,I) = 0.0
      C(J+3,I) = 0.0
      DO K = 1, N
         C(J,I)   = C(J,I)   + A(J,K)   * B(K,I)
         C(J+1,I) = C(J+1,I) + A(J+1,K) * B(K,I)
         C(J+2,I) = C(J+2,I) + A(J+2,K) * B(K,I)
         C(J+3,I) = C(J+3,I) + A(J+3,K) * B(K,I)
      ENDDO
   ENDDO
ENDDO
```

On a vector machine, the inner loop of the scalar matrix multiplication cannot be vectorized because the computation is a recurrence—that is, the interleaved load-store order of the scalar code is required to maintain the meaning of the code (assuming that reassociation of the addition is prohibited because of precision requirements). On a vector machine like the Cray T90, which has vector length 64, we need to move 64-element vector operations into the inner loop so

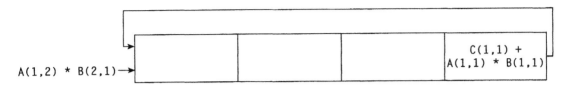

Figure 1.12 Matrix multiplication execution pipeline interlock.

```
                    ┌──────────────────────────────────────────────────────────────┐
                    │                                                                │
         ┌──────────┴──┬──────────────┬──────────────┬──────────────┐               │
         │   C(4,1) +   │   C(3,1) +   │   C(2,1) +   │   C(1,1) +   │◄──────────────┘
A(1,2) * B(2,1)──►A(4,1) * B(1,1)│A(3,1) * B(1,1)│A(2,1) * B(1,1)│A(1,1) * B(1,1)│
         └─────────────┴──────────────┴──────────────┴──────────────┘
```

Figure 1.13 Pipeline filling via outer loop unrolling.

that the vector registers on the T90 can be reused on each iteration. Thus the best code for the T90 looks like this:

```
DO I = 1, N
   DO J = 1, N, 64
      C(J:J+63,I) = 0.0
      DO K = 1, N
         C(J:J+63,I) = C(J:J+63,I) + A(J:J+63,K) * B(K,I)
      ENDDO
   ENDDO
ENDDO
```

This form of matrix multiplication extends the scalar register properties of the first code to the vector registers of the Cray. The K-loop now performs all computations necessary for one vector section of the product matrix; as a result, that section may be accumulated in a vector register just as the single element may be accumulated in the scalar form.

On a VLIW with four-way simultaneous issue, four floating-point multiply-adders, and four pipeline stages, a good version might be

```
DO I = 1, N, 4
   DO J = 1, N, 4
      C(J:J+3,I) = 0.0
      C(J:J+3,I+1) = 0.0
      C(J:J+3,I+2) = 0.0
      C(J:J+3,I+3) = 0.0
      DO K = 1, N
         C(J:J+3,I) = C(J:J+3,I) + A(J:J+3,K) * B(K,I)
         C(J:J+3,I+1) = C(J:J+3,I+1) + A(J:J+3,K) * B(K,I+1)
         C(J:J+3,I+2) = C(J:J+3,I+2) + A(J:J+3,K) * B(K,I+2)
         C(J:J+3,I+3) = C(J:J+3,I+3) + A(J:J+3,K) * B(K,I+3)
      ENDDO
   ENDDO
ENDDO
```

Here the intent is that the four multiply-adds for C(J:J+3,I) would be issued in the same cycle, followed by those indexed by I + 1 and so on. This version of the code should keep all four floating-point units busy.

The considerations that must be taken into account on symmetric multiprocessors are different from those used for vector machines. Since vector loops are executed "synchronously" by hardware, they must be the innermost loops in a given nest. Parallel loops, on the other hand, are executed asynchronously, and it is therefore desirable to move them to the outermost position to ensure that there is enough computation to compensate for the start-up and synchronization overhead. Thus, on an SMP like the Sun Starfire, the best formulation of matrix multiplication should be

```
PARALLEL DO I = 1, N
   DO J = 1, N
      C(J,I) = 0.0
      DO K = 1, N
         C(J,I) = C(J,I) + A(J,K) * B(K,I)
      ENDDO
   ENDDO
ENDDO
```

In this form, each processor can independently compute a column of the product matrix, with no need to synchronize with other processors until the product is complete. This form requires that all processors have access to the entire A matrix and one column of the B matrix, which is trivially true in SMPs, where memory is shared among all processors.

On a scalar uniprocessor with an unpipelined floating-point unit and a cache that is large enough to hold more than $3L^2$ floating-point numbers without any cache conflicts (assume the cache is fully associative), we may wish to block cache to multiply a submatrix at a time. In the following code, assume that L divides evenly into N:

```
DO II = 1, N, L
   DO JJ = 1, N, L
      DO i = II, II+L-1
         DO j = JJ, JJ+L-1
            C(j,i) = 0.0
         ENDDO
      ENDDO
      DO KK = 1, N, L
         DO i = II, II+L-1
            DO j = JJ, JJ+L-1
               DO k = KK, KK+L-1
                  C(j,i) = C(j,i) + A(j,k) * B(k,i)
               ENDDO
            ENDDO
         ENDDO
      ENDDO
   ENDDO
ENDDO
```

The idea here is that the first loop nest initializes an L by L block of C, and the second loop nest computes the values for that block. By blocking the loop on K, we are able to get reuse of L by L blocks of both A and B. In other words, on each iteration of the KK-loop we multiply an L-by L-block of A and an L-by-L block of B and add the result to an L-by-L block of C.

Two important lessons should be evident from this study of matrix multiplication:

- Explicit representation of parallelism in a source language is not sufficient to guarantee optimal use of parallel hardware. Each of the six machine types presented required a different representation of parallelism—radically different in some cases. Furthermore, getting the best form for a specific machine required detailed knowledge of the machine's architecture. This observation suggests that explicitly parallel programs need to be tailored for individual architectures; they lose efficiency when ported from one machine to another.

- While the best version of matrix multiplication is different for each machine type, all of these forms can be derived from the initial nonparallel source by relatively simple program transformations. Most can be obtained by simply interchanging the order in which the loops are executed.

Given the increasing lifetime of software and the decreasing lifetime of hardware, these lessons suggest that tailoring code to the specific machine architecture is best left to the compiler. The next section introduces the basic elements of a compiler technology designed to make this goal achievable.

1.8   Advanced Compiler Technology

It is the job of the compiler to transform a computation from a high-level representation that is easy for a human to understand into a low-level representation that a machine can execute. The high level of the human representation is rarely intended to accommodate details of machine architecture, so a naive translation process may introduce inefficiencies into the generated machine-level program. The goal of optimization phases in compilers is to eliminate these inefficiencies and to transform a computational representation into one that is well tuned for a given architecture.

A natural implication of the philosophy that compilers should be responsible for tailoring programs to specific architectures is to make compilers responsible for automatically transforming code to take advantage of parallelism. In this view, the source program is treated as a "specification," which defines the result the program is to compute. The compiler is free to transform a program in any way that makes sense, so long as the transformed program computes the same results as the original specification. While this viewpoint seems natural enough, it is often met with skepticism because of the radical transformations required to exploit parallelism. For instance, matrix multiplication required loop interchange, loop splitting, loop distribution, vectorization, and parallelization to achieve optimal results across various parallel architectures. These transformations are not usually found in classical optimizers.

This book presents the theoretical and practical ideas behind a compiler approach based upon the paradigm of aggressively transforming a sequential specification. We focus primarily on methods for uncovering parallelism in Fortran 77 programs, since Fortran is currently the lingua franca of scientific computing. We will not argue the merits of this approach versus that of starting from a parallel computation; both approaches have strong arguments in their favor. However, we will note that starting from a sequential language has the very practical advantage that it targets the bulk of existing programs. In addition, the book will demonstrate that the same theory used to uncover parallelism in sequential programs can also be applied to optimizing explicitly parallel programs.

1.8.1   Dependence

When a programmer writes an application in a sequential programming language, the results that he expects the program to compute are those obtained by first executing the initial program statement, then the second, and so on, with appropriate exceptions for control flow constructs such as branches and loops. In essence, the programmer has specified a detailed ordering on the operations he expects the computer to execute. Obviously, exploiting parallelism directly from such a specification is impossible because parallelization changes the order of operations.

The fundamental challenge that an advanced compiler must meet is determining when an execution order (one that includes parallel or vector execution) that is different from the order specified by the programmer will *always* compute the same results. In other words, sequential languages introduce constraints that are not critical to preserving the meaning of a computation; the key to transforming such programs to parallel form is finding minimal constraints needed to ensure that the transformed program will produce the correct results on every input. If these constraints can be precisely characterized, then the compiler can be allowed to reorder execution of the program in any way that does not change these constraints.

In this book we develop a set of constraints, called *dependences*, that are sufficient to ensure that program transformations do not change the meaning of a program as represented by the results it computes. These constraints are not precise; there are cases where they can be violated without changing the program meaning. However, they capture an important strategy for preserving correctness in imperative languages: they preserve the relative order of loads from and stores to each memory location in the program. (They do not preserve the relative order of reads of the same location, but this cannot affect a program's meaning.) We will see that the concept of dependence can be extended to preserve the effect of control decisions on later actions.

Specifically, dependence is a relation on the statements of the program. The pair $\langle S_1, S_2 \rangle$ is in the relation if S_2 *must* be executed after S_1 in any valid reordering of the program if the order of access to memory is to be preserved.

To illustrate the concept of dependence, consider the following simple code fragment:

```
S₁    PI = 3.14159
S₂    R = 5
S₃    AREA = PI * R ** 2
```

The results of this fragment are defined as being those that occur when the execution order $\langle S_1, S_2, S_3 \rangle$ is taken. However, nothing in the code requires that S_2 be executed after S_1; in fact, the execution order $\langle S_2, S_1, S_3 \rangle$ produces exactly the same results (i.e., the same value of the variable AREA) as the original order. In contrast, the time at which S_3 is executed is critical; if it is executed before either S_1 or S_2, an incorrect value of AREA will be computed because the input operands will not have been set. In terms of dependence, the pairs $\langle S_1, S_3 \rangle$ and $\langle S_2, S_3 \rangle$ are in the dependence relation of the fragment, but the pair $\langle S_1, S_2 \rangle$ is not.

Dependence in straight-line code is an easy concept to understand. Unfortunately, examination of straight-line code alone does not ensure effective utilization of parallelism. To achieve the highest performance, we must extend the concept of dependence to the most frequently executed parts of the program by making it possible to handle loops and arrays. The following example illustrates the complexities introduced by these extensions:

```
      DO I = 1, N
S₁       A(I) = B(I) + 1
S₂       B(I+1) = A(I) - 5
      ENDDO
```

This loop exhibits the dependence $\langle S_1, S_2 \rangle$ because on every iteration the computed value of A is immediately used in S_2, and the dependence $\langle S_2, S_1 \rangle$, because every loop iteration other than the first uses a value of B computed on the previous iteration. Detecting these dependences is difficult enough, since different loop iterations touch different elements of the arrays. However, that is only part of the problem; the cycle in the dependence graph, indicating the cyclic nature of the loop, complicates scheduling algorithms for utilizing parallelism.

Loops and arrays are only some of the constructs that the compiler must learn to deal with. IF statements also introduce problems. The fact that statements may be conditionally executed according to values available only at run time is a distinct complication in the transformation process. For that matter, the dependences of a program may be conditioned upon the values of certain key variables—information that is available only at run time.

Much of the first half of this book is devoted to the development of the theory of dependences and methods for accurately constructing them in a program.

1.8.2 Transformations

As described so far, dependence is only a passive guide for uncovering implicit parallelism within a program. However, it is far more than that. Because dependences specify how a program's execution may be reordered, dependence can also form the basis for powerful transformation systems that enhance the parallelism present within a program. For instance, the simple exchange of two arrays

```
      DO I = 1, N
         T = A(I)
         A(I) = B(I)
         B(I) = T
      ENDDO
```

cannot be directly vectorized because the scalar temporary T creates a bottleneck to the vector computation: only one element can be transferred at a time in the program as specified. If the scalar temporary is expanded into a vector temporary

```
      DO I = 1, N
         T(I) = A(I)
         A(I) = B(I)
         B(I) = T(I)
      ENDDO
```

then the loop can be directly vectorized. The legality of transformations like this one can be determined by examining the dependences of a program. (This particular transformation, called *scalar expansion*, is discussed in Chapter 5.)

The material in Chapter 5, Chapter 6, and the second half of the book discusses the application of dependence to the support of program transformations. In order to illustrate the concepts of program transformations, it is necessary to have a language in which examples can be presented. Since Fortran is by far and away the most heavily used language on parallel and vector computers today, the most logical choice of language is a version of Fortran extended with vector and parallel operations. For this purpose, we will use Fortran 90 with the addition of a parallel loop statement. The appendix contains a simple introduction to the features of Fortran 90.

1.9 Summary

This chapter has introduced the basic problems of compiling high-level languages to code that achieves acceptable performance on high-performance computer systems. It has surveyed important architectural features, including pipelining, vector parallelism, VLIW and superscalar processing, asynchronous parallelism, and memory hierarchy. For each of these we have introduced optimizations that are helpful in improving performance. These strategies include instruction scheduling, automatic vectorization, automatic parallelization, and loop transformations to improve reuse in the memory hierarchy.

Compiling systems that perform such transformations work by determining those execution orders within the total ordering that *must* be observed in order to preserve the results of the computation. Those execution orders are captured in a relation known as *dependence*—statement S_2 is said to *depend upon* statement S_1 if S_2 follows S_1 in execution in the sequential program, and it *must* follow S_1 in any transformed program that computes the same results. With this definition, a compiler is free to reorder statement instances so long as it does not change the relative order of any two statements involved in a dependence.

1.10 Case Studies

In each of the chapters in this book, we include a section on "case studies" that discusses the authors' experiences with actual implementations of the concepts described in the chapter. Most of these experiences focus on two major systems: PFC and the Ardent Titan compiler.

The PFC system was developed at Rice by the two authors under a major research contract from IBM. Initially, PFC focused exclusively on vectorization, and it served as a model for a later vectorizing compiler from IBM. PFC was built from the ground up on the twin concepts of dependence and program transformation, and it served as a framework for investigations that addressed subjects far beyond vectorization, including parallelization, memory hierarchy management, and interprocedural analysis and optimization. It was the starting point for a series of related research systems at Rice, including PTOOL, a program parallelization tool that displayed dependences (races) preventing parallelism directly in the source code; ParaScope, a parallel programming environment; and the D System, a compiler and programming environment for High Performance Fortran (HPF).

When Allen left Rice, he joined Ardent Computer Corporation to lead their compiler development effort. There he constructed a commercial-quality compiler for the Titan series of computers. The Titan compiler used many of the same algorithms that were employed in PFC. However, where PFC was primarily a source-to-source translator, the Titan compiler generated machine language for a real computer with a number of unique and challenging features. In addition, this compiler had to handle C as well as Fortran, which presents a special set of challenges that are discussed in Chapter 12.

These two systems provide a rich source of experiences that we hope will illustrate and illuminate the discussion of basic principles found in the main part of each chapter.

1.11   Historical Comments and References

The development of dependence as a basis for aggressive program transformations has been the result of the work of many research efforts. Of particular historical importance is the seminal work on automatic vectorization and parallelization done at Massachusetts Computer Associates, later known as Compass. In the early 1970s, Compass created a transformation tool for the Illiac IV known as the Parallelizer. The key papers describing the Parallelizer include theoretical technical reports by Lamport [195, 196] and an elegant paper by Loveman espousing a philosophical approach toward optimization [204].

The most influential ideas on automatic program transformations were pioneered at the University of Illinois under the direction of David Kuck. Illinois had been involved with parallelism at its very early stages via the Illiac series of computers; the direction of research turned toward automatic program transformations in the mid-1970s with the inception of the Parafrase project. As can be surmised from its name, Parafrase attempts to restate sequential programs as parallel and vector equivalents. Among the many important papers produced in this project are papers on dependence testing [32, 190, 283], loop interchange [280], auxiliary transformations [285, 259], and low-level parallelism [219]. An outgrowth of the Parafrase project was Kuck and Associates, Inc., a commercial enterprise that markets advanced program transformation systems based on dependence.

The Parallel Fortran Converter (PFC) project was begun at Rice in the late 1970s under the direction of Ken Kennedy [20]. Initially, this project focused on extending Parafrase to add new capabilities. However, due to limitations in the internal data representations, the Parafrase version was dropped, and an entirely new system was implemented. Advances in PFC include a distinct categorization of dependences that makes clear a number of areas to which dependence can be applied, efficient algorithms for a number of transformations (particularly vector code generation and loop interchange), methods for handling conditional statements within a program, and new transformations for enhancing parallelism [16, 21, 23]. The PFC project itself served as a prototype for the vectorizing compiler for the IBM 3090 Vector Feature [243] and the Ardent Titan compiler [24]; the theory underlying PFC was also the basis for the Convex vectorizing compiler.

Exercises

1.1 Produce DLX code for the expression $X * Y * 2 + V * W * 3$. Find the best schedule for this code assuming that loads take three cycles, immediate loads take one cycle, floating addition takes one cycle, and floating multiplication takes two cycles. Assume as many registers as you need, but there is only one load-store unit and one floating-point arithmetic unit. All instructions are pipelined but the machine can issue at most one instruction per cycle. What strategy did you use to find the best schedule?

1.2 Redo Exercise 1.1 under the assumption that you can issue two instructions per cycle and there are two load-store units and two floating-point arithmetic units.

1.3 Produce a version of the *N*-by-*N* matrix multiply example from this chapter that would perform well on a parallel-vector machine, such as a T90 with 32 processors.

1.4 Produce a version of an *N*-by-*N* matrix multiply that would perform well for a symmetric multiprocessor in which each processor has an unpipelined execution unit and a fully associative cache with enough room to hold a few more than $3L^2$ elements of a matrix, where *L* divides into *N* evenly.

1.5 For any shared-memory high-performance computer system available to you, implement a version of a 1,000-by-1,000 matrix multiply in Fortran or C that achieves the highest possible performance. Pay special attention to the memory hierarchy by trying to find the right block size for cache.

CHAPTER 2

Dependence:
Theory and Practice

2.1 Introduction

As we learned in Chapter 1, optimization has an important function in the acceptance of a programming language—if the optimizer does not do a good job, no one will use the language. As a result, optimization technology has become quite sophisticated. However, most of the development effort in optimization technology has focused on scalar machines. On these machines, the principal optimizations are register allocation, instruction scheduling, and reducing the cost of array address calculations.

Parallelism introduces much more complexity into the optimization process. For parallel computers, the principal optimization becomes finding parallelism in a sequential code and tailoring that parallelism to the target machine, including its memory hierarchy. The principal strategy for seeking out useful parallelism is to look for a *data decomposition* in which parallel tasks perform similar operations on different elements of the data arrays. In Fortran, this strategy naturally maps to running different iterations of DO-loops in parallel. Data decomposition is effective on scientific problems because it is *scalable*—as the problem size increases, so does the available parallelism.

Given the focus in Fortran on loop iterations, an advanced compiler must be able to determine whether Bernstein's conditions [40] (see Section 1.5.2) are satisfied for every pair of iterations. Examining loop iterations is complicated enough; adding to the complexity is the fact that most code within a data-parallel loop will reference subscripted array variables. As a result, the compiler must have the ability to analyze such references to determine whether two different iterations access the same memory location. Given that one array contains multiple elements, it is not always obvious when two iterations or statements refer to different elements of the same array. Because of this added complexity, the simple definition of dependence presented in Chapter 1, while elegant and easy to understand, is ineffective in the presence of loops and array references.

The goal of this chapter is to elaborate the definition and properties of dependence as a constraint system that preserves the order of data accesses to memory with respect to loop nests. The chapter will also establish fundamental results that form the basis for later chapters. A principal goal will be to establish the applicability of dependence to automatic parallelization and vectorization. As an illustration of the power of dependence, the chapter concludes with a vectorization algorithm that is at the heart of several commercial compilers.

2.2   **Dependence and Its Properties**

Section 1.8 outlined the fundamental approach taken in this book to uncovering parallelism. The basis of this approach is a *dependence relation*, or *dependence graph*, which includes, for a given sequential program, a collection of statement-to-statement execution orderings that can be used as a guide to select and apply transformations that preserve the meaning of the program. Each pair of statements in the graph is called a *dependence*. Given a correct dependence graph for the program, any ordering-based optimization that does not change the dependences of a program will be guaranteed not to change the results of the program.

Dependences represent two different kinds of constraints on program transformations. First there are constraints designed to ensure that data is produced and consumed in the correct order. The dependences that arise from these constraints are called *data dependences*. Revisiting the example from Chapter 1

```
S₁   PI = 3.14
S₂   R = 5.0
S₃   AREA = PI * R ** 2
```

statement S_3 cannot be moved before either S_1 or S_2 without producing potentially incorrect values for the variables PI and R. To prevent this, we will construct data dependences from statements S_1 and S_2 to statement S_3. No execution constraint between S_1 and S_2 is required because the execution order S_2, S_1, S_3 will produce exactly the same value for PI as the execution order S_1, S_2, S_3.

The other constraint that gives rise to dependences is control flow. For example, in the following code

```
S₁   IF (T.EQ.0.0) GOTO S₃
S₂      A = A / T
S₃   CONTINUE
```

statement S_2 cannot be executed before S_1 in a correctly transformed program because the execution of S_2 is conditional upon the execution of the branch in S_1.

Executing S_2 before S_1 could cause a divide-by-zero exception that would be impossible in the original version. A dependence that arises because of control flow is called a *control dependence*.

Although both data and control dependences must be considered when correctly parallelizing a program, the next few chapters will concentrate exclusively on data dependences, which are simpler to understand and illustrate most of the important principles. Chapter 7 will show how to apply these principles to control dependences, either by converting them to data dependences with a technique known as "if-conversion" or by extending the algorithms to take control dependences into account.

Returning to data dependence, if we are to ensure that data is produced and consumed in the right order, we must make sure that we do not interchange loads and stores to the same location; otherwise the load may get the wrong value. Furthermore, we must also make sure that two stores take place in the correct order so that subsequent loads will get the right value. Formalizing these notions produces the following definition of data dependence.

DEFINITION 2.1   There is a *data dependence* from statement S_1 to statement S_2 (statement S_2 *depends on* statement S_1) if and only if (1) both statements access the same memory location and at least one of them stores into it, and (2) there is a feasible run-time execution path from S_1 to S_2.

The next few sections will discuss various properties by which dependences can be classified. These properties are important for understanding the algorithms presented later in the book.

2.2.1   Load-Store Classification

Expressed in terms of load-store order, there are three ways that a dependence can arise in a program.

1. *True dependence.* The first statement stores into a location that is later read by the second statement:

    ```
    S₁   X = ...
    S₂   ... = X
    ```

    The dependence ensures that the second statement receives the value computed by the first. This type of dependence is also known as a *flow dependence* and is denoted $S_1 \delta S_2$ (read S_2 depends on S_1). The convention for graphically displaying dependence is to depict the edge as flowing from the statement that executes first (the *source*) to the one that executes later (the *sink*).

2. *Antidependence.* The first statement reads from a location into which the second statement later stores:

```
S₁   ... = X
S₂   X = ...
```

Here the dependence prevents the interchange of S_1 and S_2, which could lead to S_1 incorrectly using the value computed by S_2. In essence, this dependence is present to prevent a program transformation from introducing a new true dependence that did not exist in the original program. An antidependence such as this one is denoted $S_1 \delta^{-1} S_2$. Antidependence is also denoted $S_1 \delta^- S_2$ in some texts.

3. *Output dependence.* Both statements write into the same location:

```
S₁   X = ...
S₂   X = ...
```

This dependence prevents an interchange that might cause a later statement to read the wrong value. For example, in the code fragment

```
S₁   X = 1
S₂   ...
S₃   X = 2
S₄   W = X * Y
```

statement S_3 should not be allowed to move before statement S_1 lest Y be incorrectly multiplied by 1, rather than 2, in S_4. This type of dependence is called an *output dependence* and is denoted $S_1 \delta^o S_2$.

In the context of hardware design, dependences are often called *hazards* or *stalls*, due to their effects on pipelines. A true dependence is the same as a RAW (read after write) hazard; an antidependence is equivalent to a WAR (write after read) hazard; and an output dependence is a WAW (write after write) hazard [145].

2.2.2   Dependence in Loops

Extending the concept of dependence to loops requires some way to parameterize statements by the loop iterations in which they are executed. For example, in the simple loop nest

```
     DO I = 1, N
S₁      A(I+1) = A(I) + B(I)
     ENDDO
```

the statement S_1 on any loop iteration depends on the instance of itself from the previous iteration. The statement "S_1 depends upon itself" is true in this case, but is not precise. For instance, a simple change in a single index can cause the statement to depend on the instance two iterations previous:

```
     DO I = 1, N
S₁       A(I+2) = A(I) + B(I)
     ENDDO
```

Thus, precise characterization of dependences in loops requires that statements be parameterized by some representation of the loop iteration in which the statement occurs. To do this we will construct a vector of integers representing the *iteration number* of each loop in which the statement is nested. For a simple loop

```
     DO I = 1, N
       . . .
     ENDDO
```

the iteration number is exactly equal to the loop index: for the first iteration the iteration number is equal to 1, for the second iteration the iteration number is equal to 2, and so on. However, in the loop

```
     DO I = L, U, S
       . . .
     ENDDO
```

the iteration number is 1 when I is equal to L, 2 when I is equal to L + S, and so on.[1]

In some situations it is preferable to use a normalized version of the iteration number in which the iterations run from 1 to some upper bound in increments of 1. These notions are formalized in the following definition:

DEFINITION 2.2 For an arbitrary loop in which the loop index I runs from L to U in steps of S, the *(normalized) iteration number* i of a specific iteration is equal to the value $(I-L+S)/S$, where I is the value of the index on that iteration.

In a loop nest, the *nesting level* of a specific loop is equal to one more than the number of loops that enclose it. That is, loops are numbered from the outermost to innermost starting at 1. This leads to a natural definition of iterations in multiple loops.

---

1. Some texts define the *iteration number* as equal to the loop index I. However, this causes problems when the step size is negative. In this book we will use the normalized definition unless otherwise noted. In normalized loops, there is no difference between the two.

**DEFINITION
2.3**

Given a nest of n loops, the *iteration vector i* of a particular iteration of the innermost loop is a vector of integers that contains the iteration numbers for each of the loops in order of nesting level. In other words, the iteration vector is given by

$$i = \{i_1, i_2, \ldots, i_n\} \tag{2.1}$$

where i_k, $1 \leq k \leq n$, represents the iteration number for the loop at nesting level k.

A statement parameterized by a specific execution vector denotes the instance of that statement executed when the loop induction variables have the values in the execution vector. For example, $S[(2,1)]$ in

```
DO I = 1, 2
   DO J = 1, 2
      S
   ENDDO
ENDDO
```

represents the instance of statement S that occurs on the second iteration of the I-loop and the first iteration of the J-loop. The set of all possible iteration vectors for a statement is an *iteration space*. The iteration space of S in the above example is $\{(1,1), (1,2), (2,1), (2,2)\}$.

Because of the importance of execution order to dependence, iteration vectors need an ordering that corresponds to the execution order of their loops. Assuming the notation that i is a vector, i_k is the kth element of the vector i, and $i[1:k]$ is a k-vector consisting of the leftmost k elements of i, we can define *lexicographic order* on iteration vectors of length n as follows:

**DEFINITION
2.4**

Iteration i *precedes* iteration j, denoted $i < j$, if and only if (1) $i[1:n{-}1] < j[1:n{-}1]$ or (2) $i[1:n{-}1] = j[1:n{-}1]$ and $i_n < j_n$.

In other words, an iteration vector i precedes another iteration vector j if and only if any statement executed on the iteration described by i is executed before any statement on the iteration described by j. The equality relation on iteration vectors is easy to define—it corresponds to componentwise equality of iteration numbers. The relations $\leq$, $>$, and $\geq$ can also be defined on iteration vectors by the natural extensions to lexicographic ordering.

We now define dependence between statements in a common loop nest.

| **THEOREM** | *Loop Dependence* |
| 2.1 | |

There exists a dependence from statement S_1 to statement S_2 in a common nest of loops if and only if there exist two iteration vectors i and j for the nest, such that (1) $i < j$ or $i = j$ and there is a path from S_1 to S_2 in the body of the loop, (2) statement S_1 accesses memory location M on iteration i and statement S_2 accesses location M on iteration j, and (3) one of these accesses is a write.

This theorem follows directly from the definition of dependence. Condition (2) ensures that there is a path from the source to the sink of the dependence.

2.2.3   Dependence and Transformations

Dependence in programs is intended to be a tool for determining when it is safe to make certain program transformations. When we say that a transformation is "safe," we typically mean that the transformed program has the same "meaning" as the original program. In other words, we are not concerned with the correctness of the program originally presented to the compiler, but whether the transformed program does the same thing as the original.

But this raises the question: What program behaviors must be preserved? Certainly we don't need to preserve running time, since the entire point of these transformations is to improve performance. Informally, preservation of the observable program effects, such as the values and order of the outputs, seems to capture the essence of what we are trying to achieve.

Program Equivalence under Transformations

Dependence is traditionally associated with imperative languages, in which each statement reads from and stores into memory. In imperative programs, meaning is most logically defined in terms of the *state* of the computation. A state of a computation is the set of all values held in its memory locations; each distinct set of values (and locations) comprises a different state. Obviously, two computations that proceed through exactly the same set of states are identical, but such a strong definition of equivalence is too restrictive for optimizations because it provides little flexibility to rearrange the program steps. The real problem is that a program state specifies *all* the values of a program simultaneously. That means that programs that interchange the order of updates to different memory locations are not permitted, even though this transformation would have no effect on the outputs.

We need a definition of equivalence that is much more permissive in terms of the transformations it permits, while maintaining what the programmer expects in terms of correctness. For example, if a different algorithm that computes exactly the same answers could be substituted, that should be acceptable. Thus it should be permissible to substitute any stable sorting algorithm for bubble sort.

To achieve this effect, we should concentrate on the consistency of the observable program behavior. During most steps of a computation, internal state is externally invisible. Output statements exist precisely to make the "interesting" aspects—that is, the things the programmer is trying to compute—of internal state visible. Therefore, it is much more useful to say the following:

DEFINITION 2.5	Two computations are *equivalent* if, on the same inputs, they produce identical values for output variables at the time output statements are executed and the output statements are executed in the same order.

This definition permits different instruction sequences (some of which are more efficient than others) to compute the same outputs. Furthermore, it captures the notion that the only aspects of a computation that must be preserved by optimization are its outputs. If the term "output" is defined broadly enough, this definition will suffice for the purposes of this book.

This discussion raises the question: What about side effects of a computation? An example of a side effect is an exception, particularly one that is associated with an error. Such side effects have been a traditional source of problems for optimizing compilers, giving rise to an extensive literature on the "safety" of transformations [167]. It is clear that a compiler transformation should never introduce an error that would not have occurred in the original program. However, should transformations that eliminate error exceptions while maintaining the equivalence of outputs be permitted? The conventional answer for Fortran is "yes," but in languages like Java with stricter semantics and explicit exceptions, this may be unacceptable. Since this book focuses on Fortran and similar languages, we will permit transformations that eliminate exceptions or adjust the time at which those exceptions occur, so long as no transformation introduces an exception for a given input that would not have occurred on the original program with the same input.

Correctness of Dependence-Based Transformations

With these notions of the correctness of transformations in hand we are ready to address the role of dependence in establishing correct transformations. Most optimizations discussed in this book are "reordering transformations," defined as follows:

DEFINITION 2.6	A *reordering transformation* is any program transformation that merely changes the order of execution of the code, without adding or deleting any executions of any statements.

Since a reordering transformation does not delete any statement executions, any two executions that reference a common memory element *before* a reordering transformation will also reference the same memory element *after* that transformation. Hence, if there is a dependence between the statements before the transformation, there will also be one afterward. Note, however, that the transformation may *reverse* the order in which the statements reference the common memory location—thereby reversing the dependence (i.e., $S_1 \delta S_2$ before the transformation and $S_2 \delta S_1$ after the transformation). This will clearly lead to incorrect behavior at run time.

**DEFINITION
2.7**   A reordering transformation *preserves* a dependence if it preserves the relative execution order of the source and sink of that dependence.

Now we are ready to prove the central result concerning the role of dependences in transformations.

**THEOREM
2.2**   *Fundamental Theorem of Dependence*

Any reordering transformation that preserves every dependence in a program preserves the meaning of that program.

Proof We begin by considering loop-free programs that contain no conditional statements. Let $\{S_1, S_2, \ldots, S_n\}$ be the execution order in the original program and $\{i_1, i_2, \ldots, i_n\}$ be a permutation of the statement indices that represents the order of execution of statements in the reordered program; that is, $\{i_1, i_2, \ldots, i_n\}$ is a permutation of $\{1, 2, \ldots, n\}$ corresponding to the reordering of the statements. Assume that dependences are preserved, but that the meaning changes. This means that some output statement produces a different result from the corresponding output statement in the original program.

For the purposes of this discussion, we view output statements as simply computing another result, namely, the result being produced. In this model, the sequence of statements in the transformed program contains at least one statement, namely, the output statement, that produces an "incorrect" result in the sense that it is different from that produced by the corresponding statement in the original program. Let S_k be the first statement in the new order that produces an incorrect output. Because the statement is exactly the same as the statement in the original program, it must have found an incorrect value in one of its input memory locations. Since all the statements that have executed *before* S_k produce the same value they did in the original program, there are only three ways that S_k can see an incorrect input in a specific location *M*:

1. A statement S_m that originally stored its result into M before it was read by S_k now stores into M *after* it is read by S_k. This would mean that the reordering failed to preserve the true dependence $S_m \, \delta \, S_k$ in the original program, contrary to assumption.

2. A statement S_m that originally stored into M after it was read by S_k now writes M *before* S_k reads it. This would mean that the reordering failed to preserve an antidependence (that of $S_k \, \delta^{-1} \, S_m$), contrary to assumption.

3. Two statements that both wrote into M before it was read by S_k in the original order have had their relative order of execution reversed, causing the wrong value to be left in M. This would mean that the reordering failed to preserve an output dependence, contrary to assumption.

Since this exhausts the ways that S_k can get the wrong value, the result is proved by contradiction.

Loops. To extend this result to loops, simply note that the statement executions in the list can be viewed as statement instantiations that are indexed by the iteration vector. Then the same argument applies, providing that the correct loop iteration count is computed *before* any statement in the loop body is executed. This is necessary to ensure that the entire collection of statement instantiations is preserved. The normal convention for enforcing this restriction is to have a control dependence from a loop header to each statement in the body of the loop.

Programs with Conditionals. Because we do not yet have a definition of reordering transformations in the presence of conditionals, we will assume for now that a conditional is a single macro statement (i.e., an if-then-else statement) that is treated as a unit by reordering transformations. The result will be extended to more general transformations in Chapter 7. With that single limitation, the theorem is proved.

Theorem 2.2 leads us to the following definition:

DEFINITION 2.8   A transformation is said to be *valid* for the program to which it applies if it preserves all dependences in the program.

It should be clear from this theorem and its proof that a collection of valid transformations preserves the order of loads and stores to every memory location in the program—only input accesses can be reordered. Thus valid transformations preserve a condition that is stronger than equivalence as specified by Definition 2.1, as the following example shows:

```
L₀    DO I = 1, N
L₁       DO J = 1, 2
S₀          A(I,J) = A(I,J) + B
          ENDDO
S₁          T = A(I,1)
S₂          A(I,1) = A(I,2)
S₃          A(I,2) = T
          ENDDO
```

In this code, there is a dependence from S_0 to each of S_1, S_2, and S_3. Thus, a dependence-based compiler would prohibit interchanging the block of statements $\{S_1, S_2, S_3\}$ with loop L_1, even though the interchange leaves the same values in the array A. To see this, note that both A(I,1) and A(I,2) receive an identical update, so it does not matter whether that update occurs before or after the swap.

From Theorem 2.2 we can immediately conclude that two statements in a loop-free program can be run in parallel if there is no dependence between them. This is because the absence of dependence means that the relative ordering of the two statements is not important to the meaning of the program as represented by the outputs it produces. Unfortunately, this observation is not very helpful, since loop-free programs rarely have enough computation to be interesting. To extend this notion to loops we need to introduce concepts that help us reason about statement instances in loop nests.

2.2.4 Distance and Direction Vectors

It is convenient to characterize dependences by the distance between the source and sink of a dependence in the iteration space of the loop nest containing the statements involved in the dependence. We express this in terms of *distance vectors* and *direction vectors* [278].

DEFINITION 2.9

Suppose that there is a dependence from statement S_1 on iteration i of a loop nest to statement S_2 on iteration j; then the *dependence distance vector* $d(i,j)$ is defined as a vector of length n such that $d(i,j)_k = j_k - i_k$.

In some situations it is useful to work with a distance vector that is expressed in terms of the number of loop iterations that the dependence crosses. For that purpose we can define a normalized distance vector $d_N(i,j)$ as $d(i,j)/s$, where $s = \{s_1, s_2, \ldots, s_n\}$, the vector of loop step sizes. For the purposes of discussion in this chapter we will assume that all distance vectors are normalized. This implies that, given two iteration numbers i and j for statement instances involved in a dependence within a loop nest, $i < j$ if and only if $d(i,j) > 0$.

Distance vectors give rise to direction vectors as follows:

DEFINITION 2.10	Suppose that there is a dependence from statement S_1 on iteration i of a loop nest of n loops and statement S_2 on iteration j; then the *dependence direction vector $D(i,j)$* is defined as a vector of length n such that

$$D(i,j)_k = \begin{cases} \text{"<" if } d(i,j)_k > 0 \\ \text{"=" if } d(i,j)_k = 0 \\ \text{">" if } d(i,j)_k < 0 \end{cases}$$

One convenient mechanism for remembering the entries in direction vectors is to treat "<" and ">" as arrows. With that treatment, the arrow always points to the loop iteration that occurs first in a pair of iteration vectors for the source and sink of the dependence.

The direction vector for a dependence relates the iteration vector at the source of a dependence to the iteration vector at the sink. For example, in the loop

```
      DO I - 1, N
         DO J - 1, M
            DO K - 1, L
S₁             A(I+1,J,K-1) = A(I,J,K) + 10
            ENDDO
         ENDDO
      ENDDO
```

statement S_1 has a true dependence on itself with direction vector $(<,=,>)$, meaning that the outermost loop index at the source is less than the index at the sink, the middle loop index is equal at source and sink, and the innermost loop index is larger at the source than at the sink. Note that a dependence cannot exist if it has a direction vector whose leftmost non-"=" component is not "<" because that would mean that the sink of the dependence occurs before the source, which is impossible.

The reason for limiting distance and direction vectors and difference vectors to common loops is that these loops are the only ones that affect the relative execution order of statements. If two statement instances are contained in n common loops and the first n components of the two iteration vectors for these statements are equal, then their relative execution order is determined by textual position, regardless of any remaining components of the vectors.

Direction Vectors and Transformations

Direction vectors can be used as a basis for understanding loop reordering transformations because they summarize the relationship between the index vectors at the source and sink of a dependence. Chapter 5 will show how it is possible to determine the effect of various transformations on the direction vectors for dependences in the loop nest affected by the transformation. The following theorem explains how direction vectors can be used to test for legality of a transformation.

THEOREM
2.3

Direction Vector Transformation

Let *T* be a transformation that is applied to a loop nest and that does not rearrange the statements in the body of the loop. Then the transformation is valid if, after it is applied, none of the direction vectors for dependences with source and sink in the nest has a leftmost non- "=" component that is ">".

Proof The theorem follows directly from Theorem 2.2 because all of the dependences still exist and none of the dependences have been reversed in sense.

The principal impact of Theorem 2.3 is that if we can show how a transformation on a loop nest affects the direction vectors for dependences in that loop, we can use the theorem to determine when the transformation is legal. This will be used in Chapter 5 to establish correctness of loop interchange and several other transformations.

The Number of Dependences

A question that often arises when dealing with dependences is, How many dependences are there between a given pair of statements in a loop nest? Technically, we must say that there is one dependence for each statement instance that is the source of a dependence to another statement instance in the same loop nest. Thus, in the loop below, there is one dependence from statement S to itself for each iteration vector (i,j), such that $1 \le i \le 9$ and $1 \le j \le 10$.

```
      DO J = 1, 10
         DO I = 1, 10
S           A(I+1,J) = A(I,J) + X
         ENDDO
      ENDDO
```

This is because statement S with index values I = i and J = j creates a value in array A that is used in statement S when index I has the value $i + 1$ and index J has the value j. Thus, there is no dependence originating at statement instances on the last iteration of the I-loop because there is no subsequent iteration to consume the value. As a result of this analysis, we see that there are 90 distinct dependences in the loop.

In practice, no compiler can afford to keep track of this many dependences for each statement in each loop nest. Thus, we must seek ways of summarizing the dependences. For example, there is no difference between dependences that arise in different iterations of the outer loop, so long as it has at least one iteration. If we combine all the dependences for all these iterations, we can reduce the number of dependences to 9. Next we note that there is a great deal of symmetry of all these dependences: each one produces a value on one iteration and consumes it on the next, so all the dependences are true or flow dependences and all have a distance of 1. This suggests that we can reduce the number of dependences by keeping track only of the distinct distance vectors for each distinct dependence type. However, even this reduction can leave us with too many dependences, as the following loop nest illustrates:

```
      DO J = 1, 10
        DO I = 1, 99
S₁        A(I,J) = B(I,J) + X
S₂        C(I,J)= A(100-I,J) + Y
        ENDDO
      ENDDO
```

When $I = 1$, the loop stores into $A(1,J)$ at statement S_1. The same location is later used on the last iteration of the inner loop when $I = 99$. Thus there is a dependence from S_1 to S_2 of distance 98. When $I = 2$, it stores into $A(2,J)$, which is used when $I = 98$, yielding a distance of 96. Continuing in this manner we get even distances down to distance 0 on the iteration when $I = 50$.

On the next iteration, $I = 51$ and the distance becomes a negative 2. However, we know that no legal dependence can have a negative distance because this would indicate that the source of the dependence was executed before the sink. What this means is that the dependences for iterations where I is greater than 50 have their source and sink reversed; that is, they are antidependences from statement S_2 to statement S_1. Thus there are antidependences in the loop with all even distances up to and including 98. So there are a total of 50 different distances for true dependences from S_1 to S_2 and 49 different distances for antidependences from S_2 to S_1. Once again, this is too many.

To further reduce the number of distinct dependences that the compiler must keep track of, this book will adopt the convention that the total number of dependences between a given pair of references is equal to the number of distinct *direction vectors*, summed over all the types of dependences between those references. This is sufficient because most of the transformations that will be applied can be handled solely with a knowledge of direction vectors. To address transformations that require distances, we will keep track of distances only in those cases where the distance does not vary from iteration to iteration. In the last example above, there are only two direction vectors—$(=,<)$ and $(=,=)$—for the true dependence from S_1 to S_2. The antidependence from S_2 to S_1 has $(=,<)$ as its only direction vector. Thus, by our convention, there are a total of three distinct dependences in the loop nest.

2.2.5   Loop-Carried and Loop-Independent Dependences

The theory of data dependence described so far imposes two requirements that must be met for a statement S_2 to be data dependent on statement S_1:

1. There must exist a possible execution path such that statements S_1 and S_2 both reference the same memory location M.

2. The execution of S_1 that references M occurs before the execution of S_2 that references M.

In order for S_2 to depend upon S_1, it is necessary for some execution of S_1 to reference a memory location (as a store, if true dependence is considered) that is later referenced by an execution of S_2 (as a use, for true dependence). There are two possible ways that this pattern can occur:

1. S_1 can reference the common location on one iteration of a loop; on a subsequent iteration S_2 can reference the same location.

2. S_1 and S_2 can both reference the common location on the same loop iteration, but with S_1 preceding S_2 during execution of the loop iteration.

The first case is an example of *loop-carried dependence,* since the dependence exists only when the loop is iterated. The second case is an example of *loop-independent dependence,* since the dependence exists because of the position of the code within the loops. The following sections detail these types of dependence.

Loop-Carried Dependence

A loop-carried dependence arises because of the iteration of loops. The following Fortran segment demonstrates this idea:

```
      DO I = 1, N
S₁       A(I+1) = F(I)
S₂       F(I+1) = A(I)
      ENDDO
```

On every iteration of the I-loop other than the first, S_2 uses a value of A that was computed on the previous iteration by S_1; hence, statement S_2 has a true dependence on statement S_1. Likewise, statement S_1 uses a value of F computed by statement S_2 on the previous iteration (except for the first), and truly depends on statement S_2. Both of these dependences are carried by the loop. If any particular iteration of the loop is chosen and executed alone, no dependence exists.

DEFINITION 2.11	Statement S_2 has a *loop-carried dependence* on statement S_1 if and only if S_1 references location M on iteration i, S_2 references M on iteration j, and $d(i,j) > 0$ (that is, $D(i,j)$ contains a "<" as its leftmost non- "=" component).

The appearance of a nonzero component in $d(i,j)$ guarantees that the corresponding loop iterates at least once between the common references—hence the name "loop-carried dependence." It will be useful to classify carried dependences according to the relative order in the loop body of the statements involved.

DEFINITION 2.12	A loop-carried dependence from statement S_1 to statement S_2 is said to be *backward* if S_2 appears before S_1 in the loop body or if S_1 and S_2 are the same statement. The carried dependence is said to be *forward* if S_2 appears after S_1 in the loop body.

An important property of loop-carried dependence is the *level* of a dependence.

DEFINITION 2.13	The *level* of a loop-carried dependence is the index of the leftmost non-"=" of $D(i,j)$ for the dependence.

In other words, the level of the dependence is the nesting level of the outermost loop index that varies between the source and sink, where the outermost loop is taken to be at nesting level 1. The level of all the dependences in the previous example is 1, since $D(i,j)$ is (<) for every dependence. The level of the dependence in

```
        DO I = 1, 10
          DO J = 1, 10
            DO K = 1, 10
S₁             A(I,J,K+1) = A(I,J,K)
            ENDDO
          ENDDO
        ENDDO
```

is 3 because $D(i,j)$ is (=,=,<). Note that the dependence in this case is actually a collection of dependences, one for every iteration vector in the set {1:10,1:10,1:9}. In the future, we will associate a separate dependence between each pair of different subscripted array references. We will refer to all dependences for a single reference pair as being one dependence, but that dependence may have many direction vectors.

Dependence level is a useful concept for many reasons. One reason is that level very conveniently summarizes dependences. For example, the last fragment contains 900 total dependences. Since every iteration vector pair (i,j) that gives rise to a dependence has $d(i,j) = (0,0,1)$, dependence level conveniently characterizes all the dependences by a single property.

We can also use dependence level to help us choose which transformations to apply in a program and which to preclude. Sometimes we may decide to preclude transformations of a particular type because this guarantees the validity of other transformations that we wish to make.

DEFINITION
2.14

A dependence will be said to be *satisfied* if transformations that fail to preserve it are precluded.

To see how this definition is useful, consider the case where we wish to satisfy all dependences carried by a particular loop level.

THEOREM
2.4

Any reordering transformation that (1) preserves the iteration order of the level-k loop, (2) does not interchange any loop at level < k to a position inside the level-k loop, and (3) does not interchange any loop at level > k to a position outside the level-k loop preserves all level-k dependences.

Proof The direction vector $D(i,j)$ for any level-k dependence must have its leftmost "<" in the kth entry. That means that the directions in positions 1 through $k-1$ are all "=". Thus the source and sink of a level-k dependence are in the same iteration of loops 1 through $k-1$. Thus no reordering of the iterations of any of those loops can change the sense of the dependence, since these loops will remain at levels 1 through $k-1$ by hypothesis. In addition, no loop that is originally inside the level-k loop can become the carrier of one of its dependences because that would require that it be interchanged to the outside of that loop, which is precluded by hypothesis.

Since the order of iterations at level k is preserved, the direction in the kth position of $D(i,j)$ will remain "<". Thus the dependence must be preserved.

Theorem 2.4 tells us that we can satisfy any level-k dependence by declining to reorder the iterations of the level-k loop. This can be used to establish the validity of some powerful transformations. For example, the fragment in

```
      DO I = 1, 10
S₁       A(I+1) = F(I)
S₂       F(I+1) = A(I)
      ENDDO
```

is equivalent to

```
      DO I = 1, 10
S₂        F(I+1) = A(I)
S₁        A(I+1) = F(I)
      ENDDO
```

because all dependences are carried at level 1 and we retain the order of iteration of the level-1 loop. Statement order is irrelevant to loop-carried dependences.

Theorem 2.4 also establishes that arbitrary transformations are valid if they are made inside the deepest dependence level. For example, in the following code fragment, we can perform loop rearrangement and loop reversal on the inner two loops, once we have decided to run the outer loop sequentially in the original order.

```
      DO I = 1, 10
        DO J = 1, 10
          DO K = 1, 10
S               A(I+1,J+2,K+3) = A(I,J,K) + B
          ENDDO
        ENDDO
      ENDDO
```

The only dependence in this example is carried at level 1. Therefore, the code is equivalent to

```
      DO I = 1, 10
        DO K = 10, 1, -1
          DO J = 1, 10
S               A(I+1,J+2,K+3) = A(I,J,K) + B
          ENDDO
        ENDDO
      ENDDO
```

obtained by interchanging the J- and K-loops and reversing the K-loop, because we maintain the order of iteration of the level-1 I-loop.

Given the importance of dependence level, we will use special notation—a subscript on the dependence symbol—to represent it. That is, a level-l dependence between S_1 and S_2 will be denoted $S_1 \, \delta_l \, S_2$.

Loop-Independent Dependences

In contrast to loop-carried dependence, loop-independent dependences arise as a result of relative statement position. Thus, loop-independent dependences determine the order in which code is executed within a nest of loops, while loop-carried dependences determine the order in which loops must be iterated.

DEFINITION 2.15

Statement S_2 has a *loop-independent dependence* on statement S_1 if and only if there exist two iteration vectors i and j such that (1) statement S_1 refers to memory location M on iteration i, S_2 refers to M on iteration j, and $i = j$; and (2) there is a control flow path from S_1 to S_2 within the iteration.

Intuitively, Definition 2.15 states that a loop-independent dependence exists when two statements reference the same memory location within a single iteration of all their common loops. A very obvious example is

```
     DO I = 1,10
S₁       A(I) = ...
S₂.      ... = A(I)
     ENDDO
```

On every iteration of the I-loop, statement S_2 uses the value just computed by statement S_1, thus creating a loop-independent dependence.
    A less obvious example is

```
     DO I = 1, 9
S₁       A(I) =
S₂       ... = A(10-I)
     ENDDO
```

On the fifth iteration of the loop, statement S_1 stores into A(5) while statement S_2 fetches from A(5). That dependence is loop independent. All other dependences in the segment are carried by the loop. The reason that separate iteration vectors i and j appear in the definition is illustrated by the following:

```
     DO I = 1, 10
S₁       A(I) = ...
     ENDDO
     DO I = 1,10
S₂       ... = A(20-I)
     ENDDO
```

Statement S_2 uses the value of A(10) computed by statement S_1 on the 10th iteration of the first loop, creating a loop-independent dependence. No common loop is necessary for loop-independent dependences, since they arise from statement position.
    Note that if we preserve the order of statements involved in loop-independent dependences, we guarantee that those dependences are satisfied.

THEOREM   If there is a loop-independent dependence from S_1 to S_2, any reordering trans-
2.5   formation that does not move statement instances between iterations and
preserves the relative order of S_1 and S_2 in the loop body preserves that
dependence.

> **Proof**   By definition, S_2 and S_1 reference a location M on iteration vectors i and j such
> that $i = j$, and S_2 follows S_1. A reordering transformation that maps i into i'
> and j into j' must have $i' = j'$. Since neither statement can be moved out of its
> original loop iteration and since S_2 follows S_1, then the criteria for a loop-
> independent dependence are still met.

To see why we need to prohibit movement of statement iterations, note that
the following code

```
       DO I = 1, N
S₁        A(I) = B(I) + C
S₂        D(I) = A(I) + E
       ENDDO
```

could be transformed to

```
       D(1) = A(1) + E
       DO I = 2, N
S₁        A(I-1) = B(I-1) + C
S₂        D(I) = A(I) + E
       ENDDO
       A(N) = B(N) + C
```

This is still a reordering transformation since all instances of statements S_1 and S_2
are executed. Furthermore, the transformation preserves the order of those two
statements within the loop body. Nevertheless, by moving statement instances out
of the loop, it converts a loop-independent true dependence to a backward-carried
antidependence, making the transformation invalid.

Given the properties of loop-independent dependences established in Theorem 2.5, the natural extension of level notation utilized in loop-carried dependence
is to denote loop-independent dependence by an infinite level (that is, S_2 depends
on S_1 with a loop-independent dependence is denoted $S_1 \delta_\infty S_2$). That level indicates that no ordering of loops can preserve the dependence. Note that the direction vector for a loop-independent dependence has entries that are all "=".

Theorems 2.4 and 2.5 illustrate clearly how loop-carried and loop-independent
dependences complement each other. A loop-carried dependence is satisfied so long
as certain loops are iterated in the original order, regardless of the statement order

within a specific iteration. A loop-independent dependence is satisfied so long as the statement order is maintained, regardless of the order in which the loops are iterated.

Loop-independent and loop-carried dependences partition all possible data dependences. To see this, it is only necessary to note that the existence of a dependence $S_1 \delta S_2$ requires that S_1 be executed before S_2. This can happen in only two instances:

1. when the distance vector for the dependence is greater than 0, or

2. when the distance vector equals 0 and S_1 occurs before S_2 textually.

These are precisely the criteria for loop-carried and loop-independent dependences, respectively. If neither of these is the case and S_1 and S_2 reference a common memory element, then S_2 is executed before S_1, and the dependence is actually $S_2 \delta S_1$.

Iteration Reordering

We conclude this section with a result about the validity of iteration reordering.

THEOREM 2.6

Iteration Reordering

A transformation that reorders the iterations of a level-k loop, without making any other changes, is valid if the loop carries no dependence.

Proof Assume that the level-k loop carries no dependence but some order of its iterations fails to preserve a dependence in the original program. Consequently, there must exist a dependence in the original program that is reversed by this transformation. This cannot be a loop-independent dependence, by Theorem 2.5. Therefore, it must be a carried dependence. There are two cases:

1. The dependence is carried by a loop outside the loop in question. Thus its level must be $k - 1$ or less. Since reordering iterations at level k does not affect loops at levels 1 to $k - 1$, any dependence carried at those levels must be preserved by Theorem 2.4. Thus the dependence cannot be carried by an outer loop.

2. The dependence is carried by a loop that is inside the loop in question. Since the direction vector for the dependence must have an "=" in the kth position, reordering the loop cannot change the direction. Therefore, the direction vector must still have "<" in the leftmost position, so the transformation is valid by Theorem 2.3.

Thus the theorem is established by contradiction.

2.3 Simple Dependence Testing

Dependence testing methods will be extensively discussed in Chapter 3. However, since some intuition on how dependences are computed is necessary in order to understand how dependence-based transformations work, we present an intuitive introduction in this section.

We begin by stating the general condition for loop dependence in more concrete terms.

THEOREM 2.7

Let α and β be iteration vectors within the iteration space of the following loop nest:

```
DO i₁ = L₁, U₁, S₁
    DO i₂ = L₂, U₂, S₂
        ...
        DO iₙ = Lₙ, Uₙ, Sₙ
S₁          A(f₁(i₁,...,iₙ),...,fₘ(i₁,...,iₙ)) = ...
S₂          ... = A(g₁(i₁,...,iₙ),...,gₘ(i₁,...,iₙ))
        ENDDO
        ...
    ENDDO
ENDDO
```

A dependence exists from S_1 to S_2 if and only if there exist values of α and β such that (1) α is lexicographically less than or equal to β and (2) the following system of *dependence equations* is satisfied:

$$f_i(\alpha) = g_i(\beta) \text{ for all } i, 1 \le i \le m \tag{2.2}$$

Proof This is a direct application of Theorem 2.1. If $\alpha < \beta$, condition (1) in Theorem 2.1 holds. Otherwise if $\alpha = \beta$, condition (1) holds because there is clearly a path from S_1 to S_2 in the loop nest. Thus, condition (1) in Theorem 2.7 is equivalent to condition (1) in Theorem 2.1.

Equation 2.2 means that the index values for the array A are equal on iterations α and β, so these equations are equivalent to condition (2) of Theorem 2.1. Since S_1 is a write, condition (3) of Theorem 2.1 also holds, so the theorem must apply, establishing the desired result.

While Theorem 2.7 can be easily generalized, we will for the moment assume that the sink and source of a potential dependence are contained in exactly the same loops.

In order to develop some intuition behind dependence, we will present a simple Δ-notation, which is the basis for the Delta test to be discussed in Section

3.4.1. This notation tends to make it intuitively easier to visualize dependences in simple cases.

Recall from the previous section that a dependence exists whenever the potential source accesses a memory location M on iteration i, then some number of iterations later on iteration j the sink accesses the same location M. Given that the vast majority of subscripts are simple, with a single loop index plus or minus a constant per subscript entry, an easy way to understand dependences is to view the potential source and sink as being at distance Δ from each other. That is, assuming that the source accesses M on iteration I_0, then the sink accesses M on some later iteration $I_0 + \Delta I$, where ΔI is the number of iterations between the accesses. For the simple form of most subscripts, using this notation provides a quick, intuitive way of computing dependences.

As an illustration, consider the following loop:

```
      DO I = 1, N
S        A(I+1) = A(I) + B
      ENDDO
```

To test for true dependence, assume that the left-hand side of statement S accesses M on iteration I_0 and that the right-hand side accesses the same location ΔI iterations later. Then $A(I_0 + 1)$ and $A(I_0 + \Delta I)$ must both refer to memory location M. For this to be so, we must have

$$I_0 + 1 = I_0 + \Delta I$$

Simplifying, this yields $\Delta I = 1$. Since 1 is greater than 0 (meaning it does come later) and less than the upper bound (so it does get executed), there is a true dependence with distance 1 and direction vector ($<$). Applying the same method to tests for an antidependence yields $\Delta I = -1$, showing no dependence. Because the form of the subscript is simple, the deltas are the same for every iteration of the loop and hence the dependence distance is consistent.

In a case with multiple subscripts, such as this code fragment

```
DO I = 1, 100
   DO J = 1, 100
      DO K = 1, 100
         A(I+1,J,K) = A(I,J,K+1) + B
      ENDDO
   ENDDO
ENDDO
```

we get the following index expression equations:

$$I_0 + 1 = I_0 + \Delta I; \quad J_0 = J_0 + \Delta J; \quad K_0 = K_0 + \Delta K + 1;$$

The solutions to these equations are

$$\Delta I = 1; \quad \Delta J = 0; \quad \Delta K = -1$$

and the corresponding direction vector is $(<,=,>)$.

For a slightly more complex example, consider the following:

```
DO I = 1, 100
   DO J = 1, 100
      A(I+1,J) = A(I,5) + B
   ENDDO
ENDDO
```

Solving the system of equations resulting from this loop gives

$$\Delta I = 1 \text{ and } J_0 = 5$$

The first result tells us that the dependence distance in the I-dimension is uniformly 1, for all values of I, since I is unconstrained. The second result, on the other hand, tells us that at the source of the dependence J_0 is a constant 5. Since the distance is unconstrained, we must assume that any distance between −4 and 95 (the minimum and maximum permitted by the loop bounds) is realized.

A side observation on this example is that any time a loop index does not appear in any subscript at either the source or sink, its distance is unconstrained; that is, it can take on any legal distance. In particular, the direction corresponding to that index is "*", which denotes the union of all three directions. Thus in the following loop

```
DO I = 1, 100
   DO J = 1, 100
      A(I+1) = A(I) + B(J)
   ENDDO
ENDDO
```

the direction vector for the dependence carried by the I-loop is $(<,*)$.

As a final note, it may happen that testing with the assumption that one reference is the source and another is the sink may lead to the appearance of a ">" in the leftmost direction vector position. This does not mean that the dependence is illegal, but rather that there is a dependence of the opposite type in the reverse direction. For example, if the previous code fragment had the J-loop outermost

```
DO J = 1, 100
   DO I = 1, 100
      A(I+1) = A(I) + B(J)
   ENDDO
ENDDO
```

testing would produce the direction vector $(*,<)$ or $\{(<,<), (=,<), (>,<)\}$. The first direction corresponds to a level-1 true dependence. The second direction vector corresponds to a level-2 true dependence, and the third corresponds to a level-1 antidependence with direction vector $(<,>)$. This exists because when $J = 1$ and $I = 2$ the statement reads $A(2)$, and when $J = 2$ and $I = 1$, the statement stores into $A(2)$.

2.4 Parallelization and Vectorization

We conclude the chapter with a discussion of the application of dependence to automatic parallelization and vectorization. Although vectorization can be viewed as a special case of parallelization, we will treat it second because it involves the additional transformation of loop distribution.

2.4.1 Parallelization

The standard way to parallelize a loop is to convert each separate iteration to a parallel thread and run these threads asynchronously. In some sense, this is a reordering transformation in which the original order of iterations can be converted into an undetermined order. Furthermore, because the loop body is not an atomic operation, statements in two different iterations may run simultaneously. By Theorem 2.2, the parallelization is valid if it does not reverse the sense of any dependence. The only way we can ensure this, short of explicit synchronization, is to prohibit any dependences between the iterations we wish to run in parallel.

THEOREM 2.8

Loop Parallelization

It is valid to convert a sequential loop to a parallel loop if the loop carries no dependence.

Proof For the transformation to be valid, the transformed program must be valid for any schedule of execution. From the Iteration Reordering Theorem (Theorem 2.6) we know that if the loop carries no dependence, it is valid to arrange the iterations into any order. However, in the case of parallelism it is possible to interleave individual statements in parallel iterations. To establish the theorem, we must show that this cannot cause a dependence to be reversed.

Assume that a dependence is reversed on some schedule of a parallel loop. That means that the sink of the dependence occurs before the source in that schedule. Clearly, the dependence cannot be one that is loop independent or carried at a level within the parallel loop, because in that case, the source and sink occur within a single iteration. Since that iteration is executed by a single thread, the order of all statement instances within it is preserved. Therefore, the dependence must be carried by a loop outside the parallel loop. But by Theorem 2.4, this dependence is preserved by any reordering transformation that does not affect the order of the carrier loop. Thus the theorem is established.

2.4.2 Vectorization

Recall from Section 1.3.2 that the task of vectorization is to determine whether statements in an inner loop can be vectorized by directly rewriting them in Fortran 90. Theorem 2.8 from the previous section tells us that any single-statement loop that carries no dependence can be directly vectorized because that loop can be run in parallel. Thus the following loop

```
DO I = 1, N
    X(I) = X(I) + C
ENDDO
```

can be safely rewritten as

```
X(1:N) = X(1:N) + C
```

On the other hand, in

```
DO I = 1, N
    X(I+1) = X(I) + C
ENDDO
```

which carries a dependence, the transformation to the statement

```
X(2:N+1) = X(1:N) + C
```

would be incorrect. On each iteration, the sequential version uses a value of X that is computed on the previous iteration, while the Fortran 90 statement uses only original values of X.

Given the Loop Parallelization Theorem (Theorem 2.8), a natural question to ask is, Can any statements in loops that carry dependences be directly vectorized? This question is motivated by the following example:

```
      DO I = 1, N
S₁       A(I+1) = B(I) + C
S₂       D(I) = A(I) + E
      ENDDO
```

This loop carries a dependence ($S_1 \delta S_2$) because it stores into A on one iteration and loads from A on the next.

However, the direct transliteration of the loop into Fortran 90 has the same meaning as the sequential loop.

```
S₁   A(2:N+1) = B(1:N) + C
S₂   D(1:N) = A(1:N) + E
```

The parallel version of the second statement uses elements A(2:N) defined by the previous loop, as it does in the sequential loop. This apparent contradiction can be explained by the fact that the process of vectorization incorporated an extra transformation, called *loop distribution*. The effect is as if the loop were first transformed into two different loops

```
      DO I = 1, N
S₁       A(I+1) = B(I) + C
      ENDDO
      DO I = 1, N
S₂       D(I) = A(I) + E
      ENDDO
```

each of which can be directly vectorized. In this case the carried dependence was forward, but vectorization can take place even when the carried dependence is backward, as in the following example:

```
      DO I = 1, N
S₂       D(I) = A(I) + E
S₁       A(I+1) = B(I) + C
      ENDDO
```

Obviously, this loop can be vectorized if the statements in the loop body are interchanged because it then becomes identical to the previous case. The interchange is legal, since there are no loop-independent dependences between the statements.

On the other hand, if there is a backward-carried dependence *and* a loop-independent dependence between the statements, they cannot be vectorized because the interchange above is illegal:

```
      DO I = 1, N
S₁       B(I) = A(I) + E
S₂       A(I+1) = B(I) + C
      ENDDO
```

Here the backward loop-carried dependence cannot be eliminated by distribution because we cannot interchange the statements in the loop body due to the loop-independent dependence involving array B. This is intuitively consistent with our understanding of vectorization. To vectorize a statement, we must be able to distribute the loop around it. To do that we must be able to compute all inputs to any iteration of the distributed loop before it is entered. The cycle of dependences makes this impossible.

These observations are formalized in the following theorem, which establishes the general conditions under which statements in a loop can be vectorized.

THEOREM
2.9

Loop Vectorization

A statement contained in at least one loop can be vectorized by directly rewriting in Fortran 90 if the statement is not included in any cycle of dependences.

Proof Assume that the statement is not included in any cycle. Then the algorithm given in Figure 2.1 will correctly vectorize the statement.

Recalling earlier discussions, the key semantic difference between a statement in a Fortran 77 DO-loop and its Fortran 90 vector analog is that the vector version must fetch all inputs before storing any outputs, while the DO-loop may intermix loads and stores. Thus, if a statement contained in a loop has all its inputs available at the beginning of the loop, that statement can be correctly rewritten as an array assignment in Fortran 90.

The algorithm in Figure 2.1 groups the statements in the same loop into a totally ordered sequence of statement groups in which each statement is either part of a cycle in a dependence graph (also called a *recurrence*) or a single statement that is not part of a cycle. This reordering is equivalent to distributing loops around dependence cycles and vectorizing statements that are not part of any cycle. The distribution is correct because there can be no backward edges from later cycles to earlier ones (topological ordering guarantees that), so that all necessary inputs will be available at the start of each distributed loop. The vectorization is legal because all the input values needed by a group from outside the group are available before the group begins executing, given that the ordering is consistent with dependence. As a result, any vectorization performed by the algorithm is correct.

Theorem 2.9 establishes a sufficient condition for vectorizability, but it is much stronger than it needs to be, as we will see in the next section.

procedure *vectorize(L,D)*
    // *L* is the maximal loop nest containing the statement.
    // *D* is the dependence graph for statements in *L*.
    find the set $\{S_1, S_2, \ldots, S_m\}$ of maximal strongly connected
        regions in the dependence graph *D* restricted to *L*
        (use Tarjan's strongly connected components algorithm [256]);
    construct L_π from *L* by reducing each S_i to a single node and
        compute D_π, the dependence graph naturally induced on
        L_π by *D*;
    let $\{\pi_1, \pi_2, \ldots, \pi_m\}$ be the *m* nodes of L_π numbered in an order
        consistent with D_π (use topological sort to do the ordering);
    for *i* = 1 **to** *m* **do begin**
      if π_i is a dependence cycle **then**
        generate a DO-loop around the statements in π_i;
      else
        directly rewrite the single statement p_i in Fortran 90,
            vectorizing it with respect to every loop containing it;
    end
end

Figure 2.1 Simple vectorization.

2.4.3   An Advanced Vectorization Algorithm

The problem with the simple vectorization algorithm in Figure 2.1 is that it misses opportunities for vectorization. Consider the following simple example:

```
DO I = 1, N
   DO J = 1, M
S        A(I+1,J) = A(I,J) + B
   ENDDO
ENDDO
```

If we construct the dependence graph using the intuitive approach from Section 2.3, we see that there is a dependence from S to itself with the distance vector (1,0) and direction vector (<,=). Thus, statement S is contained in a dependence cycle, so the simple algorithm will not vectorize it.

On the other hand, the self-dependence is carried at level 1 in the nest. Theorem 2.4 tells us that we can ensure that the dependence is preserved by ensuring that no change of iteration order is made to the level-1 loop; that is, running the outer loop sequentially is enough to ensure that the dependence is preserved. This suggests that, once we have ensured that the dependence will be satisfied, we can vectorize the inner loop to yield

```
      DO I = 1, N
S         A(I+1,1:M) = A(I,1:M) + B
      ENDDO
```

In general, Theorem 2.4 tells us that a level-k dependence can be satisfied by running all loops outside of and including the loop at level k sequentially. Thus, even if a statement is in a recurrence, we may be able to vectorize it by running *some* loops sequentially.

These observations suggest a recursive approach to the problem of multidimensional vectorization: First, attempt to generate vector code at the outermost loop level. If dependences prevent that, then run the outer loop sequentially, thereby satisfying the dependences carried by that loop, and try again one level deeper, ignoring dependences carried by the outer loop. This approach is elaborated in the procedure *codegen* presented in Figure 2.2 [168, 21].

Codegen is called initially on a whole program at level 1 (the outermost level). The first step is to partition the program into *piblocks*, where a piblock is a strongly

---

procedure *codegen*(R,k,D)

    // R is the region for which we must generate code.
    // k is the minimum nesting level of possible parallel loops.
    // D is the dependence graph among statements in R.
    find the set $\{S_1, S_2, \ldots, S_m\}$ of maximal strongly connected regions in the
        dependence graph D restricted to R (use Tarjan's algorithm);
    construct R_π from R by reducing each S_i to a single node and
        compute D_π, the dependence graph naturally induced on
        R_π by D;
    let $\{\pi_1, \pi_2, \ldots, \pi_m\}$ be the m nodes of R_π numbered in an order
        consistent with D_π (use topological sort to do the numbering);
    for i = 1 **to** m **do begin**
        if π_i is cyclic **then begin**
            generate a level-k DO statement;
            let D_i be the dependence graph consisting of all
                dependence edges in D that are at level $k + 1$ or greater
                and are internal to π_i;
            codegen$(\pi_i, k+1, D_i)$;
            generate the level-k ENDDO statement;
        end
        else
            generate a vector statement for π_i in $\rho(\pi_i) - k + 1$ dimensions,
            where $\rho(\pi_i)$ is the number of loops containing π_i;
    end
end *codegen*

Figure 2.2 Multilevel vector code generation algorithm.

connected region as defined by Tarjan's algorithm [256]. The definition of a strongly connected region permits both cyclic and acyclic piblocks; however, any acyclic blocks are single statements that do not depend upon themselves. Next, the strongly connected regions are topologically sorted according to the dependence relation [185]. Finally, each region is examined in order. If the region is acyclic (thus necessarily consisting of one statement), then a parallel form of the statement is generated in the remaining dimensions. If the region is cyclic, the level-1 DO-loop is generated for that region, the level-1 dependences are deleted because they are guaranteed to be satisfied, and *codegen* is called recursively for the region with the set of dependences at level 2 and deeper.

To illustrate the power of *codegen*, consider its application to the following program fragment.

```
       DO I = 1, 100
S₁        X(I) = Y(I) + 10
          DO J = 1, 100
S₂           B(J) = A(J,N)
             DO K = 1, 100
S₃              A(J+1,K) = B(J) + C(J,K)
             ENDDO
S₄           Y(I+J) = A(J+1, N)
          ENDDO
       ENDDO
```

The dependence graph for this program is given in Figure 2.3. The program contains the following dependences:

- There is both a level-1 and a loop-independent true dependence from S_2 to S_3 by virtue of the use of B(J) in both statements. To see this we follow the simple dependence testing procedure in Section 2.3. Since the index I does not occur in either subscript, the distance vector for the outer loop is unconstrained and the direction is "*". On the other hand, the references to J at the source and the sink give rise to the equation $J_0 = J_0 + \Delta J$. This implies that $\Delta J = 0$ and the direction for the J-loop is "=". Thus the set of direction vectors associated with B(J) is (*,=) or {(<,=), (=,=), (>,=)}. The first vector gives us the level-1 true dependence, and the second gives us the loop-independent true dependence. The third direction corresponds to an antidependence in the opposite direction, discussed in the next paragraph.

- There is an antidependence from S_3 to S_2, carried by the I-loop, because S_3 uses B(J) before S_2 stores into it on the next iteration of the I-loop.

- There is a loop-independent true dependence from S_3 to S_4 by virtue of the definition of A(J+1,K) in S_3 and the use of A(J+1,N) in statement S_4. Dependence is presumed to exist because, in the absence of other information about the value of N, it must be assumed that N can lie in the range of

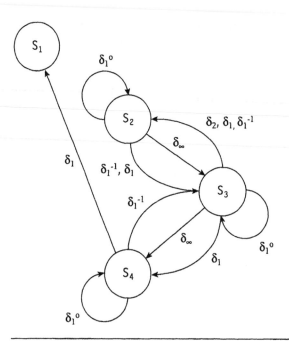

Figure 2.3 Example dependence graph.

K (between 1 and 100). Note that if we apply our dependence testing procedure to this pair of statements with S_3 as the source, we get the set of directions $(*,=)$ or $\{(<,=), (=,=), (>,=)\}$. This means that there is also a true dependence carried by the I-loop between these two references and an antidependence in the reverse direction, corresponding to the first and third direction vectors, respectively. The antidependence is discussed in the next paragraph.

- There is an antidependence from S_4 to S_3, carried by the I-loop, because S_4 uses $A(J+1,N)$ on one iteration of the I-loop; on a subsequent iteration of that loop (when the value of J is the same and $K = N$), S_3 stores into the same location. This corresponds to the third direction in the previous paragraph.

- There is a true dependence carried by the I-loop (level 1) from S_4 to S_1 because S_4 can store into $Y(I+1)$ on one iteration and S_1 reads from it on the next iteration of the I-loop. Using the simple dependence testing procedure with S_4 as the source yields the equation

$$I_0 + J = I_0 + \Delta I$$

which means that $\Delta I = J$. Since J is always greater than 0, we have the direction "<" and the dependence is true.

- There is a true dependence carried by the J-loop (level 2) from S_3 to S_2 because S_3 stores into A(J+1,K) on one iteration of the J-loop and reads from the same location via its access to A(J,N) on the next iteration. Once again, it must be assumed that N is between 1 and 100. The direction vector for this dependence is (*,<), which also gives rise to a dependence and a reverse antidependence carried by the I-loop, which are shown as extra labels in Figure 2.3.

- Statements S_2, S_3, and S_4 all have output dependences upon themselves because their left-hand sides have one less dimension than the number of loops containing them. Hence, the outer loop must cause stores into the same array element on different iterations. In the simple dependence testing procedure, we would see this because the direction for the I-loop would be "*".

Codegen called at the outermost level will produce two piblocks: one cyclic piblock consisting of S_2, S_3, and S_4, and one acyclic piblock consisting of S_1. As a result, S_1 will be vectorized, but must follow the code for the multistatement piblock, due to topological ordering constraints. Thus, the code produced at this level is

```
DO I = 1, 100
    codegen({S₂,S₃,S₄},2,D₂)
ENDDO
X(1:100) = Y(1:100) + 10
```

In order to effect the call to *codegen* at level 2, all level-1 dependences are stripped off, leaving the dependence graph depicted in Figure 2.4.

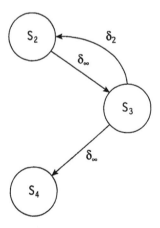

Figure 2.4 Dependence graph for $\{S_2,S_3,S_4\}$ after removing level-1 dependences.

Vector code can now be generated for S_4, but S_2 and S_3 are still in a recurrence. The code produced so far is

```
DO I = 1, 100
    DO J = 1, 100
        codegen({S2,S3},3,D3)
    ENDDO
    Y(I+1:I+100) = A(2:101,N)
ENDDO
X(1:100) = Y(1:100) + 10
```

The final call to *codegen* requires that level-2 dependence be removed, leaving the graph in Figure 2.5.

Both remaining statements can be executed as vector operations. S_2 has no dimensions for the vector execution, so it produces a simple scalar statement. The final code is

```
DO I = 1, 100
    DO J = 1, 100
        B(J) = A(J,N)
        A(J+1,1:100) = B(J) + C(J,1:100)
    ENDDO
    Y(I+1:I+100) = A(2:101,N)
ENDDO
X(1:100) = Y(1:100) + 10
```

Even though *codegen* is a simple, elegant algorithm, it is able to effect dramatic changes in a program. In the previous example, all available vectorization has been exposed, requiring a fairly dramatic change in statement order, by a straightforward application of the algorithm.

The correctness of procedure *codegen* follows quite easily from the theorems in this chapter. If a region is cyclic, then Theorem 2.4 guarantees that any level-k

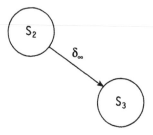

Figure 2.5 Dependence graph for $\{S_2, S_3\}$ after removing level-2 dependences.

dependences will be satisfied by running the k-loop (and by the nature of the algorithm, loops 1 through $k - 1$) sequentially. Thus, the statements within the then-clause only ignore dependences that have been satisfied by the sequential loops. Once a level has been reached where all recurrences have been eliminated by sequentially executing DO-loops, Theorem 2.9 guarantees that the remaining loops may be correctly run in parallel. Note that such a level *must* be reached (guaranteeing termination), since loop-independent dependences are inherently acyclic and all loop-carried dependences will eventually be satisfied, if only by running all loops sequentially (thereby generating code that is parallel in 0 dimensions). Finally, the topological sort guarantees that loop-independent dependences will be preserved by virtue of Theorem 2.5. Although it has not been explicitly proved, it is also true that loop-carried dependences outside of a recurrence can be preserved by topological sorting without requiring that the statements be contained in common loops.

It should be clear that, when *codegen* is applied to a loop nest, its effectiveness is limited by the precision of the dependence graph. In Chapter 3, we provide details on how to construct an effective and accurate dependence testing procedure. We return to algorithm *codegen* in Chapter 5.

2.5 **Summary**

Dependence is the principal tool used by compilers in analyzing and transforming programs for execution on parallel and vector machines. Any transformation that reorders the execution of statements in the program preserves correctness if the transformation preserves the order of source and sink of every dependence in the program. This can be used as an effective tool to determine when it is safe to parallelize or vectorize a loop.

Dependences can be characterized by several different properties. The *type* of a dependence—true, anti-, or output—tells whether it corresponds to a write before a read, a read before a write, or a write before a write. Dependences in loops have special properties. A dependence *direction vector* describes the relationship (<, =, or >) between the values of the loop indices for the nest at the source and sink of the dependence. The *distance vector* gives the number of iterations crossed by the dependence for each index in the loop nest. A dependence is said to be *loop independent* if its direction vector entries are all "=". Otherwise it is *loop carried*. The *level* of a loop-carried dependence is the nesting level of the loop that corresponds to the "leftmost non-"="" direction in the direction vector.

The usefulness of these concepts is illustrated in a simple and efficient algorithm for *vectorization*, shown in Figure 2.2. Methods for constructing the dependence graph, introduced briefly in this chapter, are discussed in detail in Chapter 3.

2.6 **Case Studies**

Procedure *codegen* was originally designed to be at the heart of the PFC vectorization system. It was implemented in PL/1 using a collection of PL/1 preprocessor macros to implement the sets, so that the actual implementation resembled the sample code in Figure 2.2 quite closely. Over the years, the procedure was generalized to include a number of the transformations that will be presented in Chapter 5. Throughout these additions, the basic structure was retained. The *codegen* structure was later adopted into both the IBM VS Fortran Vectorizer [243] and the Ardent Titan compiler [24].

The original implementation of PFC used a simplified representation of dependence that did not include full direction vectors, but rather identified the level of each carried dependence in the program and distinguished carried dependences from loop-independent ones. This representation is described in more detail in Section 3.8.

2.7 **Historical Comments and References**

The earliest expositions of data dependence and its application to vectorization and program transformation were by Lamport [195, 196] and Kuck, Muraoka, and Chen [191, 219]. In the context of the Parallelizer system, Lamport developed the concepts of iteration spaces, difference vectors, and a notion similar to direction vectors. He also had notions similar to true dependence, antidependence, and output dependence, although Kuck [189] was the first to precisely characterize and name these. Statement dependences were determined using simple but effective data dependence tests. Lamport presents an algorithm for vectorization based on a criterion that precisely partitions loops that can be correctly vectorized from those that cannot. This criterion, called "tree inconsistency," is equivalent to the notion of cycles in the dependence graph, discussed in Section 2.4.2.

In the Parafrase system, Kuck and his colleagues [191, 219] developed a notion of dependence that is much cleaner than that used in the Parallelizer: data dependences are clearly classified into true dependences, antidependences, and output dependences, and sophisticated tests are used to determine the presence or absence of dependence. Because of its clear definition of dependence, Parafrase has a simple test for detecting vector statements: any statement can be executed in vector so long as it does not depend upon itself. As a result, a transitive closure of the dependence graph is used to partition vectorizable and nonvectorizable statements. Wolfe [283] developed the approach to direction vectors as presented in this chapter, and applied them to a number of reordering transformations including loop interchange and vectorization.

Kennedy was the first to note the importance of dependence levels and the application of Tarjan's algorithm to this problem; the two algorithms presented in this book are due to him [168]. Allen precisely characterized reordering transformations as the range of transformations to which dependence could be applied. Many researchers have developed specific transformations based on dependence, including loop interchange [280, 19], loop skewing [195, 281], parallelization [52, 25], node splitting [190], and loop fusion [1, 269].

The characterization of loop-carried dependences and loop-independent dependences was first noted by Allen and Kennedy [16, 21]. The properties of each classification, as well as the refined vectorization algorithm based on the level of dependences, was also developed by Allen and Kennedy.

Dependence testing has been discussed by a number of authors [21, 32, 283, 285]. The informal testing strategy is from Goff, Kennedy, and Tseng [123]. Dependence testing is discussed in much more detail in Chapter 3.

Exercises

2.1 Using the simple procedure for dependence, construct all the dependences for the loop nest below and provide (a) direction vector(s), (b) distance vector(s), (c) loop level, and (d) types, for each one.

```
DO K = 1, 100
   DO J = 1, 100
      DO I = 1, 100
         A(I+1,J+2,K+1) = A(I,J,K+1) + B
      ENDDO
   ENDDO
ENDDO
```

2.2 Construct all direction vectors for the following loop and indicate the type of dependence associated with each.

```
DO K = 1, 100
   DO J = 1, 100
      DO I = 1, 100
         A(I+1,J,K) = A(I,J,5) + B
      ENDDO
   ENDDO
ENDDO
```

2.3 Can the loop in Exercise 2.2 be parallelized? If so give a parallel version.

2.4 Construct all the direction vectors for the dependences shown in Figure 2.3. For each direction that corresponds to a fixed distance, show that distance.

2.5 Consider the following loop:

```
        DO K = 1, 100
           DO J = 1, 100
S₁            B(1,J,K) = A(1,J-1,K)
              DO I = 1, 100
S₂               A(I+1,J,K) = B(I,100-J,K) + C
              ENDDO
           ENDDO
        ENDDO
```

Does statement S_2 depend on statement S_1? Does statement S_1 depend on statement S_2? Give the dependence type, direction vector, and array variable involved for each dependence that exists. What would procedure *codegen* produce when applied to this nest?

2.6 *Loop reversal* is a transformation that reverses order of the iterations of a given loop. In other words, loop reversal transforms a loop with header

```
        DO I = L, H
```

to a loop with the same body but with header

```
        DO I = H, L, -1
```

State and prove a sufficient condition for the validity of loop reversal. Show that your condition is not *necessary* by giving an example loop that violates the condition but nevertheless can be reversed without changing the result.

2.7 Is loop reversal valid on the I-loop in the following nest? Why or why not?

```
        DO J = 1, N
           DO I = 1, M
              A(I+1,J+1) = A(I,J) + C
           ENDDO
        ENDDO
```

2.8 The representative of a well-known parallel computing company was fond of saying, "If you want to determine whether a given loop can be parallelized, just reverse it—if you get the same answers, it can be safely converted to a parallel DO." Is this statement correct? Why or why not?

CHAPTER 3

Dependence Testing

3.1 Introduction

Dependence testing is the method used to determine whether dependences exist between two subscripted references to the same array in a loop nest. Calculating data dependence for arrays is complex because arrays contain many different locations. This chapter provides detailed descriptions of methods for high-precision dependence testing. For the purposes of this explication, control flow (other than the loops themselves) is ignored.

Recall from Chapter 2 that dependence testing in almost full generality can be illustrated by the problem of determining whether a dependence exists from statement S_1 to statement S_2 in the following model loop nest:

```
DO i₁ = L₁, U₁
    DO i₂ = L₂, U₂
        . . .
        DO iₙ = Lₙ, Uₙ
S₁          A(f₁(i₁,...,iₙ),...,fₘ(i₁,...,iₙ)) = ...
S₂          ... = A(g₁(i₁,...,iₙ),...,gₘ(i₁,...,iₙ))
        ENDDO
        . . .
    ENDDO
ENDDO
```

Let α and β be iteration vectors within the iteration space of the loop nest described above. Thus, α and β are vectors of length n, the *k*th entry of which is an integer value between the lower and upper bounds of the *k*th loop in the nest.

73

Recall from Definition 2.1 that two requirements must be met for a data dependence to exist between two statements: the two statements must both access some memory location, and there must exist a feasible control flow path between the identical accesses. Expressed in terms of this example, this definition says that a dependence exists from S_1 to S_2 if and only if there exist values of α and β such that α is lexicographically less than or equal to β (the control flow requirement) that satisfies the following system of *dependence equations* (the common access requirement):

$$f_i(\alpha) = g_i(\beta) \text{ for all } i, 1 \le i \le m \qquad (3.1)$$

Equation 3.1 is based on the simple observation that two array accesses are to the same memory location if and only if each corresponding subscript entry is identical.[1] Otherwise the two references are independent.

Dependence testing has two goals. The first goal (and the most desired result) is to prove that no dependence exists between given pairs of subscripted references to the same array variable. The mechanism used to achieve this goal is to show that Equation 3.1 has no solutions in the region of appropriate α and β. When it cannot achieve this goal, dependence testing attempts to characterize the possible dependences in some manner, usually as a minimal complete set of distance and direction vectors. Throughout all of this, testing must be conservative; that is, it must assume the existence of any possible dependence whose existence it cannot explicitly disprove.

The remainder of this chapter discusses methods for automating the solution (or proving the absence of solutions) to Equation 3.1.

3.1.1   **Background and Terminology**

Before developing methods for determining the solutions or absence of solutions to Equation 3.1, a modest amount of notation is necessary. Distance vectors, direction vectors, and their application to data dependence have already been introduced in Chapter 2. That knowledge is assumed throughout this chapter. The goal of dependence testing is to construct the complete set of distance and direction vectors representing potential dependences between an arbitrary pair of subscripted references to the same array variable. Since distance vectors may be treated as precise direction vectors, only direction vectors will be used throughout the remainder of this chapter.

Indices and Subscripts

For the purposes of dependence testing, the term *index* will be used to mean the index variable for some loop surrounding both of the references. Furthermore, it

---

1. This statement is not true if a program makes an array access outside of stated array bounds. Such accesses are illegal in Fortran; this book assumes only legal array references.

will be assumed that all *auxiliary induction variables* have been detected and replaced by linear functions of the loop indices (see Chapter 4 for more details).

The term *subscript* will be used to refer to one of the subscripted positions in a pair of array references. Since dependence tests always consider a pair of array references, we will always use the term *subscript* to refer to a *pair* of subscript positions. For example, in the pair of references to array A in the following loop nest

```
    DO i
        DO j
            DO k
S₁              A(i,j) = A(i,k) + C
            ENDDO
        ENDDO
    ENDDO
```

index i occurs in the first subscript, and indices j and k occur in the second subscript.

For the sake of simplicity, it will be assumed that all loops have a step of 1. Nonunit step values may be normalized on the fly as needed via methods discussed in Chapter 4.

Nonlinearity

In its full generality, dependence testing is obviously an undecidable problem. Subscript values can be arbitrary expressions whose values are not known until run time, making compile-time determination of dependence impossible. While some undecidable instances occur in real programs (necessitating the conservative assumption that all possible dependences exist), most subscripts are simpler— generally polynomials of induction variables—and thus are subject to some form of compile-time analysis. Even general polynomials are too complex to permit solution of Equation 3.1 using current mathematical theory. Therefore, we will make one further simplification: unless otherwise stated, it will be assumed that array subscripts are linear expressions of the loop index variables. That is, all subscript expressions are of the form

$$a_1 i_1 + a_2 i_2 + \ldots + a_n i_n + e \qquad (3.2)$$

where i_k is the index for the loop at nesting level k; all a_k, $1 \leq k \leq n$, are integer constants; and e is an expression possibly containing loop-invariant symbolic expressions. Any subscript that does not conform to this restriction will be classified as a *nonlinear subscript* and will not be tested. This restriction is not onerous, as most subscripts encountered in practice are linear. However, nonlinear subscripts occur for a variety of reasons. For example, if a variable that is read from an input medium within the loop appears in a subscript, the subscript will be nonlinear. In addition, most dependence testers will treat any subscript that contains another subscripted array reference as nonlinear. Since such subscripts are common in "irregular" or "adaptive" numerical codes, this can lead to overly conservative approximation to dependence.

Conservative Testing

With the linearity restriction, dependence testing is equivalent to the problem of finding integer solutions to systems of linear Diophantine equations, an *NP*-complete problem. Solving this problem exactly is very difficult; as a result, most dependence tests seek efficient approximate solutions. In general, the most common approximation is to test conservatively—a *conservative* test attempts to prove that there exists no solution to the dependence equation (Equation 3.1). It does not attempt to prove that a dependence actually exists. In other words, if a conservative test determines that no dependence exists, a compiler can rely on that conclusion. However, it may be the case that the references are independent, but the conservative test is unable to prove it. *Exact* tests, on the other hand, are dependence tests that will detect dependences if and only if they exist. Note that the imprecision due to conservative dependence testing will never lead the compiler to generate incorrect code, only code that is less than optimal.

Whenever a nonlinear subscript is encountered by a conservative dependence tester, it will be assumed that the subscript expressions can be equal for arbitrary distances and directions. That is, a nonlinear subscript cannot be used to refine dependence testing on any indices that it contains. Thus for the purposes of testing, a nonlinear subscript is treated as one that effectively does not exist. Other subscripts can still be used to refine the collection of directions that may occur in the dependence or even prove independence.

Complexity

Complexity refers to the number of indices appearing within a subscript—the more distinct loop indices that appear within a subscript position, the more complex dependence testing becomes. A subscript is said to be ZIV (zero index variable) if the subscript position contains no index in either reference. A subscript is said to be SIV (single index variable) if only one index occurs in that position. Any subscript with more than one index is said to be MIV (multiple index variable). For instance, consider the following loop:

```
      DO i
         DO j
            DO k
S₁             A(5,i+1,j) = A(N,i,k) + C
            ENDDO
         ENDDO
      ENDDO
```

When testing for a true dependence between the two references to A in the sample fragment, the first subscript is ZIV, the second is SIV, and the third is MIV. Remember again the convention that "subscript" in this context means a pair of corresponding subscripts.

Separability

Separability describes whether a given subscript interacts with other subscripts for the purpose of dependence testing. When testing multidimensional arrays, a subscript position is said to be *separable* if its indices do not occur in the other subscripts [16, 51]. If two different subscripts contain the same index, they are *coupled*. For example, in the following loop

```
        DO i
            DO j
                DO k
S₁                  A(i,j,j) = A(i,j,k) + C
                ENDDO
            ENDDO
        ENDDO
```

the first subscript is separable, but the second and third are coupled because they both contain the index j. ZIV subscripts are vacuously separable because they contain no loop indices.

The term "separable" derives from linear algebra and differential equations, and applies to systems of equations with distinct variables that may be solved independently. The independent solutions can then be merged to form an exact solution set.

This independence property also holds for separable subscripts. If a subscript position is separable, the loop indices it contains occur in no other subscript. Therefore, the set of directions corresponding to those indices can be tested for independently by examining that subscript position and no others. The resulting direction vectors can be merged on a positional basis with full precision. For example, in the following loop nest

```
        DO i
            DO j
                DO k
S₁                  A(i+1,j,k-1) = A(i,j,k) + C
                ENDDO
            ENDDO
        ENDDO
```

the leftmost direction in the direction vector is determined by testing the first subscript, the middle direction by testing the second subscript, and the rightmost direction by testing the third subscript. The resulting direction vector, $(<,=,>)$, is precise. The same approach applied to distances allows us to calculate the exact distance vector $(1, 0, -1)$.

When testing coupled groups, on the other hand, we must take all the subscripts in the group into account in order to get a precise set of directions. Note that imprecision in testing here means that some directions that cannot actually exist may be reported by the dependence tester.

Coupled Subscript Groups

As we indicated in the previous section, a subscript that is not separable must contain an occurrence of an index that also occurs in at least one other subscript of the same array reference pair. Any two subscripts containing the same index are said to be *coupled*.

It is important to recognize coupling because multidimensional array references with coupled subscripts can cause imprecision in dependence testing. To see this, consider the following example loop:

```
      DO I = 1, 100
S₁        A(I+1,I) = B(I) + C
S₂        D(I) = A(I,I) * E
      ENDDO
```

If we examined the subscripted references to array A separately, we would discover that we cannot eliminate the possibility of dependence of statement S_2 on statement S_1. The first subscript at the store in S_1 equals the first subscript at the use in S_2 one iteration later. The second subscript at the store equals the second subscript on the *same* iteration. Thus neither subscript alone can be used to eliminate the dependence. However, if we consider them together, we can see that no dependence can exist—the dependence cannot be simultaneously loop carried and loop independent.

It is fairly easy to see that coupling is a form of equivalence relationship. Thus, we can define a (minimal) *coupled group* as a nontrivial equivalence class under the coupling relation—a group of at least two subscripts such that (1) each subscript is coupled with at least one other subscript in the group and (2) the group cannot be partitioned into smaller groups without putting two coupled subscripts into different subgroups. The restriction to nontrivial equivalence classes is required because a coupled group of size 1 is simply a separable subscript.

When testing for a dependence of statement S on itself in the following example

```
      DO i
        DO j
          DO k
S               A(i+1,j,k-1) = A(i,j+i,k) + C
```

```
            ENDDO
        ENDDO
    ENDDO
```

the first and second subscripts form a coupled group, while the third subscript is separable.

Coupled MIV subscripts of the form $<a_1 i + c_1, a_2 j + c_2>$ are called *restricted double index variable (RDIV) subscripts*. These subscripts are similar to SIV subscripts, except that i and j are distinct indices. The testing of this special case will be discussed in Section 3.4.1.

Note that a coupled group of subscripts can be thought of as a separable entity because it can be tested precisely for a set of directions corresponding to the loop indices appearing within the group. These directions can then be merged with the directions arising from other tests in the same way that directions coming from separable subscripts are merged.

3.2 Dependence Testing Overview

While we have not explicitly said so, the major reason for classifying subscripts as ZIV, SIV, or MIV is that simpler forms of subscripts can be tested for equality (the heart of dependence) more simply and more accurately than more complicated forms. For instance, the ZIV pair A(5) and A(6) can be determined never to be equal (and thus independent) by simple examination. The more complicated MIV pair A(I+J) and A(I-J) requires more sophisticated, less accurate analysis. The key to efficient dependence testing is to apply tests that are no more complicated than the subscripts require.

This section details the nature of dependence tests for each of the subscript types discussed so far. Implicit in this discussion is a driving algorithm that locates a pair of subscripts that may cause a dependence, determines the number of common loops that surrounds those references, partitions the subscripts of the references according to type, and calls appropriate tests for uncovering direction vectors based on subscript type. The mathematically complex part of this algorithm involves the work once a specific pair of references has been identified for testing, and is the subject of the rest of this section. That part of the algorithm performs the following steps:

1. Partition the subscripts into separable and minimal coupled groups.

2. Classify each subscript as ZIV, SIV, or MIV.

3. For each separable subscript, apply the appropriate single subscript test (ZIV, SIV, MIV), based on the complexity of the subscript, to either prove independence or produce direction vectors for the indices occurring in that subscript. If independence is proved, no further testing is needed in other positions.

4. For each coupled group, apply a multiple subscript test to produce a set of direction vectors for the indices occurring within that group.

5. If any test yields independence, no further testing is needed because no dependences exist.

6. Otherwise merge all the direction vectors computed in the previous steps into a single set of direction vectors for the two references.

This algorithm takes advantage of separability by classifying all subscripts in a pair of array references either as separable or as part of some minimal coupled group. A coupled group is minimal if it cannot be partitioned into two nonempty subgroups with distinct sets of indices. Once a partition is achieved, each separable subscript and each coupled group have completely disjoint sets of indices. Each partition may then be tested in isolation and the resulting distance or direction vectors merged with no loss of precision.

3.2.1 Subscript Partitioning

The first step, that of partitioning subscripts, is detailed in the algorithm presented in Figure 3.1. *Partition* initially places each subscript pair in its own partition, then merges together partitions that refer to the same loop variable. While the algorithm may initially appear to be of time complexity $O(m^2)$, it is actually linear when a data structure that permits constant time unioning is used for partitions.

---

procedure *partition*(S,P,n_p)
    // S is a set of m subscript pairs $S_1, S_2, \ldots, S_m$ for a single reference pair
    //   enclosed in n loops with indices $I_1, I_2, \ldots, I_n$,
    // P is an output variable, containing the sets forming a partition of the
    //   subscripts into separable or minimal coupled groups,
    // n_p is the number of partitions.
    $n_p = m$;
    for $i = 1$ **to** m **do** $P_i \leftarrow \{S_i\}$;
    for $i = 1$ **to** n **do begin**
      $k \leftarrow$ \<none>
      for each remaining partition P_j **do**
        if there exists $s \in P_j$ such that s contains I_i **then**
          if $k =$ \< none > **then** $k \leftarrow j$;
          else begin $P_k \leftarrow P_k \cup P_j$; discard P_j; $n_p := n_p - 1$; **end**
    end
  end *partition*

Figure 3.1 Subscript partitioning algorithm.

3.2.2 **Merging Direction Vectors**

The merge operation described in the testing algorithm merits additional explanation. Since each separable and coupled subscript group contains a unique subset of indices, merge may be thought of as a Cartesian product. In this loop nest

```
      DO I
         DO J
S₁          A(I+1,J) = A(I,J) + C
         ENDDO
      ENDDO
```

the first position yields the direction vector (<) for the I-loop, while the second position yields the direction vector (=) for the J-loop. The resulting Cartesian product is the single vector (<,=).

A more complex example is

```
      DO I
         DO J
S₁          A(I+1,5) = A(I,N) + C
         ENDDO
      ENDDO
```

The first subscript yields the direction vector (<) for the I-loop. Since there is no variance on the J-loop (J does not appear in any subscript and N does not indirectly vary with J), both references to A access the same memory location throughout each iteration of the J-loop. Thus, if they access a common memory element, all patterns of access to that element occur. In other words, the full set of direction vectors {(<),(=),(>)} must be assumed for the J-loop. The merge yields the following set of direction vectors: {(<,<), (<,=), (<,>)}

Dependence test results for ZIV subscripts are treated specially. If a ZIV subscript proves independence, the dependence testing algorithm halts immediately. If independence is not proved, the ZIV test does not produce direction vectors, so no merge is necessary.

3.3 **Single-Subscript Dependence Tests**

Once subscripts have been partitioned and classified, it is time to apply specific tests to determine whether dependences exist and to characterize those that do. This section develops the simplest tests available: those that can be applied to single subscripts. Later sections will develop tests for coupled groups.

3.3.1   **ZIV Test**

Since ZIV subscripts contain no references to any loop induction variables, they do not vary within any loop (assuming all symbolic terms are loop invariant). Thus, if the two expressions can be proved not equal, then the corresponding array references are independent. If the expressions cannot be shown to be different, then the subscript does not contribute to any direction vector (since it contains no loop induction variable) and may be ignored. The ZIV test can be easily extended for symbolic expressions by forming the expression representing the difference between the two subscript expressions. If the difference simplifies to a nonzero constant, the subscripts are independent.

3.3.2   **SIV Tests**

A level up in complexity from ZIV subscripts are SIV subscripts. SIV subscripts are the most commonly occurring in practice, and a number of authors, notably Banerjee, Cohagan, and Wolfe [34, 77, 285], have published a single-index exact test for linear SIV subscripts. These methods are based on finding all solutions to a simple Diophantine equation in two variables. The methods presented in this section are somewhat simpler than these exact tests. These methods gain their simplicity by separating SIV subscripts into two categories: strong SIV and weak SIV.

Strong SIV Subscripts

An SIV subscript for index i is said to be *strong* if it has the form $<ai + c_1, ai' + c_2>$; that is, if it is linear and the coefficients of the two occurrences of the index i are constant and equal. Figure 3.2 gives a geometric picture of the equations corresponding to a strong SIV pair. Since the loop coefficients are identical for each reference, a strong SIV pair maps into a pair of parallel lines. The horizontal line marked A(m) indicates one point where the two subscripts access the same element. Because of the parallel nature of the lines, accesses to common elements will always be separated by the same distance in terms of loop iterations. This distance, called the *dependence distance,* can be calculated by the following:

$$d = i' - i = \frac{c_1 - c_2}{a} \tag{3.3}$$

A dependence exists between two references only if access to common elements occurs within the bounds set by the loop (given SIV, there must be only one loop involved in the two references). This access will occur only when d is an integer (if it is not an integer, references to the same element cannot occur on a loop iteration for both subscripts) and

$$|d| \le U - L \tag{3.4}$$

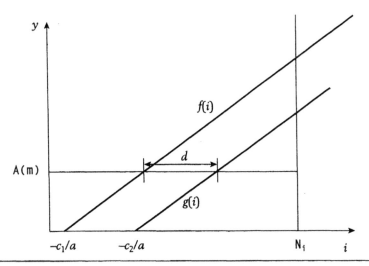

Figure 3.2 Geometric view of strong SIV tests.

where U and L are the loop upper and lower bounds (otherwise, at most one reference can occur within the iteration space of the loop). These facts provide for a very simple dependence test: calculate d; if it is an integer and its absolute value falls within the range of the loop, there exists a dependence whose direction can be determined by the sign of d.[2] Otherwise, no dependence exists.

One advantage of the strong SIV test is that it can be easily extended to handle loop-invariant symbolic expressions. The extension is to first evaluate the dependence distance d symbolically. If the result is a constant, then the test may be performed as above. Otherwise, the difference between the loop bounds can be calculated and compared with d symbolically. The following loop is an example of code that occurs occasionally:

```
        DO I = 1, N
S₁        A(I+2*N) = A(I+N) + C
        ENDDO
```

The strong SIV test can evaluate the dependence distance d as $2N - N$, which simplifies to N. This is compared with the loop bounds symbolically, proving independence since $N > N - 1$.

---

2. One notable exception here is a distance of 0, which can only give rise to a loop-independent dependence. A zero distance between references within a single statement does not indicate a dependence.

Weak SIV Subscripts

In contrast to a strong SIV subscript, a weak SIV subscript has different coefficients for the loop induction variable, and thus takes the form $<a_1i + c_1, a_2i' + c_2>$. As stated previously, weak SIV subscripts may be solved using the single-index exact test. However, it also may be helpful to view the problem geometrically, where the dependence equation

$$a_1i + c_1 = a_2i' + c_2 \qquad (3.5)$$

describes a line in the two-dimensional plane with i and i' as the axes [51]. The weak SIV test can then be formulated as determining whether there exists an integral value m between the loop bounds and integral values i and i' such that $a_1i + c_1 = a_2i' + c_2 = m$, as shown in Figure 3.3. There are two special cases that are useful to consider.

Weak-Zero SIV Subscripts

If one of the two coefficients is 0 (i.e., $a_1 = 0$ or $a_2 = 0$), the subscript is a *weak-zero SIV* subscript. If a_2 is equal to zero, the dependence equation reduces to

$$i = \frac{c_2 - c_1}{a_1} \qquad (3.6)$$

The reference in which the coefficient is zero references only one array element during the loop (the horizontal line in Figure 3.4). Given that the other coefficient is nonzero, the two lines can intersect at only one point—that defined in Equation 3.6. Thus, the test consists merely of checking that the computed value is an integer and is within the loop bounds. A symmetric test applies when a_1 is zero.

The weak-zero SIV test finds dependences caused by a particular iteration. In scientific codes, this iteration is usually the first or last of the loop, eliminating one possible direction vector for the dependence. More importantly, weak-zero dependences caused by the first or last loop iteration may be eliminated by loop peeling. Consider, for instance, the following simplified loop in the program *tomcatv* from the SPEC benchmark suite:

```
        DO I = 1, N
S₁        Y(I,N) = Y(1,N) + Y(N,N)
        ENDDO
```

The weak-zero SIV test can determine that the use of Y(1,N) causes a loop-carried true dependence from the first iteration to all other iterations. Similarly, with aid from symbolic analysis, the weak-zero SIV test can discover that the use

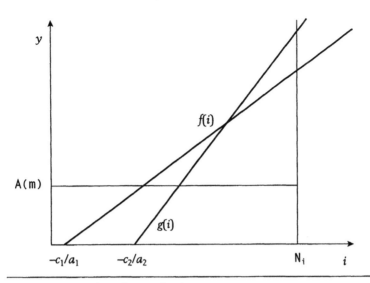

Figure 3.3 Geometric view of weak SIV subscripts.

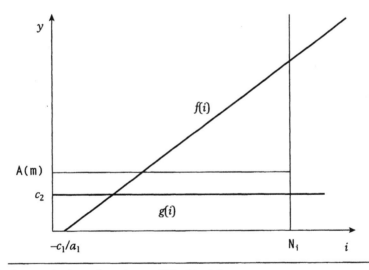

Figure 3.4 Geometric view of weak-zero SIV subscripts.

of Y(N,N) causes a loop-carried antidependence from all iterations to the last iteration. By identifying the first and last iterations as the only cause of dependences, the weak-zero SIV test can advise the user or compiler to peel the first and last iterations of the loop, resulting in the following parallel loop:

```
        Y(1,N) - Y(1,N) + Y(N,N)
        DO I - 2, N - 1
S₁         Y(I,N) - Y(1,N) + Y(N,N)
        ENDDO
        Y(N,N) = Y(1,N) + Y(N,N)
```

Weak-Crossing SIV Subscripts

Subscripts in which $a_2 = -a_1$ are called *weak-crossing SIV*. In these cases, the important property that simplifies analysis is symmetry. Given that the absolute values of the slopes of the lines are the same, they "move" away from a given point at exactly the same rate, although one moves up and the other moves down. As a result, the lines are symmetric about a vertical line through their point of intersection (see Figure 3.5).

Because of this symmetry, the ends of all dependences are on opposite sides of a crossing point—the point where the lines intersect. One common example where weak-crossing SIV subscripts occur is in Cholesky decomposition. To locate the crossing point, i is set to i' and the substitution of $a_2 = -a_1$ is made, deriving

$$i = \frac{c_2 - c_1}{2a_1} \tag{3.7}$$

Since all dependences span the crossing point, determining whether dependences exist is a simple check that the resulting i is within the loop bounds and is

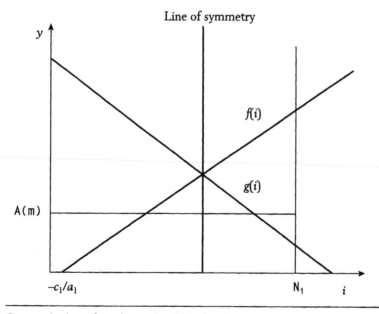

Figure 3.5 Geometric view of weak-crossing SIV subscripts.

either an integer or has a noninteger part equal to 1/2. The second part of the condition arises because each line moves symmetrically from the crossing point; if that point is not halfway between two integers, then the lines cannot intersect integers on the y-axis at integral points on the x-axis. An example will serve to illustrate this. Suppose N is equal to 4. Then we have the following values for i and $N - i + 1$:

Crossing point

i:	1	2	3	4
$N - i + 1$:	4	3	2	1

The crossing point must be exactly at 2.5 for the dependence to exist.

Weak-crossing SIV dependences may be eliminated by loop splitting. To illustrate, consider the following loop from the Callahan-Dongarra-Levine vector test suite [57]:

```
        DO I = 1, N
S₁        A(I) = A(N-I+1) + C
        ENDDO
```

The weak-crossing SIV test determines that dependences exist between the definition and use of A, and that they all cross iteration (N+1)/2 where the semantics of Fortran require truncation of nonintegral values. Splitting the loop at that iteration results in two parallel loops:

```
        DO I = 1, (N+1)/2
            A(I) = A(N-I+1) + C
        ENDDO
        DO I = (N+1)/2 + 1, N
            A(I) = A(N-I+1) + C
        ENDDO
```

Both forms of weak SIV tests are also useful for testing coupled subscripts, described in Section 3.1.1. The exact SIV test, described at the end of Section 3.3.2, can be used for precise testing of any other SIV subscript.

Complex Iteration Spaces

SIV tests as described so far have been applied to rectangular iteration spaces, where all loop bounds are independent of the loop values proper. They do not apply directly to triangular loops (where one of the loop bounds is a function of at least one other loop index) or trapezoidal loops (where both bounds are functions of at least one other loop index). However, they can be extended to apply to such loops, with some loss of precision.

To understand how to do this, consider the special case of a strong SIV subscript in a loop where the upper bound is a function of at most one other loop index.

```
     DO I - 1, N
         DO J - L₀ + L₁ * I, U₀ + U₁ * I
S₁          A(J+D) - ...
S₂          ... - A(J) + B
         ENDDO
     ENDDO
```

By the strong SIV test, we can see that there is a dependence of statement S_2 on statement S_1 carried by the J-loop if the dependence distance d is smaller in absolute value than the distance from the loop lower bound to the loop upper bound. In other words, there is a dependence if

$$|d| \leq U_0 - L_0 + (U_1 - L_1)I$$

Thus, we can assume a dependence if $|d|$ is smaller than the largest value for the quantity on the right-hand side of the inequality. If $U_1 - L_1$ is positive, this value occurs when I takes its maximum value; otherwise, it occurs when I takes its minimum value.

But this does not tell the entire story, because the dependence might not exist for every value of I. In particular, for the dependence to exist we must have

$$I \geq \frac{|d| - (U_0 - L_0)}{U_1 - L_1} \tag{3.8}$$

For other values of I, the dependence does not exist. Unless it can be shown that this inequality is violated for all values of I in its iteration range, we must assume a dependence in the loop, because there will be one for some value of I. In that sense, the dependence test is precise.

On the other hand, because the dependence does not occur for all values, we can use the expression as a mechanism for index-set splitting, discussed in Section 5.7. We can append the condition

$$I < \frac{|d| - (U_0 - L_0)}{U_1 - L_1} \tag{3.9}$$

as a *breaking condition*, which is a predicate that specifies the condition or conditions under which the dependence does not hold. The breaking condition can be used to partially vectorize a statement. For example, in the following loop

```
     DO I - 1, 100
         DO J - 1, I
```

```
S₁              A(J+20) = A(J) + B
        ENDDO
    ENDDO
```

the statement S_1 can be vectorized for every value of I such that the following breaking condition holds:

$$I < \frac{|d| - (U_0 - L_0)}{U_1 - L_1} = \frac{20 - (-1)}{1} = 21$$

Thus the loop nest can be subdivided into two nests:

```
    DO I = 1, 20
        DO J = 1, I
S₁ₐ         A(J+20) = A(J) + B
        ENDDO
    ENDDO
    DO I = 21, 100
        DO J = 1, I
S₁ᵦ         A(J+20) = A(J) + B
        ENDDO
    ENDDO
```

where the inner loop of the first nest can be vectorized. As we shall see in Section 5.7.1, index-set splitting can be used to vectorize the second loop as well.

A similar analysis holds for the weak-zero test.

```
    DO I = 1, N
        DO J = L₀ + L₁ * I, U₀ + U₁ * I
S₁          A(c) = ...
S₂          ... = A(J) + B
        ENDDO
    ENDDO
```

Here we have a dependence only if c is within the loop bounds

$$L_0 + L_1 I \le c \le U_0 + U_1 I$$

The dependence exists for all values of I for which both inequalities hold. However, we must report the dependence if the inequalities hold for any values of I in the iteration range, even though it holds only within nonempty loops for values of I given by the following inequality:

$$\frac{c - U_0}{U_1} \le I \le \frac{c - L_0}{L_1} \tag{3.10}$$

If the term in the denominator is 0 on either side of the inequality, we assume that there is no bound on that side.

Technically, if the loop index variable in one loop has an upper or lower bound that is the index for another loop that appears in another subscript in the same pair of references, the subscript positions are coupled. To see why, consider this example:

```
        DO I = 1, 100
           DO J = 1, I
S₁            A(J+20,I) = A(J,19) + B
           ENDDO
        ENDDO
```

The first subscript, tested by the triangular strong SIV test, is just like our earlier example—there can be no dependence unless $I \geq 21$. The weak-zero test applied to the second subscript tells us that the subscripts can be equal only when $I = 19$. Thus there can be no dependence even though we would assume a dependence if we tested the two subscripts separately.

An example of coupling with two SIV subscripts is as follows:

```
        DO I = 1, 100
           DO J = I, I + 19
S₁            A(I+20,J) = A(I,J) + B
           ENDDO
        ENDDO
```

Independent SIV subscript testing indicates that there is a dependence with a distance vector of (20,0). However, we note that the iteration ranges for the J-loop at the source and sink of the dependence are nonintersecting: when $I = 1$, statement S_1 stores into A(21,1:20), while at the sink, statement S_1 reads from A(21,21:40). Since there are no common memory locations in the two slices, there can be no dependence.

In practice, cases like these happen so rarely that they are not worth worrying about. However, we shall see some more powerful tests for coupled groups that can catch these cases easily.

Symbolic SIV Dependence Tests

Most of the dependence tests that have been presented so far are precise when all terms involved are compile-time constants, but are unable to cope well with symbolic quantities. There are a few exceptions: for instance, loop-invariant symbolic additive constants have been treated by assuming that the difference $(c_2 - c_1)$ may be formed symbolically and simplified, then used like a constant. Symbolic quantities appear frequently in subscripts, arising from programming practices such as passing a multidimensional array to a procedure that only expects a one-dimensional array. As a result, symbolic tests are important.

This section describes a special test for independence between references that are contained in two different loops at the same nesting level. For instance, the test can be applied in the following pair of loops.

```
        DO I = L₁, U₁
S₁          A(a₁*I+c₁) = ...
        ENDDO
        DO J = L₂, U₂
S₂          ... = A(a₂*J+c₂)
        ENDDO
```

Assume for the sake of simplicity that a_1 is greater or equal to zero. A dependence exists if the following dependence equation is satisfied:

$$a_1 i - a_2 j = c_2 - c_1 \tag{3.11}$$

for some value of i, $L_1 \le i \le U_1$, and j, $L_2 \le j \le U_2$. There are two cases to consider. First, a_1 and a_2 may have the same sign. In this case, $a_1 i - a_2 j$ assumes its maximum value for $i = U_1$ and $j = L_2$, and its minimum value for $i = L_1$ and $j = U_2$ (remember, a_1 and a_2 are nonnegative). Hence, there is a dependence only if

$$a_1 L_1 - a_2 U_2 \le c_2 - c_1 \le a_1 U_1 - a_2 L_2 \tag{3.12}$$

If either inequality is violated, the dependence cannot exist.

In the second case, a_1 and a_2 have different signs. In this case, $a_1 i - a_2 j$ assumes its maximum for $i = U_1$ and $j = U_2$, so there is a dependence only if

$$a_1 L_1 - a_2 L_2 \le c_2 - c_1 \le a_1 U_1 - a_2 U_2 \tag{3.13}$$

If either inequality is violated, the dependence cannot exist.

It should be noted that these inequalities are just special cases of the Banerjee Inequality, which will be introduced in Section 3.3.3. However, stated in this form, they obviously can be formulated for symbolic values of c_1, c_2, L_1, L_2, U_1, and U_2. Furthermore, this test may also be used to test for dependence in the same loop, with $L_1 = L_2$ and $U_1 = U_2$.

As an example of symbolic testing, consider the following loop nest:

```
        DO I = N + 1, 2 * N
S₁          A(I+N) = A(I) + B
        ENDDO
```

Substituting for the loop bounds in Equation 3.12, we get the following symbolic inequality:

$$N + 1 - 2N \le 0 - N \le 2N - (N+1)$$

which simplifies to

$$1 - N \le -N \le N - 1$$

If we assume the loop is executed for at least one iteration (otherwise the issue is moot), $1 - N$ is never smaller than $-N$, so there is no dependence. A good simplifier will catch this case and more complicated cases as well.

Breaking Conditions

Another way to look at the preceding example is that the dependence distance in the loop was the symbolic quantity N. To see this, we can form the expression for dependence distance given by the strong SIV test. It is possible to have a symbolic distance because the value of N does not change in the loop.

Now consider a loop very similar to the one from the preceding example:

```
      DO I = 1, L
S₁        A(I+N) = A(I) + B
      ENDDO
```

Since the variable N does not occur in the upper bound for the loop, we cannot determine at compile time whether the dependence distance actually exists, so we must assume that it does. However, we know that it would not exist if the loop upper bound L were no larger than the dependence distance. In other words, if L <= N, then there is no dependence from the statement S_1 to itself. The predicate "L <= N" is called a *breaking condition* for the dependence. Many dependence testers, when faced with simple cases like this, will annotate dependences that cannot be disproved at compile time with breaking conditions in hopes that run-time testing or input from the programmer can eliminate the dependence later.

In the above example, a vectorizer could generate alternative codes depending on the run-time value of the breaking condition:

```
      IF (L<=N) THEN
          A(N+1:N+L) = A(1:L) + B
      ELSE
          DO I = 1, L
S₁            A(I+N) = A(I) + B
          ENDDO
      ENDIF
```

The code could be further improved by strip-mining the loop into strips of exactly size N if the value of N is large enough to make vectorization worthwhile.

Another interesting breaking condition arises from the weak-zero SIV test, as demonstrated in the following example:

```
     DO I = 1, N
S₁      A(I) = A(L) + B
     ENDDO
```

Assuming there is no known relationship between the values of N and L, the weak-zero test cannot prove that there is no self-dependence for statement S_1. However, the dependence tester can record a breaking condition for this dependence

$$(L<1).OR.(L>N)$$

which can be used in turn to vectorize the loop conditionally.

```
     IF ((L.LT.1).OR.(L.GT.N)) THEN
        A(1:N) = A(L) + B
     ELSE
        DO I = 1, N
S₁         A(I) = A(L) + B
        ENDDO
     ENDIF
```

As before, this can be further improved by strip-mining the sequential loop.

The ZIV test also provides many opportunities for the use of breaking conditions. Consider the following loop:

```
     DO I = 1, N
S₁      A(L) = B(I) + C
S₂      B(I+1) = A(L+K) + X(I)
     ENDDO
```

Without knowledge of the values of L and K in this loop, we cannot disprove the assumption that statement S_2 depends on statement S_1. However, it is clear that there can be no dependence unless K is zero. Therefore, the predicate K.NE.0 is a breaking condition for the dependence and the recurrence.

Breaking conditions are especially useful in some libraries. For instance, in the LAPACK linear algebra library, one of the basic linear algebra subroutines has a loop fragment that looks like the following:

```
     DO I = 1, N
S₁      A(S*I) = A(S*I) + B(I)
     ENDDO
```

Here the variable S holds a stride (≥ 0) for the loop that is passed into the subroutine by a calling program. In most programs, this stride is 1. However, if in the degenerate case where S = 0, the loop becomes a reduction. In this example, the dependence tester must assume that there are three dependences from statement

S to itself—a true dependence, an antidependence, and an output dependence. However, these dependences all have the same breaking condition, $S.NE.0$, which can be used to provide alternative versions of the loop, one vector and one reduction, selectable at run time.

An Exact SIV Test

An SIV subscript position in which the subscripts are of the form

$$a_1i + a_0 \text{ and } b_1i + b_0$$

can be tested exactly by constructing all solutions of the linear Diophantine equation

$$a_1x - b_1y = b_0 - a_0 \tag{3.14}$$

This equation system has a solution if and only if the greatest common denominator of a_1 and b_1 divides $b_0 - a_0$. It is well known that the Euclidean algorithm for computing the greatest common denominator can be extended to compute values n_a and n_b such that

$$n_a a_1 + n_b b_1 = \gcd(a_1, b_1) \tag{3.15}$$

Once these values are available, all solutions of the Diophantine equations are given by the following formulas:

$$
\begin{aligned}
x_k &= n_a\left(\frac{b_0 - a_0}{g}\right) + k\frac{b_1}{g} \\[2ex]
y_k &= -n_b\left(\frac{b_0 - a_0}{g}\right) + k\frac{a_1}{g}
\end{aligned}
\tag{3.16}
$$

Here (x_k, y_k) is a solution of $a_1x - b_1y = b_0 - a_0$ for every integral value of k. Furthermore, for any solution (x,y) there exists a k such that $x = x_k$ and $y = y_k$.

A solution alone does not imply dependence. For dependence to exist, the solution must occur in the region indicated by the loop bounds. Determining whether there exists a solution that implies dependence for a particular direction vector and given loop bounds requires a search procedure that is beyond the scope of this book.

3.3.3   Multiple Induction-Variable Tests

When restricted to linear functions of loop induction variables, ZIV and SIV subscripts are relatively simple linear mappings from Z (the set of natural numbers) to Z. MIV subscripts are much more complicated, being linear mappings from Z^m to Z, where m is the number of loop induction variables appearing in the subscript. This added complexity requires more sophisticated mathematics in order to accurately determine dependences. Accordingly, this section reviews the general dependence equations, recast in terms suitable to MIV subscripts, and the appropriate mathematics as a prelude to the MIV tests proper.

To illustrate the issues, let us consider a general nest of loops:

```
DO i₁ = L₁, U₁
    DO i₂ = L₂, U₂
        ...
        DO iₙ = Lₙ, Uₙ
S₁          A(f(i₁,...,iₙ)) = ...
S₂          ... = A(g(i₁,...,iₙ))
        ENDDO
        ...
    ENDDO
ENDDO
```

Determining whether there is a dependence with direction vector $D = (D_1, D_2, \ldots, D_n)$ is equivalent to determining whether there exists an integer solution to the equation system

$$f(x_1, x_2, \ldots, x_n) = g(y_1, y_2, \ldots, y_n) \tag{3.17}$$

in the space defined by

$$L_i \leq x_i, y_i \leq U_i, \; \forall i, \; 1 \leq i \leq n \tag{3.18}$$

with the additional restriction due to the direction vector:

$$x_i \, D_i \, y_i \; \forall i, \; 1 \leq i \leq n \tag{3.19}$$

(Recall that each entry of a direction vector is one of "<", "=", or ">"). Let R denote the region defined by Equations 3.18 and 3.19. Then the equation has a solution if

$$h(x_1, x_2, \ldots, x_n, y_1, y_2, \ldots, y_n) = f(x_1, x_2, \ldots, x_n) - g(y_1, y_2, \ldots, y_n) = 0 \tag{3.20}$$

has an integer solution somewhere inside the region R.

Since integer solutions are required, this problem lies in the theory of Diophantine equations. As mentioned earlier, exactly solving Diophantine equations in a restricted space is difficult. As a result, finding simplifications that are not exact but that provide reasonable precision is useful in a compiler. One such simplification is removing the restriction that the solutions be integers, making the solution space continuous rather than discrete. In other words, searching for real solutions (or, more precisely, the absence of real solutions) to Equation 3.20 in the region R is useful. If the equation does not have a real solution, then it cannot have an integer solution, and accordingly, no dependence can exist. Assume for the moment that the functions f and g are continuous in the region R. The following theorem follows directly from elementary analysis.

THEOREM
3.1

If f and g are continuous functions on region R, there exists a real solution to Equation 3.20 if and only if

$$\min_R h \leq 0 \leq \max_R h \tag{3.21}$$

Proof Immediate from the Intermediate Value Theorem.[3]

This theorem is the basis for several dependence tests.

The remainder of this chapter assumes that both f and g are affine functions; that is, they have the form

$$f(x_1, x_2, \ldots, x_n) = a_0 + a_1 x_1 + \ldots + a_n x_n \tag{3.22}$$

$$g(y_1, y_2, \ldots, y_n) = b_0 + b_1 y_1 + \ldots + b_n y_n \tag{3.23}$$

and that the dependence problem to be solved is to find solutions in the region R to the linear Diophantine equation

$$a_0 - b_0 + a_1 x_1 - b_1 y_1 + \ldots + a_n x_n - b_n y_n = 0 \tag{3.24}$$

GCD Test

Rearranging the terms of Equation 3.24 yields the following:

$$a_1 x_1 - b_1 y_1 + \ldots + a_n x_n - b_n y_n = b_0 - a_0 \tag{3.25}$$

which is the standard form for a linear Diophantine equation. Linear Diophantine equations have been the subject of extensive study for hundreds of years. A fundamental theorem about these equations is the following:

THEOREM
3.2

GCD Test

Equation 3.25 has a solution if and only if $\gcd(a_1, \ldots, a_n, b_1, \ldots, b_n)$ divides $b_0 - a_0$.

Thus, if the gcd of all the coefficients of loop induction variables does not divide the difference of the two constant additive terms, there can be no solution to the equation anywhere—hence, no dependence can exist. On the other hand, if

---

3. Strictly speaking, the region R needs to be closed for max and min to be used in place of inf and sup. For the applications in this book, all regions will be closed.

the gcd of the coefficients does divide $b_0 - a_0$, there is a solution somewhere, although it need not be in the region of interest R.

When testing for a specific direction vector $D = (D_1, \ldots, D_n)$, some of whose directions are "=", this condition can be tightened. Assume that the direction vector for the dependence being tested is D and has only one "=" component, D_i. Then any acceptable solution must have $x_i = y_i$, making the equation

$$a_1 x_1 - b_1 y_1 + \ldots + (a_i - b_i)x_i + \ldots + a_n x_n - b_n y_n = b_0 - a_0 \qquad (3.26)$$

It is obvious that the gcd should include $(a_i - b_i)$ and exclude both a_i and b_i in this case, which is slightly more precise. In the general case, a similar replacement should be performed in any position where the direction vector being tested is "=".

With this observation, it should be clear that the strong SIV test described in Section 3.3.2 is a special case of the GCD test in Theorem 3.2.

Banerjee Inequality

Although the GCD test is extremely useful in some cases, it is inadequate as a general dependence test. The reason is that the most common gcd encountered in practice is 1, which divides everything. Furthermore, the GCD test indicates dependence whenever the dependence equation has an integer solution anywhere, not just in the region R. The equations that derive from common subscripts generally have integer solutions somewhere, even if not in the region of interest. One test that eliminates this problem by considering iteration limits is the Banerjee Inequality.

The Banerjee Inequality follows directly from Theorem 3.1 applied in the case when f and g are affine functions:

$$h(x_1, x_2, \ldots, x_n, y_1, y_2, \ldots, y_n) = a_0 - b_0 + a_1 x_1 - b_1 y_1 + \ldots + a_n x_n - b_n y_n \quad (3.27)$$

Some preliminary definitions and notation are necessary before presenting the test itself.

DEFINITION 3.1

Let $h_i^+ = \max_{R_i} h_i(x_i, y_i)$ and $h_i^- = \min_{R_i} h_i(x_i, y_i)$, where

$$h_i(x_i, y_i) = a_i x_i - b_i y_i \qquad (3.28)$$

and the region R_i is defined by

$$L_i \le x_i, \ y_i \le U_i \text{ and } x_i D_i y_i \qquad (3.29)$$

where D_i is the direction vector element for the ith position.

In other words, h_i^+ is the maximum value of the function h_i over a region and h_i^- is the minimum value. For these values to be useful, there has to be some way of calculating them. The following definitions help accomplish that.

**DEFINITION
3.2**

Let a be a real number. The *positive part* of a, denoted a^+, is given by the expression

$$a^+ = \text{if } a \geq 0 \text{ then } a \text{ else } 0 \tag{3.30}$$

The *negative part* of a, denoted a^-, is given by

$$a^- = \text{if } a \geq 0 \text{ then } 0 \text{ else } -a \tag{3.31}$$

Both a^+ and a^- are nonnegative and the following relationship holds:

$$a = a^+ - a^- \tag{3.32}$$

With these definitions, the following lemma can be proved.

**LEMMA
3.1**

Let t, s, and z denote real numbers. If $0 \leq z \leq s$, then

$$-t^- s \leq tz \leq t^+ s$$

Furthermore, there exist values z_1, z_2 such that

$$tz_1 = -t^- s \text{ and } tz_2 = t^+ s$$

Proof Case 1: $t \geq 0$. In this case $t^+ = t$ and $t^- = 0$. So the inequality is satisfied because $0 \leq tz = t^+ z \leq t^+ s$, since $0 \leq z \leq s$. In this case $z_1 = 0$ and $z_2 = s$.

Case 2: $t < 0$. In this case $t^+ = 0$ and $t^- = -t$. Thus, the inequality becomes $-t^- s \leq -t^- z = tz \leq 0$ and we have $z_1 = s$ and $z_2 = 0$.

The next step is to generalize this inequality to arbitrary bounds.

**LEMMA
3.2**

Let t, l, u, and z denote real numbers. If $l \leq z \leq u$, then

$$-t^- u + t^+ l \leq tz \leq t^+ u - t^- l$$

and there exist values z_1, z_2 such that

$$tz_1 = -t^- u + t^+ l \text{ and } tz_2 = t^+ u - t^- l.$$

Proof Assume $l \leq z \leq u$. Rearranging terms gives $0 \leq z - l \leq u - l$. Lemma 3.1 then gives us

$$-t^- (u - l) \leq t(z - l) \leq t^+ (u - l)$$

Rearranging terms again yields

$$-t^- u + (t + t^-)l \leq tz \leq t^+ u - (t^+ - t)l$$

Rearranging Equation 3.32 gives us

$$t^+ = t + t^- \text{ and } t^- = t^+ - t$$

which proves the inequality. The existence of z_1 and z_2 follows directly from Lemma 3.1.

This inequality provides the basis for proving an important result about the minimum and maximum values of h. However, before we begin, we need to introduce a little more terminology.

DEFINITION 3.3

The quantities $H_i^-(D)$ and $H_i^+(D)$, where D is a direction, are defined as follows:

$$H_i^-(<) = -(a_i^- + b_i)^+(U_i - 1) + [(a_i^- + b_i)^- + a_i^+]L_i - b_i$$

$$H_i^+(<) = (a_i^+ - b_i)^+(U_i - 1) - [(a_i^+ - b_i)^- + a_i^-]L_i - b_i$$

$$H_i^-(=) = -(a_i - b_i)^- U_i + (a_i - b_i)^+ L_i$$

$$H_i^+(=) = (a_i - b_i)^+ U_i - (a_i - b_i)^- L_i$$

$$H_i^-(>) = -(a_i - b_i^+)^-(U_i - 1) + [(a_i - b_i^+)^+ + b_i^-]L_i + a_i$$

$$H_i^+(>) = (a_i + b_i^-)^+ (U_i - 1) - [(a_i + b_i^-)^- + b_i^+]L_i + a_i$$

$$H_i^-(*) = -a_i^- U_i^x + a_i^+ L_i^x - b_i^+ U_i^y + b_i^- L_i^y$$

$$H_i^+(*) = a_i^+ U_i^x - a_i^- L_i^x + b_i^- U_i^y - b_i^+ L_i^y$$

where L_i^x, U_i^x, L_i^y, and U_i^y are used in the last two equations to handle the case where the source and sink of the dependence are in different loops with different upper and lower bounds.

This use of different upper and lower bounds in the definition for direction "*" permits the handling of cases like the following:

```
         DO I = 1, 100
            DO J = 1, 50
S₁             A(I,J) = B(I,J) + C
            ENDDO
            DO J = 51, 100
S₂             A(I,J) = A(I,J) + D
            ENDDO
         ENDDO
```

Because of the nonintersecting iteration ranges of the first and second loops, S_1 and S_2 are independent. Permitting the upper and lower bounds to be different makes it possible to catch this case using the Banerjee Inequality.

LEMMA 3.3

Let $h_i(x_i, y_i) = a_i x_i - b_i y_i$ and let R_i be as described by Equation 3.29: $L_i \le x_i, y_i \le U_i$ and $x_i D_i y_i$. Then the minimum and maximum values of h_i are given by

$$\min_R h_i = h_i^- = H_i^-(D_i) \qquad (3.33)$$

$$\max_R h_i = h_i^+ = H_i^+(D_i) \qquad (3.34)$$

where the values of H are given by Definition 3.3.

Proof   Case 1: $D =$ "=". In this case $L_i \le x_i = y_i \le U_i$. Substituting x_i for y_i in the equations:

$$L_i \le x_i \le U_i$$

$$h_i = a_i x_i - b_i y_i = (a_i - b_i) x_i$$

One application of Lemma 3.2 yields the desired inequalities. Since Lemma 3.2 guarantees that there exist points within R where the left- and right-hand side values are obtained, the result is established.

Case 2: $D =$ "<". In this case $L_i \le x_i < y_i \le U_i$. To use Lemma 3.2, the inequality needs to be translated to

$$L_i \le x_i \le y_i - 1 \le U_i - 1$$

Note that h_i (the quantity to be minimized and maximized) is given by

$$h_i = a_i x_i - b_i y_i = a_i x_i - b_i(y_i - 1) - b_i$$

An application of Lemma 3.2 to $L_i \le x_i \le y_i - 1$ can eliminate x_i:

$$-a_i^-(y_i - 1) + a_i^+ L_i - b_i(y_i - 1) - b_i \le h_i$$

$$\le a_i^+(y_i - 1) - a_i^- L_i - b_i(y_i - 1) - b_i$$

Next, Lemma 3.2 is applied to $L_i \le y_i - 1 \le U_i - 1$ to eliminate y_i:

$$-(a_i^- + b_i)^+(U_i - 1) + (a_i^- + b_i)^- L_i + a_i^+ L_i - b_i \le h_i$$

$$\le (a_i^+ - b_i)^+(U_i - 1) - (a_i^+ - b_i)^- L_i - a_i^- L_i - b_i$$

which establishes the result for this case. Once again, Lemma 3.1 guarantees that there exist points within R where the minima and maxima occur.

Case 3: $D =$ ">". In this case $L_i \le y_i < x_i \le U_i$. First the inequality is translated to

$$L_i \le y_i \le x_i - 1 \le U_i - 1$$

Rearranging h_i yields

$$h_i = a_i x_i - b_i y_i = a_i(x_i - 1) - b_i y_i + a_i$$

Applying Lemma 3.2 eliminates y_i:

$$a_i(x_i - 1) - b_i^+(x_i - 1) + b_i^- L_i + a_i \le h_i$$

$$\le a_i(x_i - 1) + b_i^-(x_i - 1) - b_i^+ L_i + a_i$$

A second application eliminates x_i:

$$-(a_i - b_i^+)^-(U_i - 1) + (a_i - b_i^+)^+L_i + b_i^-L_i + a_i \leq h_i$$
$$\leq (a_i + b_i^-)^+(U_i - 1) - (a_i + b_i^-)^-L_i - b_i^+L_i + a_i$$

which is the desired inequality.

Case 4: $D = $ "$*$". In this case $L_i^x \leq x_i \leq U_i^x$, $L_i^y \leq y_i \leq U_i^y$, with no implied relationship between x_i and y_i. Two applications of Lemma 3.2 on the expression $h_i = a_i x_i - b_i y_i$ yield the inequality

$$H_i^-(*) \leq h_i \leq H_i^+(*)$$

Since Lemma 3.2 guarantees that there exist points within R where the minima and maxima occur, the result is established for this case.

Since each of the terms in h involves a different induction variable, each term can be maximized and minimized independently. This yields the following important result.

THEOREM 3.3

Banerjee Inequality

There exists a real solution to $h = 0$ (Equation 3.20) for direction vector $D = (D_1, D_2, \ldots, D_n)$ if and only if the following inequality is satisfied on both sides:

$$\sum_{i=1}^{n} H_i^-(D_i) \leq b_0 - a_0 \leq \sum_{i=1}^{n} H_i^+(D_i) \tag{3.35}$$

Proof The dependence equation provides the following formula for h:

$$h = a_0 - b_0 + \sum_{i=1}^{n} h_i = a_0 - b_0 + \sum_{i=1}^{n} (a_i x_i - b_i y_i)$$

Lemma 3.3 can then be applied to minimize and maximize h:

$$\min_R h = a_0 - b_0 + \sum_{i=1}^{n} H_i^-(D_i)$$

$$\max_R h = a_0 - b_0 + \sum_{i=1}^{n} H_i^+(D_i)$$

Substituting these formulas into the inequality from Equation 3.21 in Theorem 3.1 and subtracting $a_0 - b_0$ from all three sides of the inequality gives the desired result.

Handling Symbolics in the Banerjee Inequality

In the previous section we introduced a method for dealing with symbolic quantities in the simple SIV and ZIV tests. Here we will show how to integrate symbolics into MIV testing using the Banerjee Inequality. Our principal concern will be the existence of symbolic upper and lower loop bounds. In this task, we will make use of three principles:

1. Unless the step is explicitly specified as –1, we can assume that the lower bound is less than or equal to the upper bound. If this is not so, the dependence test is moot.

2. The product of 0 times an unknown value (in this case a loop upper or lower bound) is always 0.

3. If a loop upper bound or lower bound is not constrained by either of the above rules, it must be assumed to take on any value. Therefore, we can make the worst possible assumption for dependence testing.

In the dependence testing strategy we will use, the first principle will typically allow us to eliminate arbitrarily small values of the loop upper bound or arbitrarily large values of the lower bound. For example, if we have the loop

```
DO I = 1, N
   DO J = 1, M
      DO K = 1, 100
         A(I,K) = A(I+J,K) + B
      ENDDO
   ENDDO
ENDDO
```

we know that N and M must be at least equal to 1. Suppose that we are testing for direction vector (=,*,*). Note that

$$a_1 = 1; a_2 = 0; b_1 = 1; b_2 = 1$$

Using these values in the Banerjee Inequality on the first subscript position (we don't need the K-loop because K does not appear in the subscript) gives

$$H_1^-(=) + H_2^-(*)$$

$$= -(a_1{-}b_1)^-U_1 + (a_1{-}b_1)^+L_1 - (a_2^-{+}b_2^+)U_2 + (a_2^+{+}b_2^-)L_2$$

$$= -(1{-}1)^-N + (1{-}1)^+1 - (0{+}1)M + (0{+}0)1 = -M$$

$$\leq b_0 - a_0 = 0 - 0 = 0$$

$$\leq H_1^+(=) + H_2^+(*)$$

$$= (a_1-b_1)^+U_1 - (a_1-b_1)^-L_1 + (a_2^++b_2^-)U_2 - (a_2^-+b_2^+)L_2$$

$$\leq (1-1)^+N - (1-1)^-1 + (0+0)M - (0+1)1 = -1$$

The right inequality is violated; therefore there is no dependence. Note that this result is achieved because of the second principle—both terms involving symbolic upper bounds have coefficients of 0. On the left, we must assume that the inequality holds because $-M$ can become an arbitrarily large negative quantity but it must be no greater than -1.

Trapezoidal Banerjee Inequality

The Banerjee test presented thus far assumes that the upper and lower bounds of all the loops in the loop nest are independent of the values of other loop induction variables. Not all loops meet this requirement, however, and it is common in practice to encounter loop nests where the iteration range of the inner loops depends on the values of outer loop indices. The following is an example:

```
      DO I = 1, 100
         DO J = 1, I - 1
S₁          A(J) = A(I+J-1) + C
         ENDDO
      ENDDO
```

In this case, no dependence can be carried by the inner loop because for a given value of I, the references on the left-hand side fall in the subarray A(1:I-1) while the references on the right fall in the subarray A(I:I*2-2). Since these two subarrays are nonintersecting, no dependence exists with direction vector (=,*). However, if we substitute the coefficient values

$$a_1 = 0; a_2 = 1; b_1 = 1; b_2 = 1$$

in the Banerjee Inequality, we get

$$H_1^-(=) + H_2^-(*)$$

$$= -(a_1-b_1)^-U_1 + (a_1-b_1)^+L_1 - (a_2^-+b_2^+)U_2 + (a_2^++b_2^-)L_2$$

$$= -(0-1)^-(100) + (0-1)^+1 - (0+1)(I-1) + (1+0)1 = -I - 100$$

$$\leq b_0 - a_0 = -1 - 0 = -1$$

$$\leq H_1^+(=) + H_2^+(*)$$

$$= (a_1-b_1)^+U_1 - (a_1-b_1)^-L_1 + (a_2^++b_2^-)U_2 - (a_2^-+b_2^+)L_2$$

$$\leq (0-1)^+(100) - (0-1)^-1 + (1+0)(I-1) - (0+1)1 = I - 3$$

which can certainly be satisfied, since I takes on values greater than or equal to 2. As a result, a dependence must be assumed.

The problem is that the Banerjee Inequality as currently formulated cannot take advantage of knowledge about values of loop induction variables in the upper bound expression. To alleviate this deficiency, we will derive a special version of the Banerjee Inequality that we call the *trapezoidal Banerjee Inequality*, so named because it handles trapezoidal loops.

Let us start by assuming that the upper and lower bound expressions can be rewritten as an affine combination of the loop induction variables:

$$U_i = U_{i0} + \sum_{j=1}^{i-1} U_{ij} i_j \qquad L_i = L_{i0} + \sum_{j=1}^{i-1} L_{ij} i_j \qquad (3.36)$$

The desired result is a modification of the Banerjee Inequality that considers these bound expressions. This result is not straightforward because the evaluation of minimum and maximum for each loop is no longer independent of the other loops. For example, evaluating the minimum and maximum at the innermost loop level can modify the coefficients associated with outer loops.

To understand how this happens, consider the evaluation of $H_i^-(<)$. Minimizing h_i according to Lemma 3.2 yields

$$H_i^-(<) = -(a_i^-+b_i)^+ \left(U_{i0} - 1 + \sum_{j=1}^{i-1} U_{ij} i_j \right)$$

$$+ [(a_i^-+b_i)^- + a_i^+] \left(L_{i0} + \sum_{j=1}^{i-1} L_{ij} i_j \right) - b_i \qquad (3.37)$$

where i_j can be either x_j or y_j, so long as it is uniformly one or the other in a single summation. Following the proof in Lemma 3.3, case 2, the lower bound of x_i is introduced in the first step to eliminate x_i and produce

$$-a_i^-(y_i-1) + a_i^+ L_i - b_i(y_i-1) - b_i \le h_i$$

$$\le a_i^+(y_i-1) - a_i^- L_i - b_i(y_i-1) - b_i$$

Thus, the summation with x_j should be used for the lower bound multiplied by a_i^+ in the left-hand side above and a_i^- in the right-hand side above. When eliminating the remaining terms it is proper to use upper and lower bounds for y_i. Thus the final expression is

$$H_i^-(<) = -(a_i^-+b_i)^+ \left(U_{i0} - 1 + \sum_{j=1}^{i-1} U_{ij}y_j \right)$$

$$+(a_i^-+b_i)^- \left(L_{i0} + \sum_{j=1}^{i-1} L_{ij}y_j \right) \tag{3.38}$$

$$+ a_i^+ \left(L_{i0} + \sum_{j=1}^{i-1} L_{ij}x_j \right) - b_i$$

This means that the coefficients of x_j and y_j, for $1 \le j < i$, used in minimizing h_j must be adjusted by the appropriate term in Equation 3.38. A similar adjustment needs to be made to coefficients on the maximum side of the inequality.

Figure 3.6 (along with Figures 3.7 through 3.10) contains the algorithm for evaluating the trapezoidal Banerjee Inequality for any direction vector. Note that it evaluates the inequality starting at the innermost loop and moving outward. At

```
boolean function Banerjee(D)
    // Al[i] is the adjusted coefficient ai used on the minimum side
    // Bl[i] is the adjusted coefficient bi used on the minimum side
    // Ar[i] is the adjusted coefficient ai used on the maximum side
    // Br[i] is the adjusted coefficient bi used on the maximum side
    // Vmin is the accumulated Banerjee left-hand side
    // Vmax is the accumulated Banerjee right-hand side
    for i := 1 to n do begin
        Al[i] := ai; Ar[i] := ai; Bl[i] := bi; Br[i] := bi;
    end;
    Vmin := 0; Vmax := 0;
    for i := n to 1 do begin
        if Di = "=" then
            ComputePositionEqual(Vmin,Vmax,Al,Bl,Ar,Br);
        else if Di = "<" then
            ComputePositionLessThan(Vmin,Vmax,Al,Bl,Ar,Br);
        else if Di = ">" then
            ComputePositionGreaterThan(Vmin,Vmax,Al,Bl,Ar,Br);
        else if Di = "*" then
            ComputePositionAny(Vmin,Vmax,Al,Bl,Ar,Br);
    end;
    if Vmin ≤ b0 - a0 and b0 - a0 ≤ Vmax then return true else return false;
end Banerjee
```

Figure 3.6 Trapezoidal Banerjee Inequality evaluation.

procedure *ComputePositionEqual*($V_{min}, V_{max}, A_l, B_l, A_r, B_r$)
    // $A_l[i]$ is the adjusted coefficient a_i used on the minimum side
    // $B_l[i]$ is the adjusted coefficient b_i used on the minimum side
    // $A_r[i]$ is the adjusted coefficient a_i used on the maximum side
    // $B_r[i]$ is the adjusted coefficient b_i used on the maximum side
    // V_{min} is the accumulated Banerjee left-hand side
    // V_{max} is the accumulated Banerjee right-hand side
    $V_{min} := V_{min} - (A_l[i] - B_l[i])^- U_{i0} + (A_l[i] - B_l[i])^+ L_{i0};$
    $V_{max} := V_{max} + (A_r[i] - B_r[i])^+ U_{i0} - (A_r[i] - B_r[i])^- L_{i0};$
    $nU := 0; nL := 0;$
    // $v(<) = -1, v(=) = 0$ and $v(>) = 1$
    for $j := 1$ **to** $i-1$ **do begin**
        $nL := nL + L_{ij}v(D_j); nU := nU + U_{ij}v(D_j);$
    end
    if $nL \leq 0$ **then**
        for $j := 1$ **to** $i-1$ **do begin**
            // Signs reversed for updates to B
            $B_l[j] := B_l[j] - (A_l[i] - B_l[i])^+ L_{ij};$
            $B_r[j] := B_r[j] + (A_r[i] - B_r[i])^- L_{ij};$
        end
    else
        for $j := 1$ **to** $i-1$ **do begin**
            $A_l[j] := A_l[j] + (A_l[i] - B_l[i])^+ L_{ij};$
            $A_r[j] := A_r[j] - (A_r[i] - B_r[i])^- L_{ij};$
        end
    end
    if $nU \leq 0$ **then begin**
        for $j := 1$ **to** $i-1$ **do begin**
            $A_l[j] := A_l[j] - (A_l[i] - B_l[i])^- U_{ij};$
            $A_r[j] := A_r[j] + (A_r[i] - B_r[i])^+ U_{ij};$
        end
    else begin
        for $j := 1$ **to** $i-1$ **do begin**
            // Signs reversed for updates to B
            $B_l[j] := B_l[j] + (A_l[i] - B_l[i])^- U_{ij};$
            $B_r[j] := B_r[j] - (A_r[i] - B_r[i])^+ U_{ij};$
        end
    end
end *ComputePositionEqual*

Figure 3.7 Trapezoidal Banerjee for direction "=".

each stage, it updates the accumulated left- and right-hand sides of the inequality, then it adjusts, as appropriate, the coefficients corresponding to outer loops. These coefficients are held in the temporary arrays $A_l[]$ and $B_l[]$, which hold coefficients

procedure *ComputePositionLessThan*($V_{min}, V_{max}, A_l, B_l, A_r, B_r$)
   // $A_l[i]$, $B_l[i]$, $A_r[i]$, $B_r[i]$ are the adjusted coefficients
   // V_{min} is the accumulated Banerjee left-hand side
   // V_{max} is the accumulated Banerjee right-hand side
   $V_{min} := V_{min} - (A_l[i]^- + B_l[i])^+ (U_{i0} - 1)$
        $+ ((A_l[i]^- + B_l[i])^- + A_l[i]^+)L_{i0} - B_l[i]$;
   $V_{max} := V_{max} + (A_r[i]^+ - B_r[i])^+ (U_{i0} - 1)$
        $- ((A_r[i]^+ - B_r[i])^- + A_r[i]^-)L_{i0} - B_r[i]$;
   for $j := 1$ **to** $i{-}1$ **do begin**
      // Signs reversed for updates to B
      $A_l[j] := A_l[j] + A_l[i]^+ L_{ij}$;
      $B_l[j] := B_l[j] + (A_l[i]^- + B_l[i])^+ U_{ij} - (A_l[i]^- + B_l[i])^- L_{ij}$;
      $A_r[j] := A_r[j] - A_r[i]^- L_{ij}$;
      $B_r[j] := B_r[j] - (A_r[i]^+ - B_r[i])^+ U_{ij} + (A_r[i]^+ - B_r[i])^- L_{ij}$;
   end
end *ComputePositionLessThan*

Figure 3.8 Trapezoidal Banerjee for direction "<".

procedure *ComputePositionGreaterThan*($V_{min}, V_{max}, A_l, B_l, A_r, B_r$)
   // $A_l[i]$, $B_l[i]$, $A_r[i]$, $B_r[i]$ are the adjusted coefficients
   // V_{min} is the accumulated Banerjee left-hand side
   // V_{max} is the accumulated Banerjee right-hand side
   $V_{min} := V_{min} - (A_l[i] - B_l[i]^+)^- (U_{i0} - 1)$
        $+ ((A_l[i] - B_l[i]^+)^+ + B_l[i]^-)L_{i0} + A_l[i]$;
   $V_{max} := V_{max} + (A_r[i] + B_r[i]^-)^+ (U_{i0} - 1)$
        $- ((A_r[i] + B_r[i]^-)^- + B_r[i]^+)L_{i0} + A_l[i]$;
   for $j := 1$ **to** $i{-}1$ **do begin**
      // Signs reversed for updates to B
      $B_l[j] := B_l[j] - B_l[i]^- L_{ij}$;
      $A_l[j] := A_l[j] - (A_l[i] - B_l[i]^+)^- U_{ij} + (A_l[i] - B_l[i]^+)^+ L_{ij}$;
      $B_r[j] := B_r[j] + B_r[i]^+ L_{ij}$;
      $A_r[j] := A_r[j] + (A_r[i] + B_r[i]^-)^+ U_{ij} - (A_r[i] + B_r[i]^-)^- L_{ij}$;
   end
end *ComputePositionGreaterThan*

Figure 3.9 Trapezoidal Banerjee for direction ">".

for the left-hand inequality, and $A_r[]$ and $B_r[]$, which hold coefficients for the right-hand inequality.

Note that the testing for direction "*" assumes that we may have different loop bounds at the source and sink of the dependence. This derives from the desire to eliminate dependences that have endpoints in separate loops with nonintersecting iteration ranges. (See the previous subsection "Banerjee Inequality" for a

procedure $ComputePositionAny(V_{min}, V_{max}, A_l, B_l, A_r, B_r)$
// $A_l[i]$, $B_l[i]$, $A_r[i]$, $B_r[i]$ are the adjusted coefficients
// V_{min} is the accumulated Banerjee left-hand side
// V_{max} is the accumulated Banerjee right-hand side
$V_{min} := V_{min} - A_l[i]^- U_{i0}^x + A_l[i]^+ L_{i0}^x - B_l[i]^+ U_{i0}^y + B_l[i]^- L_{i0}^y;$
$V_{max} := V_{max} + A_r[i]^+ U_{i0}^x - A_r[i]^- L_{i0}^x + B_r[i]^- U_{i0}^y - B_r[i]^+ L_{i0}^y;$
for $j := 1$ **to** $i-1$ **do begin**
    // Signs reversed for updates to B
    $A_l[j] := A_l[j] - A_l[i]^- U_{ij}^x + A_l[i]^+ L_{ij}^x;$
    $B_l[j] := B_l[j] + B_l[i]^+ U_{ij}^y - B_l[i]^- L_{ij}^y;$
    $A_r[j] := A_r[j] + A_r[i]^+ U_{ij}^x - A_r[i]^- L_{ij}^x;$
    $B_r[j] := B_r[j] - B_r[i]^- U_{ij}^y + B_r[i]^+ L_{ij}^y;$
end
end $ComputePositionAny$

Figure 3.10 Trapezoidal Banerjee for direction "$*$".

discussion.) In this case we assume that we have distinct upper and lower bound expressions for each of the occurrences.

$$U_i^x = U_{i0}^x + \sum_{j=1}^{i-1} U_{ij}^x x_j \qquad L_i^x = L_{i0}^x + \sum_{j=1}^{i-1} L_{ij}^x x_j \qquad (3.39)$$

$$U_i^y = U_{i0}^y + \sum_{j=1}^{i-1} U_{ij}^y y_j \qquad L_i^y = L_{i0}^y + \sum_{j=1}^{i-1} L_{ij}^y y_j \qquad (3.40)$$

Of course, these values will be the same if the two occurrences are both within the same loop.

Correctness. To show correctness of function *Banerjee* we must show that the values of V_{min} and V_{max} computed by function *Banerjee* in Figure 3.6 are such that

$$V_{min} + a_0 - b_0 \le \min_R h \quad \text{and} \quad \max_R h \le V_{max} + a_0 - b_0$$

In other words, if *Banerjee* returns *false*, no dependence can exist. For the cases $D_i = $ "$<$", $D_i = $ "$>$", and $D_i = $ "$*$", this follows directly from the proof of Theorem 3.3, with the adjustments being made to coefficients for outer loops along the lines described in the discussion of Equations 3.37 and 3.38. In fact, the inequality is precise for those directions by Lemma 3.3.

The only tricky case occurs when $D_i = $ "$=$". In this case, the following expansions for $H_i^-(=)$ and $H_i^+(=)$ are valid:

$$H_i^-(=) = -(a_i-b_i)^-\left(U_{i0} + \sum_{j=1}^{i-1} U_{ij}i_j\right) + (a_i-b_i)^+\left(L_{i0} + \sum_{j=1}^{i-1} L_{ij}i_j\right)$$

(3.41)

$$H_i^+(=) = (a_i-b_i)^+\left(U_{i0} + \sum_{j=1}^{i-1} U_{ij}i_j\right) - (a_i-b_i)^-\left(L_{i0} + \sum_{j=1}^{i-1} L_{ij}i_j\right)$$

The problem is that the source and sink of the dependence can have different upper and lower bounds because the outer loop index values at the source and sink are likely to be different (unless all outer loop directions are "="). Since the requirement is that $x_i = y_i$, the dependence cannot exist unless x_i is greater than *both* lower bounds and less than *both* upper bounds. Unfortunately, simply substituting the maximum of two summations back into the equation will not yield meaningful coefficients for the outer loops. Hence, one of the lower bounds and one of the upper bounds must be chosen, with a loss of precision.

Choosing the upper and lower bounds that preserve as much precision as possible requires an intelligent heuristic. Since the direction vector is known, the following can be evaluated:

$$nL = \sum_{j=1}^{i-1} L_{ij}v(D_j) \qquad \text{and} \qquad nU = \sum_{j=1}^{i-1} U_{ij}v(D_j)$$

where

$$v(D_i) = \begin{cases} -1 & \text{if } D_i = \text{"<"} \\ 0 & \text{if } D_i = \text{"="} \\ 1 & \text{if } D_i = \text{">"} \end{cases}$$

If $nL \leq 0$, then it is likely that the lower bound for y_i is greater than the one for x_i, so that lower bound in Equation 3.41 is used. Similarly, if $nU \leq 0$, the upper bound for x_i is likely to be lower than the upper bound for y_i, so the upper bound for x_i is used in Equation 3.41. This heuristic, which is precise if there is only one nonzero L_{ij}, is the source of the somewhat branchy adjustment in the code for *Banerjee*.

Returning to the example, the key loop constants have the following values:

$$a_1 = 0; a_2 = 1; b_1 = 1; b_2 = 1$$

$$U_{10} = 100; U_{20} = -1; U_{21} = 1; L_{10} = L_{20} = 1; L_{21} = 0$$

We leave it to the reader to verify that the trapezoidal Banerjee Inequality does not hold for this case.

Testing for All Direction Vectors

For dependence testing to be useful, it should construct the entire set of direction vectors for a dependence between a given pair of statements. Burke and Cytron originated an efficient algorithm to perform this construction [49]. The basic idea behind the algorithm is to begin by testing for the most general set of direction vectors, then successively refine the test, pruning whenever it is shown that an entire set of direction vectors cannot exist. This idea is illustrated in Figure 3.11 (the algorithm itself is reproduced in Figure 3.12). Here the procedure establishes that some dependence exists by testing for (*,*,*), then it refines the test by testing separately for directions in the first position. If any of these succeeds, it further refines the test by testing for different directions in the second position and so on.

The test, shown in Figure 3.12, is implemented by a function *try*, which is called with a direction vector of all "*"'s and an empty *dvlist* (i.e., $D := (*,*, \ldots , *)$;

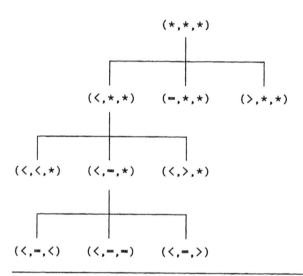

Figure 3.11 Testing for all direction vectors.

```
set function try(D,k,dvlist)
    if not Banerjee(D) then return dvlist;
    if k = n then return dvlist » {D};
    for d := "<", "=", ">" do begin
        D_i := d;
        dvlist := try(D, k+1, dvlist);
    end
end try
```

Figure 3.12 MIV direction vector test.

dvlist := *try*(D, 1, ∅);). This function then recursively calls itself whenever a test is successful.

Although this procedure has the same asymptotic complexity as exhaustive testing in the worst case, it can significantly reduce testing overhead in the average case by pruning the tree whenever a test indicates that no dependences exist along a particular branch.

3.4   **Testing in Coupled Groups**

The tests used for separable subscripts can also be used on each subscript of a coupled group: if any test proves independence, then no dependence exists. However, we have seen in Section 3.1.1 that subscript-by-subscript testing in a coupled group may yield false dependences.

A slightly stronger approach to subscript-by-subscript testing is to test each subscript separately and intersect the resulting sets of direction vectors [283]. This is effective on the example from Section 3.1.1:

```
      DO I = 1, 100
S₁       A(I+1,I) = B(I) + C
S₂       D(I) = A(I,I) * E
      ENDDO
```

Here, testing the first subscript yields the direction vector (<), while testing in the second position yields the direction vector (=). When we intersect these directions, we discover that no dependence can exist.

This method permits simple and efficient testing, but in some cases also provides a conservative approximation to the set of directions within a coupled group. That is, it may yield direction vectors that do not exist. For instance, consider the following loop:

```
      DO I = 1, 100
S₁       A(I+1,I+2) = A(I,I) + C
      ENDDO
```

Subscript-by-subscript testing with direction vector intersection would yield the single direction vector (<,<). However, a careful examination of the statement reveals that this direction vector is invalid because no dependence actually exists—the subscript pairs cannot be simultaneously equal.

To address this problem we can strengthen the dependence test to intersect distance vectors rather than direction vectors. When the SIV test is applied to the above example, the two subscripts produce two different distance vectors: (1) and (2). The intersection of these distance vectors is clearly empty. This strategy is extremely effective because such a large percentage of the dependence tests applied in practice are strong SIV tests, which produce distances.

Many researchers have worked on multiple subscript tests [202, 266, 286]. Most of the work is focused on fast methods for determining whether simultaneous linear Diophantine equations can have a solution. An overview of this work is provided in Section 3.4.2.

3.4.1   The Delta Test

In this section we discuss a simple intuitive strategy called the Delta test for testing dependence in multiple subscripts. The Delta test is designed to be exact yet efficient for common coupled subscripts. An overview of the algorithm is given in Figure 3.13.

The main idea behind the Delta test is to build on the intuition behind intersection of distance vectors. Since most subscripts found in practice are SIV and since SIV tests are simple and exact in most cases, the information gleaned from them can be used to simplify the testing of other subscripts in the same coupled group. In the Delta test, we examine each SIV subscript in the coupled group to

```
procedure Delta_test(subscripts,DVset,dV)
    // subscripts is a set of all coupled SIV and/or MIV subscripts
    // DVset is an output parameter containing all direction vectors
    // dV is an output parameter containing known distance vectors
    initialize elements of constraint vector C to < none >
    while ∃ untested SIV subscripts in subscripts do begin
        apply SIV test to all untested SIV subscripts,
            return independence or derive new constraint vector C';
        C' := C ∩ C';
        if C' = ∅ then return independence;
        else if C ≠ C' then begin
            C := C';
            propagate constraint C into MIV subscripts,
                possibly creating new ZIV or SIV subscripts;
            apply ZIV test to untested ZIV subscripts,
                return independence or continue;
        end
    end
    while ∃ untested RDIV subscripts do
        test and propagate RDIV constraints;
    test remaining MIV subscripts, and
        intersect resulting direction vectors with C;
    construct DVset and dV from C;
end Delta_test
```

Figure 3.13 Delta test algorithm.

produce constraints that can be propagated into other subscripts in the same group. Usually this propagation results in a simplification that produces a precise set of direction vectors. Since most coupled subscripts in scientific Fortran codes are SIV, the Delta test is a practical, fast, and in most cases exact multiple subscript test.

The name "Delta test" derives from the informal usage of ΔI to represent the distance between the source and sink index in the I-loop. Thus we assume that the index at the source of a dependence is a specific value of I and the index at the sink is the same value plus the distance: $I + \Delta I$.

To see how this works, consider a simple example:

```
DO I = 1, 100
    DO J = 1, 100
S₁        A(I+1,I+J) = A(I,I+J-1) + C
    ENDDO
ENDDO
```

If we apply the SIV test to the first subscript, we get a distance of 1, that is, $\Delta I = 1$. From the second subscript we have the equation

$$I_0 + J_0 = I_0 + \Delta I + J_0 + \Delta J - 1$$

which is derived by substituting the incremented value of the indices at the source for the index at the sink. If we substitute $\Delta I = 1$ into this equation we get

$$I_0 + J_0 = I_0 + 1 + J_0 + \Delta J - 1$$

We now simplify by eliminating the constant values I_0 and J_0 to get

$$\Delta J = 0$$

Thus the only legal distance vector is $(0,1)$, and the only legal direction vector is $(<,=)$.

In essence, what we have done is to factor out the I in the dependence test of the second subscript, converting the test to the following for S_1:

```
DO I = 1, 100
    DO J = 1, 100
S₁        A(I+1,J) = A(I,J) + C
    ENDDO
ENDDO
```

Note that we have used a strong SIV subscript to reduce an MIV subscript to strong SIV form.

The Delta test can detect independence if any of its component SIV tests detect independence. Otherwise, it converts all SIV subscripts into constraints, propagating them into MIV subscripts where possible. This process repeats until no new constraints are found. Constraints are then propagated into coupled RDIV subscripts. The remaining MIV subscripts are tested and the results are intersected with existing constraints. The following sections develop the Delta test in greater detail.

Constraints

In the context of this book, *constraints* are assertions on indices that must hold for a dependence to exist. Given the tie to dependence, constraints are usually derived from subscripts. As an example, the dependence equation applied to the subscript $<a_1 i + c_1, a_2 i' + c_2>$ generates the constraint $a_1 i - a_2 i' = c_2 - c_1$ for index i. Another example of a simple constraint is a dependence distance.

The *constraint vector* $\mathbf{C} = (\delta_1, \delta_2, \ldots, \delta_n)$ is a vector with one constraint for each of the n indices in the coupled subscript group. In the Delta test, constraint vectors are used to store constraints generated from SIV tests. Because of the simple nature of SIV subscripts, these constraints can be easily converted to distance or direction vectors.

A *constraint* δ may have the following form:

- *Dependence line:* a line $<ax + by = c>$ representing the dependence equation.

- *Dependence distance:* the value $<d>$ of the dependence distance; it is equivalent to the dependence line $<x - y = -d>$.

- *Dependence point:* a point $<x, y>$ representing dependence from iteration x to iteration y.

Dependence distances and lines derive directly from the strong and weak SIV tests. Dependence points result from intersecting constraints, as described in the next section.

Intersecting Constraints

Since dependence equations from all subscripts must simultaneously have solutions for any dependences to exist, intersecting constraints from each subscript can improve precision. If the intersection is the empty set, no dependence is possible. This may seem a little counterintuitive because the term "constraint" usually implies a restriction or restraint, and thus, the lack of constraints on indices for dependences would seem to imply that all dependences can exist. The important fact to remember is that constraints are actually logical expressions guaranteed to be true when some dependence exists. If there are no such logical expressions, there can be no dependence. We have already seen constraint intersection applied to both direction vectors and coupled SIV subscripts.

Dependence distances are the easiest to intersect, by simply comparing the distances. If the distances are not all equal, then they cannot simultaneously hold, and no dependences exist. For example, as we saw in the following loop nest shown earlier

```
      DO I = 1, N
S₁       A(I+1,I+2) = A(I,I) + C
      ENDDO
```

the strong SIV test applied to the first subscript shows a dependence distance of 1; applied to the second subscript, it shows a distance of 2. Intersecting the two constraints is performed by comparing them. They are not equal, producing the empty set as the constraint set and proving independence. This reflects the fact that any value i' substituted into the subscripts on the left side cannot simultaneously be both 1 and 2 less than any value of i substituted into the subscripts on the right side.

Even complex constraints from SIV subscripts may be intersected exactly. Since each dependence equation from an SIV subscript may be viewed as a line in a two-dimensional plane, intersecting constraints from multiple SIV subscripts corresponds to calculating the point(s) of intersection for lines in a plane. No dependence exists if the lines do not intersect at a common point within the loop bounds, or if the coordinates of this point do not have integer values. If all dependence equations intersect at a single *dependence point*, its coordinates are the only two iterations that actually cause dependence.

```
      DO I = 1, N
S₁       A(I,I) = A(1,I-1) + C
      ENDDO
```

In this example loop, testing the first and second subscripts in the pair of references to A derives the dependence lines <I = 1> and <I = I'- 1>, respectively. These dependence lines intersect at the dependence point <1,2>, indicating that the only dependence is from the first to the second iteration. Since calculating the intersection of lines in a plane can be performed precisely, constraint intersection is exact.

The full constraint intersection algorithm will not be given here, as it is straightforward to derive.

Constraint Propagation

The goal of constraint propagation is to use information gained from testing in one subscript to improve dependence testing in other subscripts in the same coupled group. Here we discuss several issues associated with constraints and their use in coupled testing.

SIV Constraints A major contribution of the Delta test is its ability to propagate constraints derived from SIV subscripts into coupled MIV subscripts, usually with no loss of precision. The resulting constrained subscript can then be tested with greater efficiency and precision. Although we will not present a full constraint propagation algorithm here, it is easy to construct. The goal of such an algorithm is to utilize SIV constraints for each index to eliminate instances of that index in the target MIV subscript. To make the algorithm more concrete, consider the following example:

```
    DO I
        DO J
S₁          A(I+1,I+J) = A(I,I+J)
        ENDDO
    ENDDO
```

Applying the strong SIV test to the first subscript of array A reveals a dependence distance of <1> for index I. Propagating this constraint into the second subscript to eliminate both occurrences of I results in the constrained SIV subscript <J - 1, J>. The strong SIV test applied to this subscript gives a distance of −1 on the J-loop. Since this completes testing on all subscripts, it also completes the Delta test. Merging the elements of the constraint vector gives a dependence with distance vector (1, −1).

Constraint propagation in this example is exact because both instances of index I in the constrained subscript were eliminated. Empirical studies [123] show that this is frequently the case for scientific codes. In general the algorithm may only eliminate one occurrence of an index. This results in improved precision when testing coupled groups, but is not exact. If desired, additional precision may be gained by utilizing the constraint to reduce the range of the remaining index, as in Fourier-Motzkin elimination [244].

Multiple Passes The Delta test algorithm iterates if MIV subscripts are reduced to SIV subscripts, since that action may produce new constraints. The following loop nest provides an example:

```
    DO I
        DO J
            DO K
S₁              A(J-I,I+1,J+K) = A(J-I,I,J+K)
            ENDDO
        ENDDO
    ENDDO
```

In the first pass of the Delta test, the second subscript is tested, producing a dependence distance of <1> on the I-loop. This constraint is then propagated into the first subscript, resulting in the subscript < J + 1, J >.

Since a new SIV subscript has been created, the algorithm repeats. On the second pass, the new subscript is tested to produce a distance of 1 on the J-loop. This constraint is then propagated into the third subscript to derive the subscript (K - 1,K). The new SIV subscript causes another pass that discovers a distance of −1 on the K-loop. Since all SIV subscripts have been tested, the Delta test halts at this point, returning the distance vector (1, 1, −1).

Improved Precision The Delta test may improve the precision of other dependence tests on remaining constrained MIV subscripts.

```
      DO I = 1, 100
        DO J = 1, 100
S₁        A(I-1,2*I) = A(I,I+J+110)
        ENDDO
      ENDDO
```

The Banerjee Inequalitiy applied to the subscripts in this example loop cannot by itself prove independence. The Delta test improves on this by first converting the leftmost subscript into a dependence distance constraint of <−1>. This constraint is then propagated into the rightmost subscript to produce the constrained MIV subscript < 2, J − I + 110 >, which can be successfully handled (i.e., independence detected) by the Banerjee Inequality.

```
      DO I
        DO J
S₁        A(I,2*J+I) = A(I,2*J-I+5)
        ENDDO
      ENDDO
```

Similarly, in this example loop the GCD test shows integer solutions for both subscripts. However, propagating the distance constraint < 0 > for I from the first subscript into the second subscript yields the constrained MIV subscript <2 * J, 2 * J - 2 * I + 5>. The GCD test can now detect independence since the GCD of the coefficients of all the indices is 2, which does not divide evenly into the constant term 5.

Distance Vectors The Delta test is particularly useful for producing distance vectors from MIV subscripts in coupled groups. The following loop nest, which exhibits a pattern that is fairly common in numerical codes after transformations to improve parallelism, is illustrative:

```
      DO I = 1, N
        DO J = I + 1, I + N
S₁        A(I,J-I) = A(I-1,J-I) + C
        ENDDO
      ENDDO
```

In this example, for instance, most dependence tests are unable to calculate distance vectors due to the MIV subscript in the second position. The Delta test, however, does permit accurate analysis of these subscripts. The test propagates distance constraints for I from the first subscript into the second subscript, deriving the distance vector (1, 1).

Restricted DIV Constraints The previous section showed how SIV constraints may be propagated. MIV constraints may also be propagated, but are expensive to propagate in the general case. However, in the special case of coupled RDIV subscripts (introduced in Section 3.1.1), we present a method to handle an important special case. For simplicity, only the following types of array references are considered:

```
DO i
    DO j
S₁        A(i₁+c₁,i₂+c₂) = A(i₃+c₃,i₄+c₄)
    ENDDO
ENDDO
```

When i_1 and i_2 are both instances of index i, and i_3 and i_4 are both instances of index j, a constraint between i and j is derived from the first subscript. That constraint may be propagated into the second subscript using the algorithms for SIV subscripts discussed previously. The only additional consideration is that bounds for i and j may differ.

More commonly, i_1 and i_4 are both instances of index i, and i_2 and i_3 are both instances of index j. In this case, the following set of dependence equations results:

$$i + c_1 = j' + c_3$$
$$j + c_2 = i' + c_4$$

Each dependence equation may be tested separately without loss of precision when checking for dependence. However, both equations must be considered simultaneously when determining which distance or direction vectors are possible.

These constraints can be propagated by considering instances of index i in the second reference as $i + \Delta_i$, where Δ_i is the dependence distance between the two occurrences of i. The index j is treated in the same fashion, producing the following set of dependence equations:

$$i + c_1 = j + \Delta_j + c_3$$
$$j + c_2 = i + \Delta_i + c_4$$

Adding these equations together and rearranging terms slightly yields the following equation:

$$\Delta_i + \Delta_j = c_1 + c_2 - c_3 - c_4$$

This dependence equation can then be checked when testing for a specific distance or direction vector.

To illustrate this more concretely, consider the following example loop:

```
      DO I = 1, N
        DO J = 1, N
S₁         A(I,J) = A(J,I) + C
        ENDDO
      ENDDO
```

Propagating RDIV constraints results in the dependence equation $\Delta_i + \Delta_j = 0$. As a result, distance vectors must have the form $(d,-d)$, and the only valid direction vectors are $(<,>)$ and $(=,=)$. All dependences are thus carried on the outer loop; the inner loop may be executed in parallel.

Precision and Complexity

The precision of the Delta test depends on the nature of the coupled subscripts being tested. The SIV tests applied in the first phase are exact. The constraint intersection algorithm is also exact, since the intersection of any number of lines in a plane can be calculated precisely. The Delta test is thus exact for any number of coupled SIV subscripts.

In the constraint propagation phase, weak-zero SIV constraints and dependence points may always be applied exactly, since they assign values to occurrences of an index in a subscript. Dependence distances (from strong SIV subscripts) may also be propagated into MIV subscripts without loss of precision when the coefficients of the corresponding index are equal. Fortunately, this is frequently the case in scientific codes.

When constraints can be propagated exactly and all subscripts uncoupled by eliminating shared indices, the Delta test prevents loss of precision due to multiple subscripts. At its conclusion, if the Delta test has tested all subscripts using ZIV and SIV tests, the answer is exact. If only separable MIV subscripts remain, the Delta test is limited by the precision of the single subscript tests applied to each subscript. Research has shown that the Banerjee-GCD test is usually exact for single subscripts [32, 184, 201], so the Delta test is also likely to be exact for these cases.

There are three sources of imprecision for the Delta test. First, constraint propagation of dependence lines and distances may be imprecise if an index cannot be completely eliminated from both references in the target subscripts. Second, complex iteration spaces such as triangular loops may impose constraints between subscripts not utilized by the Delta test. Finally, the Delta test does not propagate constraints from general MIV subscripts. As a result, coupled MIV subscripts may remain at the end of the Delta test. More general but expensive multiple subscript dependence tests such as the λ- or Power tests discussed in the next sections may be used in these cases.

Since each subscript in the coupled group is tested at most once, the complexity of the Delta test is linear in the number of subscripts. However, constraints may be propagated into subscripts multiple times.

3.4.2 More Powerful Multiple-Subscript Tests

Many of the earliest multiple-subscript tests utilized Fourier-Motzkin elimination, a linear programming method based on pairwise comparison of linear inequalities. Kuhn [192] and Triolet et al. [261] represent array accesses in convex regions that may be intersected using Fourier-Motzkin elimination. Regions may also be used to summarize memory accesses for entire segments of the program. These techniques are flexible but expensive. Triolet found that using Fourier-Motzkin elimination for dependence testing takes from 22 to 28 times longer than conventional dependence tests [260].

Li et al. present the λ-test, a multidimensional version of Banerjee's Inequalities that checks for simultaneous constrained real-valued solutions [202]. The λ-test forms linear combinations of subscripts that eliminate one or more instances of indices, then tests the result using Banerjee's Inequalities. Simultaneous real-valued solutions exist if and only if Banerjee's Inequalities find solutions in all the linear combinations generated.

The λ-test can test direction vectors and triangular loops. Its precision may be enhanced by also applying the GCD or single-index exact tests to the pseudosubscripts generated. However, there is no obvious method to extend the λ-test to prove the existence of simultaneous integer solutions. The λ-test is exact for two dimensions if unconstrained integer solutions exist and the coefficients of index variables are all 1, 0, or -1 [201]. However, even with these restrictions it is not exact for three or more coupled dimensions.

The Delta test may be viewed as a restricted form of the λ-test that trades generality for greater efficiency and precision.

Since testing linear subscript functions for dependence is equivalent to finding simultaneous integer solutions within loop limits, one approach has been to employ integer programming methods. However, these methods must be used with care because their high initialization costs and long running times—they are typically exponential in complexity—make them less desirable for dependence testing in a production system where the dependence test is applied many thousands of times during a single compilation. Nevertheless, if used with careful screening of special cases, they can be effective in eliminating more dependences than simpler methods. Two early examples of such strategies are Wallace's Constraint-Matrix test, a simplex algorithm modified for integer programming, and Banerjee's multidimensional GCD test, which applies Gaussian elimination modified for integers to create a compact system where all integer points provide integer solutions to the original dependence system [34].

A third strategy for adding to the power of dependence testing is to combine integer programming with Fourier-Motzkin elimination to determine whether an integral solution to the dependence equations exists. Wolfe and Tseng's Power test applies loop bounds using Fourier-Motzkin elimination to the dense system resulting from the multidimensional GCD test [286]. The Power test is expensive but well suited for providing precise dependence information such as direction vectors in imperfectly nested loops, loops with complex bounds, and in the presence of constraints not involving direction vectors.

Maydan, Hennessy, and Lam [207] present a dependence test, implemented in the SUIF system, that uses a cascade of special-case exact tests based on integer programming methods. As a backup, they use Fourier-Motzkin elimination if all special cases fail. To increase the efficiency of this test, they maintain a table of previously computed test results so that duplicate tests can be recognized quickly.

Pugh's Omega test [228] is based on an extension of Fourier-Motzkin elimination to integer programming. As such, it attempts to determine whether there exists a solution to the dependence equations rather than to find all such solutions. Although the procedure is potentially exponential, it has been shown to have low-order, polynomial complexity in many situations where cheaper methods are accurate. The Omega test can also be used to project integer programming problems onto a subset of the variables, rather than just deciding them, which makes it possible to accurately compute dependence direction and distance vectors. Over time, the Omega test has evolved into a general-purpose tool, called the Omega Calculator, for simplifying and verifying Presburger formulas. This system can be used to solve a variety of program analysis problems, including the elimination of false dependences [229].

3.5 **An Empirical Study**

To help the reader understand some of the trade-offs to be considered in real implementations of dependence testing, we present the results of a major dependence testing study conducted by Goff, Kennedy, and Tseng [123] using the dependence analysis system in PFC [20], the Rice program analysis system.

At the time of the test, PFC used the dependence analysis system described in this chapter, including subscript partitioning and the following dependence tests: ZIV (including symbolic), strong SIV (symbolic), weak SIV tests with special cases (weak-zero, weak-crossing, exact), MIV tests (GCD, Banerjee Inequality with single-loop triangularity), and the Delta test (with general constraint intersection but propagation of distance constraints only). The study measured the number of times each dependence test was applied by PFC when processing four groups of Fortran programs: RiCEPS (Rice Compiler Evaluation Program Suite), the Perfect and SPEC benchmark suites [92, 254], and two math libraries, EISPACK and LINPACK. These suites included 28 complete programs and two large subroutine libraries, containing 986 subroutines and 99,440 lines of Fortran

77 code. Table 3.1 summarizes the effectiveness of each dependence test relative to other tests by presenting the percentage contribution of each test to the total number of applications, successes, and independences. For the purpose of this table, a "success" is any test application that eliminates one or more directions. The percentages presented in this table are the results of summing over all programs.

Also displayed in Table 3.1 is the absolute effectiveness of each test; that is, the percentage of applications of each test that proved independence or was successful in eliminating one or more direction vectors.

In this study, PFC applied dependence tests 74,889 times (88% of all subscript pairs). Subscript pairs were not tested if they were nonlinear (6%), or if tests on other subscripts in the same multidimensional array had already proven independence. Over all array reference pairs tested, most subscript pairs were ZIV (45%) or strong SIV (34%). Few of the subscripts tested were MIV (5.1%). The ZIV and strong SIV tests combined for most of the successful tests (83%). The ZIV test accounted for almost all reference pairs proven independent (85%).

Goff, Kennedy, and Tseng also report that most subscripts in the programs were separable. Coupled subscripts (20% overall) were concentrated in a few programs, notably the EISPACK library, which accounted for 75% of all coupled subscripts. Most of the 8,449 coupled groups found were of size two; some coupled groups of size three were also encountered. The Delta test constraint intersection algorithm tested 6,570 coupled groups exactly (78% of all such groups). Propagation of distance constraints was applied in 376 cases (4.4% of the coupled groups), converting MIV subscripts into SIV form in all but 28 cases. The Delta test thus managed to test 6,918 coupled groups exactly (82%), using only constraint intersection and propagation of dependence distances.

The results show that the SIV and Delta tests tested most subscripts exactly. MIV tests such as the Banerjee-GCD test are only needed for a small fraction of all subscripts (5%), although they are important for certain programs. Many of the successful tests required PFC's ability to manipulate symbolic additive constants (28.5%).

In related studies, Li et al. showed that for coupled subscripts, multiple-subscript tests may detect independence in up to 36% more cases than subscript-

Table 3.1 Frequency and effectiveness of dependence tests

| | | SIV | | | | | | Symbolic used in |
Percentage	ZIV	Strong	Weak-zero	Weak-crossing	Exact	MIV	Delta	test
Of all tests	44.7	33.9	6.7	0.7	0.1	5.1	8.4	—
Of successful tests	30.9	51.8	7.6	0.6	0.2	2.6	6.0	28.5
Of proved independences	85.4	4.8	1.5	0.1	0.0	2.7	5.3	9.9
Success per application	43.9	97.0	71.7	47.9	87.7	33.0	45.4	—
Independent per application	43.9	3.2	5.2	3.9	0.0	12.4	14.3	—

by-subscript tests in libraries such as EISPACK [202]. A comprehensive empirical study of array subscripts and conventional dependence tests was performed by Shen et al. [247].

From these statistics, several conclusions are obvious. First, within the framework presented, the ZIV, strong SIV, weak-zero SIV, and MIV tests, along with some form of coupled subscript test, are essential for accurate dependence testing. The weak-crossing and exact SIV tests are almost never used, but it has been shown that they catch important special cases when they are invoked. However, they should be a lower priority in an implementation of dependence testing. Since symbolic tests were used in over 28% of the tests, not counting tests that permit symbolic loop bounds (almost every loop), handling of symbolics is also essential.

A final observation is that the MIV and complex coupled subscript tests are invoked so infrequently that it is reasonable to use a more powerful (and more expensive) test of some sort, such as the multiple-subscript tests discussed in Section 3.4.2.

3.6 Putting It All Together

Figures 3.14 and 3.15 contain a detailed version of the dependence testing algorithm originally described in Section 3.2. There are several important points to be made about this algorithm. First, this tester is called once for each pair of array references that are being tested for dependence. An assumption is made about which reference is the source and which reference is the sink. However, the dependence tester is fully capable of reporting direction vectors that have ">" as the leading direction. In that case, the calling procedure will reverse the sense of the dependence corresponding to that direction vector and reverse the direction of the dependence.

To understand this, consider the following:

```
       DO I = 1, N
S₀       T = B(I,J)
         DO J = 2, N
S₁         A(J-1) = T
S₂         T = A(J) + B(I,J)
         ENDDO
S₃       C(I) = C(I) + A(J)
       ENDDO
```

If we examine the dependence of statement S_2 on statement S_1 due to the array reference A, we might pass reference A(J-1) as R_1, the assumed source reference, and reference A(J) as R_2, the sink reference. When the tester returns, it will produce the direction vector set (*,>). Thus the complete set of direction vectors are (<,>), (=,>), and (>,>). The first direction corresponds to a true dependence

boolean procedure *test_dependence*($R_1,R_2,L,n,DVset$)

// R_1 and R_2 are the source and sink array references
//   enclosed in a collection of n loops.
// L is a collection of loop descriptors ($LD_1, LD_2, \ldots, LD_n$) where
//   each descriptor LD_i is a quadruple (I_i, L_i, U_i, s_i), representing
//   the loop index, lower bound, upper bound, and step, respectively
// *DVset* is an output variable representing the set of direction vectors
//   for the dependences that are found between these two references.

let m be the number of subscript positions in the reference pair;
allocate $S[1:m]$, an array of subscript pairs;
for $j := 1$ **to** m **do** $S[j] := (R_1[j], R_2[j])$;
for $j := 1$ **to** m **do**
    linear[j] := *analyze_subscript*($S[j]$, $nx[j]$, $In[j][0:nx[j]]$,
        $a[j][0:nx[j]]$, $b[j][0:nx[j]]$);
// *In* is an output array such that $In[i]$ is the set of loop indices in $S[j]$.

partition(S,P, n_p);
// P is an output variable containing a collection of partitions $P[1:p]$
//   where each $P[k]$ is a set of subscripts in the partition

$DVset := \{(*,*, \ldots, *)\}$;

// First test all separable subscripts.
for $k := 1$ **to** n_p **do**
    if $\|P[k]\| = 1$ **then begin**
        depExists = *test_separable*($P[k]$, *DVset*);
        if not *depExists* **then return** *false*;
    end

// Now iterate through the partitions again to test coupled groups.
for $k := 1$ **to** n_p **do**
    if $\|P[k]\| > 1$ **then begin**
        $InP := \emptyset$;
        for all $j \in P[k]$ **do** $InP := InP \cup In[j]$;
        depExists = *Delta_test*($P[k]$, *DV*, *dV*);
        if not *depExists* **then return** *depExists*;
        else *merge_vector_sets*(InP, *DVset*, *DV*);
    end
return *true*;
end *test_dependence*

Figure 3.14 Complete dependence testing algorithm.

carried by the outer loop, while the last two dependences correspond to antide-pendences carried by the inner and outer loops, respectively. After this result, the calling program would report that the set of actual dependences are a true depen-

boolean procedure *test_separable(P, DVset)*

    // *P* is the subscript partition, which must contain only one subscript
    // *DVset* is the direction vector collection so far

    let *j* be the single subscript position in *P*;
    if *linear[j]* **then begin**
        if $nx[j] = 0$ **then** *depExists = ZIV_test(a[j][0],b[j][0])*;
        else if $nx[j] = 1$ **then**
            depExists = SIV_test(In[j], a[j][0:1], b[j][0:1], DV, dV);
        else
            depExists =
                MIV_test(In[j], a[j][0:nx[j]],b[j][0:nx[j]], DV, dV);
        if not *depExists* **then return** *false*;
        else begin
            merge_vector_sets(In[j], DVset, DV);
            return *true*;
        end
    end
    else return *true*;
end *test_separable*

Figure 3.15 Separable subscript testing.

dence with direction vector (<,>), an antidependence with direction vector (=,<), and an antidependence with direction (<,<). Note that all directions have been reversed in the two antidependences, which is the correct action when the sense of a dependence is reversed.

This strategy of producing and reporting all direction vectors, even illegal ones, permits the tester to be called for each distinct pair of references only once. Thus, if the set of references in the program is $\{R_1, R_2, \ldots, R_N\}$ ordered by dependence, we might see the following loop in the driver:

    for $i := 1$ **to** N **do**
        for $j := i$ **to** N **do begin**
            depExists := test_dependence$(R_i, R_j, L, n, DVset)$;
            if *depExists* **then begin**
                // record each distinct DV as a dependence in the graph
                // reversing the sense of dependences with illegal DVs
                . . .
            end
        end

Preliminary Analysis One of the first things done by *test_dependence* is to reorganize the pair of references into a collection of subscript pairs, one for each position in the references. Once this is done, the routine *analyze_subscript* is called for each subscript position. This routine parses the subscript pair and determines whether the subscript can be expressed as a linear combination of the indices of the loops that contain the pair of references

$$<a_1i_1 + a_2i_2 +\ldots+ a_ni_n + a_0, b_1i_1 + b_2i_2 +\ldots+ b_ni_n + b_0>$$

For the subscript pair to be reported as linear, each of the values of a_i and b_i for all i must be a constant or a symbolic expression whose value does not vary in the loop nest. (Some dependence testers also require that only a_0 and b_0 be symbolic.) If the subscripts cannot be put into the correct form, *analyze_subscript* reports that the subscript is *nonlinear* and therefore cannot be tested. It does this by returning the value *false*.

The procedure *analyze_subscript*, which we will not detail here, requires that the subscript expressions be parsed and factored. This can require a substantive amount of work. In addition to the Boolean return value, the procedure returns the number of loop indices actually found in the subscript, stored in $nx[j]$, along with an array stored into $ln[j][0:nx[j]]$ that contains the level numbers of the loop indices found. It also returns the actual values for the a_i and b_i found in the subscript in the arrays $a[j][0:nx[j]]$ and $b[j][0:nx[j]]$. Thus, if the indices for levels 1, 3, and 4 are found in subscript position j, the coefficients a_1, a_3, and a_4 will be found in $a[j][1]$, $a[j][2]$, and $a[j][3]$, respectively. Thus, the representation is reasonably compact.

Once the subscripts are analyzed, we call the procedure *partition*, which is described in abstract form in Figure 3.1. Note that *partition* must return an array of partitions, each of which is a disjoint subset of subscript positions in the reference pair, where subscript positions are integers between 1 and m.

Finally, dependence testing begins in earnest. First, all the subscripts are visited and linear separable subscripts are tested using the ZIV and SIV tests as shown in procedure *test_separable* in Figure 3.15. If none of these tests yields independence, the coupled groups are tested. Except for the ZIV test, each test that does not prove independence produces a set of possible direction vectors *DV*. This set must then be merged with the aggregate set for the dependence by the procedure *merge_vector_sets*, given in Figure 3.16.

Direction Vector Merging The merging process is made easier by the fact that each of the tests is applied to a single partition of the subscripts. Recall that each partition contains a unique collection of the loop indices. That is, no partition contains a loop index that is found in any other partition. Therefore, we can be sure that when we perform the merge, all direction vectors for the dependence have the entry "*" in positions for the set of indices found in the just-tested partition. Therefore, we can essentially take the Cartesian product, producing a set of direction vectors that is of size equal to the number of vectors for the partition times the number of such vectors for the dependence so far.

procedure *merge_vector_sets*(*In,DVset,DV*)

>// *In* is the list of indices that are represented in the direction vectors
>// *DVset* is the current direction vector set that will be augmented
>// *DV* is the set of distance vectors for the indices in list *In*

>// This routine is only called when the columns of
>//   all current direction vectors for the indices in list *In* are "*"
>// Thus we can simply replicate all current direction vectors to the
>//   cardinality of *DV* and fill in the directions for each new vector.

>$nV := \| DV \|$; $nI := \| In \|$; $nDVset := \| DVset \|$
>$newDVset :=$ **new** $DVarray[nDVset*nV]$;

>$lastNewDV := 0$
>**for** $i := 1$ **to** nV **do begin**
>>**for** $j := 1$ **to** $nDVset$ **do begin**
>>>$thisDV :=$ copy of $DVset[j]$;
>>>**for** $k := 1$ **to** nI **do** $thisDV[In[k]] := DV[i][k]$;
>>>$lastNewDV := lastNewDV + 1$;
>>>$newDVset[lastNewDV] := thisDV$;
>>**end**
>**end**
>**free** *DVset*;
>$DVset := newDVset$;

end *merge_vector_sets*

Figure 3.16 Direction and distance vector merging.

We can illustrate the merge procedure with an example. Suppose we have the following code:

```
      DO I = 1, N
         DO J = 2, N
            DO K = 1, N
S              A(I,J,J+K) = A(I+1,J,J+K) + C
            ENDDO
         ENDDO
      ENDDO
```

In testing the two references in statement S, we begin with the default direction vector (*,*,*). The first subscript is separable, so the SIV test is applied to it first. This returns the direction ">" and the distance −1. The merge process simply inserts the direction into the position for I, the outer loop index, to produce (>,*,*). Next the coupled group consisting of subscripts 2 and 3 are tested. Applying the SIV test to the second subscript produces the direction "=" for the J-loop.

This means that the value of J is equal at the source and the sink. When this is substituted into the third position, the values of J can be dropped from the equation and we get the direction "=" for the K-loop as well.

Thus the direction vector for the partition, which consists of the J- and K-loops, is (=,=). When this is merged with the current direction vector set (>,*,*), the result is (>,=,=). From this we see that the self-dependence on S is an antidependence with direction vector (<,=,=). Note that the merging always takes place into positions with "*" in the current direction vector set.

Distances and Breaking Conditions   Although we have discussed the handling of direction vectors, we have not shown how these algorithms can be extended to handle distances and other annotations such as crossing thresholds and breaking conditions. In most dependence testers, these quantities are added as annotations to the direction vectors. In the previous example, the only direction whose distance is unknown is the ">" associated with a distance of −1. This information can be added as an annotation to the direction by including a Boolean variable indicating that there is an associated distance, a type indicating the kind of distance, and a value. So the direction vector would actually look something like this:

$$(>[\text{fixed}:-1],=,=)$$

Symbolic distance and breaking conditions could be handled similarly.

Note that the breaking condition for the dependence is the disjunction of the breaking conditions for all of the directions that have such conditions. Of course, the ZIV test gives rise to breaking conditions that do not relate to any specific direction. These can be attached to the direction vector as a whole. This representation takes advantage of the fact that distances and breaking conditions are less common than directions, so space need not be allocated for such annotations in every loop index position.

Scalar Dependences   A final pragmatic issue is the representation of dependences associated with scalar variables. To understand the problem, consider the following example:

```
      DO I = 1, N
        DO J = 1, N
          DO K = 1, N
S              T = T + A(I,J,K)
          ENDDO
        ENDDO
      ENDDO
```

Because the scalar variable T is not indexed by any variable, we can see that it has a dependence carried by every one of the three loops. In fact the two references to T give rise to three classes of dependence: output dependences due to the left-hand side occurrence of T, antidependences from the right-hand side occurrence to the left-hand side occurrence, and true dependences from the left-hand side occurrence to the right-hand side occurrence. The sets of direction vectors are as follows:

1. Output dependence: $(<,*,<), (<,*,>), (=,<,<), (=,<,>)$
2. Antidependence: $(<,*,<), (<,*,>), (=,<,<), (=,<,>)$
3. True dependence: $(<,*,<), (<,*,>), (=,<,<), (=,<,>)$

In other words, there are eight distinct direction vectors for each dependence. If we record a distinct dependence for each of these direction vectors as we do with dependences due to array references, the space requirements will quickly become unmanageable. In fact, this happened in an early version of PFC, in which a fairly small subroutine caused the maximum of 64,000 entries in the dependence table to be exceeded.

To avoid problems of this sort, it is better to represent scalar dependences in a summary form that indicates the set of loops that carry the dependence and whether a loop-independent dependence is possible. For the previous example, we would record that all three loops can carry a dependence but that loop-independent dependences are not possible. This can be represented as a range of loop levels plus a single Boolean variable.

3.7 Summary

Dependence testing is the process of determining whether two references to the same variable in a given set of loops might access the same memory location. If a dependence is possible, the testing procedure must identify the set of direction vectors, and in some cases the distances, that describe all possible dependences between the given pair.

In the most general case, dependence testing amounts to determining whether a system of Diophantine equations has a solution within the bounds of iteration of the loop nest in which the subscripted references appear. In most cases, this problem is simplified by focusing only on subscripts that can be described as affine combinations of the loop induction variable. Even then, however, the problem is complicated by the existence of symbolic coefficients in the linear expressions.

In this chapter we have presented a dependence testing procedure that uses a case-based analysis to ensure that the most frequent cases are handled efficiently and accurately. This procedure consists of the following steps:

1. Partition the subscripts, where a subscript is a matched pair of subscript positions in the pair of references, into separable and minimal coupled groups. A subscript is *separable* if none of the induction variables that appear in it appear in any other subscript. A coupled group is *minimal* if it

cannot be partitioned into two nonempty subgroups with distinct sets of indices. Once a partition is achieved, each separable subscript and each coupled group have completely disjoint sets of indices. Each partition may then be tested in isolation and the resulting distance or direction vectors merged with no loss of precision.

2. Classify each subscript position as ZIV (containing zero induction variables), SIV (containing a single induction variable) or MIV (containing multiple induction variables).

3. For each separable subscript, apply the appropriate single-subscript test (ZIV, SIV, MIV) based on the complexity of the subscript. This will produce independence or direction vectors for the indices occurring in that subscript. If independence is proved, no further testing is needed in other positions.

4. For each coupled group, apply a multiple-subscript test, such as the Delta test, to produce a set of direction vectors for the indices occurring within that group.

5. If any test yields independence, no further testing is needed as no dependences exist. Otherwise merge all the direction vectors computed in the previous steps into a single set of direction vectors for the two references.

The chapter presents detailed descriptions of ZIV and SIV tests and discusses in detail the GCD test and Banerjee Inequality—a fast and accurate pair of MIV tests. To be truly effective, any testing procedure must handle symbolic coefficients and trapezoidal loops. Extensions to the tests to handle these cases are also presented.

3.8 Case Studies

Both the PFC and Ardent Titan compiler implemented dependence testing along lines described in this chapter. The original PFC vectorizer tested only for subscripts carried by one of the loop contained the dependence pair. For example, if a pair were contained in three loops, it would test for the following direction vectors:

1. $(<,*,*)$ — carried by the outermost loop
2. $(=,<,*)$ — carried by the next-to-outermost loop
3. $(=,=,<)$ — carried by the innermost loop

It would also construct threshold (distance) information for each carrier loop and would test for whether interchanging the innermost with the next-to-innermost loop was legal. In a nest of three loops, this consisted of testing for the direction vector (=,<,>). All these tests were conducted using the triangular Banerjee Inequality and the GCD test.

PFC was later enhanced to include the ZIV, all SIV, and the MIV tests, along with a restricted version of the Delta test, as described in this chapter. The triangular Banerjee Inequality was restricted to at most one outer loop index included in any loop upper bound [170].

This second version of PFC computed complete direction vectors and, where possible, also computed distance vectors. A symbolic expression would be recorded as a distance if the symbolic quantities in the expression were invariant throughout the loop. These distances could be used in symbolic dependence testing.

PFC also recorded breaking conditions and used them to insert run-time dependence testing. These conditions were also used to eliminate dependences in an interactive programming tool called PTOOL [18], which used PFC as the dependence testing engine. The ParaScope Editor [31, 79, 132] also used PFC for testing dependence before incorporating its own testing system.

An important feature of PFC was its support for interprocedural analysis, which made it possible to do interprocedural dependence testing along the lines described in Chapter 11.

3.9   Historical Comments and References

The earliest work on dependence tests concentrated on deriving distance vectors from strong SIV subscripts [191, 195, 219]. Cohagan [77] described a test that analyzes general SIV subscripts symbolically. Banerjee and Wolfe [33, 283] developed the current form of the single-index exact test. Callahan describes the separability approach used in PFC [51].

For MIV subscripts, the GCD test may be used to check unconstrained integer solutions [32, 168]. Banerjee's Inequalities provide a useful general-purpose single-subscript test for constrained real solutions [33]. It has also been adapted to provide many different types of dependence information [21, 34, 49, 168, 170, 283]. Research has shown that Banerjee's Inequalities are exact in many common cases [32, 184, 201], though results have not been extended for direction vectors or complex iteration spaces.

The I-test developed by Kong et al. integrates the GCD and Banerjee tests and can usually prove integer solutions [188]. Gross and Steenkiste propose an efficient interval analysis method for calculating dependences for arrays [126]. Unfortunately, their method does not handle coupled subscripts and is unsuitable for most loop transformations since distance and direction vectors are not calculated.

Lichnewsky and Thomasset describe symbolic dependence testing in the VATIL vectorizer [203]. Haghighat and Polychronopoulos propose a flow analysis framework to aid symbolic tests [128].

Execution conditions may also be used to refine dependence tests. Wolfe's All-Equals test checks for loop-independent dependences invalidated by control flow within the loop [283]. Lu and Chen's subdomain test incorporates information about indices from conditionals within the loop body [205]. Klappholz and Kong have extended Banerjee's Inequalities to do the same [183].

Early approaches to impose simultaneity in testing multidimensional arrays include intersecting direction vectors from each dimension [283] and linearization [49, 121]; they proved inaccurate in many cases. True multiple-subscript tests provide precision at the expense of efficiency by considering all subscripts simultaneously. These tests are discussed in Section 3.4.2. The Delta test described in this chapter was developed by Goff, Kennedy, and Tseng [123].

Exercises

3.1 In each of the following examples, suppose you are testing for dependence of statement S upon itself. Which subscript positions are separable? Which are coupled? Which dependence test would be applied to each position by the dependence testing procedure described in this chapter?

a.
```
        DO K = 1, 100
          DO J = 1, 100
            DO I = 1, 100
  S             A(I+1,J+1,K+1) = A(I,J,1) + C
            ENDDO
          ENDDO
        ENDDO
```

b.
```
        DO K = 1, 100
          DO J = 1, 100
            DO I = 1, 100
  S             A(I+1,J+K+1,K+1) = A(I,J,K) + C
            ENDDO
          ENDDO
        ENDDO
```

c.
```
        DO K = 1, 100
          DO J = 1, 100
            DO I = 1, 100
  S             A(I+1,J+K+1,I) = A(I,J,2) + C
            ENDDO
          ENDDO
        ENDDO
```

3.2 In the following example compute the entire set of direction vectors for all potential dependences in the loop. Be specific about the type of dependence in each case. Describe the tests that would be used by the dependence tester in this chapter on this example.

```
            DO K = 1, 100
               DO J = 1, 100
                  DO I = 1, 100
    S₁                A(I+1,J+4,K+1) = B(I,J,K) + C
    S₂                B(I+J,5,K+1) = A(2,K,K) + D
                  ENDDO
               ENDDO
            ENDDO
```

3.3 For the following examples, construct valid breaking conditions.

a.
```
        DO I = 1, 100
    S       A(I+IX) = A(I) + C
        ENDDO
```

b.
```
        DO K = 1, 100
           DO J = 1, 100
              DO I = 1, 100
    S             A(I+1,J+1,K+1) = A(I,JX,K) + C
              ENDDO
           ENDDO
        ENDDO
```

c.
```
        DO K = 1, 100
           DO J = 1, 100
              DO I = 1, 100
    S             A(I+1,J+K+JX) = A(I,J) + C
              ENDDO
           ENDDO
        ENDDO
```

3.4 Section 3.3.2 considers the effect of a trapezoidal iteration space on the strong SIV dependence test. Show what you would get on the same example by applying the trapezoidal Banerjee Inequality from Section 3.3.3. Is it the same or different? Why?

3.5 Section 3.3.2 also considers the weak-zero SIV test in a trapezoidal region of iteration. Is the result the same as you would get by applying the trapezoidal Banerjee Inequality?

3.6 Using Lemma 3.2, show that in the region $L_i^x \leq x_i \leq U_i^x$, $L_i^y \leq y_i \leq U_i^y$

$$-a_i^- U_i^x + a_i^+ L_i^x - b_i^+ U_i^y + b_i^- L_i^y \leq a_i x_i - b_i y_i$$

$$\leq a_i^+ U_i^x - a_i^- L_i^x + b_i^- U_i^y - b_i^+ L_i^y$$

(This is case 4 in the proof of Lemma 3.3.)

CHAPTER 4

Preliminary Transformations

4.1 Introduction

Most of the dependence tests presented in Chapter 3 require that subscript expressions be linear or affine functions of loop induction variables, with known constant coefficients and at most a symbolic additive constant. If these tests are to construct an accurate dependence graph, most of the subscripts in a program must be in this form.

Unfortunately, programs are not typically written with dependence testing in mind. Programmers tend to write code that exploits the quirks of different versions of the Fortran language or its compilers. Furthermore, many idiosyncratic practices have been developed to overcome weaknesses in compiler optimization strategies. The result is often code that defeats the best dependence analyzer. The following example is typical:

```
INC = 2
KI = 0
DO I = 1, 100
   DO J = 1, 100
      KI = KI + INC
      U(KI) = U(KI) + W(J)
   ENDDO
   S(I)= U(KI)
ENDDO
```

Only two subscripts in this loop nest—W(J) and S(I)—are affine functions of the loop induction variables. In particular, the expression U(KI) (which is involved in every dependence test) cannot be tested in the form written because KI varies within the loop. If the tests from Chapter 3 are to be successfully applied to this example, the code must be transformed.

To address problems of this sort, a number of transformations can be applied prior to dependence testing with the goal of making testing more accurate. These transformations can make many more subscripts amenable to accurate testing as described in Chapter 3.

One critical transformation in this process is *induction-variable substitution*. In the example above, the variable INC is invariant within the inner loop. Therefore, the assignment to KI within the J-loop increments its value by a constant amount on each loop iteration. This increment makes KI an *auxiliary induction variable*; it is essentially another loop variable that tracks the regular loop index (J), but with a different increment or starting point. Induction-variable substitution transforms every reference to an auxiliary induction variable into a direct function of the loop index. Applying this transformation to the inner loop yields

```
      INC = 2
      KI = 0
      DO I = 1, 100
         DO J = 1, 100
            ! Deleted: KI = KI + INC
            U(KI+J*INC) = U(KI+J*INC) + W(J)
         ENDDO
S₁       KI = KI + 100 * INC
         S(I)= U(KI)
      ENDDO
```

The uses of KI within the loop have been changed to a function of the loop induction variable; the increment has been deleted (changed to a CONTINUE statement); and S_1 has been inserted to set KI to the correct value outside of the loop. Note that there is still a reference to KI in the loop, but it now contains the loop-invariant initial value for that variable.

By inserting an increment of KI in the outer loop, the transformation has made KI an auxiliary induction variable with respect to that loop. A second application of induction-variable substitution is needed to completely eliminate KI as an auxiliary induction variable:

```
      INC = 2
      KI = 0
      DO I = 1, 100
         DO J = 1, 100
            U(KI + (I-1)*100*INC+J*INC) = &
               U(KI+(I-1)*100*INC+J*INC) + W(J)
```

```
      ENDDO
      ! Deleted: KI = KI + 100 * INC
      S(I)= U(KI+I*(100*INC))
   ENDDO
   KI = KI + 100*100*INC
```

Now all subscripts are affine functions of loop induction variables, although the coefficients are all symbolic.

The next step in simplifying this program is to recognize that the values of INC and KI used within the loops are actually just constant values. *Constant propagation* of the values from outside the loop will eliminate these symbolic quantities, yielding after simplification

```
   INC = 2
   ! Deleted: KI = 0
   DO I = 1, 100
      DO J = 1, 100
         U(I*200+J*2-200) = U(I*200+J*2-200) + W(J)
      ENDDO
      S(I) = U(I*200)
   ENDDO
   KI = 20,000
```

Although this example is now in a form amenable to dependence testing, it has some useless redundancy—some of the constant-valued assignments may never be used. In particular, the assignments to KI and INC are needed only if they are used later in the program. Rather than wasting code space and execution time for these assignments, we can discover and delete them via *dead code elimination*. Assuming there are no uses of KI or INC after the loop, this would yield

```
   DO I = 1, 100
      DO J = 1, 100
         U(I*200+J*2-200) = U(I*200+J*2-200) + W(J)
      ENDDO
      S(I) = U(I*200)
   ENDDO
```

In practice, many programs contain code similar to the example above. Thus, the ability to transform code is important for dependence testing to be successful. This chapter presents methods for performing preliminary transformations on programs to make them fit the requirements of dependence tests. Because these transformations become more difficult in the presence of control flow, we will delay discussion of control until Chapter 7.

4.2   **Information Requirements**

When discussing methods for dependence testing, Chapter 3 assumed a number of properties for loops. For instance, most of the dependence tests as stated assume that loops have a step size of 1. In order to implement these tests, it is necessary to gather information regarding which loops meet these requirements and to do something about those that do not. Furthermore, implementing the transformations described in the previous section requires knowledge about the structure and use of data within a program. The necessary information includes the following:

1. *Loop stride:* Although dependence tests can be recast to accommodate non-unit strides, they are easiest to implement if the stride is 1.

2. *Loop-invariant quantities:* Compilers must be able to recognize loop-invariant variables and expressions if they are to find opportunities for auxiliary induction-variable substitution.

3. *Constant-valued assignments:* Recognition of constant-valued assignments is a critical preliminary to constant propagation.

4. *Usage of variables:* Propagating a constant-valued assignment requires knowing which statements use the variable defined by that assignment. Similarly, dead code recognition involves identifying statements whose outputs are never used.

The process of gathering this information involves well-known scalar optimization techniques. In particular, the last three items are usually computed by scalar *data flow analysis*. The remainder of this chapter provides a simple introduction to the program transformation and data flow analysis strategies needed to compute the required information.

4.3   **Loop Normalization**

To make the dependence testing process as simple as possible, many advanced compilers normalize all loops to run from a lower bound of 1 to some upper bound with a stride of 1—basically making all loops "count off" the iterations they execute, replacing references to the original loop induction variables with affine functions of the new induction variables. This transformation is called *loop normalization*.

As originally defined, the term "loop normalization" applied specifically to this one transformation. However, dependence tests require a lot of information about loops—for example, which loops surround which statements, which induction variables control which loops, and what bounds control each loop. Since this information must be gathered sometime prior to testing proper and since loop normalization must examine all loops anyway, many compilers implement loop normalization as a general normalization and information-gathering phase. As a result, the term is often applied not only to the specific transformation, but also to a general phase for gathering information about loops. We will use "loop normalization" interchangeably for either the transformation or the phase; the context should clarify the intended meaning.

Figure 4.1 presents a simple algorithm for loop normalization that can be applied to any Fortran 90 DO-loop with integer control parameters. It replaces the original loop index variable with one that is normalized and substitutes an equivalent expression in the new index variable for references to the original. Note that for simplicity we treat the lowercase variable i as a compiler-introduced variable that is different from the uppercase I even though most Fortran 90 implementations would make them the same.

Correctness To show that *normalizeLoop* has the desired effect, we only need to show that the loop bound computed in step S_1, the substituted index values computed in step S_2, and the finalization value computed in step S_3 are correct. That is, the substituted loop has the same number of iterations, and the expressions substituted for the original loop induction variable are equivalent.

In a Fortran 90 loop, the loop index is set to the loop lower bound just outside the loop and tested to ensure that it is less than the upper bound. On subsequent iterations the increment is added to the current index value, and if the result is less than or equal to the upper bound, the loop body is executed. Thus the body of the loop is executed for each value of the new induction variable i such that

$$\text{L + (i-1) * S} \le \text{U}$$

procedure *normalizeLoop*(L_0)
    // L_0 is the loop to be normalized

        let i be a unique compiler-generated loop induction variable;

S_1 : replace the loop header for L_0
        DO I ← L, U, S
      with the adjusted loop header
        DO i ← 1, (U-L+S)/S;

S_2: replace each reference to **I** within the loop by
        i * S - S + L;

S_3: insert a finalization assignment
        I ← i * S - S + L
        immediately after the end of the loop;
end *normalizeLoop*

Figure 4.1 Loop normalization algorithm.

In other words, it is executed for each value of i such that

$$i * S \leq U - L + S$$

The largest value of i within the loop iteration range must therefore be the greatest integer less than or equal to

$$(U-L+S)/S$$

where division is interpreted as producing a real number. However, integer division in Fortran produces the largest integer less than or equal to the real quotient. Therefore the loop count computed in step 1 is correct.

Next we must show that the value substituted for the original loop induction variable I has the same value as I on every iteration. Clearly, the value on the first iteration, when $i = 1$, is correct because that value is L. If the value is correct on one iteration, it must be correct on the subsequent iteration because the substituted value on the subsequent iteration is greater than the substituted value on the correct iteration by S, the loop increment. Thus the substitutions in step 2 are correct.

On exit from a Fortran loop, the loop induction variable takes on the value of that variable on the last loop iteration incremented by the step size S. By the reasoning above, this must be

$$i * S - S + L$$

where i is the exit value for the generated loop induction variable. Given that all the subscript values are the same in the normalized loop, normalization is always safe because it does not change the order of any statements in the loop. Thus all dependences are preserved. Furthermore, the values of the original induction variable after the loop are correctly reconstructed. Therefore, the transformation preserves the meaning of the original program.

Loop normalization offers a number of advantages. In addition to simplifying dependence testing it creates a loop index that is equivalent to the iteration count of the loop. This makes transformations like induction-variable substitution easier to perform.

However, loop normalization also possesses some significant disadvantages. The most prominent of these is the possibility of distorting the properties dependences. The following loop nest illustrates this:

```
      DO I = 1, M
        DO J = I, N
S₁          A(J,I) = A(J,I-1) + 5
        ENDDO
      ENDDO
```

The true dependence of S_1 on itself has a direction vector of $(<,=)$. When the inner loop is normalized, the following code is produced:

```
      DO I = 1, M
         DO J = 1, N - I + 1
S₁          A(J+I-1,I) = A(J+I-1,I-1) + 5
         ENDDO
      ENDDO
```

Since this is a safe reordering transformation, the dependence must still exist. However, the direction vector has been transformed from $(<,=)$ into $(<,>)$. This transformation is not completely harmless. Consider, for instance, attempting to interchange the I- and J-loops (loop interchange is discussed fully in Section 5.2). The effect of loop interchange on direction vectors is to swap the entries corresponding to the interchanged loops. As a result, loop interchange applied to the original direction vector of $(<,=)$ yields a new direction vector of $(=,<)$, which preserves the dependence and is obviously safe. Loop interchange applied to the normalized direction vector of $(<,>)$ yields a new direction vector of $(>,<)$, which reverses the dependence, and is obviously *not* safe. Thus normalization has made this interchange invalid, although we shall see that this problem can be overcome via another transformation.

Normalization also creates problems when the step size in the original loop is symbolic. In this case, normalization produces a symbolic coefficient in the expressions introduced for the original induction variable, making it difficult to test for dependence in any subscript in which those expressions appear. In such cases it is actually better to apply a simple version of normalization that assumes the step size is exactly 1. This loses precision but makes it possible to test the subscripts. In practice, the run-time value of symbolic subscripts is often equal to 1, as in applications that use the LINPACK library, where the generality of a user-selected stride is almost never needed.

In spite of these drawbacks, loop normalization is a useful transformation and is applied in almost all vectorizing compilers. Although it is not required, the examples in this book assume, for simplicity, that normalization has been performed. Note, however, that the dependence tests in Chapter 3 all work with arbitrary lower bounds.

4.4 Data Flow Analysis

The goal of data flow analysis is to understand how data elements are created and used in a program in order to support optimizing transformations that preserve the program's meaning. There is a voluminous literature on scalar data flow analysis (see Kennedy [169] and Muchnick [218]), which we do not presume to adequately represent here. Instead, we present a brief introduction to the methods for constructing auxiliary data structures—definition-use chains and static single-assignment form—that are useful for supporting both dependence analysis and transformations discussed later in this chapter and the rest of the book.

4.4.1   Definition-Use Chains

One ubiquitous need throughout all the described preliminary transformations was that of being able to easily get from a definition of a variable to all locations that could consume that defined value. Definition-use chains are a data structure designed precisely to ease that operation:

DEFINITION 4.1	The *definition-use graph* is a graph that contains an edge from each definition point in the program to every possible use of the variable at run time.

We use the term "definition-use graph" instead of the more traditional "definition-use chains" because "graph" more correctly characterizes the nature of the information it contains. The definition-use graph is essentially the scalar version of the true dependences within a program.

Constructing definition-use edges within a single straight-line block[1] of code is very simple. You walk through each statement in order in the basic block, noting the variables defined by each statement (also called its *definitions*) as well as the variables used by each statement (its *uses*). For each use, an edge is added to the definition-use graph to that use from the last *exposed* definition of that variable in the block—in other words, from the definition that *reaches* the use. Whenever a new definition is encountered for a variable, the new definition *kills* the existing definition, so that later uses are linked only to the new definition, not to the old. When the end of the block is reached, the local graph is complete.

In addition to the local graph, the basic block computation also produces a number of useful sets that characterize the behavior of the block. These include the following:

> *uses(b):* The set of all variables used within the block *b* that have no prior definitions within the block. In other words, these are uses that are not "satisfied" within the block, so they are exposed to any definitions that reach this block from previous blocks.

---

1. Such blocks are also called *basic blocks*. A basic block is a maximal group of statements such that one statement in the group is executed if and only if every statement is executed. In other words, there is no control flow into or out of a basic block except at its very beginning or its very end. For more information, see Kennedy [169].

defsout(b): The set of all definitions within block *b* that are not killed within the
block. In other words, these are all the definitions that can reach other
blocks outside of *b*.

killed(b): The set of all definitions that define variables killed by other definitions within block *b*. Any definitions from other blocks that try to "reach
through" *b* will be stopped if they are in *killed(b)*.

These sets provide the basic tools for constructing the definition-use graph for
the whole program, rather than individual blocks. Given these local sets, the one
missing set necessary for computation of global edges is the set *reaches(b)*—the set
of all definitions from all blocks (including *b*) that can possibly reach *b*. For any
given block *b*, all global definition-use edges can be obtained by adding an edge for
each element in *reaches(b)* to all appropriate elements of *uses(b)*. As a result, if we
can find a way to compute *reaches* for all blocks, we can build the definition-use
graph.

In order to understand how to compute *reaches* globally, it is first useful to
look at the problem on a very limited graph: one basic block *b* and some number
of predecessors, each of which can reach *b* via some form of control flow. In this
simple graph, *reaches(b)* along any one predecessor *p* is the set of all definitions
that reach *p* (*reaches(p)*) and that also are not killed inside *p* (the negation of
killed(p)), plus those definitions in *p* that reach the exit of *p* (*defsout(p)*).
Expressed more formally, *reaches(b)* can be defined by the following equation:

$$reaches(b) \ = \ \bigcup_{p \in P(b)} (defsout(p) \cup (reaches(p) \cap \neg killed(p))) \qquad (4.1)$$

This equation is obviously simple to solve over the limited graph described
above, but is not so simple over general control flow graphs. The complication is
that computing *reaches* for one block *b* may immediately change all other *reaches*
(including that for *b* itself), since *reaches(b)* is an input into other *reaches* equations. Achieving the correct solution requires simultaneously solving all individual
equations.

Fortunately, the underlying mathematics of this problem guarantee that iteratively applying Equation 4.1 at each node in the program will eventually terminate with a stable solution that is exactly the one obtained by simultaneously
solving all equations. That proof is beyond the scope of this book.[2] However, the
result yields the conceptually simple iterative method for solving systems of data
flow equations, presented in Figure 4.2. Although this approach is the most
straightforward to implement, its asymptotic worst-case bound is the most complex. The algorithm begins with a naive initial approximation to the solution—all
reaches sets for inputs to Equation 4.1 are null. The method then repeatedly iterates over all vertices until it reaches a fixed point (a point where each pass

---

2. See Kennedy [169] for more details.

procedure *iterate*(G)
    // G = (N,E) is the input control flow graph, where
    // N is the set of basic blocks and
    // E is the set of control flow edges
    // *defsout*(b) is the set of definitions in b that reaches the exit of b
    // *killed*(b) is the set of definitions that cannot reach the end of b
    //   due to an intervening assignment
    // *reaches*(b) is the set of definitions that reach block b

    for each b ∈ G **do** *reaches*(b) = ∅;

    // Iterate to a fixed point
    changed := *true*;
    while *changed* **do begin**
        changed := *false*;
        for each b ∈ N **do begin**
            newreaches := *reaches*(b);
            foreach p ∈ predecessors(b) **do**
                newreaches := *newreaches* ∪ (*defsout*(p) ∪ (*reaches*(p) ∩ ¬*killed*(p)));
            if *newreaches* ≠ *reaches*(b) **then begin**
                reaches(b) := *newreaches*;
                changed := *true*;
            end
        end
    end
end *iterate*

Figure 4.2 Iterative method for reaching definitions.

through the blocks produces no further changes). That solution is the global solution.

In many cases the convergence is accelerated if the right order is chosen for visiting the vertices in the control flow graph. The most commonly used order is depth-first order—the order in which depth-first search would visit the nodes if it starts at the program entry node.

Procedure *iterate* is not the only (or even the fastest, in the worst case) method for building global *reaches* sets, and from there, definition-use chains. In general it takes $O((N+E)N)$ set operations, where N is the number of vertices and E is the number of edges in the graph G [169, 164]. However, it is the simplest method to implement and in practice it converges very rapidly.[3] The reader inter-

---

3. To be precise, the algorithm actually requires $O((N+E)D(G))$, where $D(G)$ is the "loop connect-edness" of a graph, which is related to the depth of loop nesting in the program. For most programs $D(G)$ is much smaller than N.

ested in other methods for solving data flow problems should see the survey by Kennedy [169] or Muchnick's text [218].

Once the definition-use graph has been constructed, the problems of induction-variable substitution, constant propagation, and dead code elimination can be attacked. In a compiler, those problems are usually addressed in that order. However, in terms of difficulty of understanding, induction-variable substitution is the hardest and dead code elimination is the simplest. As a result, the remaining sections discuss these problems in inverse chronological order.

4.4.2   Dead Code Elimination

Dead code is code whose results are never used in any useful statement. "Useful statements," at a first approximation, are simply output statements since those are the only ones that perform any action directly seen by the outside world. Of course, any statements that compute values used by output statements are also useful, as are statements that compute values used by useful statements. This crude definition forms the basis of an algorithm for dead code elimination, based on finding all useful statements and eliminating all others. This algorithm, presented in Figure 4.3, starts with a set *worklist* of all absolutely useful statements (i.e., output statements, control flow statements, and input statements[4]). It then repeatedly adds statements that are necessary to compute the current members of

procedure *eliminateDeadCode(P)*

   // *P* is the procedure from which dead code is to be eliminated
   // Assume the availability of def-use chains for all the statements in *P*

   let *worklist*:= {absolutely useful statements};

   while *worklist* ≠ ∅ **do begin**
       x := an arbitrary element of *worklist*;
       mark *x* useful;
       worklist := *worklist* − {*x*};
       for all (*y*,*x*) ∈ *defuse* **do**
           if *y* is not marked useful **then** *worklist* := *worklist* ∪ {*y*};
   end
   delete every statement that is not marked useful;
end *eliminateDeadCode*

Figure 4.3 Dead code elimination.

---

4. If any input statement is not executed, even if its results are not useful, other input statements can easily receive the wrong values.

worklist until no more statements are necessary. At that point, *worklist* contains all useful statements from the program, and all others may be removed.

The power of this algorithm is often demonstrated on carelessly written user benchmarks. In a benchmark, the programmer usually cares about the time required by the computation, rather than the results of the computation. In the past, some benchmark designers have remembered to print out the execution time, but forgotten to print out any results. When processed by a compiler that performs dead code elimination, the entire computation becomes dead, resulting in extremely fast execution times—the generated code will typically read the clock once, read it again, take the difference, and print it out.

It should be pointed out that dead code elimination algorithms like the one in Figure 4.3 often have trouble with expressions that determine control flow. Even though these expressions do not produce values used in other statements, they control the execution of every statement that can be bypassed depending on the outcome of the test determining flow of control. Simple dead code elimination systems mark every conditional statement as absolutely useful, then delete conditionals if all statements they control are deleted. A more sophisticated approach is to augment definition-use chains with *control dependence* edges, described in Chapter 7. If this is done, the algorithm in Figure 4.3 will produce accurate results. The next section presents a more complicated definition-use based algorithm: constant propagation.

4.4.3   Constant Propagation

Constant propagation attempts to replace all variables that can be proven to have constant values at run time with those constant values. One way of analyzing this problem is in terms of a lattice of constant values depicted in Figure 4.4. The lattice represents the information that can be gathered about variables. At the top level ("unknown"), no information is available regarding a particular variable. The middle level represents a variable having one known constant value—the situation desired by constant propagation. Note that this level is infinitely wide, since any integral constant (assuming we are propagating integers; we can equally well place floating numbers in this level) can appear. The bottom level represents a variable that is known to take on more than one value, or whose constant value cannot be known at compile time. While this lattice has infinite width, it has finite depth, since the longest downward chain has length two.

The basic idea of the constant propagation algorithm is to begin with each variable approximated by the top element of the lattice. Whenever a statement with constant output is found, its output variable value is lowered to the constant value. Then, definition-use edges are employed to locate all instructions that use the output value. At each use, the input variable's approximate value is adjusted by taking the meet of the old and new value in the lattice. The full algorithm is given in Figure 4.5.

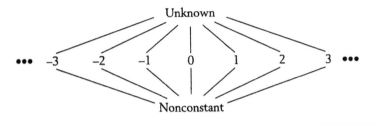

Figure 4.4 Constant propagation lattice.

procedure *propagateConst*(P)

    // P is the procedure in which constants are to be propagated
    // *valin*(w, s) is the best approximate value of input w to s
    // *valout*(v, s) is the best value of output v from s
    // μ(s)(inputs to s) is the result of symbolic interpretation
    //   of statement s over the lattice values of its inputs. The
    //   output is the lattice value of the output of the statement

    for all statements s in the program **do begin**
        for each output v of s **do** *valout*(v, s) := *unknown*;
        for each input w of s **do**
            if w is a variable **then** *valin*(w, s) := *unknown*;
            else *valin*(w, s) := the constant value of w;
    end;

    worklist := {all statements of constant form, e.g., X = 5};

    while *worklist* ≠ ∅ **do begin**
        choose and remove an arbitrary statement x from *worklist*;
        let v denote the output variable for x;
        // Symbolic interpretation of the statement x
        newval := μ(x)(*valin*(v, x), for all inputs v to x);
        if *newval* ≠ *valout*(v, x) **then begin**
            valout(v, x) := *newval*;
            for all (x, y) ∈ *defuse* **do begin**
                oldval := *valin*(v, y);
                valin(v, y) := *oldval* ∧ *valout*(v, x);
                    if *valin*(v, y) ≠ *oldval* **then** *worklist* := *worklist* ∪ {y};
            end
        end
    end
end *propagateConst*

Figure 4.5 Constant propagation algorithm.

Intuitively, constant propagation starts with a set of all assignments that assign a variable to be a constant value. One element is selected from that set; definition-use edges are used to find all inputs that the definition can reach. For each of these inputs, the definition-use edges are traced backward to find all definitions that can reach a specific input. If all definitions have the same constant value, the input is replaced with that value; otherwise, it is not known to be constant. If the input is replaced, that may create a new constant assignment; if it does, the assignment is added to the *worklist* set.

The time required by constant propagation is $O(N+E)$, where N is the number of statements in the program and E is the number of edges in the definition-use graph. To see this, note that a statement can be put on the worklist at most two times because it is only added to the worklist if its output value is lowered in the lattice. Since the longest downward chain has no more than two edges, the output value can be lowered at most two times. Hence, the body of the main loop is executed $O(N)$ times. The innermost forall loop iterates over definition-use edges that emanate from a single statement. In the aggregate, the body of this loop is executed at most twice for each edge, since the source of the edge can be taken from the worklist no more than two times. Thus the innermost forall body takes $O(E)$ time and the entire procedure takes $O(N+E)$.

4.4.4   Static Single-Assignment Form

One problem with the constant propagation algorithm in Figure 4.5 is that the number of definition-use edges can grow very large in the presence of control flow. Figure 4.6 presents an example that illustrates this problem. Statements S_1, S_2, and S_3 all define the variable X. These definitions all reach the uses in statements S_5, S_6, and S_7 by passing through statement S_4. Because each definition can reach every use, the number of definition-use edges is proportional to the square of the number of statements. In this particular case, there are nine edges: (S_1,S_5), (S_1,S_6), (S_1,S_7), (S_2,S_5), (S_2,S_6), (S_2,S_7), (S_3,S_5), (S_3,S_6), and (S_3,S_7). Since constant propagation takes time $O(N+E)$ and E can be proportional to N^2, the time required for the overall algorithm can be quadratic in the number of statements.

One way to reduce the number of operations is to put a special pseudo-operation in the node for statement S_4:

```
X = X
```

Because this definition kills the values of X that are created in statements S_1, S_2, and S_3, the total number of definition-use edges in the modified program is six: (S_1,S_4), (S_2,S_4), (S_3,S_4), (S_4,S_5), (S_4,S_6), and (S_4,S_7).

This idea can be combined with a method for providing unique names for each scalar variable range to produce *static single-assignment form* (commonly abbreviated SSA), a variation on the definition-use graph with the following properties:

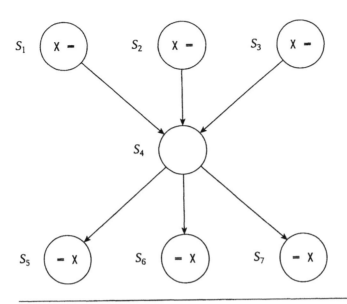

S_1 (X ◂) S_2 (X ◂) S_3 (X ◂)

S_4 ( )

S_5 (◂ X) S_6 (◂ X) S_7 (◂ X)

Figure 4.6 Definition-use example.

1. Each assignment creates a different variable name.
2. At points where control flow joins, a special operation is inserted to merge different incarnations of the same variable.

The static single-assignment graph for the example in Figure 4.6 is given in Figure 4.7. It is no coincidence that this graph resembles the original control flow graph, since merge nodes are inserted at points where control flow paths merge.

The static single-assignment form representation of the definition-use graph has a number of advantages for analysis, the most important of which is the improved performance of algorithms like constant propagation and the reduced size of the graph.

Construction of SSA typically proceeds in two major phases:

1. identification of the points where merge functions, called φ-*functions*, are needed and
2. variable renaming to create a unique name for each definition point.

Before we can identify points where φ-functions are to be inserted we need to consider our goals. To keep the graph small, we should introduce a φ-function only at those points where it is essential for preserving desired properties of the graph, the most important of which is that only one definition reach each variable use. Thus we will want to insert a φ-function for a given variable x at the beginning of a block that has more than one predecessor if every path to one of those predecessors contains a definition that some path to one of the other predecessors

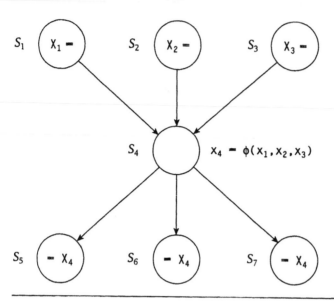

Figure 4.7 Static single-assignment form for Figure 4.6.

bypasses. A ϕ-function for x is needed at the beginning of that block to ensure that subsequent uses cannot be reached by more than one definition of x.

Dominance Frontiers. To identify the desired insertion points, we will introduce the concepts of dominators and dominance frontiers.

DEFINITION 4.2	A node x in directed graph G with a single exit node *predominates* (or *dominates*) node y in G if any path from the entry node of G to y must pass through x. Node x *strictly dominates* y if x dominates y and $x \neq y$.

The problem of computing dominators in a directed graph has been explored by a number of researchers [198, 138]. The simplest way to compute dominators is as a data flow problem. Let *dominators(b)* be the set of vertices that predominate the vertex b. By convention we will always assume that $b \in$ *dominators(b)*. Then the following set of data flow equations is sufficient to compute dominators:

$$dominators(x) = \{x\} \cup \bigcap_{y \in preds(x)} dominators(y) \qquad (4.2)$$

This can be solved by a variant of the iterative method presented in Figure 4.2, in which all the *dominators* sets are initialized to the universal set so that a maximum fixed point is reached (see Figure 4.8).

```
procedure iterateDom(G)
    //G = (N,E) is the input control flow graph, where
    // N is the set of basic blocks and
    // E is the set of control flow edges
    // dominators(b) is the set of dominators for block b

    for each b ∈ N do
        if predecessors(b) = ∅ then dominators(b) :={b}; else dominators(b) := N;

    changed := true;
    while changed do begin
        changed := false;
        for each b ∈ N do begin
            newDoms := dominators(b);
            for each p ∈ predecessors(b) do
                newDoms := newDoms ∩ dominators(p);
            newDoms := newDoms ∪ {b};
            if newDoms != dominators(b) then begin
                dominators(b) := newDoms;
                changed := true;
            end
        end
    end
end iterateDom
```

Figure 4.8 Iterative dominators construction.

This algorithm inherits the asymptotic running time of the iterative method—$O((N+E)N)$ set operations. However, for the special case where the control flow graph is *reducible* (that is, it contains no multiple-entry loops), as most well-structured graphs are, it is easy to see that the algorithm converges in a single pass, assuming that the vertices of the graph are processed in depth-first order. This is because the dominator set for the source of a back edge in a reducible graph is a superset of the dominators for the sink. Thus back edges do not reduce the dominator sets of their sink nodes further. Hence, for reducible graphs, this algorithm requires only $O(N+E)$ set operations.

DEFINITION 4.3 The *immediate dominator* of a given vertex x in graph G is the vertex $y \in$ dominators$(x) - \{x\}$ such that if $z \in$ dominators$(x) - \{x\}$ then $z \in$ dominators(y).

In other words, the immediate dominator of a vertex x must strictly dominate x, and it must be strictly dominated by every other dominator of x.

Once the dominators sets are available, it is straightforward to construct the immediate dominator tree. Observe that, since the immediate dominator y of x

must be dominated by every dominator of x except x itself, then the immediate dominator of x must be the member of *dominators*$(x) - \{x\}$ that has the largest dominator set. Based on this observation, we can construct a two-pass procedure for building the immediate dominator tree, in which each pass takes no more than $O(N^2)$ time.

1. Annotate every vertex x with the number of vertices in its dominator set.

2. For each vertex x, set *idom*(x) to be the vertex in *dominators*$(x) - \{x\}$ that has the largest dominator set.

Lengauer and Tarjan have developed an algorithm that directly constructs the immediate dominator relationship in $O(E\alpha(N,E))$ time in the worst case, where N and E are the number of nodes and edges in the control flow graph, respectively, and α is a very slowly growing function related to an inverse of Ackerman's function [198]. The function α grows so slowly that this algorithm is effectively linear in the size of the input graph. Harel has improved the algorithm to linear in the worst case [198].

DEFINITION 4.4

The *dominance frontier DF(x)* for a given block x is the set of blocks y such that some predecessor of y is dominated in the control flow graph by x, but y itself is not strictly dominated by x.

Figure 4.9 gives an algorithm for computing the dominance frontier for every block in a control flow graph.

We must show that algorithm *ConstructDF* correctly constructs the dominance frontiers. That is, $y \in DF(x)$ after execution of the algorithm if and only if y is in the dominance frontier of x.

To see this, assume that y is in the dominance frontier of x. If it is a successor of x, but not dominated by x, it is added to $DF(x)$ in step L_3. Assume it is not a successor of x. Then there exists some sequence $\{x_1, x_2, \ldots, x_n\}$ of dominators in the dominator tree such that

$$x \text{ idom } x_1 \text{ idom } x_2 \ldots \text{ idom } x_n$$

where y is a successor of x_n but x is not a strict dominator of y. Note that none of the vertices x_i can dominate y because then all the predecessors of x_i in the dominator tree, including x, must dominate y, which contradicts an assumption. Since the vertices are processed in reverse dominator order, x_n will be processed first and y will be added to $DF(x_n)$ by L_3. Subsequently, when other elements up the dominance chain are processed, y will be added to each of their dominance frontiers by L_4. Thus y will eventually be added to $DF(x)$.

On the other hand, if the algorithm adds a vertex to $DF(x)$, that vertex must be in the dominance frontier for x. Clearly, this is true for statements added in L_3

procedure *ConstructDF(G,DF)*
    // G is the input control flow graph
    // *DF(x)* is the set of blocks in the dominance frontier of x
    // *idom(y)* is the immediate dominator of block y in the
    // control flow graph G.

L_1:   find the immediate dominator relation *idom* for the control flow graph G; (For a
        control flow graph with a single entry, this relation forms a tree, with the
        entry node as the root.)
        let l be a reverse topological listing of the dominator tree such that, if x domi-
        nates y, then x comes *after* y in l;

L_2:   **while** $l \neq \varnothing$ **do begin**
        let x be the first element of l;
        remove x from l;

L_3:   **for all** control flow successors y of x **do**
        if *idom(y)* $\neq x$ **then** *DF(x)* := *DF(x)* $\cup$ {y};

L_4:   **for all** z such that *idom(z)* $= x$ **do**
        for all $y \in DF(z)$ **do**
            if *idom(y)* $\neq x$ **then** *DF(x)* := *DF(x)* $\cup$ {y};
    end
end *ConstructDF*

Figure 4.9 Dominance frontier construction algorithm.

because this loop simply implements the dominance frontier definition. Suppose some vertex y is added incorrectly to $DF(x)$ by step L_4. (We can assume that y is the first such vertex incorrectly added.) Thus, there exists a z such that x idom z and y is in $DF(z)$. Since z is processed before x, y must have been correctly added to its dominance frontier by assumption. But the only way that it could be incorrect to add y to $DF(x)$ would be if x idom y. However, if it does, it must be the immediate dominator, since if any of the nodes between y and x dominated y, then y could not be in the dominance frontier of z. But this cannot be, because if x is the immediate dominator of y, then it is never added to $DF(x)$ in L_4.

Not counting the construction of predominators, algorithm *ConstructDF* requires $O(\max(N+E, |DF|))$ time in the worst case. To see this, observe that the topological sort takes $O(N+E)$ time, while the header of the loop at label L_2 is executed once for every node in the control flow graph or $O(N)$ times. The loop at L_3 is entered once for each control flow successor of each node, for a total of $O(E)$ times and, since its body can be implemented in constant time, the total time required by the loop is $O(E)$.

The loop at label L_4 is more complicated. The loop is executed once for each edge in the dominator tree, but since each node has at most one immediate predominator, the loop header is executed only $O(N)$ times. The inner loop is executed at most once for each element of the dominance frontier of the given node x, so the loop nest takes $O(|DF|)$ time.

Note that *ConstructDF* takes time proportional to the size of the maximum of its input and output. Since an algorithm must take time that is at least as great as either of these, this algorithm is optimal.

Determining Insertion Locations. Once we have dominance frontiers available, we can determine all the locations for φ-functions by the procedure in Figure 4.10. This algorithm is based upon the simple observation that if block x contains a definition of variable y, then a φ-function for y must be inserted at the head of

procedure *LocatePhi(G,DF,PutPhiHere)*

// G is the input control flow graph
// DF is the dominator frontier graph, where
// $DF(x)$ is the set of blocks in the dominance frontier of block x,
//   i.e., the successors of x in the DF-graph.
// $Def(x)$ is the set of variables defined in block x.
// $PutPhiHere(x)$ is the set of variables for which φ-functions
//   must be inserted at the beginning of block x.

find the set $\{S_1, S_2, \ldots, S_m\}$ of maximal strongly connected regions in the dominance frontier graph DF (use Tarjan's depth-first search algorithm);

construct DF_π from DF by reducing each S_i to a single node an edge (x,y) in DF becomes an edge (S_x, S_y) in DF_π, where S_x is the region containing x and S_y is the region containing y; (*Note:* delete edges that go from a region to itself.)

let $\{\pi_1, \pi_2, \ldots, \pi_m\}$ be the m nodes of DF_π numbered in an order consistent with D_π (use topological sort to do the ordering);

for $i := 1$ **to** m **do begin**
    set $Def(\pi_i)$ to be the union of $Def(x)$ for all x in π_i;
    set $PutPhiHere(\pi_i)$ to empty;
end

for $i := 1$ **to** m **do**
    for each π_j in $DF_\pi(\pi_i)$ **do**
        $PutPhiHere(\pi_j) := PutPhiHere(\pi_j) \cup Def(\pi_i)$;
for $i := 1$ **to** m **do begin**
    if π_i is a strongly connected region or a self-loop **then**
        $PutPhiHere(\pi_i) := PutPhiHere(\pi_i) \cup Def(\pi_i)$;
    for each $x \in \pi_i$ that has a predecessor outside π_i **do**
        $PutPhiHere(x) := PutPhiHere(\pi_i)$;
end
end *LocatePhi*

Figure 4.10 Determining locations for φ-functions.

every block in *DF(x)* because there is an alternate path to each of those blocks that does not pass through x and hence contains a different definition for y. Once a ϕ-function for y is inserted in a block z, then, by transitivity, we must also insert a ϕ-function for y in every element of *DF(z)*.

There is an additional observation that will make the algorithm more efficient. It is possible for there to be a cycle in the DF-graph. The simplest example is given by a two-vertex loop in which a single vertex outside the loop branches directly to each vertex in the loop. Then each of the vertices is in the dominance frontier of the other. Dealing with such loops is simple, however, because if a ϕ-function must be placed in any node in the loop, one must be placed in every node in the loop that is a loop entry, by virtue of the transitivity requirement stated above. Thus we can treat strongly connected regions in the DF-graph as single vertices for the purpose of propagation.

It should be clear from the observations that this algorithm computes the correct locations for ϕ-functions and takes time linear in the number of nodes in the DF-graph. It should be observed that the DF-graph can be considerably larger than the control flow graph. In fact, in the worst case it can be proportional to the square of the size of the control flow graph, although this behavior is rare [97]. Recently, it has been shown that the locations of ϕ-functions can be determined in time proportional to the size of the control flow graph [253].

It should be pointed out that the number of ϕ-functions can be significantly reduced by not placing any such functions at the beginning of join nodes where the target variable is dead. A straightforward enhancement of the algorithm in Figure 4.10, coupled with the construction of sets of live variables at each block through iterative analysis, will suffice to accomplish this.

All that remains in the construction of the SSA form is to rename the variables and build the SSA edges. This can be accomplished in a straightforward manner by assigning a uniquely indexed name to the value produced at each definition point, including ϕ-functions. Then an application of the *reaches* propagation algorithm described in Section 4.4.1 can determine which value reaches each use because only one definition can reach any use once the ϕ-functions are inserted.

Although SSA form does not significantly modify the structure of the dead code elimination and constant propagation algorithms described earlier, the algorithms for forward substitution of expressions and induction-variable substitution, treated in the next section, will benefit significantly from its special properties.

4.5 Induction-Variable Exposure

Dead code elimination and constant propagation are both transformations that rely on fairly simple patterns in the definition-use graph. Induction-variable substitution is more complicated and requires recognition of fairly complex patterns. As a result, induction-variable substitution typically involves a sophisticated framework for analyzing programs. Given the existence of this framework, as well as the fact that the original need for induction-variable substitution arises from the necessity of transforming common programming practices into a form more amenable for dependence testing, an induction-variable substitution phase generally does more than just replace auxiliary induction variables. One common addition is forward substitution of region-invariant expressions into subscripts.

In this section we will present algorithms for forward substitution and loop induction-variable substitution. We will then tie the material together with a discussion of how they can be made to work together.

4.5.1   Forward Expression Substitution

The following is an example where forward substitution is useful:

```
      DO I = 1, 100
         K = I + 2
S₁       A(K) = A(K) + 5
      ENDDO
```

Here the programmer has done some of the work of the compiler by performing common subexpression elimination on his code, compressing the two subscript calculations into a single variable. Unfortunately, a dependence tester will have problems calculating dependences arising from the references to array A because of the use of K, which is not an induction variable yet varies in the loop, in subscripts of A. Substituting K forward to produce

```
      DO I = 1, 100
S₁       A(I+2) = A(I+2) + 5
      ENDDO
```

yields a form that dependence testing can easily handle. Furthermore, if this example is being compiled for a vector machine, the generated code will be much more efficient. Assuming the first form could be determined to be vectorizable (it is), it would be vectorized by expanding K into a temporary vector and using that temporary vector as a scatter-gather index for A. The second form yields a much simpler vector operation.

Performing induction-variable substitution and forward expression substitution requires not only definition-use edges but also some control flow analysis. For a statement to define an induction variable, it must be executed on every iteration of the loop. Similarly, before a definition can be forward-substituted, it is necessary to guarantee that the definition is always executed on a loop iteration before the statement into which it is substituted. These properties are easy to determine if we use the SSA graph effectively and if we have a simple procedure to determine which statements are inside the given loop and which are not.

To determine whether a given statement is inside a given loop, we need to maintain a separate data structure for each statement that determines the collection of loops inside which the statement is nested. Then a statement S is in a given loop L if L is in the nest of loops containing S. In particular, if the level of the loop is k, we need only test whether the level-k loop containing S is equal to L. This is easy to do if we maintain a stack of loop identifiers containing each statement.

Using this mechanism, we can develop a simple procedure for forward substitution that handles any expression involving only loop-invariant quantities and the loop induction variable. The SSA graph makes it easy to determine whether a given expression meets this requirement. Given a statement S that is a candidate for forward substitution, we simply examine each SSA edge into S. If the edge comes from a statement in the loop, then that statement must be the ϕ-node for the loop induction variable at the beginning of the loop body. Otherwise, the quantity contains an expression other than the loop induction variable that changes in the loop, and we must preclude forward substitution.

Actually the above statement is not precisely correct. There could be a loop-invariant assignment before the actual use, as follows:

```
      DO I = 1, N
         ...
S₁       IC = IB ! IB is loop invariant
         ...
S₂       IX = IC + 5
         ...
      ENDDO
```

The expression "IC + 5" can be forward-substituted because IC is assigned a loop-invariant value IB. However, the procedure we propose will avoid the stated problem by dealing with statements in the loop in order. Thus the assignment to IC will be forward-substituted into the statement S_2 before the right-hand side of S_2 is considered for forward substitution.

Returning to the forward substitution algorithm, the following fragment illustrates how the standard loop induction variable is incremented after a DO-loop is expanded into simpler code:

```
      DO I = 1, N
         ...
      ENDDO
```

becomes

```
      I = 1
L     IF (I > N) GO TO E
         ...
      I = I + 1
      GO TO L
E
```

where L and E are unique numeric labels. The update of the induction variable occurs at the very end of the loop, after all statements that use it. Therefore, every use of the standard loop induction variable must have an edge from the ϕ-node that merges values of that induction variable right after loop entry.

Once it is determined that a statement S can be forward-substituted, the procedure can be carried out by examining each edge out of the target statement to another statement in the loop that is not a ϕ-node. For each such edge, we substitute the right-hand side of S for every occurrence of the left-hand side of S in the statement at the sink of the SSA edge. Figure 4.11 presents an algorithm for forward expression substitution that follows this approach.

As we indicated earlier, this algorithm must be applied to statements in the loop in order from beginning to end. By doing this, chains of forward substitutions can reduce the number of variables used in the loop, at the expense of additional expression complexity in the loop. This ordered application is a part of the transformation driver presented in Figure 4.16 (in Section 4.5.3).

ForwardSub also requires one property of the SSA graph that is worth noting. The first loop in the algorithm traces all edges coming into a statement from outside. The second loop in the graph traces all edges going out of a statement into other statements. Any data structure chosen to implement the SSA graph must possess this bidirectional property for this algorithm to work.

The return value is used to determine whether to try induction-variable substitution on the statement. This return value will be of use in the driver routine to be presented in Section 4.5.3. The return value will be true only if forward substitution is not tried because some input to S is defined in the loop. Note that the routine will never return true if the statement S is deleted or moved.

4.5.2   Induction-Variable Substitution

Having dealt with forward substitution, it is now time to focus on induction-variable substitution. The first task is to recognize auxiliary induction variables.

**DEFINITION
4.5**

An auxiliary induction variable in a DO-loop headed by

$$DO \ I \ = \ LB, \ UB, \ S$$

is any variable that can be correctly expressed as

$$cexpr * I + iexpr_L$$

at every location L where it is used in the loop, where *cexpr* and *iexpr$_L$* are expressions that do not vary in the loop, although different locations in the loop may require substitution of different values of *iexpr$_L$*.

---

boolean procedure *ForwardSub(S,L)*
    // *S*, the candidate statement for forward substitution
    // *L* is the loop within which the substitution is being performed
    // Assume the SSA graph and information about statement nesting
    // Returns *true* if substitution eliminates all uses of the defined variable in the loop
    //   otherwise, returns *false* indicating that IV substitution should be tried

    // *ForwardSub* carries out substitution of every statement in *L*
    //   whose right-hand side variables include only
    //   the induction variable for *L* or variables that are invariant in *L*.

    if *S* applies a ϕ-function **or** *S* has side_effects **then return** *true*;

    // Substitute the statement into all qualified uses in the loop.
    all_nonloop_uses_gone = *true*;
    all_loop_uses_gone = *true*;
    for each SSA edge *e* emanating from *S* **do begin**
       S_t = target_stmt(*S*);
       if S_t is within loop *L* **then**
          if operation(S_t) $\neq \phi$ **then begin**
             replace target(*e*) with rhs(*S*);
             // update SSA edges
             for each SSA edge *ie* into rhs(*S*) **do**
                add new edge from source_stmt(*ie*) to S_t;
             remove edge *e*;
          end
          else *all_loop_uses_gone* = *false*;
       else *all_nonloop_uses_gone* = *false*;
    end
    if *all_loop_uses_gone* **and** *all_nonloop_uses_gone* **then begin**
       delete(*S*);
       return *true*;
    end
    else if *all_loop_uses_gone* **then begin**
       move *S* outside loop;
       return *true*;
    else return *false*; // cannot be fully substituted, but try IV-sub
    end *ForwardSub*

Figure 4.11 Forward expression substitution algorithm.

In the simplest form, an auxiliary induction variable will be defined by a statement like

$$K = K \pm cexpr \tag{4.3}$$

where once again, *cexpr* is loop invariant.

Induction-variable recognition can be done with a great deal of generality. Some programs define collections of induction variables, as the following example illustrates:

```
DO I = 1, N
   J = K + 1
   ...
   K = J + 2
ENDDO
```

Here both J and K are auxiliary induction variables of the loop.

We can use the procedure from Section 4.5.1 that determines whether a statement is within a given loop L to help us determine whether a given statement S defines an induction variable. Statement S may define an auxiliary induction variable for L if S is contained in a simple cycle of SSA edges that involves only S and one other statement, a ϕ-node, in the loop. This ϕ-node is required on loop entry to merge the values of the loop induction variable initialized outside the loop with the values incremented inside the loop. If the cycle contains other ϕ-nodes inside the loop, it cannot be an induction variable, as it is not updated on every iteration.

As an example, consider the following loop:

```
DO I = 1, N
   A(I) = B(K) + 1
   K = K + 4
   ...
   D(K) = D(K) + A(I)
ENDDO
```

It has the SSA graph defined in Figure 4.12, in which the indexed variable names have been omitted for simplicity. The figure shows only the portion of the SSA graph involving definitions and uses of the variable K within the loop. The cycle with a single ϕ-node is the telltale sign of an auxiliary induction variable.

If it satisfies the cycle condition, which assures that the induction variable is defined on every iteration of the loop, the only remaining requirement is that the defining expression be of the correct form. For the purposes of this book, we will present a simple recognition algorithm that finds induction variables only of the form represented in Equation 4.3. This recognition algorithm is given in Figure 4.13.

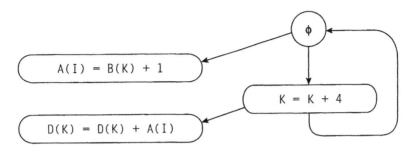

Figure 4.12 Sample SSA graph for induction-variable recognition.

boolean procedure *isIV(S,iV,cexpr,cexpr_edges,iV)*

    // *S* is the candidate statement that may define an auxiliary *IV*
    // *isIV* returns true if the *S* defines an induction variable
    // *iV* is the induction variable
    // *cexpr* is an expression that is added to the induction variable in *S*
    // *cexpr_edges* is the set of SSA edges from outside the loop to *cexpr*
    // *isIV* examines assignment statement *S* to determine whether
    //   it defines an induction variable within the loop containing it.
    // The procedure recognizes only induction-variable updates
    //   of the form I = I ± *cexpr*, where *cexpr* is constant in the loop.

  is_iv = false;
  if *S* is part of a cycle in the SSA graph inside the loop
    involving only itself and a φ-node in the loop header
  then begin
    let *iV* be the variable on the left-hand side of *S*;
    let *cexpr* be rhs(*S*) with *iV* eliminated;
    if *iV* is added to rhs(*S*) **and**
        cexpr is either added to or subtracted from rhs(*S*)
    then begin
      loop_invariant := *true*;
      cexpr_edges := ∅;
      or each edge *e* coming into *cexpr* **do**
        if source(*e*) is inside the current loop
          then *loop_invariant* := *false*;
          else *cexpr_edges* := *cexpr_edges* ∪ {*e*};
      if *cexpr* is subtracted from rhs(*S*) **then** *cexpr* := − *cexpr*;
      if *loop_invariant* **then** *is_iv* := *true*;
    end
  end
  return *is_iv*;
end *isIV*

Figure 4.13 Induction-variable recognition.

Procedure *isIV* begins by ensuring that the candidate statement *S* is executed on every iteration of the loop (if it were not, it would be involved in a cycle that included a ϕ-node at the end of the loop as well) and that the variable it defines is updated on every loop iteration (the self-edge requirement). Next, it ensures that the potential induction variable is added to the right-hand side and does not have a multiplicative coefficient and that a constant amount (*cexpr*) is either added to or subtracted from the induction-variable candidate on each iteration. If the loop-invariant part is subtracted, it is negated, so that the substitution phase can assume that addition is the controlling operation.

Figures 4.14 and 4.15 present an algorithm for carrying out the replacement of uses of an induction variable, once it is identified.

The substitution algorithm uses two different expressions for the auxiliary induction variable being replaced. For statements that occur prior to *S* in the loop, the multiplier to be used is one less than the current iteration number. For statements after *S*, the multiplier is the current iteration number (*I* is the loop index; *L* is its lower bound; *U* is its upper bound; and *S* is its stride).

4.5.3   Driving the Substitution Process

Having developed individual algorithms for applying forward substitution and induction-variable substitution, it is now time to develop a driving algorithm to tie the individual transformations together. There are a couple of key considerations. First, since induction-variable substitution performed on an inner loop may produce a new induction on an outer loop (see, for instance, the examples in Section 4.1), induction-variable substitution should be performed from the inside out. Second, substituting loop-invariant expressions forward may create some new inductions, meaning it should be performed first. These observations are both encapsulated in the algorithm *IVDrive*, presented in Figure 4.16.

There are two final comments worth noting on induction-variable substitution. The first regards the interaction between loop normalization (Section 4.3) and induction-variable substitution. When induction-variable substitution is performed on an unnormalized loop, extremely inefficient code can result.

Consider, for instance, the following very general example:

```
DO I = L, U, S
   K = K + N
   ... = A(K)
ENDDO
```

Applying induction-variable substitution as described in Figure 4.14 yields

```
DO I = L, U, S
   ... = A(K+(I-L+S)/S*N)
ENDDO
K = K + (U-L+S)/S * N
```

procedure *IVSub(S,L)*

> // *S* is the candidate statement that may define an auxiliary *IV*
> // *L* is the loop with respect to which the substitution is performed
> // *IVSub* examines assignment statement *S* to determine whether
> //   it is an induction variable, and replaces it if so.
>
> **if not** *isIV(S,iV,cexpr,cexpr_edges)* **then return**;
> // *iV* is the auxiliary induction variable defined
> // *cexpr* is the constant expression added to *iV*
> // *cexpr_edges* is the set of edges that defined vars used in *cexpr*
>
> let the header for the innermost loop containing *S* be
>
> > DO I = L, U, S
>
> let S_h denote the φ-node in the loop header for *iV*;
>
> // SSA ensures that only one edge comes into S_h from outside the loop
> let S_o denote the source of the single edge to S_h from outside the loop;
>
> **for each** edge *e* out of S_h to a node in the same loop **do begin**
> > // target(*e*) comes *before* *S* in the loop body
> > replace target_expr(*e*) with
> > > "target_expr(*e*) + ((I-L)/S) * *cexpr*";
> >
> > *update_SSA_edges(e,cexpr_edges,S_o)*;
>
> **end**
>
> **for each** edge *e* out of *S* to a node in the same loop **do begin**
> > // target(*e*) comes *after* *S* in the loop body
> > replace target_expr(*e*) with
> > > target_expr(*e*) + ((I-L+S)/S) * *cexpr*;
> >
> > *update_SSA_edges(e,cexpr_edges,S_o)*;
>
> **end**
>
> **if** there are edges from *S* to vertices outside the loop **then begin**
> > move *S* outside loop,
> > > changing *cexpr* to ((U-L+S)/S) * *cexpr*;
> >
> > add an edge from S_o to *S*; delete the edge from S_h to *S*;
>
> **end**
> **else** delete *S* and the edge from S_h to *S*;
> delete S_h and the edge from S_o to S_h;
> **return**;
> **end** *IVSub*

Figure 4.14 Induction-variable substitution algorithm.

procedure *update_SSA_edges(e,cexpr_edges,S_o)*

    // *e* is the edge along which *iV* substitution has been performed
    // *cexpr_edges* is the set of edges into the update expression
    //   from outside the loop
    // S_o is the unique definition point of *iV* outside the loop.

    for each edge *ie* ∈ *cexpr_edges* **do**
       add a new edge from source(*ie*) to target(*e*);
    add an edge from S_o to target(*e*);
    delete edge *e*;
end *update_SSA_edges*

Figure 4.15 Update SSA graph after induction-variable substitution.

procedure *IVDrive(L)*
    // *L* is the loop being processed, assume SSA graph available
    // *IVDrive* performs forward substitution and induction-variable
    // substitution on the loop *L*, recursively calling itself where necessary.

    for each do loop *D* nested at the top level within *L* **do** *IVDrive(D)*;

    for each statement *S* in *L* in order **do begin**
       case(kind(*S*))
          assignment:
             all_uses_removed:= *ForwardSub(S,L)*;
             if not *all_uses_removed* **then** *IVSub(S,L)*;

          default:
       end case
    end
end *IVDrive*

Figure 4.16 Induction-variable substitution driver.

Integer divides and multiplies are not implemented in hardware on many machines; even when they are, they are very inefficient instructions to use. By introducing both an integer divide and an integer multiply in the loop, induction-variable substitution has produced much less efficient code. Normally, an optimization known as strength reduction is applied to attempt to reduce most common uses of integer multiply, but the form that appears inside the loop cannot be eliminated by this transformation. Furthermore, the nonlinear nature of the new subscript means that dependence testing will fail for it. The summary is that it is fruitless to apply induction-variable substitution to this loop.

However, if the loop is normalized prior to induction-variable substitution,

```
I = 1
DO i = 1, (U-L+S)/S, 1
   K = K + N
   ... = A(K)
   I = I + 1
ENDDO
```

the code resulting from induction-variable substitution is much more palatable:

```
I = 1
DO i = 1, (U-L+S)/S, 1
   ... = A(K+i*N)
ENDDO
K = K + (U-L+S)/S * N
I = I + (U-L+S)/S
```

This code has only one integer multiply within the loop, which strength reduction can easily eliminate. Furthermore, the subscript can easily be handled by dependence tests described in Chapter 3. The summary is that loop normalization should be applied before induction-variable substitution to make the latter transformation more effective.

The second comment involves the simplicity of the induction-variable substitution algorithm presented here. The algorithm presented in Figure 4.14 is a simple version designed to demonstrate the general principles involved. Often there will be more complicated auxiliary induction variables in the loop, as demonstrated by the following example:

```
DO I = 1, N, 2
   K = K + 1
   A(K) = A(K) + 1
   K = K + 1
   A(K) = A(K) + 1
ENDDO
```

Induction-variable recognition in cases like this is still quite simple—the statements involved in defining the induction variable will form an SSA graph cycle within the loop, as shown in Figure 4.17. The cycle will have only one ϕ-node, the one that is obligatory at the beginning of the loop. Of course, the regular restrictions apply—only addition and subtraction of loop-invariant quantities are permitted. Note that, once again, the indexed variable names, usual in SSA graphs, have been omitted in Figure 4.17 for simplicity.

Once such variables are recognized, induction-variable substitution is easily adapted to handle the more complex case. First, the statements defining the induction variable are numbered $\{S_0, S_1, \ldots, S_n\}$ beginning with the ϕ-node. Then,

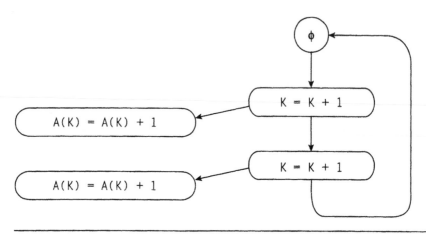

Figure 4.17 SSA graph for complex induction-variable substitution.

each is assigned a different substitution formula depending on the aggregate value of the induction variable right after the execution of the particular statement S_i. The details of this implementation are straightforward.

An alternative strategy is to enhance forward substitution to recognize region invariance. When this is done, the first assignment to K can be propagated forward, yielding

```
DO I = 1, N, 2
   A(K+1) = A(K+1) + 1
   K = K + 1 + 1
   A(K) = A(K) + 1
ENDDO
```

At this point, normal induction-variable substitution will complete elimination of K. The extensions to forward substitution to recognize this case are straightforward [20].

4.6 **Summary**

We have presented a number of transformations that support dependence testing by putting more subscripts into a standard form.

  - *Loop normalization* is a transformation that makes a loop run from a standard lower bound to an upper bound in steps of one. It is used in many compilers to simplify dependence testing, although it has a number of drawbacks.

- *Constant propagation* replaces unknown variables with constants known at compile time. It is performed by an algorithm on a graph representation of data flow within the program.

- *Induction-variable substitution* eliminates auxiliary induction variables, replacing them with linear functions of the standard loop induction variable. A simple variant of the induction-variable substitution algorithm performs expression folding in loop nests.

These transformations are supported by a number of data flow analysis strategies, including iterative solution of data flow algorithms and the construction of definition-use chains or static single-assignment (SSA) form.

4.7 Case Studies

The original PFC implementation performed loop normalization on all loop nests. After that, it applied induction-variable recognition, forward substitution, and induction-variable substitution, following the algorithms presented in this chapter. Since the implementation predated the development of SSA, all the algorithms employed definition-use chains. This added a bit of extra complexity to some of the procedures but was nevertheless effective.

PFC's induction-variable substitution phase was extremely systematic and could handle multiple updates to the same induction variable within the same loop. It processed loops from innermost to outermost, treating the initialization and finalization statements generated by inner loop processing as candidates for further substitution in outer loops. It turned out that the induction-variable substitution phase was critical to the success of vectorization in general within the PFC system.

PFC also carried out systematic dead code elimination after each major transformation phase. This made the code much cleaner and easier to understand. Because the dead code eliminator did not include control dependence edges, it marked all control structures as absolutely useful. This made it necessary to include a postpass that deleted loops and if statements with empty clauses.

The Ardent Titan compiler used a similar set of algorithms for Fortran, but had the additional task of dealing with optimization of C. This put additional burdens on induction-variable substitution. Because the C front end did not do a sophisticated analysis for side effects on expressions with the ++ operator, the intermediate code it generated provided many opportunities for induction-variable substitution. For example, source code such as

```
while(n) {
   *a++ = *b++;
   n--;
}
```

would have been translated by the C front end into

```
while(n) {
    temp_1 = a;
    a = temp_1 + 4;
    temp_2 = b;
    b = temp_2 + 4;
    *temp_1 = *temp_2;
    temp_3 = n;
    n = temp_3 - 1;
}
```

This loop is easy to vectorize (it is, after all, only a vector copy) once all the garbage is cleared away. Before this can happen, the key assignment must be converted into a form like

```
*(a+4*i) = *(b+4*i);
```

where i is the generated loop induction variable. The problem is that this form can be produced only by substituting the assignments to temp_1 and temp_2 forward into the star assignment. This substitution cannot be made, however, until the updates to a and b are moved forward. As a result, naive techniques cannot handle this loop.

Although the theory has produced very general techniques for handling this problem—strategies that employ partial redundancy elimination, for example [215, 75]—for pragmatic reasons, particularly space concerns, the Titan compiler designers chose not to use them. Instead the compiler used a simple heuristic solution: whenever a statement is rejected for substitution only because a later statement redefines a variable used by that statement, the later statement is marked as "blocking" the first statement. When a blocking statement is substituted forward, all the statements it blocks are reexamined for substitution. Thus, backtracking is only required when it is guaranteed to yield some substitution. Furthermore, most of the analysis necessary to substitute the statement need not be repeated. As a result, backtracking is rarely invoked, but when it is invoked, it is extremely efficient.

An extensive discussion of transformations (especially vectorization) in C is postponed until Chapter 12.

4.8 Historical Comments and References

Loop normalization was performed by many vectorizing compilers starting with the Parafrase system [190]. There is an enormous literature of data flow analysis [15, 125, 164, 169, 182, 218, 264]. The construction of definition-use chains, along with the constant propagation and dead code elimination algorithms described here, were conceptually developed by John Cocke. The formulation used here is due to Kennedy [169], as modified by Wegman and Zadeck [272].

The data flow approach to dominator construction is a traditional approach (see Muchnick [218], for example). The algorithm for construction of immediate dominators from dominator sets, however, is new and asymptotically superior to the method presented by Muchnick. However, the Lengauer-Tarjan [198] and Harel [138] methods for direct construction of the immediate dominator relationship are asymptotically more efficient than the methods described here.

The construction of SSA form is due to Cytron, Ferrante, Rosen, Wegman, and Zadeck [97], although the formulation of the computation of locations for insertion of ϕ-functions based on the DF-graph is a variant of their approach. A linear time algorithm for SSA construction has been developed by Sreedhar and Gao [253].

Induction-variable substitution in various forms has been in every vectorizing compiler. The induction-variable substitution algorithm presented here is adapted to SSA form from the PFC system as described by Allen, Kennedy, and Callahan [16, 21, 20]. A more sophisticated approach has been presented by Wolfe [284, 285].

Exercises

4.1 Based on the testing strategies from Chapter 3, which property of an unnormalized loop causes the most difficulty—the nonunit starting index or the nonunit stride. Why?

4.2 Normalize the following loop by hand:

```
DO I = 1000, 1, -2
   A(I) = A(I) + B
ENDDO
```

4.3 Apply normalization, induction-variable substitution, and constant folding by hand to the following loop:

```
IS = 5
DO I = 1, 100
   IS = IS + 10
   DO J = 2, 200, 3
      A(IS) = B(I) + C(J)
      IS = IS + 1
   ENDDO
ENDDO
```

4.4 Develop data flow equations similar to those in Equation 4.1 for the *live analysis* problem. The goal is to compute the set *live(b)* of variables that are "live" on entry to basic block *b*, for every block *b* in the program. A variable is live at a point in the program if there is a control flow path from that point to a use of the variable, and that path contains no definition of the variable prior to its use. *Hint:* Consider two cases—the case of variables that are live because of a use in the same block and the case of variables that are live due to a use in some later block.

4.5 Consider the loop nest, where L1, L2, H1, and H2 are all unknown:

```
     DO J = L1, H1, 7
        DO I = L2, H2, 10
S          A(I+J+3) = A(I+J) + C
        ENDDO
     ENDDO
```

What are the prospects of eliminating direction vectors, other than (=,=) associated with dependences from statement S to itself? Why? *Hint:* What happens if you normalize and use MIV tests from Chapter 3?

CHAPTER 5

Enhancing Fine-Grained Parallelism

5.1 Introduction

This chapter and the next cover the use of dependence to automatically parallelize sequential code. Following the historical development, we begin with parallelism that has no minimum granularity. This kind of parallelism is useful in vector machines and machines with instruction-level parallelism, such as VLIW and superscalar processors. Because most of the theory was developed first on vector machines, the discussion will concentrate on vectorization. The treatment of granularity-sensitive parallelism will be postponed until Chapter 6.

In Chapter 2, we presented the parallelization algorithm *codegen*, shown in Figure 2.2, for automatically finding fine-grained parallelism in a Fortran program. That algorithm finds essentially all the parallelism possible using only the transformations of loop distribution and statement reordering. In this chapter, we expand on the basic code generation algorithm by exploring other transformations, such as loop interchange, needed to increase the amount of fine-grained parallelism to a level that makes automatic vectorization practical and effective.

We illustrate the power of two of these advanced transformations on a fairly typical sequential coding of matrix multiplication:

```
DO J = 1, M
   DO I = 1, N
      T = 0.0
      DO K = 1, L
         T = T + A(I,K) * B(K,J)
      ENDDO
      C(I,J) = T
   ENDDO
ENDDO
```

171

When *codegen* is applied to this loop nest, it will uncover no vector operations, even though matrix multiplication can be easily parallelized by hand. The problem in this case is the use of the scalar temporary T, which introduces several dependences carried by *each* of the loops in the nest. Most of these dependences can be eliminated by *scalar expansion*, in which the scalar T is replaced by an array temporary T$:

```
DO J = 1, M
    DO I = 1, N
        T$(I) = 0.0
        DO K = 1, L
            T$(I) = T$(I) + A(I,K) * B(K,J)
        ENDDO
        C(I,J) = T$(I)
    ENDDO
ENDDO
```

The I-loop can now be fully distributed around the statements it contains:

```
DO J = 1, M
    DO I = 1, N
        T$(I) = 0.0
    ENDDO
    DO I = 1, N
        DO K = 1, L
            T$(I) = T$(I) + A(I,K) * B(K,J)
        ENDDO
    ENDDO
    DO I = 1, N
        C(I,J) = T$(I)
    ENDDO
ENDDO
```

Finally, the I- and K-loops are *interchanged* to move the vector parallelism to the innermost position. After this interchange, all of the inner I-loops can be vectorized to produce

```
DO J = 1, M
    T$(1:N) = 0.0
    DO K = 1, L
        T$(1:N) = T$(1:N) + A(1:N,K) * B(K,J)
    ENDDO
    C(1:N,J) = T$(1:N)
ENDDO
```

The transformations of scalar expansion and loop interchange have created parallelism where none previously existed. Experience has shown that automatic parallelization cannot be made effective enough to be practical without transformations like these.

5.2   **Loop Interchange**

Loop interchange—switching the nesting order of two loops in a perfect nest—is one of the most useful transformations available for improving program performance. An example of its value in vectorization is given by the following:

```
      DO I = 1, N
         DO J = 1, M
S           A(I,J+1) = A(I,J) + B
         ENDDO
      ENDDO
```

The innermost loop in this example carries a true dependence from S to itself. As a result, the vector code generation algorithm *codegen* given in Figure 2.2 would fail to produce any vectorization. If the loops are interchanged, however,

```
      DO J = 1, M
         DO I = 1, N
S           A(I,J+1) = A(I,J) + B
         ENDDO
      ENDDO
```

the dependence is carried by the outer loop, leaving the inner loop dependence-free. When *codegen* is applied to this nest, the inner loop will vectorize to produce the following result:

```
      DO J = 1, M
S        A(1:N,J+1) = A(1:N,J) + B
      ENDDO
```

In this example, loop interchange enhances vectorization by moving a vectorizable loop to the innermost position. For coarse-grained parallelization, discussed in Chapter 6, this process is reversed, moving a parallel loop to the outermost position to increase granularity and decrease synchronization overhead.

To see that loop interchange is a reordering transformation, think of a loop as creating parameterized instances of the statements within it. Loop interchange changes the order in which the parameterized instances are executed but does not create any new instances. In the code below, let S(I,J) denote the instance of statement S with parameters I and J. In other words, S(I,J) is the instance of S executed on the iteration with iteration vector (I,J).

```
DO J = 1, M
   DO I = 1, N
      S
   ENDDO
ENDDO
```

Using the new notation, we can see that S(1,2)is executed after S(2,1) in the code as written, but will be executed before S(2,1) if the loops are interchanged. Thus, it is indeed a reordering transformation. Because it is a reordering transformation, the legality of loop interchange can be determined by using data dependence: any loop interchange that reorders the endpoints of some dependence is illegal.

5.2.1   Safety of Loop Interchange

Not all loop interchanges are legal, as the following example illustrates:

```
DO J = 1, M
   DO I = 1, N
      A(I,J+1) = A(I+1,J) + B
   ENDDO
ENDDO
```

In the original execution order, A(2,2)is assigned when I = 2 and J = 1; it is used one iteration of the J-loop later, when I = 1 and J = 2. If the loops are interchanged, A(2,2)is assigned on the second iteration of the outer loop (iteration vector (2,1)) after being used on the first (iteration vector (1,2)). As a result, loop interchange in this example violates a dependence by causing the use of A(2,2)to get the wrong value.

This kind of violation is illustrated graphically in Figure 5.1. This diagram shows various kinds of dependences that can arise from statement S(2,1). The arrows emanating from that statement go to statements that execute after it. The gray arrow represents the dependence described previously that is reversed by loop interchange; if the J-loop is run as the inner loop, the tail of that edge is executed before the source. The black arrows depict dependences that are preserved regardless of the order in which the loops are iterated.

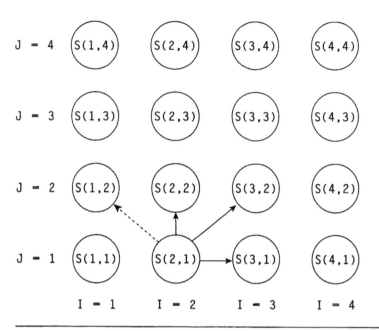

Figure 5.1 Legality of loop interchange.

Two classes of dependences relevant to the safety of loop interchange are defined below:

DEFINITION 5.1	A dependence is *interchange preventing* with respect to a given pair of loops if interchanging those loops would reorder the endpoints of the dependence.

DEFINITION 5.2	A dependence is *interchange sensitive* if it is carried by the same loop after interchange. That is, an interchange-sensitive dependence moves with its original carrier loop to the new level.

In Figure 5.1, the gray dependence is interchange preventing; the horizontal and vertical arrows represent interchange-sensitive dependences. Regardless of which loop is iterated "faster," the horizontal dependence will be carried by the I-loop and the vertical dependence will be carried by the J-loop. The remaining arrow (that from S(2,1) to S(3,2)) represents a dependence that is always carried by the outer loop in the pair. Such dependences are often called *interchange insensitive*.

Direction vectors are an important tool for reasoning about the effects of loop interchange because of the result in Theorem 5.1. From this result and the fact that interchange-preventing dependences are reversed by interchange, it is easy to

see that the direction vector corresponding to an interchange-preventing dependence is (<,>). After interchange, such a dependence becomes (>,<), which
clearly accesses data in a different order. To extend these observations to interchange testing for a loop nest containing several dependences, we need one more
definition.

THEOREM
5.1

Let $D(i,j)$ be a direction vector for a dependence in a perfect nest of n loops.
Then the direction vector for the same dependence after a permutation of the
loops in the nest is determined by applying the same permutation to the elements of $D(i,j)$.

Proof By Definitions 2.9 and 2.10, the components of the direction vector are determined by the relative values of the components of the iteration vectors i and j
at the source and the sink of the dependence, according to the following
equation:

$$D(i,j) = \begin{cases} \text{``<'' if } i_k < j_k \\ \text{``='' if } i_k = j_k \\ \text{``>'' if } i_k > j_k \end{cases}$$

Since the loop permutation simply permutes the components of the iteration
vectors, then the corresponding direction vector must be permuted in exactly
the same way.

DEFINITION
5.3

The *direction matrix* for a nest of loops is a matrix in which each row is a direction vector for some dependence between statements contained in the nest
and every such direction vector is represented by a row.

Note that this definition permits identical direction vectors to be represented
by a single row. We illustrate this definition with the following loop nest:

```
DO I = 1, N
    DO J = 1, M
        DO K = 1, L
            A(I+1,J+1,K) = A(I,J,K) + A(I,J+1,K+1)
        ENDDO
    ENDDO
ENDDO
```

The direction matrix is

$$\begin{bmatrix} < & < & = \\ < & = & > \end{bmatrix}$$

The first row in this matrix represents the true dependence from A(I+1,J+1,K) to A(I,J,K); the second row is the true dependence into A(I,J+1,K+1).

It is easy to see how to extend Theorem 5.1 to direction matrices. Since the effects of permuting loops on a particular dependence can be reflected by permuting the entries in the direction vector, the effects of the same permutation on all dependences can be reflected by permuting columns in the direction matrix. For instance, if the outermost loop in the example is moved to the innermost position, letting the other two loops drift outward accordingly, the following direction matrix results:

$$\begin{bmatrix} < & = & < \\ = & > & < \end{bmatrix}$$

The second row in the matrix now has a ">" as the leftmost non-"=" symbol. This dependence is illegal, reflecting the fact that the described transformation is invalid.

THEOREM 5.2   A permutation of the loops in a perfect nest is legal if and only if the direction matrix, after the same permutation is applied to its columns, has no ">" direction as the leftmost non-"=" direction in any row.

Theorem 5.2, which follows directly from Theorems 5.1 and 2.3, provides a simple and effective procedure for testing the safety of any loop interchange—construct direction vectors for all dependences in the loop nest, enter them into a direction matrix, and perform the desired permutation to see if it yields an illegal direction matrix.

5.2.2 Profitability of Loop Interchange

The vectorization algorithm *codegen* presented in Figure 2.2 works by vectorizing all loops that are nested inside the loop carrying the innermost dependence cycle. For loop interchange to enhance the vectorization uncovered by that algorithm, it should increase the number of loops inside that cycle. In other words, to be effective loop interchange must change the dependence pattern in loop nests to which it is applied.

Theorem 5.2 tells us that the effects of a specific loop interchange on dependences in the loop nest can be seen by modifying the direction matrix; in other words, the resulting dependence pattern can be determined without having to modify the program itself. Therefore, to establish profitability, we can analyze potentially profitable loop permutations and then check to see if they are legal by permuting the direction matrix.

The architecture of the target machine is usually the principal factor in determining the most profitable interchange pattern. Thus the right loop nesting cannot be determined in a machine-independent fashion. To see how the best interchange pattern varies with target architectures, consider the following example:

```
      DO I = 1, N
        DO J = 1, M
          DO K = 1, L
S             A(I+1,J+1,K) = A(I,J,K) + B
          ENDDO
        ENDDO
      ENDDO
```

S has a true self-dependence with direction vector $(<,<,=)$. If this nest is processed by *codegen* from Figure 2.2, the inner two loops will be vectorized (the dependence is carried by the outer loop). The resulting Fortran 90 code is

```
      DO I = 1, N
S       A(I+1,2:M+1,1:L) = A(I,1:M,1:L) + B
      ENDDO
```

This form may be effective for SIMD machines with a large number of synchronous functional units (e.g., the Connection Machine), but it is not the most effective for vector register machines. This is because the vector register size is typically less than the iteration count of a single loop so that vectorizing more than one loop produces little added benefit. On the other hand, choosing the right memory access pattern can make a big difference on these machines.

On most vector machines, it is best to vectorize loops with stride-1 memory access because memory technology is most efficient at delivering blocks of contiguous data. Since Fortran stores arrays in column-major order (the leftmost dimension is the one with contiguous memory access), this means that it is best to vectorize the first dimension—the I-loop in the current example. If the I-loop is shifted to the innermost position while keeping the relative order of the other two loops, the resulting direction vector is $(<,=,<)$. The I-loop in this form carries no dependence, and *codegen* vectorizes it to produce

```
      DO J = 1, M
        DO K = 1, L
S         A(2:N+1,J+1,K) = A(1:N,J,K) + B
        ENDDO
      ENDDO
```

If the target is an MIMD parallel machine with vector execution units, this loop ordering is good, but not the best possible. The I-loop is still the best vector loop, but the K-loop, which is the only remaining possibility for parallel execution, is not in the optimal position. If it is moved to the outermost position, yielding a direction vector of (=,<,<), it can be run in parallel and will cut down synchronization costs by a factor of M. The resulting code is

```
PARALLEL DO K = 1, L
    DO J = 1, M
        A(2:N+1,J+1,K) = A(1:N,J,K) + B
    ENDDO
END PARALLEL DO
```

It should be evident from these examples that the direction matrix can be used to determine the best loop permutation for a particular target machine. However, exhaustively trying all permutations is usually not the most efficient approach; it is much better to predict the best ordering for the given target, then use the direction matrix to confirm the safety of that ordering. Such a "predictive approach" turns out to be beneficial not just in loop interchange, but also in other transformations as well. The following section shows how loop interchange can be incorporated into the *codegen* algorithm and tuned to vector machines.

5.2.3   Loop Interchange and Vectorization

For vectorization, a simple observation leads to a powerful and practical loop interchange scheme. The observation is this: a loop that carries no dependences cannot carry any dependences that prevent interchange with other loops nested inside it. Furthermore, such a loop cannot possibly carry any dependences that are sensitive to the interchange. The absence of interchange-preventing dependences implies that shifting that loop to a position at a deeper nesting level is always legal; the absence of dependences at the original level guarantees that the loop will not carry any dependences in its new, more deeply nested position. As a result, this process of inward shifting can be continued until the loop is in the innermost position with the assurance that it will not carry any dependences there. Since a dependence-free loop is also a recurrence-free loop, and since the goal of vectorization is to have recurrence-free inner loops, this method of interchange is ideal for vectorization algorithms. The following theorem states these observations more formally.

THEOREM   In a perfect loop nest, if loops at levels i through $i + n$ carry no dependence—
5.3   that is, all dependences are carried by loops at levels less than i or greater than $i + n$—it is always legal to shift these loops inside of the loop at level $i + n + 1$. Furthermore, these loops will not carry any dependences in their new position.

Proof   To establish the truth of this theorem we consider two cases. First, if the dependence is carried by the outer loop, as shown in the first two rows of the direction matrix below, then no matter what permutation is applied to the inner columns, the transformation is legal because the outermost "<" will still ensure that the source is executed before the sink.

Loops
i to $i + n$

On the other hand, if the dependence is carried by an inner loop as shown in the last two rows of the illustration, then the entries in all columns corresponding to levels i to $i + n$ must all be "=" direction, because the outermost non-"=" is at a level greater than $i + n$. Once again, these loops can be shifted to the inside, and the carrier loop will be preserved.

Theorem 5.3 provides a basis for moving a block of loops to the innermost position. Because this form of interchange basically "shifts" a block inside another loop, it is known as a *loop shift*. An excellent example of how this result can be used to carry out loop interchange is given by the following common encoding of matrix multiplication:

```
        DO I = 1, N
          DO J = 1, N
            DO K = 1, N
S               A(I,J) = A(I,J) + B(I,K) * C(K,J)
            ENDDO
          ENDDO
        ENDDO
```

Statement S has true, anti-, and output dependences on itself, all carried by the K-loop and all with direction vector $(=,=,<)$. If *codegen* is applied directly to this loop nest, it will produce no vectorized statements because the recurrence exists at the innermost loop. At each stage, starting with the outermost loop, the recursive code generator will discover that the current level carries a recurrence, thus requiring a sequential DO, even though the outer two loops carry no dependence.

However, based on the observations at the beginning of the section, it is easy to see that, since the outermost dependence is carried at level 3, loops 1 and 2 carry no dependences and can be shifted inside of 3 where they will still carry no dependences. The resulting loop nest,

```
    DO K = 1, N
       DO I = 1, N
          DO J = 1, N
S                A(I,J) = A(I,J) + B(I,K) * C(K,J)
          ENDDO
       ENDDO
    ENDDO
```

has the direction vector ($<$,$=$,$=$). When *codegen* is applied to this nest, it will find that the inner two loops are free of both dependences and recurrences, and thus can be vectorized in two dimensions:

```
    DO K = 1, N
       FORALL (J=1,N)
          A(1:N,J) = A(1:N,J) + B(1:N,K) * C(K,J)
       END FORALL
    ENDDO
```

The FORALL loop is used here for clarity. While the two-dimensional vector statement can be written in Fortran 90 without use of the FORALL construct, the resulting code is difficult to understand.

This observation can be incorporated into the algorithm *codegen* in Figure 2.2 by a simple device—instead of generating a sequential DO for the loop at level k, shift the outermost remaining loop that carries a dependence to level k, then generate the sequential loop for that loop. This is always legal by Theorem 5.3. In the next section we will present a revised version of *codegen* that incorporates this modification in a more general framework.

A Code Generation Framework

Figure 5.2 shows a generalized parallel code generation algorithm that incorporates both loop shifting and recurrence breaking. It will be used as the framework for code generation in most of the rest of this chapter.

This version contains two changes from the original. First, if a region is cyclic, there is a test to see if this is the innermost loop in the nest. If it is, then recurrence breaking is attempted. Otherwise, it attempts to select a loop for sequentialization in the routine *select_loop_and_interchange*. Recall that in the original algorithm, the outermost loop of a cyclic nest was always selected. However, in this version, we could implement the loop-shifting heuristic by using the procedure in Figure 5.3. This procedure would achieve the desired result on the example presented earlier in this section.

procedure *codegen(R,k,D)*

// *R* is the region for which code must be generated.
// *k* is the minimum nesting level of possible parallel loops
// *D* is the dependence graph among statements in *R*

find the set $\{S_1, S_2, \ldots, S_m\}$ of maximal strongly connected regions in the dependence graph *D* restricted to *R* (use Tarjan's algorithm);

construct R_π from *R* by reducing each S_i to a single node and compute D_π, the dependence graph naturally induced on R_π by *D*;

let $\{\pi_1, \pi_2, \ldots, \pi_m\}$ be the *m* nodes of R_π numbered in an order consistent with D_π (use topological sort to do the numbering);

for *i* = 1 **to** *m* **do**

    if π_i is cyclic **then**

        if *k* is the deepest loop in π_i
        then *try_recurrence_breaking(π_i, D, k)*;
        else begin

            select_loop_and_interchange(π_i, D, k);

            generate a level-*k* DO statement;

            let D_i be the dependence graph consisting of all dependence edges in *D* that are at level *k* + 1 or greater and are internal to π_i;

            codegen (π_i,k+1,D_i);

            generate the level-*k* ENDDO statement;
        end
    else
        generate a vector statement for π_i in $\rho(\pi_i) - k + 1$ dimensions, where $\rho(\pi_i)$ is the number of loops containing π_i;
end *codegen*

Figure 5.2 Code generation framework with loop selection and recurrence breaking.

General Loop Selection and Interchange

In practice, the loop-shifting algorithm presented in Figure 5.3 is very effective. Not only is it simple to implement, usually requiring only a small number of lines of code, but it also does best on codes that employ the most common style for

procedure *select_loop_and_interchange*(π_i,D,k)

    if the outermost carried dependence in π_i is at level $p > k$ **then**
        shift loops at level k, $k + 1$, . . . , $p - 1$ inside the level-p loop,
        making it into the level-k loop;
  return;
end *select_loop_and_interchange*

Figure 5.3 Loop selection to implement simple loop-shifting interchange.

coding subscripts. However, the algorithm is not perfect. It would, for instance, miss the vectorization opportunity in

```
      DO I = 1, N
         DO J = 1, M
S            A(I+1,J+1) = A(I,J) + A(I+1,J)
         ENDDO
      ENDDO
```

In this example, there are two true dependences of S on itself, with the direction matrix

$$\begin{bmatrix} < & < \\ = & < \end{bmatrix}$$

Since both loops carry dependences, the loop-shifting algorithm will fail to uncover any vector loops. However, a brief examination of the direction matrix will show that interchanging the two loops frees the new inner loop of carried dependences, allowing it to be vectorized. The resulting vector code is

```
      DO J = 1, M
         A(2:N+1,J+1) = A(1:N,J) + A(2:N+1,J)
      ENDDO
```

Furthermore, this vector loop runs over contiguous memory, which has the benefits discussed previously. Given the difference in execution speeds between the interchanged, vectorized version and the noninterchanged, nonvectorized version, modifications to *codegen* to handle cases such as this are extremely useful.

As mentioned previously, one obvious although not necessarily efficient way of handling any loop interchange is to examine all legal permutations of the direction matrix for the optimal form and then generate a loop ordering corresponding to that permutation. This approach will be reconsidered later, when the full context of all transformations has been presented. For vectorization, the desired result is to achieve an algorithm that obtains more vectorization than obtained by loop shifting, but with less work than examining all permutations.

A general scheme for doing this is to replace the *loop-shift* code in Figure 5.3 with general *loop selection*: select a loop at nesting level $p \geq k$ that can be safely moved outward to level k and shift the loops at level $k, k + 1, \ldots, p - 1$ inside it. For this strategy to be effective, there needs to be some rationale for selecting the loop at level p. In particular, it should at least carry a dependence.

There are many different heuristics that have been tried in addition to loop selection. In this section, we will discuss a heuristic that does slightly better than loop shifting by examining the direction matrix. The basic strategy is as follows:

1. If the level-k loop carries no dependence, then let p be the smallest integer such that the level-p loop carries a dependence. (This case has the same effect as the loop-shifting heuristic.)

2. If the level-k loop carries a dependence, let p be the outermost loop that can be shifted outward to position k and that carries a dependence d whose direction vector contains an "=" in every position but the pth. If no such loop exists, let $p = k$.

The advantage of this heuristic is that it will sequentialize any loop that must be sequentialized anyway because it carries a dependence that cannot be satisfied by sequentializing some other loop. Thus it will correctly handle the example above on which simple loop shifting fails. Figure 5.4 shows the code that implements this more complicated heuristic.

Having fully explored loop interchange with respect to vectorization, we turn to recurrence breaking in *codegen*.

5.3 Scalar Expansion

As the original coding of matrix multiplication in Section 5.1 showed, Fortran 77 programs frequently use scalar temporaries in computations involving vectors and arrays. A typical example is the following fragment, which swaps the contents of two vectors.

```
        DO I = 1, N
S₁        T = A(I)
S₂        A(I) = B(I)
S₃        B(I) = T
        ENDDO
```

The dependence graph for this loop, shown in Figure 5.5, reveals that this loop is not vectorizable as is.

procedure *select_loop_and_interchange(R,k)*
 // k is the current nesting level in region R
 // R is strongly connected when only edges at level k
 // and deeper are considered.
 let N be the deepest loop nesting level;
 let p be the level of the outermost carried dependence;
 if p = k **then begin**
  not_found = *true*;
  while(*not_found* and p ≤ N) **do**

   if the level-p loop can be safely shifted outward to level k **and**
    there exists a dependence d carried by the loop such that
    the direction vector for d has "=" in every position but p
   then *not_found* := *false*;
   else p := p + 1;
  end
  if p > N **then** p = k;
 end
 if p > k **then** shift loops at level k, k +1, . . . , p − 1 inside the level-p loop;
end *select_loop_and_interchange*

Figure 5.4 Loop selection heuristic.

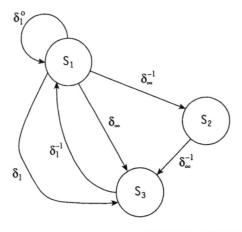

Figure 5.5 Dependence graph for vector swap.

  By its very nature a vector swap must read elements of an array and then over-write the same elements. Therefore, the loop-independent antidependences (S_1 δ_∞^{-1} S_2 and S_2 δ_∞^{-1} S_3) due to arrays A and B cannot be eliminated. The other dependences all arise because of the scalar T. Since T is used to hold a value while its original location is being overwritten, the true loop-independent dependence will be difficult to remove or change. However, the other scalar dependences all arise because the same location is used as temporary storage on different iterations. In particular, the loop-carried true dependence $S_1 \delta_1 S_3$ is present because of the inclusive nature of the definition of dependence given in Section 2.2—S_1 stores into a location read by S_3 on a later iteration. If each iteration has a separate location to use as a temporary, these dependences disappear, leaving the obviously vectorizable dependence graph in Figure 5.6.

To transform the program so that it corresponds to this loop nest, references to the scalar T must be replaced with references to a compiler-generated temporary array T$ that has a separate location for each loop iteration. This transformation, known as *scalar expansion*, produces the following code:

```
      DO I = 1, N
S₁        T$(I) = A(I)
S₂        A(I) = B(I)
S₃        B(I) = T$(I)
      ENDDO
      T = T$(N)
```

The assignment to T after the loop captures the "last" value of T$ computed in the loop. Procedure *codegen* applied to this loop yields

```
S₁    T$(1:N) = A(1:N)
S₂    A(1:N) = B(1:N)
S₃    B(1:N) = T$(1:N)
      T = T$(N)
```

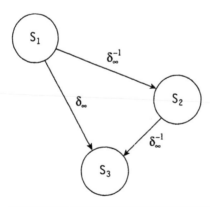

Figure 5.6 Revised dependence graph for vector swap.

In Section 6.2.1 we will discuss *privatization*, a slightly different way to achieve the same result by declaring the location T to be private to each iteration of a parallel loop. Neither scalar expansion nor scalar privatization is cost-free, since extra memory is required and more complex addressing is necessary. As a result, neither transformation should be used unless it increases the amount of vectorization or parallelization uncovered.

To illustrate that scalar expansion (like vectorization) is not always profitable, consider the following code fragment, typical of many loops encountered in finite difference computations:

```
DO I = 1, N
   T = T + A(I) + A(I-1)
   A(I) = T
ENDDO
```

Because there is a use of T before the first assignment to it, the scalar expansion algorithm must be careful to insert initialization code (symmetric to the finalization in the previous example). Correctly expanded, the code becomes

```
      T$(0) = T
      DO I = 1, N
S₁       T$(I) = T$(I-1) + A(I) + A(I-1)
S₂       A(I) = T$(I)
      ENDDO
      T = T$(N)
```

The dependence graph for this fragment is presented in Figure 5.7. Even with the scalar expanded, no vectorization is possible.

It should be obvious to the reader from these two examples that scalar expansion can always be safely carried out. The actual process of expansion, which we will describe shortly, is a straightforward and somewhat tedious procedure that can be applied to any loop nest. As we have seen, however, scalar expansion is not always profitable, and the principal challenge is determining when it is worth the costs incurred.

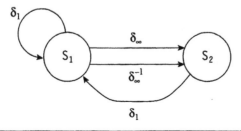

Figure 5.7 Dependence graph where expansion is not profitable.

One obvious approach is to expand all scalars, generate the optimal vectorization, then shrink all unnecessarily expanded scalars. While this approach is feasible, it would be better to avoid the unnecessary work of expanding, testing, and shrinking scalars by determining when the transformation is guaranteed to be profitable. As with loop interchange, we will attempt instead to *predict* the effects of scalar expansion on the dependence graph before actually transforming the program. By doing so, the benefits can be computed prior to the expensive process of modifying loops, saving the work of undoing unnecessary transformations.

A method for determining the effects of scalar expansion on dependences follows directly from the observations at the beginning of this section. Some dependences arise from the reuse of memory locations, whereas others arise from the reuse of values. Dependences due to the reuse of values must always be preserved, since any transformation that removes one of those will change the results of a computation. Dependences that arise from the reuse of memory locations, on the other hand, can be deleted by expanding the corresponding scalar. If the edges that are *deletable* by scalar expansion can be determined in advance, then scalar expansion can be carried out by removing deletable edges, computing the strongly connected regions in the new graph, and expanding scalars only if the new graph has vectorizable statements.

A critical concept for determining deletable edges is introduced by the following definition.

DEFINITION
5.4

A definition X of a scalar S is a *covering definition* for loop L if a definition of S placed at the beginning of L reaches no uses of S that occur past X. Whenever there are multiple covering definitions of a loop, the term "covering definition" will refer to the earliest.

In the following, S_1 is a covering definition for T in the loop:

```
      DO I = 1, 100
S₁       T = X(I)
S₂       Y(I) = T
      ENDDO
```

Any definition of T placed at the beginning of the loop is immediately killed by S_1, so that the use in S_2 can never be reached.

Similarly, S_1 is also a covering definition in the following example:

```
      DO I = 1, 100
         IF (A(I).GT.0) THEN
S₁          T = X(I)
S₂          Y(I) = T
         ENDIF
      ENDDO
```

Even though the assignment to T may not be executed on every iteration of the loop, it is executed on every iteration that uses T. As a result, any definition placed at the beginning of the loop cannot reach past S_1.

A covering definition does not always exist:

```
     DO I - 1, 100
         IF (A(I).GT.0) THEN
S₁          T - X(I)
         ENDIF
S₂       Y(I) - T
     ENDDO
```

Since S_2 is executed unconditionally and S_1 is executed conditionally, a definition placed at the loop start always has a chance of reaching S_2. As a result T has no covering definition. In terms of static single-assignment form, discussed in Section 4.4.4, there exists no covering definition for a variable T if the edge out of the first assignment to T goes to a ϕ-function later in the loop that merges its values with those for another control flow path through the loop.

For the purpose of scalar expansion, it will be useful to consider a more general interpretation of a covering definition that extends to a collection of definitions along different paths going through the loop. We will say that there is a collection C of covering definitions for the T in a given loop if either (1) there exists no ϕ-function at the beginning of the loop that merges versions of T from outside the loop with versions that are defined within the loop or (2) the ϕ-function within the loop has no SSA edge to any ϕ-function, including itself. An example of this kind of loop is as follows:

```
     DO I - 1, 100
         IF (A(I).GT.0) THEN
S₁          T - X(I)
         ELSE
S₂             T - -X(I)
         ENDIF
S₃       Y(I) - T
     ENDDO
```

Here S_1 and S_2 form a collection of covering definitions because there is no ϕ-function required at the beginning of the loop, although one is required just prior to statement S_3.

With this expanded definition, any single loop with a definition of T can be converted to one with a collection of covering definitions by inserting dummy assignments along paths where T is uncovered, according to the following procedure on the SSA graph, which also computes the collection C of covering definitions.

1. Let S_0 be the ϕ-function for T at the beginning of the loop, if there is one, and null otherwise. Make C empty and initialize an empty stack.

2. Let S_1 be the first definition of T in the loop. Add S_1 to C.

3. If the SSA successor of S_1 is a ϕ-function S_2 that is not equal to S_0, then push S_2 onto the stack and mark it.

4. While the stack is nonempty,

   a. pop the ϕ-function S from the stack;

   b. add all SSA predecessors that are not ϕ-functions to C;

   c. if there is an SSA edge from S_0 into S, then insert the assignment T = T as the last statement along that edge and add it to C;

   d. for each unmarked ϕ-function S_3 (other than S_0) that is an SSA predecessor of S, mark S_3 and push it onto the stack;

   e. for each unmarked ϕ-function S_4 that can be reached from S by a single SSA edge and that is not predominated by S in the control flow graph, mark S_4 and push it onto the stack.

This procedure simply continues looking for parallel paths to a ϕ-function following the first assignment, until no more exist. However, in step 4e, it avoids stacking ϕ-functions dominated by the current ϕ-function because there can be no unconsidered path to such a node.

When applied to the earlier loop that had no covering definition, this procedure would produce

```
      DO I = 1, 100
         IF (A(I).GT.0) THEN
S₁          T = X(I)
         ELSE
S₂            T = T
         ENDIF
S₃       Y(I) = T
      ENDDO
```

Covering definitions are important because they determine the way that scalars are expanded and therefore which edges are deletable. Here is a procedure for carrying out scalar expansion for T in a normalized loop, once covering definitions have been identified.

1. Create an array T$ of appropriate length.

2. For each S in the covering definition collection C, replace the T on the left-hand side by T$(I).

3. For every other definition of T and every use of T in the loop body reachable by SSA edges that do not pass through S_0 (the ϕ-function at the beginning of the loop), replace T by T$(I).

4. For every use prior to a covering definition (direct successors of S_0 in the SSA graph), replace T by T$(I-1).

5. If S_0 is not null, then insert T$(0) = T before the loop.

6. If there is an SSA edge from any definition in the loop to a use outside the loop, insert T = T$(U) after the loop, where U is the loop upper bound.

The early examples in this chapter showed how expressions with covering definitions would be expanded. The following is an expansion for the previous loop, which originally had no covering definition:

```
      DO I = 1, 100
         IF (A(I).GT.0) THEN
S₁          T$(I) = X(I)
         ELSE
            T$(I) = T$(I-1)
         ENDIF
S₂       Y(I) = T$(I)
      ENDDO
```

Given this definition of covering definitions, we can now identify all deletable dependences.

THEOREM 5.4

If all uses of a scalar T before any member of the collection of covering definitions are expanded as T$(I-1) and all other uses and definitions are expanded as T$(I), then the edges that will be deleted with the scalar expansion are (1) backward-carried antidependences, (2) all carried output dependences, (3) forward loop-carried and loop-independent antidependences, and (4) redundant forward-carried true dependences.

To see the truth of this result, consider each dependence class in turn:

1. *Backward-carried antidependences:* Every member of the collection of covering definitions is upwards exposed in the loop body; all carried antidependences must have one of these covering definitions or a later definition as a target. Likewise, since the antidependence is backward, its source also occurs after the covering definitions. Thus the endpoint references are both expanded as T$(I), but since each iteration uses a different location, the endpoints use different locations within the array and the dependence is broken.

2. *Backward-carried output dependences:* By a minor change to the previous argument.

3. *Forward-carried output dependences:* Since all definitions occur after one or more of the covering definitions, all definitions are expanded as T$(I) and the reuse across loop iterations is broken. Note that this case includes the self-output dependence of the covering definition.

4. *Forward antidependences into the covering definition:* The use prior to the covering definition will be expanded as T$(I-1); the covering definition will be expanded as T$(I). Since the use now refers to a location that is different from the one assigned on any current or future iteration, the antidependence is broken.

5. *Loop-carried true dependences from a covering definition to a use after the covering definition:* The covering definitions kill any interiteration value transfer.

To illustrate these principles more concretely, consider again the dependence graph for the vector swap presented in Figure 5.6. Figure 5.8 presents that dependence graph with the deletable edges clearly marked with Ds. Edge D_1 is a backward-carried antidependence and is deletable according to the first case. Edge D_2 is a forward-carried output dependence and is deletable by the third case. Edge D_3 is a forward-carried true dependence, deletable by the fifth case.

The fourth principle is not intuitive from the previous examples, but a new one should clarify it.

```
      DO I = 1, 100
S₁        A(I) = T
S₂        T = B(I) + C(I)
      ENDDO
```

The dependence graph for this fragment, with deletable edges marked, is shown in Figure 5.9. Edges D_1 and D_3 are forward antidependences, which disappear according to case 4. The code after scalar expansion is

```
      T$(0) = T
      DO I = 1, 100
S₁        A(I) = T$(I-1)
S₂        T$(I) = B(I) + C(I)
      ENDDO
      T = T$(100)
```

The antidependence has disappeared, since the store is always one iteration ahead of the use. With statement reordering, this example can in fact be vectorized (just as the transformed graph indicates) as

```
      T$(0) = T
S₂    T$(1:100) = B(1:100) + C(1:100)
S₁    A(1:100) = T$(0:99)
      T = T$(100)
```

It is worth noting that Theorem 5.4 applies only when scalars are expanded in one loop. It can be extended to accommodate expansion in multiple loops, but

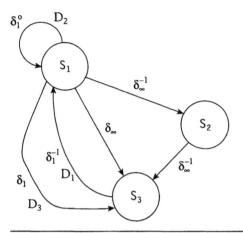

Figure 5.8 Deletable edges in vector swap.

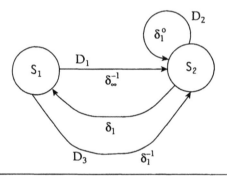

Figure 5.9 Loop-independent deletable edges.

this process is more complicated and provides far less benefit than the initial expansion in one loop.

With the ability to predict the results of scalar expansion in the dependence graph, *codegen* is easily modified to expand scalars. Figure 5.10 contains a version of the procedure *try_recurrence_breaking,* which is invoked from the code generation framework given in Figure 5.2. It is worth noting that the only scalars that must be expanded in the step "expand scalars indicated by deletable edges" are those indicated by deletable edges that either cross into or cross out of a vector piblock.

One obvious drawback of scalar expansion is an increase in the memory requirements for the program. If not carefully managed, this penalty can overcome the benefits gained by vectorization and parallelism. Fortunately, there are several techniques that can ameliorate storage problems caused by scalar expansion. One is to simply expand scalars in a single loop, gaining the greatest marginal

procedure *try_recurrence_breaking*(π_i, D, k)

    if k is the deepest loop in π_i **then begin**
        remove deletable edges in π_i;
        find the set $\{SC_1, SC_2, \ldots, SC_n\}$ of maximal strongly connected
           regions in D restricted to π_i;
        if there are vector statements among SC_i **then begin**
           expand scalars indicated by deletable edges;
           codegen(π_i, k, D restricted to π_i);
        end
    end
end *try_recurrence_breaking*

Figure 5.10 Recurrence breaking via scalar expansion at the deepest nesting level.

benefit for the least cost. Expanding in more than one loop greatly increases memory requirements, with only a small additional payoff in performance. The second technique is to strip-mine the loop before scalar expansion, and to expand only the strip loop.

For instance, strip-mining the following

```
DO I = 1, N
    T = A(I) + A(I+1)
    A(I) = T + B(I)
ENDDO
```

for a vector register machine with a register size of 64 (and assuming that N is an even multiple of 64) yields

```
DO I = 1, N, 64
    DO j = 0, 63
        T = A(I+j) + A(I+j+1)
        A(I+j) = T + B(I+j)
    ENDDO
ENDDO
```

Expanding in the strip loop is much more manageable and gives

```
DO I = 1, N, 64
    DO j = 0, 63
        T$(j) = A(I+j) + A(I+j+1)
        A(I+j) = T$(j) + B(I+j)
    ENDDO
ENDDO
```

The size of the temporary is now small and known at compile time. Furthermore, given that the vector register size is 64, T$ can be allocated to a vector register, requiring no extra memory whatsoever. Essentially, the scalar temporary that was intended to be allocated to a scalar register has been expanded to a vector temporary allocated to a vector register.

The third technique for alleviating storage requirements is *forward substitution*. Returning to the previous example, another method for eliminating any extra storage (and also the need for scalar expansion) is to forward-substitute T into its only use, yielding

```
DO I - 1, N
    A(I) - A(I) + A(I+1) + B(I)
ENDDO
```

In this example, forward substitution is obviously a desirable approach, since there is only one use of the temporary. In general, however, a trade-off must be made: as the temporary is used more, the cost of memory to hold the expanded scalar must be measured against the extra computation required to recompute the substituted expression. This type of substitution can be easily accommodated during induction-variable substitution (see Section 4.5).

5.4 Scalar and Array Renaming

Scalar expansion effectively eliminates some dependences that arise from reuse of memory locations, albeit at the cost of extra memory. In fact, reuse of memory locations, while reducing program size, leads to many "artificial" dependences that can be eliminated by utilizing extra memory. The following fragment provides another example of scalar dependences that can be eliminated:

```
       DO I - 1, 100
S₁        T - A(I) + B(I)
S₂        C(I) - T + T
S₃        T - D(I) - B(I)
S₄        A(I+1) - T * T
       ENDDO
```

If the dependence graph is naively constructed, the dependence $S_1 \delta S_4$ may appear. Furthermore, even a sophisticated construction will add the output dependence $S_1 \delta^o S_3$, which cannot be broken by scalar expansion. Although the first dependence exists according to the definition of dependence, this dependence cannot correspond to the passing of a value because S_3 always blocks the output of S_1 from reaching S_4. The second dependence exists only because the memory location was reused. The second dependence indicates that there are really two separate variables that just happen to inhabit the same memory location. If they are placed in separate memory locations, as in

```
        DO I - 1, 100
S₁        T1 = A(I) + B(I)
S₂        C(I) - T1 + T1
S₃        T2 - D(I) - B(I)
S₄        A(I+1) - T2 * T2
        ENDDO
        T - T2
```

the artificial dependences disappear, permitting the loop to be completely vectorized:

```
S₃   T2$(1:100) - D(1:100) - B(1:100)
S₄   A(2:101) - T2$(1:100) * T2$(1:100)
S₁   T1$(1:100) - A(1:100) + B(1:100)
S₂   C(1:100) - T1$(1:100) + T1$(1:100)
     T - T2$(100)
```

To see that *scalar renaming*, rather than scalar expansion, has enabled the vectorization, consider the unrenamed fragment with scalars expanded:

```
        DO I - 1, 100
S₁        T$(I) - A(I) + B(I)
S₂        C(I) - T$(I) + T$(I)
S₃        T$(I) - D(I) - B(I)
S₄        A(I+1) - T$(I) * T$(I)
        ENDDO
```

The dependence graph for this example, presented in Figure 5.11, is still cyclic.

The definition-use graph can be used as a basis for scalar renaming. Figure 5.12 describes an algorithm that partitions scalars into different equivalence classes, each of which can be renamed to a different value. Simply stated, the algorithm repeatedly picks a definition, adds in all uses that it reaches, adds in all definitions that reach any of those uses, and so on, until a fixed point is reached. In the worst case, all definitions and uses end up in the same partition, meaning that no renaming can be done.

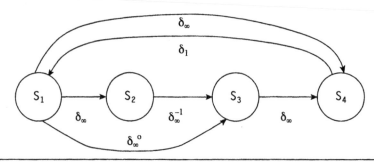

Figure 5.11 Recurrence not broken by scalar expansion alone.

procedure *rename(S,D)*

> // S is the scalar that is being considered for renaming
> // D is the definition-use graph for the loop
> // *rename* partitions all definitions and uses of S into equivalence
> //   classes, each of which can occupy different memory locations.
>
> *partitions* = ∅;
> *defs_to_examine* = ∅;
> let *unmarked_defs* = all definitions of S;
>
> **while** (*unmarked_defs* != ∅) **do begin**
>> choose and remove an element s of *unmarked_defs*;
>> add s to *defs_to_examine*;
>> create a new partition p;
>>
>> **while** (*defs_to_examine* != ∅) **do begin**
>>> choose and remove an element s of *defs_to_examine*;
>>> add s to p;
>>>
>>> **for each** use u reached by s **do begin**
>>>> add u to p;
>>>>
>>>> **for each** def d ∈ *unmarked_defs* that reaches u **do begin**
>>>>> remove d from *unmarked_defs*;
>>>>> add d to *defs_to_examine*;
>>>> **end**
>>> **end**
>>> name all elements of p the same;
>> **end**
> **end**
> **end** *rename*

Figure 5.12 Scalar renaming.

This algorithm assumes that if the same variable appears on both the left- and right-hand side of an assignment, the definition on the left is distinct from the use on the right. Note that a slightly different version of this algorithm works on SSA form (see Section 4.4.4). In this case, a φ-node would be treated as both a definition and use of the same variable. All other instructions that define and use the same variable would be treated as a distinct definition and use.

Having established an algorithm that safely renames scalars, the last issue to consider is when scalar renaming is profitable. In general, scalar renaming will break recurrences in situations that are similar to the one presented in Figure 5.11, where a loop-independent output dependence or antidependence is a critical element of a cycle. However, scalar renaming is essentially free of bad side effects; the amount of increased memory is very small at worst, and is typically nonexistent, since each named scalar will likely be allocated to a register. Further-more, the essential operations of scalar renaming are usually performed by most optimizing compilers while determining live ranges for register allocation.

While scalar renaming is essentially free, the analogous transformation of *array renaming* is not. Just as scalar memory locations are sometimes reused for different values, array locations are sometimes reused, creating unnecessary anti-dependences and output dependences. Consider, for instance:

```
DO I = 1, N

    A(I) = A(I-1) + X
        δ∞
    Y(I) = A(I) + Z
            δ∞⁻¹
    A(I) = B(I) + C

ENDDO
```

This loop contains a recurrence, and thus does not vectorize using the algo-rithm described so far. The recurrence here is similar to the one in the scalar renaming example: A(I) is used for two different things within the loop. The def-inition in the last statement and the use in the first statement involve one "value," while the definition in the first statement and the use in the second involve another. If A(I) is replaced by A\$(I) in the latter value set, the code computes equivalent results and becomes

```
DO I = 1, N

    A$(I) = A(I-1) + X
        δ∞
    Y(I) = A$(I) + Z
                        δ₁
    A(I) = B(I) + C

ENDDO
```

Just as in the scalar renaming case, the critical antidependence and output dependence have been eliminated. This breaks the recurrence, allowing vectoriza-tion of the loop.

```
A(1:N) = B(1:N) + C
A$(1:N) = A(0:N-1) + X
Y(1:N) = A$(1:N) + Z
```

Obviously, both the safety and the profitability of array renaming are more complex than in the case of scalar renaming. Scalar renaming can be accomplished in the presence of control flow with relative ease because scalar "kills" can be identified; identifying array kills is more complicated. Moreover, array renaming appears to require extra memory proportional to the size of the array (although we will shortly show how to avoid this)— a cost that can severely impact a program's performance. As a result, array renaming requires a more careful implementation.

As far as vectorization is concerned, the benefit provided by array renaming is the removal of loop-independent antidependences and loop-independent output dependences between the renamed references and the array proper. When one of those dependences is critical to the existence of a cycle, array renaming breaks that cycle, possibly producing vector statements.

Ideally, the profitability of array renaming could be determined in advance by examining the dependence graph and determining the minimal set of "critical edges" that break a recurrence and that also can be removed by array renaming. Unfortunately, this problem as stated is *NP*-complete and is thus not amenable to an exact, efficient solution. However, just as with scalar expansion, if the edges that are removed by array renaming can be identified, the effects of array renaming can be predicted by examining the dependence graph without actually carrying out the change in the program itself, which is the expensive part of the transformation.

Just as with scalar renaming, array renaming is effective at increasing parallelism when the same array location is redefined within a loop. Array renaming is more complicated because determining that two array references access the same element is difficult even in the absence of control flow, and it is very difficult when control flow changes occur.

Fortunately, in the absence of control flow, the dependence graph can be used to partition array references (where possible) into renameable regions. Figure 5.13 presents an algorithm for partitioning the graph into renameable regions under the following simplifying assumptions:

1. There is no control flow in the loop body.

2. Each reference or use of the array A is of the form A(I+c), where c is a constant.

The actual name space construction can be handled by a fusion algorithm such as the one that will be presented in Section 6.2.5.

To establish that this algorithm works, we must show that each use $u = A(I+c_u)$ is assigned to exactly one name space. In particular, it is assigned to the name space associated with the definition that is "closest" to the u in the iteration space of the loop. Let $d_x = A(I+c_x)$ be the definition such that the distance $c_x - c_u$ is minimized. If this distance is 0, then d_x must appear before u in the loop body. If more than one definition has the same minimal distance, pick the definition that is later in the loop body (or closest to u in the loop body if the distance is 0). We

procedure *array_partition(l,D,A)*

// *l* is the loop under consideration
// *D* is the dependence graph
// *array_partition* identifies collections of references to array A
//   that refer to the same value,
//   making all output and antidependences deletable.

let $\{d_1, d_2, \ldots, d_n\}$ be the collection of definitions of the array A;
let the artificial definition d_0 represent all definitions outside the loop;
treat the dependence graph as a collection of individual references;
nameSpace(d_0) := {all references that are not the sink of a dependence
   with source within the loop};
for each definition d_i **do begin**
   nameSpace(d_i) := $\{d_i\}$;
   for each true dependence δ out of d_i within the loop **do begin**
      let *u* be the sink reference of δ;
      if there exists no path in the dependence graph from d_i to *u* that
         traverses an output dependence or an antidependence
         (loop independent or carried by loop *l*)
      then add *u* to *nameSpace*(d_i);
   end
end
end *array_partition*

Figure 5.13 Partitioning algorithm for array renaming in simple loops.

---

claim that there cannot be a dependence path from d_x to *u* through some other definition d_y because either the dependence from d_y to *u* would have a smaller distance or d_y would come after d_x in the loop, contrary to assumption. Thus, each use in the loop is in the name space for the closest preceding definition, or it is in the default *nameSpace*(d_0).

Once name spaces are available, code generation is straightforward. Each name space is given a separate name, with one of the name spaces retaining the original array name. However, one problem remains: How do we get the final values back into the original array? The trick is to minimize the amount of copying at the beginning or the end. The strategy we use is to pick the name space for the definition that will assign most of the locations last and use the original name for that. This may result in a number of copies being generated at the beginning. We will also use the original name for the default name space, although this will leave some antidependences in the code. Here is a rough outline of the procedure:

1. Let $\{c_1, c_2, \ldots, c_m\}$ be the additive constants that are found in definitions within the loop, in increasing order, with no duplicates, and let $\{e_1, e_2, \ldots, e_n\}$ be the additive constants that are found in uses within the loop, in

increasing order, with no duplicates. Let e_k be the first constant in a use such that either $e_k > c_m$ or $e_k = c_m$ and there is a use of $A(I+e_k)$ before any definition of $A(I+c_m)$. Then let *nameSpace*(d_0) consist of $\{A(I+e_k), A(I+e_{k+1}), \dots, A(I+e_n)\}$.

2. Let d_1 be the last dependence in the loop body with the constant c_1. Associate the original array name with *nameSpace*(d_1); because no other definition overwrites the value written by d_1, this ensures that the maximum number of values are written out to the correct array. Choose arbitrary names for each of the other name spaces associated with definitions in the loop.

3. Also use the original array name for *nameSpace*(d_0) because the references in this name space can never be part of a true recurrence carried by the loop. However, node splitting may be needed to eliminate some antidependences (see the next section).

4. Insert finalization code for each value in the original array that is not assigned to the original array. If we adopt the convention that d_i is the definition associated with the last assignment to $A(I+c_i)$, and A$i is the name associated with *nameSpace*(d_i), then we need to insert a sequence of loops for $i = 2$ to m at the end of the loop as follows:

```
DO j = c_{i-1} + 1, c_i
   A(U+j) = A$i(U+j)
ENDDO
```

where U is the original loop upper bound.

5. Finally, we need to insert initialization code for any uses in the name spaces for any of the final definitions $\{d_i\}$ that occur on subsequent iterations. Let $A(I+g_i)$, where $g_i < c_i$, be the use in the name space for $A(I+c_i)$ with the smallest additive coefficient. Then we need to insert the loop

```
DO j = g_i + 1, c_i
   A$i(j) = A(j)
ENDDO
```

We illustrate these points with an example:

```
      DO I = 1, 100
S_1       A(I+2) = A(I+1) + B1
S_2       A(I+1) = A(I+3) + B2
S_3       A(I-1) = A(I) + B3
      ENDDO
```

Here the name space for the definition of $A(I+2)$ in S_1 includes the use of $A(I+1)$ in the same statement; the name space for the definition of $A(I+1)$ in S_2 includes the use of $A(I)$ in S_3; and the name space for the definition of $A(I-1)$ in

S_3 contains only itself. The default name space for inputs to the loop includes only the use of A(I+3) in S_2. If we follow the algorithm and use the original array name for the definition in S_3 and the use in S_2, we will get transformed code, including initializations that, after reducing single-iteration loops to single statements, look like this:

```
      A$1(1) = A(1)
      A$2(2) = A(2)
      DO I = 1, 100
S₁      A$2(I+2) = A$2(I+1) + B1
S₂      A$1(I+1) = A(I+3) + B2
S₃      A(I-1) = A$1(I) + B3
      ENDDO
      DO j = 0, 1
         A(100+j) = A$1(100+j)
      ENDDO
      A(102) = A$2(102)
```

5.5 Node Splitting

There are special cases when, after applying the renaming algorithm in the previous section, we are still unable to eliminate a critical antidependence. This is because, in the interest of avoiding copying, we have two different name spaces with the same name in the same statement. Consider the following example:

```
DO I = 1, N
       ┌─────────────────────────────┐
       │    A(I) = X(I+1) + X(I)      │
 δ₁    │            ╱ δ∞⁻¹            │
       │    X(I+1) = B(I) + 10        │
       └─────────────────────────────┘

ENDDO
```

If the renaming algorithm is applied to this loop, the two different references to X in the first statement are in two different name spaces because the first reference refers to values of X on loop entry (e.g., X(I+1)) and the second (e.g., X(I)) to values that are computed within the loop, except on the first iteration. Furthermore, our naming algorithm attempts to give both name spaces the name of the original array. This leaves the antidependence and the recurrence intact.

When a recurrence contains such a critical antidependence (that is, an antidependence without which the recurrence would not exist), it may be broken through a technique known as *node splitting*. Node splitting creates a copy of a node from which an antidependence emanates; if there are no dependences coming into the node, the recurrence will be broken. Node splitting makes a copy of the X array to provide access to the old values, permitting the statements to be reordered. (This optimization can be performed automatically in the renaming operation when needed by simply giving the default *nameSpace*(d_0) a generated name and initializing it outside the loop.)

```
DO I = 1, N
        X$(I) = X(I+1)
        A(I) = X$(I) + X(I)       δ∞⁻¹
        X(I+1) = B(I) + 10
ENDDO
```

δ₁

When *codegen* is applied to the transformed code, it can now linearize the dependences (since the cycle has been broken), yielding the following vector code:

```
X$(1:N) = X(2:N+1)
X(2:N+1) = B(1:N) + 10
A(1:N) = X$(1:N) + X(1:N)
```

Carrying out the node-splitting transformation is straightforward, once the antidependence to be broken has been identified. The only requirement for the antidependence is that the source reference must use only "old" values of the array. Antidependences with constant thresholds always meet this requirement. Figure 5.14 lists a straightforward algorithm for splitting a node, given the antidependence to be deleted. This algorithm just replaces the reference with a scalar (assuming that scalar expansion will be called later) and updates the dependence graph to reflect the program changes.

It should be easy to see that *node_split* eliminates the antidependence by moving the source to a statement that cannot possibly be involved in any recurrence cycle. Even though node splitting can be implemented by a kind of array renaming, it can often be applied to more general loops than renaming. For example, consider a variant of our original example:

```
DO I = 1, N
        X$ = X(I+1)
        A(I) = X$ + X(I)          δ∞⁻¹
        X(I+1) = A(I) + 10
ENDDO
```

δ₁

procedure *node_split(D)*

> // *node_split* takes a constant, loop-independent antidependence,
> // splits the node associated with it, and adjusts the dependence
> //   graph accordingly.

> let T$ be a new scalar not already used in the program;
> create a new assignment x: T$ = *source(D)* and insert it before *source(D)*;
> replace *source(D)* with T$;
> add a loop-independent true dependence from x to *source(D)*;
> change *source(D)* to be x;

end *node_split*

Figure 5.14 Node splitting.

The array renaming algorithm in Section 5.4 cannot be applied here because of the reference to X(2), yet node splitting works well.

While node splitting is straightforward to apply, it is not easy to determine that it is profitable in a specific situation. The following example shows that node splitting does not always break a recurrence:

```
 DO I = 1, N
```

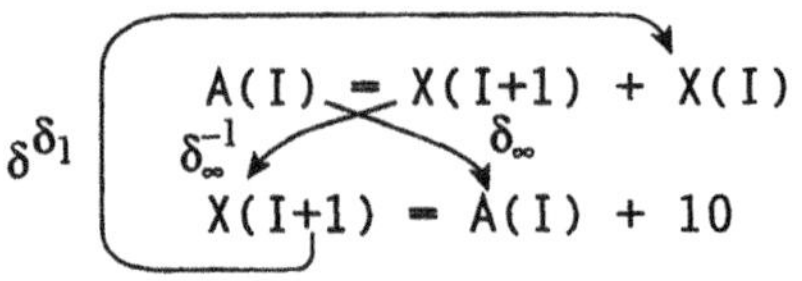

```
 ENDDO
```

Applying the transformation from Figure 5.14 yields

```
DO I = 1, N
```

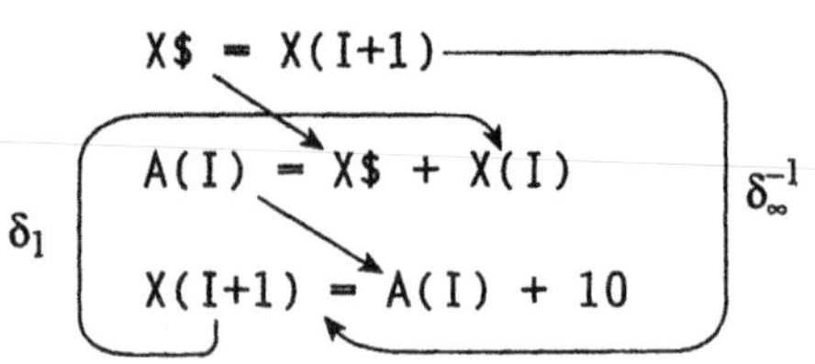

```
ENDDO
```

Scalar expansion will enable the generated assignment to X$ to be vectorized, but the remaining statements are still bound in a recurrence. The problem here is that the antidependence was not critical to the recurrence. For node splitting to generate effective vectorization, the dependence that is split must be "critical" to the recurrence; that is, breaking that dependence must break the recurrence. Unfortunately, the problem of determining a minimal set of such critical dependences in a given recurrence is *NP*-complete. Therefore, there are no efficient methods for finding an optimal solution. In other words, doing a perfect job of node splitting is probably too ambitious for a compiler writer to undertake in a production compiler.

Fortunately, a perfect job is probably unnecessary given the approach of Figure 5.14 because the major expense of the transformation occurs when the temporary scalars are expanded. If scalar expansion is performed only when profitable vectorization is guaranteed and if the profitability algorithm knows that artificially generated assignments do not create profitable vectorization, then node splitting can be performed wherever possible with little danger of degrading performance.

These observations suggest a simple strategy for node splitting: Select antidependences in a recurrence, delete them, and see if the result is acyclic. If so, apply node splitting to eliminate those antidependences.

We leave as an exercise for the reader (Exercise 5.4) to establish the correctness of node splitting—that is, when node splitting is applied along an antidependence critical to a recurrence, the recurrence will be broken. It is important to note, however, that even though the recurrence is broken, it is possible that no vectorization will result because the recurrence may simply break into a group of smaller recurrences.

5.6 Recognition of Reductions

Many operations that are not directly vectorizable occur commonly enough in programs to merit the use of special hardware in a vector architecture. For instance, summing the elements of a vector or array is an extremely common operation, but is not directly vectorizable. The process of obtaining a single element by combining the elements of a vector is known as *reduction*—because the operation reduces the vector to one element. Summing a vector is known as a *sum reduction*. Finding the maximum/minimum element in a vector is a *max/min reduction*. Counting the number of true elements in a vector is a *count reduction*.

Because reductions occur in many important programs, many machines have special hardware or software procedures to compute them. For example, consider sum reduction:

```
S = 0.0
DO I = 1, N
    S = S + A(I)
ENDDO
```

If floating-point addition is assumed to be both commutative and associative (an assumption that is almost never strictly true, but that is usually close enough not to upset programmers too much), the reduction can be rearranged as a number of parallel partial sums followed by a final addition. On a target machine with a four-stage addition pipeline, a natural transformation is to decompose the reduction into four separate sum reductions:

```
S = 0.0
DO k = 1, 4
   SUM(k) = 0.0
   DO I = k, N, 4
      SUM(k) = SUM(k) + A(I)
   ENDDO
   S = S + SUM(k)
ENDDO
```

Distributing the k-loop breaks the reduction naturally into three parts: initialization, computation, and finalization.

```
S = 0.0
DO k = 1, 4
   SUM(k) = 0.0
ENDDO
DO k = 1, 4
   DO I = k, N, 4
      SUM(k) = SUM(k) + A(I)
   ENDDO
ENDDO
DO k = 1, 4
   S = S + SUM(k)
ENDDO
```

Given that the target has a four-stage pipeline, we want to interchange the loops in the computation nest, yielding

```
DO I = 1, N, 4
   DO k = I, min(I+3,N)
      SUM(k-I+1) = SUM(k-I+1) + A(I)
   ENDDO
ENDDO
```

The inner loop does not carry a dependence and can be vectorized to produce

```
DO I = 1, N, 4
   SUM(1:4) = SUM(1:4) + A(I:I+3)
ENDDO
```

If a vector computation is viewed abstractly as occurring simultaneously (which is not the way it actually occurs), this form simultaneously adds four elements of A to four different partial sums. These partial sums are accumulated throughout the outer loop (usually into a set of special registers called *accumulators*). Figure 5.15 displays this graphically, in terms of a four-stage pipeline.

Even with the short vector length, this form is a speedup over the analogous scalar computation. However, notice that if the result for SUM(1) can be fed back into the pipeline as soon as it is available (as is depicted at the left of Figure 5.15), the computation can be run at essentially vector speed—as soon as results come out of one end of the pipeline, they are fed into the beginning. Once the four partial sums are available in SUM(1:4), the total sum can be computed by three floating-point additions, two of which may be overlapped. Similar techniques can be used to compute product, min/max, and other reductions.

The Fortran 90 intrinsic function SUM is intended to provide the fastest possible sum reduction permitted by commutativity and associativity. Thus, if the compiler recognizes the sum reduction loop and replaces it with the appropriate intrinsic call

```
S = SUM(A(1:N))
```

efficient code should result on any machine with sum reduction hardware. The Fortran 90 intrinsic functions PRODUCT, MINVAL, and MAXVAL play the same role for multiplication, minimum, and maximum, respectively.

The problem for the writer of advanced compilers, then, is to recognize and replace reductions where possible with the equivalent fast intrinsic routine. Reductions have three essential properties:

1. They reduce the elements of some vector or array dimension down to one element.

2. Only the final result of the reduction is used later; use of an intermediate result voids the reduction.

3. There is no variation inside the intermediate accumulation; that is, the reduction operates on the vector and nothing else.

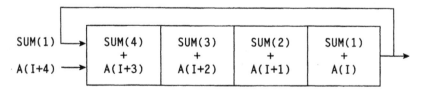

Figure 5.15 Pipeline for sum reduction.

Fortunately, these properties are easily determined from dependence graphs. Consider the following dependence graph for the sum reduction loop presented earlier.

```
DO I = 1, N
```

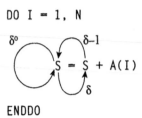

$$S = S + A(I)$$

```
ENDDO
```

This pattern of self-true dependence, output dependence, and antidependence is necessary for a reduction to exist. The true dependence reflects the fact that the statement adds to the partially accumulated result on each iteration; the output dependence reflects the fact that only the last value is used; and the antidependence reflects the fact that the partial accumulations are going to be rewritten. These dependences all are necessary to satisfy the first property of a reduction.

The second and third properties are indicated by the absence of other true dependences. To illustrate a fragment that does not meet these requirements, consider the following:

```
       DO I = 1, N
S₁         S = S + A(I)
S₂         T(I) = S
       ENDDO
```

Intermediate values of the reduction are used by S_2—values that cannot be obtained if the reduction is performed as a single operation.

The third property is symmetric to the use of intermediate values, but has to do with values feeding into the reduction. This condition is satisfied by the absence of true dependences feeding into the reduction.

The simplest way of verifying the second and third properties is to identify reductions when loops are being distributed. If both requirements are met, a reduction will fall out as a single statement recurrence when loop distribution is applied. If either requirement is violated, the reduction, by nature of its accumulation into a single element, will pull other statements into a recurrence with it.

Because reductions rarely take full advantage of vector hardware, some care has to be taken when recognizing reductions to ensure that recognizing the reduction does not obscure a more efficient form for the loop. Consider the following example:

```
DO I = 1, N
   DO J = 1, M
      S(I) = S(I) + A(I,J)
```

```
      ENDDO
   ENDDO
```

The inner loop is a sum reduction and the code could be replaced by

```
DO I = 1, N
   S(I) = S(I) + SUM (A(I,1:M))
ENDDO
```

However, the outer loop performs the reduction across all elements of S. As a result, it can be directly vectorized with loop interchange, giving

```
DO J = 1, M
   S(1:N) = S(1:N) + A(1:N,J)
ENDDO
```

This form will be more efficient on most vector machines, assuming proper scalarization and memory optimizations are performed as described in Chapters 8 and 13. Thus, it is important not to indiscriminately transform code by inserting equivalent reductions early in the vector code generation process. Instead, insertion of reductions should wait until all other options are understood.

5.7 Index-Set Splitting

There are a number of situations where a loop contains a recurrence that cannot be broken by the methods we have discussed so far, but where the dependence pattern holds for only part of the range of iteration of the loop. When this happens, an *index-set splitting* transformation, which subdivides the loop into different iteration ranges, may be used to achieve partial parallelization. In this section we will discuss several such transformations.

5.7.1 Threshold Analysis

Recall that the threshold of a dependence is the value of its leftmost nonzero distance. In other words, the threshold is the number of iterations of the carrier loop that occur between the access to the source of the dependence and the access to the sink of the dependence. Since both accesses must be made for the dependence to exist, one method for generating vector code is to break loops into sizes that are smaller than the thresholds of the dependences. For example, the following loop does not carry a dependence because its upper bound is right at the threshold of the dependence:

```
DO I = 1, 20
   A(I+20) = A(I) + B
ENDDO
```

As a result, it can be directly rewritten as a vector statement:

```
A(21:40) = A(1:20) + B
```

If the number of iterations is increased, however, the dependence material-izes, and the loop cannot be vectorized, as in the following version:

```
DO I = 1, 100
   A(I+20) = A(I) + B
ENDDO
```

This problem can be easily overcome if we strip-mine the loop into sections no larger than 20:

```
DO I = 1, 100, 20
   DO j = I, I + 19
      A(j+20) = A(j) + B
   ENDDO
ENDDO
```

Because of the threshold effect, the inner loop is dependence-free; the outer loop carries all dependences. Accordingly, the inner loop can be vectorized:

```
DO I = 1, 100, 20
   A(I+20:I+39) = A(I:I+19) + B
ENDDO
```

Unfortunately, this transformation is not very useful in practice because depen-dences in real programs typically have small thresholds—in particular, the most common threshold is one iteration. Nevertheless, the analysis is useful in some spe-cial classes of programs—for example, programs that simulate dynamic storage allocation by assigning different abstract arrays to different sections of one major array and subroutines that receive multidimensional arrays as one-dimensional vectors.

Although constant thresholds are the most common, *crossing thresholds* occur in practice with a frequency that makes them worth analyzing. Crossing thresh-olds, briefly introduced in Section 3.3.2, occur in dependences in which the dis-tance varies, but all dependences cross a single specific iteration. The following loop is an example:

```
       DO I = 1, 100
S₁        A(101-I) = A(I) + B
       ENDDO
```

The dependence of S_1 upon itself varies in distance from 99 at $I = 1$ down to 1 at $I = 50$. After that the references cross, and the true dependence becomes an antidependence. All dependences, whether true dependences or antidependences, have their source before iteration 50 and their sink after iteration 50. As a result, if the loop is strip-mined at length 50, all dependences will remain with the outer loop, leaving a recurrence-free inner loop:

```
DO I = 1, 100, 50
    DO j = I, I + 49
        A(101-j) = A(j) + B
    ENDDO
ENDDO
```

When *codegen* is applied to the transformed loop, the following vector code results:

```
DO I = 1, 100, 50
    A(101-I:51-I) = A(I:I+49) + B
ENDDO
```

Crossing thresholds can be computed in a natural way by the dependence analyzer, as shown in Section 3.3.2.

Given the ease with which these simple cases can be implemented and the small amount of compile time required to test for them, some amount of index splitting based on thresholds is practical in a production compiler, even though the occasions on which it can be profitably applied will be few. In particular, later chapters will show practical applications of threshold analysis in contexts other than vectorization.

5.7.2 Loop Peeling

A more frequent occurrence is a loop with a carried dependence whose source is a single iteration:

```
DO I = 1, N
    A(I) = A(I) + A(1)
ENDDO
```

The computation on each iteration uses the value of $A(1)$ computed on the first iteration. This carried dependence can be converted into a loop-independent dependence originating outside the loop by *peeling* the first iteration into the loop prolog:

```
A(1) = A(1) + A(1)
DO I = 2, N
   A(I) = A(I) + A(1)
ENDDO
```

The resulting loop carries no dependence and can be directly vectorized:

```
A(1) = A(1) + A(1)
A(2:N) = A(2:N) + A(1)
```

Loop peeling can involve iterations other than the first and last; in such cases, the loop must be split across the iteration that causes the dependence. For instance, assuming that N is exactly divisible by 2 in the following:

```
DO I = 1, N
   A(I) = A(N/2) + B(I)
ENDDO
```

The desire is to use loop splitting to convert the loop-carried dependence into a loop-independent one between two loops. Doing so yields

```
M = N/2
DO I = 1, M
   A(I) = A(N/2) + B(I)
ENDDO
DO I = M + 1, N
   A(I) = A(N/2) + B(I)
ENDDO
```

This is clearly another form of crossing threshold, and the loop size can be easily determined at dependence testing time. In this case, the test that determines the transformation is the *weak-zero test*, described in Section 3.3.2.

5.7.3   Section-Based Splitting

A variation on loop peeling is illustrated by the following loop nest, where once again, we assume that N is exactly divisible by 2:

```
     DO I = 1, N
        DO J = 1, N/2
S₁         B(J,I) = A(J,I) + C
        ENDDO
        DO J = 1, N
```

```
S₂          A(J,I+1) = B(J,I) + D
        ENDDO
      ENDDO
```

There are two dependences of interest in this example: a loop-independent dependence from S_1 to S_2 (due to B) and a dependence from S_2 to S_1 carried by the I-loop (due to A). As a result, the J-loops can be vectorized, but the outer loop is bound in a recurrence. Since S_1 defines only a portion of B (B(1:N/2)), a natural way of breaking the loop-independent dependence is to partition the second loop into a loop that uses the results of S_1 and a loop that does not. The following illustrates such a partition:

```
      DO I = 1, N
        DO J = 1, N/2
S₁          B(J,I) = A(J,I) + C
        ENDDO
        DO J = 1, N/2
S₂          A(J,I+1) = B(J,I) + D
        ENDDO
        DO J = N/2+1, N
S₃          A(J,I+1) = B(J,I) + D
        ENDDO
      ENDDO
```

S_3 is now independent of the other two statements, so *codegen* will distribute the I-loop and, depending on the topological sort, it might move S_3 to the beginning.

```
      DO I = 1, N
        DO J = N/2 + 1, N
S₃          A(J,I+1) = B(J,I) + D
        ENDDO
      ENDDO
      DO I = 1, N
        DO J = 1, N/2
S₁          B(J,I) = A(J,I) + C
        ENDDO
        DO J = 1, N/2
S₂          A(J,I+1) = B(J,I) + D
        ENDDO
      ENDDO
```

This permits vectorization of S_3 in two dimensions, while the remainder will vectorize only in the J-dimension:

```
       M = N/2
S₃     A(M+1:N,2:N+1) = B(M+1:N,1:N) + D
       DO I = 1, N
S₁        B(1:M,I) = A(1:M,I) + C
S₂        A(1:M,I+1) = B(1:M,I) + D
       ENDDO
```

This kind of transformation requires sophisticated knowledge and analysis of array sections flowing along dependence edges. For instance, this example was predicated on the knowledge that only a portion of B was defined and used within the I-loop. As with thresholds, this analysis is probably too complex and costly to be applied to all loops. However, in the context of procedure calls, such analysis can be worthwhile. Chapter 11 will illustrate the development of this type of analysis for determining interprocedural effects.

5.8 Run-Time Symbolic Resolution

In many codes, symbolic variables complicate dependence testing by appearing in subscripts. In those cases, a dependence analyzer must make conservative assumptions. For instance, in

```
DO I = 1, N
   A(I+L) = A(I) + B(I)
ENDDO
```

the unknown variable L prevents vectorization. If L is greater than zero, the statement contains a self-true dependence and obviously cannot be vectorized. However, if L is less than or equal to zero, the statement contains either no dependence or a self-antidependence, which does not preclude vectorization. Since it is very possible that L is set at run time, making compile-time determination impossible, a restructuring phase will normally have to assume that both the true dependence and the antidependence exist. One way to temper this conservatism is to annotate dependence edges with *breaking conditions*, which are logical expressions that will break the dependence if true (see Section 3.3.2). For instance, in the example, the true dependence has a breaking condition (L.LE.0), and the antidependence has a breaking condition (L.GT.0).

When breaking conditions are present in a loop, the loop can often be vectorized by making the vector version conditional, enclosing it in an IF statement that guarantees enough dependences do not exist to break the recurrence. In the previous example, breaking the true dependence is enough to break the recurrence, so that the loop can be vectorized as follows:

```
IF (L.LE.0) THEN
    A(L:N+L) = A(1:N) + B(1:N)
ELSE
    DO I = 1, N
        A(I+L) = A(I) + B(I)
    ENDDO
ENDIF
```

One very common application of breaking conditions is in computations with variable strides. These strides are particularly prevalent in very general library packages, such as LINPACK [106], that support operations on arbitrary arrays. For instance, the following is similar to DAXPY (a common linear algebra operation that forms the basis of LINPACK):

```
DO I = 1, N
    A(I*IS-IS+1) = A(I*IS-IS+1) + B(I)
ENDDO
```

If IS happens to be zero (which is virtually never true in practice), the loop is a reduction and has a loop-carried true dependence, output dependence, and anti-dependence. If IS is anything other than zero, there are no dependences, and the loop can be completely vectorized. This type of construct is easy to detect in dependence analyzers and produces the following code when breaking conditions are examined:

```
M = N*IS-IS+1
IF (IS.NE.0) THEN
    A(1:M:IS) = A(1:M:IS) + B(1:N)
ELSE
    A(1) = A(1) + SUM(B(1:N))
ENDIF
```

In this case, the breaking condition allows vector code to be generated in both its true and false form, since the loop becomes a sum reduction when the dependences are known to exist.

In general, a loop can contain an arbitrary number of breaking conditions. Just as identifying a minimal number of dependences that will break a recurrence with array renaming is *NP*-complete, identifying the minimal number of breaking conditions necessary to break a recurrence is also *NP*-complete. As a result, attempting to handle very general cases of breaking conditions is probably impractical in a production compiler. However, the simple examples presented in this section are extracted from important numerical packages, justifying an approach that handles at least these cases. Thus we recommend an analysis similar to the one presented for node splitting to identify when a critical dependence can be conditionally eliminated via a breaking condition.

5.9 **Loop Skewing**

All the program transformations presented so far have focused on uncovering parallel loop iterations. While most programs have very regular parallelism that can be expressed in terms of parallel loops, several important examples do not. *Loop skewing* is a transformation that reshapes an iteration space to make it possible to express the existing parallelism with conventional parallel loops. Consider, for example, the following loop:

```
     DO I - 1, N
        DO J - 1, N
                          (=,<)
                      ┌─────────────┐
S:         A(I,J) = A(I-1,J) + A(I,J-1)
                      └────────┘
                        (<,-)

        ENDDO
     ENDDO
```

Even a simple glance at the dependences reveals that neither loop can be run in parallel; both the I- and the J-loops carry dependences. However, the fragment does contain parallelism, which is most easily visualized graphically. Figure 5.16 displays the dependences for this example spread across the iteration space. Obviously, neither loop can be run in parallel, since dependence arcs span both axes. Any attempt to move a line of parallelism down either axis will fail, since the dependences force sequential execution on any line parallel to an axis. However, there are *diagonal* lines of parallelism, proceeding from the upper left to the lower right. For instance, iterations S(1,2) and S(2,1) can be run in parallel, once iteration S(1,1) completes. Similarly, S(1,3), S(2,2), and S(3,1) can be executed in parallel, once S(1,2) and S(2,1) complete. In other words, a diagonal line of parallelism can be moved up the iteration space, starting from the lower left and proceeding up to the upper right. The problem is that this parallelism does not directly apply to either loop.

One way to rotate the diagonal line of parallelism into one that tracks a loop is to remap the iteration space, much as eigenvalues are uncovered in linear algebra. A mapping that works in this example is to create a new index variable j as follows:

$$j = J + I$$

Using j to replace J given the inverse mapping

$$J = j - I$$

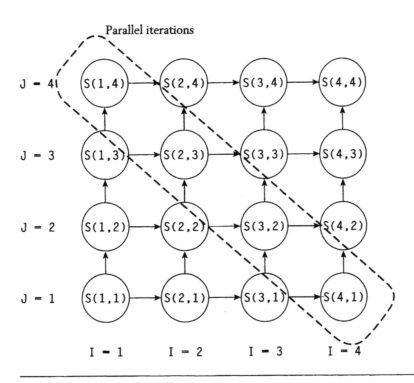

Figure 5.16 Dependence pattern prior to loop skewing.

yields the following, when substituted in the original example:

```
DO I = 1, N
    DO j = I + 1, I + N
                (=,<)
S:          A(I,j-I) = A(I-1,j-I) + A(I,j-I-1)
                (<,<)
    ENDDO
ENDDO
```

Note that the change in iteration space affects the direction vector for the dependence carried by the I-loop, depicted as the lower dependence in the example. In order for the left subscript positions to be equal, the value of I used in the store must be one less than the value used on the right. When this constraint is propagated into the right subscript positions, it forces j to be one greater in the use than in the store, making the directions "<" for both loops. In terms of delta notation:

$$\Delta I = 1 \text{ and } j - I = j + \Delta j - I - \Delta I$$
$$\text{therefore, } \Delta j = \Delta I = 1$$

The new dependence pattern, mapped into the new shape for the iteration space, is depicted in Figure 5.17, in which nodes are labeled with the indices from the original loop—that is, I and J.

Since both loops still carry dependences, it is not yet clear that loop skewing has done anything more than confuse naive readers. However, by noting that the dependence carried by the outer loop is now interchange sensitive (the diagonally oriented dependences in the figure), a parallel loop can be produced: interchanging the two loops pulls all dependences to the new outer loop, leaving the inner loop dependence-free. The example after loop interchange becomes

```
DO j - 2, N + N
    DO I - max(1,j-N), min(N,j-1)
        A(I,j-I) - A(I-1,j-I) + A(I,j-I-1)
    ENDDO
ENDDO
```

The loop bounds that result after loop interchange in this example are typical of those created by loop skewing and loop interchange; the skewed loop produces a trapezoidal iteration space that yields complex loop bounds after interchange. When this form is presented to *codegen*, the following vector code results:

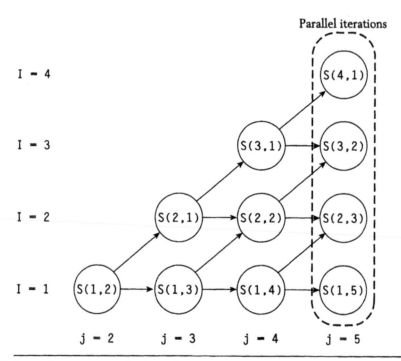

Figure 5.17 Dependence pattern after loop skewing.

```
DO j = 2, N + N
   FORALL (I=max(1,j-N),min(N,j-1))
      A(I,j-I) = A(I-1,j-I) + A(I,j-I-1)
   END FORALL
ENDDO
```

The FORALL statement is required because the vector statement is not directly expressible in triplet notation.

While the vectorization gained through loop skewing in this example probably improves performance, this form of vector code has some disadvantages. The primary disadvantage is the varying vector length—the vector length starts at one, runs up to N, then back down to one, for an average length of N/2. If the vector start-up time is large and N is small, this vector form could easily run slower than the scalar. Another disadvantage is that the vector bounds must be recomputed on each iteration of the outer loop.

To apply loop skewing more generally, assume that we have a loop nest in which both the outer loop on index I and the inner loop on index J are normalized. We wish to skew the inner loop so that the distances of dependences carried by the inner loop position are k more than in the original loop. To do this, we introduce a new inner loop index

$$j = J + k * I \tag{5.1}$$

and transform the loop to use this value. This means that the loop bounds must be changed and instances of J in the original loop be replaced by instances of the expression $j - k * I$. The safety of this transformation follows from the fact that we are not reordering any computation—we are only relabeling the iteration space. The proof that this transformation achieves the desired effect on direction vectors will be left as an exercise.

The effect of skewing a loop on J with respect to a loop on I by a factor of k is to modify the dependence distances corresponding to loop J. Specifically, if a given dependence has a distance ΔI corresponding to the loop on I and distance ΔJ corresponding to the loop on J and both of these distances are constant throughout the loop, then the dependence distance Δj of the inner loop after skewing is given by

$$\Delta j = \Delta J + k * \Delta I \tag{5.2}$$

To see this, let $f_1(I,J)$ be the (multidimensional) subscript expression at the source of the dependence and $f_2(I,J)$ be the expression at the sink. We know that

$$f_1(I,J) = f_2(I+\Delta I, J+\Delta J)$$

Substituting $j - k * I$ for J on all sides of the equation, we get

$$f_1(I, j-k*I) = f_2(I+\Delta I, j-k*I-k*\Delta I+\Delta j)$$

But since the distance is consistent for every value of I and J, we know that the difference between the second parameter to f_2 and the second parameter to f_1 must be exactly ΔJ. Thus

$$\Delta J = \Delta j - k \star \Delta I$$

from which Equation 5.2 follows immediately.

Equation 5.2 tells us that loop skewing can be used to produce a dependence-free loop out of two loops that each carry dependences, so long as all dependences have a consistent distance. To do so, apply the method described earlier in this section—skew the inner loop with respect to the outer loop so that the dependences carried by the outer loop have distances of at least 1 in the inner loop position. This may involve skewing by a large constant, if some dependences carried by the outer loop start out with negative distances in the position corresponding to the inner loop. Once all the distances for the inner loop are positive, exchange this loop to the outside and it will now carry all dependences, permitting the new inner loop to be parallelized. One final example will illustrate the complexity:

```
DO I = 1, N
   DO J = 1, N
      A(I,J) = A(I-1,J) + A(I,J-1) + A(I-1,J+1)
   ENDDO
ENDDO
```

This differs from the example at the beginning of this section by the addition of the third reference on the right-hand side, which gives rise to a dependence with direction vector (< , >) and distance vector (1 , -1). In order to be able to interchange the inner and outer loops after skewing, we must skew by 2 in order to make the distance of this third dependence positive in the position corresponding to J.

```
DO I = 1, N
   DO j = 2 * I + 1, 2 * I + N
      A(I,j-2*I) = A(I-1,j-2*I) + A(I,j-2*I-1) $
                 + A(I-1,j-2*I+1)
   ENDDO
ENDDO
```

As we have already seen, loop skewing is not without cost. The loops that result from this transformation are highly trapezoidal. The penalties arising from such an irregular loop are greatest on vector machines; they are less problematic on asynchronous multiprocessors. However, even on those architectures, loop skewing must be applied with care to avoid significant load imbalances.

5.10   **Putting It All Together**

This chapter has presented a number of transformations for uncovering or enhancing parallelism: loop interchange, scalar expansion, scalar renaming, array renaming, node splitting, reduction recognition, index-set splitting, symbolic resolution, and loop skewing. The positive aspect of having such a large number of transformations is that they provide several alternatives for exploiting parallelism. The negative side is that it is a complex task to choose the right transformation from among so many alternatives, and automating the transformation selection process is even harder. There are at least two considerations that must be addressed in choosing transformations: making sure that the selected transformation actually improves the program over its original form, and making sure that the selected transformation does not conflict or interfere with other transformations that offer more overall benefit for the program.

Many examples of the first problem have been presented throughout this chapter. Virtually every transformation has been dealt with from two perspectives: establishing when the transformation is *safe* and establishing that the transformation is *profitable*. Safety has always been definitively established. Profitability, on the other hand, has been somewhat more difficult because determining the most profitable transformation often requires the solution of an *NP*-complete problem.

However, when dealing with vector machines, one clear test for profitability has always been available: pick the transformation that results in the most vectorization. This is determined by carrying out the transformation—preferably just in the graph, but if necessary in the program as well—and repartitioning the dependence graph into strongly connected regions. In the abstract, more vectorization is always better. However, in practice, real machine architectures always have problem areas that cloud this determination (see Section 5.11 for some examples).

The second problem—that of avoiding interference between transformations—is more complicated. One example of such an interference was presented in Section 5.6, where premature insertion of a sum reduction blocked loop interchange. Loop skewing abounds with examples of interference: the complexity of the loop interchange in Section 5.9 is an excellent example.

One final example that illustrates why naive approaches to program transformation will not work is provided by the following simple sum reduction:

```
DO I = 1, N
   S = S + A(I)
ENDDO
```

In this form, this loop is easily reduced to a sum reduction call, which should be optimal on any architecture. However, a naive compiler might attempt scalar expansion before reduction recognition (even though Section 5.3 would show this expansion to be pointless), producing the following code:

```
S$(0) = S
DO I = 1, N
    S$(I) = S$(I-1) + A(I)
ENDDO
S = S$(N)
```

This loop is still a reduction, but it is *much* harder to recognize as a sum reduction. In this form, it is more likely to be recognized as a simple linear recurrence and replaced with a solving subroutine. While this result is better than scalar code, it is less efficient than direct substitution of a sum reduction.

In developing an algorithm to tie all the transformations together, two points must be considered. First, any approach to generating effective code must view the transformed code globally, not just locally. That is, it is difficult (if not impossible) to decide when considering a transformation on one loop whether that transformation is in fact the most effective to apply. That determination requires knowledge of at least the whole loop nest. The following provides an example of the type of scope required:

```
DO I = 1, M
    DO J = 1, N
        A(I,J) = A(I-1,J-1) + B(INDEX(I),J)
    ENDDO
ENDDO
```

Loop interchange can be used to vectorize either loop, but not both—one must be run in scalar. When focused on either loop, a transformation algorithm can easily determine whether that loop can be vectorized. However, it is difficult to determine that vectorizing one loop precludes vectorization of the other. In this example, the J-loop is the more profitable loop to vectorize, even though the I-loop is stride one, because the gather operation required on B to vectorize the I-loop is inefficient on most machines.

This principle extends well beyond vector machines. Determining the best code to generate is difficult enough when a global view is taken; it is downright impossible with a purely local approach.

Second, determining which transformations are best for a given program requires knowledge of the architecture of the target machine. On a highly parallel machine such as the Connection Machine, extracting all possible parallelism is essential, and the focus must be on transforming the program to create as many parallel loops as possible. On less parallel systems, such as a single-CPU superscalar architecture, choosing one appropriately parallel loop is far more important than generating a large number of parallel loops. It is impossible to give one strategy for tying program transformations together that satisfies both extremes (or most of the points in between).

In order to illustrate the principles involved in a global transformation strategy, this section examines an algorithm tuned for vector register architectures. For illustration purposes, these architectures have the clear advantages of possessing moderate parallelism whose benefits are usually easy to determine and can be easily represented at source level as Fortran 90 vector operations. We will assume that finding one good vector loop is the principal goal; the benefits of vectorizing additional loops are too small to justify the effort. This assumption is true for most vector register architectures in commercial use today.

Given the target architecture, the process of generating vector code from a scalar source program falls naturally into three phases:

1. *Detection:* finding all loops for each statement that can be run in vector
2. *Selection:* choosing from among viable candidates the best loop for vector execution for each statement
3. *Transformation:* carrying out the transformations necessary to vectorize the selected loop

This strategy fits in well with the transformations presented in this chapter. The detection phase involves modifying the dependence graph to reflect all possible transformations, without carrying them out in the program proper. Since the transformations described here only enhance parallelism (no transformation blocks parallelism), modifying the dependence graph in this fashion has no detrimental effects. The selection phase is highly machine dependent and involves detailed analysis of the subscripts and loops. The final transformation phase uses the original dependence graph to drive the program modifications necessary to achieve the best vector loops.

The detection phase is more fully detailed in the procedure *mark_loop* in Figure 5.18. This algorithm deletes all dependences from the graph that may be removed by scalar expansion, array renaming, node splitting, and symbolic resolution. Loop interchange is handled by searching for loops that carry no dependences. Index-set splitting and loop skewing are saved as final resorts—they are applied when no other vectorization can be found. Reductions are recognized during the marking process, since they are most easily found after loop distribution has been performed.

After these changes are made in the dependence graph, a variant of *codegen*, called *mark_gen*, is invoked on the result (see Figure 5.19). However, rather than generating vector code or performing loop interchange, *mark_gen* simply marks loops detected as vector and all statements involved.

This procedure uses simple loop shifting as its interchange strategy. However, it can easily be adapted to employ a more sophisticated loop selection heuristic such as the one presented in Figure 5.4.

The second phase of the global code generation algorithm selects the best vector loop for each statement from among all possible vector loops for that statement. This phase involves examining each statement locally for machine-specific criteria such as those discussed in Section 5.11. However, some nonlocal analysis

procedure *mark_loop(S,D)*

> // *mark_loop* takes a set of statements *S* and the associated
> //   dependence graph *D* (with all deletable edges marked) and
> //   marks all loops on all possible vector statements

> **for each** edge *e* in *D* that is deletable by array renaming, scalar
>   renaming, node splitting, or symbolic resolution **do begin**
>   add *e* to list *deletable_edges*;
>   delete *e* from *D*;
> **end**

> *mark_gen(S,1,D)*;

> **for each** statement *x* in *S* that has no vector loops marked **do**
>   attempt index-set splitting and loop skewing, marking vector
>   loops found;

> **for each** edge *e* in *deletable_edges* **do**
>   restore *e* to *D*;

end *mark_loop*

Figure 5.18   Vector loop detection.

is necessary to ensure that the transformations are applied consistently. For example, in scalar expansion a single scalar must be expanded across the same loop for each renamed partition. While it might be tempting to expand

```
DO I = 1, M
   DO J = 1, N
      T = A(I,J) + B(I,J)
      C(J,I) = T + B(J,I)
   ENDDO
ENDDO
```

as follows (which maximizes results for the individual statements by creating stride-one access)

```
DO I = 1, M
   DO J = 1, N
      T$(I) = A(I,J) + B(I,J)
      C(J,I) = T$(J) + B(J,I)
   ENDDO
ENDDO
```

the result is obviously incorrect. If the statements are examined individually with no global perspective, this type of code can easily be the result.

procedure *mark_gen(S,k,D)*

    find the set $\{S_1, S_2, \ldots, S_m\}$ of maximal strongly connected regions in the
        dependence graph D restricted to R (use Tarjan's algorithm);

    for $i = 1$ **to** m **do begin**

        if S_i is cyclic **then**

                if the outermost carried dependence is at level $p > k$ **then begin**
                    mark all loops at level $k, k + 1, \ldots, p - 1$ as vector for all statements in S_i;
                    mark_gen(S_i, p, D_i);
                end

                else if S_i is a reduction **then begin**
                    mark loop k as vector for S_i;
                    mark statements in S_i as being reductions at level k;
                end

                else begin
                    let D_i be the dependence graph consisting of all dependence edges
                        in D that are at level $k + 1$ or greater and are internal to π_i;

                    mark_gen(S_i, k+1, D_i);
                end

        else
                mark statements in S_i as vector for loops k and deeper;
    end
    end *mark_gen*

Figure 5.19 Variant of *codegen* to mark vector loops and statements.

        Once a consistent set of best vector loops has been found for each statement, the task remaining is to carry out the transformations in the program—in other words, to make the program correspond to the dependence graph. The dependence graph provides a simple mechanism for efficiently uncovering a simple path to recognizing the proper transformations to vectorize the selected loops. The original graph is restored (that is, deletable edges are restored), and *codegen* is reinvoked. Whenever *codegen* finds a "best vector" loop that does not vectorize, then it knows it must invoke a transformation. Because the transformation is known, the edges that identify the potential program transformation are easy to locate during this process. As a result, *codegen* can efficiently search for the proper set of transformations that yield the desired result. Figures 5.20 and 5.21 detail a version of *codegen* that implements this process; it is initially invoked at the outermost loop level. If it returns with no vector code generated, but best vector loops have been marked, then loop skewing or index-set splitting is necessary.

procedure *transform_code(R,k,D)*

find the set $\{S_1, S_2, \ldots, S_m\}$ of maximal strongly connected regions in the dependence graph D restricted to R (use Tarjan's algorithm);

construct R_π from R by reducing each S_i to a single node and compute D_π, the dependence graph naturally induced on R_π by D;

let $\{\pi_1, \pi_2, \ldots, \pi_m\}$ be the m nodes of R_π numbered in an order consistent with D_π (use topological sort to do the numbering);

for $i = 1$ **to** m **do**

  if k is the best vector loop for some statement in π_i **then**
    if π_i is cyclic **then begin**
      select_and_apply_tranformation(π_i,k,D);
      // retry the vectorization on new dependence graph
      transform_code(π_i,k,D);
    end
    else
      generate a vector statement for π_i in loop k;
  else begin
    generate a level-k DO statement;

    let D_i be the dependence graph consisting of all dependence edges in D that are at level $k + 1$ or greater and are internal to π_i;

    transform_code(π_i,k+1,D_i);

    generate the level-k ENDDO statement
  end
end *transform_code*

Figure 5.20 Driver for program transformations.

5.11 Complications of Real Machines

While the selection phase of vector code generation, which determines the best vector loop, may appear to be the simplest of the phases, in fact, it is one of the more difficult ones because it must include considerations about the architecture of the target machine. When generating code for a fine-grained parallel machine, a major concern is ensuring that the operations selected in the innermost loop match the functional units available. When targeting coarse-grained multiprocessors, ensuring that the parallel decomposition provides enough computation to overcome synchronization overhead while keeping the load balanced is a difficult problem.

Given these problems, you might assume that vector machines are the simplest to target, and that the small discussion provided in the previous section more

procedure *select_and_apply_transformation*(π_i, *k*, *D*)

    if loop *k* does not carry a dependence in π_i **then**
        shift loop *k* to innermost position;
    else if π_i is a reduction at level *k* **then**
        replace with reduction and remove edges
            associated with the reduction;
    else // transform and adjust dependences
        if array renaming is possible **then**
            apply array renaming and adjust dependences,
                employing node splitting where needed;
        else if node splitting is possible **then**
            apply node splitting and adjust dependences;
        else if scalar expansion is possible **then**
            apply scalar expansion and adjust dependences;
        else
            apply skewing or index-set splitting and adjust dependences;
end *select_and_apply_transformation*

Figure 5.21 Selection of transformations.

than covers the topic. In fact, the opposite is true; determining the best vector loop (or even one that is guaranteed to execute faster after vectorization) is a very difficult proposition. This section presents a number of issues that must be considered when trying to determine the best vector loop for a particular machine. These considerations are typical of the kinds of issues that arise when targeting real, rather than ideal, machines.

Memory-Stride Access. One of the difficult balances to achieve in machine architectures is that of CPU performance versus memory performance. This balance is especially tricky in vector machines, where heavily pipelined CPUs can require operands every clock cycle for the number of cycles necessary to complete a (possibly long) vector operation. Memory components that are fast enough to feed such a CPU are far more expensive than the CPU logic and are hard to justify given that vector machines do far more than just vector memory operations.

    To avoid incurring prohibitive costs, system designers commonly use components that are not as fast as the CPU but are designed to provide equivalent speed on most operations. Two standard architectural features include multiple memory banks and prefetching. With memory banks, all of memory is partitioned into some number of banks (usually a small power of two—eight and sixteen are common). While an access within a single bank will take longer than a single cycle, accesses to different banks may be overlapped, providing an operand every cycle after the start-up delay (much the same way that pipelined functional units operate). Of course, this rate of access can only be sustained when successive accesses are made to different banks; repeatedly accessing the same memory bank produces the analog of pipeline interlock, with the equivalent slowdown in access rate. Since contiguous memory addresses are usually assigned to banks in round-robin fashion (that is, address x is placed in bank 0; address $x + 1$ is placed in bank 1; and so on), stride-one access is guaranteed to perform well on such a system because each successive access is guaranteed to go to a different bank. On the other hand, vector accesses with strides equal to the memory bank size perform very poorly, since they repeatedly access the same memory bank. On a system that uses memory banks in this way, it is critical to vectorize operations in a way that avoids bank conflicts. Note that making the stride equal to one does not *always* guarantee the absence of bank conflicts; if memory is banked along word boundaries, vector accesses to halfword elements perform better with a stride of two.

When hardware prefetching is employed, an access to a particular word causes some number of following words to be accessed as well. With unit vector strides, this technique automatically pulls the next few operands from memory, allowing the processing unit to proceed at full speed. Prefetching is less effective with nonunit strides, since only part (or none) of the prefetched operands are used. When choosing a best vector loop, prefetching definitely favors small vector strides.

Scatter-Gather. One memory factor that is closely related to stride is scatter-gather operation. A *gather* occurs when a program uses a vector index to gather sparse operands together, as in

```
DO I = 1, N
    A(I) = B(INDEX(I))
ENDDO
```

Analogously, a scatter spreads compressed operands out to uncompressed memory locations:

```
DO I = 1, N
    A(INDEX(I)) = B(I)
ENDDO
```

Since gathers and scatters both involve varying, unknown strides, they are always less efficient than direct memory access, for the same reasons that strides other than one are problematic. Scatter-gather is very common in scientific codes, so vectorizing such constructs is important; however, it is also important to recognize that vectorized scatter or gather loops usually execute much less efficiently than direct memory access.

Loop Length. All vector units incur some overhead in initially filling the pipeline and, accordingly, require some number of operations for the segmented execution speedup to overcome start-up cost. The longer the vectorized loop (when only one is vectorized), the more effectively the vector unit is able to amortize the start-up overhead. When loop lengths are all known at compile time (a situation that is rarely true), the compiler can evaluate the vectorized efficiency of each loop. When loop bounds are symbolic, trading off loop lengths versus strides and other parameters is very difficult. With no additional input from the programmer, compilers must generally assume that all loops with unknown bounds are long enough for efficient vector execution. This assumption can provide very unpleasant inefficiencies in many areas. For instance, graphics programs often have loops of length four; physics and chemistry codes often have loops of length three (one for x, y, and z directions). When such programs are naively vectorized, the resulting transformed code often runs much slower than the original program.

Operand Reuse. The best method for optimizing memory access is to minimize the number of accesses to memory. Vectorizing so that operands are reused from registers is one obvious way of achieving this goal. Some examples of this consideration have been presented in this chapter; many more will be presented in Chapter 8 and Chapter 13.

Nonexistent Vector Operations. Not all arithmetic operations can be effectively segmented, and not all architectures provide support for vector versions of all instructions. One common example of an arithmetic operation that is difficult to pipeline is a floating-point divide. A floating-point divide is a complex instruction, requiring many iterations of a basic instruction sequence. Because of this iterative process, divides rarely speed up when vectorized, and many architectures do not waste instruction bits supporting vectorized divides. As a result, vectorizing a loop that performs a vector divide is something a compiler must carefully consider. In the following example

```
DO I = 1, M
   DO J = 1, N
      A(I,J) = B(J) / C(I)
   ENDDO
ENDDO
```

the J-loop is the preferred vector loop on most machines, despite stride and memory considerations. When the J-loop is vectorized, the divide can be efficiently performed by computing the scalar inverse and changing the divide into a multiply (assuming the programmer is willing to accept a small inaccuracy in his result):

```
DO I = 1, M
   T = 1.0 / C(I)
   DO J = 1, N, 32
      A(I,J:J+31) = B(J:J+31) * T
   ENDDO
ENDDO
```

If the I-loop is vectorized, most machines will show no speedup.

Conditional Execution. Because vector units continually repeat the same operation, they perform best when working on a regular series of operands. Disrupting that regularity by introducing conditionals (so that some operations are skipped) greatly decreases vector efficiency. Most vector units are able to execute conditional operations via a set of *mask registers* that control whether the result of an individual operation overwrites the result register. However, even mask registers rarely permit conditional setting (that is, mask registers cannot be set under the control of mask registers), so that only a single level of IF nesting is supported. Even a single level of conditional execution is less efficient than pure vector execution, and should be avoided where possible. Thus, in the following

```
DO I = 1, M
   DO J = 1, N
      IF (A(J).GT.0) THEN
         B(J,I) = B(J,I) + 1.0
      ENDIF
   ENDDO
ENDDO
```

the better loop to vectorize is probably the I-loop, since it can be transformed into

```
DO J = 1, N
   IF (A(J).GT.0) THEN
      DO I = 1, M
         B(J,I) = B(J,I) + 1.0
      ENDDO
   ENDIF
ENDDO
```

removing the conditional execution from the vector pipeline.

As these examples indicate, even the apparently simple task of selecting a best vector loop is not easy. When this task is further complicated by the presence of coarse parallelism (in the form of multiple CPUs) or by the presence of less regular fine-grained parallelism, the job of the compiler becomes very difficult indeed.

5.12 **Summary**

This chapter has developed the theory behind a number of dependence-based transformations designed to enhance the parallelism found in a program. These transformations, all of which are loop oriented, focus either on rearranging a program to obtain better parallelism or on breaking recurrences to create parallelism:

- *Loop interchange,* which is critical not only to vectorization but to most of the methods presented in this book, adjusts the nesting order of loops so as to get parallel loops into the optimal position. Because sequentializing an outer loop makes more vectorization possible in inner loops, the essence of a good loop interchange strategy is to select the right outer loop for sequentialization.

- *Scalar expansion* removes dependences by expanding a scalar into a vector, permitting parallelism when scalar bottlenecks restrict execution order, at the expense of additional memory.

- *Array renaming, scalar renaming,* and *node splitting* likewise delete dependences by the use of additional memory.

- Reductions form an important part of many codes, causing *reduction recognition* to be an integral part of any advanced compiler.

- *Index-set splitting, symbolic resolution,* and *loop skewing* are other parallelism-exposing techniques applicable to special cases.

These transformations must be applied carefully in the context of other operations in the same loop nest to ensure that the maximum amount of parallelism is achieved. The chapter presents a driving procedure for these transformations on vector machines. The procedure consists of three phases: *identification* of loops that can be vectorized, *selection* of the best loop for vectorization, and *transformation* of the code to vectorize the selected loops. The chapter concludes with a discussion of aspects of real vector machines that should be considered in selecting the best vector loop for each statement.

5.13 Case Studies

Since vectorization was a principal focus of both the PFC system and the Ardent Titan compiler, this section discusses their capabilities in detail. In addition, it presents the results of a study of how well PFC and a number of commercial compilers performed on a set of loops designed to test breadth of vectorization coverage.

5.13.1 PFC

The PFC system, developed at Rice by the authors, vectorized code using the loop-shifting strategy of Figures 5.2 and 5.3. If no vectorization was found by the time *codegen* reached the innermost level, it would attempt general loop interchange of the two innermost loops. Instead of having to compute and examine the entire direction matrix, this approach can be implemented by attributing dependence edges with a single property—that of being interchange preventing (or not) with the next inner loop. This attribute is easily calculated during dependence testing by looking for the explicit direction pair "<,>" at the level of the loop carrier and the loop just inside it.

To expose more vectorization, PFC did a reasonably complete job of scalar expansion, scalar renaming, and node splitting. It employed sophisticated versions of index-set splitting, including threshold analysis, crossing thresholds, and peeling. It also included a simple form of run-time resolution. It did not attempt either loop skewing or array renaming.

Given that the PFC system produced Fortran 90 rather than code for any target machine, specific machine considerations were not integral to its functioning. Therefore, the selection of transformations to apply was done by ad hoc methods. Specifically, if *codegen* produced no vectorization by the time it reached the innermost loop and interchanging the inner loops did not help, transformations would be attempted to break dependences, in a specific order, beginning with scalar expansion.

5.13.2 Ardent Titan Compiler

The flexibility of the vector register file on the Ardent Titan allowed for a wide range of vectorization strategies. At one extreme, the register file could be treated as four vector registers of length 2K. Using that paradigm, the Titan would have essentially been a vector memory machine, and the proper strategy would have been to vectorize as many loops to create the longest possible vector operations.

The alternative chosen was more reasonable and allowed for the potential of vector register reuse—something the four vector registers does not allow. The Ardent compiler partitioned the vector register file into roughly 64 vector registers each of length 32.[1] This length was sufficient to amortize the vector start-up costs but allowed an ample number of registers for reuse, and left some room for the operating system to make context switching more efficient.

The small vector start-up costs and the short vector lengths allowed an important simplification in the Titan vectorization strategy. Rather than trying to vectorize the maximum possible number of loops, the Ardent compiler focused on running only one loop in vector. There were several reasons behind this decision:

1. Given the decision to set the length of the vector registers to 32, the odds were good that vectorizing one loop would provide enough operations to fill the vector unit.

2. Given the asynchronicity of the vector unit, scheduling a large number of small vector operations could be accomplished just as quickly as firing off one longer vector operation, with the right compiler scheduling. As a result, even if one vectorized loop happened not to fill the vector registers, there would be little loss of performance.

---

1. There is some fudging here because scalar registers got special treatment.

3. Vectorizing only one loop simplified a lot of representation problems. When only one loop is vectorized, the resulting linearized vector operation can always be represented simply as a triple. Not all multiply-vectorized loops can, and deciding on one loop meant the optimizer could avoid a lot of expensive analysis determining whether a statement could be correctly vectorized in multiple loops or not.

4. Limiting vectorization to only one loop would simplify a lot of compile-time search issues regarding optimal loop order. Many of the problems involving ordering vector loops are exponential in the number of loops. Even though loop nests tend not to be very deep, even a small nesting depth can cause potential compile-time problems with an exponential solution. These problems don't arise when the limit on the exponent is one.

With this strategic decision, the philosophy behind the Ardent optimizer became one of vectorizing the best loop, as opposed to the philosophy of vectorizing the most loops. This shift led to variations in virtually all of the code generation algorithms. Specifically, it produced the code generation strategy described in Section 5.10.

While a concern at the time was that limiting vectorization to one loop might negatively impact later retargets to other vector machines, this turned out not to be the case. The Ardent optimizer was later retargeted to an architecture that was essentially a vector memory architecture, and the resulting code was excellent.

The last key decision in terms of vectorization strategy involved the overall approach to vectorization. The algorithms presented in this book approach vectorization from a purely semantic point of view, determining when a vector operation is semantically equivalent to its scalar analog. Unfortunately, that is not sufficient for most real machines, since it is also necessary that the machine be able to *execute* the vector operation. The Titan I, for instance, did not have a vector divide instruction, so while it was nice from a theoretical point of view when the compiler vectorized a divide, it did not result in any program speedup.[2]

Faced with the hard realities of fixed hardware, the Titan vectorizer either had to (1) avoid vectorizing operations that were not available on the hardware, or (2) convert such vectorized operations into a sequence of acceptable operations. The approach taken was the second one: vectorize loops from a purely semantic viewpoint, then have a machine-dependent "devectorization" pass following that converted nonexistent vector operations into valid instructions. The reasoning at the time was that the compiler would eventually be retargeted to other architectures, and performing a clean vectorization (parameterized according to machine constraints such as strip size and available parallelism) followed by a less-clean devectorization was the easiest way to retarget.

As it turned out, this was also the most efficient approach in other ways, particularly in terms of final code. For instance, even though the Titan did not have a

---

2. In the sense that the executable immediately dumped core when the CPU attempted to execute the vector divide, it did speed up.

vector divide, it could in some cases essentially vectorize a divide of a vector by a scalar by computing the inverse of the scalar and then doing a vector multiply of the result times the vector (assumes that $x/a == x * 1/a$).[3] This type of transformation is difficult to recognize in a prevectorization pass, since you do not know whether the divisor is a scalar until you know which loop has vectorized. It is trivial to implement in a postvectorization pass.

5.13.3   Vectorization Performance

To illustrate the performance of the vectorization technologies used in PFC and described in this chapter, we present a study of the effectiveness of various compilers on the Callahan-Dongarra-Levine benchmark suite, a collection of 100 loops that exercise various capabilities of vectorizing compilers. The tests, which can be found in source form at *www.mkp.com/ocma/*, are grouped into four categories:

1. *Dependence,* which explores the precision of dependence testing
2. *Vectorization,* which tests for the presence of various vectorizing transformations, such as loop distribution, loop interchange, scalar expansion, and crossing thresholds
3. *Idioms,* which test how well each compiler recognizes common reductions, packing, searches, and some specialized recurrences
4. *Completeness,* which tests the handling of complex language constructs such as flow of control, equivalencing, and intrinsics

The actual performance of PFC and a large variety of commercial compilers is given in Table 5.1. The PFC experiments were conducted by Ervan Darnell of the PFC project, while all other data is from the paper by Callahan, Dongarra, and Levine [57]. Among the commercial compilers, the Ardent Titan compiler, the Convex C series compiler, and the IBM 3090 VF compiler [243] were all directly based on the methods and algorithms from PFC. Within each group, three columns are shown: the column labeled "V" indicates the number of loops that were completely vectorized and the column labeled "P" gives the number of loops partially vectorized. The difference between 100 and the sum of these two columns indicates the number of loops that were not vectorized.

As Table 5.1 shows, PFC did very well on the vectorization and completeness groups, due to the systematic approach it took to program transformations (e.g., array renaming and crossing thresholds), handling of conditional statements (see Chapter 7), and interprocedural analysis (see Chapter 11). In the dependence analysis group, PFC did moderately well, but at the time of the experiment, it did

---

3. Numerical purists will readily recognize that without some guarantees on the scalar, the results are not exactly equivalent.

Table 5.1 Performance on Callahan-Dongarra-Levine tests

Vectorizing compiler	Total		Dependence		Vectorization		Idioms		Completeness	
	V	*P*	*V*	*P*	*V*	*P*	*V*	*P*	*V*	*P*
PFC	70	6	17	0	25	4	5	0	23	2
Alliant FX/8, Fortran V4.0	68	5	19	0	20	5	10	0	19	0
Amdahl VP-E, Fortran 77	62	11	16	1	21	8	11	1	14	1
Ardent Titan-1	62	6	18	0	19	5	9	0	16	1
CDC Cyber 205, VAST-2	62	5	16	0	20	5	7	0	19	0
CDC Cyber 990E/995E	25	11	8	0	6	8	3	1	8	2
Convex C Series, FC 5.0	69	5	17	0	25	4	11	0	16	1
Cray series, CF77 V3.0	69	3	20	0	18	3	9	0	22	0
CRAX X-MP, CFT V1.15	50	1	16	0	12	1	10	0	12	0
Cray Series, CFT77 V3.0	50	1	17	0	8	1	7	0	18	0
CRAY-2, CFT2 V3.1a	27	1	5	0	3	1	8	0	11	0
ETA-10, FTN 77 V1.0	62	7	18	0	18	7	7	0	19	0
Gould NP1, GCF 2.0	60	7	14	0	19	7	8	0	19	0
Hitachi S-810/820	67	4	14	0	24	4	14	0	15	0
IBM 3090/VF, VS Fortran	52	4	12	0	19	3	5	1	16	0
Intel iPSC/2-VX, VAST-2	56	8	15	0	17	8	6	0	18	0
NEC SX/2, F77/SX	66	5	17	0	21	5	12	0	16	0
SCS-40, CFT x13g	24	1	7	0	6	1	5	0	6	0
Stellar GS 1000, F77	48	11	14	0	20	9	4	1	10	1
Unisys ISP, UFTN 4.1.2	67	13	21	3	19	8	10	2	17	0

not employ the full suite of tests described in Chapter 3. By contrast, PFC performed rather poorly on the idioms. This was due to a design decision on the PFC project not to invest substantive resources on the special-case pattern matching required to do well here.

The compilers directly based on PFC—from Ardent, Convex, and IBM—also did relatively well, although the IBM vectorizer suffered in dependence testing because it performed this test on low-level intermediate code rather than on source programs. The Ardent compiler did very well in spite of the fact that it was evaluated after only a year and a half of development.

All in all, these results demonstrate that the transformations and testing described in this book provide fairly comprehensive coverage of the challenges facing vectorizing compilers. There is, however, another message in the Callahan-Dongarra-Levine tests. The compilers that did best were those that paid meticulous attention to details. The idioms are an example of this, but we present one other example—test 171, a test that PFC failed, but that most compilers handled correctly:

```
subroutine s171(a,b,n)
  integer n
  real a(*), b(*)
  do 1030 i = 1, n
     a(i*n) = a(i*n) + b(i)
1030 continue
```

PFC failed this test because of its poor handling of symbolic coefficients in subscripts. It did not vectorize the loop because of the possibility that $n = 0$. However, it missed the fact that, because n is also the loop upper bound, the loop will degenerate in that case. This and other examples illustrate that, even with the right framework, success depends on systematic pursuit of the special cases that occur in practice. A goal of this chapter is to provide a general framework that significantly simplifies that pursuit.

5.14 Historical Comments and References

The earliest papers on dependence-based program transformations include papers by Lamport [195, 196] and Kuck [190]. Lamport developed a form of loop interchange for use in vectorization, as well as the *wavefront* method for parallelization, an early form of loop skewing. Lamport also discussed the importance of scalar expansion, although he provided no method for implementing it. Loop interchange was further developed by Wolfe [278, 280, 283]; the extensions described in this chapter are due to Allen and Kennedy [16, 19, 20]. The use of the direction matrix to drive interchange is new to this book but is essentially a variant of the use of direction vectors by Wolfe [280] and the distance matrix approach used by Lamport and further developed by Wolf and Lam [277].

Wolfe's master's thesis [278] discusses a mechanism for scalar expansion. His technique mechanically expands all scalars, regardless of profitability, and relies on later passes to contract out unprofitable expansion. A Ph.D. thesis by Pieper [224] surveys a number of different approaches to scalar expansion and compares their efficacy in real programs.

The various techniques for renaming to eliminate dependences are discussed in general in a number of places [20], as is index splitting. In particular, Padua's thesis provides a precise algorithm for scalar renaming [221]. The algorithms for array renaming and node splitting are drawn from a paper by Allen and Kennedy [21], but modified for this book. Loop skewing in its current form was introduced by Wolfe [281] as a practical way of performing Lamport's wavefront transformation. Useful surveys of program transformations include those by Padua and Wolfe [222], Kuck et al. [190], Wolfe's Ph.D. thesis [283], and a subsequent textbook by Wolfe [285].

The strategies for global selection of vector transformations presented here were developed by Allen as a part of his work on the Ardent Titan compiler.

Exercises

5.1 Apply the loop-shifting code generation heuristic to the following example:

```
DO I = 1, N
    DO J = 1, N
        DO K = 1, N
            A(I,J+1) = A(I,J) + B(K,J)
        ENDDO
    ENDDO
ENDDO
```

5.2 Adapt the array-renaming algorithm from Section 5.4 to handle code with control flow in the loop body. *Hint:* Take advantage of a method similar to the one for scalar expansion to ensure that a definition occurs on all branches.

5.3 Prove that the loop skewing substitution in Equation 5.1 has the desired effect of adding k to the inner loop distance for dependences carried by the outer loop. What effect does it have on dependences carried by the inner loop?

5.4 Show that the node-splitting algorithm of Figure 5.14, when presented with a critical antidependence, breaks the dependence cycle after scalar expansion is applied.

5.5 Apply the code generation algorithm of Section 5.10 to the following loop nest:

```
DO I = 1, N
    DO J = 1, N
        DO K = 1, N
            T = A(K,J) + A(K+1,J)
            A(K+1,J) = T + B(K)
            A(K+1,J) = A(K+1,J) + C(K)
        ENDDO
    ENDDO
ENDDO
```

Which transformations does it employ?

5.6 What vector code should be generated for the following loop?

```
DO I = 1, 100
    A(I) = B(K) + C(I)
    B(I+1) = A(I) + D(I)
ENDDO
```

CHAPTER 6

Creating Coarse-Grained Parallelism

6.1 Introduction

Chapter 5 discussed program transformations designed to enhance the parallelism in inner loops. Those transformations improve performance on vector and super-scalar architectures, where parallelism is fine-grained and found primarily in inner-most loops. In this chapter we turn to the problem of finding parallelism for multiple asynchronous processors with a shared global memory. These processors are typified by the symmetric multiprocessor (SMP)—found in workstations from companies like Sun, Silicon Graphics, and Compaq—and the distributed shared-memory (DSM) systems typified by the SGI Origin 2000 and the HP/Convex SPP-2000.

Coarse-grained parallelism at the level of multiple processors requires a different focus; on such architectures, parallelism is employed by creating a thread on each of the processors, executing in parallel for a period of time with occasional synchronization, and synchronizing via a barrier at the end. The key to achieving high performance on such systems is to find and package parallelism with a granularity large enough to compensate for the overhead of parallelism initiation and synchronization. As a result, the focus is to find parallel loops with significant amounts of computation within their bodies. This usually means parallelization of outer loops rather than inner loops, and it often means parallelization of loops with subroutine calls, a subject discussed in Chapter 11.

When generating parallel code for coarse-grained architectures, many delicate trade-offs must be managed. One of the most difficult is minimizing communication and synchronization overhead while balancing the load evenly across all the processors. At one extreme, the absolute minimal overhead is accomplished when the entire program is run on one processor; since there is no parallelism, there is no overhead involved in interprocessor communication and synchronization. Of course, the load balance and corresponding parallel speedup are very poor. At the other extreme, the best load balance is obtained when a program is decomposed into the smallest possible parallel elements, with the elements distributed evenly among the idle processors. With very small parallel program elements, no processor is stuck working on one large element while other processors are idle, awaiting work. However, the synchronization and communication overhead is maximized in this case. This overhead almost always outweighs the benefits obtained by the perfect load balance. Somewhere in between these two extremes lies the most effective parallel decomposition—a parallelizing compiler is faced with the challenge of locating that sweet spot.

Chapter 1 introduced the PARALLEL DO statement (see Section 1.5.1), which represents a loop whose iterations can be correctly run in any order. The literature has also called this type of loop a DOALL. An alternative form of coarsely parallel loop is a DOACROSS, which pipelines parallel loop iterations (basically using multiple processors as a high-level vector processor) with cross-iteration synchronization. This chapter will focus on the generation of PARALLEL DO loops because any loop that can utilize parallelism effectively as a DOACROSS loop can be distributed into a series of PARALLEL DO loops, although the pipeline parallelism may be lost. Section 6.6.2 discusses the introduction of pipeline parallelism in more detail.

The remainder of this chapter describes transformations that can be applied to programs to create new opportunities for parallelism, thus enhancing this simple code generation algorithm into a sophisticated, aggressive code generation strategy. Many of these transformations have already been presented in the context of vectorization; this chapter presents the (often minor) adaptations necessary for coarse-grained parallelism.

6.2   Single-Loop Methods

When attempting to enhance the parallelism extracted from a single loop, there are two general strategies that should be tried. If the loop is a sequential loop (i.e., it carries a dependence), finding some way to make it parallel is the obvious way to enhance parallelism. Any transformation that eliminates loop-carried dependences (e.g., loop distribution) can be used to achieve this goal. Once a loop is parallel, increasing the granularity of the exposed parallelism is generally useful. This section discusses various transformations for achieving each of these goals.

6.2.1   Privatization

Section 5.3 introduced the transformations of scalar expansion and scalar privatization. Scalar expansion is effective in vectorization because it eliminates many dependences—both loop carried and loop independent—associated with the original scalar. Since deleting loop-carried dependences can enable the conversion of sequential loops into parallel loops, both scalar expansion and scalar privatization are important transformations in increasing coarse-grained parallelism.

The mechanics of scalar expansion and the conditions for determining its safety were discussed in Section 5.3. These are the same regardless of whether they are applied to vectorization or to parallelization. In this section we will concentrate on privatization, which determines that a variable assigned within the loop is used only in the same iteration in which it is assigned. Such variables can be replicated across the iterations, eliminating carried dependences that might superficially bar parallelization.

As an example, consider the simple code fragment from Section 5.3 in which the values in two arrays are exchanged:

```
      DO I = 1, N
S₁       T = A(I)
S₂       A(I) = B(I)
S₃       B(I) = T
      ENDDO
```

The dependence pattern for this loop is given in Figure 6.1. Because of the carried anti- and output dependences, the loop is not parallelizable as it is currently formulated.

Fortunately, all of the carried dependences are due to assignments and uses of the scalar variable T. As we pointed out in Section 5.3, all of these carried dependences go away if each iteration has its own copy of the variable T, as in the transformed and parallelized code below:

```
      PARALLEL DO I = 1, N
         PRIVATE t
S₁       t = A(I)
S₂       A(I) = B(I)
S₃       B(I) = t
      END PARALLEL DO
```

In the example above, making the transformation so that each iteration has a private copy of T is correct because all uses of T within the body of the loop get a value that is assigned earlier in the same iteration—in other words, there are no upwards-exposed uses in the loop body. This condition is made formal by the following definition.

DEFINITION 6.1

A scalar variable *x* defined within a loop is said to be *privatizable* with respect to that loop if and only if every path from the beginning of the loop body to a use of *x* within that body must pass through a definition of *x* before reaching that use.

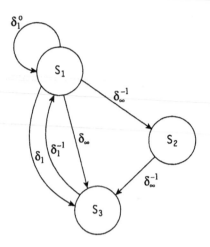

Figure 6.1 Dependence graph for array swap.

Privatizability can be determined by standard data flow analysis as described in Section 4.4. First we solve a set of data flow equations on the loop body to determine the variables $up(x)$ that are upwards-exposed at the beginning of each block x:

$$up(x) = use(x) \cup (\neg def(x) \cap \bigcup_{y \in succs(x)} up(y))   \quad (6.1)$$

where $use(x)$ is the set of variables that have upwards-exposed uses in block x and $def(x)$ is the set of variables that are defined in block x. If b_0 is the entry block of the loop body, then a variable defined in the loop is privatizable if and only if it is not in $up(b_0)$. The set of all privatizable variables in a loop body B is given by

$$private(B) = \neg up(b_0) \cap (\bigcup_{y \in B} def(y))   \quad (6.2)$$

An alternative method for determining whether a specific scalar variable is privatizable is provided by the SSA graph discussed in Section 4.4.4.

THEOREM
6.1

A variable x defined in a loop may be made private if and only if the SSA graph for the variable does not have a ϕ-node at the entry to the loop.

This statement is true because the standard SSA construction inserts a dummy initialization to a variable that is not explicitly assigned in the program. Therefore, we can assume that every scalar variable is assigned outside the loop body. If a given variable x has an upwards-exposed use, then the definition outside the loop can reach that use. In addition, any definition inside the loop can also reach that use by a path that crosses iterations. Thus the values created by two distinct definitions must be resolved by the insertion of a φ-node during SSA construction for the loop. Clearly, a φ-node is not needed if there is no upwards-exposed use in the body. Thus there is a φ-node at the beginning of the loop if and only if there is an upwards-exposed use.

If all the dependences carried by a given loop involve a privatizable variable, then the loop can be parallelized by making all those variables private.

Although privatization is clearly preferable to scalar expansion for eliminating carried dependences in coarse-grained loops, scalar expansion can help in some cases where privatization is not applicable. One such situation is demonstrated by the following example:

```
DO I = 1, N
   T = A(I) + B(I)
   A(I-1) = T
ENDDO
```

Because there are loop-carried dependences due to both T and A, privatization will not produce any parallelism. However, expanding T allows the loop to be distributed, yielding two parallel loops with a barrier in between:

```
PARALLEL DO I = 1, N
   T$(I) = A(I) + B(I)
ENDDO
PARALLEL DO I = 1, N
   A(I-1) = T$(I)
ENDDO
```

Scalar expansion applied in this manner can require a large amount of storage (particularly if expansion is applied in multiple loops), necessitating some discretion in its use.

Good privatization is critical to the task of parallelizing most applications. Many applications cannot be parallelized without privatizing arrays as well as scalars. Consider the problem of array privatization for arrays of a single dimension. Since we do not construct SSA graphs for subscripted variables, the simple test for privatizability given by Theorem 6.1 cannot be used for arrays. Unfortunately, the existence of a carried dependence is not sufficient to establish that an array is not privatizable, as the following example shows:

```
       DO I = 1, 100
S₀       T(1) = X
L₁       DO J = 2, N
S₁          T(J) = T(J-1) + B(I,J)
S₂          A(I,J) = T(J)
         ENDDO
       ENDDO
```

Although it may not be immediately obvious, every use of a location in the array T in the body of the I-loop is preceded by an assignment in that same loop. However, a standard dependence analyzer will construct a dependence carried by the I-loop from statement S_1 to itself because the T(J-1) refers to the same location as T(J) on different iterations of the I-loop. Thus, in order to privatize the array T, we must determine that there is no upwards-exposed use of any location in T.

If we are dealing with a single loop, we can perform the analysis in a manner similar to the data flow analysis for scalars. Suppose we treat all the distinct instances of the subscripted variable T as individual scalar references. Thus, T(1) would be treated as distinct from T(J) and T(J-1). If we then solve the upwards-exposed use problem for the loop body, the result will be those references that we must assume are used before being defined in the loop body. If this method is applied to the inner loop of the example above

```
L₁    DO J = 2, N
S₁        T(J) = T(J-1) + B(I,J)
S₂        A(I,J) = T(J)
      ENDDO
```

it determines that the reference T(J-1) is upwards-exposed. Note that B(I,J) is also upwards-exposed in the loop, but we will focus exclusively on T for the moment since it is the only variable both used and defined in the entire loop nest.

To extend this analysis to nests of loops, we need some way of determining the set of references that are upwards-exposed in an inner loop. To compute this, we construct a representation of which variables are upwards-exposed from the loop due to iteration J of the loop. The set of variables upwards-exposed on iteration J is simply the set of variables that are upwards-exposed from the body of the loop on iteration J less the set of variables that are defined on some previous iteration.

For the inner loop above, we have already seen that T(J-1) is upwards-exposed on iteration J. Clearly, the set of variables defined on some previous iteration is given by the union of the definition sets of all previous iterations. In the case above this is clearly T(2:J). The union of these differences for all values of J gives the entire set of upwards-exposed locations in T.

$$up(L_1) = \bigcup_{J=2}^{N} \{T(J-1)\} - T(2:J)$$

It is easy to see that the expression T(J-1)-T(2:J) is empty except when J is equal to 2. Thus the entire set of upwards-exposed locations for the inner loop is {T(1)}.

Once the subloops have been handled, the algorithm for determining which variables are privatizable operates using the single-loop method, with the inner loop serving as a single statement that uses every variable in its upwards-exposed list before defining every variable that must be defined on some iteration of the loop. In our example, L_1 defines T(2:N).

The end result of this analysis applied to the example is that T(1) is defined in the statement just prior to L_1, so there are no upwards-exposed locations in the outer loop. Thus the entire array can be made private in the I-loop, and the outer loop can be parallelized:

```
         PARALLEL DO I = 1, 100
            PRIVATE t
S₀          t(1) = X
L₁          DO J = 2, N
S₁             t(J) = t(J-1) + B(I,J)
S₂             A(I,J) = t(J)
            ENDDO
         ENDDO
```

Note that this code assumes no use of the array T (here t and T are considered distinct) after the loop. If there is such a use, the privatization transformation needs to insert a conditional assignment to copy values from t to T on exit from the loop. In the example, this would yield

```
         PARALLEL DO I = 1, 100
            PRIVATE t(N)
S₀          t(1) = X
L₁          DO J = 2, N
S₁             t(J) = t(J-1) + B(I,J)
S₂             A(I,J) = t(J)
            ENDDO
            IF (I==100) T(1:N) = t(1:N)
         ENDDO
```

6.2.2 Loop Distribution

The fine-grained parallelization algorithm *codegen* (Figure 2.2) depends implicitly on loop distribution to transform carried dependences into loop-independent dependences. For example, when the J-loop is distributed across the carried dependence from statement S_1 to statement S_2 in

```
      DO I = 1, 100
         DO J = 1, 100
S₁          A(I,J) = B(I,J) + C(I,J)
S₂          D(I,J) = A(I,J-1) * 2.0
         ENDDO
      ENDDO
```

the nest becomes

```
DO I = 1, 100
    DO J = 1, 100
S₁      A(I,J) = B(I,J) + C(I,J)
    ENDDO
    DO J = 1, 100
S₂      D(I,J) = A(I,J-1) * 2.0
    ENDDO
ENDDO
```

In the original code, the dependence from S_1 to S_2 due to array A crosses iterations of the J-loop, and is thus carried by the loop. With loop distribution, the dependence is no longer carried by any loop.

Loop distribution can be used to convert a sequential loop to multiple parallel loops. However, because it converts loop-carried dependences to loop-independent dependences between the distributed loops, this transformation implicitly inserts a synchronization barrier between the dependence endpoints (at the end of the first parallel loop). This decreases the granularity of parallelism and creates extra communication and synchronization overhead. Thus, it is worth attempting other transformations that can eliminate dependences without decreasing granularity before resorting to loop distribution. In the next several sections we will discuss some of these transformations.

6.2.3 Alignment

Loop distribution transforms loop-carried dependences by executing the sources of all dependences before executing any sinks. Before distribution, values were computed on one iteration of a loop and used on a later iteration. After distribution, the values are computed in one loop and used in a different loop. An alternative approach to achieve the same effect is to realign the loop to compute and use the values on the same iteration. The following example, adapted from the distribution example in Section 6.2.2, illustrates this idea:

```
DO I = 2, N
    A(I) = B(I) + C(I)
    D(I) = A(I-1) * 2.0
ENDDO
```

This loop cannot be run in parallel because the value of A computed on iteration I is used on iteration I + 1. The two statements can be *aligned* to compute and use the values in the same iteration by adding an extra iteration and adjusting the indices of one of the statements to produce

```
DO i = 1, N
    IF (i.GT.1) A(i) = B(i) + C(i)
    IF (i.LT.N) D(i+1) = A(i) * 2.0
ENDDO
```

The resulting loop carries no dependences so it can be run in parallel. This transformation is called *loop alignment*. The idea of loop alignment is illustrated Figure 6.2.

More generally, loop alignment is carried out by increasing the number of loop iterations and executing the statements on slightly different subsets of those iterations, so that the carried dependence becomes a loop-independent dependence. Loop alignment does incur some overhead—one extra loop iteration and extra work required to test the conditionals. This overhead can be reduced by executing the last iteration of the first statement with the first iteration of the second statement; that is,

```
DO i = 2, N
    j = i - 1; IF (i.EQ.2) j = N
    A(j) = B(j) + C(j)
    D(i) = A(i-1) * 2.0
ENDDO
```

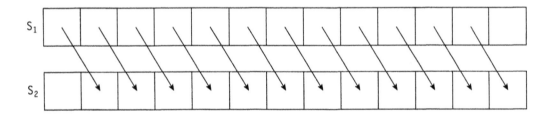

After alignment:

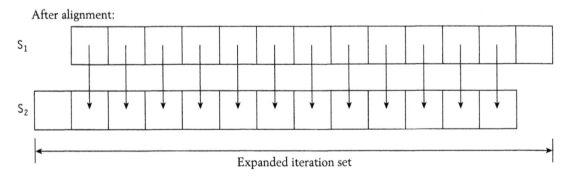

Expanded iteration set

Figure 6.2 Illustration of loop alignment.

For every iteration other than the first, j is one less than i, so that the assignment is to $A(i-1)$. On the first iteration, $j = N$, so the assignment to the last location of A is correctly executed. As a result, the total number of loop iterations is restored to its original count, but there is still the overhead of the conditional assignment to j.

Alternatively, the conditional statements can be eliminated by peeling off the first and last executions for each of the statements, yielding

```
D(2) = A(1) * 2.0
DO I = 2, N - 1
   A(I) = B(I) + C(I)
   D(I+1) = A(I) * 2.0
ENDDO
A(N) = B(N) + C(N)
```

This form permits efficient parallelism with the added overhead of two statements, one before and one after the loop, that cannot be executed in parallel.

Is it possible to use alignment to eliminate all carried dependences in a loop? Clearly, the answer is no if the carried dependence is involved in a recurrence, as the following example shows:

```
DO I = 1, N
   A(I) = B(I) + C
   B(I+1) = A(I) + D
ENDDO
```

In this example, the references to B create a carried dependence. For alignment to be successful in this case, we would need to interchange the order of the two statements in the loop body. However, the loop-independent dependence involving A prevents interchanging the statements before alignment, so our hope is that we can do the alignment and statement interchange in a single step to eliminate the carried dependence:

```
DO I = 1, N + 1
   IF (I.NE.1) B(I) = A(I-1) + D
   IF (I.NE.N+1) A(I) = B(I) + C
ENDDO
```

Although B is now aligned, the references to A are misaligned, creating a new carried dependence. Looking at this example, it is reasonable to believe that loop alignment cannot eliminate carried dependences in a recurrence. To argue more formally that this is the case, let us suppose that we have a recurrence and we wish to transform the program to convert all carried dependences into loop-independent dependences. For the transformation to be valid, every dependence must be preserved in the transformed code. This means that each statement in the recurrence must have a dependence from it to some other statement in the recurrence and, by the statement of the lemma, that dependence must be loop independent. This requirement clearly cannot hold for the final statement in the reordered code, since any dependence from it must be backward, and therefore cannot be loop independent.

Intuitively, it is fairly clear why a recurrence is a problem for alignment. Each recurrence has a fixed aggregate threshold; that is, each statement in the recurrence is involved in the computation of the instance of itself a fixed number iterations forward in the loop. Decreasing the thresholds of forward dependences within the body of the loop must necessarily increase the thresholds of backward-carried dependences. Thus the thresholds of all dependences in the loop cannot simultaneously reduce the thresholds to zero.

But what about carried dependences that are not involved in a recurrence? Can they always be converted by alignment without introducing new carried dependences? The answer is again no, because of the possibility of an *alignment conflict*—two or more dependences that cannot be simultaneously aligned. Consider the following example:

```
DO I = 1, N
   A(I+1) = B(I) + C
   X(I) = A(I+1) + A(I)
ENDDO
```

This loop contains two dependences involving the array A, one loop-independent dependence and a loop-carried dependence. If the statements are aligned to eliminate the carried dependence, the following code results:

```
DO I = 0, N
   IF (I.NE.0) A(I+1) = B(I) + C
   IF (I.NE.N) X(I+1) = A(I+2) + A(I+1)
ENDDO
```

The original loop-carried dependence has been eliminated, but the process of eliminating it has transformed the original loop-independent dependence into a loop-carried dependence. The loop still cannot be correctly run in parallel. Fortunately, another transformation—*code replication*—can be used to eliminate alignment conflicts in many cases.

6.2.4 Code Replication

An alignment conflict occurs because two or more dependences (or chains of dependences) emanating from the same source and entering the same sink have different thresholds. Whenever the source or sink is adjusted to align one of the dependences, the others are offset by its threshold, thereby misaligning them.

If the dependences in an alignment conflict can be adjusted to have different sources or different sinks, then the individual dependences can be separately aligned without conflict. One way to split a dependence source is to replicate the computation at that source. For instance, in the alignment conflict example from the previous section, the value of A(I) used in the second statement on every iteration after the first comes from the first statement (hence the loop-carried dependence). Since the input operands to the first statement do not change inside the loop, it is possible to recompute the value of A(I) on the iteration needed. The following revision of the alignment conflict example eliminates the carried dependence through replication:

```
DO I = 1, N
   A(I+1) = B(I) + C

   ! Replicated statement
   IF (I.EQ.1) THEN
      t = A(I)
   ELSE
      t = B(I-1) + C
   END IF

   X(I) = A(I+1) + t
ENDDO
```

The first iteration has to be separated, since A(1) comes from the values extant before loop entry rather than from any statement in the loop. This loop has no carried dependences and can be run in parallel, assuming that the variable t is privatized. Since the essential aspect of the transformation applied here involves redundantly repeating some computation, the transformation is called *code replication*.

Is the combination of code replication, loop alignment, and statement reordering sufficient to eliminate all carried dependences in nonrecurrence loops? The following theorem shows the answer to be yes.

THEOREM
6.2

Alignment, replication, and statement reordering are sufficient to eliminate all carried dependences in a single loop that contains no recurrence and in which the distance of each dependence is a constant independent of the loop index.

We establish this theorem by constructing an algorithm to produce the desired result. Given the fact that the loop is free of any cycles, its dependence graph can be represented as a directed acyclic *alignment graph* $G = (V, E)$. The vertices (V) represent statements; the edges (E) represent dependences and are labeled with the dependence distance.

In an alignment graph, the alignment of any statement at any point in time is held in an *offset*, which represents the number of iterations between the statement's current alignment and its original placement in the loop. An example should clarify this concept.

```
     DO I = 1, N
S₁       A(I+2) = B(I) + C
S₂       X(I+1) = A(I) + D
S₃       Y(I) = A(I+1) + X(I)
     ENDDO
```

The initial alignment graph for this example is shown in Figure 6.3. The dependence distances are represented in the *d* fields; the offsets (which are all zero before any transformations are effected) are held in *o* fields. Before demonstrating the effects of alignment, a definition is useful:

**DEFINITION
6.2**

If $o(v)$ denotes the offset of vertex v, and $d(e)$ the distance for dependence edge e, an alignment graph $G = (V, E)$ is said to be *carry-free* if for each edge $e = (v_1, v_2)$

$$o(v_1) + d(e) = o(v_2)$$

The alignment graph in Figure 6.3 is not carry-free. Since the overall goal is to create a parallel loop, the goal of an alignment and replication algorithm is to produce, through offset adjustment and vertex replication, a carry-free alignment graph. Given such a graph, generating code for the adjusted loop is straightforward.

The basic approach of the alignment and replication algorithm presented in Figure 6.4 is as follows:

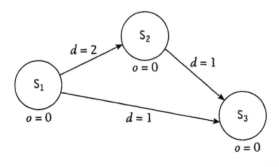

Figure 6.3 An alignment graph.

procedure *Align(V,E,d,o)*

    // V and E are the vertex and edge sets, respectively
    // d is the dependence distance table
    // o is the offset table, an output variable
    // W is a worklist for the algorithm

    while $V \neq \varnothing$ **do begin**
       select and remove an arbitrary element v_0 from V;
       $W := \{v_0\}$; $o(v_0) := 0$;
       while $W \neq \varnothing$ **do begin**
          select and remove an arbitrary element v from W;
          for each edge e incident on v **do**
             if $e = (w,v)$ **then**
                if $w \in V$ **then**
                begin
                    $W := W \cup \{w\}$; $V := V - \{w\}$;
                    $o(w) := o(v) - d(e)$;
                end
                else if $o(w) \neq o(v) - d(e)$ **then begin** // conflict
                    create a new vertex w';
                    replace the edge $e = (w,v)$ *with* $e' = (w',v)$;
                    for each edge into w **do**
                       replicate the edge, replacing w with w';
                    $W := W \cup \{w'\}$; $o(w') := o(v) - d(e)$;
                end
             else // $e = (v,w)$
                if $w \in V$ **then**
                begin
                    $W := W \cup \{w\}$; $V := V - \{w\}$;
                    $o(w) := o(v) - d(e)$;
                end
                else if $o(w) \neq o(v) + d(e)$ **then begin** // conflict
                    // always replicate the upstream vertex
                    create a replicated vertex v';
                    replace the edge $e = (v,w)$ *with* $e' = (v',w)$;
                    for each edge into v **do**
                       replicate the edge, replacing v with v';
                    $W := W \cup \{v'\}$; $o(v') := o(w) - d(e)$;
                end
       end
      end
    end *Align*

Figure 6.4 Alignment and replication algorithm.

1. Create a worklist initially containing an arbitrary unvisited vertex in the graph.
2. While the worklist is nonempty, repeat the following three steps:
   a. Pick and remove a node from the worklist.
   b. Align with that node any nodes that are adjacent to it in the alignment graph, replicating code when different alignments are required.
   c. Put each of these nodes on the worklist.
3. If there are other unvisited vertices, return to step 1.

If we apply this algorithm to the alignment graph in Figure 6.3, choosing S_3 as the root, we get the modified graph in Figure 6.5.

All that remains is to show how code is generated from an alignment graph. Note that the offset indicates where in the alignment space each statement should start. Here is a naive alignment for the loop that generated Figure 6.3.

```
     DO I = 1, N + 3
S₁       IF (I.GE.4) A(I-1) = B(I-3) + C
S₁'      IF (I.GE.2.AND.I.LE.N+1) THEN
             t = B(I-1) + C
         ELSE
             t = A(I+1)
         ENDIF
S₂       IF (I.GE.2.AND.I.LE.N+1) X(I) = A(I-1) + D
S₃       IF (I.LE.N) Y(I) = t + X(I)
     ENDDO
```

As with an earlier example, we can repack this code as follows:

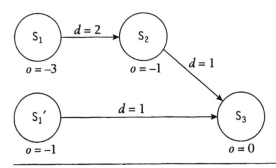

Figure 6.5 Modified alignment graph.

```
        DO I = 1, N
           i1 = I - 3; IF (i1.LE.0) i1 = i1 + N
S₁         A(i1+2) = B(i1) + C
           i2 = I - 1; IF (i2.LE.0) i2 = i2 + N
S₁'        IF (i2.GE.2) THEN
              t = A(i2) + D
           ELSE
              t = X(I)
           ENDIF
S₂         X(i2+1) = A(i2) + D
S₃         Y(I) = t + X(I)
        ENDDO
```

Figure 6.6 gives the algorithm to generate the unpacked version of the aligned code. We leave as an exercise the adaptation of this algorithm to produce the packed form using the conditional assignment to compute loop indices.

6.2.5 Loop Fusion

To this point, we have developed mechanisms for transforming a loop to increase parallelism without resorting to loop distribution. As we discussed in Section 6.2.2, we are reluctant to distribute because it results in finer granularity and more synchronization overhead. But what if a loop has some statements that can be run in parallel but others that cannot? We need to explore ways to restructure existing loops to separate potentially parallel code from code that must be sequentialized, and loop distribution is the obvious mechanism for doing so. Effective use of loop distribution requires the answers to two questions:

1. How can we effectively select the portion of the loop to run in parallel and separate that from the sequential code?

2. How can we avoid losing too much granularity of parallelism?

When we considered fine-grained parallelism, we had the luxury of using maximal loop distribution, which attempts to put each statement in a loop to itself. After loop distribution, some loops can be run in parallel and others cannot because they are part of a recurrence. When we are generating code for asynchronous parallelism, this approach is problematic because the granularity of the generated loops will be too fine. On the other hand, it neatly separates the parallel from the sequential code. One way to recover granularity is to recombine, or "fuse," the parallel loops into larger parallel loops. This idea can be illustrated in the following example:

```
     DO I = 1, N
S₁      A(I) = B(I) + 1
S₂      C(I) = A(I) + C(I-1)
S₃      D(I) = A(I) + X
     ENDDO
```

procedure *GenAlign(V,E,o)*

> // *V* and *E* are the vertex and edge sets, respectively
> // *o* is the offset table, an output variable

> *hi* := maximum offset of any vertex in *V*;
> *lo* := minimum offset of any vertex in *V*;
> let *Ivar* be the original loop induction variable;
> let *Lvar* be the original loop lower bound;
> let *Uvar* be the original loop upper bound;

> generate the loop statement "`DO` *Ivar* = *Lvar* – *hi, Uvar* + *lo*";

> topologically sort the vertices of *V*, breaking ties by taking the vertex
>   with smallest offset first;

> **for each** *v* ∈ *V* in sorted order **do begin**
>   **if** *o(v)* = *lo* **then** prefix the statement associated with *v* with
>   "`IF  (`*Ivar*`.GE.`*Lvar–o(v)*`)`";
>   **else if** *o(v)* = *hi* **then** prefix the statement associated with *v* with
>   "`IF  (`*Ivar*`.LE.`*Uvar–o(v)*`))`";

>   **else** prefix the statement associated with *v* with
>   "`IF  (`*Ivar*`.GE.`*Lvar–o(v)*` .AND.` *Ivar*`.LE.`*Uvar–o(v)*`))`";
>   **if** *v* is a replicated node **then begin**
>   replace the statement S after the `IF` by
>   `THEN`
> t_v = RHS(S) with *Ivar* + *o(v)* substituted for *Ivar*
>   `ELSE`
> t_v = LHS(S) with *Ivar* + *o(v)* substituted for *Ivar*
>   `ENDIF`
>   where t_v is a unique scalar variable;
>   replace the reference at the sink of every dependence from
>   *v* by the variable t_v;
>   **end**
>   **end**

> generate the loop ending statement "`ENDDO`";
> **end** *GenAlign*

Figure 6.6 Generation of aligned and replicated code.

Since there is a carried dependence from S_2 to itself, alignment, replication, or skewing cannot parallelize the loop. Loop distribution converts the loop into three separate loops:

```
L₁   DO I = 1, N
         A(I) = B(I) + 1
     ENDDO
L₂   DO I = 1, N
         C(I) = A(I) + C(I-1)
     ENDDO
L₃   DO I = 1, N
         D(I) = A(I) + X
     ENDDO
```

It is easy to see that loops L_1 and L_3 carry no dependence and therefore can be made parallel. However, since each is a single-statement loop, it is unlikely that the resulting parallelism will be beneficial unless the loop upper bounds are large enough to make it worthwhile to aggregate groups of iterations by strip mining.

To increase the granularity of parallelism, we will attempt to merge different parallel regions into a larger loop. To visualize how this might be done, we will represent the loops resulting from full distribution as a directed graph in which vertices represent loops and edges represent dependences between statements in different loops. Figure 6.7 illustrates this abstraction for the previous example. In this diagram the double circles are used to indicate parallel subloops that arise from distribution, and single circles indicate sequential subloops.

From Figure 6.7 it is evident that loops L_1 and L_3 can be merged to increase the granularity of parallelism because they were originally in the same loop and there is no dependence from L_2 to L_3 that would prevent the merger. The following parallel code results from merging L_1 and L_3:

```
L₁   PARALLEL DO I = 1, N
         A(I) = B(I) + 1
L₃       D(I) = A(I) + X
     ENDDO
L₂   DO I = 1, N
         C(I) = A(I) + C(I-1)
     ENDDO
```

This transformation is known as *loop fusion*. As usual with reordering transformations, there are instances where loop fusion is invalid. In particular, just as there are interchange-preventing dependences, there are also *fusion-preventing* dependences—dependences that are reversed when two loops are fused. Such dependences cannot arise from subloops created from loop distribution, since it

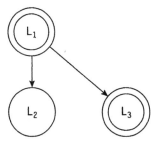

Figure 6.7 Interloop dependence graph.

must obviously be valid to fuse such subloops (they were originally one loop, so it cannot be illegal to remerge them into one loop). However, such dependences are possible in originally distinct loops, as the following example demonstrates:

```
      DO I - 1, N
S₁      A(I) - B(I) + C
      ENDDO
      DO I - 1, N
S₂      D(I) - A(I+1) + E
      ENDDO
```

The dependence from S_1 to S_2 due to A is loop independent—all values of A used in S_2 are created by statement S_1, with the sole exception of the one used on the last iteration. If the loops are fused,

```
      DO I - 1, N
S₁      A(I) - B(I) + C
S₂      D(I) - A(I+1) + E
      ENDDO
```

the loop-independent dependence has become a *backward* loop-carried antidependence. As evidence of this fact, none of the values of A used by S_2 are created by S_1 in the fused loops.

As discussed in Section 6.2.2, loop distribution converts some loop-carried dependences into loop-independent dependences. Since it seems reasonable that loops created by distribution can be correctly remerged, the loop-independent dependences that are converted from loop-carried dependences during distribution cannot prevent fusion—they will be correctly reconverted to loop-carried dependences by fusion. What distinguishes these from the carried dependence in the previous example is that they are all *forward*-carried dependences. If the two loops in the example were as follows

```
        DO I = 1, N
S₁        A(I) = B(I) + C
        ENDDO
        DO I = 1, N
S₂        D(I) = A(I-1) + E
        ENDDO
```

they could be correctly fused to produce

```
        DO I = 1, N
S₁        A(I) = B(I) + C
S₂        D(I) = A(I-1) + E
        ENDDO
```

because in both cases S_1 creates all values of A used in S_2 except for the first.

The problem with the earlier fusion example was that fusing the two loops converted a forward true dependence to a backward-carried antidependence. In other words, the source and sink of the dependence were reversed. This is clearly a violation of the ordering constraint given by the Fundamental Theorem of Dependence (Theorem 2.2). Thus, any forward loop-independent dependence that becomes carried and reverses endpoints after fusion is said to be fusion preventing.

DEFINITION
6.3

A loop-independent dependence between statements in two different loops (i.e., from S_1 to S_2) is *fusion preventing* if fusing the two loops causes the dependence to be carried by the combined loop in the reverse direction (from S_2 to S_1).

Obviously, fusion-preventing and parallelization-inhibiting dependences represent safety and profitability considerations that must be factored into a general code generation algorithm for parallelism. Another safety consideration is ordering: it must be possible to combine the loops without violating any ordering constraints implied by dependences. The following modification to the original example illustrates this condition:

```
        DO I = 1, N
S₁        A(I) = B(I) + 1
S₂        C(I) = A(I) + C(I-1)
S₃        D(I) = A(I) + C(I)
        ENDDO
```

Once again, distributing loops as fully as possible will create three subloops. However, the interloop dependence graph has changed and is shown in Figure 6.8.

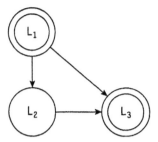

Figure 6.8 A fusion prevented by the ordering constraint.

Fusing loops L_1 and L_3 must cause either L_3 to be executed before L_2 (if the fused loops are executed first) or L_1 to be executed after L_2 (if the fused loops are executed second). Either ordering violates a dependence. The topological ordering imposed by dependences must be obeyed both in fusion and in distribution.

Summarizing, there are two *safety constraints* for loop fusion:

1. *Fusion-preventing dependence constraint:* Two loops cannot be validly fused if there exists a fusion-preventing dependence between them.

2. *Ordering constraint:* Two loops cannot be validly fused if there exists a path of loop-independent dependences between them that contains a loop or statement that is not being fused with them.

While it will not be explicitly proved, these two constraints constitute the only safety considerations necessary for loop fusion (other than the minor, but obvious requirements that the loops have the same bounds, etc.).

While fusion-prevention and ordering constraints are the primary determinants of the safety of loop fusion, they are not sufficient to guarantee profitability. A minimal requirement for profitability that should be valid for any machine architecture is that fusion should not destroy parallelism—there should be at least as many parallel statements after loop fusion as before, or the fusion is not profitable. Such a requirement might appear to be trivially met by fusion; in fact, that is not the case.

As an example where fusion decreases parallelism, consider the following pair of loops:

```
L₁   DO I = 1, N
        A(I) = B(I) + 1
     ENDDO
L₂   DO I = 1, N
        C(I) = A(I) + C(I-1)
     ENDDO
```

L_1 contains no carried dependences and may be run in parallel; L_2 is a recurrence and must be run sequentially. The two loops may be legally fused, but since L_2 must be run sequentially, fusing the loops forces L_1 to be run sequentially, eliminating the opportunity for parallelism. Any time a sequential loop is fused into a parallel loop, parallelism is lost, prompting the following constraint on fusion:

1. *Separation constraint:* A sequential loop should not be fused with a parallel loop because the result would necessarily be sequential, reducing the total amount of parallelism.

However, the separation constraint alone is not sufficient to guarantee the profitability of fusion in the context of parallelism. It is possible to fuse two parallel loops and end up with a sequential loop, as in the following example:

```
        DO I - 1, N
S₁        A(I+1) - B(I) + C
        ENDDO
        DO I - 1, N
S₂        D(I) - A(I) + E
        ENDDO
```

Either loop can be run alone in parallel, but if the loops are fused together

```
        DO I - 1, N
S₁        A(I+1) - B(I) + C
S₂        D(I) - A(I) + E
        ENDDO
```

the merged loop carries a dependence, which inhibits parallelism. Although these dependences can be handled by alignment and replication (since there cannot possibly be a recurrence or the fusion would have been invalid), we will assume for the sake of simplicity that fusion should be prevented in this case. Thus we introduce a new definition to cover this case.

DEFINITION 6.4   An edge between statements in two different loops is said to be *parallelism inhibiting* if, after fusing the two loops, the dependence would be carried by the combined loop.

This definition is the basis of the second profitability constraint:

2. *Parallelism-inhibiting dependence constraint:* Two parallel loops should not be fused if there exists a parallelism-inhibiting dependence between them.

Having spent a lot of time discussing how fusion *cannot* be used for exploiting parallelism, it is now time to formulate a fusion procedure that shows how fusion *can* be used.

Typed Fusion

We will begin with a code generation model that maintains a strict separation between parallel and sequential code; in other words, it attempts to create the largest possible parallel loops via loop fusion, but does not attempt to determine when sequential loops might be run in parallel with other sequential loops or with parallel loops. In this model, each parallel loop would be terminated by a barrier, and all sequential code that must follow that parallel loop or precede the next would appear immediately after the barrier. In this model, the central task of code generation can be stated in abstract terms:

> *Given a graph in which the edges represent dependences and the vertices represent loops, use correct and profitable loop fusion to produce an equivalent program with the minimal number of parallel loops.*

We can generalize this problem to the problem of *typed fusion:*

DEFINITION 6.5

A *typed fusion problem* is a quintuple $P = (G,T,m,B,t_0)$, where

1. $G = (V,E)$ is a graph,

2. T is a set of *types,*

3. $m:V{\rightarrow}T$ is a mapping such that $m(v)$ for $v \in V$ is the *type* of v,

4. $B \subseteq E$ is a set of *bad edges*, and

5. $t_0 \in T$ is the objective type.

A *solution* to the typed fusion problem P is a graph $G' = (V',E')$, where V' is derived from V by fusing vertices of the distinguished type t_0 subject to these constraints:

1. *Bad edge constraint:* No two vertices joined by a bad edge may be fused.

2. *Ordering constraint:* No two vertices joined by a path containing a vertex of type $t \neq t_0$ may be fused.

An *optimal solution* to the typed fusion problem has a minimal number of edges.

It is easy to see that typed fusion is a model for the parallel fusion problem, with vertices corresponding to loops, edges corresponding to dependences, types corresponding to *parallel* and *sequential,* bad edges corresponding to fusion-preventing or parallelism-inhibiting edges, and the distinguished type *parallel*. An optimal solution to the problem has the smallest number of parallel loops and therefore the coarsest granularity possible.

In Figures 6.9 through 6.12 we present the algorithm *TypedFusion*, due to Kennedy and McKinley [177], which produces an optimal greedy fusion of the

procedure *TypedFusion*($G,T,type,B,t_0$)
  // $G = (V,E)$ the original typed graph
  // T is a set of types
  // *type*(n) is a function that returns the type of a node
  // B is the set of bad edges
  // t_0 is a specific type for which we will find a minimal fusion
  // Initialization
  lastnum := 0; *lastfused* := 0; *count*[*] := 0; *fused* := 0; *node*[*] := 0;
  for each edge $e = (m,n) \in E$ **do** *count*[n] := *count*[n] + 1;
  for each node $n \in V$ **do begin**
    maxBadPrev[n] := 0; *num*[n] := 0; *next*[n] := 0;
    if *count*[n] = 0 **then** $W := W \cup \{n\}$;
  end
  // Iterate over working set, visiting nodes, fusing nodes of type t_0
  while $W \neq \emptyset$ **do begin**
    let n be an arbitrary element in W; $W := W - \{n\}$; $t := type(n)$;
L_1:   **if** $t = t_0$ **then begin** // A node of the type being worked on
      // Compute node to fuse with.
S_1:   **if** *maxBadPrev*[n] = 0 **then** p := *fused*;
       else p := *next*[*maxBadPrev*[n]];
       if $p \neq 0$ **then begin** // Fuse with node at p
         x := *node*[p]; *num*[n] := *num*[x];
         update_successors(n,t); // visit successors before fusing
         fuse x and n and call the result x,
            making all edges out of n be out of x;
       end
       else begin // Make this the first node in a new group
         create_new_fused_node(n);
         update_successors(n,t);
       end
     end
     else begin // $t \neq t_0$
       create_new_node(n);
       update_successors(n,t);
     end
  end
end *TypedFusion*

Figure 6.9 Typed fusion algorithm.

procedure *create_new_node(n)*

    lastnum := lastnum + 1;
    num[n] := lastnum;
    node[num[n]] := n;
end *create_new_node*

Figure 6.10 Create a new node in the reduced graph.

procedure *create_new_fused_node(n)*

    create_new_node(n);

    // append node *n* to the end of *fused*
    if *lastfused =* 0 **then begin**
        fused := lastnum;
        lastfused := fused;
    end
    else begin
        next[lastfused] := lastnum;
        lastfused := lastnum;
    end
end *create_new_fused_node*

Figure 6.11 Create and initialize a new fusion group.

procedure *update_successors(n,t)*

l2: **for each** node *m* such that $(n,m) \in E$ **do begin**
    count[m] := count[m] −1;
    if *count[m] =* 0 **then** $W := W \cup \{m\}$;

    if $t \neq t_0$ **then**
        maxBadPrev[m] := MAX(*maxBadPrev[m], maxBadPrev[n]*);
    else // $t = t_0$
        if *type(m)* $\neq t_0$ **or** $(n,m) \in B$ **then** // bad edge
            maxBadPrev[m] := MAX(*maxBadPrev[m], num[n]*);
        else // equal types and not fusion preventing
            maxBadPrev[m] := MAX(*maxBadPrev[m], maxBadPrev[n]*);
    end
end *update_successors*

Figure 6.12 Visit successors, add to worklist, and update *MaxBadPrev*.

nodes of a given type t_0 in a graph that contains bad edges and nodes of several types. This algorithm is fast in that it takes $O(N+E)$ steps in the worst case, where N is the number of vertices and E is the number of edges in the graph G. Since any algorithm must traverse the graph at least once, this is clearly the minimum possible.

The basic idea of this algorithm is that, as each node is visited for the first time, the algorithm determines in constant time the exact node of the same type into which it would be fused by the greedy algorithm. If no such node exists, the node is assigned a separate node number. In essence, the algorithm in Figures 6.9 through 6.12 carries out greedy fusion for the single selected type.

DEFINITION 6.6

We define a *bad path* for type t to be a path that begins with a node of type t and contains either a bad edge between two nodes of type t or a node of type different from t.

The algorithm treats a bad path as if it were a bad edge. Only nodes of the same type are considered for fusion. The principal data structure used for this computation is *maxBadPrev[n]*, computed for each vertex n in the graph. For a given vertex n in the original graph, *maxBadPrev[n]* is the vertex number in the fused graph of the highest numbered vertex of the same type as n that cannot be fused with n because there is a bad path from that vertex (or some vertex in the collection it represents) to n. Obviously, n cannot fuse with *maxBadPrev[n]*. We will show that it also cannot fuse with any node numbered lower than *maxBad-Prev[n]*. Therefore the first node it can fuse with is the first node of the same type as n that comes after *maxBadPrev[n]* in the reduced graph numbering. By always fusing n with this node, *TypedFusion* implements a greedy strategy.

In addition to *maxBadPrev[n]*, the algorithm uses the following intermediate quantities:

- *num[n]* is the number of the first visit to a node in the collection of nodes that n is fused with t_0. In other words, it is the numbering of the fused node containing n in the output graph.

- *node[i]* is an array that maps numbers to nodes such that *node[i]* is the representative node of the *i*th collection in the output graph. *Note:* *node[num[x]] = x*.

- *lastnum* is the most recently assigned node number.

- *fused* is the number of the first node of type t_0 in the graph.

- *lastfused* is the number of the most recently visited node of type t_0.

- *next[i]*, where i is the number of a node on the *fused* list, is the number of the next node in the *fused* list.

- *W* is a working set of nodes ready to be visited.

The algorithm works a bit like topological sort. It begins by initializing all these data structures, putting nodes with no predecessors on the worklist W. Then in loop L_1, it repeatedly removes a node from the worklist. If that node is not of the desired type t_0, it simply creates a new node for the output graph. On the other hand, if it *is* of type t_0, the algorithm finds the earliest node to fuse it with by the algorithm described previously or, if no such node exists, it creates a new fusion group and adds that group to the end of the list of fused nodes.

As each node is processed, all the dependence successors are visited (in the routine *update_successors*) so that the *maxBadPrev* values are updated for those successors. This procedure also adds a successor to the worklist W whenever it detects that all its predecessors have been processed.

TypedFusion achieves an optimal $O(E+V)$ time bound by choosing, as each new node of the selected type is visited, the correct node with which to fuse in constant time. This occurs in statement S_1. If we can show that this chooses the correct node to fuse with, an analysis similar to that used for topological sort will establish the desired time bound.

Correctness. To establish correctness, we must show that the constraints in the problem definition are observed. First, the algorithm clearly fuses only nodes of the distinguished type t_0. To show that it obeys the bad edge constraint, we must establish that it never fuses two nodes joined by a bad edge. To show that it satisfies the ordering constraint, we must show that it never fuses two nodes joined by a path that passes through a node of different type. These will both be established by the correctness of the selection procedure—if *maxBadPrev*[n] is correctly computed, we will never fuse with a node from which there is a bad path (containing a node of a different type or a bad edge). A careful examination of the routine *update_successors* in Figure 6.12 reveals that at every successor m of a vertex n that is visited, *maxBadPrev*[m] is computed as the maximum of its existing value and *maxBadPrev*[n] or, if *type*(n) = t_0 and (n,m) is a bad edge or *type*(m) ≠ t_0, the number of the fused node n. This clearly produces the correct value.

To establish that the algorithm produces the greedy solution we must show that it merges a vertex n of type t_0 with the earliest fused node it can be merged with. This is so because there must be a bad path to n from any fused node of type t_0 prior to *maxBadPrev*[n]. Clearly, there is a bad path from *maxBadPrev*[n] to n. Let x be some fused node of type t_0 prior to *maxBadPrev*[n]. Then there must be a bad path from x to *maxBadPrev*[n] because otherwise those two could have been fused. Since n fuses with the first node after *maxBadPrev*[n] in the list of fused nodes, that must be the first node it *can* fuse with.

Optimality. To show that the algorithm produces a solution with the fewest possible fused nodes, we must show that the greedy solution has this property. Although we will not prove this result formally, we will outline an informal argument. Suppose there is a collection C of fusion groups that satisfies the problem specification but that has fewer fusion groups than the greedy collection C_G computed by *TypedFusion*. Then there must be a first group in C that differs from the correspondingly numbered group in C_G. This group must be a subset of the greedy group because we put everything in the greedy group that could not be fused with an earlier group. Thus we could move all vertices in the greedy group into the corresponding group in C to make some later group in C be the first that differs from C_G. If we continue this process we can only *reduce* the size of C to be the same as C_G because we are moving elements from later groups in C to earlier ones. Thus C cannot be smaller than C_G.

Complexity. As we said before, the complexity of this algorithm is $O(E+V)$, where E is the number of edges in the original graph and V is the number of vertices. This can be seen by an analysis similar to that for topological sort. Each vertex is taken off the worklist W at most once, so all the constant-time work in the routine and calls to other routines within loop L_1 will take $O(N)$ time. The only place where nonconstant time is taken is in *update_successors*, where each successor of a given node is visited. Since each edge is traversed at most once over the entire calculation, the total amount of work taken by this process is bounded by the number of calls $O(N)$ plus the number of edges in the graph $O(E)$. Thus the asymptotic time bound is $O(N+E)$.

To see how this partitioning algorithm works, consider the example in Figure 6.13. When the algorithm is applied to the nodes of type *parallel*, indicated by the double circle, it produces the intermediate annotations shown in Figure 6.14. Each parallel node is annotated by a tuple of the form

$$(maxBadPrev, p) \rightarrow num$$

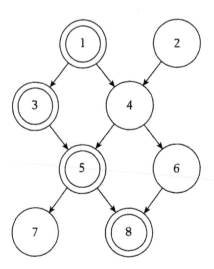

Figure 6.13 An example subloop graph.

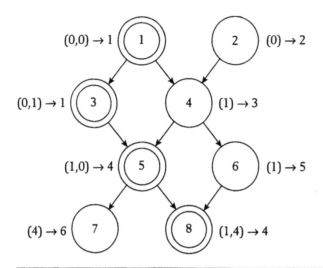

Figure 6.14 Annotated version of the example graph for $t_0 = $ *parallel*.

where p is as computed in the algorithm and *num* is the final number assigned to the node. The vertices of the original graph represented by a node are shown in the circle. Nodes of type *sequential* are annotated with a singleton, as computed by the algorithm for nodes of type other than t_0:

$$(maxBadPrev) \rightarrow num$$

The result after fusion is shown in Figure 6.15, with new node numbers shown to the side.

Note that we could now apply the algorithm *TypedFusion* a second time with $t_0 = $ *sequential* to fuse all of the sequential loops. We do not necessarily need to fuse them, but it is useful to know how many sequential "epochs" are needed. The final result is shown in Figure 6.16.

The desired schedule is

1. parallel loop containing original loops 1 and 3
2. sequential loop containing original loops 2, 4, and 6
3. parallel loop containing original loops 5 and 8
4. sequential loop containing the original loop 7

Unordered and Ordered Typed Fusion

Once we have developed the notion of typed fusion, we can envision many applications for it. An important example will be given later in the chapter. For now consider the problem of dealing with incompatible loop headers. It may not be

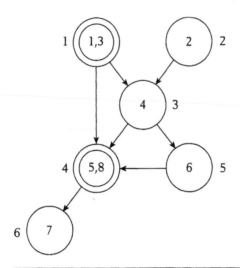

Figure 6.15 Example after fusing parallel loops.

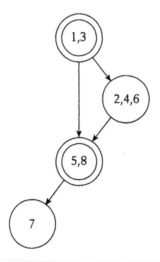

Figure 6.16 Example after fusing sequential loops.

convenient or profitable to go to the trouble to fuse two loops that have loop headers that are not compatible because they have different iteration ranges. If we let each loop header be a different type, we can restrict fusion to compatible loop headers by applying the algorithm *TypedFusion* once for each type.

It is natural to ask, Does this always produce the minimum total number of nodes? To understand this issue, consider the simple dependence graph in Figure 6.17, which illustrates a *type conflict*. Although we can fuse either type separately,

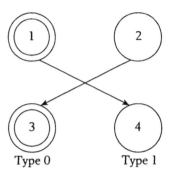

Type 0   Type 1

Figure 6.17 A type conflict.

we cannot fuse both types because the fusion of one type creates a bad path for the other type. Thus we must select which of the two types we wish to fuse.

The example in Figure 6.18 shows how order can make a difference in the quality of the fusion. If we were to choose to fuse type 1 before either type 0 or type 2, we would create bad paths for both types 0 and 2, preventing all other fusions. However, if we choose to fuse type 0 first, we will create a bad path only for type 1, permitting the two type 2 nodes to fuse as well. The first approach yields a total of 5 nodes, while the second yields 4, a clearly better result.

Is there any way to determine the order in which to fuse types that are otherwise undistinguished? The answer is yes, but it is costly. Kennedy and McKinley have proved that the problem is *NP*-hard in the number of types [176, 177]. Fortunately, type conflicts are fairly rare, so a good heuristic for choosing order may be effective.

The situation is much simpler for the *ordered typed fusion problem*, in which the types can be prioritized according to some criterion, so that it is always more important to minimize the number of nodes of a higher-priority type, no matter how many bad paths for lower-priority types are created. In this case a simple

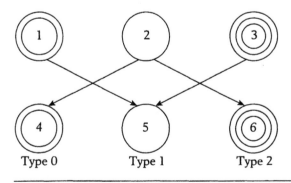

Type 0   Type 1   Type 2

Figure 6.18 An order-sensitive fusion problem.

algorithm that calls *TypedFusion* for each type in descending priority order will produce an "optimal" result—one that, for each type, is as good as possible given the fusions for higher-priority types.

An important ordered typed fusion problem that occurs frequently in practice has vertices representing three types of constructs:

1. a parallel loop

2. a sequential loop

3. a single statement not contained in any loop

Obviously, it is always best to fuse parallel loops. Since there is no gain in "fusing" two statements, which simply means putting them together, and there is a reduction in overhead for fusing two sequential loops, fusing of loops is always to be preferred. Thus there is a clear priority order for these three types.

In reality, total orders for types are hard to come by. It is far more typical to find a partial order for types. In other words, in fusion problems that arise in practice, there will usually be only a few priority rules that favor one type over another. We can deal with these problems by using topological sort to establish a total priority order for the graph and then calling *TypedFusion* in descending priority order.

Cohort Fusion

A somewhat different problem is presented if you wish to not only parallelize loops but also run two sequential loops in parallel or a sequential loop in parallel with a parallel loop. In a sense, the problem here is to find all the loops that can be run in parallel with one another either by fusion or because they have no dependences between them. This model combines some of the features of data and task parallelism.

The principal idea behind the algorithm is to identify at each stage a *cohort*, which is a collection of loops that can be run in parallel. This collection may contain a number of parallel loops, all of which can be fused into a single parallel loop, along with some number of sequential loops that can be run at the same time as the parallel loop.

DEFINITION 6.7   A *parallel cohort* is a collection of sequential and parallel loops that satisfies two conditions: (1) there are no fusion-preventing or parallelism-inhibiting edges between any two parallel loops in the cohort, and (2) there are no execution constraints (i.e., dependence edges) existing between any parallel loop and any sequential loop in the cohort.

In other words, the only interloop dependence edges that can exist in a cohort are edges between two sequential loops and edges between two parallel loops that are neither fusion preventing nor parallelism inhibiting. If one sequential loop in the cohort depends on another, it can be fused with its predecessor so long as the edge joining them is not fusion preventing.

In general, fusing sequential loops in a cohort is probably not desirable unless the loops are connected by a dependence. If there are no execution constraints between two sequential loops, they may be run in parallel (as a whole) with each other. Fusing the loops forces the pair to be executed on the same processor at the same time, resulting in a loss of parallelism. If there is a dependence edge between two sequential loops, then fusing the two loops may save some execution time due to memory hierarchy (see Chapter 8) or from simplified execution control. However, the time saved is probably relatively small.

This problem can be solved by two applications of *TypedFusion*. In the first, all nodes are treated as a single type, and the following edges are defined to be bad:

1. fusion-preventing edges
2. parallelism-inhibiting edges
3. edges that have a parallel loop at one endpoint and a sequential loop at the other

This pass will produce a minimal number of cohorts and thus a minimum number of barriers. A second application of *TypedFusion* can be used to fuse all of the parallel loops within each cohort, although this is overkill, since the parallel loops in a cohort can all be fused by definition.

Although this method minimizes the number of barriers, it could be unsatisfactory because of the handling of sequential loops in the system. It is possible that a very large sequential loop would dominate a cohort generated by this algorithm, when a better load balance would be achieved by splitting the sequential loop between two cohorts, dividing iterations in the right proportion.

6.3 Perfect Loop Nests

So far, this chapter has presented several techniques for uncovering parallelism in a single loop and one technique (loop interchange) for arranging the order of loops to enhance parallelism. This section will begin to combine these techniques, with the aim of developing a general algorithm for uncovering parallel loops in arbitrary loop nests. The first step toward that goal is the development of techniques for handling perfect loop nests.

6.3.1 Loop Interchange for Parallelization

Because of its ability to radically affect the execution order of a large number of statements at one time, loop interchange is a valuable transformation. Parallelization presents a different set of problems for loop interchange (and transformations in general), as pointed out in Section 1.5.2. Specifically, the need to balance parallelism versus communication and synchronization costs requires that parallel regions possess sufficient granularity to overcome the overheads of starting and synchronizing parallel computation. In other words, a successful parallel decomposition must be of fine enough granularity to provide reasonable load balance, but with communication and synchronization costs reduced enough to avoid dominating the resultant parallelism.

Since loops generally execute enough times to provide reasonable load balance, applying this principle to loop nests generally implies parallelizing outer loops. The implication of this principle with respect to loop interchange is that dependence-free loops should be moved to the *outermost* possible position, so long as doing so does not cause them to carry a dependence. This is in stark contrast to vectorization, where the goal is to move dependence-free loops to the innermost position. The following example should illustrate the distinction.

```
DO I = 1, N
   DO J = 1, M
      A(I+1,J) = A(I,J) + B(I,J)
   ENDDO
ENDDO
```

The outer (I) loop carries a recurrence, while the inner (J) loop is free of dependences. For vectorization, this loop ordering is reasonable, since it permits the inner loop to be vectorized. For coarse-grained parallelism, however, this ordering is problematic because only the inner loop can be parallelized, which could require N barrier synchronizations at run time—one for each iteration of the sequential outer loop.

On the other hand, if the parallel loop is interchanged to the outermost position (where it still remains free of dependences)

```
PARALLEL DO J = 1, M
   DO I = 1, N
      A(I+1,J) = A(I,J) + B(I,J)
   ENDDO
END PARALLEL DO
```

only one synchronization will be required during execution of the loop nest.

Of course, it is not always possible to move a parallel loop outward and have it remain free of dependences. For instance, if this example is changed slightly

```
DO I = 1, N
   DO J = 1, M
      A(I+1,J+1) = A(I,J) + B(I,J)
   ENDDO
ENDDO
```

(making the direction vector of the dependence (<,<) rather than (<,=)), loop interchange will not be effective. The dependence in this modified example is not interchange sensitive, and the outer loop will still carry the dependence after interchange. Without the aid of additional transformations, inner loop parallelism, along with the resulting number of synchronizations, is the best we can do.

```
DO I = 1, N
   PARALLEL DO J = 1, M
      A(I+1,J+1) = A(I,J) + B(I,J)
   END PARALLEL DO
ENDDO
```

We have seen in Chapter 5 that loop skewing combined with loop interchange can produce inner loop parallelism on this example, but inner loop parallelism will not be satisfactory for coarse-grained parallelism unless we have enough loop iterations in the inner loop to have each processor run a large block of iterations.

The question that naturally follows from these examples is, When can a loop be moved to the outermost position in a nest and guaranteed to be parallel? This question is answered by the following theorem.

THEOREM 6.3   In a perfect nest of loops, a particular loop can be parallelized at the outermost level if and only if the column of the direction matrix for that nest contains only "=" entries.

Proof   *If.* Clearly, a loop with all "=" entries in its direction matrix column can be parallelized at the outermost level; it can be moved to the outermost position because the loops inside it will remain in the same relative order and thus all direction vectors in the matrix will still have all "<" entries in their outermost non-"=" positions. Since it has only "=" entries, this loop will carry no dependences at any level, including the outermost. Thus it can be parallelized by Theorem 2.8.

Only if. Now we must show that these are the only loops that can be parallelized at the outermost level. Consider any other case. If the column contains a ">", the loop cannot be moved to the outermost position, because the dependence in that row will be reversed (see Theorem 5.2). If the column contains a "<," it cannot be parallelized at the outermost level because it will always carry a dependence at that level. Since there are no other possible entries, it must be the case that a loop can be moved to the outermost position and parallelized only if its column contains only "=" entries.

This theorem suggests a general code generation strategy for perfect loop nests based on the direction matrix:

1. While the direction matrix contains columns with only "=" entries, choose any loop that has such a column (the outermost such loop is a logical selection, but any will do), move it to the outermost position, and parallelize it, then eliminate its column from the direction matrix. Continue this process until all such columns have been removed.

2. Once all equality columns have been eliminated, pick the loop with the greatest number of "<" entries, move it to the outermost remaining position, and generate a sequential loop for it. Eliminate this column; also eliminate any rows that represent dependences carried by this loop (these rows will be the ones containing "<" entries in the newly outermost position). The row elimination may create new all-"=" columns, so repeat the algorithm starting with step 1.

Later sections will generalize this algorithm substantially. However, this simple version illustrates the operation model of all algorithms we will present: repeated selection of a loop (either parallel or sequential) to be in the outermost position. If a sequential loop is selected, it should be the loop that uncovers the most parallelism in the remaining loops.

The following three-loop nest illustrates this approach:

```
DO I = 1, N
   DO J = 1, M
      DO K = 1, L
         A(I+1,J,K) = A(I,J,K) + X1
         B(I,J,K+1) = B(I,J,K) + X2
         C(I+1,J+1,K+1) = C(I,J,K) + X3
      ENDDO
   ENDDO
ENDDO
```

The direction matrix for this nest is

$$
\begin{bmatrix}
< & = & = \\
= & = & < \\
< & < & <
\end{bmatrix}
$$

Since there are no columns with all "=" entries, none of the loops can be parallelized at the outermost level. Both the I and the K loops will carry two dependences in the outermost position, so either loop can logically be selected to be run sequentially in the outermost position. Choosing the I loop leaves a direction matrix [= <], which permits the loop on J to be parallelized and forces the K loop to be sequential.

```
DO I - 1, N
    PARALLEL DO J - 1, M
        DO K - 1, L
            A(I+1,J,K) = A(I,J,K) + X1
            B(I,J,K+1) = B(I,J,K) + X2
            C(I+1,J+1,K+1) - C(I,J,K) + X3
        ENDDO
    END PARALLEL DO
ENDDO
```

While this simple algorithm uncovers a reasonable amount of parallelism, it should be obvious that additional transformations such as loop distribution can increase the total parallelism available. For example, if the loop nests were distributed into three separate loops, each loop would have two dimensions of parallelism. The profitability of such a distribution depends on the minimum effective granularity for the target machine.

6.3.2 Loop Selection

Given a perfect loop nest, the principal challenge with respect to generation of parallelism is to generate the most parallelism with adequate granularity. The key to meeting that challenge is selecting the proper loops to run in parallel. Section 6.3.1 provided an introduction to that challenge by showing how loop interchange could be used to enhance parallelism. This section will extend the methods developed there and demonstrate how difficult the problem of loop selection is.

Recall the informal parallel code generation strategy from Section 6.3.1:

1. while there are loops that can be run in parallel, move them to the outermost position and parallelize them, then

2. select a sequential loop, run it serially, and find what new parallelism may have been revealed.

Figure 6.19 provides a more formal specification of this approach.

The key step that determines the success of this algorithm is step S: the heuristic selection of the loop to be run sequentially. To illustrate the importance of this selection, consider the following example

```
DO I - 2, N + 1
    DO J - 2, M + 1
        DO K - 1, L
            A(I,J,K+1) = A(I,J-1,K) + A(I-1,J,K+2)
        ENDDO
    ENDDO
ENDDO
```

procedure *parallelizeNest(N,success)*

// *N* is the loop nest to be parallelized
// *success* is returned as true if at least one loop is parallelized
// *M* is the direction matrix for the loop nest
// *L* is a worklist of the (perfectly nested) loops in *N*

compute the direction matrix *M* for the nest;
let *L* be a list of the loops in the nest *N*;

success := *false*;

while *L* ≠ Ø **do begin**
    while there exist columns in *M* with all "=" directions **do begin**
        success := *true*;
        l := loop corresponding to the outermost all-"=" column;
        remove *l* from *L*;
        generate a parallel loop for *l* at the outermost position;
        eliminate the column corresponding to *l* from *M*;
    end;

    if *L* ≠ Ø **and** ¬*success* **then begin**
        // select a loop (heuristically) to sequentialize.
        // it must be movable to the outermost position and
        // it should lead to the uncovering of parallelism

S: *select_loop_and_interchange(L)*;

        let *l* be the outermost loop in *L*; remove *l* from *L*;
        generate a sequential loop for *l*;
        remove the column corresponding to *l* from *M*;
        remove all rows corresponding to dependences carried by
            loop *l* from *M*;
    end
  end
  if ¬*success* **then** restore the original loop; // try again in *Parallelize*
end *parallelizeNest*

Figure 6.19 Algorithm to parallelize a loop nest.

which has the direction matrix

$$\begin{bmatrix} = & < & < \\ < & = & > \end{bmatrix}$$

No column contains only "=" entries, so no loop can be immediately run in parallel. In addition, the inner loop has a ">" direction, which prevents it from moving to the outermost position. As a result, the selection heuristic must be invoked as the first step in parallelizing this nest. In this case the choice is clear—the outermost loop must be sequentialized at some point because it must cover the ">" entry for the inner loop. Once this is done, neither of the remaining loops can be immediately parallelized, causing another invocation of the selection heuristic. Running either of these loops sequentially will permit the other to be run in parallel, so one parallel loop will eventually result.

```
DO I = 2, N + 1
    DO J = 2, M + 1
        PARALLEL DO K = 1, L
            A(I,J,K+1) = A(I,J-1,K) + A(I-1,J,K+2)
        ENDDO
    ENDDO
ENDDO
```

Is it possible to derive a selection heuristic that provides optimal code? Deriving such a heuristic is probably not possible, as it is not very difficult to show that selecting the proper loop is an *NP*-complete problem (see Exercise 6.2). For the moment, assume the simple approach of selecting the loop with the most "<" directions, on the theory that such a loop eliminates the maximum number of rows from the direction matrix. Applying such a strategy to the following direction matrix would fail:

$$
\begin{bmatrix}
< & < & = & = \\
< & = & < & = \\
< & = & = & < \\
= & < & = & = \\
= & = & < & = \\
= & = & = & <
\end{bmatrix}
$$

Even though the outer loop carries the most dependences, it will do no good to sequentialize it because the three inner loops will need to be sequentialized as well. However, if the three inner loops are sequentialized, the outer loop can be moved to the innermost position and parallelized.

One way to avoid the problem highlighted by the example is to favor the selection of loops that must be sequentialized before parallelism can be uncovered. Thus, if there exists a loop that can legally be moved to the outermost position and there is a dependence for which that loop has the only "<" direction, sequentialize that loop. If there are several such loops, they will all need to be sequentialized at some point in the process.

To show that loop selection is *NP*-complete, it is useful to visualize the loops as bit vectors with a "1" in each position corresponding to a dependence that would be carried by this loop in the outermost position. Illustrating with the previous direction matrix:

$$
\begin{bmatrix}
1 & 1 & 0 & 0 \\
1 & 0 & 1 & 0 \\
1 & 0 & 0 & 1 \\
0 & 1 & 0 & 0 \\
0 & 0 & 1 & 0 \\
0 & 0 & 0 & 1
\end{bmatrix}
$$

Then the problem of loop selection corresponds to finding a minimal basis among the loops, with "logical or" as the combining operation. In turn, this is the same as the minimum set cover problem, which is known to be *NP*-complete. This is the reason that loop selection is best done by a heuristic.

We conclude this section with a simple example to illustrate some of the principles involved in heuristic loop selection. Consider the code below, which is intended to resemble a stencil calculation:

```
DO I = 2, N
   DO J = 2, M
      DO K = 2, L
         A(I,J,K) = A(I,J-1,K)+ A(I-1,J,K-1) &
            + A(I,J+1,K+1) + A(I-1,J,K+1)
      ENDDO
   ENDDO
ENDDO
```

This code has four dependences, one for each of the right-hand side references. Note that the third reference gives rise to an antidependence. The direction matrix is given below, where the dependence vectors for the right-hand side are in order from top to bottom:

$$
\begin{bmatrix}
= & < & = \\
< & = & < \\
= & < & < \\
< & = & >
\end{bmatrix}
$$

The interesting thing to observe about this example is that the innermost loop cannot be moved to the outermost position because it has a ">" entry. Therefore, this entry must be covered by some entry in an outer sequential loop. This will necessitate that the outermost loop be sequentialized. In addition, the next outermost loop must also be sequentialized because the first row of the direction matrix represents a dependence that cannot be satisfied by sequentializing any other loop. Any heuristic should be designed to discover these facts. In this case, the heuristic described earlier would select the J-loop for sequentialization because the first direction vector has its only non-"=" in that loop. Then it will select the I-loop to cover the inner loop. The result is

```
DO J = 2, M
    DO I = 2, N
        PARALLEL DO K = 2, L
            A(I,J,K) = A(I,J-1,K) + A(I-1,J,K-1) &
                + A(I,J+1,K+1) + A(I-1,J,K+1)
        ENDDO
    ENDDO
ENDDO
```

It should be clear that this level of complexity would be difficult for a programmer to manage.

6.3.3   Loop Reversal

Consider a variation on the example at the beginning of Section 6.3.2:

```
DO I = 2, N + 1
    DO J = 2, M + 1
        DO K = 1, L
            A(I,J,K) = A(I,J-1,K+1) + A(I-1,J,K+1)
        ENDDO
    ENDDO
ENDDO
```

This code has a direction vector in which all the directions in the innermost loop are ">":

$$\begin{bmatrix} = & < & > \\ < & = & > \end{bmatrix}$$

This provides an opportunity to improve the parallelization. Although we cannot immediately move the inner loop to the outermost loop position, we can reverse the direction of iteration of the inner loop (i.e., run from L to 1 by –1), which reverses the directions for that loop in every dependence. Once this transformation, known as *loop reversal*, is performed, we can move the loop to the outermost position, resulting in the following direction matrix:

$$\begin{bmatrix} < & = & < \\ < & < & = \end{bmatrix}$$

Since all dependences are now carried by the outer loop, running it sequentially allows the two inner loops to be run in parallel. The code that results is

```
DO K = L, 1, -1
   PARALLEL DO I = 2, N + 1
      PARALLEL DO J = 2, M + 1
         A(I,J,K) = A(I,J-1,K+1) + A(I-1,J,K+1)
      END PARALLEL DO
   END PARALLEL DO
ENDDO
```

This example shows that loop reversal can increase the range of options available to the loop selection heuristic—it is no longer forced to cover every ">" direction if it can change these directions by reversing the loop.

6.3.4 Loop Skewing for Parallelization

In Chapter 5, loop skewing was used to create inner loop parallelism by converting "=" directions to "<" directions. This conversion can also be beneficial when generating asynchronous parallelism. Consider the following example:

```
DO I = 2, N + 1
   DO J = 2, M + 1
      DO K = 1, L
         A(I,J,K) = A(I,J-1,K) + A(I-1,J,K)
         B(I,J,K+1) = B(I,J,K) + A(I,J,K)
      ENDDO
   ENDDO
ENDDO
```

The direction matrix for this example is

$$\begin{bmatrix} = & < & = \\ < & = & = \\ = & = & < \\ = & = & = \end{bmatrix}$$

Expressing the dependences more precisely as a distance matrix produces

$$\begin{bmatrix} 0 & 1 & 0 \\ 1 & 0 & 0 \\ 0 & 0 & 1 \\ 0 & 0 & 0 \end{bmatrix}$$

Since every loop carries a dependence, there is no obvious way to immediately generate parallelism. *Loop skewing*, described in Section 5.9, can be used to convert "=" directions to "<" on an inner loop. When the inner loop is then moved to the outside and sequentialized, it may make many other loops parallel.

The innermost loop in the example can be skewed with respect to the two outer loops by using the substitution

$$k = K + I + J$$

which yields the code

```
DO I = 2, N + 1
   DO J = 2, M + 1
      DO k = I + J + 1, I + J + L
         A(I,J,k-I-J) = A(I,J-1,k-I-J) + A(I-1,J,k-I-J)
         B(I,J,k-I-J+1) = B(I,J,k-I-J) + A(I,J,k-I-J)
      ENDDO
   ENDDO
ENDDO
```

The transformed direction matrix for this code is

$$
\begin{bmatrix}
= & < & < \\
< & = & < \\
= & = & < \\
= & = & =
\end{bmatrix}
$$

Note that the innermost loop now consists of "<" entries in every position corresponding to a carried dependence, so that if it is moved to the outermost position and sequentialized, it will leave the inner loops with no carried dependences. Applying this transformation to the code yields a nest in which both inner loops can be parallelized:

```
DO k = 5, N + M + 1
   DO I = MAX(2,k-M-L-1), MIN(N+1,k-L-2)
      DO J = MAX(2,k-I-L), MIN(M+1,k-I-1)
         A(I,J,k-I-J) = A(I,J-1,k-I-J) + A(I-1,J,k-I-J)
         B(I,J,k-I-J+1) = B(I,J,k-I-J) + A(I,J,k-I-J)
      ENDDO
   ENDDO
ENDDO
```

As we shall see, skewing has two properties that are critical to parallelization. First, it can be used to transform the skewed loop into one that can be interchanged to the outermost position without changing the meaning of the program.

Second, it can be used to transform the skewed loop in such a way that, after outward interchange, it will carry all dependences formerly carried by the loop with respect to which it is skewed.

Both of these properties hold for the same reason. We know from previous discussion that a loop can be moved to the outermost position if all the direction matrix entries in its column are either "=" or "<". If a loop has a ">" direction in some dependence, then that dependence must be carried by an outer loop. Therefore, if we skew the target loop with respect to that outer loop by a sufficiently large constant k, we can convert the direction to one that is "=" or "<", which establishes the first property.

The second property follows from the same argument. For each dependence that is carried by some outer loop, there is a positive distance in the column for the carrier loop. Skewing by a large enough factor with respect to that carrier loop ensures that the distance matrix column for the skewed loop will contain only entries that are greater than 0. Hence, this loop will carry all dependences when it is moved to the outermost position.

These observations lead us to a selection heuristic for algorithm *Parallelize* in Figure 6.19 that incorporates loop skewing. The strategy employed in this heuristic is to try to sequentialize at most one outer loop to find parallelism in the next loop. Furthermore, it attempts to parallelize the loop in the outermost position if possible. This is accomplished by first trying to find a loop that covers the current outermost loop and that can be interchanged to the outermost position. If such a loop can be found, it can be sequentialized to make parallelization of the current outer loop possible on the next step.

If the first attempt fails, then we will try skewing. If we can skew some loop with respect to the outer loop and interchange it to the outermost position, we will do so. If not, we try to find a pair of loops that can move to the two outermost positions where the inner loop can be skewed with respect to the outer loop. Finally, if this fails, we choose to sequentialize the loop that can be moved to the outermost position and covers the most other loops. This selection heuristic is presented in Figure 6.20.

Note that *select_loop and interchange* does not attempt skewing with respect to more than one loop, but it can be easily extended to do this. How skewing is applied by the algorithm can be illustrated on the following code:

```
DO K = 1, L
    DO J = 1, M
        DO I = 1, N
            A(I+1,J+1,K+1) = A(I,J,K+1) + A(I,J+1,K) &
                            + A(I+1,J+1,K)
        ENDDO
    ENDDO
ENDDO
```

The direction matrix for this loop is

procedure *select_loop_and_interchange*(L)

// L is the input loop nest
// upon return the outermost loop is selected for sequentialization

let $\{l_1, l_2, \ldots, l_k\}$ be a collection of remaining loops in L;

if any of $l_2, \ldots, l_k$ (say, l_p) can be moved to the outermost position
   and l_p covers l_1 in that position
then interchange l_p to the outermost position;
else if l_1 covers one of $l_2, \ldots, l_k$ **then** leave l_1 in the outermost position;

else begin
   let l_t and l_s be the outermost pair of loops such that
      (1) l_t may be legally moved to the outermost position
      (2) l_s may be legally moved to the next outermost position (within l_t)
      (3) both l_t and l_s have only constant distances in the distance matrix;
   if such a pair exists **then begin** // try skewing
      interchange l_t to the outermost position;
      skew l_s with respect to l_t in such a way that
         (a) l_s may be interchanged outside of l_t and
         (b) each entry in the distance matrix for l_s corresponding to loops
            that l_t carries in the outermost position is at least 1;
      interchange l_s to the outermost position;
  end
  else begin // find a covering loop for sequentialization
      // select a loop that has a chance of uncovering parallelism
      l := the outermost loop that
         (a) can be moved to the outermost position and
         (b) must be sequentialized (if such a loop exists) and
         (c) has the most "<" directions in its column;
      interchange l to the outermost position;
  end
end
end *select_loop_and_interchange*

Figure 6.20 Selection heuristic with loop skewing.

$$\begin{bmatrix} = & < & < \\ < & = & < \\ < & = & = \end{bmatrix}$$

Clearly, all distances are constant (1 or 0). The outermost loop covers neither of the other loops, so we chose to skew the middle loop with respect to the outer loop by making the substitution

$$j = J + K$$

All references to J in the loop will be replaced by

$$j - K$$

After these substitutions, the transformed loop nest becomes

```
DO K = 1, L
    DO j = K + 1, K + M
        DO I = 1, N
            A(I+1,j-K+1,K+1) = A(I,j-K,K+1) + &
                A(I,j-K+1,K) + A(I+1,j-K+1,K)
        ENDDO
    ENDDO
ENDDO
```

The revised direction matrix for this loop is

$$
\begin{bmatrix}
= & < & < \\
< & < & < \\
< & < & =
\end{bmatrix}
$$

When this is interchanged to the outermost position, both inner loops can be parallelized, although the inner loop may be left sequential to optimize for memory hierarchy performance (as we will see in the next section).

```
DO j = 2, L + M
    PARALLEL DO K = MAX(1,j-M), MIN(L,j-1)
        DO I = 1, N
            A(I+1,j-K+1,K+1) = A(I,j-K,K+1) + &
                A(I,j-K+1,K) + A(I+1,j-K+1,K)
        ENDDO
    ENDDO
ENDDO
```

While the loop selection heuristic in Figure 6.20 finds parallelism in the next to outermost loop, the resulting parallelism is not necessarily well balanced. In our example, the loop on K executes a variable number of iterations between 1 and L. However, in the case of asynchronous parallelism, this is not so great a problem as it was with vector parallelism because most parallel loops are self-scheduled and can deal with varying amounts of work. We shall return to this subject in Section 10.5.

6.3.5   Unimodular Transformations

Loop interchange, loop skewing, and loop reversal are all examples of a very general set of transformations known as *unimodular transformations*. The term "unimodular" is borrowed from linear algebra, where it describes a mapping (or matrix) that permutes its domain without changing the size of the domain.

DEFINITION
6.8

A transformation represented by a matrix T is *unimodular* if

1. T is square,

2. all the elements of T are integral, and

3. the absolute value of the determinant of T is 1.

If matrices T_1 and T_2 are both unimodular, then their product $T_1 \cdot T_2$ is also unimodular (the product of two square matrices is square; both must have integral elements, and the sum and product of integers is integral; and the determinant of the product of two matrices is the product of the determinants of the matrices). In other words, any composition of unimodular transformations is unimodular.

Unimodular transformation theory has been used to support powerful goal-directed parallelization strategies (see Banerjee [36] and Wolf and Lam [277]). Many of these strategies are more formal versions of the methods that use the direction matrix, so we will not discuss them further here.

6.3.6 Profitability-Based Parallelization Methods

Because of the need for a minimum granularity for parallelism to be profitable and because there are many alternatives to be considered in parallel code generation, practical methods must employ some method for estimating the cost of different code arrangements. One study we conducted at Rice used a particularly effective strategy for discovering parallelizable loops in Fortran. The strategy succeeded on loops that could not be parallelized by existing commercial compilers. Unfortunately, once these loops were parallelized, the code ran substantially slower than before because of insufficient granularity of parallelism.

Therefore, some form of performance estimation will be needed to make parallel code generation effective. We will consider the use of a static performance estimation function that can be applied to any code fragment to estimate the running time of that fragment. It is not so important that such a function be accurate, but rather that it be good for selecting the better of two alternative code arrangements. In developing a static estimator, key considerations will be the cost of memory references in the code fragment and whether the granularity associated with a parallel loop is sufficient to make parallelization profitable.

One way to use such a cost function in code generation for a loop nest is to consider all possible permutations and parallelizations and pick the best one. This is impractical for two reasons. First, the total number of alternatives is exponential in the number of loops in a nest, and the cost of evaluating the cost estimate is usually significant, making this strategy unacceptably slow. Second, many of the loop upper bounds in a loop nest will not be known at compile time. Thus, it may be impossible to precisely estimate the running time. This might be overcome by generating a variety of loop arrangements and selecting the best one at run time, but the number of such arrangements is likely to cause an explosion in code size.

For these reasons, it is common to consider only a subset of the possible code arrangements, based on properties of the cost function itself. As an illustration, we present a code generation heuristic that uses the cost of memory references as the primary consideration in selecting the right permutation for a perfect loop nest. This method is based on work by Kennedy and McKinley [175].

We begin by developing a measure C_L of the cost of a particular loop when it is innermost in the nest. This cost is essentially an upper bound on the number of cache misses generated by the loop when it is innermost. We shall call this measure *loop cost*. To evaluate loop cost for a given loop, we perform three steps:

1. Subdivide all the references in the loop body into *reference groups*. Two references are in the same reference group if there is a loop-independent dependence or a constant-distance carried dependence from one to the other. Intuitively, a cache miss for the first of two references in the same reference group will be the only one experienced by the group because the second reference will find the desired line in cache.

2. For each reference group, determine whether subsequent accesses to the same reference are (a) loop invariant, (b) unit stride, or (c) nonunit stride. For case (a) assign the group a reference cost of 1 because only one cache miss will be experienced for the entire loop. For case (b) assign the group a reference cost equal to the number of iterations of the loop divided by the cache line size (in data items of the type referenced) because of reuse within the cache line. For case (c), assume no reuse within a cache line and assign a cost equal to the number of iterations in the loop.

3. Assign the loop a cost equal to the sum of the reference costs times the aggregate number of times the loop will be executed if it is innermost in the loop nest. This is essentially equal to the product of the loop bounds for the outer loops.

As an example, consider the matrix multiplication inner loop:

```
DO I = 1, N
   DO J = 1, N
      DO K = 1, N
         C(I,J) = C(I,J) + A(I,K) * B(K,J)
      ENDDO
   ENDDO
ENDDO
```

When the K-loop is innermost the reference cost for C is 1 because it is loop invariant. The reference cost for A is N because it is nonunit stride, and the reference cost for B is N/L, where L is the cache line size, because of the unit stride. Hence the total loop cost for the K-loop is $N^3(1+1/L) + N^2$. When the J-loop is innermost, the cost is $2N^3 + N^2$ because the C and B references are nonunit stride and the A reference is invariant. When the I-loop is innermost, we have two unit-stride reference groups and one invariant for a cost of $2N^3/L + N^2$. Thus, the I-loop has the lowest loop cost and is the preferred innermost loop, from the perspective of cache reuse. Of course, this comparison of symbolic values assumes that the upper bounds are large. (Otherwise, the number of iterations would be small and thus the loop ordering would be unimportant.) Table 6.1 summarizes the loop costs.

To find a best total order, we simply order the loops from innermost to outermost by increasing loop cost, on the theory that inner loop reuse could also be outer loop reuse if the cache is big enough. This would imply that the following loop order should be selected for best cache performance:

```
DO J - 1, N
   DO K - 1, N
      DO I - 1, N
         C(I,J) - C(I,J) + A(I,K) * B(K,J)
      ENDDO
   ENDDO
ENDDO
```

Even if the outer loop cache reuse is not achieved, it might be induced by strip mining.

Once a desired loop order is established by the loop cost heuristic, the next step is to put the loops into a permutation that is as close as possible to the desired order, although it may not be possible to achieve exactly the desired loop order because some permutations will be illegal. An algorithm for doing this is given in Figure 6.21.

It is easy to show that if any legal permutation has the desired innermost loop in the innermost position, this algorithm will find a permutation that has the desired loop innermost [176]. This memory-based loop interchange algorithm is but one heuristic approach to folding profitability information into a code generation scheme without suffering exponential execution time. Experiments have shown that it is quite effective in practice [176].

Table 6.1 Summary of loop costs

Inner loop index	Cost
I	$2N^3/L + N^2$
J	$2N^3 + N^2$
K	$N^3(1+1/L) + N^2$

procedure *select_permutation*(O,P)

// Input: A desired loop permutation order $O = (i_1, i_2, \ldots, i_n)$ and
//   the original direction matrix D for the loop.
// Output: A nearby permutation P.

$P := \emptyset;$
for $i := 1$ **to** n **do begin**
    select the leftmost loop l in O such that $(P_1, P_2, \ldots, P_{i-1}, l)$ has no
        illegal direction vector prefixes;
    remove l from O;
    append l to the end of P, so that it becomes P_i;
end
end *select_permutation*

Figure 6.21 Selecting a nearby permutation.

Once we have the loops in an optimal memory order, a parallel code generation system may wish to mark the inner loop sequential if it would perform very
well in cache—that is, it shows stride-one access that would be lost if it were parallelized. This marking would prevent the loop from being parallelized and moved
away from the innermost position. If this is the only parallel loop, a compromise
might be to strip-mine the loop and interchange the iterate-by-strip loop to the
outside for parallel execution. Of course, this will only work if the loop has
enough iterations to simultaneously exploit stride-one access and provide a sufficient degree of parallelism to obtain significant speedup.

It is fairly easy to adapt the code generation algorithm *ParallelizeNest* to incorporate this strategy, so we will not present a revised algorithm here.

6.4 Imperfectly Nested Loops

When loops are imperfectly nested at the outermost level and the outermost loop
cannot be directly parallelized, maximal loop distribution can be an effective
transformation because it produces a collection of loops, each of which may be
perfectly nested. In the case where an imperfectly nested loop is produced, it is
because of a tight recurrence involving a statement and an inner loop, in which
case it may simply be better to sequentialize the outer loop and move on.

In this section, we consider code generation strategies in which maximal
loop distribution is tried first and then multilevel loop fusion is used to increase
granularity.

6.4.1 **Multilevel Loop Fusion**

The problem of fusion becomes even more difficult when dealing with loop nests because each loop nest could have a different optimal permutation. If we assume that we will only fuse loops that were originally fused in the loop nest before distribution, then different loop permutations can interfere with loop fusion. For example, consider the following loop nest:

```
DO I = 1, N
   DO J = 1, M
      A(I,J+1) = A(I,J) + C
      B(I+1,J) = B(I,J) + D
   ENDDO
ENDDO
```

After distribution, it is clear that each statement will do better with a different outer loop:

```
PARALLEL DO I = 1, N
   DO J = 1, M
      A(I,J+1) = A(I,J) + C
   ENDDO
END PARALLEL DO

PARALLEL DO J = 1, M
   DO I = 1, N
      B(I+1,J) = B(I,J) + D
   ENDDO
END PARALLEL DO
```

Although each nest has outer loop parallelism, the two nests are trickier to fuse because the outer loops have different headers with different loop iteration bounds. In addition, because the subscript positions for the loop indices differ, it may be unwise to fuse the nests because of memory hierarchy considerations.

It has been shown that loop fusion in the presence of loop interchange is *NP*-complete [52] in the number of loops. The following loop illustrates one of the reasons that this problem is so hard:

```
DO I = 1, N
   DO J = 1, M
      A(I,J) = A(I,J) + X
      B(I+1,J) = A(I,J) + B(I,J)
      C(I,J+1) = A(I,J) + C(I,J)
      D(I+1,J) = B(I+1,J) + C(I,J) + D(I,J)
   ENDDO
ENDDO
```

This nest distributes over all four statements to yield the four loops:

```
DO I = 1, N ! Can be parallel
   DO J = 1, M ! Can be parallel
      A(I,J) = A(I,J) + X
   ENDDO
ENDDO

DO I = 1, N ! Sequential
   DO J = 1, M ! Can be parallel
      B(I+1,J) = A(I,J) + B(I,J)
   ENDDO
ENDDO

DO I = 1, N ! Can be parallel
   DO J = 1, M ! Sequential
      C(I,J+1) = A(I,J) + C(I,J)
   ENDDO
ENDDO

DO I = 1, N ! Sequential
   DO J = 1, M ! Can be parallel
      D(I+1,J) = B(I+1,J) + C(I,J) + D(I,J)
   ENDDO
ENDDO
```

The problem with this loop can be illustrated by the graph in Figure 6.22. In this diagram, each subloop is represented by a node labeled by the variable that is assigned in that subloop. Inside each node the loop indices of the loops that can be parallel are listed.

The problem is to determine which loop to fuse into the A-loop. The A-loop produces values that are used in both the B- and C-loops. Hence we would like to fuse with each of those loops. However, we cannot fuse with both without giving up parallelism. If we fuse the A-loop with the B-loop, we will need to make the loop on J parallel in the resulting nest. But then a subsequent fusion with the C-loop would force both the I- and J-levels of the result to be sequential. So we must choose.

The problem is that we cannot determine the optimal choice by simply examining the successors. Although they both look equally good at this point, it is definitely advantageous to fuse with the C-loop. To see why, suppose we fuse with the B-loop instead. The resulting loop could not be fused with the C-loop for the reason we just described. Furthermore, it cannot be fused with the D-loop because we cannot fuse two loops if there is a path in the dependence graph from one to the other that passes through a loop that is not fused into the group. In this case, the path through the C-loop forces us to keep the D-loop separate. The result has two barriers and three parallel loops:

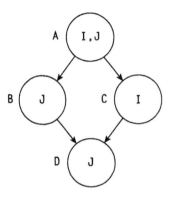

Figure 6.22 Two-level fusion example.

```
PARALLEL DO J - 1, M
    DO I - 1, N
        A(I,J) - A(I,J) + X
        B(I+1,J) - A(I,J) + B(I,J)
    ENDDO
END PARALLEL DO

PARALLEL DO I - 1, N
    DO J - 1, M
        C(I,J+1) - A(I,J) + C(I,J)
    ENDDO
END PARALLEL DO

PARALLEL DO J - 1, M
    DO I - 1, N
        D(I+1,J) - B(I+1,J) + C(I,J) + D(I,J)
    ENDDO
END PARALLEL DO
```

On the other hand, if we fuse the A- and C-loops, we can then fuse the B- and D-loops, which would leave only one barrier and two loop nests.

```
PARALLEL DO I - 1, N
    DO J - 1, M
        A(I,J) - A(I,J) + X
        C(I,J+1) = A(I,J) + C(I,J)
    ENDDO
END PARALLEL DO

PARALLEL DO J - 1, M
    DO I - 1, N
```

```
            B(I+1,J) = A(I,J) + B(I,J)
            D(I+1,J) = B(I+1,J) + C(I,J) + D(I,J)
        ENDDO
    END PARALLEL DO
```

This version is clearly superior in terms of its data reuse and number of processors. The problem is that lookahead is required to determine what to do in situations where fusion decisions need to be made. As it happens, lookahead of arbitrary length can be required.

Because of these problems, most parallel code generation systems use some heuristic to determine how to fuse loops with multiple levels. An interesting heuristic is to fuse with the loop that cannot be fused with one of its successors. The rationale behind this heuristic, which incidentally solves the example problem, is that if a successor cannot be fused with its successor, then you are going to need at least one barrier anyway. So why immediately choose to have two by putting another barrier in front of that successor? This heuristic was used in the parallel code generation system for PFC.

6.4.2 A Parallel Code Generation Algorithm

In this section we develop a code generation algorithm for the general case—a loop nest with hierarchy. The main problem here is to decide when to use loop distribution and fusion and which loops to fuse once parallelization of the separate nests is done.

As usual, we begin with a top-down scheme that attempts to parallelize the outermost loop nest. If it succeeds in finding sufficient parallelism, no further effort is required. Otherwise, the outer loops are distributed in an attempt to find more parallelism on inner loops. The resulting routine—*Parallelize*—is shown in Figure 6.23. To handle perfect nests, it employs the routine *ParallelizeNest* presented in Figure 6.19, with the loop selection heuristic from Figure 6.20. We assume that *ParallelizeNest* is modified to reorder loops to improve memory hierarchy performance, as discussed in Section 6.3.6, and marks inner loops sequential if the loop needs to run on a single processor to use cache effectively.

Parallelize first invokes *ParallelizeNest* to attempt the perfect-nest strategies discussed in Section 6.3. If this fails, it tries distributing the loop into a collection of subnests, parallelizing each one recursively, and fusing as many of the resulting nests as possible. If the loop cannot be distributed, it sequentializes the outermost loop and calls itself recursively on all top-level loops in the body of that loop. When this process is complete, it attempts to merge as many of the resulting nests as possible.

A key component of this algorithm is the routine *Merge* in Figure 6.24, which fuses the parallelized loops back together whenever possible. *Merge* uses a method

procedure *Parallelize(l,D_l)*

> // *l* is the loop nest to be parallelized
> // *D_l* is the dependence graph restricted to statements in *l*;
>
> *ParallelizeNest(l, success)*;
> **if** ¬*success* **then begin**
>
> > **if** *l* can be distributed **then begin**
> > > distribute *l* into loop nests $l_1, l_2, \ldots, l_n$;
> > > **for** $i := 1$ **to** n **do begin**
> > > > let D_i be the set of dependences between statements in l_i;
> > > > *Parallelize(l_i, D_i)*;
> > > **end**
> > > *Merge($\{l_1, l_2, \ldots, l_n\}$)*;
> > **end**
> >
> > **else begin**
> > > // either *l* carries a recurrence or it encloses a single statement
> > > // that must run on one processor for memory performance
> > > // Note that *ParallelizeNest* has generated a sequential loop
> > > // for each statement in the nest. However, it has not tried to
> > > // distribute the loop immediately inside the outer loop;
> > >
> > > **for each** outer loop l_o nested in *l* **do begin**
> > > > let D_o be the set of dependences between statements in l_o
> > > > > less dependences carried by *l*;
> > > > *Parallelize(l_o,D_o)*;
> > > **end**
> > > let *S* be the set of outer loops and statements loops left in *l*;
> > > **if** $\|S\| > 1$ **then** *Merge(S)*;
> > **end**
> **end**
> **end**
> **end** *Parallelize*

Figure 6.23 A general code generation algorithm.

---

similar to the one used in the algorithm for sequential-parallel fusion given in Figure 6.9. The basic idea is to classify the various loop nests by *type*, where each type represents the outermost loop in the original nest that can be made outermost in the distributed nest without changing one of the critical performance factors, such as parallelism, granularity, or memory performance in the innermost position. Furthermore, two loops are of different types if the canonical outermost loop is parallel in one and sequential in the other. As an example, consider the following loop nest:

procedure *Merge(S)*

// *S* is the set of loop nests to be fused
// *Note:* single statements may be considered loops of a special type

let $\{t_1, t_2, \ldots, t_m\}$ be the collection of loop types;
fuse the outermost loops in *S* of each type in order
 using *TypedFusion* as given in Figure 6.9;
for each fused group *G* **do begin**
 let $\{l_1, l_2, \ldots, l_k\}$ be the loop nests inside fused group *G*;
 Merge($\{l_1, l_2, \ldots, l_k\}$);
end
end *Merge*

Figure 6.24 Loop fusion for a collection of loop nests.

```
DO J = 1, M
   DO I = 1, N
      A(I+1,J+1) = A(I+1,J) + C
      X(I,J) = A(I,J) + C
   ENDDO
ENDDO
```

Neither loop in this nest can be parallelized, so the outer loop is distributed:

```
DO J = 1, M
   DO I = 1, N
      A(I+1,J+1) = A(I+1,J) + C
   ENDDO
ENDDO
DO J = 1, M
   DO I = 1, N
      X(I,J) = A(I,J) + C
   ENDDO
ENDDO
```

Each of these loops can be parallelized, the second in two dimensions, although the code generator is likely to sequentialize the inner loop of the second nest to ensure that it has acceptable memory performance:

```
PARALLEL DO I = 1, N
   DO J = 1, M
      A(I+1,J+1) = A(I,J+1) + C
   ENDDO
ENDDO
```

```
PARALLEL DO J = 1, M
    DO I = 1, N ! Left sequential for memory hierarchy
        X(I,J) = A(I,J) + C
    ENDDO
ENDDO
```

The type of the first loop nest is (I-loop, parallel). The type of the second loop nest is (J-loop, parallel). Thus these loops have different types and cannot be merged at the outermost level.

A slightly more complicated nest is the following, which is similar to the example from Section 6.4.1:

```
DO J = 1, M
    DO I = 1, N
        A(I,J) = A(I,J) + X
        B(I+1,J) = A(I,J) + B(I,J)
        C(I,J+1) = A(I,J) + C(I,J)
        D(I+1,J) = B(I+1,J) + C(I,J) + D(I,J)
    ENDDO
ENDDO
```

After distribution and parallelization, this becomes

```
L1  PARALLEL DO J = 1, M
        DO I = 1, N ! Sequentialized for memory hierarchy
            A(I,J) = A(I,J) + X
        END PARALLEL DO
    ENDDO

L2  PARALLEL DO J = 1, M
        DO I = 1, N
            B(I+1,J) = A(I,J) + B(I,J)
        ENDDO
    END PARALLEL DO

L3  PARALLEL DO I = 1, N
        DO J = 1, M
            C(I,J+1) = A(I,J) + C(I,J)
        ENDDO
    END PARALLEL DO

L4  PARALLEL DO J = 1, M
        DO I = 1, N
            D(I+1,J) = B(I+1,J) + C(I,J) + D(I,J)
        ENDDO
    ENDDO
```

The first, second, and fourth loops will be classified as a single type. The fusion graph is shown in Figure 6.25.

A greedy fusion algorithm will merge loops L_1 and L_2, leaving loop L_4 separate. In addition, the recursive call to *Merge* will also fuse the inner sequential loops. The result is

```
L₁   PARALLEL DO J = 1, M
        DO I = 1, N
           A(I,J) = A(I,J) + X
           B(I+1,J) = A(I,J) + B(I,J)
        ENDDO
     END PARALLEL DO

L₃   PARALLEL DO I = 1, N
        DO J = 1, M
           C(I,J+1) = A(I,J) + C(I,J)
        ENDDO
     END PARALLEL DO

L₄   PARALLEL DO J = 1, M
        DO I = 1, N
           D(I+1,J) = B(I+1,J) + C(I,J) + D(I,J)
        ENDDO
     ENDDO
```

As we pointed out in Section 6.4.1, it is possible to have fewer parallel loops in this example. However, we are prepared to accept this result because it has better memory performance and the problem of minimizing the number of parallel loops is *NP*-complete.

There are two final points to be made about *Parallelize*. First, it is often useful to apply it to a collection of loop nests at the outermost level in a given program

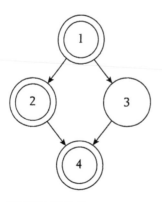

Figure 6.25 Parallel and sequential subgraphs.

procedure *DriveParallelize(L,D)*

    // *L* is a list of loop nests (and single statements) at the outermost level
    // *D* is the dependence graph for the collection of statements in *L*
    for each loop nest $l \in L$ **do begin**
        let D_l be the set of dependences between statements in *l*;
        Parallelize(l,D_l);
    end
    if $\|L\| > 1$ **then** Merge(*L*);
end *DriveParallelize*

Figure 6.26 Driver for parallelization process on a set of loops and statements.

or procedure. To do this, a simple driver is needed, which could be included at the top level of *Parallelize* or left to stand alone. The driver is shown in Figure 6.26. It will be used in the extended example in Section 6.5.

The second observation is that *Parallelize*, as written, always favors paralleliz-ing a whole loop, even if it is not the outermost loop, before trying any kind of dis-tribution. This may not turn out to be the optimal strategy on every machine. It is possible that a better result could be obtained by trying both strategies, scoring them according to some metric, and then choosing the best one. We leave it as an exercise (Exercise 6.4) to revise *Parallelize* to accomplish this.

6.5 **An Extended Example**

We will conclude the treatment of code generation in loop nests with a discus-sion of a particular sample code. The code we choose is a subroutine of Erle-bacher, a NASA differential equation solver written by Thomas M. Eidson. The original code is given in Figure 6.27. Notice that the loops are already maximally distributed.

If we apply the general multilevel code generation algorithm in Figure 6.23 to each of these nests, the J-loop will be parallelized in each of the nests, while the loops on index I will be left serial to ensure that sequential access takes place on a single processor. Since the outermost loops that result are all compatible—they are all parallel and run from J = 1 to JMAXD—the outer loops will all be merged by the first application of *TypedFusion* to produce the code in Figure 6.28.

TypedFusion is then applied to the loops at the next level, all of which are sequential. This produces the fusion graph shown in Figure 6.29. Here loops L_1, L_3, and L_4 (with the outer loop on I) are assigned one type and loops L_2 and L_5 (with the outer loop on K) are assigned another. This second pass produces the final program shown in Figure 6.30, with a single parallel loop at the outermost position and all inner loops using stride-one access of the key arrays.

```
L₁   DO J = 1, JMAXD
        DO I = 1, IMAXD
           F(I,J,1) = F(I,J,1) * B(1)
        ENDDO
     ENDDO

L₂   DO K = 2, N - 1
        DO J = 1, JMAXD
           DO I = 1, IMAXD
              F(I,J,K) = (F(I,J,K)-A(K)*F(I,J,K-1)) * B(K)
           ENDDO
        ENDDO
     ENDDO

L₃   DO J = 1, JMAXD
        DO I = 1, IMAXD
           TOT(I,J) = 0.0
        ENDDO
     ENDDO

L₄   DO J = 1, JMAXD
        DO I = 1, IMAXD
           TOT(I,J) = TOT(I,J) + D(1) * F(I,J,1)
        ENDDO
     ENDDO

L₅   DO K = 2, N - 1
        DO J = 1, JMAXD
           DO I = 1, IMAXD
              TOT(I,J) = TOT(I,J) + D(K) * F(I,J,K)
           ENDDO
        ENDDO
     ENDDO
```

Figure 6.27 Subroutine *tridvpk* from Erlebacher.

6.6 Packaging of Parallelism

Often the performance of parallelized code depends not only on how much parallelism is found but also on how it is packaged. We have already seen in Section 6.3.6 one trade-off between parallelism and performance of the memory hierarchy. In this section we consider trade-offs between parallelism and granularity of synchronization. As we said in the introduction, there is a cost, which varies from machine to machine, associated with every synchronization operation. If there were no costs for initiation and synchronization of parallel threads, then it

```
L₁    PARALLEL DO J = 1, JMAXD
         DO I = 1, IMAXD
            F(I,J,1) = F(I,J,1) * B(1)
         ENDDO

L₂    DO K = 2, N - 1
         DO I = 1, IMAXD
            F(I,J,K) = (F(I,J,K)-A(K)*F(I,J,K-1)) * B(K)
         ENDDO
      ENDDO

L₃    DO I = 1, IMAXD
         TOT(I,J) = 0.0
      ENDDO

L₄    DO I = 1, IMAXD
         TOT(I,J) = TOT(I,J) + D(1) * F(I,J,1)
      ENDDO

L₅    DO K = 2, N - 1
         DO I = 1, IMAXD
            TOT(I,J) = TOT(I,J) + D(K) * F(I,J,K)
         ENDDO
      ENDDO
   ENDDO
```

Figure 6.28 Subroutine *tridvpk* from Erlebacher after single-nest parallelization.

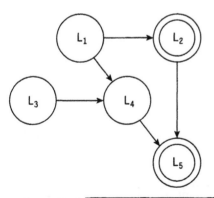

Figure 6.29 Fusion graph for Erlebacher.

would always be best to package the parallelism at the finest granularity. Then the zero-cost scheduler would always keep all processors busy until all the work was done. The maximum load imbalance would be equal to the largest granule of

```
PARALLEL DO J = 1, JMAXD
  DO I = 1, IMAXD
    F(I,J,1) = F(I,J,1) * B(1)
    TOT(I,J) = 0.0
    TOT(I,J) = TOT(I,J) + D(1) * F(I,J,1)
  ENDDO

  DO K = 2, N - 1
    DO I = 1, IMAXD
      F(I,J,K) = (F(I,J,K)-A(K)*F(I,J,K-1)) * B(K)
      TOT(I,J) = TOT(I,J) + D(K) * F(I,J,K)
    ENDDO
  ENDDO
ENDDO
```

Figure 6.30 Final code for subroutine *tridvpk* from Erlebacher.

work executed on the parallel processor, and the amount of time spent in overhead would be zero.

Because the cost of thread initiation and synchronization is greater than zero
on every real system, the trade-off becomes more complicated. Larger granularity
work units mean that scheduling and synchronization need to be done less frequently at the cost of less parallelism and often poorer load balance. These trade-
offs need to be managed by the compiler differently for each target platform.

In this section we will discuss two tools for managing the trade-off between
parallelism and synchronization. Strip mining is a strategy for increasing granularity directly by reducing the total number of available parallel processes. Pipelining,
on the other hand, presents a way to achieve parallelism through explicit synchronization, when no other method is available. As we will see, pipelining involves
yet another trade-off between granularity and parallelism.

6.6.1 Strip Mining

Many dependence-free loops whose iterations can be correctly executed in parallel may not be *efficiently* executed in parallel if naively scheduled. Quite commonly, there may not be enough work in a single loop iteration to justify scheduling that iteration as a single entity. In such a case, grouping the iterations into sets,
each of which is treated as a schedulable unit, will provide more efficient use of
parallelism. The analogous transformation for vectorization is strip mining—converting the available parallelism into a form more suitable for the hardware. The
following simple loop will illustrate the advantages of this transformation for
parallelism:

```
DO I = 1, N
    A(I) = A(I) + B(I)
ENDDO
```

If there are exactly P processors available to execute the loop, then the best load balance and synchronization minimization is achieved by

```
k = CEIL(N/P)
PARALLEL DO I = 1, N, k
    DO j = I, MIN(I+k-1,N)
        A(j) = A(j) + B(j)
    ENDDO
END PARALLEL DO
```

In loops such as this one, where each iteration clearly requires the same amount of computation, finding the proper balance is easy once the number of loop iterations and the number of available processors are known. Since those values are frequently not known until run time, this strip mining is often done by special hardware (as was the case on the Convex C2 and C3).

In cases where execution time varies among iterations, such as in the following

```
DO I = 1, N
    DO J = 2, I
        A(I,J) = A(I,J-1) + B(I)
    ENDDO
ENDDO
```

providing an effective balance is much more difficult. Rather than strip-mining the parallel (outer, in this case) to an exact division among processors, it is usually preferable to choose a smaller block size. By doing so, processors that do less work (and thus finish quicker) can pick up some of the excess while more heavily loaded processors are still working, thereby providing some load balance. Smaller block sizes are also advantageous when processors begin work at staggered times, since that permits processors that begin work first to pick up more of the load. Several different schemes for dynamic scheduling of parallel processes have been proposed. These techniques will be discussed later in this chapter.

6.6.2 Pipeline Parallelism

An alternative form of coarsely parallel loop is a DOACROSS, which pipelines parallel loop iterations (basically using multiple processors as a high-level vector processor) with cross-iteration synchronization. For instance, the following loop

```
      DOACROSS I = 2, N
S₁      A(I) = B(I) + C(I)
        POST(EV(I))
        IF (I.GT.2) WAIT(EV(I-1))
S₂      C(I) = A(I-1) + A(I)
      ENDDO
```

can perform all instantiations of S_1 in parallel just as with a PARALLEL DO, but pipelines individual iterations of S_2 as the necessary results become available. In this example POST(EV(I)) signals that the event EV(I) has occurred and WAIT(EV(I)) blocks until the event is posted. By convention, all events are initialized to the nonposted state.

A more elaborate example is the pipelined version of the wavefront parallelization of finite difference relaxation. The sequential version of this loop nest is

```
DO I = 2, N - 1
   DO J = 2, N - 1
      A(I,J) = 0.25 * (A(I-1,J) + A(I,J-1) &
         + A(I+1,J) + A(I,J+1))
   ENDDO
ENDDO
```

We have already seen how to parallelize this using loop skewing, which can be thought of as a way of implementing pipelining. Now we will show how to implement it via a DOACROSS loop. In this implementation, we will run the outer loop in parallel and the inner loop sequentially. The important thing is to ensure that we do not begin to compute A(I+1,J) until we have computed A(I,J). As above, we will use a two-dimensional array of events to ensure that the computation is correctly synchronized.

```
POST(EV(1,1))
DOACROSS I = 2, N - 1
   DO J = 2, N - 1
      WAIT(EV(I-1,J-1))
      A(I,J) = 0.25 * (A(I-1,J) + A(I,J-1) &
         + A(I+1,J) + A(I,J+1))
      POST (EV(I,J))
   ENDDO
ENDDO
```

The execution of this parallel loop is depicted in Figure 6.31. Note that the arrows in this diagram represent a post-wait synchronization on a common event.

If there is substantial overhead involved in the synchronization, we may wish to group iterations together to reduce the frequency of synchronization. For

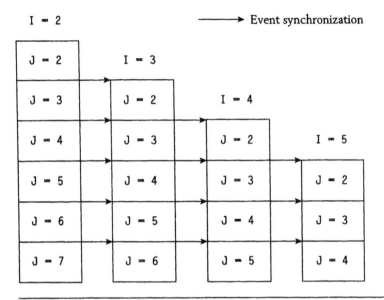

Figure 6.31 Pipelined parallelism.

example, if we wanted to synchronize less often, we could group the iterations into pairs as follows:

```
POST (EV(1,1))
DOACROSS I = 2, N - 1
  K = 0
  DO J = 2, N - 1, 2
    K = K + 1
    WAIT(EV(I-1,K))
    DO m = J, MIN(J+1,N-1)
      A(I,m) = 0.25 * (A(I-1,m) + A(I,m-1) &
        + A(I+1,m) + A(I,m+1))
    ENDDO
    POST (EV(I,K+1))
  ENDDO
ENDDO
```

Notice that we have paid for the lower frequency of synchronization by reducing the degree of parallelism. The difference can be seen in Figure 6.32. Although the last iteration of the I-loop starts much later, in this example, if the synchronization cost is large, the reduced synchronization frequency could pay for the cost in starting-time delay.

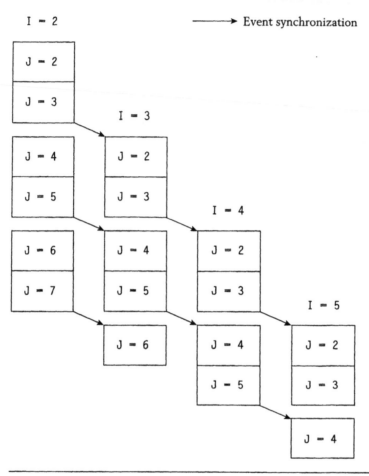

Figure 6.32 Pipelined parallelism with coarse granularity.

Because the value of DOACROSS is highly machine dependent (its execution efficiency relies heavily on processor synchronization), it should be used only when pipeline parallelism is the only possible way to improve performance.

6.6.3 Scheduling Parallel Work

Successfully scheduling parallel loop iterations across multiple processors is difficult and has been one of the major barriers to general acceptance of parallel programming. At one level, most of the primitives necessary are simple and already implemented on many operating systems. On Unix machines, for instance, all that is necessary is a lightweight thread (usually obtained by a variant of the system fork call) that shares address, data space, and stack, but has its own "thread-local" storage (usually created in the paging mechanism using copy-on-write semantics). The lightweight thread must be able to create its own stack to support subroutine calls; this is often done out of thread-local storage.

A fairly standard technique for scheduling parallel loop iterations in such an environment is to keep the loop variable in a synchronized, shared location. Loop iterations are dispensed to individual processors as the processors become free, in much the same fashion as customers are served in a "take-a-number" bakery (hence the name "bakery counter" scheduling). Under such a scheme, a parallel program executes a system call that procures the processors available for work at start-up time. As it obtains the processors, the program sends all but the "chief processor" (the start-up processor) into a low-priority idle pen, waiting for work. The chief processor then continues executing serially through the program. Upon finding a parallel loop, the chief processor initializes the loop variable and sets a jump vector for the idle pen that frees the contained processors by sending them to the start of the appropriate parallel loop (each thread has a copy of the same code space). Each processor goes to the bakery counter via synchronization to obtain a loop iteration to perform. This continues round-robin until all work is done, at which point the slave processors reenter the idle loop and the chief processor continues through the serial regions. In general, the bakery counter method provides reasonable balance between reducing synchronization overhead and balancing work across processors. However, there are cases when it can be very inefficient—for instance, if a processor assigned to an iteration is interrupted by the operating system for a long time to do other work. In such a case, that one iteration will hold up the rest of the computation.

The bakery counter algorithm illustrates the fundamental conflict involved in successfully scheduling parallelism—achieving the proper resolution between load balance and synchronization. To achieve the best load balance, the work in a parallel process should be broken into the smallest possible units (the finest granularity) possible. That way, there are the maximal number of units to dispense at any given time, maximizing the probability that processors will find new work to do as they complete tasks. This decreases the chance that one processor will get bogged down completing a task while others are waiting idly for work.

There is a cost involved in decreasing the granularity of parallelism, however; that cost is synchronization overhead. Dispensing a unit of work to a processor involves some synchronization—in the bakery counter scheme, that synchronization is the lock on the shared loop variable. As the granularity is made finer, there are more units to be dispensed; each time a unit is dispensed, more synchronization overhead is introduced. Obviously, executing a parallel process as one single thread (sequential execution) introduces no overhead; executing every instruction in a parallel process as an independent thread obviously introduces the maximal amount of overhead. Strictly minimizing overhead would argue for sequential execution, which, of course, provides the worst load balance. In other words, the lowest overhead is achieved at the point where the load balance is the worst, and the best load balance is achieved at the point of highest overhead. Somewhere in between are the points that make effective use of processors without introducing too much overhead; finding those points is the key to effective parallel scheduling.

To illustrate concretely how critical this balance is, consider the following parallel triangular matrix operation:

```
DO PARALLEL I = 1, 100
    DO J = 2, I
        A(J,I) = A(J-1,I) * 2.0
    ENDDO
ENDDO
```

The first parallel loop iteration performs no multiplications, the second performs one, the third performs two, and so on, with the last iteration doing N multiplications. If you were to schedule this on a machine with four processors, one way to achieve the minimal synchronization overhead would be to do the parallel loop in four chunks, each doing $N/4$ iterations. The problem, of course, is that the first processor will do roughly $N/8$ multiplies, the second processor will do roughly $3/8\ N$ multiplies, the third will do $5/8\ N$ multiplies, and the last will do $7/8\ N$ multiplies. In other words, the first three processors will sit idle while the last processor does most of the work. Breaking to the finest granularity—each processor doing one loop iteration at a time—provides the best load balance, but also the maximal synchronization overhead.

Balancing these two conflicting effects is the key to useful parallelism. As a general rule, any effective system for achieving this balance is going to involve dynamic scheduling of processors (as opposed to static scheduling), since the amount of parallelism and availability of processors is known only at run time. The bakery counter algorithm is an example of dynamic scheduling; it is also an example of *self-scheduling*, in that each processor determines what task to execute next (as opposed to having one global control unit control execution). Dynamic self-scheduling algorithms are essential for achieving load balance without creating too much overhead. Guided self-scheduling—the one dynamic self-scheduled approach that has been put forth with the goal of achieving this balance—is discussed in the next section.

6.6.4 Guided Self-Scheduling

As noted earlier, the key tension in effectively scheduling loop-level parallelism is balancing the load so as to keep all processors busy while not incurring enough overhead to destroy the benefits of parallelism. There are a number of sources of overhead in parallel computations, including accesses to loop variables, synchronized accesses to global variables, and extra cache misses required for auxiliary processors. It is very easy for this overhead to dominate any benefits derived from parallel execution. For instance, making the simple assumption that overhead is a constant factor σ_0 per processor (leading to a total overhead of $p\sigma_0$ for p processors) shows that parallel execution will *always* be slower than serial execution if

$$\sigma_0 \geq (NB)/p \qquad\qquad (6.3)$$

where N is the number of loop iterations and B is the time it takes for one iteration to execute. In other words, just the overhead of firing up p processors with a per-processor overhead of $1/p$ times the total execution time leads to an execution time greater than that obtained serially, meaning no benefit is possible from parallelism. It is not difficult at all to incur overheads of this magnitude, particularly as the number of processors p increases.

Guided self-scheduling (GSS) incorporates some level of static scheduling to guide dynamic self-scheduling. Fundamentally, GSS attempts to do two things: (1) minimize the amount of synchronization overhead and (2) keep all processors busy at all times. GSS reduces synchronization overhead by scheduling groups of iterations to a processor, rather than single iterations as in the bakery counter method. However, while parceling out a group of iterations to one processor, it tries to ensure there is enough work left to keep all other processors busy until the scheduled processor completes its task. The result is a dynamic load balance where in the early stages of processing a parallel region, large chunks of work are dispensed to processors; toward the end of a parallel region, small chunks are dispensed. The hope is that none of the early chunks are so large as to distort the load balance beyond the repair of later iterations.

More formally, GSS proceeds by first invoking loop transformations such as loop interchange and loop coalescing to obtain the largest possible parallel loop. It then dispenses ranges of iterations to processors in a bakery counter fashion, where the number of iterations dispensed at time t is

$$x = \left\lceil \frac{N_t}{p} \right\rceil \qquad\qquad (6.4)$$

and N_{t+1} is set to $N_t - x$. That is, each processor takes $1/p$th of the remaining iterations at any given time, getting a reasonable chunk to work on, but leaving enough to ensure that other processors will remain busy while it works. Using GSS to schedule a loop that takes 20 iterations on a machine with four processors would result in the allocation shown in Table 6.2.

The processors specified and the time taken assumes that all loop iterations take exactly the same amount of time to complete and that there are no external interruptions. With those assumptions, P1 performs 6 iterations, P2 performs 5 iterations, P3 performs 4 iterations, and P4 performs 5 iterations—not quite a perfect balance, but given that in reality there will be some spreading due to synchronization overhead, a good balance. The total number of synchronizations executed will be 9, as opposed to the 20 required by the bakery counter.

A formal description of GSS is given in Figure 6.33. The algorithm performs a number of static preliminary transformations (loop coalescing, loop interchange,

Table 6.2 Iteration allocation under GSS

Step(t)	Processor	Number remaining	Number allocated	Iterations done
1	P1	20	5	1–5
2	P2	15	4	6–9
3	P3	11	3	10–12
4	P4	8	2	13, 14
5	P4	6	2	15, 16
6	P3	4	1	17
7	P2	3	1	18
8	P4	2	1	19
9	P1	1	1	20

// Given an arbitrary nest of loops L with at least one DOALL
// to be scheduled for p processors.

Distribute the loops in L wherever possible.
Interchange DOALLs to outmost position possible.
Coalesce all inner loops into the outer, where possible.

Schedule each parallel loop as follows:
$N_t := N$; // The total number of parallel loop iterations
while $N_t > 0$ **do begin**
    if there is an idle processor **then begin**
        schedule it for $x := (N_t + p - 1)/p$ iterations;
        $N_t := N_t - x$;
    end
end

Figure 6.33 Guided self-scheduling.

loop distribution) to make the parallel loop as large as possible, then sets up the static information necessary for run-time allocation. Obviously, GSS does not (and cannot) produce an optimal schedule for every possible variant of a parallel loop—for instance, in the example illustrated in Table 6.2, if the first five loop iterations are all very long in executing and the remaining iterations are very short, it would obviously be better to parcel them out individually. However, with reasonable bounds as to what "optimal" means, GSS can be shown to obtain the optimal schedule and the minimum number of synchronization points under any initial processor configuration.

The ceiling operator has been rewritten as $(N_t + p - 1)/p$, which is equivalent. Note that the last four allocations are all for a single-loop iteration. This is not just coincidence in this particular case; GSS in its simplest form (also called GSS(1)) guarantees that the last $p - 1$ allocations will all be single-loop iterations. These allocations can be eliminated by minor changes to the basic GSS algorithm. Specifically, if the number of iterations parceled out at each synchronization step is made $(N_t+2p-1)/p$, then the iteration flow becomes (6,5,4,3,2) for the example. This variation is known as GSS(2); in general, GSS(k) guarantees that there are no blocks of iterations of size less than k handed out. The basic GSS algorithm can be converted into GSS(k) by adjusting the coefficient of p in the formula for the number of iterations parceled out. Some minor adjustments are also necessary for the termination condition, as only GSS(1) is guaranteed to exactly hit zero iterations remaining; others may overshoot.

Guided self-scheduling provides an excellent balance between static and dynamic scheduling by using compile-time information to guide scheduling at run time. In particular, the compiler can adjust the value of k for different loops according to the number of iterations and expected run time of each iteration— the larger the ratio of the number of iterations to the number of processors, the higher k should be. While no general method can schedule for an arbitrary parallel loop perfectly, GSS does provide the balance of the bakery counter algorithm with much less synchronization overhead.

6.7 **Summary**

In preparing programs for execution on symmetric multiprocessors, the principal challenge is to manage the trade-off between parallelism and granularity. If there is insufficient parallelism, the processors will not be effectively used. On the other hand, if the computation is too fine-grained, the start-up and synchronization costs of parallel execution will outweigh the performance gains. Thus the challenge is to find parallelism at the coarsest possible granularity.

We have presented mechanisms for addressing this problem in three contexts:

- In *single loops*, a number of transformations, including privatization, alignment, and replication, can be used to eliminate carried dependences and thereby obviate the need for loop distribution, which reduces granularity. If loop distribution is needed, it can be followed by aggressive loop fusion to minimize the impact of granularity reduction.

- In *perfect loop nests*, loop interchange, loop reversal, and loop skewing can be used to uncover parallelism and move it to the outermost position possible. In many cases the decisions on how to organize the loops for optimal performance are driven not only by the goal of maximizing parallelism but also by concerns for architectural issues such as performance of the memory hierarchy.

- In *general loop nests*, which are not necessarily perfectly nested, multilevel loop distribution, followed by parallelization of the resulting loop nests and aggressive application of loop fusion, can be used to extract the parallelism available and package it for high efficiency.

In a truly effective compiler, all of these strategies will be needed, and they must collaborate with other strategies for performance improvement, especially memory hierarchy management.

6.8   Case Studies

The research efforts at Rice on PFC and ParaScope and on the Ardent Titan compiler both focused on enhancing coarse-grained parallelism as a major goal. This section provides a review of the approaches used in both projects.

6.8.1   PFC and ParaScope

The PFC system performed parallelization along the lines described in this chapter. For nested loops it would attempt to get the parallel loop to the outermost possible position. Inner loops or loops that were not perfectly nested would be distributed, parallelized, and then fused together again as described in Section 6.2.5. Typed fusion was not employed for this task, however.

Because PFC was constructed originally as a vectorizer, it did not carry out dependence analysis outside of loop nests. This was a problem for parallelization, where it was important to consider dependences across loop nests within a subroutine. Over the years, this problem was ameliorated by treating the subroutine as having a single loop around the entire body for the purposes of dependence analysis, but never testing for dependences carried by that loop.

In support of her dissertation, Kathryn McKinley carried out experiments using the ParaScope system, a successor of PFC that used the dependence information from PFC to determine safety and profitability of transformations [209]. The driver for the transformations was fairly close to the one in Figure 6.23 and was fully automated, as were the legality and safety tests. However, the transformations themselves were carried out by hand following the instructions produced by the driver, using the ParaScope Editor, an interactive transformation system. Thus the results closely simulate what a fully automatic system might achieve. In McKinley's tests, the automatic system was compared to speedups obtained on 19 processors of a Sequent Symmetry SMP by hand code from users experienced in parallel programming, none of whom were members of the PFC or ParaScope implementation teams. The results are shown in Figure 6.34.

Note that there was no hand parallelization for the LINPACKD benchmarks at the time of the experiment. The speedups for the benchmark "Control" were obtained on a configuration with only eight processors. For further details on this experiment, see McKinley's dissertation [209].

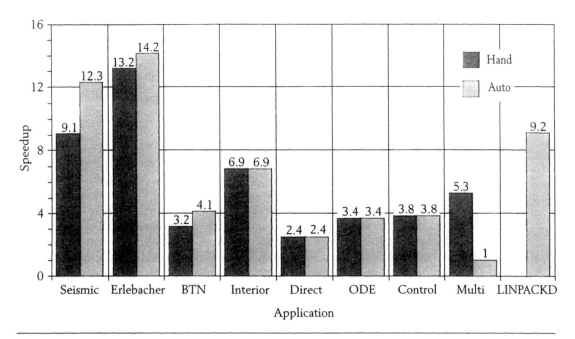

Figure 6.34 Parallelization speedups on the Sequent Symmetry using PFC/ParaScope.

Figure 6.34 shows that, without significant algorithmic changes, the automatic parallelization strategies described in this section are competitive with hand coding by moderately sophisticated users on symmetric multiprocessors of modest size. The one major failure occurred on benchmark "Multi," where the user employed a critical section to synchronize updates to a shared variable. The automatic system was unable to discern that this would produce the same results because it is technically a reordering of memory accesses.

6.8.2   Ardent Titan Compiler

The Ardent Titan had multiple vector processors. For simplicity, it would attempt to vectorize only one loop and parallelize only one loop. Once this decision was made, loop interchange became a somewhat simpler matter. In the ideal case (that is, in a loop nest that yields a vector loop and a parallel loop), the goals of loop interchange on the Titan were the following:

1. Move the vector loop to the innermost position. By the definition of vectorization, this transformation was guaranteed to be legal. Also, since this loop would be "tripled" during parallel code generation, it would disappear during *codegen*.

2. Move the parallel loop to the outermost possible position.

3. Move the best loop for obtaining reuse just outside the "tripled" loop—the real innermost position in the generated code. Given that the vector register file was the only form of "cache" on the vector unit, the goal was to get vector registers reused where possible. This was the biggest win on the Titan, and the remaining second-order effects of getting other loops in the right position weren't considered important enough to justify the compile-time cost.

Focusing on this strategy simplified both dependence testing and code generation. This limited form of loop interchange did not require full dependence matrices. To determine whether a given outer loop could be vectorized, the Ardent compiler would use only the simple innermosting test—a loop that carried no dependence could always be innermosted and vectorized. Moving the parallel loop to the outermost position was accomplished by repeatedly exchanging the parallel loop with the loop just outside it, where legal—this was simple to incorporate into the code generation process. As a result, the test for outermosting became simply an interchange inward test. If the next loop outside did not carry a dependence, it could obviously be moved inward. If it did carry a dependence, the important criterion was that it carried the dependence with it as it interchanged inward (since otherwise the parallelism would be destroyed with the outward move). Thus, the important criterion for outermosting was that if the outer loop contained a dependence, the dependence would move inward with an interchange. This was exactly the same criterion required for the third condition above—getting a loop that fostered reuse into the innermost position. As a result, the only special testing required for loop interchange was one of "interchange-inhibiting" in the vectorization sense, although those were exactly the dependences the Titan optimizer would interchange.

Many of the loop transformations that are employed in parallelization are things that users can perform. For instance, loop distribution is easy to perform at a source level, and most sophisticated users can recognize when they can safely distribute loops. Loop fusion is a transformation that users tend to naturally implement—when they write a loop, they put as much into it as possible. Relying on this view, the Ardent team decided not to implement loop fusion in the Ardent compiler. The factors in this decision included the following:

1. *Size of the dependence graph:* To perform arbitrary loop fusion, dependence graphs have to be calculated across nonoverlapping loop nests as well as intervening statements. These can get to be very large very quickly.

2. *Simplicity and speed of dependence tests:* Many decisions regarding loop interchange and scalar expansion had already simplified the properties of dependence that the compiler required. Removing the requirement for calculating fusion prevention eliminated one more decision.

3. *Applicability:* As stated earlier, the expectation was that loop fusion applied to general programs would probably provide little benefit, as the natural

inclination for most programmers is to fuse.[1] On the one occasion where we did expect to fuse disjoint loops (unroll-and-jam), the safety could be dynamically calculated as necessary.

It is important to note that this restriction was not avoiding loop fusion altogether, but simply fusion of loops that were originally disjoint. The Ardent optimizer expected to fuse loops that had been distributed from the same loop, as occurs in *codegen*, but this type of fusion does not require any safety calculations. The fact that the loops were originally one guarantees that they can be safely merged. Note also that the Ardent compiler did not support Fortran 90, which requires fusion to achieve performance from array statements.

The overall parallel code generation strategy for the Ardent Titan compiler can be summarized by two principles:

1. Vectorize at most one loop and parallelize at most one loop.
2. Effect no auxiliary transformation (e.g., scalar expansion, if-conversion, loop interchange) unless the transformation is guaranteed to enhance vectorization, parallelism, or memory reuse.

The first principle implied that the code generation algorithm had to focus on finding the best vector and parallel loops, rather than all vector and parallel loops. The second principle implied that code generation had to drive auxiliary transformations on a demand basis, implementing the transformations only when required. While these two principles may at first appear difficult to incorporate into the general *codegen* algorithm, they in fact blend in easily to the general scheme with only minor modifications. The resulting overall approach taken by the Ardent optimizer became

1. All dependence edges were attributed with a "deletability" property, extending the notion introduced for scalar expansion. When this property was true, it implied that the edge could be removed by some transformation.
2. Control edges were explicitly in the graph for control flow, and back edges were inserted as well to force all statements in a control region to remain together throughout *codegen*. The loops produced by distribution were attributed with the separate properties of being "parallelizable" and being "vectorizable" at a given level. When evaluating "parallelizable" in Tarjan's algorithm, carried control edges were ignored.
3. A first pass of code generation was made to find all possible vector and parallel loops. This information was gathered by temporarily removing all deletable edges from the graph, calling the *codegen* algorithm, and rather than generating parallel or vector code at any step, merely recording that

---

1. This, of course, did not consider the possibility of machine-generated code, which violates all known sanity requirements and is the bane of compiler writers everywhere. It is also true that there are always some programmers that violate all reasonable programming practices.

the loop at the level could or could not be run in vector or in parallel. This pass essentially evaluated the effects of all possible recurrence-breaking transformations, but by implementing them only in the graph, rather than in the source.

4. After determining all possible parallel and vector loops, code generation scored the loops to determine the best vector and parallel loop. Considerations included stride-one access, lack of scatter-gathers, loop length, and global consistency.

5. Code generation was effected with a final *codegen* pass, focused on the best vector and parallel loop. When this *codegen* encountered a best vector or parallel loop that did not vectorize or parallelize, it knew it had to effect some recurrence-breaking transformation, and it could choose appropriately. Similarly, fusing like regions was simple in this scheme.

Figure 6.35 contains a high-level algorithmic overview of the code generation strategy employed by the Ardent optimizer.

As a simple example of the effectiveness of this strategy, consider matrix multiplication. The standard coding found in textbooks on linear algebra puts the sum reduction loop in the innermost position, as shown in the following code:

```
DO I = 1, 512
   DO J = 1, 512
      C(I,J) = 0.0
      DO K = 1, N
         C(I,J) = C(I,J) + A(I,K) * B(K,J)
      ENDDO
   ENDDO
ENDDO
```

procedure *generate*(*T*)

   // *T* is the intermediate representation that is to be parallelized

   compute the dependence graph *D* for *T* making *deletable*(*e*) true for all edges *e*
      that can be broken by some transformation;

   compute D_d from *D* by removing all edges *e* such that *deletable*(*e*) is true;

   mark(D_d, *S*);   // Store in *S* all loops for all statements that can be
             // done in vector or in parallel

   score(D_d, *S*); // Store best vector and parallel loops for each stmt

   codegen(*D*, *S*, *T*); // Actually generate code
end *generate*

Figure 6.35 Ardent Titan code generation overview.

All other things being equal, the Ardent compiler would choose the I-loop because it ensures that the vector statement will have a stride of one, which has the best possible load/store performance on the Titan. Because the Titan has vector registers of length 32, it will strip that loop to length 32 and move it to the innermost position. The only other loop that is fully parallel is the J-loop, which would be moved to the outermost position. The resulting code is extremely well matched to the Titan architecture:

```
PARALLEL DO J = 1, 512
    DO I = 1, 512, 32
        C(I:I+31,J) = 0.0
        DO K = 1, N
            C(I:I+31,J) = C(I:I+31,J) + A(I:I+31,K) * B(K,J)
        ENDDO
    ENDDO
ENDDO
```

6.9 Historical Comments and References

Scalar privatization was introduced by Cytron and Ferrante [95] and Allen et al. [14] in the context of the PTRAN automatic parallelization project. The need for array privatization was established in a study of the Perfect benchmark suite by Eigenmann et al. [108], and methods for performing the optimization were described by Li [199]. The original treatment of alignment and distribution was due to Allen, Callahan, and Kennedy [25].

Loop interchange methods have been widely used. The treatment by Wolfe introduced the use of direction vectors for this purpose [280]. The topic was further explored by Allen and Kennedy [19]. The formulation based on the direction matrix is new, but can be viewed as a variant of unimodular transformations, as discussed by Wolf and Lam [277]. Loop skewing is a variant of the wavefront method introduced by Lamport [195]. The transformation itself was introduced by Wolfe [281].

Loop fusion for optimization of array and stream operations has a long history [124, 118, 163]. Methods combining loop distribution and fusion were originally discussed by Allen, Callahan, and Kennedy [25]. The typed fusion algorithm and its application to single-level multilevel loop parallelization are due to Kennedy and McKinley [176]. Kennedy and McKinley also described strategies for managing the trade-off between memory hierarchy performance and parallelism presented in Section 6.3.6 [175].

Cytron developed the notion of DOACROSS and the treatment of pipeline parallelism in the context of the Cedar project [93, 94]. The bakery counter algorithm for multiprocessor scheduling is a venerable strategy that has been widely cited in the operating systems literature. Guided self-scheduling is due to Poly-chronopoulos and Kuck [226, 225].

Excellent general treatments of the subject of dependence and parallelization can be found in the works by Allen et al. [14], Amarasinghe et al. [28], Kuck et al. [190], and Wolfe [283, 285].

Exercises

6.1 Construct the direction matrix for the following loop nests and show how each should be parallelized to achieve maximum granularity. Describe the transformations that will lead to this parallelization.

a.
```
DO J = 1, M
    DO I = 1, N
        A(I+1,J+1) = A(I,J+1) + C
        B(I+1,J+1) = B(I,J+1) + A(I+1,J) + D
    ENDDO
ENDDO
```

b.
```
DO K = 1, L
    DO J = 1, M
        DO I = 1, N
            A(I+1,J+1,K+1) = A(I,J+1,K+1) + A(I+1,J-1,K) &
                + A(I+1,J,K+1)
        ENDDO
    ENDDO
ENDDO
```

c.
```
DO K = 1, L
    DO J = 1, M
        DO I = 1, N
            A(I+1,J+1,K+1) = A(I,J+1,K+1) + A(I+1,5,K)
        ENDDO
    ENDDO
ENDDO
```

6.2 Show that the following problem is *NP*-complete: given a direction matrix for a nest with N loops and $M > N$ dependences, find the minimal number of loops that covers all remaining loops.

6.3 Show how to incorporate loop reversal into the routine *ParallelizeNest* given in Figure 6.19 with the selection heuristic from Figure 6.20.

6.4 Develop a version of the routine *Parallelize* that tries both whole-loop parallelization (without finalizing transformations) and outer loop distribution (if whole-loop parallelization does not produce a parallel outer loop), then chooses the best one according to some scoring metric. The metric need not be shown.

6.5 Adaptive scheduling partitions the amount of computation to achieve load balancing. An orthogonal direction is the partitioning of data. For example, a parallel Web server receives requests for a large number of data files. Can you extend the idea of adaptive scheduling to partition data among parallel server machines?

CHAPTER 7

Handling
Control Flow

7.1 Introduction

To this point in the book, we have focused on transformations of programs that have no control flow other than loops. In other words, we have ignored the problems created by conditional branches. These problems are extremely difficult to handle because control flow creates a new type of constraint on program transformations—one that is not handled by data dependence.

To illustrate the execution constraints imposed by control flow, consider the following loop:

```
      DO 100 I = 1, N
S₁       IF (A(I-1).GT.0.0) GOTO 100
S₂          A(I) = A(I) + B(I) * C
100 CONTINUE
```

If we consider only data dependences, we see that S_1 has a loop-carried dependence upon S_2, due to the reference to A and no other data dependences. As a result, data dependence alone would indicate that both statements could be vectorized. However, since we do not know how to vectorize an IF with a GOTO, we will implement that as a loop, yielding

```
S₂  A(1:N) = A(1:N) + B(1:N) * C
    DO 100 I = 1, N
S₁     IF (A(I-1).GT.0.0) GOTO 100
100 CONTINUE
```

Here the loop with the IF statement must come after the vector statement because of the dependence from S_2 to S_1 in the original code.

It is easy to see that this code is incorrect. In the original version, statement S_2 executes only on iterations where $A(I-1)$ is greater than zero; in the transformed version, the statement executes unconditionally. Obviously we have missed some constraint that would prevent us from interchanging the order of S_1 and S_2. What is needed to prevent this erroneous transformation? According to Theorem 2.8, statements can be vectorized so long as they are not part of a cycle in the dependence graph. Therefore, we must have omitted a dependence from S_1 to S_2. That dependence—a *control dependence*—arises because S_2 is conditionally executed depending on the outcome of S_1.

In this chapter we will develop the notion of control dependence and extend the results of previous chapters to programs that include conditional control. The chapter also presents mechanisms for computing and handling control dependences.

Basically, there are two principal strategies for dealing with control. The first is to eliminate control dependences by converting them to data dependences. This is the strategy that was generally adopted for automatic vectorization. The mechanism for accomplishing this transformation, known as *if-conversion*, will be discussed in the next section.

The second strategy is to deal with control dependence as an extension of data dependence and to include control dependence edges in the dependence graph. This strategy, which has been adopted for automatic parallelization, primarily because it leads to simpler code, is described in Section 7.3. Although this strategy attempts to avoid systematic if-conversion, we will see that situations arise requiring an analog of if-conversion to generate correct code.

7.2 If-Conversion

The problem described in the introductory section becomes much easier to deal with if we rewrite the example problem without the use of a GOTO:

```
DO I = 1, N
    IF (A(I-1).LE.0.0) A(I) = A(I) + B(I) * C
ENDDO
```

In this form, the conditional guard can be viewed as another input to the statement, making the recurrence obvious.

If we look at a slightly more complicated example

```
      DO 100 I = 1, N
S₁        IF (A(I-1).GT.0.0) GOTO 100
S₂        A(I) = A(I) + B(I) * C
S₃        B(I) = B(I) + A(I)
100 CONTINUE
```

once again, it is fairly difficult to tell whether anything can be done to vectorize either S_2 or S_3 in this example.

But if we convert the example to conditional assignment statements

```
      DO 100 I = 1, N
S₂      IF (A(I-1).LE.0.0) A(I) = A(I) + B(I) * C
S₃      IF (A(I-1).LE.0.0) B(I) = B(I) + A(I)
100 CONTINUE
```

an analysis of the data dependences tells us that the second statement can be vectorized. Rewriting the example in vectorized form using the Fortran 90 WHERE statement yields

```
      DO 100 I = 1, N
S₂      IF (A(I-1).LE.0.0) A(I) = A(I) + B(I) * C
100 CONTINUE
S₃  WHERE (A(0:N-1).LE.0.0) B(1:N) = B(1:N) + A(1:N)
```

Given the simplicity and clarity introduced by the transformation from branches to conditional execution, a natural question to ask is whether this transformation can be generalized to apply to all forms of statements and program constructs. In other words, can control dependence be converted into data dependence by converting statements to a guarded form where the conditionals controlling a statement's execution are considered as inputs to the statement? As this chapter will demonstrate, the answer is yes. The resulting transformation, known as *if-conversion*, is widely used in vectorizing compilers. If-conversion provides a theoretically elegant method for handling control dependences by converting all such dependences into data dependences, necessitating only one form of dependence.

7.2.1 Definition

Section 7.1 introduced the concept of if-conversion with a simple example. Succinctly stated, if-conversion is the process of removing all branches from a program. Of course, branches cannot simply be removed without replacing them with something else, if correct execution is to be maintained. If-conversion assumes a target notation of *guarded execution*, in which every statement implicitly contains a logical expression controlling its execution. The statement is executed only if its guard evaluates to true.

To illustrate guarded execution, consider again the first example in this chapter, but without the loop:

```
S₁  IF (A(I-1).GT.0.0) GOTO 100
S₂      A(I) = A(I) + B(I) * C
100 CONTINUE
```

Expressed in guarded notation, with branches removed, this fragment becomes

```
S₁   M = A(I-1).GT.0.0
S₂   IF (.NOT.M) A(I) = A(I) + B(I) * C
100 CONTINUE
```

The guard on the second statement (.NOT.M) is most naturally expressed in Fortran as an IF statement. When no guard is explicitly stated, the assumption is that the guard is true and the statement is always executed.

The goal of if-conversion is to remove all branches from a program by replacing the statements in the program with an equivalent set of guarded statements. Given the Fortran 90 WHERE statement, if-conversion is obviously valuable in vectorization, since guarded execution translates naturally into WHERE statements so long as data dependences permit.

While if-conversion in the simple example above is a fairly straightforward process, it can become extremely complex. In order to present the process clearly, it is useful to categorize branches into different classifications.

7.2.2   Branch Classification

For the purpose of analysis, every branch can be categorized as one of three types:

1. A *forward branch* transfers control to a target that occurs after the branch but at the same loop nesting level.

2. A *backward branch* transfers control to a statement occurring lexically before the branch but at the same level of nesting.

3. An *exit branch* terminates one or more loops by transferring control to a target outside a loop nest.

The first example in this chapter illustrates a forward branch. Backward branches are similar, but go backward to implicitly create a loop rather than forward. Backward branches are often used in Fortran 66 and Fortran 77 to encode while loops, as in

```
10   I = NEXT(I)
     A(I) = A(I) + B(I)
     IF (I.LT.1000) GOTO 10
```

The defining property of exit branches, and the property that most determines how they are removed, is the fact that the branch exits a loop. It does not matter in which direction the branch exits the loop (that is, whether the branch exits in a forward direction or in a backward direction). Exit branches are often used in "search loops," such as the following:

```
    DO I = 1, N
        IF (ABS(A(I)-B(I)).LE.DEL) GOTO 200
    ENDDO
    ...
200 CONTINUE
```

In this "search loop," the exit occurs when a pair of values from the arrays A and B is found to be sufficiently close together in value.

The one category not covered in this taxonomy are branches that jump into loops. While technically illegal in Fortran, they can arise in C and other languages. These branches will not be treated in this book (see Allen et al. [23] for a full treatment).

If-conversion is actually a composition of two different transformations:

1. *Branch relocation* moves branches out of loops until the branch and its target are nested in the same number of DO-loops—the procedure converts each exit branch into either a forward branch or a backward branch.

2. *Branch removal* eliminates forward branches by computing guard expressions for action statements under their control and conditioning execution on those expressions.

The following sections present these two techniques in more detail.

7.2.3 Forward Branches

The simplest transformation in if-conversion is branch removal, which eliminates forward branches within a loop by inserting the appropriate guards. The basic idea behind branch removal is to sweep through a program, maintaining a Boolean expression that represents the logical conditions that must be true for the current statement to be executed. When a new branch is encountered, its controlling expression is conjoined into the current logical guard. When the target of a branch is encountered, its controlling expression is disjoined into the current logical guard.

Earlier examples have illustrated very simple branch removal, involving only one GOTO. Branch removal in general can be quite complex, as the following example shows:

```
        DO I = 1, N
$c_1$     IF (A(I).GT.10) GOTO 60
20          A(I) = A(I) + 10
$c_2$       IF (B(I).GT.10) GOTO 80
40            B(I) = B(I) + 10
60          A(I) = B(I) + A(I)
80          B(I) = A(I) - 5
        ENDDO
```

In order to perform branch removal on this loop, it is necessary to determine the guarding condition that holds at every assignment statement. Statement 20 is clearly executed if and only if the conditional in C_1 is false. Similarly, statement 40 is executed if and only if both the conditionals from C_1 and C_2 are false. Statements 60 and 80 are not so simple. Statement 60 can be reached by direct fall-through (C_1 and C_2 both false) or by transfer from statement C_1 (C_1 true). Statement 80 can be reached by fall-through from 60 (hence under the same conditions) or by direct transfer from C_2 (C_1 false and C_2 true). Correct branch removal should thus produce the following:

```
      DO I = 1, N
         m1 = A(I).GT.10
20       IF(.NOT.m1) A(I) = A(I) + 10
         IF(.NOT.m1) m2 = B(I).GT.10
40       IF(.NOT.m1.AND..NOT.m2) B(I) = B(I) + 10
60       IF(.NOT.m1.AND..NOT.m2.OR.m1) A(I) = B(I) + A(I)
80       IF(.NOT.m1.AND..NOT.m2.OR.m1.OR..NOT.m1.AND.m2) &
            B(I) = A(I) - 5
      ENDDO
```

On first glance, the guarding conditions at the end of the loop appear complicated. However, when the conditions are simplified symbolically, the control flow becomes more apparent and much less complex. Statement 80 is in fact unconditionally executed, and statement 60 is executed if the first branch is taken or if the second branch is not. After simplification, the loop looks like this:

```
      DO I = 1, N
         m1 = A(I).GT.10
20       IF(.NOT.m1) A(I) = A(I) + 10
         IF(.NOT.m1) m2 = B(I).GT.10
40       IF(.NOT.m1.AND..NOT.m2) B(I) = B(I) + 10
60       IF(m1.OR..NOT.m2) A(I) = B(I) + A(I)
80       B(I) = A(I) - 5
      ENDDO
```

This form vectorizes trivially, once data dependences are calculated and scalar expansion (see Section 5.3) is applied. The result is represented in Fortran 90 WHERE statements:

```
      m1(1:N) = A(1:N).GT.10
20    WHERE(.NOT.m1(1:N)) A(1:N) = A(1:N) + 10
      WHERE(.NOT.m1(1:N)) m2(1:N) = B(1:N).GT.10
40    WHERE(.NOT.m1(1:N).AND..NOT.m2(1:N)) B(1:N) = B(1:N) + 10
60    WHERE(m1(1:N).OR..NOT.m2(1:N)) A(1:N) = B(1:N) + A(1:N)
80    B(1:N) = A(1:N) - 5
```

There are a couple of points worth noting in this example. First, a close examination of the transformed loop seems to indicate that the uninitialized values of the variable m2 can be used in statements 40 and 60. That is, in fact, true; however, the uninitialized values cannot have any adverse effect. On any specific iteration, m2 is not set when m1 is true. Statement 40 can be executed only when m1 is false and m2 is true. Since m1 being false forces m2 to be correctly set, there is no possibility of statement 40 being executed incorrectly due to an uninitialized setting of m2. Similarly, statement 60 is executed when m1 is true or m2 is false. If m1 is true, m2 is not set, but the statement should be executed regardless of the value of m2. If m1 is false, so that m2 alone controls the statement's execution, m2 is correctly initialized.

The second point involves the complexity of the Boolean guards. Obviously, some form of Boolean simplification is important to obtain reasonable code. Simplification will be discussed in Section 7.2.7.

Figure 7.1 provides a more formal specification of forward branch removal. It does not discuss block IF-THEN-ELSEs, under the assumption that those are easily removed, and it assumes that only labeled statements can be reached with a branch. In the notation used in the algorithm, conditions are strings in Fortran 90 notation. This is to ensure that the reader keeps in mind that the conditions are ones that will be used to modify the program at compile time by generating textual code after simplification.

Correctness. We now turn to a discussion of the correctness of branch removal. Recall that in Section 2.2.3, we defined a transformed program to be equivalent to an original program if (1) the value of output variables in both programs is identical at the point of output, (2) the output statements are executed in the same order, and (3) the transformed program introduces no error exceptions that would not have occurred in the original program. Under this definition, we must establish three things to show correctness:

1. The guard for the statement instance in the new program is true if and only if the corresponding statement in the old program is executed, unless the statement has been introduced to capture a guard variable value, which must be executed at the point the conditional expression would have been evaluated.

2. The order of execution of statements in the new program with true guards is the same as the order of execution of those statements in the original program.

3. Any expression with side effects is evaluated exactly as many times in the new program as in the old program.

The first of these conditions can be established by an induction on statement order. Our goal is to establish that the guard at each statement expresses exactly the set of conditions under which the statement in the original program would be

procedure *remove_branches(B)*

// Input: a single loop with a list of body statements B
// Output: a loop without conditional transfers.

current := ".TRUE.";
for each labeled statement S in B **do** *cond(S)* := ".FALSE.";

for each statement S in B in order **do begin**
  if S is labeled
    then *current* := *Simplify (current* || ".OR." || *cond(S)*);
  if S is a conditional transfer: IF(C) GO TO L
  then begin
    let S_L be the statement labeled by L;
    let m be a new compiler-generated logical variable,
      initialized to *true*;
    convert it to "IF(*current*) m := C";
    cond(S_L) := *cond(S_L)* || ".OR." || *current* || ".AND.m");
    current := *current* || ".AND..NOT.m";
  end
  else if S is of the form: IF(C)S, where S is not a transfer
    then convert it to "IF(C.AND.*current*) S";
  else
    convert S to IF(*current*)S";
end *remove_branches*

Figure 7.1 Forward branch removal.

---

executed. At the first statement, the empty guard is trivially correct. Suppose the guards at all previous statements are correct. We must show that the guards at the current statement are correct. The guard at the current statement is formed by taking the disjunction of the terms attached to it by virtue of previous branches—*cond(S_L)*—and the current condition passed by the previous statement. This reflects the fact that control may reach this statement either by a branch or from the previous statement.

Each of the conditions attached to the statement due to branches must be correct because each such condition is the conjunction of the current condition for that branch, which is correct by induction, and the variable that is used to capture the value of the conditional expression controlling the branch. Therefore, *cond(S_L)*, the disjunction of all such conditions, is true if and only if some statement for which the guard condition is true branches to S_L.

Thus we need only show that the fall-through current condition is correct. By induction the current condition at the previous statement is correct. Therefore, unless that statement is a conditional branch, the current condition is the same at the current statement and must also be correct. If it is a conditional branch, then the fall-through current condition is simply the conjunction of the current condition and the negation of the variable that captures the condition controlling the branch. Thus the current condition passed to the current statement from the previous statement is the conjunction of the current condition at that statement and the negation of the variable that captures the value of the expression controlling the branch. Thus that current condition is true if and only if the previous statement is executed and the branch is not taken, which is clearly correct.

The second condition above is trivially true because no reordering of statements is done. The third condition is established by the first plus the observation that the conditions controlling each conditional branch are each evaluated once at the point where the branch would have been located. All other statements are executed exactly in the same position and iteration that they would be in the original program.

Note that unconditional forward branches can be handled in the above code by simply treating them as conditional branches with constant condition *true*.

7.2.4 Exit Branches

Exit branches are more complicated to eliminate than are forward branches. The reason is that forward branches only affect the guarding condition of statements following the branch; exit branches affect both statements that follow and statements that precede the branch. Consider the following simple fragment:

```
      DO I = 1, N
         S₁
         IF (p(I)) GOTO 100
         S₂
      ENDDO
100   S₃
```

If the first loop iteration on which $p(I)$ is true is I_0, then execution of the loop is effectively terminated at that point. When the loop is converted to guarded execution, the DO-loop proper will execute all iterations, including the one for I_0 and beyond, since there cannot be a branch to prematurely terminate the loop. In this form, S_2 will not be executed for iterations i through N and S_1 will not be executed for iterations $i + 1$ through N. The fact that exit branches affect all statements within a loop makes their elimination more complicated than simple forward branches.

Since the most complicated aspect of exit branches is the fact that they terminate a loop, eliminating that property is the key to obtaining guarded execution. If the branch can be relocated outside of all loops that it terminates, the resulting branch becomes a simple forward branch. To illustrate how this relocation can be performed, consider the following example:

```
        DO J - 1, M
          DO I - 1, N
            A(I,J) = B(I,J) + X
S           IF (L(I,J)) GOTO 200
            C(I,J) - A(I,J) + Y
          ENDDO
          D(J) - A(N,J)
200       F(J) - C(10,J)
        ENDDO
```

The branch of interest, statement S, exits one loop. If S can be converted from an exit branch to a forward branch, a transformation that yields something similar to the following must be carried out:

```
        DO J - 1, M
          DO I - 1, N
            IF (C₁) A(I,J) - B(I,J) + X
Sₐ          Code to set C₁ and C₂
            IF (C₂) C(I,J) - A(I,J) + Y
          ENDDO
Sᵦ        IF (.NOT.C₁.OR..NOT.C₂) GOTO 200
          D(J) - A(N,J)
200       F(J) - C(10,J)
        ENDDO
```

In this form, the original exit branch has been moved out of the loop to become statement S_b. It now is a simple forward branch, which can be removed using the algorithm in Figure 7.1. The problem, then, is to find the proper conditions to guard the statements inside the inner loop.

Simply stated, the statements in the inner loop are going to be executed only if the exit branch was not taken on any previous iteration. In other words, once an iteration is executed on which the condition guarding the exit branch is true, no future iterations are executed. Thus, we need to iteratively compute a variable that becomes false on any iteration on which the guard on the exit branch becomes true and stays false after that. That variable is the correct guard for all other statements in the loop. Such a variable is trivial to compute—it is simply the conjunction of the negation of the guard on the exit branch for all previous iterations:

$$lm = \bigcap_{k=1}^{I} \neg L(k, J) \qquad (7.1)$$

When this transformation is applied to the previous example, the following code results:

```
    DO J = 1, M
       lm = .TRUE.
       DO I = 1, N
          IF (lm) A(I,J) = B(I,J) + X
          IF (lm) m1 = .NOT. L(I,J)
          lm = lm .AND. m1
          IF (lm) C(I,J) = A(I,J) + Y
       ENDDO
       m2 = lm
       IF (m2) D(J) = A(N,J)
200    F(J) = C(10,J)
    ENDDO
```

Note that the variable m1 is introduced to ensure that the evaluation of the condition L(I,K), which might have side effects, is done only if the original program would have performed the evaluation. Forward-substituting the variable m2 and expanding lm to a two-dimensional array yields

```
    DO J = 1, M
       lm(0,J) = .TRUE.
       DO I = 1, N
          IF (lm(I-1,J)) A(I,J) = B(I,J) + X
          IF (lm(I-1,J)) m1 = .NOT.L(I,J)
          lm(I,J) = lm(I-1,J) .AND. m1
          IF (lm(I,J)) C(I,J) = A(I,J) + Y
       ENDDO
       IF (lm(N,J)) D(J) = A(N,J)
200    F(J) = C(10,J)
    ENDDO
```

When *codegen* is applied to this fragment, the following vectorized loops result:

```
    DO J = 1, M
       lm(0,J) = .TRUE.
       DO I = 1, N
          IF (lm(I-1,J)) m1 = .NOT.L(I,J)
          lm(I,J) = lm(I-1,J) .AND. m1
       ENDDO
    ENDDO
    WHERE(lm(0:N-1,1:M)) A(1:N,1:M) = B(1:N,1:M) + X
    WHERE(lm(0:N-1,1:M)) C(1:N,1:M) = A(1:N,1:M) + Y
    WHERE(lm(N,1:M)) D(1:M) = A(N,1:M)
200 F(1:M) = C(10,1:M)
```

Such an aggressive approach produces four vectorized loops, which may appear to be extremely efficient. However, it is not the most efficient result possible. Instead of expanding 1m in both loops, a more efficacious approach expands it only in the inner loop:

```
DO J = 1, M
   1m(0) = .TRUE.
   DO I = 1, N
      IF (1m(I-1)) A(I,J) = B(I,J) + X
      IF (1m(I-1)) m1 = .NOT.L(I,J)
      1m(I) = 1m(I-1) .AND. m1
      IF (1m(I)) C(I,J) = A(I,J) + Y
   ENDDO
   IF (1m(N)) D(J) = A(N,J)
200    F(J) = C(10,J)
ENDDO
```

After vectorization this becomes

```
DO J = 1, M
   1m(0) = .TRUE.
   DO I = 1, N
      IF (1m(I-1)) m1 = .NOT.L(I,J)
      1m(I) = 1m(I-1) .AND. m1
   ENDDO
   WHERE (1m(0:N-1)) A(1:N,J) = B(1:N,J) + X
   WHERE (1m(1:N)) C(1:N,J) = A(1:N,J) + Y
   IF (1m(N)) D(J) = A(N,J)
200    F(J) = C(10,J)
ENDDO
```

An intelligent reduction recognition algorithm will realize that the remaining I-loop is actually a "FirstTrue" reduction—that is, a function that finds the index of the first true element of a vector. On a machine with the appropriate hardware (which is typically very simple and easy to add), the following code is appropriate:

```
DO J = 1, M
   n = FirstTrueX(L(1:N,J)) - 1
   A(1:n+1,J) = B(1:n+1,J) + X
   C(1:n,J) = A(1:n,J) + Y
   IF (n.GT.N) D(J) = A(N,J)
200    F(J) = C(10,J)
ENDDO
```

where the built-in vector function FirstTrueX returns the index in the logical parameter array of the first .TRUE. value or, if there are no true values, the length of the parameter array plus 1. This code is much more effective on most vector machines than the two-dimensional vectorized version. The reason is that the two-dimensional form works on varying length vectors—that is, the WHERE statements operate over the entire length of the I-loop, while in actuality, the vectors can be scheduled densely (that is, executed unconditionally) over the loop until the point where the exit branch is taken, then skipped entirely after that.

The basic procedure used in branch relocation, as in forward branch elimination, is to compute the precise Boolean guard expression that governs the execution of each statement in the loop from which the exit branch is to be eliminated. The algorithm is given in Figure 7.2. Computation of the exit branch condition x in the loop is left unguarded so that when it is expanded to a vector or an array, the result will be correct, as in the examples. This cannot cause a difference in meaning because the statement itself is designed to have no side effects.

procedure *relocate_branches*(l)

> // l is the DO statement for the loop
> // lg is the *loop guard expression* that will be used to guard each
> // statement within the loop.

S_1:   **for each** DO statement d in the loop l **do**
>   *relocate_branches*(d);
> set $lg = null$;

S_2:   **for each** exit branch "IF(p) GO TO S" **do begin**
>   create a new loop exit flag x;
>   insert the assignment "x = .TRUE." prior to l;
>   if $lg = null$ **then** $lg := $ "x"; **else** $lg := lg \parallel$ " .AND.x";
>   insert the branch "IF (.NOT.x) GO TO S" after the loop;
>   create a new Boolean variable m and replace the exit branch
>   by the pair of statements
>   "m = .NOT.p" followed by "x = x.AND.m";
> **end**

> **for each** non-DO statement s in the loop l **do**
>   if guard(s) = *null* **begin**
>   if the variable assigned in s is not a flag in lg
>   **then** guard(s) := lg;
>   **end**
>   **else** guard(s) := guard(s) .AND.lg;

end *relocate_branches*

Figure 7.2 Branch relocation algorithm.

The procedure *relocate_branches* eliminates exit branches both within the loop on which it is called and also on any contained loops. The key to interior elimination is the recursive call in statement S_1, where the procedure removes exit branches from contained loops. This recursive call must be executed before the body of code starting at statement S_2. The reason is that an interior branch that exits multiple loops may exit the loop l as well, and thus must be removed by the body of code at statement S_2.

Correctness. For the algorithm *relocate_branches* from Figure 7.2 to be useful, it must be the case that (1) an application of the algorithm to a loop does not change the meaning of the program—that is, it does not reorder, add, or delete statement instances—and (2) the algorithm eliminates all exit branches from a loop on which it is called.

First we establish that *relocate_branches* removes all exit branches, which is the simpler case. By definition, the loop at statement S_2 locates all exit branches within the loop proper and replaces those branches with assignments. The new branches that are created by the algorithm are created outside the examined loop, so they cannot be exit branches for that loop. The recursive call to *relocate_branches* has removed all exit branches within inner loops by simple induction. As a result, there can be no exit branches within any loop on which *relocate_branches* has been called.

Establishing that the meaning is preserved requires more effort. Since no statements are added or deleted within the loop, establishing correctness requires showing that statements within the loop are executed in the same order up until the time the exit branch would have been taken and not executed after that. On any iteration on which the condition controlling an exit branch becomes true, the guard variable x corresponding to that branch is set to false at the exact point where the exit branch was originally located. Since the loop guard expression is simply the conjunction of the exit guard variables corresponding to exit branches in the loop, the loop guard expression becomes false as soon as any variable becomes false and it stays that way. Because the loop guard expression is conjoined to the guard of every statement in the loop body, the guard expression of every statement becomes false at the same point, so no more statements within the loop will be executed. Since the statements within the loop are all executed in the same order, and conditions within exit branches are evaluated at exactly the points where they would be evaluated in the original program, the statement execution order within the loop is preserved and exactly the same statements are executed.

There remains the issue of whether the conditional branches at the end of the loop are correct. Note that only one exit branch guard variable can be set to false because, as soon as one is set, none of the others can be assigned due to the loop guard expression being false. Therefore, only one of the conditional branches immediately after the loop can be executed. If none of the conditions are true, then execution will fall through to the statement that was originally the first one after the loop. This completes the argument for correctness.

This argument for correctness does not apply to the value of the induction variable that controls the exited loop; if the exit branch is taken, the loop induction variable will contain a different value after application of *relocate_branches*. To handle this situation correctly (which is necessary, since exit branches are often used to terminate search loops with the loop variable holding the located value), the loop induction variable I can be replaced by a compiler-generated variable i in the loop control expressions. Then the statement that replaces the loop guard

```
IF(1g) x =.NOT.p
```

could be replaced by the block conditional

```
IF(1g) THEN
   x =.NOT.p
   I = i
ENDIF
```

so that the last value of the loop induction variable is captured. This also requires that the value be captured after all the moved branches inserted immediately after the loop by *relocate_branches*.

7.2.5 Backward Branches

So far, two types of forward branches have been covered—those that exit loops and those that do not. The one remaining possibility—those that enter loops—is essentially forbidden by the Fortran standard. As a result, it might seem that Section 7.2.4 completes handling of all forward branches and that the last remaining type of branch to be covered is backward branches. However, backward branches complicate the handling of forward branches, by creating the remaining possibility of forward branches into loops. In general, backward branches are complicated for at least two reasons:

1. They create implicit loops. Backward control flow is the basic element of a loop, and loops cannot be simulated by simple guards (as simple forward branches can). Removing backward branches requires some other mechanism for representing backward control flow.

2. They complicate the removal of forward branches by creating loops into which forward branches may jump.

The following example illustrates this complication:

```
        IF (P) GOTO 200
        ...
    100 S₁
        ...
    200 S₂
        ...
        IF  (Q) GOTO 100
```

Applying the forward if-conversion algorithm in Figure 7.1 would produce

```
        m1 = .NOT. P
        ...
    100 IF (m1) S₁
        ...
    200 S₂
        ...
        IF  (Q) GOTO 100
```

If the forward branch to 200 is taken followed by the backward branch to 100, the guard variable m1 will be .FALSE., thereby preventing execution of statements until 200 is reached again. However, those statements would be executed in the original program.

Because of these complications, backward branches cannot be simply handled in isolation. Instead, they must be transformed in conjunction with the forward branches that impinge upon their control flow. The simplest approach is to isolate backward branches and leave all code under their control (known as *implicitly iterative regions*) untouched. Such an approach prevents removal of forward branches into an implicitly iterative region, a severe limitation. As a result, this approach is probably too simple to be effective in a production compiler that is focused on Fortran 77.

In a 1983 paper, Allen et al. [23] demonstrated how to eliminate all backward branches from a Fortran program through a variant of if-conversion. Although the details of this procedure are beyond the scope of this book, we will present the basic idea here.

The key problem in the previous example is the guard for statement S_1. To be correct, that guard must reflect two facts:

1. S_1 is executed on the first pass through the code only if P is false.

2. S_1 is always executed when the backward branch is taken.

Because the first pass through the code is singled out, it is clear that one set of conditions must be used to guard the first pass through an implicitly iterative region and a different set used to guard subsequent passes. One way to do this is to introduce a backward branch guard bb, which is true when its associated backward branch is taken. Illustrating in the previous example:

```
    m = P
    ...
    bb = .FALSE.
100 IF (.NOT.m.OR (m.AND.bb)) S₁
    ...
200 S₂
    ...
    IF (Q) THEN
        bb = .TRUE.
        GOTO 100
    ENDIF
```

The backward branch variable bb becomes true only when the backward branch is taken. S_1 is executed whenever

1. the forward branch is not taken, so that m is .FALSE.

2. the backward branch is taken.

If the forward branch is not taken, the first condition will hold regardless of how bb is set. If the forward branch is taken, both bb and m will be .TRUE., causing the guarding condition to be true.

In general, there are two ways that the target of a backward branch can be reached from the start of a program:

1. It can *fall through* from the previous statement, in which case the condition for execution is encoded by the current condition from the predecessor, or

2. it can branch around the statement and then reach it via a backward branch, in which case the correct guard is the logical conjunction of the condition for branching around and the condition for branching back.

Thus, if the current condition just prior to target y is denoted by cc, the branch condition denoted by m, and the backward branch condition denoted by bb, the guard at y should be

cc.OR.(m1.AND.bb)

This condition is identical to that presented in the example.

The paper by Allen et al. [23] goes on to discuss how to deal with forward branches into implicitly iterative regions caused by backward branches . It also shows how to convert implicitly iterative regions to Fortran 90 WHILE loops. However, modern programming practice discourages the use of GOTO statements, particularly for the creation of implicitly iterative regions. Furthermore, Fortran 90 includes WHILE loops, which obviate the need for many implicitly iterative constructs. For these reasons, this book will henceforth assume that the only control flow constructs in programs presented to the compiler are explicit loops and forward unconditional or conditional branches. This assumption significantly simplifies the compiler's task.

7.2.6　Complete Forward Branch Removal

We are now ready to present a complete forward branch removal algorithm. This procedure, which is given in detail in Figure 7.3, processes the statements in its input statement list in order of appearance in the list of statements presented to it and maintains the *current condition*, which is to be used to guard the statement currently being processed.

At each statement, depending on the type of statement, the algorithm will perform the following steps:

1. If the statement is a branch target, the current condition must be computed in simplified form. To do that, it must combine the set of conditions associated with branches to that target with the current condition passed from the lexical predecessor of the statement. This is done by the simplification algorithm discussed in the next section. Processing of the statement then proceeds to step 2 below.

2. If the current statement is of any type except DO, ENDDO, or CONTINUE, which the if-conversion leaves unguarded, the current condition—either as computed in step 1 or inherited from the lexically previous statement in case the current statement is not a branch target—is conjoined to the guard for the current statement. If the current statement is unguarded, the current condition becomes its guard.

3. If the current statement is a DO, first invoke *relocate_branches* on the loop to eliminate any exit branches it may contain. This may generate some statements before the loop that should be guarded by the current condition. In addition, this may cause new statements to be inserted in the statement list after the revised loop. The branch removal procedure is applied recursively to the body of the loop that emerges after branch relocation.

4. If the current statement is a conditional branch, two copies of the current condition are made. The compiler-generated variable associated with the new condition is conjoined to the beginning of one of these copies, and the result is appended to the list associated with the branch target statement. The negation of the variable is conjoined to the beginning of the other condition, which becomes the current condition for the next statement in the program.

5. If the current statement is an unconditional branch, the current condition is appended to the list of conditions for the branch target statement. The current condition for the next statement is set to empty (false). If that statement is not a branch target, it cannot be reached.

6. Continue processing at step 1 with the next statement.

procedure *remove_branches(R,current)*
      // *R* is the collection of statements under consideration
      // *current* is the current condition at the beginning of the list

      for each statement *S* in *R* that is a potential branch target **do**
         cond(S) := ".FALSE.";

S_1:   **for each** loop *l* in *R* **do** *relocate_branches(l)*;

      for each statement *S in R* **do begin**
        if *S* is a branch target **then**
          current := *Simplify* (*current* || ".OR." || *cond(S)*);

        case *statement_type(S)* **in**
If: **begin** // IF (*P*) GOTO L — forward
           let m be a new compiler-generated logical variable,
              initialized to *true*;
           insert the assignment "IF(*current*) m := *P*";
           let S_L denote the statement at label *L*;
           $cond(S_L)$:= $cond(S_L)$ || ".OR." || *current* || ".AND.m";
           current := *current* || ".AND..NOT.m";
           delete statement *S*;
        end
Goto: **begin** // GOTO L
           let S_L denote the statement at label *L*;
           $cond(S_L)$:= $cond(S_L)$ || ".OR." || *current*;
           current := ".FALSE.";
           delete statement *S*;
        end
Loop: **begin** // DO B ENDDO — a loop
           remove_branches(B, current);
           // Because *relocate_branches* was applied first, the current
           // condition after the loop will be the same as before it
        end
Other: **begin** // All other statement types except continue
           if *S* is of the form "IF (*P*) S_1" **then**
              replace it with "IF (*current*.AND.*P*) S_1";
           else replace it with "IF (*current*) S";
        end
        end case
      end
end *remove_branches*

Figure 7.3 Complete forward branch removal.

The correctness of this procedure follows directly from the correctness of the algorithms for forward branch removal (Figure 7.1) and branch relocation (Figure 7.2), along with a simple induction on the recursion. All that remains to complete the algorithm is the simplification procedure, which is discussed in the next section.

7.2.7   Simplification

As has been evidenced in several of the examples presented so far, simplification of statement guards is an important aspect of if-conversion. Straightforward application of the algorithms presented results in clumsy, complex guarding conditions, and since the guards are repeatedly evaluated at run time, simplifying them as much as possible at compile time is obviously important. Unfortunately, it is not difficult to show that Boolean simplification is NP-complete. Given a Boolean simplification procedure that reduces expressions to simplest terms, a general Boolean expression will be unsatisfiable if and only if it simplifies to false. As a result, satisfiability can be reduced to simplification, and satisfiability is known to be NP-complete. It is also easy to show that if-conversion can produce arbitrary expressions, so there are no shortcuts available for simplifying the output of conversion algorithms.

Since the Boolean simplifier is called each time a potential branch target is processed, efficiency is an important consideration. While control flow within normal programs is rarely complex, it can be deep enough (particularly with Fortran assigned GOTOs) to cause exponential simplification times even in small programs. Note that the complexity of guard expressions at a particular statement is proportional to the number of branches that can affect the execution of that statement.

The most widely used simplification procedure, due to Quine and McCluskey [230, 208], operates in three phases:

1. It reduces the original logical expression to a disjunction of *minterms*, each of which is a conjunction including every logical variable in the original expression in either negated or nonnegated form.

2. It computes a collection of *prime implicants*—terms that exactly represent a disjunction of minterms in the original expression but are not contained in any other implicant. The strategy for computing implicants is to combine pairs of minterms that are identical in every factor except for a single variable that appears negated in one of the minterms and unnegated in the other.

3. It selects a minimal legal subset of the prime implicants, where a subset is legal only if it covers the original expression. That is, the disjunction of a legal selection of prime implicants is true if and only if the original Boolean expression is true.

To illustrate this process, we introduce an example that we will use throughout this section:

```
      DO I = 1, N
1        IF (P) GO TO 10
2           A(I) = B(I)
3           IF (Q) GO TO 20
10             C(I) = 0
20       A(I) = A(I) + C(I)
      ENDDO
```

After if-conversion with no simplification, this becomes

```
      DO I = 1, N
1        m1 = P
2           IF(.NOT.m1) A(I) = B(I)
3           IF(.NOT.m1) m2 = Q
10             IF((.NOT.m2.AND..NOT.m1).OR.m1) C(I) = 0
20       IF(((.NOT.m2.AND..NOT.m1).OR.m1).OR.m2) &
             A(I) = A(I) + C(I)
      ENDDO
```

Let us begin by applying the Quine-McCluskey procedure to statement 20.
The first stage reduces the guard to a collection of minterms:

$$(\neg m2 \wedge \neg m1) \vee (m2 \wedge m1) \vee (\neg m2 \wedge m1) \vee (m2 \wedge \neg m1)$$

To find the prime implicants, we successively reduce terms. The second and third
minterms $(m2 \wedge m1) \vee (\neg m2 \wedge m1)$ can be reduced to $m1$, while the first and last
minterms $(\neg m2 \wedge \neg m1) \vee (m2 \wedge \neg m1)$ can be reduced to $\neg m1$. In turn, these
can be reduced to the single prime implicant .TRUE. that represents the entire
expression. Therefore, the guard on statement 20 is empty. A similar analysis will
show that the guard on statement 10 can be reduced to a pair of prime implicants:

$$(\neg m2 \wedge \neg m1) \vee (m2 \wedge m1) \vee (\neg m2 \wedge m1) = \neg m2 \vee m1$$

Unfortunately, the Quine-McCluskey algorithm is known to be exponential in
the size of the original expression, making it impractical for general if-conversion.
However, we will show that by redefining the simplification problem to meet the
minimal needs of if-conversion, the exponential behavior can be eliminated.

A faster algorithm can be derived by sacrificing economy of representation
and instead concentrating on the real reason for simplification: the determination
of when a compiler-generated branch variable can be factored out of the current
guard condition. To illustrate the difference, let us return to our example. If we

simplify the guard expressions for both statement 10 and statement 20 using Quine-McCluskey, we get

```
    DO I = 1, N
1      m1 = P
2          IF(.NOT.m1) A(I) = B(I)
3          IF(.NOT.m1) m2 = Q
10             IF(.NOT.m2.OR.m1) C(I) = 0
20     A(I) = A(I) + C(I)
    ENDDO
```

Here it should be clear that the simplification of the guard on statement 20 is much more important than the simplification of the guard on statement 10 because we *eliminate* variables from the guard expression at statement 20, while at statement 10 we have a simpler expression in exactly the same variables. If we decline to simplify at statement 10, we get the slightly more complicated form

```
    DO I = 1, N
1      m1 = P
2          IF(.NOT.m1) A(I) = B(I)
3          IF(.NOT.m1) m2 = Q
10             IF((.NOT.m2.AND..NOT.m1).OR.m1) C(I) = 0
20     A(I) = A(I) + C(I)
    ENDDO
```

The significant aspect of this example is the fact that variable m1 does not simplify out of the guard until the branch target for m2 is reached, even though the branch target for variable m1 is reached at statement 10. In general, logical branch variables can only be simplified out of an expression in the reverse order that they are introduced by the algorithm. In other words, the most recently introduced logical variable will simplify out first. Thus, m1 cannot be eliminated until statement 20 (the branch target for m2) is reached. At that time, both variables can be eliminated by simplification, and the resulting statement is unguarded.

This discussion suggests that a good way to streamline simplification is to worry only about simplifying the variable that has been most recently introduced. That is, rather than attempting to simplify all variables in the current condition at a given statement, the simplifier should instead concentrate on eliminating the last variable introduced. This form of simplification would result in the last version of the example; the more complex guard on statement 10 in that example illustrates the price paid for the streamlining. The main difference is that the streamlined algorithm simplifies only when it is possible to eliminate a variable from a guard and hence eliminate an input to the guarded statement. This is the critical task for simplification in support of if-conversion.

With this observation, it is now possible to specify a fast simplification algorithm. This algorithm will maintain conditions as a disjunction of *terms*, each of which represents a conjunction of *factors*, where a factor is a variable that may or may not be negated. Within a term, the factors will appear in inverse order of introduction, so that the most recently introduced variable will appear first in the term. The most recently introduced factor is called the *key factor*—it contains the variable that must be simplified out of the term before any other variables can be considered for elimination.

The simplification algorithm, which is given in detail in Figure 7.4, is designed under the assumption that it is used in the procedure *remove_branches* given in Figure 7.3. Recall that *remove_branches* processes the statements in order of appearance in the program and maintains a *current condition*, which is the condition that should be used to guard the current statement.

The simplifier is called only when a potential branch target is encountered. It must combine the set of conditions associated with branches to that target with the current condition passed from the lexical predecessor of the statement. These conditions can be collected into a set of terms, each of which as a key factor. If there exists a pair of terms whose key factors contain the same variable, it must be the case that the two terms are identical except for that factor, where the variable must be negated in one term and not in the other. (To see this, remember that the two terms represent distinct paths in which the last branch was on the variable in the key factor—since the paths are distinct, the two paths must have gone in different directions at that branch.) If such a pair can be found, the terms are replaced in the collection by a single term consisting of either of the original terms with the key factor stripped off. In other words, the key factor has been eliminated. The first factor in the new term becomes the new key factor. This step is repeated until no two terms contain the same variable in their key factors. When this happens, the disjunction of the collection of terms remaining is the new current condition.

To illustrate this algorithm more concretely, consider again the previous example. At the time statement 1 is processed, the current condition is .TRUE., which is represented by an empty condition. After statement 1 is processed, statement 10 has the condition "m1" on its target list and the current condition is ".NOT.m1". At statement 3, the condition

$$m2.AND..NOT.m1$$

is added to the list for statement 20 and

$$.NOT.m2.AND..NOT.m1$$

becomes the new current condition. As a result, as statement 10 is processed (invoking statement 4 of the algorithm), the two conditions to consider are the current condition and the condition on the target, that is,

".NOT.m2.AND..NOT.m1" and "m1"

These two conditions are disjoined to create the new current condition. Since the key variables are different, no further simplification is possible. Finally, we reach statement 20, with the terms

> "m2.AND..NOT.m1," ".NOT.m2.AND..NOT.m1," and "m1"

The first two terms have the same variable in their key factors and are combined to yield

> ".NOT.m1" and "m1"

which have the same variable in their key factors. The result simplifies to .TRUE., which is the desired result. Note that no simplification is performed on statement 10.

The streamlined simplification algorithm for use in the forward if-conversion procedure is given in Figure 7.4.

---

procedure *Simplify*(*cond*)
    // *cond* is a disjunction of terms, each term having a key variable
    // *seen* is a set of variables that have been seen as key variables
    //   in the current condition
    // *sofar* is the set of terms that have been added so far to the list
    //   for the output condition.
    // *worklist* is the collection of terms currently under consideration for
    //   the output current condition.

    seen := ∅; *sofar* := ∅;
    worklist := the set of terms in *cond*;
    while *worklist* ≠ ∅ **do begin**
        let *t* be an arbitrary element of *worklist*;
        worklist := *worklist* – {*t*};
        let *k* be the variable in the key factor for *t*;
        while *k* ∈ *seen* **do begin**
            take the term *q* corresponding to *k* from *sofar*;
            sofar := *sofar* – {*q*};
            t := the term resulting when the key factor is stripped from *q*;
            k := the variable in the key factor at the beginning of *t*;
        end
        sofar := *sofar* ∪ {*t*};
        seen := *seen* ∪ {*k*};
    end
    return the disjunction of terms in *sofar*;
end *Simplify*

Figure 7.4 Simplification.

At each branch target, this algorithm does an amount of work proportional to the number of terms in the current condition. To see this, note that the outer loop is executed once for each term in the current condition. At each step of the inner loop one term of the current condition is eliminated, so the total number of iterations of the inner loop over the entire algorithm is limited by the number of terms in the original current condition as well.

Note that the number of terms in the current condition is roughly proportional to the number of control flow paths past the current point in the program—the number of edges severed by a cut through the control flow graph at this point. If we are applying an if-conversion only to forward branches, this number is bounded by the number of statements in the program. Thus, for the case of forward branches, the total cost of simplification over the entire program is no worse than $O(N^2)$, where N is the number of statements in the program.

7.2.8   Iterative Dependences

Once an if-conversion has been applied to a program, all dependences due to action statements, branch statements, and placeholder statements are representable as data dependences. However, those statements do not account for all control dependences. Iterative statements can also create control dependences, as the next example illustrates:

```
20 DO I = 1, 100
40     L = 2 * I
60     DO J = 1, L
80         A(I,J) = 0
       ENDDO
   ENDDO
```

If the assumption is made that the iterative statements do not carry any control dependences, the example could be incorrectly vectorized as

```
20 DO I = 1, 100
40     L = 2 * I
   ENDDO
80 A(1:100,1:L) = 0
```

The original example zeroes out a triangular section of the result array. The vectorized example zeroes out a rectangular section. The vectorized result fails to duplicate the variant boundary based on the outer loop. This variance is overlooked because there are dependences that are missing from the dependence graph. These dependences must capture the notion that a DO statement controls the number of times a particular statement is executed. To model this, we will introduce the notion that each statement in a loop has an implicit iteration range input that will be represented in the example code by inclusion in parentheses at the end. Thus,

$$A(I,J) = 0 \text{ (irange2)}$$

denotes that the statement is controlled by iteration range irange2, which is a compiler-generated scalar designed to hold the iteration range for the level-2 loop.

The iteration range variable for a given loop will be assigned at a point corresponding to the point where the iteration range would be evaluated in the original program. In Fortran, the loop bounds are evaluated just prior to entering the loop, so the assignment should be nested just outside the loop it controls. In the case of a conditional loop, such as a WHILE loop, the control condition is evaluated on each pass through the loop; therefore, the assignment for a WHILE loop should be nested at the same level as the statements within the loop.

Using this strategy, the example that started this discussion would be converted to

```
20   irange1 = (1,100)
     DO I = irange1
40      L = 2 * I (irange1)
60      irange2 = (1,L) (irange1)
        DO J = irange2
80         A(I,J) = 0 (irange2)
        ENDDO
     ENDDO
```

Before determining dependences, the compiler should forward-substitute any constants and loop-independent variables, using methods similar to those in Chapter 4. This would reduce the program to

```
20   DO I = 1, 100
40      L = 2 * I (1,100)
60      DO J = 1, L (1,100)
80         A(I,J) = 0 (1,L) (1,100)
        ENDDO
     ENDDO
```

For the purposes of dependence testing, constant inputs are ignored, so the dependence pattern constructed would be the one given in Figure 7.5. Note that the antidependences carried by the level-1 loop are due to the fact that the scalar upper bound L of the inner loop is used implicitly by both the loop statement and the assignment at statement 80.

When the standard vectorization procedure is applied to this dependence graph, it produces the following code

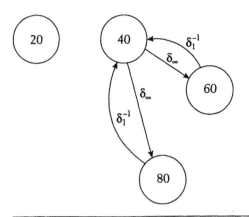

Figure 7.5 Iterative dependence example.

```
20   DO I - 1, 100
40       L = 2 * I
80       A(I,1:L) = 0
     ENDDO
```

in which the inner loop is eliminated because it is empty.

To achieve maximum performance, it is desirable to move the range computations out of as many loops as possible and to forward-substitute whenever we can. This is demonstrated by the following example:

```
10   READ 5, L, M
     DO I = 1, L
20       N = 2 * I
         DO J = 1, M
             DO K = 1, N
30               A(I,J,K) = 0.0
             ENDDO
         ENDDO
     ENDDO
```

After conversion, this becomes

```
10   READ 5, L, M
     irange1 = (1,L)
     DO I = irange1
20       N = 2 * I (irange1)
         irange2 = (1,M) (irange1)
         DO J = irange2
             irange3 = (1,N) (irange2)
```

```
                 DO k - irange3
30                   A(I,J,K) - 0.0 (irange3)
                 ENDDO
             ENDDO
         ENDDO
```

When forward substitution is performed following the methods in Section 4.5.1, we get the following code:

```
10   READ 5, L, M
     DO I - 1, L
20      N = 2 * I (1,L)
        DO J - (1,M), (1,L)
           DO k - (1,N) (1,M) (1,L)
30             A(I,J,K) - 0.0 (1,N) (1,M) (1,L)
           ENDDO
        ENDDO
     ENDDO
```

The dependence graph for this example is given in Figure 7.6.
When the vectorization algorithm is applied to this example, it will produce

```
READ 5, L, M
DO I - 1, L
   N - 2 * I
   A(I,1:M,1:N) - 0.0
ENDDO
```

Iterative dependences arising from while loops can be handled similarly, except that the condition is evaluated within the loop. For example:

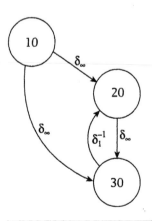

Figure 7.6 Iterative dependence example.

```
DO I = 1, L
   M = I * 2
   J = 0
   DO WHILE (J.LT.M)
      J = J + 1
      A(I,J) = 0
   ENDDO
ENDDO
```

The conversion in this case would produce

```
irange1 = (1,L)
DO I = irange1
   M = I * 2 (range1)
   J = 0 (irange1)
   irange2 = (J.LT.M) (irange1)
   DO WHILE (irange2)
      irange2 = (J.LT.M) (irange2)
      J = J + 1 (irange2)
      A(I,J) = 0 (irange2)
   ENDDO
ENDDO
```

Because the condition irange2 is recomputed each time the inner loop is executed, no vectorization is possible without further modifications. In an effort to convert the inner while loop to an iterative loop, we introduce the compiler generation induction variable jtemp:

```
irange1 = (1,L)
DO I = irange1
   M = I * 2 (range1)
   J = 0 (irange1)
   irange2 = (0.LT.M) (irange1)
   DO jtemp = 1, nolimit WHILE (irange2)
      irange2 = (J.LT.M) (irange2)
      J = J + 1 (irange2)
      A(I,J) = 0 (irange2)
   ENDDO
ENDDO
```

Now induction-variable substitution and forward expression folding will yield the following code:

```
DO I = 1, L
   M = I * 2 (1,L)
   J = 0 (1,L)
   irange2 = (0.LT.M) (1,L)
   DO jtemp = 1, nolimit WHILE (irange2)
      irange2 = ((jtemp-1).LT.M) (irange2)
      A(I,jtemp-1) = 0 (irange2)
   ENDDO
ENDDO
```

Now irange2, which controls the inner loop statements, is simply the test (jtemp-1.LT.M), which can be folded back into the loop control condition to produce a completely iterative loop:

```
DO I = 1, L
   M = I * 2 (1,L)
   J = 0 (1,L)
   irange2 = (1,M+1) (1,L)
   DO jtemp = 1, M+1
      A(I,jtemp-1) = 0 (irange2)
   ENDDO
ENDDO
```

This version of the loop can be vectorized in the second dimension, producing

```
DO I = 1, L
   M = I * 2 (1,L)
   A(I,0:M) = 0
ENDDO
```

In addition to illustrating how to deal with iterative dependences for WHILE loops, this example shows a general procedure for converting WHILE loops to iterative loops using transformations that are variants of those discussed in Chapter 4.

7.2.9 If-Reconstruction

While if-conversion is an extremely useful transformation, it has negative performance implications when vectorization is not possible. Consider, for instance, the following example:

```
DO 100 I = 1, N
   IF (A(I).GT.0) GOTO 100
   B(I) = A(I) * 2.0
```

```
         A(I+1) = B(I) + 1
100 CONTINUE
```

After if-conversion, the loop becomes

```
      DO 100 I = 1, N
         m1 = (A(I).GT.0)
         IF (.NOT.m1) B(I) = A(I) * 2.0
         IF (.NOT.m1) A(I+1) = B(I) + 1
100 CONTINUE
```

Because of a recurrence, this loop cannot be correctly vectorized. In the untransformed example, there is only one conditional evaluation. Based on the results of that evaluation, either a branch is taken or the two assignments are unconditionally executed. In the transformed example, the one conditional is again evaluated, but in addition, conditionals are executed before each assignment. On loop iterations where the branch would not be taken, the transformed example incurs extra overhead evaluating conditionals before each assignment. On loop iterations where the branch would be taken, the transformed code executes a sequence of branches where the original code would execute one. That is, when executed on a typical machine (where "typical machine" is one that does not have conditional execution but does have branches), the transformed example would generate assembly code similar to the following loop:

```
      DO 100 I = 1, N
         m1 = (A(I).GT.0)
         IF (m1) GOTO 10
            B(I) = A(I) * 2.0
10       IF (m1) GOTO 20
            A(I+1) = B(I) + 1
20       CONTINUE
100 CONTINUE
```

Because of the extra overhead associated with the guarded execution, if-conversion will degrade the performance of this example. To avoid this degradation in loops that do not vectorize, we can apply an inverse transformation pass known as *if-reconstruction*. Simply stated, if-reconstruction converts guarded execution into a sequence of conditional branches.

The goal of if-reconstruction is to replace sections of guarded code with a minimal set of branches that enforce the guarded execution. If the order of statements out of *codegen* in a nonvectorized loop is the same as the input order, then reconstructing a set of branches no worse than the original loop is fairly easy. However, *codegen* often changes the order of statements. Furthermore, programmers do not always use a minimal number of branches when coding. Both of these mean that more intelligent methods are necessary to determine sections of code controlled by equivalent conditions. Forward branches can be handled by a simple topological walk through the dependence graph, maintaining like guards as long as possible. Exit branches have the property of locking statements tightly in a recurrence, so that regions are easily found. However, many common recurrences that can be handled by vector hardware are often coded as exit branches (for instance, searches for first and last elements that are true in a conditional vector). An important part of the reconstruction process is recognizing these recurrences and converting them to code that effectively uses the vector unit. This kind of recurrence recognition was discussed in Section 7.2.4.

While if-reconstruction can remove most of the inefficiencies introduced by if-conversion, the process of if-conversion, Boolean simplification, and if-reconstruction represents a substantive amount of work by the compiler—useless work when no vectorization results. Moreover, some form of control dependence is necessary for transformations such as scalar expansion. These disadvantages make an alternative to if-conversion desirable. The next section explores such an alternative.

7.3   Control Dependence

Although if-conversion neatly solves the problem of vectorization in the presence of conditional branches, it has a number of undesirable side effects. The most problematic of these is that it unnecessarily complicates the code when vectorization is not possible. It would be much more desirable to analyze the code to determine that vectorization or parallelization is possible, then convert I F statements only when it is required to generate parallel code. Unfortunately, this cannot be done with if-conversion because the transformation must be done in advance to ensure that data dependences characterize all of the constraints that must be met to preserve correctness.

In this section we explore a different approach in which the constraints established by control flow are characterized by a different class of dependence called *control dependence*. Intuitively, a control dependence exists if the statement at the source of the dependence is a conditional branch that can determine whether or not the statement at the sink of the dependence is executed. In the remainder of this section we will formalize this intuitive definition and show how it can be used in vectorization and parallelization.

We begin with a concrete definition of control dependence:

**DEFINITION
7.1**

A statement *y* is said to be *control dependent* on another statement *x* if (1) there exists a nontrivial path from *x* to *y* such that every statement $z \neq x$ in the path is postdominated by *y*, and (2) *x* is not postdominated by *y*.

The intuition behind this definition is that x must be a conditional branch such that if the branch is taken in one direction, y must be executed, while if it goes the other way, control can avoid y.

Because a basic block is defined as the maximal group of statements such that all are executed if and only if any one is executed, it is convenient to discuss control dependence as being a property of basic blocks. There is no change in control flow within a basic block, so every statement in a block has the same control dependences. Consider the example in Figure 7.7.

In this figure, each node represents a basic block, and each edge represents a possible transfer of control. The set of blocks on which a given block is control dependent is specified by each node. It is interesting to note that neither block 4 nor block 5 depends on block 1, because block 1 cannot force execution of either block 4 or 5 by transferring to one of its successors. Furthermore, block 6 does not depend on block 3 because there is no way to avoid executing block 6 once control reaches block 3.

Control dependence graphs (that is, graphs that represent the control dependences between blocks) can be much larger than their associated control flow graphs, as shown in Figure 7.8. In this example, each node on the left-hand side of the diagram is control dependent on only one other node. However, each node on the right-hand side is control dependent on node 1 plus every even-numbered node that can reach it. Thus the total number of control dependences for a graph with $2n + 2$ nodes is n for the left-hand side plus

$$\sum_{i=1}^{n}(i+1) = \frac{n(n+1)}{2} + n$$

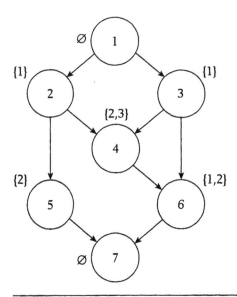

Figure 7.7 Control dependence example.

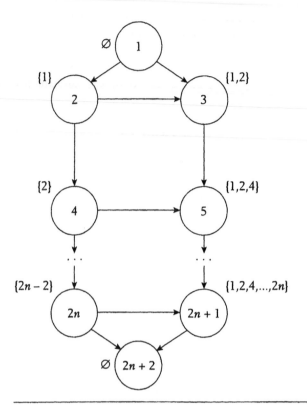

Figure 7.8 Quadratic growth of the control dependence graph.

for a total of

$$\frac{n(n+1)}{2} + 2n = \frac{n(n+5)}{2}$$

or $O(n^2)$ control dependences.

7.3.1 Constructing Control Dependence

Before a control dependence graph can be used in vectorization, it must be constructed. The algorithm *ConstructCD* in Figure 7.9, due to Cytron et al. [97], is the fastest known method for the general construction of a control dependence graph from a control flow graph.

procedure *ConstructCD(G,CD)*
    // G is the input control flow graph
    // CD(x) is the set of blocks on which x is control dependent
    // ipostdom(x) is the immediate postdominator of block x in the
    //   control flow graph G.

L_1:   find the immediate postdominator relation *ipostdom* for the control flow graph
        G; (For a control flow graph with a single exit, this relation forms a tree,
        with the exit node as the root.);
       let *l* be a topological listing of the postdominator tree such that,
         if x postdominates y, then x comes *after* y in *l*;

L_2:   **while** $l \neq \emptyset$ **do begin**
       let x be the first element of *l*;
       remove x from *l*;

L_3:   **for all** control flow predecessors y of x **do**
          if *ipostdom(y)* $\neq$ x **then** CD(x) = CD(x) $\cup$ {y};

L_4:   **for all** z such that *ipostdom(z)* = x **do**
          for all y $\in$ CD(z) **do**
             if *ipostdom(y)* $\neq$ x **then** CD(x) = CD(x) $\cup$ {y};
   end
end *ConstructCD*

Figure 7.9 Control dependence construction algorithm.

Algorithm *ConstructCD* depends on the construction of a postdominator tree.

DEFINITION 7.2   A node x in directed graph G with a single exit node *postdominates* node y in G if any path from y to the exit node of G must pass through x.

Figure 7.10 contains the postdominator tree for the control flow graph shown in Figure 7.7. Note that all vertices are postdominated by the exit vertex 7.

The problem of computing postdominators in a directed graph has been explored by a number of researchers. The commonly used Lengauer-Tarjan algorithm [198] requires $O(E\alpha(N,E))$ time in the worst case, where N and E are the number of nodes and edges in the control flow graph, respectively, and α is a very slowly growing function related to an inverse of Ackerman's function. In fact, α grows so slowly that for all practical effects, this algorithm is effectively linear in the size of the input graph. More recently, Harel has published an algorithm that achieves a linear time bound [138]. We prefer using the iterative algorithm given in Figure 4.8, modified to compute postdominators. Cooper, Harvey, and Kennedy

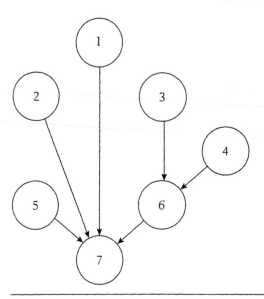

Figure 7.10 Postdominator tree for Figure 7.7.

have shown that this is highly efficient on graphs arising from real programs if the set data structures are implemented cleverly [84].

Correctness. To prove that Algorithm *ConstructCD* correctly constructs the control dependence relation, we must show that, after execution, $y \in CD(x)$ if and only if x is control dependent on y.

Note that the algorithm processes nodes in an order that is consistent with the postdominator relationship. This ensures that if x postdominates z, then z will have been processed before x is processed. Thus we can prove the theorem by an induction that assumes that when x is processed, the property is true for all vertices that it postdominates. The completion of this proof is left to the reader as Exercise 7.4.

Complexity. Not counting the construction of postdominators, algorithm *ConstructCD* requires $O(\max(N+E, |CD|))$ time in the worst case. To see this, note that the topological sort takes $O(N+E)$ time, while the header of the loop at label L_2 is executed once for every node in the control flow graph or $O(N)$ times. The loop at label L_3 is entered once for each control flow predecessor of each node, for a total of $O(E)$ times, and since its body can be implemented in constant time, the total time required by the loop is $O(E)$.

The loop at label L_4 is more complicated—it is executed once for each edge in the postdominator tree, but since each node has only one postdominator, the loop header is executed only $O(N)$ times. The inner loop is executed at most once for each edge in the control dependence graph, so the loop nest takes $O(|CD|)$ time. The overall time bound follows immediately.

Since this time bound is the maximum of the size of its input and its output, there can be no algorithm that is asymptotically better in performance.

7.3.2 **Control Dependence in Loops**

Although loops can be handled by the standard algorithm by converting them to a control flow graph and then applying *ConstructCD*, there are advantages to treating them as a special case. For instance, it is sometimes useful to have a loop control node to which we can attach information about the iteration of the loop. This node can then be used to represent the loop in all sorts of transformations. For example, loop distribution can be handled by cloning the loop node.

In the representation we employ here, we will use a loop control node to represent the loop. We can think of this node as evaluating the loop control expression that determines the next iteration. The question immediately arises: Which statements in the program are control dependent on the loop control node? Recall that a control dependence exists from S_1 to S_2 if one branch out of S_1 forces execution of S_2 and the other does not. Clearly, the loop control node forces execution of one iteration of the loop body, so all statements within the loop that are not control dependent on another statement in the loop are clear candidates. In general, there should be an edge from the loop control vertex to every vertex in the loop that will be executed if the loop body is executed.

This is illustrated by the following example:

```
10    DO I = 1, 100
20        A(I) = A(I) + B(I)
30        IF (A(I).GT.0) GOTO 50
40            A(I) = -A(I)
50        B(I) = A(I) + C(I)
      ENDDO
```

The control dependence graph for this loop is given in Figure 7.11. The false label attached to the control dependence between statement 30 and 40 is used to indicate that the statement is forced if the if-condition is false. We note that by analogy with the while statement the loop control dependences are annotated with true, indicating that the while condition is true. Thus if the while condition is false, the statements are not executed.

The thing that is special about the loop control statement is that it establishes a collection of statement instances that can be executed. In the case of a DO-loop with a fixed iteration range from 1 to 100 by 1, the loop control variable can be thought of as spawning 100 instances of each statement in the loop body. The correct execution of those statement instances is discussed in the next section.

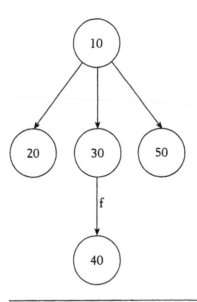

Figure 7.11 Control dependence example.

7.3.3   An Execution Model for Control Dependences

In the following sections we will argue that the transformations involving control dependence are correct. However, to address the problem of correctness, we must have an execution model for a program annotated with control and data dependences, and we must show that this model is correct. We have seen that data dependence indicates that statements must be executed in a particular order. Control dependence essentially says the same thing; however, it is a bit more complicated because it also tells us *whether* a statement is executed.

Recall that in Chapter 2 we developed a model that allowed us to reorder statements or statement instances if it did not reverse the order of the source and sink of the dependence. Without flow of control, there were only statements and loops. We could therefore think of the program execution as a collection of statement instances $S(i)$, each of which is indexed by iteration vector i for the nest of loops containing the statement. In this model $S(i)$ could be executed whenever every statement instance that it depended on had already been executed. In other words, if $S(i)$ depended on $S_0(j)$, where $j \leq i$, then $S_0(j)$ must execute before $S(i)$. We can think of this as an execution model in which a statement can be executed at any time after all it depends on have been executed.

Control dependence introduces the extra possibility that S_2 could depend on S_1 but S_1 is never executed. In the execution model above, S_2 would not be able to execute either. This situation is illustrated by the following pseudocode:

```
        DO I = 1, N
S₀         IF (P) GOTO 100
             S₁
100        S₂
        ENDDO
```

On those iterations where the branch is taken, execution of $S_2(I)$ should not wait until $S_1(I)$ has been executed, because that will never happen. Although the dependence is real on other iterations, the path from $S_1(I)$ to $S_2(I)$ is not executed on those iterations, so there is no dependence.

We can address this problem by thinking of each statement instance as having an execution variable $S(i).doit$. Statement instances that are not control dependent on any other statement instances have their *doit* flags initialized to true. The *doit* flags for all other statements are initially set to false. Then we can execute a statement instance $S(i)$ if its *doit* flag is set to true and every statement instance it depends upon either has a false *doit* flag or has been executed.

In this model, how does a *doit* flag for a statement get set to true? The rule is simple: all those statements that are control dependent on the conditional and whose execution is forced by the sense of the condition have their *doit* flags set to true.

This leads us to annotate control dependence with the truth value of the condition that forces execution. All those statements that are control dependent on a conditional and have their execution forced if the condition is true have their control dependence edge annotated with true, and all those forced by a false condition have their edge annotated with false. Thus the control dependences in the previous example loop body are shown in Figure 7.12.

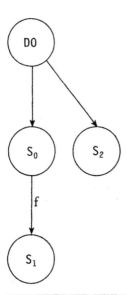

Figure 7.12 Control dependence example.

We observe that if the *doit* flag for a given statement S is set to true, then there exists a sequence of control statements $S_0, S_1, \ldots, S_m = S$ such that S_0 is not control dependent on any other statement and, hence, is executed unconditionally in the original program and that the decision taken at S_k forces the execution of S_{k+1} for each k, $0 \le k < m$. Thus the sequence of control dependences defines a unique execution path that must have been taken in the original program.

All that remains to the specification of the execution model is to define the behavior of loop control nodes in the execution of a control dependence graph. We begin with the simple case of a loop node that is not contained in a control or data dependence cycle carried by the loop it heads. If this is the case, then when the *doit* flag for the loop node is set to true, the range of iteration of the loop can be completely evaluated. When this happens, the execution of the loop header creates a collection of statement instances, one for each statement on each iteration of the loop. It then sets the *doit* flags of every statement instance that represents a statement that is control dependent on the loop header to true. The *doit* variables of all other statement instances on this step are set to false. Statement instances with true *doit* flags are eligible for execution as before.

In the case where there is a dependence cycle, where the evaluation of the iteration range depends on quantities computed in the loop, the execution of the DO node is more complex. If the range of iteration is nonempty, it creates a new statement instance of itself adjusting the range to be the remainder of the iterations. That DO node is given a *doit* flag of true if the dependence back to the DO node is a data dependence, and false if it is a control dependence. It then creates statement instances for each statement in the loop, setting the *doit* flags for all statements control dependent on the loop header to true, and the others to false. Execution then proceeds normally.

The correctness of this model is given by the following.

THEOREM
7.1

Dependence graphs that are executed according to the execution model given in this section are equivalent in meaning to the programs from which they are created.

Proof

Note that the execution model requires that no statement instance executes before a statement that it depends upon. Thus, we need only concern ourselves with the additional complexities of control dependences. The essence of this proof is to establish that the dependence graph executed under the graph execution model executes exactly the same set of statements as the original program. To do this, we must show that a statement in the graph has its *doit* flag set to true if and only if it is executed in the original program.

Assume the contrary, that some statement instance $S_x(i_0)$ gets the wrong *doit* flag. Then there exists some sequence of statement instances $S_0, S_1, \ldots, S_m$, such that S_0 is control dependent on no other statement (and therefore always executed) and $S_m = S_x(i_0)$. Furthermore, assume without loss of generality that S_m is the first statement in the sequence to get the wrong *doit* flag. Further assume without loss of generality that this is the shortest sequence leading to a wrong *doit* flag. The sequence therefore represents a sequence of control decisions along an execution path in the original program leading to $S_m = S_x(i_0)$. Since all of the decisions on the path are the same except the last one, made at S_{m-1}, we must consider the decision made at S_{m-1}. Given that all the data dependences are honored, all statements that S_{m-1} depends upon, either directly or indirectly, along the execution path must have already been executed by the time the decision at S_{m-1} is made—their *doit* flags must all have been set correctly because otherwise there would have been a sequence of decisions of length $m - 1$ leading to a statement with the wrong *doit* flag, contradicting the assumption that the shortest such path is of length m.

By a similar argument, no statement that is not executed in the original program can be executed in the graph and affect the control decision at S_{m-1} because it would also have a wrong flag and the sequence of decisions leading to it would be shorter than m, contradicting the assumption. Therefore, the decision made at statement S_{m-1} must be identical to the one in the original program.

This proof carries through to graphs including DO nodes without any change so long as you note that statements in the above proof can be statement instances.

This theorem gives us a tool to establish that transformations that preserve data and control dependences are correct. In addition, it will serve as the basis for a code generation procedure for dependence graphs.

7.3.4 **Application of Control Dependence to Parallelization**

Having the capability of creating a control dependence graph, the next problem is how to apply it to parallel code generation. More specifically, there are two concrete problems that have to be solved:

1. Adapting the transformations used in code generation (i.e., loop distribution, loop fusion, loop interchange) to work with control dependence.

2. Converting the abstraction of statements, data dependence, and control dependence back into executable code (in other words, reconstructing the control flow from the control dependence graph).

The following sections discuss each of these issues.

Control Dependence and Transformations

When examining control dependence, it is useful to start by restricting consideration to loop-independent control dependences—that is, those that arise due to forward branches within a loop. Backward branches create implicit loops, which are transformed separately, and exit branches create a complex series of loop-carried dependences as discussed in Section 7.2.4. For simplicity, this section discusses only forward branches, which create only loop-independent control dependences, and control dependences due to loops.

As we learned in Chapter 2, most loop transformations are unaffected by loop-independent dependences, regardless of whether the dependence is a data dependence or a control dependence. Loop reversal, for instance, has no effect on a loop-independent dependence. Similarly, loop skewing, strip mining, index-set splitting, and loop interchange do not affect loop-independent dependences. The two loop-based transformations that do affect loop-independent dependences are loop fusion and, in the case of control dependence, loop distribution. Loop fusion is invalid when it converts a loop-independent dependence between two loops into a loop-carried dependence within one. However, when exit branches are excluded, this type of control dependence is not possible (the branch must exit one loop to enter the other). This leaves loop distribution as the one that can invalidly impact control dependences. If the source and target of a loop-independent control dependence are distributed into two separate loops, the loop-independent dependence will invalidly become loop carried. For example, in the following code

```
        DO I - 1, N
S₁        IF (A(I).LT.B(I)) GOTO 20
S₂          B(I) - B(I) + C(I)
20      CONTINUE
        ENDDO
```

the only dependence is a control dependence from S_1 to S_2. Distributing the two statements into separate loops is clearly wrong

```
        DO I - 1, N
S₁        IF (A(I).LT.B(I)) GOTO 20
        ENDDO
        DO I - 1, N
S₂          B(I) - B(I) + C(I)
        ENDDO
20      CONTINUE
```

since it is clearly incorrect to skip all iterations of S_2 simply because one iteration of S_1 happens to take the branch. The situation is analogous to splitting a scalar dependence across two loops without expanding the scalar.

Given that the central element of all code generation algorithms presented so far was maximally distributing a single loop into the finest granularity possible, handling loop distribution correctly is critical if control dependence is to be successfully incorporated into that framework.

Loop distribution can be thought of as cloning a loop control statement and partitioning the statements that were control dependent on the original into two groups, one for each of the new loops. Since any group of statements involved in a recurrence cannot be split between the two resulting loops, we have a clear condition for when it is legal. The tricky part is what to do when a control dependence crosses between distributed loops. Of course, you could clone the conditional statement, but this runs the risk that you might evaluate the same expression, with associated duplication of side effects, twice. What is really needed is some mechanism for capturing the *doit* flags for the controlled statements in some representation for use across the arrays. To put it another way, since it is possible to have a loop-independent control dependence span two minimal distributed loops, one of which can be vectorized and one of which cannot, the essential transformation required is the ability to save the results of a conditional computation until they are needed—just as with scalars and scalar expansion.

This suggests a transformation similar to if-conversion that would save the result of the conditional expression evaluation in a logical array that could be interrogated later. For instance, assuming that you desired to distribute the previous example (more likely, you would not), it could be correctly accomplished as

```
        DO I = 1, N
S₁          e(I) = A(I).LT.B(I)
        ENDDO
        DO I = 1, N
S₂          IF (e(I).EQ..FALSE.) B(I) = B(I) + C(I)
        ENDDO
```

While the basic transformation applied here is the same as if-conversion, there is an important difference involving how it is applied. If-conversion blindly converts all control dependences, resulting in a uniform data dependence representation during loop distribution. This transformation is applied after loops have been fully distributed and fused again, to patch up control dependences broken by the transformation process.

A more complex illustration of the problem that control dependences present for loop distribution is provided by the example code in Figure 7.13.

The control flow graph for this example is given in Figure 7.14, and the corresponding control dependence graph is shown in Figure 7.15. When data dependences are added, marked by the dotted arrows in Figure 7.16, the breakdown into piblocks becomes apparent.

The dashed regions in Figure 7.16 indicate the loop structure suggested by full distribution, followed by fusion into maximal "like" regions. Loop 1 is a parallel loop, loop 2 is sequential, and loop 3 is parallel. To correctly effect this

```
    DO I = 1, N
1       IF (A(I).NE.0) THEN
2          IF (B(I)/A(I).GT.1) GOTO 4
        ENDIF
3       A(I) = B(I)
        GOTO 8
4       IF (A(I).GT.T) THEN
5          T = (B(I) - A(I)) + T
        ELSE
6          T = (T + B(I)) - A(I)
7          B(I) = A(I)
        ENDIF
8       C(I) = B(I) + C(I)
    ENDDO
```

Figure 7.13 An example for loop distribution in the presence of control dependence.

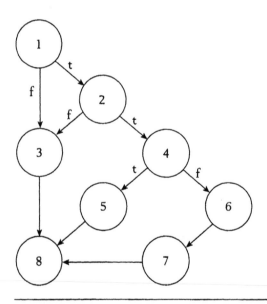

Figure 7.14 Control flow graph for Figure 7.13.

transformation, the control flow edges that cross the partition boundaries must be transformed into a persistent form. This persistence can be created by using arrays called *execution variables* to capture the branch decisions made at the source of loop-crossing arcs. The example above requires two execution variables: E2(I), to hold the result of branches at statement 2, and E4(I), to hold the result of

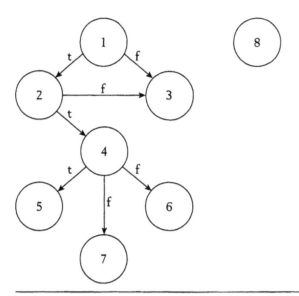

Figure 7.15 Control dependence graph for Figure 7.13.

branches at statement 4. To understand the values that an execution variable may take on, consider the cases that may hold at each of these two statements. At statement 2, three cases may hold:

1. statement 2 is executed and the true branch to statement 4 is taken,

2. statement 2 is executed and the false branch to statement 3 is taken, or

3. statement 2 is never executed because the false branch is taken at statement 1.

These three conditions can hold at any statement that is the source of a loop-crossing control dependence. This corresponds to the requirement in our execution model that three conditions must hold for a *doit* variable to be set for a given statement S—a control dependence exists from some statement S_0 to S, S_0 has its *doit* flag set, and the value of the conditional expression is the label on the branch to S (i.e., it forces execution of S).

Therefore, it seems natural to model these conditions by using three values for an execution variable element: *true, false,* or *undefined* (sometimes represented by the symbol "⊤"), corresponding to the three conditions above. Once it is determined which execution variables will be needed, all such variables are initialized to ⊤. Then the program is converted to set the execution variables at appropriate places in the code. The algorithm in Figure 7.17 performs the conversion. Note that this algorithm does not generate parallel code, but selectively converts control dependences to data dependences, changing some statements in the process.

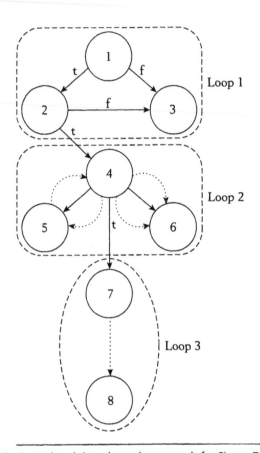

Figure 7.16 Control and data dependence graph for Figure 7.13.

Correctness. To establish correctness of algorithm *DistributeCDG* in Figure 7.17, we must show that it produces a dependence graph that has the same meaning as the original graph. This follows directly from the correctness of the execution model established in Theorem 7.1 and from the observation that the *doit* flag in the new graph for a statement after distribution will be set if and only if it was set in the original program. To establish this, we observe that the only problem is when a control dependence crosses partition boundaries. In that case, there is one *doit* flag per statement instance in the loop. Since the statement instances in the two loops are identical, we must show that the execution variable array captures the correct *doit* flags for the statement indices controlled by the control dependence edge that crosses the loops.

Thus, our goal is to show that in the revised program the *doit* flag for each corresponding instance of S will be set if and only if the *doit* flag for S is set in the original, nondistributed version of the loop. First note that the two loop control

procedure *DistributeCDG*(G, G_{cd}, P)
    // G is the input control flow graph
    // G_{cd} is the input control dependence graph
    // $P = \{P_1, P_2, \ldots, P_k\}$ is a list of partitions corresponding to loops after distribution
    // Output: modified G_{cd} with execution variables

L_1:   **for each** partition P_i **do begin**
        for each $n \in P_i$ such that there exists an edge $(n,o)_l \in G_{cd}$, where
           l is the true/false label of the control dependence edge, such that $o \notin P_i$
        do begin
           insert "$EV_n(I)$ = T" into P_i at the beginning;
           let *test* be the branch condition for n;
           if there exists an edge $(n,m)_l \in G_{cd}$, where $m \in P_i$ **then**
              replace n with
                 "$EV_n(I)$ = *test*"
                 "IF ($EV_n(I)$.EQ..TRUE.)";
                 // Conditions now depend on this latter test
           else
              replace n with "$EV_n(I)$ = *test*";
           for each $P_k \neq P_i$ containing a successor of n **do begin**
              create a new, unique statement N:
                 "IF ($EV_n(I)$.EQ. .TRUE.)";
              add N to P_k;
              insert data dependences for EV_n;
              for each $(n,q)_l$ such that $q \in P_k$ **do begin**
                 // Update control dependences
                 delete $(n,q)_l$ from G_{cd};
                 add $(N,q)_{true}$ to G_{cd};
              end
           end
        end
      end
      make a copy of the original DO-node, copying all dependences in, and insert a
        control dependence edge from this new DO node to every statement in P_i;
end *DistributeCDG*

Figure 7.17 Execution variable and guard creation.

statements have exactly the same sets of control predecessors, so that both loops are executed if the original loop would have been executed. Furthermore, the two sets of statement instances generated by the two loops are identical.

If. Assume that on iteration i, the control predecessor S_c is executed in the original program. Then its *doit* flag will be set to true, as will the *doit* flags of all the control successors that are forced by the label equal to the condition controlling the branch. In the transformed graph, the label will be captured in the execution variable $EV(i)$ and passed to another conditional, which tests for the correct truth value before setting the *doit* flag of the controlled statement. Thus the *doit* flag for statement S will be set correctly in the transformed program.

Only if. If the control predecessor S_c did not execute in the original program on iteration i, the execution array element $EV(i)$ will be set to T and the comparison test on that variable in the second loop of the transformed program will always produce false, ensuring that the statement will not be executed. On the other hand, if the wrong truth value is produced by the evaluation of the conditional, then the test for that truth value in the other loop will fail and the *doit* flag for the statement will not be set. This completes the argument.

Applying the algorithm *DistributeCDG* to the example in Figure 7.13 with appropriate code generation yields the program shown in Figure 7.18. "Appropriate code generation" is the subject of the next section.

```
      PARALLEL DO I = 1, N
        E2(I) = T;
   1    IF (A(I).NE.0) THEN
   2        E2(I) = (B(I)/A(I).GT.1)
        ENDIF
   3    IF(E2(I).NE..TRUE.) A(I) = B(I)
      ENDDO
      DO I = 1, N
        E4(I) = T;
        IF (E2(I).EQ..TRUE.) THEN
           E4(I) = (A(I).GT.T)
   4       IF (E4(I).EQ..TRUE.) THEN
   5          T = (B(I) - A(I)) + T
           ELSE
   6          T = (T + B(I)) - A(I)
           ENDIF
        ENDIF
      ENDDO
      PARALLEL DO I = 1, N
        IF (E4(I).EQ..FALSE.) THEN
   7       B(I) = A(I)
        ENDIF
   8    C(I) = B(I) + C(I)
      ENDDO
```

Figure 7.18 Example code from Figure 7.13 after loop distribution.

Generating Code

While control dependence graphs can represent arbitrary control flow, real machines can only execute a fairly limited set of control flow operations. It is not obvious that, once loop distribution and other transformations have been carried out, a dependence graph with control dependence can be mapped back into an executable form. To illustrate how difficult this problem can be, assume for the moment a target machine that can execute Fortran's control flow operations, so that the target language is Fortran. The following example

```
      DO I = 1, N
S₁       IF (p1) GOTO 3
         S₂
         GOTO 4
3        IF (p3) GOTO 5
4        S₄
5        S₅
      ENDDO
```

creates the control dependence graph shown in Figure 7.19. This figure also shows the partitions desired after distribution and fusion.

Loop distribution according to the partitions in Figure 7.19 produces the control dependence graph in Figure 7.20. Nodes 1a and 1b are two new nodes, data dependent on node 1, generated in the second partition by the distribution algorithm.

When code is generated for these two partitions, the first partition becomes

```
      DO I = 1, N
         E1(I) = p1
         IF (E1(I).EQ.FALSE) THEN
            S₂
         ENDIF
         S₅
      ENDDO
```

The second partition is not so simple. Statement 4 is control dependent on two different conditional nodes, so it cannot be put in a single structured conditional statement without some transformation. A simple way to solve this problem is to use a variant of if-conversion. The only nonconditional statement in the graph for the second partition is statement 4. If we compute the set of conditions on which it depends in the manner of if-conversion, we would get the following code:

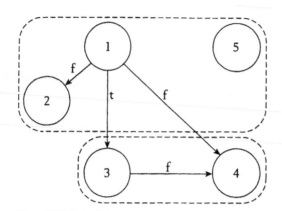

Figure 7.19 Control dependence graph for sample code fragment.

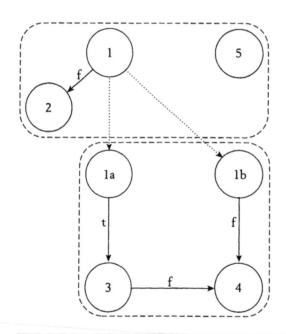

Figure 7.20 Control dependence graph for sample code fragment after distribution.

```
DO I = 1, N
   IF((E1(I).EQ..TRUE.).AND..NOT.p3).OR.
      (E1(I).EQ..FALSE.)) THEN
         S4
   ENDIF
ENDDO
```

However, things are not always this straightforward. Consider a simple variant of the same original loop:

```
      DO I = 1, N
S₁        IF (p1) GOTO 3
          S₂
          GOTO 5
3         IF (p3) THEN
             S₄
             GOTO 6
          ENDIF
5         S₅
6         S₆
      ENDDO
```

The control dependence graph after distribution (according to the dashed lines in the diagram) is given in Figure 7.21. Suppose further that there is a data dependence from S_4 to statement S_5. Code generation for this case is harder

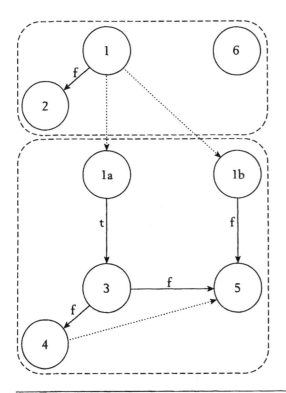

Figure 7.21 Control dependence graph for sample code fragment.

because we can generate a structured IF statement for S_4 but not for S_5. To solve this problem we will use a variant of if-conversion that generates a separate IF statement for each statement that has multiple control dependence predecessors. The code resulting from this strategy might be as follows:

```
DO I = 1, N
   P1a3 = (E1(I).EQ..TRUE.).AND..NOT.p3
   IF(P1a3) S4
   IF (P1a3.OR.(E1(I).EQ..FALSE.)) S5
ENDDO
```

It should be easy to see that generating code for graphs in which every vertex has at most one control dependence predecessor is easy—simply generate each statement in the true or false branch of the controlling conditional. To exploit this observation, our general code generation algorithm for loop-free dependence graphs with control dependences will operate in two phases. The first phase will transform the control dependence graph into a *canonical form* consisting of a set of control dependence trees having the following properties:

1. Each statement is control dependent on at most one other statement (i.e., each statement is a member of at most one tree).

2. The trees can be ordered so that all data dependences between trees flow from trees earlier in the order to trees that are later in the order.

In phase two, we will apply a simple recursive procedure that generates code for a canonical-form collection of trees.

We will motivate the discussion with the dependence graph shown in Figure 7.22. In this diagram, the solid lines represent control dependences and the dashed lines represent data dependences. We assume that each node from which control dependences emanate is an IF statement that evaluates some predicate and the other nodes are simple statements. In each case the node label is the statement number.

From Figure 7.22, several things are clear. First, statements 3 and 7 have multiple control dependence predecessors. These vertices must first be separated out so that their trees are in order. The desired effect is shown in Figure 7.23, in which initialization statements 1a, 5a, 6a, and 8a have been generated to capture the result of evaluating the predicates in statements 1, 5, 6, and 8. This strategy is used to avoid duplicate predicate evaluations. Each of these initialization assignments will have a compiler-generated logical variable on the left-hand side.

The new vertices "1|5&6" and "5&6|8" are the composite nodes controlling vertices 3 and 7, which previously had multiple control dependence predecessors. Note also that node 6 has no statement under its control so it can be deleted. Node 5, on the other hand, cannot be deleted because it now contains the initialization statement for the predicate in node 6.

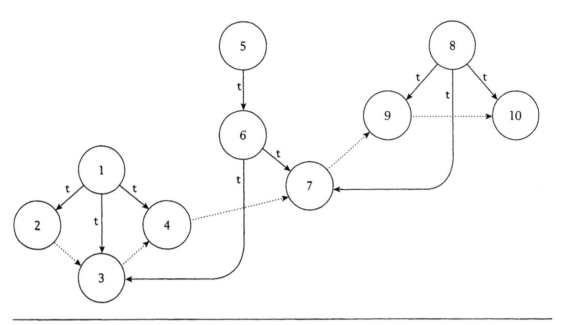

Figure 7.22 An example control dependence graph.

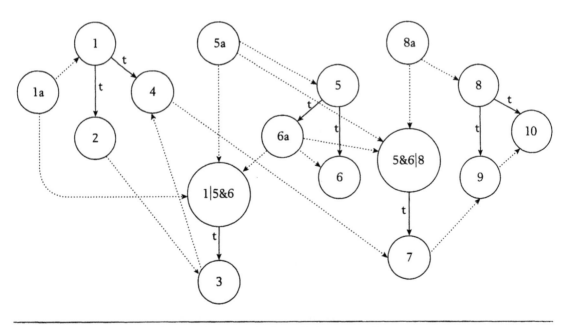

Figure 7.23 Example control dependence graph after splitting out vertices.

The next step is to see if the trees can be linearly ordered. As it happens, this cannot be done because of the data dependences from statement 2 to statement 3 and from statement 3 to statement 4. This requires further splitting of the trees to create separate trees for statements 2 and 4. The result of doing this is shown in Figure 7.24, which is in the desired canonical form. Code can now be generated for the trees in an order consistent with data dependence: 1a, 1, 5a, 5, 1|5&6, 1b, 8a, 5&6|8, and 8.

One remaining issue is how to do the second splitting step, where control dependence successors of control statements are organized into groups of statements that can be part of the same conditional statement. Statements can be grouped together if there is no dependence path between them that passes through a statement that is not a child of the same conditional node with the same label. From this description, it is easy to see that grouping is a typed fusion problem, which can be solved using the typed fusion algorithm from Section 6.2.5 if each statement is typed by a pair (p, l), where p is its unique control dependence predecessor and l is the truth label of the edge from p to the statement.

The code for the control dependence splitting pass is given in Figure 7.25. Once this pass is complete, we have a control dependence graph consisting of an ordered collection of trees in which each vertex has at most one control dependence predecessor.

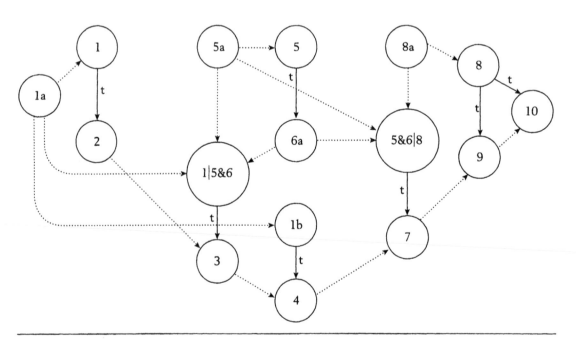

Figure 7.24 Example control dependence graph after splitting for data dependence.

procedure *CDGsplit*(G_{cd},P)

    // G_{cd} is the input control dependence graph

    // P is the collection of statements in the loop body

    for each vertex *v* in P that has multiple CDG predecessors **do begin**

        let $\{c_1, c_2, \ldots, c_m\}$ be the set of CDG predecessors for *v*;

        create an initialization vertex e_i for each condition c_i for which

            an initialization does not exist and insert it into the dependence graph

            at the level of the original predicate;

        create a new vertex *w* labeled by the condition $c_1|c_2| \ldots |c_m$, if one does not

            already exist, otherwise let *w* be that vertex (create the vertex as a child of

            the deepest common ancestor);

        insert a data dependence edge from each e_i to *w*;

        make *v* a control dependence successor of *w*;

    end

    delete all conditional vertices that have no remaining successors

        (iterate to eliminate vertices whose successors are deleted);

    for each vertex *v* that is the control dependence successor of

        some other vertex *w* in the graph **do**

            make the type of *v* be (c_w, l_{wv}), where c_w is the condition

            associated with *w* and l_{wv} is the label of the edge between *w* and *v*;

    for each distinct type *t* **do begin**

        apply typed fusion to the graph for type *t*;

        if there is more than one cluster of type *t* **then**

            create a new tree for each cluster after the first,

                generating new condition evaluation nodes as needed, along with

                appropriate data dependences (create each new tree at the

                deepest possible level);

    end

  end *CDGsplit*

Figure 7.25 Control dependence splitting algorithm.

We can now use a simple recursive procedure for code generation. These procedures are given in Figures 7.26 and 7.27. This collection of procedures generates code for each of the subtrees forming the control dependence graph in an order consistent with data dependence. The routine to generate code for a set of statements that are control dependent on a given vertex with the same label is shown in Figure 7.27. Since there is only one control dependence predecessor per statement in the canonical form, the control dependence predecessor of the set is ignored and the procedure simply calls *gencode* recursively for each statement in the set.

procedure *CDGgenCode*(G_{cd}, *P*)

// G_{cd} is the input control dependence graph in canonical form
// *P* is the collection of statements in the loop body

let *S* be the set of statements in *P* that have no control or data
   dependence predecessors;
while $S \neq \emptyset$ **do begin**
   let *n* be an arbitrary element of *S*;
   delete *n* from *S*;
   gencode(*n*);
   add to *S* any vertex that has no control dependence predecessors and all of
      whose data dependence predecessors have been processed by *gencode*;
end

end *CDGgenCode*

procedure *gencode*(*n*)
   if *n* is of the form IF(*p*) **then begin**
      let *T* be the set of statements *m* such that $(n,m)_{true} \in G_{cd}$;
      let *F* be the set of statements *m* such that $(n,m)_{false} \in G_{cd}$;
      if $T \neq \emptyset$ **then begin**
         generate "IF(*p*) then";
         genset(*T*, *n*);
         if $F \neq \emptyset$ **then begin**
            generate "ELSE";
            genset(*F*,*n*);
         end
         generate "ENDIF";
      end
      else if $F \neq \emptyset$ **then begin**
         generate "IF (.NOT. *p*) THEN";
         genset(*F*, *n*);
         generate "ENDIF";
      end
   end
   else // *n* is not a conditional
      generate *n*;
end *gencode*

Figure 7.26 Code generation from control dependence graphs.

We make two final points about the code generation algorithm. First, the running time of the code generation process should be roughly linear in the size of the original dependence graph, including both data and control dependences. The only portion of the algorithm that is not strictly linear is the repeated application

procedure *genset(S,n)* // version for structured code

```
    // Generate code for each statement in set S, in order
    // n, the control dependence predecessor, is ignored
    while S ≠ ∅ do begin
        let m be any element of S such that
            code has already been generated for all its data dependence predecessors;
        delete m from S;
        gencode(m);
    end
end genset
```

Figure 7.27   Procedure to generate code for a set of nodes from structured code.

of typed fusion, which could take time proportional to the size of the split graph (which can only be a linear factor larger than the original) times the number of distinct types. The number of types can be reduced by only using fusion on types that correspond to more than one statement.

As a second observation, this algorithm attempts to perform a limited if-conversion to generate code. In implementing it we must be careful not to do brute-force if-conversion if the result is to be satisfactory. This explains why, in the splitting algorithm, we must attempt to create duplicate nodes at the deepest possible level in the control dependence trees. When we generate a new condition to control a vertex that previously had multiple CDG predecessors, we attempt to generate that vertex as a child of the deepest common ancestor of those predecessors. When we apply typed fusion, we should generate copies of a condition as children of the least common ancestor of the original and any vertex on a path between the original vertex and the duplicate. This least common ancestor can be computed by a straightforward modification to the typed fusion algorithm.

We illustrate the code generation procedure by presenting an outline of the code that would be generated by this procedure for the control flow graph of Figure 7.24:

```
p₁ = pred1
IF (pred1) S₂
p5 = pred5
IF (p5) p6 = pred6
IF (p1.OR.(p5.AND.p6)) S₃
IF (p1) S₄
p8 = pred8
IF ((p5.AND.p6).OR.p8) S₇
IF (p8) THEN
    S₉
    S₁₀
ENDIF
```

In this code, the italicized *pred* variables represent predicate expressions. Each expression is evaluated exactly once. Note that in the interests of brevity simple I F statements have been used where only one statement is controlled by a condition.

7.4 Summary

Two distinct approaches to handling control flow in loops were presented:

1. *If-conversion* eliminates all branches by converting every statement in the program to a guarded conditional statement, where the guard reflects the exact set of conditions under which the statement will be executed. If the guards are viewed as inputs, this has the effect of converting control dependences to data dependences, making it possible to apply the code generation procedures from previous chapters to code with branches in a straightforward way. This transformation was effective in vectorizing compilers.

2. *Control dependence* is a variant of dependence arising from control flow. A statement S is *control dependent* on a statement S_0 if S_0 is a conditional branch and the decision at S_0 can force the execution of S in one direction and bypass it in the other. Control dependence can be used in analysis algorithms just like data dependence. However, it complicates the code generation process.

Code generation in the presence of conditional branches was a major topic in this chapter.

7.5 Case Studies

The original versions of both PFC and the Ardent Titan compiler used systematic if-conversion to handle control flow in loops. The PFC system implemented the complete if-conversion strategy discussed in this chapter, including the conversion of implicit loops to while loops. The success was mixed. PFC was able to vectorize extensively in loops where the only control flow was forward and within the loop. In other cases, not much benefit was achieved.

Two later versions of PFC, intended for parallelization, introduced if-reconstruction and then the execution variable scheme described here, although distribution was never implemented in its full generality.

If-conversion can consume lots of compile time. First there is the cost of the conversion itself—the fast simplification algorithm described in Section 7.2.7 was the result of a bad experience in which the exponential behavior of the Quine-McCluskey procedure was realized. Even with that code installed in PFC, if-conversion was slow. In addition, conditional operations, once vectorized, require a choice of execution form (execute the operation conditionally under masked hardware or compress the operands into a dense vector), and conditional vector operations can easily run more slowly than the scalar equivalent, depending on how many elements are actually executed. Furthermore, loads and stores of guard variables and arrays, along with the implicitly created vector masks, can cause memory hierarchy and storage problems.

Masked vector operations are not always easy or fast to perform on vector machines: mask hardware may make it easy to set or test mask bits, but usually provides no support for loads and stores or logical operations that directly operate on masks. For instance, the masks controlling the Titan vector unit were a special set of bits that could not be directly accessed via any instruction. The results of appropriately flagged vector compares and logical operations would set the mask bits; subsequent flagged vector operations would use them. To save a vector mask to memory, it was necessary to do a conditional vector move of a vector of all ones to a zeroed register (so that ones popped into the register where the mask was true) and store that to memory. Similarly, restoring a vector mask meant loading the values from memory and doing a compare against a vector of all ones. Once the vector operation that set a mask was gone, the mask could not be directly reset by another logical operation; instead it had to be pulled out into a vector register and operated on there. The result was that conjunction or disjunction of guard variables were very expensive to implement as vector operations.

Given all these considerations, plus the fact that the Titan had multiple processors for effectively speeding up conditional code, the Ardent compiler performed very limited if-conversion. Basically, only well-structured IF-THEN-ELSEs or branch patterns that formed structured IF-THEN-ELSEs were converted to guarded form. Any proper nesting of these was converted as well, although this turned out to be useless on the Titan—once the guard condition represented more than one IF, the resulting execution, even if perfectly vectorized, was always slower than scalar. Since only structured conditionals were converted, simplification was not necessary, and if-reconstruction was trivial. All other branching constructs (including jumps into loops, which are permitted in C) were handled with a variant of control dependence that is described in Chapter 12.

7.6 Historical Comments and References

The first handling of control flow changes for vector machines was by Towle and involved maintaining a conservative set of bit vectors to approximate simple control flow. If-conversion and the Boolean simplification scheme described in this chapter were developed by Allen et al. [23]; the key observations involved in Boolean simplification were developed by Warren and Kennedy for PFC. Besaw [41] implemented if-conversion with a similar Boolean simplifier in the Univac vectorizing compiler. Limited forms of if-conversion were the basis for conditional handling in many vectorizing compilers [270, 196].

Control dependence has a long history in compiler literature, although the primary development of it in terms of program transformations began with a paper by Ferrante, Ottenstein, and Warren [112]. The algorithm for construction is due to Cytron et al. [97].

The algorithms for distributing loops in the presence of control flow were developed by Kennedy and McKinley [174, 209], improving on earlier work by Callahan and Kalem [58] and Dietz [102]. Towle [259] and Baxter and Bauer [39] build condition arrays from a form of control dependence in vectorization. The code generation algorithm presented here is based on one by Kennedy and McKinley [174, 209], but generates structured code and overcomes a shortcoming that would produce incorrect code in some cases. The problem of "restructuring" unstructured code has been attacked by many researchers, including Ferrante, Mace, and Simons [110, 111], who discuss loop fusion, dead code elimination, and branch deletion in the presence of control dependence.

Exercises

7.1 Construct the control dependence graph corresponding to the control flow graph given in Figure 7.28.

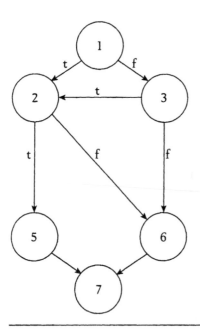

Figure 7.28 Control flow graph for Exercise 7.1.

7.2 The loop distribution transformation in the presence of control dependence uses execution variables that can take one of the three values: *true, false,* and *undefined.* Why are all three conditions needed instead of just *true* and *false?* Give an example where the value *undefined* is needed for correctness.

7.3 Consider the control dependence graph given in Figure 7.29, where the dashed regions indicate the desired regions after distribution. Show the control dependence graph after distributing the statements into two loops and the code that would be generated for the resulting loops by the procedure described in Section 7.3.4, subsection "Generating Code."

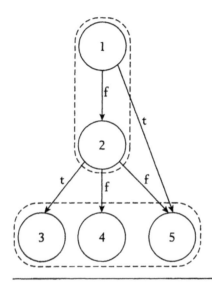

Figure 7.29 Control dependence graph for Exercise 7.3.

7.4 Prove that algorithm *ConstructCD* in Figure 7.9 correctly constructs the control dependence relationship. That is, after execution, $y \in CD(x)$ if and only if x is control dependent on y. *Hint:* The proof should be carried out by an induction on the order of processing of vertices in the algorithm, which ensures that, before a vertex x is processed, all its postdominators have been processed.

CHAPTER 8

Improving Register Usage

8.1 Introduction

Increasingly, the performance of a modern computer system is determined by the performance of its memory hierarchy. While on-chip operation speeds have been dramatically improving, the performance of memory has mostly remained constant. As a result, the latencies to main memory in terms of processor cycles have been increasing. These latencies must be ameliorated if the machine performance is to keep pace with the performance of the processor.

In this chapter, we will discuss the first of several ways to improve performance of the memory hierarchy through compiler transformations. Every computer system currently in use has some kind of processor register set. Registers are particularly important on RISC architectures, where all operations except loads and stores require that the operands be taken from processor registers and all results be assigned to registers.

Most modern machines also feature some sort of cache memory; however, some do not. Examples of machines without cache include vector processors and the Tera MTA series, in which each thread has its own register set. We will postpone the discussion of compiler management of cache until Chapter 9.

8.2 Scalar Register Allocation

In most compiler courses, we teach students that the problem of scalar register allocation has essentially been solved by the register coloring techniques pioneered by Chaitin and his colleagues at IBM research [69, 68] and refined by Chow and Hennessy at Stanford [76] and by Briggs et al. at Rice [45].

These techniques attempt to allocate all of the uses of each scalar variable in a single "live range"—the program region through which the given variable is live—to a register. To accomplish this, the compiler typically carries out the following steps:

1. It identifies the live ranges of variables and gives each a unique name.

2. It builds an interference graph to model which pairs of live ranges cannot be assigned to the same register.

3. Using a fast heuristic coloring algorithm, it attempts to color the resulting interference graph with a number of colors equal to the number of registers available.

4. If the coloring fails, it forces at least one live range out of registers and repeats the attempt to color beginning at step 3.

This approach is used in the C and Fortran compilers for every RISC processor known to the authors. In practice, this method is very effective. In most small routines it produces a perfect allocation, in which every nonarray variable is assigned to a register throughout every one of its live ranges. Thus, conventional wisdom says that nothing more can be done to improve register usage on a uniprocessor.

However, conventional wisdom fails to consider floating-point registers, which are typically used to hold temporarily individual elements of array variables. You can think of a floating-point register as containing a very small window of information, equal to one word, in the array it represents. To achieve the highest performance, we must try to make as much use as possible of the data in the window before moving on to another element, because each reuse of the element in the window eliminates the need for a load instruction that might take tens or even hundreds of cycles.

To see the importance of these techniques, consider a simple example that can be viewed as an abstraction of the calculation that occurs in matrix multiplication:

```
DO I = 1, N
   DO J = 1, M
      A(I) = A(I) + B(J)
   ENDDO
ENDDO
```

Before this example was widely understood, almost every industrial compiler would fail to recognize that A(I) can be left in a register throughout the inner loop, even though it is easy to see that the address of A(I) does not change in that loop. The reason for this failure is that uniprocessor compilers only do a good job allocating *scalar* variables to registers—an array access is treated as an expression to be evaluated on each iteration of the loop. Even though the compiler can use strength reduction to recognize that the address does not change, few compilers extend strength reduction to eliminate the load instruction.

Now consider a slight variation of the previous program:

```
DO I = 1, N
   T = A(I)
   DO J = 1, M
      T = T + B(J)
   ENDDO
   A(I) = T
ENDDO
```

This version uses a scalar variable as a temporary resting place for the value of A(I) during the execution of the inner loop. All compilers that use a coloring scheme of any kind will properly assign this scalar variable to a register. Thus, the second loop will be much faster than the first, even though it differs only superficially.

This observation led to the development of an optimization, known as *scalar replacement*, that converts array references to scalar references to improve the effectiveness of the compiler's coloring-based register allocator. Although it is designed as a compiler optimization, scalar replacement can be understood and evaluated as a source-to-source transformation.

In the next few sections, we will present a number of such source-to-source transformations that improve the performance of a uniprocessor memory hierarchy, along with algorithms for implementing them.

8.2.1 Data Dependence for Register Reuse

So far, this book has focused on data dependence as a safety constraint for reordering transformations. In that context, dependence is an execution constraint that must be observed because two different statement instances may access the same memory location. Viewed in that light, the fewer dependences a program has, the better, since fewer constraints mean the compiler has more room to reorder statements. For register (and data) reuse, we use dependence in a different way. An exact data dependence represents two different statement instances that access the same memory location. Thus dependences can be viewed as indicating memory locations that are frequently reused and, as a result, should be kept in the fastest portion of the memory hierarchy. In that light, the more dependences a program has, the better, since more dependences mean more reuse. These two variations on the usage of dependence make it applicable to the optimization of a wide range of programs.

To see how data dependence can be used in register allocation, consider the various kinds of data dependences:

- A *true* or *flow* dependence indicates that a value is computed at the source and used at the sink. If the value can be kept in a register until the sink is reached, it does not need to be fetched from memory. Similarly, a cache miss can be saved if the block containing the referenced location stays in cache until the sink.

- An *antidependence*, in which the use of a variable precedes the assignment to it, does not have an application to improvement of register allocation. However, it can save a cache miss if the block that is brought in at the source stays in cache until the sink.

- An *output dependence* can also be useful in cache management, but it has a special use in register usage improvement as well. Consider:

S_1 A(I) =

. . .

S_2 = A(I)

. . .

S_3 A(I) =

Here there is an output dependence between S_1 and S_3, along with a true dependence between S_1 and S_2. The true dependence allows us to eliminate a load in statement S_2, but the output dependence tells us that, after the use in S_2, the value of A(I) is dead and need not be stored.

- For the purposes of memory hierarchy, we will use a fourth kind of dependence, called *input dependence*, in which the source and sink both use the same location.

S_1 = A(I)

. . .

S_2 = A(I)

The input dependence from S_1 to S_2 imposes no execution constraint, but it does present an opportunity to eliminate a load at the second reference. It is straightforward to modify a standard dependence testing procedure to compute input dependence.

Recall that the type of memory access is one characterization of dependences, leading to the reuse principles listed above. However, there is a second characterization: loop carried and loop independent. That characterization also leads to reuse principles, as described in the next section.

8.2.2   Loop-Carried and Loop-Independent Reuse

It is fairly obvious that loop-independent dependences can be a guide for reusing values. For instance, a loop-independent true dependence such as

S_1 A(I) =
S_2 = A(I)

can be rewritten as

S_1 t =
S_2 = t

so long as the dependence is known to be exact and there are no intervening stores. Normal scalar register allocation should do a good job on the second form. Similarly, loop-independent output dependences can be used to eliminate unnecessary stores and loop-independent input dependences can be used to avoid unnecessary loads.

On first examination, loop-carried dependences do not seem to provide such an obvious mechanism for reuse. However, closer examination shows that backward loop-carried dependences with small thresholds can serve the same function as loop-independent dependences. For instance

S_2 = A(I)
S_1 A(I+1) =

can be rewritten as

S_2 = t
S_1 t =

and again, a good scalar register allocator should do the right thing. In this simple examination, loop-carried dependences only seem to work with sinks that occur before the source (including the source statement proper), since otherwise the new value computed on the next iteration will overwrite the value needed from the previous iteration. However, it can be extended beyond this, as later sections will show. The analogous transformation works with both input and output dependences as well.

There are constraints that must be applied to loop-carried dependences if they are to be useful in register reuse. Recall that each carried dependence has a *threshold*, which is the dependence distance for the loop that carries the dependence. This threshold is said to be *consistent* if it is constant throughout the loop— that is, the threshold is the same on each iteration. A loop-carried dependence with a consistent threshold is called a *consistent dependence*. To be useful for memory management, a carried dependence must be consistent. In practice, carried dependences with thresholds that are small compile-time constants are the best candidates for elimination of memory references because they require the fewest registers to hold the value between source and sink of the dependence. Note that consistency is also required for loop-independent dependences to be useful for memory management.

```
DO I = 1, N
   DO J = 1, M
```

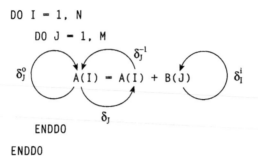

```
   ENDDO
ENDDO
```

Figure 8.1 Reduction example with dependences.

8.2.3 A Register Allocation Example

While the principles described in the previous section are simple, they are very powerful in practice. The following sum reduction loop indicates just how powerful these principles can be:

```
DO I = 1, N
   DO J = 1, M
      A(I) = A(I) + B(J)
   ENDDO
ENDDO
```

Here we find a true dependence and an output dependence from the statement to itself, both arising from the reference to A(I) and both carried by the J-loop. In addition, there is an antidependence from the statement to itself, also carried by the J-loop. Finally, there is an input dependence arising from the reference to B(J) carried by the I-loop. These dependences are depicted in Figure 8.1.

In this example, the true dependence carried by the J-loop indicates that a load can be saved if A(I) is kept in a register until the next loop iteration, while the output and antidependence show that both the initial load and the store on each iteration may be moved out of the loop entirely.

The loop that results after this transformation would require only one load per iteration, for B(J):

```
DO I = 1, N
   T = A(I)
   DO J = 1, M
      T = T + B(J)
   ENDDO
   A(I) = T
ENDDO
```

As indicated earlier, we use assignment of subscripted array variables to scalars to represent loads because most scalar register allocation procedures would put all scalar variables in registers, at least within a single subroutine.

8.3 **Scalar Replacement**

This section develops an algorithm for performing scalar replacement based on the simple principles developed earlier. The first step in the process involves pruning the dependence graph of extraneous dependences, so that each dependence can be used as a precise measure of gain in memory reuse. Later sections then extend the principles to handle more general dependences.

8.3.1 **Pruning the Dependence Graph**

In this section we will present an algorithm for pruning the dependence graph so that each dependence edge represents a possible elimination of a load or a store. The problem is illustrated by the following code:

```
     DO I = 1, N
S₁      A(I+1) = A(I-1) + B(I-1)
S₂      A(I) = A(I) + B(I) + B(I+1)
     ENDDO
```

The dependence patterns for A and B in this example are interesting. The assignment to $A(I+1)$ in statement S_1 reaches the use of $A(I)$ in statement S_2 but not the use of $A(I-1)$ in statement S_1 because it is killed by the assignment in statement S_2. The location used in S_2 at the reference to $B(I+1)$ is reused in S_2 an iteration later and again in S_1 on a third iteration.

The dependences before and after pruning are shown in Figure 8.2. The edges remaining after pruning are shown as solid lines. The dashed edges would be produced by dependence testing the normal way, but would not remain after pruning.

It is important to notice that each reference has at most one predecessor in the pruned graph, and each edge represents a potential memory access savings. The source of all edges in a group is called the *generator* of that group. The three generators in this example are the two left-hand sides of the assignment statements and the use of $B(I+1)$ in statement S_2.

If we assign all the references associated with a generator to a unique temporary, we will get the following code after scalar replacement:

```
            t0A = A(0); t1A0 = A(1); tB1 = B(0); tB2 = B(1)
            DO I = 1, N
    S₁          t1A1 = t0A + tB1
                tB3 = B(I+1)
    S₂          t0A = t1A0 + tB3 + tB2
                A(I) = t0A;
                t1A0 = t1A1; tB1 = tB2; tB2 = tB3
            ENDDO
            A(N+1) = t1A1
```

This code has only one load and one store in the main loop. The original code had five use references, all but one of which is eliminated because of the three edges in the pruned graph. In addition, a store has been eliminated because of the output dependence from A(I+1) to A(I), which makes a store of A(I+1) necessary only after the last iteration.

To prune the graph as depicted in Figure 8.2, we must eliminate two kinds of edges:

1. Flow and input dependence edges that do not represent a potential reuse because the value at the source is killed by an intervening assignment to the same location. The flow dependence from A(I+1) to A(I-1) in statement S₂ is an example of this kind of pruned dependence.

2. Input dependence edges that are redundant because of another reference, usually the generator, that has dependences to both endpoints. The input dependence from B(I) in S₂ to B(I-1) in S₁ is an example of this second type of pruned dependence.

Note that output dependences and antidependences cannot directly give rise to register reuse and are always pruned.

This suggests a three-phase algorithm for pruning edges.

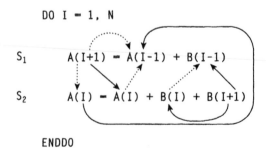

```
            DO I = 1, N


    S₁          A(I+1) = A(I-1) + B(I-1)



    S₂          A(I) = A(I) + B(I) + B(I+1)




            ENDDO
```

Figure 8.2 Effect of pruning.

Phase 1: Eliminate killed dependences. This phase prunes all dependences with a store to the location involved in the dependence occurring between the endpoints of the dependence. If the dependence to be pruned is a flow dependence, a killing store can be identified by the existence of an output dependence from the source of the dependence to an assignment from which there is a flow dependence to the sink of the dependence.

S_1 A(I+1) =

     . . .

S_2 A(I) =

     . . .

S_3 . . . = A(I)

Here the flow dependence from S_1 to S_3 will be pruned.

   If the dependence to be pruned is an input dependence killed by a store in the loop, it will have an antidependence from the source to the assignment from which there is a flow dependence to the sink.

S_1 . . . = A(I+1)

     . . .

S_2 A(I) =

     . . .

S_3 . . . = A(I-1)

Here the input dependence from S_1 to S_3 will be pruned.

Phase 2: Identify generators. In this phase all generators are identified. In the pruned graph, a generator is any assignment reference with at least one flow dependence emanating from it to another statement in the loop or a use reference with at least one input dependence emanating from it and with no input or flow dependence into it.

Phase 3: Find name partitions and eliminate input dependences. Starting at each generator, mark each reference reachable from the generator by a flow or input dependence as part of the name partition for that variable. A *name partition* is a set of references that can be replaced by a reference to a single scalar variable. Any input dependences between two elements of the same name partition may be eliminated unless the source of the dependence is the generator itself.

   A somewhat surprising consequence of this analysis is that the entire process of finding name partitions can be mapped to a typed fusion problem (Section 6.2.5) if we treat each reference as a vertex and each edge as joining two references. In this formulation, we use the name of the array in the reference as the type and define output dependences and antidependences as bad edges. Once the

```
DO I = 1, N
```
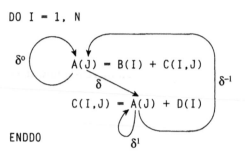
```
ENDDO
```

Figure 8.3 Reference in a dependence cycle.

typed fusion algorithm is run, each fused node represents a distinct name partition, and the initial node added to the fused node is the generator.

There are two additional complications that must be dealt with in this framework. First, there may be some references that are within a dependence cycle in
the loop. Note that the distinction here between references and statements is
important. Here is an example:

```
DO I = 1, N
    A(J) = B(I) + C(I,J)
    C(I,J) = A(J) + D(I)
ENDDO
```

In this example, the typed fusion algorithm will not visit reference A(J) because
it is in a cycle of dependences as shown in Figure 8.3.

To deal with this, we note that the references in any such cycle can all be
assigned to a single scalar throughout the loop. No replicated scalars are required:

```
DO I = 1, N
    tA = B(I) + C(I,J)
    C(I,J) = tA + D(I)
ENDDO
A(J) = tA
```

The final assignment can be moved out of the loop because of the output dependence of the assignment on itself. (Note that this code assumes $N \geq 1$.) If there
were an upwards-exposed use of A(J), an assignment to tA would need to be
inserted before the loop.

The second complication is the possibility of an *inconsistent* dependence. For a
dependence to represent reuse, it must be *consistent*, in that it has a constant
threshold throughout the iteration of the loop. Here is an example illustrating
dependences that are not consistent:

```
      DO I - 1, N
S         A(2*I) - A(I) + B(I)
      ENDDO
```

Even though there is a flow dependence from S to itself due to the references on A, this threshold changes on each iteration so the dependence is inconsistent and not suitable for reuse. Inconsistent dependences can be handled by marking them as bad edges in the typed fusion framework above. This will force a store and a load along any inconsistent dependence between references to the same array. Similarly, in references in a dependence cycle, the cycle should be broken by a bad edge, forcing a store and load. For example, consider the following loop:

```
      DO I - 1, N
S₁        A(I) - A(I-1) + B(I)
S₂        A(J) - A(J) + A(I)
      ENDDO
```

Here the reference to $A(I)$ in S_1 can be replaced by a scalar, but the reference to $A(I-1)$ must be loaded because it must be assumed that the store to $A(J)$ contaminates $A(I)$. This results in the following code:

```
      DO I - 1, N
S₁        tAI - A(I-1) + B(I)
          A(I) - tAI
S₂        A(J) - A(J) + tAI
      ENDDO
```

This code could be improved substantially by index-set splitting:

```
      tAI = A(0); tAJ - A(J)
      JU - MAX(J-1,0)
      DO I - 1, JU
S₁        tAI = tAI + B(I); A(I) - tAI
S₂        tAJ - tAJ + tAI
      ENDDO
      IF (J.GT.0.AND.J.LE.N) THEN
          tAI - tAI + B(J); A(J) = tAI
          tAJ - tAI ! can be forward-substituted
          tAJ = tAJ + tAI; tAI - tAJ
      ENDIF
      DO I - JU + 2, N
          tAI = tAI + B(I); A(I) - tAI
          tAJ - tAJ + tAI
      ENDDO
      A(J) = tAJ
```

The second code has two fewer loads and one less store per iteration.

The name partitions are the principal input to scalar replacement. However, before we present that algorithm, we present in Section 8.3.5 a practical refinement designed to overcome the limitations of existing scalar register allocators.

8.3.2   Simple Replacement

We now turn to the development of a general procedure for scalar replacement. We begin with a pruned dependence graph, developed as described in the previous section. In this graph, each true or input dependence represents an opportunity for eliminating exactly one load or store. If the dependence is loop independent, there is typically no problem replacing the second reference with a reference to a generated scalar. For example, in the following code, the transformation is straightforward:

```
DO I = 1, N
    A(I) = B(I) + C
    X(I) = A(I) * Q
ENDDO
```

In the pruned dependence graph, there will be a loop-independent dependence edge from the first statement in the loop body to the second. In this case, scalar replacement will require capturing the result of the computation in the first statement in a scalar t,[1] inserting a copy from the scalar to A(I), and replacing the reference to A(I) in the second statement by a reference to t, to produce

```
DO I = 1, N
    t = B(I) + C
    A(I) = t
    X(I) = t * Q
ENDDO
```

If t is assigned to a register in this loop, as we would expect with most compilers, there will be one less load on each iteration than in the original.

8.3.3   Handling Loop-Carried Dependences

This general procedure will work for any dependence or collection of dependences that spans less than a single-loop iteration—the first and last statements in the collection are either on the same iteration or, if they are on two successive

---

1. In the discussion that follows we will always denote compiler-introduced scalar variables intended for assignment to a register by a lowercase scalar variable such as t.

iterations, the last statement does not occur lexically after the first statement in the collection. As an example, consider the following:

```
DO I = 1, N
   A(I) = B(I-1)
   B(I) = A(I) + C(I)
ENDDO
```

Introducing two scalars, tA and tB, and inserting an initialization of tB before the loop, we get the following result:

```
tB = B(0)
DO I = 1, N
   tA = tB
   A(I) = tA
   tB = tA + C(I)
   B(I) = tB
ENDDO
```

Note that the scalars tA and tB would be combined by a good scalar register allocator into a single register. However, we will let the scalar compiler make that decision because it may be tied to timing issues that are too machine specific to address here.

8.3.4 Dependences Spanning Multiple Iterations

Scalar replacement becomes more complicated if the generating dependence crosses one or more full loop iterations:

```
DO I = 1, N
   A(I) = B(I-1) + B(I+1)
ENDDO
```

In this example, there is an input dependence from B(I+1) to B(I-1) because the same memory location referenced as B(I+1) on one iteration is referenced two iterations later as B(I-1). Thus, the distance for the dependence is two iterations.

The problem with the dependences that span more than a single iteration is that eliminating the load will require more than one temporary variable. This is because the value computed on any particular iteration will need to be preserved in a register beyond the point where the corresponding value for the next iteration is first referenced. In the current example, which spans two iterations, we will use three different scalar temporaries defined as follows:

```
t1 = B(I-1)
t2 = B(I)
t3 = B(I+1)
```

These relations may be thought of as "loop invariants" that must hold on each iteration of the loop. Now we are ready to consider the code that should be generated to eliminate the load at the dependence sink:

```
t1 = B(0)
t2 = B(1)
DO I = 1, N
   t3 = B(I+1)
   A(I) = t1 + t3
   t1 = t2
   t2 = t3
ENDDO
```

8.3.5 Eliminating Scalar Copies

While this code achieves the desired reduction in loads, it does so at the expense of introducing two scalar copy instructions that will be translated to register-register copies by the compiler. While such copies are fairly cheap, they do require instruction issue slots, degrading performance unnecessarily. Since these copies implement a permutation of values on machine registers, we can eliminate the need for copies by unrolling to the cycle length of the permutation, which would produce the following code:

```
t1 = B(0)
t2 = B(1)
mN3 = MOD(N,3)
DO I = 1, mN3
   t3 = B(I+1)
   A(I) = t1 + t3
   t1 = t2
   t2 = t3
ENDDO
DO I = mN3 + 1, N, 3
   t3 = B(I+1)
   A(I) = t1 + t3
   t1 = B(I+2)
   A(I+1) = t2 + t1
   t2 = B(I+3)
   A(I+2) = t3 + t2
ENDDO
```

The first loop, which is called a *preloop*, ensures that the number of iterations remaining when the main loop is entered is a multiple of three, so that no special testing for loop-ending conditions is needed in the main loop. The preloop is exactly the same as the naive solution discussed earlier. Now, however, the main loop is entered after at most two iterations of the preloop and requires no register-register copies while performing fewer loop-ending tests. It is fairly straightforward to prove that the final loop calculates the desired answer.

8.3.6 Moderating Register Pressure

Ideally, the scalar replacement procedure should be applied systematically to all name partitions in a loop. In practice, however, such an application will produce many scalar quantities that compete for a limited set of floating-point registers. This can cause an overload that many scalar register allocators are unable to deal with. As a result, it is often better for the scalar replacement system to limit the number of scalars to less than the number of available scalar registers.

To accomplish this, the system can attach two parameters to each name partition *R*:

1. The *value* of the name partition $v(R)$, which is simply the number of memory loads or stores saved by replacing every reference in R with references to register-resident scalars

2. The *cost* of the name partition $c(R)$, which is the number of registers needed to hold all the scalar temporary values that would be required to eliminate the references in R

Given the number of available registers n, the desired solution is the subcollection of reference sets $\{R_1, R_2, \ldots, R_m\}$ such that

$$\sum_{i=1}^{m} c(R_i) \leq n$$

that maximizes the total number of memory accesses

$$\sum_{i=1}^{m} v(R_i)$$

that are eliminated. It is easy to see that this is a packing problem known as the knapsack problem. In its most general form, bin-packing is *NP*-complete. However, the 0-1 knapsack problem can be solved in polynomial time by a dynamic programming algorithm, as shown in Figure 8.4.

It is well known that this procedure takes $O(nM)$ steps. However, if this is too time-consuming to include in a compiler, a good heuristic exists. If we order the

procedure *Pack(v,c,M,n,L,m)*

// $v[1:M]$ is the set of values for each of the M name partitions.
// $c[1:M]$ is the set of costs for each of the M name partitions.
// n is the number of registers available for array quantities.

// $L[1:m]$ lists the indices of name partitions in the best packing.

// $BP[0:n,0:M]$ is a profitability matrix such that
// $BP[i,j]$ is the value of the best possible packing of a bin of
//   size i using only reference sets 1 to j.

for $j := 0$ **to** M **do begin** $BP[0,j] := 0$; $last[0,j] := 0$ **end**
for $i := 1$ **to** n **do begin** $BP[i,0] := 0$; $last[i,0] := 0$ **end**

for $j := 1$ **to** M **do begin**
  for $i := 1$ **to** n **do begin**
    $BP[i,j] := BP[i,j-1]$; $last[i,j] := last[i,j-1]$;
    if $i - c[j] \geq 0$ **then**
      if $BP[i,j-1] < BP[i-c[j], j] + v[j]$ **then begin**
        $BP[i,j] := BP[i-c[j], j] + v[j]$;
        $last[i,j] := j$;
      end
  end
end
// Now unpack the list of included indices and save in *l*

$l := last[n,M]$; $m := 0$; $isize := M$;
while $l \neq 0$ **do begin**
  $m := m + 1$; $L[m] := l$;
  $sizeleft := sizeleft - c[l]$;
  $l := last[sizeleft, l-1]$;
end
end *Pack*

Figure 8.4 Register pressure moderation.

reference sets in decreasing order of the ratio $v(R)/c(R)$ of value to cost, we can select elements from the beginning of the list until the registers are full. In practice, the heuristic does extremely well.

8.3.7 Scalar Replacement Algorithm

We are now ready to present a simple scalar replacement algorithm (Figures 8.5–8.9) for loops that do not include conditional flow of control. This algorithm can be roughly divided into four phases as follows:

procedure *ScalarReplace*(L,G,n)

    // L is the loop nest over which we must generate code.
    // G is the augmented dependence graph among statements in L.
    // n is the number of registers available for array quantities.

    apply typed fusion to the dependence graph, with output dependences,
        antidependences, and inconsistent dependences marked as bad edges
        to produce a collection P of name partitions;

    use bin packing to choose the subset $\{p_1, p_2, \ldots, p_m\}$ of P to maximize
        the number of memory references saved while using no more than n registers;

    for $i := 1$ **to** m **do begin**
        if p_i is a noncyclic partition **then**
            ScalarReplacePartition(p_i, k_i);
        else begin
            ScalarReplaceCyclicPartition(p_i);
            $k_i := 1$;
        end
        for each inconsistent dependence δ in the loop **do**
            InsertMemoryRefs(δ);
    end

    // k_i is the number of temporaries introduced by scalar replacement
    let K be the least common multiple of $\{k_1, k_2, \ldots, k_m\}$;
    // unroll the loop to K loop bodies to eliminate scalar copies
    UnrollLoop(K);
end *ScalarReplace*

Figure 8.5 Scalar replacement.

1. First use typed fusion to find the collection of name partitions as described in Section 8.3.1. All the references in a collection will be replaced by a single temporary, or a set of temporaries replicated to cover multiple iterations.

2. Apply register pressure moderation to select the name partitions that fit into the available registers and maximize the number of saved memory references. This can be done by bin packing or by using the related heuristic as described in Section 8.3.6.

3. Replace each selected name partition with references to scalars:

    a. If it is a noncyclic partition, replace using a collection of unique temporaries, one per iteration spanned by the set as seen in Section 8.3.4. Output dependences are used to move stores out of loops where possible. Input dependences are used to move loads out of loops where possible.

procedure *ScalarReplacePartition(g,k)*

    // g is the set of dependences in the name partition.

    let k be the total number of iterations spanned by the set g;
    introduce unique temporary variables $\{t_1, t_2, \ldots, t_k\}$;

    let I be the index of the loop to which replacement is being applied;
    let $R(I+l)$ denote the reference in the group with subscript $I + l$
        in the position with the index I;
    let j be the largest additive value to I for a subscripted reference in g;
    // this means that $j - k + 1$ is the smallest additive value

    for each subscripted reference $R(I+l)$ in g **do begin**
        replace the subscripted reference by t_{j-k+1};
        if the reference is on the left-hand side of an assignment **then**
            if there is no output dependence to another assigned
                reference in the loop **then**
                insert the assignment "$R(I+l) = t_{j-k+1}$" as the statement
                    after the one containing the reference;
            else begin // there is an output dependence
                let $R(I+q)$ be the sink reference of the output dependence;
                if $q < l$ **then**
                    for $i := q + 1$ **to** l **do**
                        insert the assignment "$R(N+i) = t_{j-k+i}$"
                          after the loop; // N = loop upper bound
        end
    end

    let l be the largest additive value to I in a subscripted reference in the group to
        which there is a flow dependence from outside the loop;

    for $i := 1$ **to** $j - k + l$ **do**
        insert "$t_i = R(i)$" before the beginning of the loop;
    for $i := 1$ **to** $k - 1$ **do**
        insert "$t_i = t_{i+1}$" just before the end of the loop;

end *ScalarReplacePartition*

Figure 8.6 Scalar replacement of a noncyclic set of dependences.

    b. If it is a cyclic partition, simply replace all references with a single temporary.

    c. For each inconsistent dependence, either use index-set splitting to ensure that the right values are passed, or insert loads and stores within the loop.

  4. Finally, unroll the loop to the least common multiple of the number of iterations spanned by sets in the selected group to eliminate register-to-register copies as shown in Section 8.3.4.

procedure *ScalarReplaceCyclicPartition(g)*

 // *g* is the set of dependences in the name partition.

 if the reference involved *g* is not loop invariant **then**
  return without doing any replacement;
 let *R* be the loop-invariant reference for the name partition;
 let t be a unique temporary variable;
 for each subscripted reference *R* in *g* **do** replace *R* by t;
 if at least one reference is on the left-hand side of an assignment **then**
  insert "*R* ← t" right after the loop;
 if there is an upwards-exposed use of *R* in the loop **then**
  insert "t ← *R*" right before the loop;

end *ScalarReplaceCyclicPartition*

Figure 8.7   Scalar replacement of a cyclic set of dependences.

procedure *InsertMemoryRefs(δ)*

 // δ is the inconsistent dependence
 if δ links a loop-variant name partition with a loop-invariant one **then**
 begin // use index-set splitting to eliminate the problem
  split the loop into three parts:
   a) the iterations up to but not including the iteration
    containing the loop-invariant reference involved in δ
   b) the iteration containing the reference
   c) the iterations after the one containing the reference;
  scalar-replace the resulting three loops;
 end
 else if the dependence is a flow dependence **then begin**
  insert a store of the temporary for the source
   into the corresponding reference;
  let *R* be the earliest reference in the name partition of the sink
   that follows the source in the loop;
  insert a load of the temporary for *R* from *R* just before the ref
   if there is not one there already;
 end
 else if the dependence is an input dependence **then begin**
  let R_2 be the first reference to the sink after the current source ref;
  let R_1 be the last reference to the source before R_2;
  insert a store of the temporary for R_1 to R_1 right after R_1 if not redundant;
  insert a load of the temporary for R_2 from R_2 before R_2 if not redundant;
 end
end *InsertMemoryRefs*

Figure 8.8   Inserting memory references for inconsistent dependences.

procedure *UnrollLoop(K)*

> // K is the unroll factor
> split the loop into two loops, a preloop:
>> DO I = 1, MOD(N,K)
>
> and a main loop:
>> DO I = MOD(N,K) + 1, N;
>
> eliminate all register-to-register copies from the main loop;
> unroll the main loop to contain K copies of the body and have it
>> step by K:
>>> DO I = MOD(N,K) + 1, N, K;
>>
>> // As in all unrolling indices I is replaced by I + p in the pth copy
>> // of the loop body
>
> replace each reference to a unique generated constant t_j in the qth
>> copy of the loop body, where the first loop body is the 0th copy,
>> by a reference to $t_{MOD(j+q-1,k)+1}$ where k is the maximum index
>> for the temporary group of which t_j is a member;

end *UnrollLoop*

Figure 8.9 Unrolling to eliminate copies.

8.3.8   Experimental Data

To illustrate the effectiveness of scalar replacement, we report on the results of its application to a number of popular benchmark kernels and programs. The results shown here are from Carr's dissertation [64, 67]. In his experiments, he ran two versions of the program—the original and the version produced by scalar replacement applied to the original. Both versions were compiled and run on an IBM RS/ 6000 model 540. Speedup is computed by dividing the running time of the original by the running time of the version after scalar replacement.

Figure 8.10 shows the speedups achieved on the well-known Livermore loops. The figure shows only the loops for which a speedup occurred; for all other loops, there was no change. We can see that the improvements range from a modest 1.03 to an astounding 2.67, all over a compiler with a very good register allocator. Note that, unless the compiler on the target machine is exceedingly naive, scalar replacement can never result in a loss of performance.

Carr also tested scalar replacement on a number of well-known kernel programs, including LU decomposition as implemented in LAPACK [29], several of the NAS kernels, and some kernels he found locally at Rice (Table 8.1). The results, shown in Figure 8.11, include kernels for LU decomposition with and without pivoting and cover both the point algorithm and a blocked version. Each of these kernels contains invariant array references that require dependence analysis to detect, so these speedups would not be possible with a scalar-only compiler.

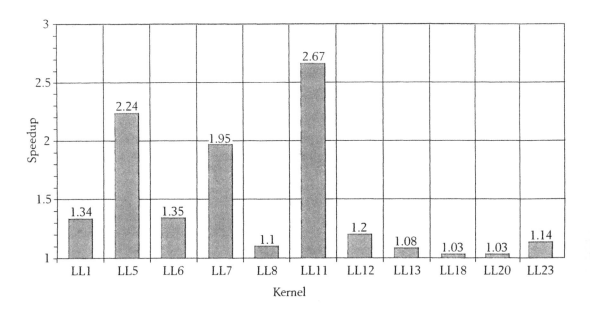

Figure 8.10 Scalar replacement on Livermore loops.

Table 8.1 Test kernels for memory transformations

Suite	Kernel	Description
Lin Alg	MM	Matrix multiplication
	LU	LU decomposition
	LUP	LU decomposition with pivoting
	BLU	Block LU decomposition
	BLUP	Block LU decomposition with pivoting
NAS	Vpenta	Pentadiagonal matrix inversion
	Emit	Vortex creation
	Gmtry	Gaussian elimination for vortex solution
Geophysics	Fold	Convolution
	Afold	Convolution
Local	Seval	B-spline evaluation
	Sor	Successive overrelaxation

The two exceptional performances, on Seval and Sor, were due to almost all of the running time being concentrated in a single computation-intensive loop, which scalar replacement successfully optimized.

Carr also ran scalar replacement on a number of benchmark applications (Table 8.2). These programs were taken from the well-known suites SPEC and

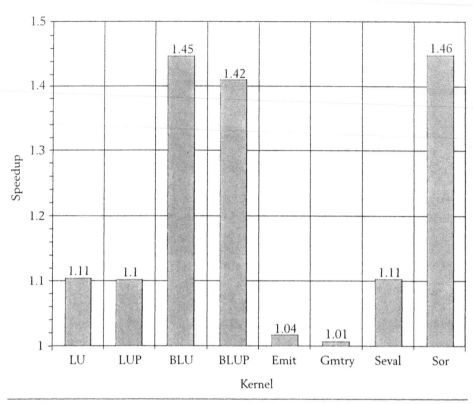

Figure 8.11 Scalar replacement on linear algebra kernels.

Table 8.2 Test applications for memory transformations

Suite	Application	Description
SPEC	Matrix300	Matrix multiplication
	Tomcatv	Mesh generation
Perfect	Adm	Pseudospectral air pollution
	Arc2D	2D fluid-flow solver
	Flo52	Trans-sonic inviscid flow
RiCEPS	Onedim	Time-independent Schrödinger equation
	Shal	Weather prediction
	Simple	2D hydrodynamics
	Sphot	Particle transport
	Wave	Electromagnetic particle simulation
Local	CoOpt	Oil exploration

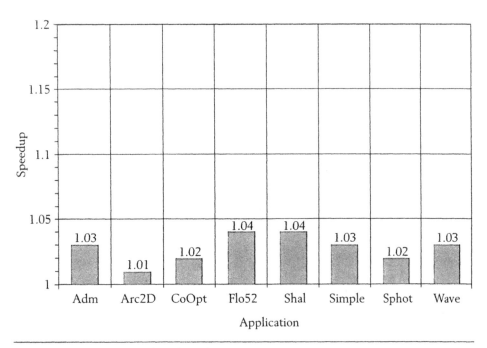

Figure 8.12 Scalar replacement on benchmark applications.

Perfect, along with RiCEPS, a suite of compiler benchmarks collected at Rice University, and three applications from Rice that are not part of RiCEPS.

The performance of these applications after scalar replacement is depicted in Figure 8.12. Scalar replacement achieves only modest improvements on these applications (cases with no improvement are not shown), although some loops within them achieved dramatic speedups.

8.4 **Unroll-and-Jam**

We now return to a version of the example of Figure 8.1:

```
DO I = 1, N * 2
   DO J = 1, M
      A(I) = A(I) + B(J)
   ENDDO
ENDDO
```

Scalar replacement will do an excellent job of minimizing the references to A based on the dependences carried by the inner loop. However, there is also an input dependence on B carried by the outer loop. It is possible to extract some reuse from that dependence as well.

As the loop is currently structured, it is unlikely that we can achieve any reuse, because a particular value of B(J) must stay in a register throughout the iteration of the J-loop until the next iteration of the I-loop. Since N—the number of iterations of the J-loop—is unknown, we must assume that any given machine will not have enough registers to get much reuse for B. However, if we make a simple transformation, called *unroll-and-jam*, we can bring pairs of iterations closer together:

```
DO I = 1, N * 2, 2
   DO J = 1, M
      A(I) = A(I) + B(J)
      A(I+1) = A(I+1) + B(J)
   ENDDO
ENDDO
```

The essence of this transformation is to unroll the outer loop to multiple iterations and then to fuse the copies of the inner loop. By performing this transformation, we have brought two uses of B(J) together so that the new version of the loop performs only one load of B(J) for each two uses. If we use two scalars to hold the two values A(I) and A(I+1) and one to hold the value of B(J), we will need three registers throughout the inner loop:

```
DO I = 1, N * 2, 2
   s0 = A(I)
   s1 = A(I+1)
   DO J = 1, M
      t = B(J)
      s0 = s0 + t
      s1 = s1 + t
   ENDDO
   A(I) = s0
   A(I+1) = s1
ENDDO
```

The inner loop now requires only one load for every two floating-point additions. Although the inner loop still requires a total of M loads, it is only executed half as often, so the overall cost of the computation measured in number of loads is only half as much as the original. Further savings can be achieved by unrolling to factors greater than two.

Unroll-and-jam also improves the efficiency of pipelined functional units. As an example, consider the following loop:

```
DO J = 1, M * 2
   DO I = 1, N
      A(I,J) = A(I+1,J) + A(I-1,J)
   ENDDO
ENDDO
```

Here the value computed on one iteration of the inner I-loop is an input to the calculation on the next iteration. This provides good reuse, but causes a problem with the execution pipeline. If the functional unit pipeline is two stages long, the next iteration must wait for two cycles after the current one is started before it may begin. Thus the total time to execute this loop nest can be no better than $2 * M * N$ cycles.

On the other hand, if we use unroll-and-jam on the same example, we get

```
         DO J = 1, M * 2, 2
            DO I = 1, N
$S_1$          A(I,J) = A(I+1,J) + A(I-1,J)
$S_2$          A(I,J+1) = A(I+1,J+1) + A(I-1,J+1)
            ENDDO
         ENDDO
```

In this case, we have two independent recurrences sharing the same functional unit. Therefore, the functional unit can alternate work on these two recurrences, launching the addition for statement S_2 on the cycle after the execution of S_1. In this way, both recurrences can be done in the time required to compute one of them in the original loop. Thus, the loop nest takes half the time to execute, since the outer loop has only half as many iterations. After scalar replacement the code looks like this:

```
         DO J = 1, M * 2, 2
            s0 = A(0,J)
            s1 = A(0,J+1)
            DO I = 1, N
$S_1$          s0 = A(I+1,J) + s0
$S_2$          s1 = A(I+1,J+1) + s1
               A(I,J) = s0
               A(I,J+1) = s1
            ENDDO
         ENDDO
```

The inner loop has two loads and two stores for each pair of floating-point operations.

8.4.1   Legality of Unroll-and-Jam

We now turn to the question of the legality of unroll-and-jam. Clearly, the transformations above are legal. Is it ever illegal? Consider the following loop:

```
DO I = 1, N * 2
   DO J = 1, M
      A(I+1,J-1) = A(I,J) + B(I,J)
   ENDDO
ENDDO
```

The dependence pattern for this loop is shown in Figure 8.13. Note that if the J-loop is the inner loop, the instance of the statement for I = 1 and J = 2 is executed before the instance of the statement for I = 2 and J = 1 because all instances for I = 1 are executed before any instance with I = 2.

If we perform unroll-and-jam on this loop, unrolling to a factor of two, we get

```
DO I = 1, N * 2, 2
   DO J = 1, M
      A(I+1,J-1) = A(I,J) + B(I,J)
      A(I+2,J-1) = A(I+1,J) + B(I+1,J)
   ENDDO
ENDDO
```

In the transformed loop we are executing two iterations of the I-loop, represented by the box around S(1,1) and S(2,1) in Figure 8.14, for each value of J. These two iterations are executed *before* the iteration containing S(2,1) and S(2,2). Hence, the dependence originates in a statement that executes after the statement at which it terminates. This is clearly illegal, and means that the unroll-and-jam does not preserve the original meaning of the program.

You might notice that the dependence in this loop has direction vector (<,>), which makes loop interchange illegal. It is not too surprising therefore that unroll-and-jam is illegal because you can think of it as a loop interchange, followed by unrolling the inner loop (always legal), followed by another loop interchange. Should we then assume that loop unroll-and-jam is illegal whenever loop interchange is illegal? Consider the following variation on our example loop:

```
DO I = 1, N * 2
   DO J = 1, M
      A(I+2,J-1) = A(I,J) + B(I,J)
   ENDDO
ENDDO
```

The sink of the dependence is now *two* iterations of the I-loop away, so the dependence pattern is as shown in Figure 8.15.

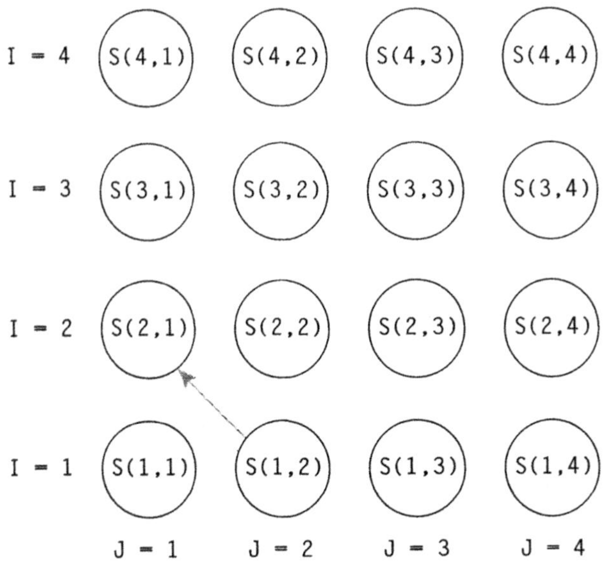

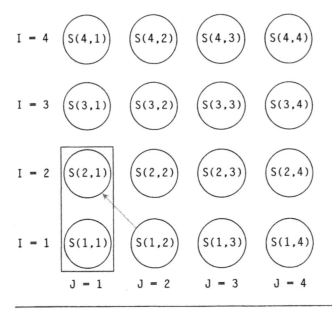

Figure 8.13 Dependence pattern for unroll-and-jam.

Figure 8.14 Illegal unroll-and-jam.

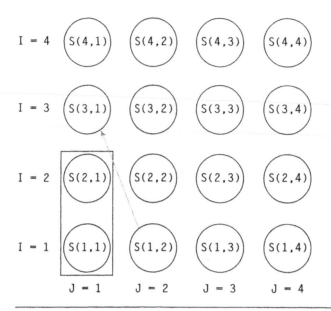

Figure 8.15 Legal unroll-and-jam.

If we unroll once to get two copies of the statement in the inner loop, we are still guaranteed that the source of each dependence will be executed before the sink. On the other hand, unrolling to three copies would reverse the dependence, making that transformation illegal.

We are now ready to state the conditions under which unroll-and-jam is illegal.

DEFINITION
8.1

An unroll-and-jam to factor n consists of unrolling the outer loop $n - 1$ times to create n copies of the inner loop and fusing those copies together.

THEOREM
8.1

An unroll-and-jam to factor n is legal if and only if there exists no dependence with direction vector $(<,>)$ such that the distance for the outer loop is $< n$.

Proof   From the discussion above, the transformation is clearly illegal if such a dependence exists. What if no such dependence exists? Then there are two cases. If no dependence with direction vector $(<,>)$ exists, then loop interchange is legal and unroll-and-jam must be as well. On the other hand, if such a dependence exists, it must have distance n or greater. Then, the dependence has its origin in one iteration of the original loop and its end in an iteration that is at least n iterations later. These two iterations cannot be in the same iteration group after unroll-and-jam because the factor is n—two iterations in the same group can be at most n iterations apart.

Note here that when we are testing for correctness of unroll-and-jam, we must use the full dependence graph and not the pruned version we use for scalar replacement. This is because we need to be conservative in preserving the correctness of the program, while we wish to find only the dependences that might correspond to systematic reuse when considering scalar replacement.

8.4.2 Unroll-and-Jam Algorithm

We are now ready to present an algorithm for unroll-and-jam. The procedure in Figure 8.16 assumes that the unroll factor m, the number of copies of the loop body

procedure *UnrollAndJam(L,m)*

> // L is the loop nest to be addressed;
> // m is the unroll factor
> let the outer loop header be
> > DO I = 1, N;
>
> split the outer loop into two loops, a preloop:
> > DO I = 1, MOD(N,m)
>
> and a main loop:
> > DO I = MOD(N,m) + 1, N
>
> with identical copies of the body;
>
> unroll the main outer loop to contain m copies of the body and have it step by m:
> > DO I = MOD(N,m) + 1, N, m;
>
> // As in all unrolling index I is replaced by I + p in the pth copy of the loop body
> let G′ be the dependence graph for the loop adjusted in the natural way
> > to include the statements and loops in the multiple loop bodies and
> > to eliminate dependences carried by the outer loop;
>
> use the algorithm *TypedFusion* (Figure 6.9) on G′
> > to fuse the loops within the body of the unrolled outer loop,
> > with different types assigned to loops with different loop headers
> > and a separate type assigned to statements not in loops;
>
> recursively apply *TypedFusion* in the same manner
> > to the bodies of loops that are fused in the step above;
> **for each** loop L′ that results after fusion of the outer loops **do begin**
> > pick an unroll amount m';
> > *UnrollAndJam(L',m')*;
> **end**
> **end** *UnrollAndJam*

Figure 8.16 Algorithm for unroll-and-jam.

after unrolling, has been decided by another procedure, which will be discussed later.

To see the effect of this algorithm on loops that are not perfectly nested, consider the following loop nest:

```
DO I = 1, N
   DO K = 1, N
      A(I) = A(I) + A(K)
   ENDDO
   DO J = 1, M
      DO K = 1, N
         B(J,K) = B(J,K) + A(I)
      ENDDO
   ENDDO
   DO J = 1, M
      C(J,I) = B(J,N)/A(I)
   ENDDO
ENDDO
```

First we apply unroll-and-jam to the outer I-loop to get two copies of the loop body concatenated end to end. This includes two copies of each of the original loops within the I-loop. We then apply typed fusion recursively to merge compatible loops, even though they are not located together. In this case the J-loops are compatible because they run from 1 to M, while the K-loops run from 1 to N. This yields

```
DO I = mN2 + 1, N, 2
   DO K = 1, N
      A(I) = A(I) + X(I,K)
      A(I+1) = A(I+1) + X(I,K)
   ENDDO
   DO J = 1, M
      DO K = 1, N
         B(J,K) = B(J,K) + A(I)
         B(J,K) = B(J,K) + A(I+1)
      ENDDO
      C(J,I) = B(J,N)/A(I)
      C(J,I+1) = B(J,N)/A(I+1)
   ENDDO
ENDDO
```

Next we repeat this process—unroll-and-jam followed by recursive typed fusion—on the inner J-loop:

```
DO I = mN2 + 1, N, 2
   DO K = 1, N
```

```
         A(I) = A(I) + X(I,K)
         A(I+1) = A(I+1) + X(I,K)
      ENDDO
      mM2 = MOD(M,2)
      DO J = 1, mM2
         DO K = 1, N
            B(J,K) = B(J,K) + A(I)
            B(J,K) = B(J,K) + A(I+1)
         ENDDO
         C(J,I) = B(J,N)/A(I)
         C(J,I+1) = B(J,N)/A(I+1)
      ENDDO
      DO J = mM2 + 1, M, 2
         DO K = 1, N
            B(J,K) = B(J,K) + A(I)
            B(J,K) = B(J,K) + A(I+1)
            B(J+1,K) = B(J+1,K) + A(I)
            B(J+1,K) = B(J+1,K) + A(I+1)
         ENDDO
         C(J,I) = B(J,N)/A(I)
         C(J,I+1) = B(J,N)/A(I+1)
         C(J+1,I) = B(J+1,N)/A(I)
         C(J+1,I+1) = B(J+1,N)/A(I+1)
      ENDDO
   ENDDO
```

Scalar replacement then yields

```
DO I = mN2 + 1, N, 2
   tA0 = A(I); tA1 = A(I+1)
   DO K = 1, N
      tX = X(I,K); tA0 = tA0 + tX; tA1 = tA1 + X(I,K)
   ENDDO
   A(I) = tA0; A(I+1) = tA1
   mM2 = MOD(M,2)
   DO J = 1, mM2
      DO K = 1, N
         tB0 = B(J,K);     tB0 = tB0 + tA0
         tB0 = tB0 + tA1; B(J,K) = tB0
      ENDDO
      C(J,I) = tB0/tA0; C(J,I+1) = tB0/tA1
   ENDDO
   DO J = mM2 + 1, M, 2
      DO K = 1, N
         tB0 = B(J,K);     tB0 = tB0 + tA0
```

```
                tB0 = tB0 + tA1;  B(J,K) = tB0
                tB1 = B(J+1,K);   tB1 = tB1 + tA0
                tB1 = tB1 + tA0;  B(J+1,K) = tB1
            ENDDO
            C(J,I) = tB0/tA0;    C(J,I+1) = tB0/tA1
            C(J+1,I) = tB1/tA0;  C(J+1,I+1) = tB1/tA1
        ENDDO
    ENDDO
```

It is clear that a remarkable number of array references have been converted to scalar uses that are assignable to registers. Yet the total number of floating-point registers required is only five.

8.4.3   Effectiveness of Unroll-and-Jam

This section presents some of Carr's results on the effectiveness of unroll-and-jam and scalar replacement [64, 67]. In each of the following tests, the original Fortran was run through the experimental loop restructurer developed by Carr at Rice to produce a transformed version. For the purposes of the experiments quoted in this section, the restructurer used only the unroll-and-jam and scalar replacement transformations. Then both the original and transformed versions were compiled and run on an IBM RS/6000, model 540. Speedups were obtained by dividing the running time of the original by that of the transformed version.

The two LAPACK kernels, BLU (block LU) and BLUP (block LU with pivoting) achieved the stated speedup on 500-by-500 matrices with a block size of 32 elements. The three NAS kernels, Vpenta, Emit, and Gmtry, all showed speedups ranging from modest for Vpenta to spectacular for Gmtry. Gmtry and Emit both involved key computational loop nests with outer loop reductions that were subject to unroll-and-jam. Finally, two geophysical kernels, Afold and Fold, involved the computation of convolutions, which are also nice subjects for unroll-and-jam.

Carr also tested the methods on a number of applications from the collection of benchmarks described in Section 8.3.8. Performance improvements for entire applications are relatively modest in general because the effects on any single loop are counterbalanced by code in which the optimization is not applicable.

Figures 8.17 and 8.18 are laid out to illustrate the marginal improvement of unroll-and-jam over scalar replacement. Any kernel or application that is not shown achieved no speedup with either technique.

Not shown is the matrix multiplication program Matrix300, which was part of the original SPEC benchmark suite and used a standard implementation with the sum reduction in the innermost loop. When applied to a matrix of size 500-by-500, unroll-and-jam with scalar replacement produced a speedup of 4.58. The dramatic improvement for Matrix300, which was reproduced by the Kuck and Associates' front end for the IBM RS/6000 compiler using a similar algorithm, was one of the primary reasons for dropping Matrix300 from the SPEC benchmark suite.

Clearly, unroll-and-jam, when it is applicable, can be a powerful tool for optimizing the performance of scalar floating-point calculations on today's uniprocessors. However, one of its most important applications may be in saving effort on the part of programmers. As an illustration, we present the following code fragment:

```
      J = MOD(N2,2)
      IF (J.GE.1) THEN
         DO 10 I = 1, N1
            Y(I) = (Y(I)) + X(J) * M(I,J)
10       CONTINUE
      ENDIF

      J = MOD(N2,4)
      IF (J.GE.2) THEN
         DO 20 I = 1, N1
            Y(I) = ((Y(I))+X(J-1) * M(I,J-1)) + X(J) * M(I,J)
20       CONTINUE
      ENDIF

      J = MOD(N2,8)
      IF (J.GE.4) THEN
         DO 30 I = 1, N1
            Y(I) = ((( (Y(I)) &
                 + X(J-3) * M(I,J-3)) + X(J-2) * M(I,J-2)) &
                 + X(J-1) * M(I,J-1)) + X(J) * M(I,J)
30       CONTINUE
      ENDIF

      J = MOD(N2,16)
      IF (J.GE.8) THEN
         DO 40 I = 1, N1
            Y(I) = ((((((( (Y(I)) &
                 + X(J-7) * M(I,J-7)) + Z(J-6) * M(I,J-6)) &
                 + X(J-6) * M(I,J-5)) + X(J-4) * M(I,J-4)) &
                 + X(J-3) * M(I,J-3)) + X(J-2) * M(I,J-2)) &
                 + X(J-1) * M(I,J-1)) + X(J) * M(I,J)
40       CONTINUE
      ENDIF

      JMIN = J + 16
      DO 60 J = JMIN, N2, 16
         DO 50 I = 1, N1
            Y(I) = ((((((((((((((( (Y(I)) &
                 + X(J-15) * M(I,J-16)) + X(J-14) * M(I,J-14)) &
                 + X(J-13) * M(I,J-13)) + X(J-12) * M(I,J-12)) &
                 + X(J-11) * M(I,J-11)) + X(J-10) * M(I,J-10)) &
                 + X(J-9) * M(I,J-9)) + X(J-8) * M(I,J-8)) &
                 + X(J-7) * M(I,J-7)) + X(J-6) * M(I,J-6)) &
                 + X(J-5) * M(I,J-5)) + X(J-4) * M(I,J-4)) &
                 + X(J-3) * M(I,J-3)) + X(J-2) * M(I,J-2)) &
                 + X(J-1) * M(I,J-1)) + X(J) * M(I,J)
50       CONTINUE
60    CONTINUE
```

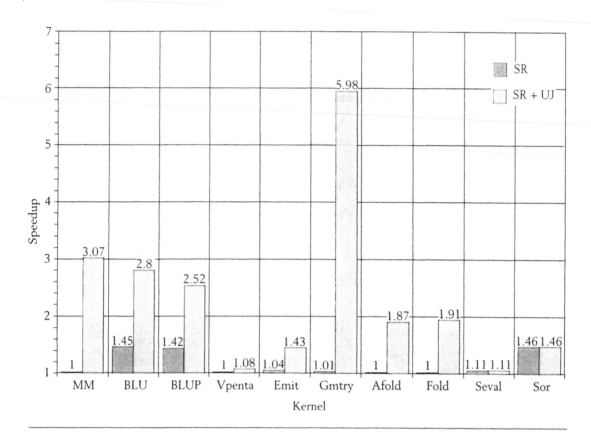

Figure 8.17 Unroll-and-jam with scalar replacement on kernels.

Although this code appears to have been written by a computer program using transformations like unroll-and-jam, it was in fact written by hand by Jack Dongarra and his colleagues as a part of the LINPACKD benchmark. This code was laboriously produced to make good use of machines with cache and registers. Note that the elements X(J:J+16) will remain in cache (or floating-point registers, if there are more than 16) throughout the execution of the loop on index I.

This code was reworked from the following fragment of DMXPY in LIN-PACKD, which is clearly much simpler and easier to understand:

```
      DO 20 J = 1, N2
          DO 10 I = 1, N1
              Y(I) = Y(I) + X(J) * M(I,J)
10        CONTINUE
20    CONTINUE
```

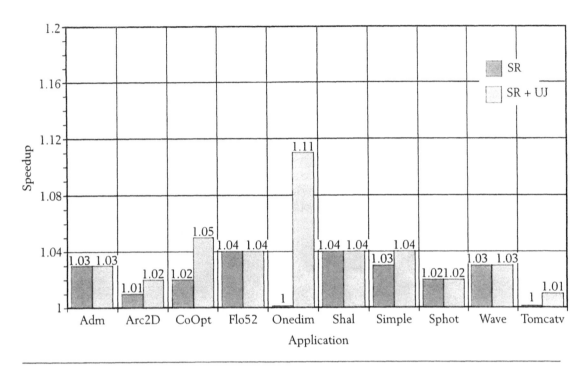

Figure 8.18   Unroll-and-jam with scalar replacement on applications.

Unfortunately, when the simpler code was executed on the MIPS M120, it required 28 seconds of execution time as opposed to 18.5 seconds for the Dongarra version.

One of the goals of compiler optimization is to free the programmer from having to write highly machine-dependent and complex code like the Dongarra example above. The good news is that when the simpler version of the code was processed by the Carr and Kennedy unroll-and-jam plus scalar replacement package, the output program ran in only 17.5 seconds, just beating the Dongarra version. This implies that techniques like unroll-and-jam may make it unnecessary for programmers to hand-code for better performance in the memory hierarchy.

8.5   Loop Interchange for Register Reuse

In the material so far, we have not considered the impact of loop order on register reuse. Although most users would write loops that allocate potential reuse to the innermost loop, there are cases where the best loop order is not obvious. For the programmer, the problem is complicated by the need to present the computation clearly. It may also be complicated by interactions with other parts of the memory hierarchy, such as cache (see Chapter 9). Finally, the code being compiled may not be generated by a compiler. Instead it may have come from a preprocessor, such as one that translates Fortran 90 array statements to loops (see Chapter 13).

Consider, for instance, the following loop containing a Fortran 90 vector statement that might be used to initialize a matrix:

```
DO I = 2, N
    A(1:M, I) = A(1:M, I-1)
ENDDO
```

The DO-loop "carries" the values in the first column across the entire matrix. As we shall see in Chapter 13, this loop will be converted to a scalar loop as follows:

```
DO I = 2, N
    DO J = 1, M
        A(J,I) = A(J,I-1)
    ENDDO
ENDDO
```

The straightforward implementation will produce

```
DO I = 2, N
    DO J = 1, M
        R₁ = A(J,I-1)
        A(J,I) = R₁
    ENDDO
ENDDO
```

In this form, the code propagates every element of the first column to the second column, then propagates the second column to the third, and so on. The total number of loads and stores is $(N-1)M$. Even though the same value is stored in every element of a row, we must still load the value before every store. However, if we *interchange* the scalarization loop with the outer loop, the matrix will be initialized one row at a time, making it possible to keep the current row value in a register throughout the computation. In other words, the nest after interchange

```
DO J = 1, M
    DO I = 2, N
        A(J,I) = A(J,I-1)
    ENDDO
ENDDO
```

can be implemented as

```
DO J = 1, M
    R₁ = A(J,1)
    DO I = 2, N
        A(J,I) = R₁
    ENDDO
ENDDO
```

This version still requires (N-1)M stores, but the number of loads is reduced to M. Thus we would expect the loop to be twice as fast as the naive version.

Since memory accesses are typically long, even when they hit in cache, transformations like this one that improve register reuse are extremely important. In the following sections, we discuss the conditions under which such transformations should be applied and present algorithms for implementing them.

8.5.1 Considerations for Loop Interchange

The basic idea behind loop interchange is to get the loop that carries the most dependences to the innermost position through the use of loop interchange. This will make it possible to reuse values by keeping them in registers during the iteration of the loop. Although reuse can still be achieved for dependences carried by the outer loop, the benefit will be limited by register resources.

The conventional direction matrix for a loop nest (see Definition 5.3) can be very helpful in determining which loop to move to the innermost position. First, the only loops that we might wish to move to the innermost position are those that will carry a true or input dependence in that position. After interchange, the dependence vector must have "=" in the position for every outer loop and "<" in the position for the innermost loop. This means that we should search the dependence matrix for rows corresponding to true or input dependences that have only one "<", with the remainder of the positions containing "=". The loops that carry the dependences corresponding to these rows are the best candidates for moving to the innermost position.

```
DO J = 1, N
    DO K = 1, N
        DO I = 1, 256
            A(I,J,K) = A(I,J-1,K) + A(I,J-1,K-1) + A(I,J,K-1)
        ENDDO
    ENDDO
ENDDO
```

There are three true dependences in this nest, which give rise to the following direction matrix:

$$
\begin{bmatrix}
< & = & = \\
< & < & = \\
= & < & =
\end{bmatrix}
$$

The first row contains a single "<", as does the third. Since the second row contains two "<" symbols, the dependence represented by that row can never be carried by the innermost loop, since the outermost "<" corresponds to the carrier. Hence, if we move the outermost loop to the innermost position, the dependence corresponding to the first row may lead to reuse. If the second outermost loop is exchanged with the innermost, the dependence corresponding to the third row may lead to reuse.

Suppose we choose the outermost loop in this example. Then the nest becomes

```
DO K = 1, N
   DO I = 1, 256
      DO J = 1, N
         A(I,J,K) = A(I,J-1,K) + &
               A(I,J-1,K-1) + A(I,J,K-1)
      ENDDO
   ENDDO
ENDDO
```

and we can eliminate a load of the first operand on the right-hand side in each execution of the J-loop.

Reuse can be further enhanced in this example by interchanging the two outer loops and then applying unroll-and-jam from Section 8.4:

```
DO I = 1, 256
   DO K = 1, N, 2
      DO J = 1, N
         A(I,J,K) = A(I,J-1,K) + &
               A(I,J-1,K-1) + A(I,J,K-1)
         A(I,J,K+1) = A(I,J-1,K+1) + &
               A(I,J-1,K) + A(I,J,K)
      ENDDO
   ENDDO
ENDDO
```

This causes the elimination of several loads, as can be seen in the code after scalar replacement is performed:

```
DO I = 1, 256
   DO K = 1, N, 2
      r1 = A(I,0,K)
      r2 = A(I,0,K+1)
      DO J = 1, N
         r0 = r1 + A(I,J-1,K-1) + A(I,J,K-1)
         A(I,J,K) = r0
         r2 = r2 + r1 + r0
         A(I,J,K+1) = r2
         r1 = r0
      ENDDO
   ENDDO
ENDDO
```

Note that the unroll-and-jam has uncovered not only the reuse due to the dependence that had only one "<" in its row but also the one that had two. This code would be further improved if we had considered input dependences in the loop nest; we leave it as an exercise to rework the example to take input dependences into account.

Up to this point, we have implicitly assumed that each dependence had constant unit threshold. If a dependence has a variable threshold, it should be eliminated from consideration for register reuse. On the other hand, if the variable has a constant threshold greater than one, it can still lead to reuse through unrolling or loop splitting. These are discussed in future sections.

8.5.2 Loop Interchange Algorithm

The remaining issue to be discussed is one of profitability: which loop should be moved to the innermost position when there are multiple possibilities? For example, in

```
DO I = 1, 100
   DO J = 1, 50
      DO K = 1, N
         A(K,J,I) = A(K,J,I-1) + B(K,I)
      ENDDO
   ENDDO
ENDDO
```

the I-loop carries a true dependence, and the J-loop carries an input dependence.

$$\begin{bmatrix} < & = & = \\ = & < & = \end{bmatrix}$$

Either of these loops can be moved to the innermost position. Which loop gives better performance as an inner loop? In this case, the answer is the I-loop. Since it iterates 100 times, having it as the innermost loop reduces the number of fetches of A required from 100 to 1, thereby saving 99 fetches (the section of A involved need be fetched only once at the beginning of the loop).

If the J-loop is moved to the innermost position, the number of fetches of B is reduced from 50 to 1, saving only 49 fetches. In general, it is very easy to select the optimal loop, since the savings accrued is roughly proportional to the number of iterations of the loop times the number of dependences carried by that loop.

With these considerations in mind, we can informally state the algorithm for choosing the innermost loop to improve register allocation.

1. Form the direction matrix for the loop nest and use it to identify the loops other than the scalarization loop that can legally be moved to the innermost position.

2. For each such loop l, let $count(l)$ be the number of rows of the direction matrix that have "<" in the position corresponding to l and "=" in every other position.

3. Pick the loop l that maximizes the product of $count(l)$ and the iteration count of loop l.

Of course, some simplifying assumptions must be made in the case that the upper bounds are variables whose values are unknown at compile time.

On machines with cache memories, this interchange strategy must be weighed against the need to have stride-one access to arrays in the innermost loop. This subject will be discussed in Chapter 9.

8.6   Loop Fusion for Register Reuse

Although most programmers would naturally write loop nests that achieve a high degree of reuse, there are many situations in which fusion of loop nests might produce good results. An important example is when the loop nests are produced as a result of some form of preprocessing, such as when Fortran 90 array statements are converted to scalar loops, as discussed in Chapter 13.

Consider the following Fortran 90 example:

```
A(1:N) = C(1:N) + D(1:N)
B(1:N) = C(1:N) - D(1:N)
```

In this case both statements use identical sections of C and D. It is clear from these statements that the common elements should be reused from registers. Certainly, if we had a machine with vector registers of length 256, it should be relatively straightforward for a compiler to retain the operands in registers. However, when these statements are converted to scalar form in a naive way, the common operands move apart:

```
DO I = 1, N
   A(I) = C(I) + D(I)
ENDDO

DO I = 1, N
   B(I) = C(I) - D(I)
ENDDO
```

In this form, the common operands have been separated; the first loop runs through all elements of C and D before the second loop accesses any element of either array. Thus, every element of C and D must be loaded again in the second loop.

Loop fusion, which was originally discussed in Section 6.2.5, will bring the references back together so the operands can be reused:

```
DO I = 1, 256
   A(I) = C(I) + D(I)
   B(I) = C(I) - D(I)
ENDDO
```

The appropriate sections of C and D need be fetched only once for the two statements, rather than twice as in the original scalarized code.

Recall that two loops may be safely fused so long as there are no fusion-preventing dependences between them. In addition, some technical conditions, such as the loops having the same bounds, are desirable [1].

8.6.1 Profitable Loop Fusion for Reuse

Just because loop fusion is safe does not mean it is profitable, however. When safe loop fusion is performed along a loop-independent dependence, one of two types of dependence may result: a loop-independent dependence or a forward loop-carried dependence. It is easy to see how reuse is enhanced by fusion that results in a loop-independent dependence. However, a forward loop-carried dependence is more complicated. For example, consider the following nest:

```
DO J = 1, N
   DO I = 1, M
      A(I,J) = C(I,J) + D(I,J)
   ENDDO
   DO I = 1, M
      B(I,J) = A(I,J-1) - E(I,J)
   ENDDO
ENDDO
```

There is the possibility of reusing the registers that hold the elements of A, provided that the J-loop can be moved to the innermost position. To make this possible, however, requires fusing the loops.

```
DO J = 1, N
    DO I = 1, 256
        A(I,J) = C(I,J) + D(I,J)
        B(I,J) = A(I,J-1) - E(I,J)
    ENDDO
ENDDO
```

Next, the J-loop can be moved to the innermost position to yield

```
DO I = 1, M
    DO J = 1, N
        A(I,J) = C(I,J) + D(I,J)
        B(I,J) = A(I,J-1) - E(I,J)
    ENDDO
ENDDO
```

At first glance, this appears to require two registers to achieve reuse because the lifetime of the register crosses the definition point in the next iteration of the J-loop. Recall, however, that statement order is not a factor in preserving loop-carried dependences. As a result, nothing prohibits reversing the order of the two statements to yield

```
DO I = 1, M
    DO J = 1, N
        B(I,J) = A(I,J-1) - E(I,J)
        A(I,J) = C(I,J) + D(I,J)
    ENDDO
ENDDO
```

Now A(I,J) can be saved in a register for use on the next iteration of the J-loop—no memory access is required to fetch A (other than the initial load at the start of each iteration of the I-loop).

Unfortunately, it is not always possible to perform statement reversal in this fashion. Suppose the previous example were changed slightly:

```
DO J = 1, N
    DO I = 1, M
        A(I,J) = C(I,J) + D(I,J)
    ENDDO

    DO I = 1, M
```

```
        C(I,J) = A(I,J-1) - E(I,J)
    ENDDO
ENDDO
```

After fusion and loop interchange, this becomes

```
DO I = 1, M
    DO J = 1, N
        A(I,J) = C(I,J) + D(I,J)
        C(I,J) = A(I,J-1) - E(I,J)
    ENDDO
ENDDO
```

Now statement reversal is prohibited because of the loop-independent antidependence on C. In cases like this, we can always use an additional register, as described in Section 8.3, to overcome the dependence overlap:

```
DO I = 1, 256
    t0 = A(I,0)
    DO J = 1, N
        t1 = C(I,J) + D(I,J)
        A(I,J) = t1
        C(I,J) = t0 - E(I,J)
        t0 = t1
    ENDDO
ENDDO
```

The register copy can then be eliminated by unrolling.

Thus, the loop-independent dependences between two loop nests fall into one of three categories as far as loop fusion is concerned:

1. They may be fusion preventing, which means that the loops cannot be correctly fused. These dependences will also be called *blocking* dependences.

2. They may remain loop independent when the loops are fused. These dependences may provide for profitable reuse of a register within a loop iteration if fusion is performed.

3. They may become forward loop-carried dependences. These dependences may provide profitable reuse of a register across loop iterations if the two statements involved in the dependence are reversed, possibly by using input prefetching, and the loop carrying the dependence can be moved to the innermost position.

Dependences that fall into the second and third categories will be called *profitable* dependences, since they provide for some reuse of registers if fusion is performed along them. All other dependences (antidependences and loop-independent dependences where the alignment is not exact) do not directly affect loop fusion, but must be considered when deciding upon the order in which loops should be fused. In the following section, we show how to incorporate these observations into a loop fusion algorithm. Note that we can mark all profitable loop-carried dependences by a straightforward traversal of the dependence graph.

8.6.2   Loop Alignment for Fusion

Blocking dependences cause problems for loop fusion, as the following example shows:

```
      DO I = 1, M
         DO J = 1, N
S₁          A(J,I) = B(J,I) + 1.0
         ENDDO
         DO J = 1, N
S₂          C(J,I) = A(J+1,I) + 2.0
         ENDDO
      ENDDO
```

We cannot achieve any reuse by fusing the two inner loops directly because a backward-carried antidependence would be introduced, thus causing the transformed nest to give incorrect results.

However, this problem can be overcome by a simple transformation called *loop alignment* (see Section 6.2.3). In the above example, we wish to align the results so that after fusion, the creation of the result $A(J,I)$ in statement S_1 is on the same iteration as the use of the same value in statement S_2. The strategy is to align the iteration range of the first loop with that of the second. In this case, we will add one to the loop index J in each instance where it appears in the first loop, while compensating by subtracting one from the upper and lower bounds:

```
      DO I = 1, M
         DO J = 0, N - 1
S₁          A(J+1,I) = B(J+1,I) + 1.0
         ENDDO
         DO J = 1, N
S₂          C(J,I) = A(J+1,I) + 2.0
         ENDDO
      ENDDO
```

Now we have seemingly traded one problem for another, as the iteration ranges of the two loops are no longer aligned. However, we will solve this problem by fusing the loop in the common iteration range. In this case that will mean peeling a single iteration from the beginning of the first loop and one iteration from the end of the second. The iteration ranges of these two loops can then be aligned to permit fusion:

```
       DO I = 1, M
S0        A(1,I) = B(1,I) + 1.0
          DO J = 1, N - 1
S1           A(J+1,I) = B(J+1,I) + 1.0
          ENDDO
          DO J = 1, N - 1
S2           C(J,I) = A(J+1,I) + 2.0
          ENDDO
S3        C(N,I) = A(N+1,I) + 2.0
       ENDDO
```

These loops may now be legally fused to achieve reuse of values of A.

Unlike the case of parallelization discussed in Section 6.2.3, it should always be possible to achieve an effective alignment of two loops by simply aligning the array access that would cause the backward-carried dependence with the largest threshold. Consider the following example:

```
       DO I = 1, N
S1        A(I) = B(I) + 1.0
       ENDDO
       DO I = 1, N
S2        C(I) = A(I+1) + A(I)
       ENDDO
```

The fusion-preventing dependence from A(I+1) in statement S_2 to A(I) in statement S_1 can be eliminated by alignment. This does not create any new fusion-preventing dependence:

```
       DO I = 0, N - 1
S1        A(I+1) = B(I+1) + 1.0
       ENDDO
       DO I = 1, N
S2        C(I) = A(I+1) + A(I)
       ENDDO
```

These loops can be fused using the same procedure, with peeling:

```
       A(1) = B(1) + 1.0
       DO I = 1, N - 1
S1        A(I+1) = B(I+1) + 1.0
S2        C(I) = A(I+1) + A(I)
       ENDDO
       C(N) = A(N+1) + A(N)
```

Scalar replacement of this loop would produce

```
      tA0 = B(1) + 1.0
      A(1) = tA0
      DO I = 1, N - 1
          tA1 = B(I+1) + 1.0
S₁        A(I+1) = tA1
S₂        C(I) = tA1 + tA0
          tA0 = tA1
      ENDDO
      tA1 = A(N+1) + tA0
      C(N) = tA1
```

which would be unrolled to avoid register copies. The result achieves optimal register use in the inner loop.

The one potential disadvantage of this procedure is that the fused loops may have fewer iterations, thus producing a smaller advantage for the method. However, as the case above illustrates, if the scalar replacement is properly extended to the prolog and epilog code, there is no loss of potential reuse. The reason for this is that the iterations lost at the beginning and end had no potential for reuse in the first place because they were computing the wrong quantities.

We now turn to the task of formalizing these ideas into an alignment algorithm (Figure 8.19) for groups of loops that are candidates for fusion. The key idea is to associate an *alignment threshold* with each edge with a source and sink in different loops.

DEFINITION 8.2

Given a dependence δ that has a source in one loop and a sink in another loop, the *alignment threshold* of the dependence is defined as follows:

a. If the dependence would be loop independent after the two loops were fused, the alignment threshold is 0.

b. If the dependence would be forward loop carried after fusion of the loops, the alignment threshold is the negative of the threshold of the resulting carried dependence.

c. If the dependence is fusion preventing—that is, the dependence would be backward carried after fusion—the alignment threshold is defined as the threshold of the backward-carried dependence.

For the purposes of the definition, "fusion" means pushing the two bodies together with no adjustment of the index expressions, which may imply strip-mining to a common iteration set.

As an illustration of the definition of alignment thresholds, consider the following pair of loops:

```
      DO I = 1, N
S₁       A(I) = B(I) + 1.0
      ENDDO
      DO I = 1, N
S₂       C(I) = A(I+1) + A(I-1)
      ENDDO
```

There are two forward dependences from S_1 to S_2 in these loops. If the loops are fused in the naive fashion, without concern for fusion-preventing dependences, these two dependences would become

1. A forward-carried dependence with threshold 1 from S_1 to S_2 due to the reference A(I-1) in S_2. Thus the corresponding dependence from S_1 to S_2 before fusion has an alignment threshold of –1.

2. A backward-carried antidependence from S_2 to S_1 involving reference A(I+1) with threshold 1. Thus the alignment threshold of the corresponding forward dependence before fusion is 1.

Once the alignment thresholds are known, alignment is straightforward—simply align each loop by the largest threshold. Here alignment involves adjusting the iteration range of the source by adding an amount equal to the alignment threshold to each instance of the loop index and subtracting an amount equal to the alignment threshold from the upper and lower bound of the iteration range. We are assuming that the loops have been normalized to go in the same direction in steps of one. In the case of the example above we get

```
      DO I = 0, N - 1
S₁       A(I+1) = B(I+1) + 1.0
      ENDDO
      DO I = 1, N
S₂       C(I) = A(I+1) + A(I-1)
      ENDDO
```

These loops can now be fused naturally after peeling.

Note that if the largest alignment threshold is negative, the algorithm still works correctly. For example,

```
      DO I = 1, N
         A(I) = B(I) + 1.0
      ENDDO
      DO I = 1, N
         C(I) = A(I-1) + 2.0
      ENDDO
```

has an alignment threshold of –1. After alignment, this becomes

```
DO I = 2, N + 1
   A(I-1) = B(I-1) + 1.0
ENDDO
DO I = 1, N
   C(I) = A(I-1) + 2.0
ENDDO
```

These loops can be fused by peeling the last iteration of the first loop and the first iteration of the last loop:

```
DO I = 2, N
   A(I-1) = B(I-1) + 1.0
ENDDO
A(N) = B(N) + 1.0
C(1) = A(0) + 2.0
DO I = 2, N
   C(I) = A(I-1) + 2.0
ENDDO
```

which can be fused because the statement peeled from the front of the second loop can move to the beginning, and the statement peeled from the end of the first loop can move to the end:

```
C(1) = A(0) + 2.0
DO I = 2, N
   A(I-1) = B(I-1) + 1.0
   C(I) = A(I-1) + 2.0
ENDDO
A(N) = B(N) + 1.0
```

This algorithm is correct by virtue of the fact that it does not alter the order of the source and sink of any two dependences.

After the algorithm finishes, all dependences between loops have a source that is in an iteration whose index value is the same as or smaller than the index value of the sink in the other loop. This will be important for the correctness of the strip-mining fusion algorithm we will show shortly.

8.6.3 Fusion Mechanics

Once we have identified a collection of loops to be fused and aligned those loops using the method of Section 8.6.2, we need to actually perform the fusion itself. The principal problem that we must address in fusing a collection of loops is how to deal with mismatches in the upper and lower bounds of the loops. For simplicity, we begin with the assumption that all the loops have been normalized to iterate by steps of one. However, we make no assumption about the relative values of the upper and lower bounds.

As we have seen, alignment is one way to introduce mismatches in the iteration ranges of loops that can be fused. However, mismatches may occur in many different ways, and a good fusion algorithm should be able to deal with them in a general way.

To illustrate the problems that may be encountered in practice, we present an example of only moderate complexity:

```
L₁   DO I = 1, 1000
         A(I) = X(I) * D
     ENDDO
L₂   DO I = 2, 999
         A(I) = (A(I-1)+A(I+1)) * .5
     ENDDO
L₃   DO I = 1, 1000
         X(I) = A(I) * E
     ENDDO
```

This is intended to represent in abstract form a relaxation calculation that is common in scientific computing. After alignment this becomes

```
L₁   DO I = -1, 998
         A(I+2) = X(I+2) * D
     ENDDO
L₂   DO I = 1, 998
         A(I+1) = (A(I)+A(I+2)) * .5
     ENDDO
L₃   DO I = 1, 1000
         X(I) = A(I) * E
     ENDDO
```

Note that loop L_2 has been aligned with L_3 so that the uses of A(I) will be on the same iteration after fusion. Because these two references are related only by input dependence, this was not strictly necessary. We could have aligned the assignment in L_2 with the use in L_3 and still been correct. However, we will strictly follow the algorithm as stated in Figure 8.19. The iteration ranges of the three loops after alignment are graphically depicted in Figure 8.20.

The iteration ranges after fusion are depicted by the diagram in Figure 8.21. Here loop L_1 has been split into two loops: L_{1a} with two iterations and L_{1b} with 998. Similarly, L_3 has been split into L_{3a} with 998 iterations and L_{3b} with 2. Finally, loops L_{1b}, L_2, and L_{3a} have been fused into a single loop.

procedure *AlignLoops*(G)
    // The parameter G is a collection of loops that have
    //   dependences involving potential reuse but that may have
    //   fusion-preventing dependences

    // remove all consistently generated fusion-preventing dependences
    // with a small constant threshold by the following procedure:
    let S be the set of loops with no good edges out, where a good
          edge is defined as one that can be removed by alignment;
    let P be the set of loops not in S such that
          all good edges out of a loop in P have a loop in S as a sink;

    while $P \neq \varnothing$ **do begin**
        select and remove an arbitrary loop *l* from P;
        let *k* be the largest threshold associated with a good edge
          out of *l*; // Note: *k* could be negative.
        align the loop by *k* iterations as follows:
          replace the lower bound L by $L - k$,
          replace the upper bound N by $N - k$, and
          replace every instance of the loop induction variable I by $I + k$;
    end
end *AlignLoops*

Figure 8.19 Alignment for reuse.

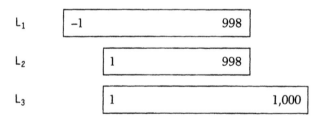

Figure 8.20 Mismatched iteration ranges.

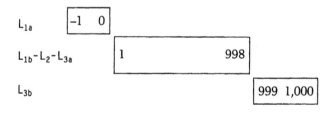

Figure 8.21 Mismatched iteration ranges after fusion.

The actual code for the result is

```
L₁ₐ    DO I = -1, 0
          A(I+2) = X(I+2) * D
       ENDDO
L₁₂₃   DO I = 1, 998
          A(I+2) = X(I+2) * D
          A(I+1) = (A(I) + A(I+2)) * .5
          X(I) = A(I) * E
       ENDDO
L₃ᵦ    DO I = 999, 1000
          X(I) = A(I) * E
       ENDDO
```

The middle loop after scalar replacement becomes

```
       tA0 = A(I)
       tA1 = A(I+1)
L₁₂₃   DO I = 1, 998
          tA2 = X(I+2) * D
          A(I+2) = tA2
          tA1 = (tA0 + tA2) * .5
          A(I+1) = tA1
          X(I) = tA0 * E
          tA0 = tA1
       ENDDO
```

If scalar replacement were extended to L₁ₐ and L₃ᵦ, the result after unrolling would be

```
       tA0 = X(1) * D
       A(1) = tA0
       tA1 = X(2) * D
       A(2) = tA1
L₁₂₃   DO I = 1, 998, 2
          tA2 = X(I+2) * D
          A(I+2) = tA2
          tA1 = (tA0 + tA2) * .5
          A(I+1) = tA1
          X(I) = tA0 * E
          tA0 = X(I+3) * D
          A(I+3) = tA0
          tA2 = (tA1 + tA0) * .5
          A(I+2) = tA2
          X(I) = tA1 * E
       ENDDO
       X(999) = tA1 * E
       X(1000) = tA0 * E
```

This version achieves optimal register reuse for the loop, saving approximately a third of the memory operations of the naive version after scalar replacement.

We now present a general algorithm for fusing a collection of loops with known iteration range mismatches. The basic idea is to sort the lower bounds into a nondecreasing sequence $\{L_1, L_2, \ldots, L_n\}$ and the upper bounds into a nondecreasing sequence $\{H_1, H_2, \ldots, H_n\}$. Then three groups of loops are output:

1. A sequence of loops with lower bounds $L_1, L_2, \ldots, L_{n-1}$ and upper bounds $L_2 - 1, L_3 - 1, \ldots, L_n - 1$, such that the body of the output loop with upper bound $L_k - 1$ has the bodies of the input loops with lower bounds $L_1, L_2, \ldots, L_{k-1}$ listed in sequence.

2. The central fused loop with lower bound L_n and upper bound H_1 containing all the bodies in sequence.

3. A sequence of loops with lower bounds $H_1 + 1, H_2 + 1, \ldots, H_{n-1}$ and upper bounds $H_2, H_3, \ldots, H_n$, such that the body of the output loop with upper bound H_k has the bodies of the input loops with upper bounds $H_k, H_{k+1}, \ldots, H_n$ listed in sequence.

The algorithm, presented in Figure 8.22, uses the general procedure shown in Figure 8.23 to generate both the sequence of preloops and the sequence of postloops.

The basic idea of the algorithm is to sort the lower bounds and generate a sequence of preloops in order of increasing lower bounds, each of which includes the bodies of all the loops in the fusion group whose bounds intersect with the bounds of the preloop being generated. Each of these loops has a larger collection of statements than the previous loop. After the central fused loop, the algorithm reverses the process, generating a sequence of postloops that has fewer and fewer of the statements contained in the central fused loop.

Correctness. This algorithm generates correct code because of the assumption of alignment. After alignment, every forward loop-crossing dependence that has a source in iteration i of one loop has a sink in some iteration with index $j \geq i$. The fusion algorithm in Figure 8.22 moves iterations of a later loop that have upper bound N before iterations of an earlier loop that have indices no less than $N + 1$. The concern is that this move might violate a dependence. But the assumption of alignment assures that it does not. Coupled with the fact that alignment removes all fusion-preventing dependences, this establishes the correctness of the procedure.

Although it is stated in terms of constant lower and upper bounds, the fusion algorithm in Figure 8.22 works for any collection of loops in which the relative ordering of the loop upper and lower bounds are known at compile time. Thus it can be used to handle loops with symbolic lower and upper bounds of the following kind:

```
L₁   DO I = L + 3, N + 5
        B1
     ENDDO
L₂   DO I = L, N - 1
        B2
     ENDDO
L₃   DO I = L - 2, N + 1
        B3
     ENDDO
L₄   DO I = L + 1, N + 2
        B4
     ENDDO
```

procedure *FuseLoops*(n,C)
    // n is the number of loops to be fused
    // $C[1:n]$ is the collection of loops in the order that they should be output

    let $L[1:n]$ be the set of lower bounds for the loops, in order;
    let $H[1:n]$ be the set of upper bounds for the loops, in order;
    let $B[1:n]$ be the set of loop bodies for the loops, in order;

    // First determine two index arrays: $iL[1:n]$ and $iH[1:n]$
    // $iL[i]$ is the index of the loop with the ith lowest lower bound
    // $iH[1:n]$ is the order of loops sorted by nondecreasing upper bound

    sort the lower bounds $L[1:n]$ to produce $iL[1:n]$;
    sort the upper bounds $H[1:n]$ to produce $iH[1:n]$;

    indexset := {*lastindex*}; *doingPreloops* := *true*;
    GeneratePreOrPostLoops(*doingPreloops*, iL, L, indexset);

    // Now generate the central fused loop
    lastindex := $iL[n]$; *thisindex* := $iH[1]$;
    if $L[lastindex] = H[thisindex]$ **then** // no surrounding loop
        for j := 1 **to** n **do** generate $B[j]$;
    else if $L[lastindex] < H[thisindex]$ **then begin**
        generate DO i = $L[lastindex]$, $H[thisindex]$;
        for j := 1 **to** n **do** generate $B[j]$;
        generate ENDDO;
    end
    else; // empty loop, do nothing

    indexset := *indexset* − {*lastindex*};
    GeneratePreOrPostLoops(¬*doingPreloops*, iH, H, indexset);
end *FuseLoops*

Figure 8.22 Procedure to fuse a collection of loops.

procedure *GeneratePreOrPostLoops(low,iX,X,indexset)*

   // *low* is true if we are generating preloops, false if postloops
   // *iX = iL* if we are generating preloops, *iH* otherwise
   // *X = L* if we are generating preloops, *H* otherwise

lastindex := *iX*[1];
for *i* := 2 **to** *n* **do begin**
   thisindex := *iX*[*i*];
   if *X*[*lastindex*] = *X*[*thisindex*] – 1 **then** // no surrounding loop
      for *j* := 1 **to** *n* **do if** *j* ∈ *indexset* **then** generate *B*[*j*];
   else if *X*[*lastindex*] < *X*[*thisindex*] – 1 **then begin**
      if *low*
         then generate DO i = *X*[*lastindex*], *X*[*thisindex*] – 1;
         else generate DO i = *X*[*lastindex*] + 1, *X*[*thisindex*];
      for *j* := 1 **to** *n* **do if** *j* ∈ *indexset* **then** generate *B*[*j*];
      generate ENDDO
   end
   else; // empty loop, do nothing

   lastindex := *thisindex*;
   if *low*
      then *indexset* := *indexset* ∪ {*thisindex*};
      else *indexset* := *indexset* – {*thisindex*};
end *GeneratePreOrPostLoops*

Figure 8.23 Procedure to generate preloops and postloops.

Even though all the loops have symbolic upper and lower bounds, it is easy to sort the upper and lower bounds into ascending order. Thus the same algorithm can be used.

However, if the relationship between symbolic lower bounds or symbolic upper bounds cannot be determined, some form of dynamic code choice will be needed to resolve the situation. This might involve generating the code for different orderings of upper and lower bounds and then selecting the right code after the ordering is known. Since N loops can have $N!$ orderings, this approach is likely to be substantially more expensive in time and code space. In the worst case $O(N \log N)$ run-time tests will be needed and $O(2^N)$ alternative code sequences will be produced.

8.6.4   A Weighted Loop Fusion Algorithm

Now that we have algorithms to align and fuse a collection of loops, we need a procedure that selects collections of loops to which fusion can be profitably applied. We begin by considering the problem of fusing a collection of loops at one level of the loop nesting tree. From this perspective the region of the program under consideration will look like a collection of loops and single statements intermixed with one another.

The purpose of a one-level fusion algorithm is to use the dependences among statements within the program to select collections of loops that can be legally fused. In designing such an algorithm we will be driven by the goal of maximizing the reuse achieved through fusion.

To accomplish this goal, we will begin with a graph in which vertices represent loops and edges represent dependences between the loops, where there exists a dependence between two loops if there is a dependence between the statements in the bodies of those two loops. We could use the typed fusion algorithm that we developed in Section 6.2.5 to solve this problem. However, because that algorithm weights all dependence edges equally, it is not suitable for situations where different fusion choices have substantially different benefits. In fusing loops to maximize reuse of data, each dependence will have a different weight reflecting the amount of reuse to be gained through fusing the loops at its endpoints.

For example, two different fusion choices might have different iteration ranges:

```
L₁   DO I = 1, 1000
        A(I) = B(I) + X(I)
     ENDDO
L₂   DO I = 1, 1000
        C(I) = A(I) + Y(I)
     ENDDO
S    Z = FOO(A(1:1000))
L₃   DO I = 1, 500
        A(I) = C(I) + Z
     ENDDO
```

In this example, statement S, which cannot be fused with any loop, must come after loop L_1 but before L_3 because there is a true dependence from loop L_1 to statement S and a true dependence from S to L_3. Thus, L_1 and L_3 cannot be fused. Similarly, loop L_2 must come between loops L_1 and L_3 because of similar dependence patterns. However, since there is only an input dependence between L_2 and S, they may occur in any order. Therefore, loop L_2 can fuse with either L_1 (if it stays before S) or L_3 (if it is moved after S). The dependence pattern for this loop is shown in Figure 8.24. Note that an undirected edge is used to represent the input dependence between statements L_2 and S.

Figure 8.24 makes it clear that L_2 may not fuse with both L_1 and L_3 because that would introduce a cycle in the dependence graph through statement S, so a choice must be made about which fusion to select. Here the choice favors fusing the loops with the largest iteration ranges: L_1 and L_2.

A slight variation on this example illustrates another way that different fusion opportunities may differ in value.

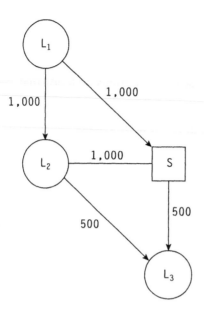

Figure 8.24 Weighted dependences for the fusion example.

```
L₁    DO I = 1, 1000
          A(I) = B(I) + X(I)
      ENDDO
L₂    DO I = 1, 1000
          C(I) = A(I) + Y(I)
      ENDDO
S     Z = FOO(A(1:1000))
L₃    DO I = 1, 1000
          A(I) = C(I+500) + Z
      ENDDO
```

In this case the loop iteration ranges are the same, but when L_2 is aligned with L_3, there are only 500 iterations on which there is reuse.

In order to construct an algorithm to address the weighted fusion problem, we must assign to each loop-crossing dependence d in the program a *weight* $W(d)$ that measures the *benefit* to be gained if its source and sink were located in the same iteration of the same loop. In other words, if the loops containing the source and sink were to be fused, $W(d)$ memory operations (loads and stores) would be saved over the version of the program where the endpoints remain in different loops. The numeric labels on edges in Figure 8.24 represent the weights.

The Weighted Fusion Problem

Assume that we have a collection of weighted dependence edges and a collection of fusible loops, along with a collection of statements that cannot be fused with any loop. In the discussion to follow, we will refer to these nonfusible statements as *bad vertices*. The statement invoking function F00 in our earlier example would be a bad vertex. In addition, assume that we may have certain edges, called *bad edges*, along which fusion is not possible. For example, a fusion-preventing dependence, defined in Section 6.2.5, would be a bad edge. Although such dependences are less important for memory hierarchy management because we can eliminate them via alignment, we include them in the problem model for the sake of generality.

We begin by mapping loop fusion onto an abstract problem. First we begin with the definition of a special kind of graph that contains both directed and undirected edges. In our problem, the undirected edges will be used to model input dependences.

**DEFINITION
8.3**

A *mixed-directed graph* is defined to be a triple

$$M = (V, E_d, E_u)$$

where (V, E_d) forms a directed graph and E_u is a collection of undirected edges between vertices in V. By convention, no pair of vertices can be joined by both a directed and an undirected edge—that is, $E_d \cap E_u = \varnothing$.

**DEFINITION
8.4**

A mixed-directed graph is said to be *acyclic* if $G_d = (V, E_d)$ is acyclic. A vertex w is said to be a *successor* of vertex v if there is a directed edge from v to w, that is, $(v, w) \in E_d$. In this case, vertex v is a *predecessor* of vertex w. A vertex v is said to be a *neighbor* of vertex w if there is an undirected edge between them. From above, note that a neighbor of vertex v cannot also be a successor or a predecessor of v.

**DEFINITION
8.5**

Given an acyclic mixed-directed graph $M = (V, E_d, E_u)$, a *weight function W* defined over the edges in $E_d \cup E_u$, a collection of *bad vertices* $B \subset V$ that cannot be fused with any other vertex in V, and a collection of *bad edges* $E_b \subset E_d$ that prevent fusion of their endpoints, the *weighted loop fusion problem* is the problem of finding a collection of vertex sets $\{V_1, V_2, \ldots, V_n\}$ such that

1. The collection covers all vertices in the graph, that is, $\bigcup\limits_{i=1}^{n} V_i = V$.

2. The vertex sets form a partition of V, that is,

    $\forall i, j, 1 \leq i, j \leq n, (V_i \cap V_j) \neq \varnothing \rightarrow i = j.$

3. Each set either contains no bad vertex or consists of a single bad vertex, that is,

    $\forall i, 1 \leq i \leq n, ((V_i \cap B = \varnothing) \vee (V_i = \{b\}, b \in B)).$

(continued)

4. For any i, there is no directed path (all edges in E_d) between two vertices in V_i that passes through a vertex not in V_i.

5. If each of the vertex sets V_i is reduced to a single vertex with the corresponding natural edge reduction, the resulting graph is acyclic.

6. For any i, there is no bad edge between two vertices in V_i.

7. The total weight of edges between vertices in the same vertex set, summed over all vertex sets, is maximized.

Note that condition (3) implies that bad vertices are never fused, either with normal vertices or with other bad vertices.

Fast Greedy Weighted Fusion

Finding the optimal solution to the weighted fusion problem has been shown to be *NP*-hard [176], so we will need to resort to heuristic approaches if we want to be able to solve really large problems. One heuristic that has proved highly effective for problems of this sort is the *greedy* strategy, which iteratively selects the edge of highest weight and fuses the endpoints of that edge, along with all edges on a path between them into the same vertex set. The *greedy weighted fusion problem* is to find a solution that the greedy heuristic would find.

In the remainder of this section we will present an algorithm developed by Kennedy [171] that produces a solution to this problem in $O(EV+V^2)$ time. Because the implementation of this algorithm is complicated and has many details, we will present only enough to illustrate the basic ideas. We will begin with an outline of the implementation to illuminate some of the algorithmic issues. The algorithm can be thought of as proceeding in six stages:

1. Initialize all the quantities and compute initial successor, predecessor, and neighbor sets. This can be implemented in $O(V+E)$ time.

2. Topologically sort the vertices of the directed acyclic graph. This takes $O(E_d+V)$ time.

3. Process the vertices in V to compute for each vertex the set *pathFrom*[v], which contains all vertices that can be reached by a path from vertex v, and the set *badPathFrom*[v], a subset of *pathFrom*[v] that includes the set of vertices that can be reached from v by a path that contains a bad vertex or a bad edge. This phase can be done in time $O(E_d+V)$ set operations, each of which takes $O(V)$ time.

4. Invert the sets *pathFrom* and *badPathFrom*, respectively, to produce the sets *pathTo*[v] and *badPathTo*[v] for each vertex v in the graph. The set *pathTo*[v] contains the vertices from which there is a path to v; the set *badPathTo*[v] contains the vertices from which v can be reached via a bad path. This can be done in $O(V^2)$ time.

5. Insert each of the edges in $E = E_d \cup E_u$ into a priority queue *edgeHeap* by weight. If the priority queue is implemented as a heap, this takes $O(E \log E)$ time. Note that since $\log E \leq \log V^2 = 2 \log V$, the complexity of this stage can be rewritten as $O(E \log V)$.

6. While *edgeHeap* is nonempty, select and remove the heaviest edge (v,w) from it. If $w \in badPathFrom[v]$, then do not fuse—repeat step 6. Otherwise, do the following:

   a. Collapse v, w, and every edge on a directed path between them into a single node.

   b. After each collapse of a vertex into v, adjust the sets *pathFrom*, *badPathFrom*, *pathTo*, and *badPathTo* to reflect the new graph. That is, the composite node will now be reached from every vertex that reaches a vertex in the composite, and it will reach any vertex that is reached by a vertex in the composite.

   c. After each vertex collapse, recompute *successor*, *predecessor*, and *neighbor* sets for the composite vertex, and recompute weights between the composite vertex and other vertices as appropriate.

A more detailed version of the algorithm is given in Figure 8.25. Note that phases 1 through 5 can be implemented in $O(EV+V^2+E \log V) = O(EV+V^2)$ time. It would be good if the total time for phase 6 could be limited to this asymptotic bound as well. To understand whether this is possible, we need to examine the steps in these phases more carefully.

Initialization. Code for the initialization routines is given in Figures 8.26 and 8.27. Note that we are computing not only *pathFrom* and *badPathFrom* sets but also the inverse sets *pathTo* and *badPathTo*, where $x \in pathTo[y]$ if and only if $y \in pathFrom[x]$. These sets are needed for the update operations that will be performed after collapses.

Collapsing a Region to a Single Node. Once it has selected an edge (v,w) along which to collapse, the greedy weighted fusion algorithm must perform the collapse. The code in loops L_2 and L_3 in Figure 8.25 determine the region R that must be collapsed. To do this it must identify every vertex that is on a path from v to w. As we see in the algorithm in Figure 8.25, this is done by performing the following steps:

1. Let *worklist* initially contain all successors x of v such that $w \in pathFrom[x]$.

2. While *worklist* is not empty, remove the first vertex x from it and add x to the collapse region R. In addition add to *worklist* all successors y of x such that $w \in pathFrom[y]$, unless one of those vertices has already been added to R. (Note that the implementation of the membership test in *worklist.ever*, which determines if a vertex has ever been in the worklist, will be described in conjunction with the fast set implementation below.)

procedure *WeightedFusion(M,B,W)*

// $M = (V,E_d,E_u)$ is an acyclic mixed-directed graph
// B is the set of bad vertices
// W is the weight function
// *pathFrom[v]* contains all vertices reachable from v;
// *badPathFrom[v]* contains vertices reachable from v
//   by a path containing a bad vertex
// *edgeHeap* is a priority queue of edges

P_1:   *InitializeGraph(V,E_d,E_u)*;

topologically sort the vertices using directed edges;

edgeHeap := $\varnothing$;
P_2:   *InitializePathInfo(V, edgeHeap)*;

L_1:   **while** *edgeHeap* $\neq \varnothing$ **do begin**
select and remove the heaviest edge $e = (v,w)$ from *edgeHeap*;
if $v \in$ *pathFrom[w]* **then** swap v and w;
if $w \in$ *badPathFrom[v]* **then**
    continue L_1; // cannot or need not be fused
// Otherwise fuse v, w, and vertices between them

P_3:   *worklist* := $\varnothing$; R := $\varnothing$; // R is the collapse region
L_2:   **for each** $x \in$ *successors[v]* **do**
        if $w \in$ *pathFrom[x]* **then** *worklist* := *worklist* $\cup$ $\{x\}$;
    if *worklist* = $\varnothing$ **then** add w to *worklist*; // (v,w) undirected

L_3:   **while** *worklist* $\neq \varnothing$ **do begin**
        extract a vertex x from *worklist*; R := $R \cup \{x\}$;
        if $x \neq w$ **then**
            for each $y \in$ *successors[x]* **do begin**
                if $w \in$ *pathFrom[y]* and $y \notin$ *worklist.ever* **then**
                    worklist := *worklist* $\cup$ $\{y\}$;
            end
    end L_3

Collapse(v,R); // perform all updates to data structures as well
end L_1
end *WeightedFusion*

Figure 8.25 Greedy weighted fusion.

The complexity of the overall process is easiest to understand if we divide the cost into traversals of edges within the region of collapse R and traversals of edges to vertices outside of R. Suppose we charge the cost of traversing the edge (x,y) to the vertex y if $y \in R$. Since each vertex can be merged into another at most once, procedure *InitializeGraph*(V,E_d,E_u)

    for each $v \in V$ **do begin**
      successors[v] := $\varnothing$;
      predecessors[v] := $\varnothing$;
      neighbors[v] := $\varnothing$;
    end

    for each $(x,y) \in E_d$ **do**
      successors[x] := *successors*[x] $\cup$ {y};
      predecessors[y] := *predecessors*[y] $\cup$ {x};
    for each $(x,y) \in E_u$ **do begin**
      neighbors[x] := *neighbors*[x] $\cup$ {y};
      neighbors[y] := *neighbors*[y] $\cup$ {x};
    end
end *InitializeGraph*

Figure 8.26 Initialize *predecessors*, *successors*, and *neighbors*.

procedure *InitializePathInfo*($V,edgeHeap$)

    // v is the vertex into which merging is taking place
    // x is the vertex currently being merged.

L_1:   **for each** $v \in V$ in reverse topological order **do begin**
      rep[v] := v;
      pathFrom[v] := {v};
      if $v \in B$ **then** *badPathFrom*[v] := {v} **else** *badPathFrom*[v] := $\varnothing$;
      for each $w \in$ *successors*[v] **do begin**
        pathFrom[v] := *pathFrom*[v] $\cup$ *pathFrom*[w];
        badPathFrom[v] := *badPathFrom*[v] $\cup$ *badPathFrom*[w];
        if (v,w) is a bad edge **or** $w \in B$ **then**
          badPathFrom[v] := *badPathFrom*[v] $\cup$ *pathFrom*[w];
        add (v,w) to *edgeHeap*;
      end
      for each $w \in$ *neighbors*[v] **do**
        if $w \in$ *pathFrom*[v] **then begin**
          delete w from *neighbors*[v];
          delete v from *neighbors*[w];
          successors[v] := *successors*[v] $\cup$ {w};
        end
        add (v,w) to *edgeHeap*;
      end
      invert *pathFrom* to compute *pathTo*;
      invert *badPathFrom* to compute *badPathTo*;
    end *InitializePathInfo*

Figure 8.27 Initialize *path* sets.

the total cost of such edge traversals is $O(V)$ over the entire program. Next consider those vertices y that are successors of some node in the region of collapse, but are not themselves in that region. Such vertices become successors of the composite region represented by v. If we charge the cost of traversing edges out of x to such an outside vertex y to the edge (x,y), an edge can accumulate $O(V)$ charges over the course of the algorithm. Thus the total cost of outside edge traversals over the course of the algorithm is $O(EV)$.

Finally, the procedure *Collapse*, shown in Figure 8.28, is called for that region R. It merges all vertices in R into the source vertex v. This is accomplished by performing the following steps:

1. Topologically sort the vertices using only the edges internal to the region of collapse.

2. For each vertex in topological order, do the following:

   a. Merge x into v;

   b. Reconstruct *pathFrom*, *badPathFrom*, *pathTo*, and *badPathTo* sets for the entire graph. Note that if some vertex u reaches x and v reaches another vertex z, then, after merging x into v, u reaches z.

   c. Create new successor, predecessor, and neighbor lists for the composite v by merging *successors*[x], *predecessors*[x], and *neighbors*[x] into *successors*[v], *predecessors*[v], and *neighbors*[v] as appropriate.

```
procedure Collapse(v,R)
    topologically sort R with respect to edges in R ∪ {v};
L₄:    for each x ∈ R in topological order do begin
        // fuse x into v;
        rep[x] := v;
        // update pathFrom and pathTo sets
        UpdatePathInfo(v,x);
        // update the graph representation
        UpdateSuccessors(v,x,R);
        UpdatePredecessors(v,x,R);
        UpdateNeighbors(v,x,R);
        // delete vertex x
        delete x, predecessors[x], successors[x],
            neighbors[x], pathFrom[x], badPathFrom[x],
            pathTo[x], and badPathTo[x];
        delete x from successors[v];
    end L₄
end Collapse
```

Figure 8.28 Collapse a region into a vertex.

The topological sort takes time linear in the number of vertices and edges in R, so its cost is bounded by $O(E+V)$ over the entire program.

    The total number of times a vertex can be collapsed into another vertex is bounded by $V - 1$, so the trick to getting the time bound we want will be bounding the work in the update steps 2b and 2c. For the purposes of this discussion, we will consider these steps in reverse order.

Updating Successors, Predecessors, and Neighbors. First, let us consider the cost of updating successors. The code for this operation is given in Figure 8.29. This procedure is invoked once for each vertex x that is collapsed into another vertex v. Thus, it can be invoked at most $O(V)$ times during the entire run of the algorithm. For each such vertex, the procedure visits each successor. Since no vertex is ever collapsed more than once, the total number of successor visits is bounded by E. All operations in the visit take constant time, except for the reheap operation on *edgeHeap*, which takes $\lg E = \lg V$ time.

```
procedure UpdateSuccessors(v,x)

    // v is the vertex into which merging is taking place
    // x is the vertex currently being merged.

    // Make successors of x be successors of v and reweight
    for each y ∈ successors[x] do begin
        if y ∈ successors[v] then begin
            W(v,y) := W(v,y) + W(x,y);   // charge to deleted edge (x,y)
            reheap edgeHeap;
            delete (x,y) from edgeHeap and reheap;
        end
        else if y ∈ neighbors[v] then begin
            successors[v] := successors[v] ∪ {y};
            W(v,y) := W(v,y) + W(x,y); // charge to deleted edge (x,y)
            reheap edgeHeap;
            delete (x,y) from edgeHeap and reheap;
            delete y from neighbors[v];
            delete x from neighbors[y];
        end
        else begin   // y has no relationship to v
            successors[v] := successors[v] ∪ {y};
            replace (x,y) with (v,y) in edgeHeap;   // no charge
        end
        delete x from predecessors[y];
    end
end UpdateSuccessors
```

Figure 8.29 Update *successors*.

One wrinkle that must be dealt with is the case where the edge from x to y is not deleted but rather moved so that it now connects v to y. This is the third case in the if statement within *UpdateSuccessors*. If we are not careful, it is possible that the same edge will be visited many times as collapses are performed. However, note that the third case does no reweighting and no reheaping is required to deal with it. Therefore, the total cost contributed by the third case in the if statement is at most $O(EV)$. The cost of operations in the other two cases can be charged to the edge being deleted, so the total cost is bounded by $O(E \log V)$.

Thus the cost associated with all invocations of *UpdateSuccessors* is $O(EV+E \log V+V) = O(EV)$. *UpdatePredecessors* and *UpdateNeighbors* are similar in structure and analysis [172].

Updating Path Information. We now turn to the problem of updating *pathFrom*, *badPathFrom*, *pathTo*, and *badPathTo* sets (step 2c) after a collapse. This step must be performed before the *successor, predecessor,* and *neighbor* sets are updated because it uses the old relationships to perform the update.

The key difficulty with this step is that any vertex that reaches the vertex x that is being collapsed into v now transitively reaches any vertex reached by v. This problem is illustrated by Figure 8.30.

If we were to recompute the *pathFrom* sets from scratch after each collapse, it would take a total of $O(EV^2+V^3)$ time, since a single application of the *pathFrom* computation takes $O(EV+V^2)$ time.

To reduce this time bound we must ensure that we do no more work than is required. The basic strategy is to compute *newPathSinks*, the set of vertices reached from v but not from x, and *newPathSources*, the set of vertices that reach x but not v.

Once we have these sets, we will update the *pathFrom* sets of every vertex in *newPathSources* and we will update the *pathTo* set of every vertex in *newPathSinks*. One way to do this would be the following:

```
for each b ∈ newPathSources do
    pathFrom[b] := pathFrom[b] ∪ newPathSinks;
for each b ∈ newPathSinks do
    pathTo[b] := pathTo[b] ∪ newPathSources;
```

The problem with this approach is that it might take $O(V^2)$ time because there could be $O(V)$ vertices in *newPathSinks* $\cup$ *newPathSources* and the set operations each take $O(V)$ time. Thus the total time would be bounded by $O(V^3)$, making it more expensive than any other part of the algorithm.

One reason the cost is high is the possibility that we are doing unnecessary work. Since we only increase the size of the *pathTo* and *pathFrom* sets, if we use bit matrices of size V^2 to represent these sets and we only turn on bits once, we will limit the total amount of work to $O(V^2)$. However, in the strategy above, we may attempt to turn on the same bit many times. This is because vertices in *newPathSources* might already reach vertices in *newPathSinks* if there is an edge between the two sets that bypasses v and x (Figure 8.31).

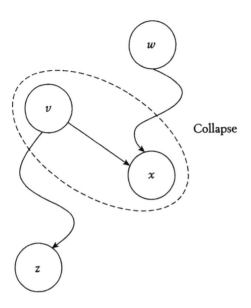

Figure 8.30 Illustration of the path update problem.

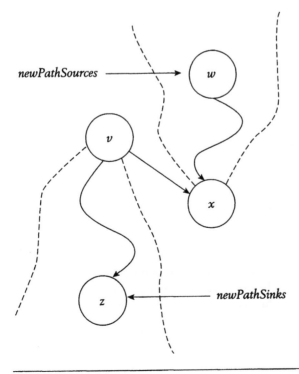

Figure 8.31 Solving the path update problem.

To avoid such redundant work we will back up through the vertices in *new-PathSources*, taking care not to turn on any *pathTo* bit more than once. Similarly, we will move down through *newPathSinks* to turn on *pathFrom* bits at most once. The key procedure is *UpdateSlice*, shown in Figure 8.32.

Note that *UpdateSlice* is designed to be used to update both the *pathFrom* and *badPathFrom* information on separate calls, by passing a different parameter to *pathFrom*. In addition, *UpdateSlice* can be called to compute *pathTo* and *badPathTo* by changing the definition of *cesors* and *pcesors* (reversing the graph and the roles of most of the sets). Thus, in each call, the parameter *pathFrom* can represent *pathFrom* (or *badPathFrom*) or *pathTo* (or *badPathTo*) sets, depending on the direction of the traversal. It can be shown that at most eight calls to *UpdateSlice* are needed to update all of the path information. For collapses along directed edges, four calls will suffice.

Since the effect of the calls in different directions is symmetric, we will analyze the cost of a single call to update all the *pathFrom* sets in *newPathSources*. For each vertex w in the slice, represented by *newPathSources*, we will compute a set *newPathFrom*[w] that represents the set of new vertices reached from w after the collapse. As each vertex is processed, we will visit all its predecessors. At each predecessor y, we will examine each vertex z in *newPathFrom*[w] to see if it is in *path-From*[y]. If z is not in *pathFrom*[y], we will add it to *pathFrom*[y] and to *newPath-From*[y]. The algorithm is given in Figure 8.32.

Correctness. The correctness of procedure *UpdateSlice* can be established by induction on the order in which elements are removed from the worklist. Since the first element off the worklist is x, we are certain that its *newPathFrom* set is correctly computed because it must be the original *newPathSinks* by the way we have computed it. Now assume that *pathFrom*[b] and *newPathFrom*[b] are computed correctly for every vertex that comes off the worklist before vertex w. Furthermore, assume that vertex w has an incorrect *pathFrom* set when it comes off the worklist. This can only be because *pathFrom*[w] has some bit off that should be on. This bit must correspond to some vertex in *newPathSinks*. But this means that none of the successors of w have that bit turned on in either their *pathFrom* or *newPathFrom* sets, but since there must be a path from w to the vertex represented by that bit, then some predecessor, which necessarily came off the worklist before w, must have the bit for that vertex set incorrectly as well, a contradiction.

Complexity. To show that the algorithm stays within the desired time limits, we must consider several aspects of the implementation. First, we will describe, in the paragraph below, entitled "A Fast Set Implementation," how to represent sets of integers so that membership testing, insertion, and initialization take constant time (initialization is the hard part). If we use this representation, we can initialize each *newPathFrom* set and the *worklist* to the empty set in constant time. Since the procedure is entered at most $O(V)$ times and there are at most $O(V)$ vertices in a slice, the cost of loop L_1 is bounded by $O(V^2)$. By the same reasoning, since each vertex in *newPathSources* is put on the worklist at most once, the body of loop L_2

procedure *UpdateSlice(x,pathFrom,newPathSources,newPathSinks,cesors,pcesors)*

    // *x* is the vertex that is being collapsed
    // *pathFrom* is the set that is being updated
    // *newPathSources* is the set of vertices that can reach *x*
    //   but not the vertex it is being collapsed into
    // *newPathSinks* is the set of vertices reachable from the vertex being
    //   collapsed into but not from *x*
    // *cesors* is the successor set (if traversing backward from *x*)
    // *pcesors* is the predecessor set (if traversing backward from *x*)

    // Update *pathFrom* sets backing up from *x* in *newPathSources*
    //   adding vertices in *newPathSinks*

S_0:   *newPathFrom*[*x*] := *newPathSinks*;
L_1:   **for each** *b* ∈ *newPathSources* − {*x*} **do** *newPathFrom*[*b*] := ∅;
    worklist := {*x*};
L_2:   **while** *worklist* ≠ ∅ **do begin**
        pick an element *w* from the front of *worklist* and remove it;
L_3:   **for each** *y* ∈ *pcesors*[*w*] **such that** *y* ∈ *newPathSources* **do begin**
            if *y* ∉ *worklist.ever* **then** add *y* to *worklist*;
L_4:   **for each** *z* ∈ *newPathFrom*[*w*] **do**
S_1:   **if** *z* ∉ *pathFrom*[*y*] **then begin**
                    pathFrom[*y*] := *pathFrom*[*y*] ∪ {*z*};
                    newPathFrom[*y*] := *newPathFrom*[*y*] ∪ {*z*};
                end
        end L_3
    end L_2
end *UpdateSlice*

Figure 8.32 Update *pathFrom* sets for a slice of vertices reaching or reached from *x*.

is executed at most $O(V^2)$ times. Loop L_3 visits each predecessor of a vertex, so its body should be executed at most $O(EV)$ times.

    Unfortunately, the work done in the body of L_3 includes the loop L_4. We must have some way of bounding the work done by the body of loop L_4, which consists of a single if statement S_1. The true branch of the if statement is taken only if the collapse has made *y* reach *z* and this is the first time that fact is noticed. We charge the constant time of this branch to the entry in the *pathFrom* matrix that is being set to true. Thus the true branch of the if statement can be executed only $O(V^2)$ times over the entire algorithm.

    This leaves the false branch. Although this branch is empty, the test itself represents a constant time cost for the false branch. How many times can the test be executed with the false outcome? Since *z* ∈ *newPathFrom*[*w*], it means that the immediate successor *w* of *y* within the *newPathFrom* set has just had its *pathFrom* bit for z set to true. Thus we will charge this test to the edge between y and w. Since a given *pathFrom* bit can be set at most once in the algorithm, each edge can be charged at most V times, once for each vertex that can be reached from the sink of that edge. Thus, the total cost of the charges for the false test over the entire algorithm is $O(EV)$.

These considerations establish that *pathFrom* and *badPathFrom* can be updated in $O(EV+V^2)$ time over the entire algorithm. An identical analysis establishes the same time bound for the updates to *pathTo* and *badPathTo*.

A Fast Set Implementation.   A naive implementation of this algorithm might use a list and associated bit vector for all sets. Unfortunately, initialization of the bit vector to represent the empty sets would require $O(V)$ time. This is unacceptable in the procedure *UpdateSlice* because it would make the total cost of loop L_1 be $O(V^3)$, which would dominate the algorithm. Thus we need to find a representation that permits a constant-time initialization while keeping constant-time membership and insertion. In addition we would like to be able to iterate over the entire set in time proportional to its size.

These goals can be achieved by using a well-known but rarely discussed strategy for avoiding the initialization costs for a set represented by an indexed array. The essential idea of this algorithm (included in the book by Aho, Hopcroft, and Ullman [10] as an exercise) is to use two integer arrays of length V for the set representation. The array Q will contain all the vertices in the queue in order from element $Q[next]$ to element $Q[last]$. The array In will serve as the bit array for element testing—$In[v]$ will contain the location in Q of vertex v.

To enter a new vertex y at the end of the queue requires the following steps:

$$last := last + 1;\ Q[last] := y;\ In[y] := last;$$

Note that this leaves the element $In[y]$ pointing to a location in Q that is within the range $[0:last]$ and contains y. Thus the test for whether a vertex z is a member of Q is

$$next \leq In[z] \leq last \text{ and } Q[In[z]] = z;$$

and the test, required in Figure 8.25, of whether z has *ever* been a member of Q is

$$0 \leq In[z] \leq last \text{ and } Q[In[z]] = z;$$

Figure 8.33 gives a graphical description of the queue representation. Note that vertex 4 cannot be mistaken for a member because no element of Q in the right range points back to 4.

Using this representation we can perform all queue operations in constant time including initialization. This data structure will be used for many of the set representations in the algorithm.

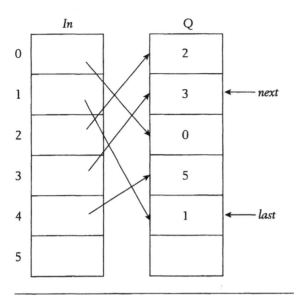

Figure 8.33 Fast queue representation.

Final Observations. To sum up, the total cost of the algorithm is $O(EV+V^2)$ for the first five phases, $O(EV)$ for phase 6a and $O(EV+V^2)$ for phase 6b. Thus the entire algorithm takes time $O(EV+V^2)$.

A critical aspect of any fusion algorithm is the recomputation of weights between a collapsed vertex and some successor or predecessor. In the algorithm as presented, the cost of a combined edge is computed by adding the costs of the edges incident on the two original vertices. In many cases this is not the best method. For example, in the fusion for reuse problem, we might have a use of the same array variable in three different loops. Suppose that the loops each execute 100 iterations. The graph for the three loops might look like Figure 8.34.

In this example, merging vertices x and y and reweighting by addition would compute an aggregate weight of 200 between x and z. In reality, the total additional reuse available after merging is 100. In this case, using *maximum* as the reweighting operation would be more appropriate.

A nice feature of the algorithm presented is that edge reweighting is done at most $O(E)$ times. This means we can use a relatively expensive reweighting algorithm without substantively affecting the asymptotic time bound. For example, suppose there are A different arrays in the program. If we associate a length A array with each vertex that indicates the volume of usage of each array in that loop, then reweighting could be done by taking the maximum of the usage counts of the arrays in the two vertices being collapsed and then summing the minimums of the weights between corresponding arrays in each successor of the composite vertex. This array-by-array computation could be done in $O(A)$ time. So the entire fusion algorithm would take time $O((E+V)(V+A))$. If $A = O(V)$, then the

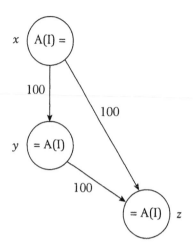

Figure 8.34 Weight computation example.

algorithm has the same asymptotic time bound as the fusion algorithm that uses addition for reweighting.

Although the algorithm should produce good answers in practice, Figure 8.35 shows that it will not always produce the optimal result. In this case the highest weight edge is (a,f), with a weight of 11. If we collapse this edge, the final merge set will be $\{a,b,c,d,f\}$ and the total weight of all edges will be 16. However, by merging c and d with b, we have precluded merging c and d with e because of the bad vertex on a path from b to e. If we merged c and d with e and f instead, the total weight saved would be 22, a better result.

8.6.5   Multilevel Loop Fusion for Register Reuse

Next we turn to the multiple-loop nesting problem. The basic strategy for multi-level fusion is to fuse at the outermost level first, then recursively fuse the bodies of the resulting loops.

This exceedingly simple approach has one important complication. When aligning loops for fusion at an outer loop level, we must align only the indices containing the outer loop index, under the assumption that the inner loop index will be aligned separately.

To illustrate this principle, consider the following example, which is intended to represent a two-dimensional relaxation:

```
DO J = 1, 1000
   DO I = 1, 1000
      A(I,J) = B
```

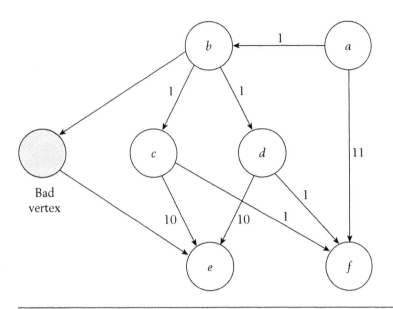

Figure 8.35 Nonoptimality of greedy weighted fusion.

```
        ENDDO
    ENDDO
    DO J = 2, 999
        DO I = 2, 999
            A(I,J) = A(I+1,J) + A(I-1,J) + A(I,J+1) + A(I,J-1)
        ENDDO
    ENDDO
```

Alignment of the outer loop should consider only the indices where J appears. Thus, the alignment would produce

```
    DO J = 0, 999
        DO I = 1, 1000
            A(I,J+1) = B
        ENDDO
    ENDDO
    DO J = 2, 999
        DO I = 2, 999
            A(I,J) = A(I+1,J) + A(I-1,J) + A(I,J+1) + A(I,J-1)
        ENDDO
    ENDDO
```

After fusion, this becomes

```
DO J = 0, 1
   DO I = 1, 1000
      A(I,J+1) = B
   ENDDO
ENDDO
DO J = 2, 999
   DO I = 1, 1000
      A(I,J+1) = B
   ENDDO
   DO I = 2, 999
      A(I,J) = A(I+1,J) + A(I-1,J) + A(I,J+1) + A(I,J-1)
   ENDDO
ENDDO
```

Now, when alignment is applied to the body of the second loop, the only reference we need to be concerned about is A(I,J+1), so no alignment is needed. Another round of fusion produces

```
DO J = 0, 1
   DO I = 1, 1000
      A(I,J+1) = B
   ENDDO
ENDDO
DO J = 2, 999
   A(1,J+1) = B
   DO I = 2, 999
      A(I,J+1) = B
      A(I,J) = A(I+1,J) + A(I-1,J) + A(I,J+1) + A(I,J-1)
   ENDDO
   A(1000, J+1) = B
ENDDO
```

After scalar replacement, the inner loop will become

```
DO J = 2, 999
   tA1 = tB ! moved into a register earlier
   A(1,J+1) = tA1
   tA0 = A(1,J)
   DO I = 2, 999
      tA1 = tB
      A(I,J+1) = tA1
      tA0 = A(I+1,J) + tA0 + tA1 + A(I,J-1)
      A(I,J) = tA0
   ENDDO
   A(1000, J+1) = B
ENDDO
```

procedure *CompleteFusion*(R)

> // The parameter R is a region of code that contains some loops
> // and some assignment statements contained in no loop.
>
> **if** there are no loops in R **then return**;
>
> use *WeightedFusion* to select sets of loops for fusion;
> **for each** set S in the collection **do begin**
> > align the loops in S along the indices of the outer loops;
> > use *FuseLoops* to produce a collection of fused loops;
>
> **end**
>
> **for each** loop l in R after fusion **do** *CompleteFusion*(body(l));
> **end** *CompleteFusion*

Figure 8.36 Multilevel loop fusion.

This code has a savings of two references on each iteration (out of a total of six) so the code should run 1.5 times faster than naive code. Half of the improvement is due to the two-level loop fusion. Unroll-and-jam can produce further improvements.

The complete fusion algorithm is given in Figure 8.36.

8.7 **Putting It All Together**

We now turn to a discussion of how the various transformations that enhance register usage fit together, illustrating the principles with a complete treatment of matrix multiplication.

8.7.1 **Ordering the Transformations**

Before turning to an extended example of the register improvement strategies, we should comment on the order of transformations discussed in this chapter. One goal for that ordering is to change the original code as little as possible. That is, we should not make any change unless it improves the code's performance and, given two alternatives that provide roughly equal performance improvements, we should choose the one that changes the code least. Keeping the code as close as possible to the original helps programmers understand the changes more easily.

That having been said, we present the recommended order of transformations for register allocation:

1. *Loop interchange:* Loop interchange should be done first because it brings reuse to the innermost loop, which should be a priority. Fusion might interfere with this process.

2. *Loop alignment and fusion:* This can achieve extra reuse across loops, particularly when compiling code generated by a preprocessor, such as a Fortran 90 front end (see Section 13.2).

3. *Unroll-and-jam:* This achieves outer loop reuse when there are dependences carried by other than the inner loop after interchange is finished.

4. *Scalar replacement:* This sets up the standard coloring-based register allocator by replacing array references that can be reused with scalar variables.

The use of all four of these steps will be illustrated on the example in the next section.

8.7.2   An Example: Matrix Multiplication

We will illustrate the use of the register allocation transformations on our canonical example of matrix multiplication. We will begin with a version of the algorithm that is well suited to vector machines. Code that has been rearranged to vectorize well is very common in scientific programs. These codes are rarely rewritten to take advantage of the scalar uniprocessors when moved to those machines.

```
      DO I = 1, N
         DO J = 1, N
S₀          C(J,I) = 0.0
         ENDDO
         DO K = 1, N
            DO J = 1, N
S₁             C(J,I) = C(J,I) + A(J,K) * B(K,I)
            ENDDO
         ENDDO
      ENDDO
```

This code achieves long vector operations in both nests by having the loop with index J, which iterates over successive column elements, in the innermost position.

The dependences involving the two statements in this loop are illustrated in Figure 8.37. As we see from this diagram, the loop on K carries the most dependences involving statement S_1.

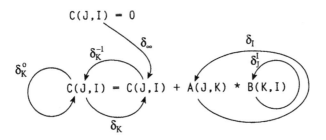

Figure 8.37 Matrix multiplication dependences.

Clearly, we should interchange the K-loop to the innermost position around statement S_1, to produce

```
DO I = 1, N
    DO J = 1, N
        C(J,I) = 0.0
    ENDDO
    DO J = 1, N
        DO K = 1, N
            C(J,I) = C(J,I) + A(J,K) * B(K,I)
        ENDDO
    ENDDO
ENDDO
```

Now we use loop fusion on the body of the I-loop to produce

```
DO I = 1, N
    DO J = 1, N
        C(J,I) = 0.0
        DO K = 1, N
            C(J,I) = C(J,I) + A(J,K) * B(K,I)
        ENDDO
    ENDDO
ENDDO
```

Next we apply unroll-and-jam with a factor of two to each of the outer loops, to get the following code:

```
DO I = 1, N, 2
    DO J = 1, N, 2
        C(J,I) = 0.0
        C(J+1,I) = 0.0
        C(J,I+1) = 0.0
```

```
            C(J+1,I+1) = 0.0
            DO K = 1, N
               C(J,I) = C(J,I) + A(J,K) * B(K,I)
               C(J+1,I) = C(J+1,I) + A(J+1,K) * B(K,I)
               C(J,I+1) = C(J,I+1) + A(J,K) * B(K,I+1)
               C(J+1,I+1) = C(J+1,I+1) + A(J+1,K) * B(K,I+1)
            ENDDO
         ENDDO
      ENDDO
```

With scalar replacement this becomes

```
DO I = 1, N, 2
   DO J = 1, N, 2
      s0 = 0.0; s1 = 0.0; s2 = 0.0; s3 = 0.0
      DO K = 1, N
         r1 = A(J,K);          r2 = B(K,I)
         r3 = A(J+1,K);        r4 = B(K,I+1)
         s0 = s0 + r1 * r2; s1 = s1 + r3 * r2
         s2 = s2 + r1 * r4; s3 = s3 + r3 * r4
      ENDDO
      C(J,I) = s0;    C(J+1,I) = s1
      C(J,I+1) = s2; C(J+1,I+1)= s3
   ENDDO
ENDDO
```

If each of the scalar variables is assigned to a register, eight registers are required, but the computation requires four loads for eight flops in the inner loop. In addition, there are enough operations to fill an addition pipeline of up to four stages. In general, if the unroll factor is m, this strategy achieves a rate of m^2 flops to $2m$ loads in the inner loop.

8.8 Complex Loop Nests

In practice, loops in real programs are often much more complicated than the ones used as examples in this chapter so far. For example, to do a good job on dense linear algebra, a transformation system will need to handle loops that contain if statements, triangular and trapezoidal loops, and specialized loop nests such as those found in LU decomposition. This section describes some of the methods for handling such loop nests.

8.8.1   Loops with If Statements

Unfortunately, the strategy for scalar replacement described in Section 8.3 does not extend naturally to conditional code. Consider the following example:

```
      DO I = 1, N
5         IF (M(I).LT.0) A(I) = B(I) + C
10        D(I) = A(I) + E
      ENDDO
```

The true dependence from statement 5 to statement 10 due to the assignment and use of A(I) does not reveal that the assignment to A(I) is conditional. Using only dependence information, a naive scalar replacement scheme might produce the following code:

```
      DO I = 1, N
5         IF (M(I).LT.0) THEN
              a0 = B(I) + C
              A(I) = a0
          ENDIF
10        D(I) = a0 + E
      ENDDO
```

This code is erroneous because a false predicate leaves a0 undefined, resulting in an incorrect value of a0 at statement 10.

The solution to this problem is fairly straightforward: we can ensure that a0 has the proper value by inserting a load of a0 from A(I) on the false branch of the if statement:

```
      DO I = 1, N
5         IF (M(I).LT.0) THEN
              a0 = B(I) + C
              A(I) = a0
          ELSE
              a0 = A(I)
          ENDIF
10        D(I) = a0 + E
      ENDDO
```

The danger of inserting instructions in this manner is that it might increase running time on some paths through the program. In this case, however, this is not a problem—if the true branch is taken, a load of A(I) is avoided, while if the false branch is taken, a load is inserted and another is eliminated. In either case, running time is not increased except for the insertion of an extra branch.

A goal of our algorithm will be to produce no increase in running time as a result of these transformations. One optimization strategy that has a similar goal is *partial redundancy elimination*, which seeks to eliminate the latter of two identical computations performed on a given execution path. A computation is *redundant* if, on every path leading to it, an identical computation occurs earlier. In this case we say that it is *anticipated* on every path. It is *partially redundant* if the computation is anticipated only on some of the execution paths leading to it. To remove a partially redundant calculation *e*, the compiler must replicate it along every path to *e* on which it is not anticipated. An essential property of partial redundancy elimination as described in the literature [215] is that it can be carried out in a way that is guaranteed not to increase the number of computations along any path.

In adapting partial redundancy elimination to scalar replacement, we are really interested in inserting initializations for variables that are uninitialized on every path to a use. To do this we see that, at a given point *p* in the program, a variable is potentially uninitialized if it is *live*—there is an assignment-free path to a use—and there exists a path from the entry block of the program that does not contain an initialization. Our goal is to insert an initialization expression on every path that does not contain one. Furthermore, we will insert the initialization at the end of the last block that is not on any path that has been initialized.

Assume for the sake of simplicity that each **if** statement in the program has a (possibly empty) **else** branch. This artificial condition can be forced by inserting empty nodes when building the control flow graph for the loop. We introduce the following variables:

- $live_{out}(b)$ is the set of temporaries that are live on exit from block *b*. $live_{in}(b)$ is the set of variables that are live on entry to *b*.

- $alive_{out}(b)$ is the set of variables that are absolutely live, that is, live on every path from the exit of *b* to the exit node of the graph. $alive_{in}(b)$ contains the set of variables that are absolutely live on entry to *b*.

- $init_{in}(b)$ is the set of variables that have always been initialized on entry to *b*. $init_{out}(b)$ is the set of variables that have always been initialized on exit from *b*.

- $pinit_{in}(b)$ is the set of variables that are *partially initialized* on entry to *b*, that is, variables that have been initialized on some path to the entry of *b*. $pinit_{out}(b)$ is the set of variables that are partially initialized at the exit of *b*.

We wish to insert an initialization in any block in which the variable is not partially initialized, but is partially initialized at a successor. Furthermore, the variable should be absolutely live on exit from the block. These conditions ensure that we never insert a load at a point where it will be redundant on any path.

The following equations define the variables *alive*, *init*, and *pinit*:

$$alive_{out}(b) = \bigcap_{c \in succ(b)} alive_{in}(c)$$
$$alive_{in}(b) = (alive_{out}(b) - killed(b)) \cup used(b)$$

$$(8.1)$$

$$init_{in}(b) = \bigcap_{a \in pred(b)} init_{out}(a)$$
$$init_{out}(b) = init_{in}(b) \cup assigned(b)$$

$$(8.2)$$

$$pinit_{in}(b) = \bigcup_{a \in pred(b)} pinit_{out}(a)$$
$$pinit_{out}(b) = pinit_{in}(b) \cup assigned(b)$$

$$(8.3)$$

Now we can state the conditions for insertion. The set $insert_{out}(b)$ is the set of temporaries whose initializations must be inserted at the end of b. The set $insert_{in}(b)$ is the set of variable initializations that must be inserted at the beginning of b. First, we must insert a variable at the beginning of the block if it is used in the block but is not initialized on any path to the block:

$$insert_{in}(b) = used(b) - pinit_{in}(b) \tag{8.4}$$

We will insert an initialization at the end of a block if the variable has not been initialized on any path to the block, it is absolutely live on exit from the block, and at some successor to the block it is partially available:

$$insert_{out}(b) = alive_{out}(b) \cap \neg pinit(b) \cap (\bigcup_{c \in succ(b)} pinit(c)) \tag{8.5}$$

At each insert point, we insert the assignment to the temporary of the subscripted reference that corresponds to the temporary. This reference can be saved during the original scalar replacement.

8.8.2 Trapezoidal Loops

Many loops that are encountered in real programs do not display the regular, rectangular structure on which the transformations shown in this chapter are effective. In particular, many loops have upper and lower bounds that vary with the indices of outer loops in the same nest. In this section we show how to adapt transformations that enhance register usage to handle these trapezoidal loops.

Triangular Unroll-and Jam

Both unroll-and-jam and loop blocking can be applied to trapezoidal loops using the techniques of previous sections if we partition these loops appropriately. For example, consider the following example loop:

```
DO I = 2, 99
   DO J = 1, I-1
      A(I,J) = A(I,I) + A(J,J)
   ENDDO
ENDDO
```

We would like to transform this loop using unroll-and-jam so that we can get reuse not only of the current value of A(I,I) but also of A(J,J). The problem is that unroll-and-jam cannot be directly used with a triangular loop.

If we do the outer loop unroll by a factor of two, we get

```
DO I = 2, 99, 2
   DO J = 1, I-1
      A(I,J) = A(I,I) + A(J,J)
   ENDDO
   DO J = 1, I
      A(I+1,J) = A(I+1,I+1) + A(J,J)
   ENDDO
ENDDO
```

We now notice that we can jam the first two loops together if we peel out the last iteration of the second inner nest. This would produce

```
DO I = 2, 99, 2
   DO J = 1, I-1
      A(I,J) = A(I,I) + A(J,J)
      A(I+1,J) = A(I+1,I+1) + A(J,J)
   ENDDO
   A(I+1,I) = A(I+1,I+1) + A(I,I)
ENDDO
```

If we now perform scalar replacement, we get

```
tI = A(2,2)
DO I = 2, 99, 2
   tI1 = A(I+1,I+1)
   DO J = 1, I-1
      tJ = A(J,J)
      A(I,J) = tI + tJ
      A(I+1,J) = tI1 + tJ
   ENDDO
   A(I+1,I) = tI + tI1; tI = tI1
ENDDO
```

which requires a load and two stores on each iteration of the inner loop—an improvement over the naive version of two loads per iteration, assuming that the

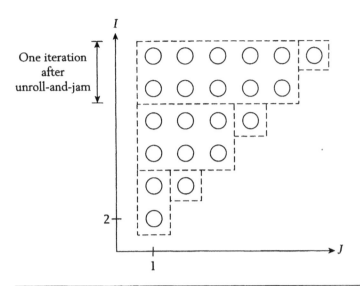

Figure 8.38 Triangular unroll-and-jam.

reuse of A(J,J) in the inner loop is detected even by the naive allocator. This strategy is illustrated in Figure 8.38. Here we see that the triangular loop is being chopped up into rectangular blocks of two J-loop iterations per block and triangular loops of fewer than two iterations (i.e., one iteration).

This approach can be generalized to unroll amounts of more than two, but the code is more complex. It is illustrative to look at the result of an outer loop unroll amount of three. Here we have adjusted the loop bounds to be evenly divisible by three, knowing that this will be taken care of by a preloop in practice.

```
DO I = 2, 100
    DO J = 1, I - 1
        A(I,J) = A(I,I) + A(J,J)
    ENDDO
ENDDO
```

If we unroll to three iterations of the outer loop, we get

```
DO I = 2, 100, 3
    DO J = 1, I - 1
        A(I,J) = A(I,I) + A(J,J)
    ENDDO
    DO J = 1, I
        A(I+1,J) = A(I+1,I+1) + A(J,J)
    ENDDO
    DO J = 1, I + 1
```

```
          A(I+2,J) = A(I+2,I+2) + A(J,J)
      ENDDO
  ENDDO
```

Fusing again, we get

```
DO I = 2, 100, 3
    DO J = 1, I - 1
        A(I,J) = A(I,I) + A(J,J)
        A(I+1,J) = A(I+1,I+1) + A(J,J)
        A(I+2,J) = A(I+2,I+2) + A(J,J)
    ENDDO
    DO J = I, I
        A(I+1,J) = A(I+1,I+1) + A(J,J)
    ENDDO
    DO J = I, I + 1
        A(I+2,J) = A(I+2,I+2) + A(J,J)
    ENDDO
ENDDO
```

Unrolling the last two inner loops, we get

```
DO I = 2, 100, 3
    DO J = 1, I - 1
        A(I,J) = A(I,I) + A(J,J)
        A(I+1,J) = A(I+1,I+1) + A(J,J)
        A(I+2,J) = A(I+2,I+2) + A(J,J)
    ENDDO
    A(I+1,I) = A(I+1,I+1) + A(I,I)
    A(I+2,I) = A(I+2,I+2) + A(I,I)
    A(I+2,I+1) = A(I+2,I+2) + A(I+1,I+1)
ENDDO
```

The resulting code after scalar replacement would be

```
tI = A(2,2); tI1 = A(3,3)
DO I = 2, 100, 3
    tI2 = A(I+2,I+2)
    DO J = 1, I - 1
        tJ = A(J,J);                A(I,J) = tI + tJ
        A(I+1,J) = tI1 + tJ; A(I+2,J) = tI2 + tJ
    ENDDO
    A(I+1,I) = tI1 + tI;
    A(I+2,I) = tI2 + tI
    A(I+2,I+1) = tI2 + tI1
```

```
      tI = tI1; tI1 = tI2
   ENDDO
```

which saves three loads per iteration of the inner loop.

Trapezoidal Unroll-and-Jam

To understand how to extend the methods of the previous section to trapezoidal loops, let us consider an important example—simple *convolution*. This loop appears in many seismic analysis applications, particularly in the oil industry. The following version was taken from an actual code for geophysical seismic analysis and constituted the bulk of the running time for that code:

```
DO I = 0, N3
   DO J = I, MIN(N3,I+N2)
      F3(I) = F3(I) + F1(J) * W(I-J)
   ENDDO
   F3(I) = F3(I) * DT
ENDDO
```

Clearly, the variable F3(I) will be held in a register throughout the iterations of the inner loop. Also, it is pretty easy to see the reuse of the variable F1(J) that can be achieved through the use of unroll-and-jam. However, unroll-and-jam can also provide reuse of the variable W(I-J).

Before we apply unroll-and-jam to this loop nest, we partition it into two parts—the part in which I + N2 ≤ N3 and the rest—so that the inner loop in each loop nest has a consistent upper bound:

```
DO I = 0, N3 - N2
   DO J = I, I + N2
      F3(I) = F3(I) + F1(J) * W(I-J)
   ENDDO
   F3(I) = F3(I) * DT
ENDDO
DO I = N3 - N2 + 1, N3
   DO J = I, N3
      F3(I) = F3(I) + F1(J) * W(I-J)
   ENDDO
   F3(I) = F3(I) * DT
ENDDO
```

The second of these loop nests is no longer trapezoidal, since the upper bound is simply N3. Therefore, we will henceforth restrict our attention to the first loop nest. Unrolling the outer loop once, we get

```
DO I = 0, N3 - N2, 2
   DO J = I, I + N2
      F3(I) = F3(I) + F1(J) * W(I-J)
   ENDDO
   F3(I) = F3(I) * DT
   DO J = I + 1, I + N2 + 1
      F3(I+1) = F3(I+1) + F1(J) * W(I-J+1)
   ENDDO
   F3(I+1) = F3(I+1) * DT
ENDDO
```

Fusion of the common iterations of the inner loop then produces

```
DO I = 0, N3 - N2, 2
   F3(I) = F3(I) + F1(I) * W(0)
   DO J = I + 1, I + N2
      F3(I) = F3(I) + F1(J) * W(I-J)
      F3(I+1) = F3(I+1) + F1(J) * W(I-J+1)
   ENDDO
   F3(I+1) = F3(I+1) + F1(I+N2+1) * W(-N2)
   F3(I) = F3(I) * DT
   F3(I+1) = F3(I+1) * DT
ENDDO
```

Scalar replacement on this loop will then yield

```
DO I = 0, N3 - N2, 2
   f3I = F3(I); f3I1 = F3(I+1)
   f1I = F1(I); wIJ0 = W(0)
   f3I = f3I + f1I * wIJ0
   DO J = I + 1, I + N2
      f1J = F1(J); wIJ1 = W(I-J)
      f3I = f3I + f1J * wIJ1
      f3I1 = f3I1 + f1J * wIJ0
      wIJ0 = wIJ1
   ENDDO
   f1J = F1(I+N2+1); wIJ1 = W(-N2)
   f3I1 = f3I1 + f1J * wIJ1
   F3(I) = f3I * DT; F3(I+1) = f3I1 * DT
ENDDO
```

Note that the reuse of W(I-J) takes place in the next iteration on the second statement instance because loop index J is subtracted in the subscript expression.

Table 8.3 Convolution timing

Original code	15.59 sec
Transformed code	7.02 sec
Speedup	2.22

In experiments on a MIPS M120, conducted by Carr and Kennedy, the improved code achieved the timings shown in Table 8.3 on arrays of only 100 elements.

8.9 Summary

We have shown a variety of dependence-based techniques to increase the reuse of array values in uniprocessor CPU registers on modern uniprocessors. These methods are particularly useful for floating-point registers because these are often used to hold single elements from array data structures. Therefore, traditional coloring-based register allocation strategies are ineffective for these registers. The methods include the following:

- *Scalar replacement*, which exposes reuse of subscripted variables to scalar compilers with good register allocation
- *Unroll-and-jam*, which transforms programs to exploit register reuse in outer loops
- *Loop interchange*, to shift loops carrying the most reuse to the innermost position
- *Loop fusion* with *alignment*, to bring uses from different loops in a program together in a single loop

These techniques have been shown to be applicable to loops that include control flow and have trapezoidal iteration ranges. An important contribution of this chapter is the introduction of a fast algorithm that uses the greedy heuristic to solve the weighted fusion problem, which naturally arises from profitability concerns for loop fusion.

8.10 Case Studies

The original implementation of the strategies developed by Carr, Callahan, and Kennedy [55, 64, 65, 67] was carried out in the PFC system and later migrated to ParaScope. All of the effectiveness studies presented in Sections 8.3.8 and 8.4.3

were done within this infrastructure. The principal implementation concern was the inclusion of testing for input dependence. Although the testing itself is easy to do using a straightforward modification of dependence analysis, the total number of input dependences is likely to be large enough to cause problems for the compiler. Scalar dependences in particular can cause huge blowups in the size of the dependence graph because they can be carried at every level of a loop nest. In PFC, we ameliorated this problem by using a summary representation for scalar dependences that summarized all levels in a single edge representation. This strategy can be extended to summarize all the direction vectors quite easily. With these changes, the dependence graphs were still large, but the size was manageable.

Scalar replacement and the related transformations were particularly important on the original Ardent Titan because floating-point operations were carried out in the vector unit, which bypassed cache for all loads and stores. In other words, floating-point quantities were never cached, so it was critical to make effective use of registers. The compiler implemented a scalar replacement pass along the lines described in this chapter except that it did not construct input dependence, so it missed a substantive number of opportunities for improvement. Nevertheless, the Titan compiler's scalar replacement phase, along with unroll-and-jam and store elimination based on output dependences, yielded spectacular results. Table 10.1 in Section 10.5 presents a study of the leverage from dependence analysis on the Livermore loops. On the six kernels where scalar replacement was a key optimization, the marginal improvements with dependence, and hence scalar replacement, turned on ranged from 7.4% all the way up to 200%. These results, and the specific kernels improved, correlate well with the PFC results on the Livermore loops reported in Figure 8.10.

Neither the original PFC implementation nor the Ardent Titan compiler performed loop fusion with alignment to improve register allocation. Although alignment and fusion have been studied as a cache improvement strategy [103, 105], we are aware of no study that isolates the improvement solely due to better scalar replacement after fusion.

8.11   Historical Comments and References

Allen and Kennedy pioneered the use of dependence for optimization of register use on vector machines in the paper "Vector Register Allocation" [22] and in Allen's dissertation [16]. John Cocke proposed the technique of unroll-and-jam for use in the RS/6000, one of the first machines with extremely long latencies for cache misses. The idea was first published in the original paper by Callahan, Cocke, and Kennedy [55]. The idea of using scalar replacement to achieve register reuse on uniprocessors was due to Carr and Kennedy [67]. Carr implemented scalar replacement and unroll-and-jam and reported on its effectiveness in a series of papers with Callahan and Kennedy [65, 66]. Algorithms for pruning the dependence graph were developed by Brandes [43], Rosene [237], and Carr [64]. Handling of complex loop nests was also due to Carr and Kennedy [66].

Loop alignment was originally discussed by Allen, Callahan, and Kennedy as a way to eliminate carried dependences in parallelization [25]. The applicability of alignment to improve opportunities for register reuse after fusion is new, although it has been studied as a mechanism for cache reuse improvement [103, 105].

The greedy weighted fusion algorithm presented in this chapter is due to Kennedy [171, 172]. Kennedy and McKinley [176] developed the original proof that weighted fusion is *NP*-complete and presented a heuristic strategy based on repetitive application of Goldberg and Tarjan's maximum flow algorithm for networks [176]. The resulting algorithm takes time $O(kEV \log (V^2/E))$, where $k \leq V$ is the number of required applications of the max-flow algorithm. It is not clear whether the solutions it produces are better or worse than those produced by greedy weighted fusion. Gao, Olsen, Sarkar, and Thekkath [118] produced a solution to the 0-1 fusion problem in which the only weights for edges are 0 or 1. This approach, designed to support the locality optimization of *array contraction* [242], used an $O(EV)$ prepass to reduce the size of the graph, then successively applied max-flow on the reduced graph $G_R = (E_R, V_R)$. The overall algorithm takes time $O(EV+V_R{}^2E_R \log V_R)$. Thus the Gao algorithm produces a heuristic solution to a subproblem of weighted fusion in a time that is asymptotically worse than greedy weighted fusion. However, it is difficult to compare these algorithms because the solutions they produce may differ due to the different heuristics used. Meggido and Sarkar have experimented with an optimal algorithm for loop fusion, showing that it has reasonable running times for small examples [211]. All of the alternative algorithms to greedy weighted fusion use addition as the reweighting operator, which makes them less attractive for memory hierarchy where more complex reweighting strategies are desirable.

Exercises

8.1 Hand-transform the following program with scalar replacement. Suppose array A is used only in this loop. Does the program need array A after scalar replacement? Can you formulate the conditions when an array can be removed from a program?

```
DO I = 1, N
    A(I) = B(I) + 3.0
    SUM = SUM + A(I)
ENDDO
```

8.2 Hand-transform the following loop nest to achieve high register reuse. What transformations did you use? What is the ratio of floating-point operations to loads before and after the transformation? How many registers did you assume?

```
DO I = 1, N
    DO J = 1, N
        A(I+1,J+1) = A(I,J+1) + A(I+1,J) + B(J)
    ENDDO
ENDDO
```

8.3 Run the loop nest from Exercise 8.2 on your favorite machine (using the Fortran compiler) for different values of N, including some that are extremely large (larger than cache). Report and explain the results.

8.4 Can two loops that access the same array A(1:N) always be fused using loop alignment? If yes, prove it. If no, give a counterexample.

8.5 Consider a simple algorithm for greedy weighted fusion that iteratively selects the heaviest edge and then traces forward along all paths from the sink to the source to determine if fusion is legal. What is the asymptotic complexity of this algorithm (i.e., why is it not just as good as the fast greedy weighted fusion algorithm presented in Section 8.6.4)?

8.6 Rework the example from Section 8.5.1 to improve performance by taking input dependence into account. Hint: this can save one additional load per iteration.

CHAPTER 9

Managing
Cache

9.1 Introduction

Although there are many commonalities between register reuse and cache reuse, there are significant differences as well. First, there is a difference in the atomicity of storage. A register contains exactly one word, while caches are organized into blocks (or *lines*) that usually contain multiple words. Thus, reuse in registers arises from subsequent accesses to the same data item. This kind of reuse, often referred to as *temporal reuse*, also helps in cache management. On the other hand, when a cache block is loaded, misses are not required for accesses to different items in the same block. This kind of reuse—of items located close enough to one another to occupy the same cache block—is called *spatial reuse*.

A second class of differences between enhancing register and cache reuse arises because of the way caches are implemented. For example, on most caches, a store into an uncached block generates a miss, forcing the referenced block to be loaded into cache before the store can complete. A store into a register requires no such load. An immediate consequence of this property is that antidependences are important for enhancing cache reuse—if the use can be brought close enough to the subsequent store, the cache miss on store may be avoided.

Finally, cache operations were originally intended to be synchronous; that is, the processor stalled while waiting for a miss to be serviced. This severely degraded performance when several misses occurred in sequence. These performance problems led machine designers to make it possible for many cache operations to be simultaneously active. A common implementation employs a *prefetch* operation that can be invoked as a machine instruction. Prefetch instructions do not block the processor unless there is a reference to the referenced cache block before loading has completed. Prefetch operations only provide opportunities for performance improvement; it is up to the compiler to generate prefetches at the right moment to actually capitalize on those opportunities. This is the topic of Section 9.5.

The two types of cache reuse, temporal and spatial, give rise to two general strategies for performance improvement. Spatial reuse is highest when iterations of a loop access memory sequentially—that is, when each iteration of a loop accesses a memory location adjacent to the location used in the previous iteration. Thus, having the right loop as the inner loop in a nest is critical to good cache performance for machines with long cache blocks. For example, in the following Fortran loop nest

```
DO I = 1, N
   DO J = 1, M
      A(I,J) = A(I,J) + B(I,J)
   ENDDO
ENDDO
```

the inner loop iterates over rows. Fortran arrays are stored in column-major order, so for the reference A(I,J), iterating the I-loop with J fixed yields contiguous access. Therefore, performance on machines with multiword cache blocks should be improved by interchanging the two loops:

```
DO J = 1, M
   DO I = 1, N
      A(I,J) = A(I,J) + B(I,J)
   ENDDO
ENDDO
```

The correct choice for an inner loop is not usually so clear-cut. Section 9.2 discusses strategies for loop interchange to enhance spatial reuse.

A somewhat different problem arises in the case of temporal reuse. Assume for the moment that we are dealing with a machine on which each data item occupies a single cache line. On such a machine, temporal reuse is the only type of reuse. Now consider the example from Section 8.1:

```
DO I = 1, N
   DO J = 1, M
      A(I) = A(I) + B(J)
   ENDDO
ENDDO
```

If we concentrate on cache effects, we can see that references to A(I) cause a single cache miss—on the first access—for each distinct value of I. On the other hand, for M large enough, *every* access to B(J) will cause a miss because almost every cache uses a "least recently used" replacement strategy. The implication is that if M is larger than the number of words in the entire cache, then B(1) is likely to be evicted from the cache by accesses that occur in late iterations of the J-loop. In this case, the total number of misses caused by the loop nest is N * M.

Performance can be improved by strip-mining the inner loop so that a single strip of length S fits in the cache and then moving the loop that iterates over the strips to the outermost position. The result is

```
DO J = 1, M, S
   DO I = 1, N
      DO jj = J, MIN(M,J+S-1)
         A(I) = A(I) + B(jj)
      ENDDO
   ENDDO
ENDDO
```

If S is small enough, the inner loop will give rise to no misses on accesses to B(jj) other than the first, for a total of M misses. However, we now have additional misses for A(I)—one miss for each element of A for each iteration of the J-loop, for a total of N * M/S misses. This is far fewer than the number of misses in the original loop for any reasonable value of S.

This transformation is known as *strip-mine-and-interchange*, and the general approach is called *cache blocking*. Section 9.3 discusses blocking strategies in more detail.

9.2 Loop Interchange for Spatial Locality

Consider a perfectly nested loop nest with at least two loops. A central issue is, Which loop in the nest should be innermost? This is important because the innermost loop determines which array dimension is accessed sequentially. When we discussed loop interchange for enhancing register reuse in Section 8.5, we simply tried to get the most dependences in the inner loop. For cache, however, the problem is complicated by spatial reuse—generally, the best results are achieved by getting stride-one access to sequential storage locations.

Since Fortran arrays are stored in column-major order, the loop iterating over the column is the only one that can give stride-one access. Moving this loop to the innermost position will improve spatial locality, reducing the miss rate to one per cache line (assuming the subscript coefficient is one). As an example consider the following loop:

```
DO I = 1, N
   DO J = 1, M
      A(I,J) = B(I,J) + C
   ENDDO
ENDDO
```

As it stands, the loop nest will result in a miss on every access to A and every access to B, for a total of 2NM misses, because the innermost loop is striding over the noncontiguous dimension. If the loops are interchanged:

```
DO J = 1, M
   DO I = 1, N
      A(I,J) = B(I,J) + C
   ENDDO
ENDDO
```

the number of misses will be reduced by a factor of b, the length of a cache line in words, for a total of 2NM/b misses.

Unfortunately, the situation is often not so clear-cut, as the following code demonstrates:

```
DO I = 1, N
   DO J = 1, M
      D(I) = D(I) + B(I,J)
   ENDDO
ENDDO
```

This loop nest will miss on accesses to the array D at most once for each of the iterations of the outer loop. In fact, since D(I) is accessed on each iteration of the inner loop, it and the entire cache line it occupies will remain in cache until the next iteration of the outer loop. Therefore, the actual number of misses is N/b, where b is the length of a cache line in words. On the other hand, the same loop nest will suffer NM misses for accesses to array B.

Loop interchange might reduce the number of these misses. Interchanging would reduce the number of misses for B to NM/b, but this would lose the natural locality in array D, so that it would now incur a miss every b accesses. As a result the total number of misses for the revised loop would be 2NM/b. If we compare these two, we see that the interchanged loop will be better if

$$N/b + NM - 2NM/b > 0$$

which reduces to

$$M(b–2) + 1 > 0$$

Thus, interchange is profitable if the cache line size in words is at least 2.

Although a detailed analysis of all possible permutations of loops would be expensive, a simple heuristic approach to establishing loop order for maximum reuse will often yield excellent results. The following approach evaluates the memory cost of each loop in a nest as if it were the innermost loop in the nest. This evaluation is done without regard to whether loops can be moved to the innermost position, so a later rearrangement phase attempts to align the loops into an order close to the order suggested by the heuristic.

The basic idea of the approach is to attach a cost to each reference in the loop nest under the assumption that the loop evaluated is positioned innermost. Given a loop nest $\{L_1, L_2, \ldots, L_n\}$, we will define the *innermost memory cost* function $C_M(L_i)$ for each loop L_i in the nest in three stages. First we will identify the references in the loop nest and assign a memory cost in terms of cache misses that each reference would incur if it were situated in only the given loop:

1. A reference that does not depend on the loop induction variable is assigned a cost of 1.

2. A reference in which the induction variable of the given loop strides over a noncontiguous dimension is given a cost N, equal to the number of iterations of the loop.

3. A reference in which the induction variable strides over a contiguous dimension in small steps of size s is assigned a cost of

$$\frac{N}{\left(\frac{b}{s}\right)} = \frac{Ns}{b}$$

where N is the loop trip count and b is the cache line size.

Once these costs are established, the costs are multiplied by factors associated with each of the other loops as follows:

1. For a reference that does not vary with the loop index of the given loop, the cost is left unchanged (multiplied by 1).

2. For a reference that varies with the loop index of the given loop, the cost is multiplied by the trip count of the loop.

Once the cost is established for each reference, the innermost memory cost for the given loop is computed by summing the individual costs for each reference.

For this scheme to work, we need to carefully define what we mean by a reference, to avoid overcounting multiple references to the same cache line. Thus, we will treat two references r_1 and r_2 as part of the same *reference group* with respect to a given inner loop L if either of the following two conditions holds:

1. There is a loop-independent dependence between the two references or a dependence carried by loop L that has a small threshold, where the definition of "small" may vary, but thresholds of 2 are always acceptable. This condition will ensure that we do not overcount references that will hit the same cache line due to temporal reuse.

2. The two references are to the same array and differ only by a small constant in the contiguous dimension, where "small" means less than the size

of the cache line. This is to avoid overcounting of references to the same cache line due to spatial reuse. In general, this condition must be generalized to start a new reference group when two references differ in the contiguous dimension by more than a cache line. Thus if the cache line is four elements and there are references to A(I), A(I+2), and A(I+4) in the same loop body, these must be treated as two reference groups.

With this modification the cost function remains the same, except costs are computed for a single reference in each reference group and summed to determine the innermost cost for a given loop.

Once the innermost memory cost is computed for each loop in the nest, a *desired loop order* is established by putting the loop with the lowest innermost memory cost at the innermost position, contained by each of the other loops from innermost to outermost in order of increasing innermost loop cost.

As an example of the application of this heuristic, consider the cost associated with our sample loop:

```
DO I = 1, N
   DO J = 1, M
      D(I) = D(I) + B(I,J)
   ENDDO
ENDDO
```

There are two reference groups, one for D(I) and one for B(I,J). We consider the costs for each loop separately:

1. When the J-loop is innermost, we have a cost of 1 for D(I) and a cost of M for B(I,J). Both costs are multiplied by N to arrive at a total cost after summing of $N + MN$.

2. If the I-loop is innermost, we have a cost of N/b for each of the two reference groups. Both costs are multiplied by M for the outer loop to yield a total cost of $2MN/b$.

If cache lines are more than two words long, the second ordering, with the I-loop innermost, should be chosen, which is the outcome produced by our deeper analysis. Note that the heuristic overcounts the number of misses for the first case because it fails to note that the constant reference in the innermost loop will get spatial reuse in the next innermost loop if that loop is over the contiguous dimension.

Once we have established a desired order $O = \{\sigma(1), \sigma(2), \ldots, \sigma(n)\}$, where $L_{\sigma(i)}$ is the loop that is desirable for the ith outermost position according to our heuristic, we need to rearrange the loops to conform to the desired order. To do this we make use of the observation that if one loop achieves more reuse than another loop in the innermost position, it is likely to achieve more reuse in outer positions as well. Thus we want to place the loop in an order closest to the one found most desirable by the heuristic.

To do this we will follow the procedure given in Figure 9.1, which repeatedly shifts to the current position in P the outermost remaining loop in the desired order that would be legal in that position. This approach clearly results in a legal loop order because that property is maintained throughout the algorithm.

This procedure has the property that if there exists a legal permutation of the loops in N where $L_{\sigma(n)}$ is in the innermost position, then *PermuteLoops* will produce a permutation with $L_{\sigma(n)}$ innermost. To see this, note that if the original loop is legal, each step of the algorithm produces a legal ordering because a loop is shifted only if the column of the direction matrix has a "<" in the position corresponding to every non-"=" direction that is not covered by a direction in the same row for a loop that was previously shifted to an outer loop position. Suppose that *PermuteLoops* does not choose $L_{\sigma(n)}$ as the innermost loop, but instead shifts it out to position P_m, where $m < n$. Then it must have passed over every loop that is outside $L_{\sigma(n)}$ in the desired order, which can only happen if each of those were illegal to shift into position m in P. In other words, each of the loops outside of $L_{\sigma(n)}$ contains a ">" direction in some position where $L_{\sigma(n)}$ has a "<" and none of the loops selected to be outside of position m covers. But this cannot be true because then there could be *no* legal permutation with $L_{\sigma(n)}$ innermost—it would always need to be outside all those loops.

From this observation we can see that *PermuteLoops* places in the innermost position the loop that carries the most reuse, as measured by the cost, that can legally be placed there. This means that if the cost model is accurate, it is choosing the optimal legal inner loop.

procedure *PermuteLoops*(N,O,n,P)

    // $N = \{L_1, L_2, \ldots, L_n\}$ is the loop nest to be permuted
    // $O = \{\sigma(1), \sigma(2), \ldots, \sigma(n)\}$ are the loop indices in the desired order
    // n is the number of loops in the nest
    // $P = \{P_1, P_2, \ldots, P_n\}$ is the final loop nest after permutation

    $j := 1;$ // the index of the current position to be filled in P
    $P := N;$ // start with the original permutation.
    while $O \neq \emptyset$ **do begin**
        let k be the leftmost element of O such that L_k can be shifted to
            position j within P without introducing any illegal direction
            vectors in the direction matrix for the nest;
        remove k from O;
        shift L_k to P_j;
        $j := j + 1;$
    end
end *PermuteLoops*

Figure 9.1 Algorithm for loop permutation.

To illustrate the method, we return once again to matrix multiplication as presented in many of the textbooks:

```
DO I = 1, N
   DO J = 1, N
      C(I,J) = 0
      DO K = 1, N
         C(I,J) = C(I,J) + A(I,K) * B(K,J)
      ENDDO
   ENDDO
ENDDO
```

This code would be distributed into two loop nests:

```
DO I = 1, N
   DO J = 1, N
      C(I,J) = 0
   ENDDO
ENDDO
DO I = 1, N
   DO J = 1, N
      DO K = 1, N
         C(I,J) = C(I,J) + A(I,K) * B(K,J)
      ENDDO
   ENDDO
ENDDO
```

In the initialization loop nest, the cost for the current configuration is N^2, while the cost with the I-loop innermost would be N^2/b. Thus the initialization would be permuted to

```
DO J = 1, N
   DO I = 1, N
      C(I,J) = 0
   ENDDO
ENDDO
```

Table 9.1 Memory analysis of matrix multiplication

Loop	C(I,J)	A(I,K)	B(K,J)	Total
I	N^3/b	N^3/b	N^2	$2N^3/b + N^2$
J	N^3	N^2	N^3	$2N^3 + N^2$
K	N^2	N^3	N^3/b	$N^3(1 + 1/b) + N^2$

In the body of the computation, there are three reference groups, one for C, one for A, and one for B. Table 9.1 gives the costs for running each of these loops in the innermost position.

This analysis leads us to select the I-loop as the innermost loop, the K-loop as next innermost, and the J-loop as outermost:

```
DO J = 1, N
   DO K = 1, N
      DO I = 1, N
         C(I,J) = C(I,J) + A(I,K) * B(K,J)
      ENDDO
   ENDDO
ENDDO
```

In experiments run on the three different machines—a Sun Sparc 2, an Intel i860, and an IBM RS/6000, this permuted loop was over two times faster than the original $N = 512$ [210]. On the RS/6000, on which latencies are similar to those expected on future machines, the improvement was nearly a factor of 10.

9.3 Blocking

Once loop interchange has selected the best loop ordering, we can attempt to improve performance by *blocking* (also called *tiling*) some of the loops. Consider the example from the previous section after loop interchange is performed:

```
DO J = 1, M
   DO I = 1, N
      D(I) = D(I) + B(I,J)
   ENDDO
ENDDO
```

As pointed out previously, this loop will incur $2NM/b$ misses. The performance can be further improved by strip-mine-and-interchange (introduced in Section 9.1), as the following shows:

```
DO I = 1, N, S
   DO J = 1, M
      DO ii = I, MIN(I+S-1,N)
         D(ii) = D(ii) + B(ii,J)
      ENDDO
   ENDDO
ENDDO
```

Assume for the moment that each column of B begins on a new cache line. Then if S is chosen to be a multiple of b, accesses to B(ii,J) will achieve full spatial reuse, missing NM/b times. Assume also that storage for D begins on a new cache line. Then if S is chosen small enough so that the line containing D(ii) stays in cache between separate iterations of the J-loop, accesses to D will benefit from both spatial locality and temporal locality, producing a total of N/b misses. Under these assumptions, the total number of misses is

$$\left(1 + \frac{1}{M}\right)\frac{NM}{b}$$

which should be fairly close to NM/b for large M.

Consider now what happens if we strip-mine the outer loop and interchange inward the loop that iterates over a single strip. This corresponds to performing strip-mine-and-interchange on the outer loop:

```
DO J = 1, M, T
    DO I = 1, N
        DO jj = J, MIN(J+T-1,M)
            D(I) = D(I) + B(I,jj)
        ENDDO
    ENDDO
ENDDO
```

Assume once again that each column of B begins on a new cache line. If T is chosen small enough so that the cache line containing B(I,jj) stays in cache between separate iterations of the I-loop, accesses to B will benefit from spatial locality so that the total number of misses is again NM/b. However, the number of misses on D will be different because there will be one miss per cache line, or N/b misses, during the execution of the inner two loops. Since these loops are executed a total of M/T times, the total miss count for D is NM/(bT), a factor of T better than the unblocked version. Thus the total time for the blocked version is

$$\left(1 + \frac{1}{T}\right)\frac{NM}{b}$$

Since we expect that M will be much larger than T, this is greater than the cost for the previous inner-loop strip mine under the same assumption of aligned rows.

9.3.1   Unaligned Data

The analysis of these two cases changes if columns of B do not begin on new cache lines. Assume that whole arrays are allocated starting at the beginning of cache lines, but multidimensional arrays are contiguous, so each new column may begin anywhere in a cache line. In the original blocking

```
DO I = 1, N, S
   DO J = 1, M
      DO ii = I, MIN(I+S-1,N)
         D(ii) = D(ii) + B(ii,J)
      ENDDO
   ENDDO
ENDDO
```

the inner loop over contiguous sections of B may incur one additional miss per iteration because the row might begin late in a cache line and end early in the last cache line. Therefore, the total number of additional misses on accesses to B is at most one per column for each iteration of the outer I-loop, or NM/S. The total number of misses is therefore no greater than

$$(1+1/M+b/S)NM/b$$

In the second blocking

```
DO J = 1, M, T
   DO I = 1, N
      DO jj = J, MIN(J+T-1,M)
         D(I) = D(I) + B(I,jj)
      ENDDO
   ENDDO
ENDDO
```

dropping the column alignment assumption produces at most one extra miss on B for each iteration of the loop on I, for a total of M/T extra misses. Thus the overall miss total for this version is

$$\left(1 + \frac{1}{T} + \frac{b}{TN}\right)\frac{NM}{b}$$

Since T is chosen to be a multiple of b and M is much larger than T, the third term in parentheses is far smaller than the second term, so the result is fairly close to

$$\left(1 + \frac{1}{T}\right)\frac{NM}{b}$$

Thus, if the block size S for the first case is approximately the same as the block size T for the second case, the first case no longer exhibits superior performance. However, an examination of the code shows that in the first approach the cache must hold S/b different blocks of D, while in the second case a cache of the same size must be able to hold T different blocks of B. This implies that S can be a factor of b larger than T, so the revised cost for the first alternative is

$$\left(1 + \frac{1}{M} + \frac{1}{T}\right)\frac{NM}{b}$$

If N and M are comparable in size, then this is slightly worse than the performance of the second alternative. In other words, alignment considerations have led us to switch our preference to the second alternative.

These considerations illustrate the complexity of choosing the optimal loop order when blocking is also being done—the best loop order for interchange solution may not be the best order from the perspective of blocking. The specific lesson from this example is that if columns of multidimensional arrays are not aligned with cache boundaries, it may pay to have the constant access innermost after blocking rather than the contiguous access because this moves the extra misses out of the inner loop.

In the next few sections we will explore several strategies for blocking a nested loop. However, we will first explore the answers to two questions:

1. When is blocking legal?
2. When is it profitable?

9.3.2   Legality of Blocking

The basic algorithm for blocking is called *strip-mine-and-interchange*. Basically, it consists of strip-mining a given loop into two loops, one that iterates within contiguous strips and an outer loop that iterates strip-by-strip, then interchanging the by-strip loop to the outside of other containing loops. The basic algorithm is given in Figure 9.2.

It is clear that the strip-mining step is always legal because it does not change the execution order in any way. However, the interchange of the by-strip loop is not necessarily legal. Conditions for the legality of loop interchange are described in Section 5.2.1. Basically, the interchange is legal if every direction vector for a dependence carried by any of the loops $L_o \ldots L_{k+1}$ has either an "=" or a "<" in the kth position, so that the direction matrix after shifting is still legal.

In fact, this legality test is overly conservative because strip-mine-and-interchange can be applied in certain circumstances where interchange would be illegal, as Figure 9.3 illustrates. If the strip size is less than or equal to the threshold of the dependence that might prevent interchange, then the strip-mine-and-interchange is legal, even though the interchange would not be. In Figure 9.3, there is an interchange-preventing dependence carried by the outer J-loop with a distance of 3, which would not prevent strip-mine-and-interchange with a strip size of 3 or less. However, given that dependence distances tend to be much shorter than useful strip sizes, it is simpler and just as effective to use the conservative test.

procedure *StripMineAndInterchange(L,m,k,o,S)*

// $L = \{L_1, L_2, \ldots, L_m\}$ is the loop nest to be transformed
// L_k is the loop to be strip-mined
// L_o is the outer loop that is to be just inside the by-strip loop
// after interchange
// S is the variable to use as strip size; its value must be positive

let the header of L_k be
   DO I = L, N, D;

split the loop into two loops, a *by-strip* loop:
    DO I = L, N, S * D
and a *within-strip* loop:
      DO i = I, MIN(I+S*D-D,N), D
around the loop body;

interchange the by-strip loop to the position just outside of L_o;

end *StripMineAndInterchange*

Figure 9.2 Algorithm for strip-mine-and-interchange.

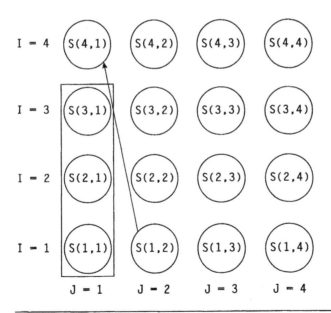

Figure 9.3 Legality of strip-mine-and-interchange.

9.3.3   Profitability of Blocking

In general, blocking is profitable if there is reuse between iterations of a loop that is not the innermost loop. If the reordering described in Section 9.2 is applied, it is likely that the search for reuse can be carried out by starting from the next-to-innermost loop and working outward.

Reuse in an outer loop occurs under two circumstances:

1. there is a small-threshold dependence of any type, including input, carried by the loop, or

2. the loop index appears, with small stride, in the contiguous dimension of a multidimensional array and in no other dimension.

In the first case, the reduction in misses for each reference that is the target of at least one carried dependence is proportional to N, the trip count of the loop. In the second case, if the reference is not the target of any dependence covered by the first case, the reduction in misses is proportional to b, the cache line size.

There is also a cost associated with strip-mine-and-interchange, as there will be misses introduced in the by-strip loop. There are two kinds of possible costs in each reference group:

1. For each reference that was the target of a dependence carried by the inner loop, M/S misses may be introduced, where M is the inner loop count and S is the strip size. (We assume that S is an integral multiple of b.)

2. For each reference that was not the target of carried dependence but included the inner loop index in the contiguous dimension, M/S misses may be introduced because of the possibility that strip boundaries are not aligned with cache lines. (If strip boundaries are aligned with cache, no extra misses are introduced.)

Thus, the total number of extra misses introduced is approximately $R_0 M/S$, where R_0 is the number of independent references in the inner loop. The total savings is

$$R_1 N + R_2 N \left(1 + \frac{1}{b}\right) = (R_1 + R_2)N - \frac{R_2 N}{b}$$

where R_1 is the number of references that are targets of a dependence carried by the outer loop and R_2 is the number of references that are contiguous but not targets of any carried dependence. If N and M are comparable in size, then the total number of references that incur savings at the outer loop level would need to be smaller than the number of savings-carrying references at the innermost level by a factor comparable to the strip size for strip-mine-and-interchange to fail the profitability test. Hence, many researchers encourage strip-mining to improve reuse in any loop where it is possible [276].

9.3.4   A Simple Blocking Algorithm

The observations of the previous section lead us to a very simple blocking algorithm, given in Figure 9.4. Essentially, this algorithm simply continues applying strip-mine-and-interchange until there are no more of the original loops carrying any reuse.

Let's see how this algorithm performs on the inner loop of matrix multiplication after loop interchange:

```
DO J = 1, N
   DO K = 1, N
      DO I = 1, N
         C(I,J) = C(I,J) + A(I,K) * B(K,J)
      ENDDO
   ENDDO
ENDDO
```

After the innermost loop is chosen, it is clear that the next innermost—the loop on K—also carries reuse because of the reuse of C(I,J) and the contiguous reference to B(K,J). We therefore strip-mine the I-loop, moving the by-strip loop all the way to the outside:

```
DO I = 1, N, S
   DO J = 1, N
      DO K = 1, N
         DO ii = I, MIN(I+S-1,N)
            C(ii,J) = C(ii,J) + A(ii,K) * B(K,J)
         ENDDO
      ENDDO
   ENDDO
ENDDO
```

The J-loop also carries a small amount of reuse due to the self-input dependence on A(ii,K). This can be exposed by applying strip-mine-and-interchange to the K-loop:

```
DO K = 1, N, T
   DO I = 1, N, S
      DO J = 1, N
         DO kk = K, MIN(K+T-1,N)
            DO ii = I, MIN(I+S-1,N)
               C(ii,J) = C(ii,J) + A(ii,kk) * B(kk,J)
            ENDDO
         ENDDO
      ENDDO
   ENDDO
ENDDO
```

procedure *BlockLoops(L,m)*

    // $L = \{L_1, L_2, \ldots, L_m\}$ is the loop nest to be transformed, arranged into the
    //   best memory order using the algorithm of Section 9.2;

    for $i := m + 1$ **to** 1 **by** −1 **do begin**
        if there is reuse in L_i **then begin**
            let $o \geq i - 1$ be the index of the outermost loop
                beyond which L_{i-1} can be shifted;
            if $o \geq i$ **then begin**
                let S_{i-1} be a new variable;
                StripMineAndInterchange(L,m,i−1,o,S_{i-1});
            end
        end
    end

end *BlockLoops*

Figure 9.4 Simple blocking.

Table 9.2 Memory analysis of blocked matrix multiplication

Loop	C(I,J)	A(I,K)	B(K,J)	Total
ii	S/b	S/b	1	$2S/b + 1$
kk	S/b	ST/b	T/b	$S/b + ST/b + T/b$
J	NS/b	ST/b	NT/b	$NS/b + ST/b + NT/b$
I	N^2/b	NT/b	$N^2 T/(Sb)$	$N^2/b + NT/b + N^2 T/(Sb)$
K	$N^3/(Tb)$	N^2/b	$N^3/(Sb)$	$N^3/(Tb) + N^3/(Sb) + N^2/b$

The total number of misses in this loop can be estimated using variants of the cost formulas from Section 9.2. In the inner loop, we have a total of S/b misses for C and A, and 1 miss for B. Assuming S is small enough, the kk-loop multiplies the number of misses for C by 1, the number of misses for A by T, and the number of misses for B by T/b. The J-loop multiplies the number of misses for C and B by N, and the number of misses for A by 1. The outer two loops multiply miss counts by N^2/ST. The total misses for the three reference groups are summarized in Table 9.2.

If $S = T$, this is an improvement over the best interchanged version, which suffered approximately $2N^3/b + N^2$ misses, by a factor of S. Furthermore, this is asymptotically the best possible complexity for a cache that can hold an S-by-S block.

9.3.5   **Blocking with Skewing**

There are loops that cannot be tiled because interchange is not possible. Here is a simple example:

```
DO I = 1, N
   DO J = 1, M
      A(J+1) = (A(J)+A(J+1))/2
   ENDDO
ENDDO
```

The direction matrix for this loop is

$$\begin{bmatrix} = & = \\ = & < \\ < & = \\ < & < \\ < & > \end{bmatrix}$$

This produces the pattern of dependences shown in Figure 9.5.

The loop permutation procedure leaves the loops as they are, but they cannot be blocked because the loops cannot be interchanged. If we wish to increase the amount of reuse in this nest, the inner loop can be skewed with respect to the outer loop

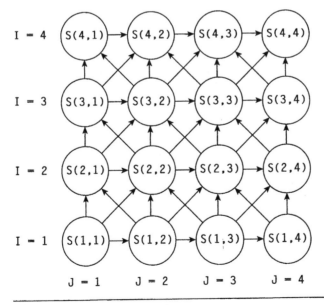

Figure 9.5 Dependence pattern in example.

```
DO I = 1, N
  DO j = I, M + I - 1
    A(j-I+2) = (A(j-I+1) + A(j-I+2))/2
  ENDDO
ENDDO
```

which makes it possible to interchange the loops. Therefore, strip-mine-and-interchange can also be applied. This is the loop after the strip-mine step:

```
DO I = 1, N
  DO j = I, M + I - 1, S
    DO jj = j, MIN(j+S-1,M+I-1)
      A(jj-I+2) = (A(jj-I+1) + A(jj-I+2))/2
    ENDDO
  ENDDO
ENDDO
```

Interchanging the by-strip loop outward produces

```
DO j = 1, M + N - 1, S
  DO I = MAX(1,j-M+1), MIN(j,N)
    DO jj = j, MIN(j+S-1,M+I-1)
      A(jj-I+2) = (A(jj-I+1) + A(jj-I+2))/2
    ENDDO
  ENDDO
ENDDO
```

This form takes advantage of reuse in the outer loop. While the original loop nest generated MN/b misses, the revised version generates something approximating

$$(S/b+1)(M+N)/S = (M+N)(1/b+1/S)$$

which is an order of magnitude improvement. The effect of blocking is illustrated in the modified dependence diagram in Figure 9.6.

In practice, opportunities for the use of skewing for the purpose of blocking are rarely seen [275], although it can be very profitable when applicable. We suggest that skewing be used in those situations where no blocking is possible to get reuse in a second dimension. This is the approach taken in the algorithm of Figure 9.7.

9.3.6   Fusion and Alignment

Loop fusion, which was discussed in depth in Section 8.6, is also extremely useful in conjunction with cache blocking to improve memory hierarchy management.

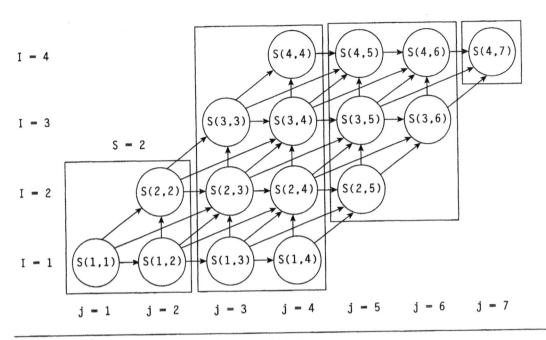

Figure 9.6 Dependence pattern after skewing and blocking.

procedure *BlockLoopsWithSkewing(L,m)*

  // $L = \{L_1, L_2, \ldots, L_m\}$ is the loop nest to be transformed, arranged into the
  //   best memory order using the algorithm of Section 9.2;

  for $i := m + 1$ **to** 1 **by** –1 **do begin**
    if there is reuse in L_i **then begin**
      let $o \geq i - 1$ be the index of the outermost loop
        beyond which L_{i-1} can be shifted;
      if $o \geq i$ **then begin**
        let S_{i-1} be a new variable;
        StripMineAndInterchange(L,m,i–1,o,S_{i-1});
      else if $i = m + 1$ **then begin** // use skewing
        skew L_{i-1} with respect to L_i;
        let S_{i-1} be a new variable;
        StripMineAndInterchange(L,m,i–1,o,S_{i-1});
      end
    end
  end

end *BlockLoopsWithSkewing*

Figure 9.7 Blocking with skewing.

In many cases, two loops, each of which can be blocked to improve memory hierarchy performance, can be fused first and then blocked, sometimes doubling the performance in the process.

As shown in Section 8.6.2, *alignment* can be used to increase the opportunities for fusion. We illustrate this with a simple example, intended to represent an initialization of a two-dimensional array, followed by a relaxation on the interior.

```
        DO I = 1, N
          DO J = 1, N
S₁          A(J,I) = AINIT(J,I)
          ENDDO
        ENDDO
        DO I = 2, N -1
          DO J = 2, N - 1
S₂          A(J,I) = (A(J+1,I+1) + A(J-1,I-1)) * 0.5
          ENDDO
        ENDDO
```

Following the strategy from Section 8.6.2, we can align the two loops so that the second reference in statement S_2 aligns with the assignment in statement S_1:

```
        DO I = 0, N - 1
          DO J = 0, N - 1
S₁          A(J+1,I+1) = AINIT(J+1,I+1)
          ENDDO
        ENDDO
        DO I = 2, N - 1
          DO J = 2, N - 1
S₂          A(J,I) = (A(J+1,I+1) + A(J-1,I-1)) * 0.5
          ENDDO
        ENDDO
```

Now we can legally fuse the two loop nests to get

```
        DO I = 0, 1
          DO J = 0, N - 1
            A(J+1,I+1) = AINIT(J+1,I+1)
          ENDDO
        ENDDO
        DO I = 2, N - 1
          A(1,I+1) = AINIT(1,I+1)
          A(2,I+1) = AINIT(2,I+1)
          DO J = 2, N - 1
S₁          A(J+1,I+1) = AINIT(J+1,I+1)
S₂          A(J,I) = (A(J+1,I+1) + A(J-1,I-1)) * 0.5
          ENDDO
        ENDDO
```

When the inner loop is blocked, every cache block in A incurs only one miss, where the original incurred two misses per iteration.

9.3.7 Blocking in Combination with Other Transformations

Blocking can be combined with other transformations discussed in this book to effect extremely powerful optimizations. We discuss three of these here.

Blocking with Register Usage Enhancement

The blocking transformations described here are fairly easy to combine with scalar replacement and unroll-and-jam described in Chapter 8. Because register management can only make use of temporal locality, it is more specialized than cache management, which also includes nontemporal spatial locality. Furthermore, cache management takes more dependences into account than register management; for example, an antidependence gives rise to cache reuse (in most cache designs) but not register reuse. Thus register management should be applied to the loops that remain after cache management has been completed. Nevertheless, because cache management attempts to optimize both temporal and spatial locality, the loops that are useful for register management should be near the innermost position after the cache management transformations have been completed.

Multiple Levels of Memory Hierarchy

In addition to registers, it is common to find multiple levels of cache in a modern computing system. Furthermore, different memories may have widely varying access times. Parallel computer systems, discussed in the next subsection, are a major source of "nonuniform" memory access times. On a typical parallel computer system, access times to remote memories can take integral factors longer than accesses to local memory. For example, on a 64-node, 128-processor SGI Origin 2000, access to a remote memory takes three times as long as access to a local memory on the average [251]. In such situations, it may be useful to block for more than one level of cache. However, unless the fastest level of cache is not much faster than the next level, or the fastest level is too small to be useful, it is essential that blocking first target the fastest cache, then attack other cache levels. In this case, a by-strip loop resulting from strip-mine-and-interchange might be strip-mined to get further reuse in a large secondary cache. Alternatively, if the primary cache were too small to effectively achieve reuse in each dimension, the larger cache could then be used to capture some of the unexploited reuse.

It is also possible to view secondary storage as part of the memory hierarchy. Experiments have shown that, using transformations similar to the ones described for optimizing cache, a typical out-of-core computation can be improved by a factor of 200 or more [173].

Blocking with Parallelization

There are two key issues that arise when cache management and parallelization are combined.

1. If the dimension of parallelism is the dimension of sequential access, increasing parallelism may interfere with the performance of the memory hierarchy.

2. If the data to be used by each processor is not properly aligned on a cache line boundary, two or more processors may contend for a cache line that contains data that both need to use, even though the processors are not actually accessing the same data. This phenomenon is referred to as *false sharing* and is a significant problem for shared-memory parallel machines.

Since poor single-node performance is one of the most frequently cited reasons for inadequate performance on a parallel machine, it seems prudent that enhancing data locality be given a high priority in generating code for parallel computers. This suggests that, if multiple dimensions of parallelism are available, the dimension of stride-one access should be avoided when parallelizing.

If the semantics of the language permit it, false sharing can also be reduced by noncontiguous allocation of data. For example, in multidimensional arrays, if the columns are to be used on different processors, it will help to ensure that each column begins on a new cache line. This violates sequence and storage association restrictions in Fortran, but those features are, by all accounts, on their way out of the language.

If the stride-one dimension must be chosen for parallelization, then the computation should be blocked on cache line boundaries to avoid false sharing. HPF-style CYCLIC(k) distributions should only be used if k specifies a number of words that is an integral multiple of the cache line size.

In the future, it is likely that parallelism will make the memory hierarchies deeper, which will increase the overall importance of the kinds of transformations discussed in this chapter.

9.3.8   Effectiveness

In general, blocking to improve cache performance, when applicable, can be remarkably effective. Porterfield reported that a single strip-mine-and-interchange reduced the number of cache misses in matrix multiplication from 932,576 to 40,000, almost completely eliminating evictions in the program [227]. Wolf reports similar improvements for the same program.

The problem is applicability of the transformation in real programs. Both Porterfield and Wolf report that simple impediments to blocking transformations often foiled their systems, leaving many programs that should be blockable with no benefits at all. The good news is that for applications where it works, it works very well indeed. For example, on the NASA kernel Gmtry, discussed in Section 8.3.8, Wolf's tiling algorithm achieved a factor of three improvement, while on Vpenta it realized a 50% improvement.

Porterfield also reports that fusion with alignment can be extremely powerful, even without blocking. On the program WANAL1, a wave analysis application, the combination of loop interchange, alignment, and fusion eliminated nearly half the misses. More recently, Ding has shown dramatic improvements through fusion on bandwidth-limited machines [103].

These successes indicate that blocking and fusion are promising ways to improve cache performance. However, a compiler must have a complete arsenal of transformations to use them effectively.

9.4 Cache Management in Complex Loop Nests

Up to now we have focused on blocking rectangular loop nests. Unfortunately, not all loop nests encountered in practice display such nice regularity. In this section we focus on the problems presented by trapezoidal loop nests and the specialized loop nests commonly encountered in linear algebra.

9.4.1 Triangular Cache Blocking

This general procedure developed in the previous sections can be applied to strip mining to improve cache performance for triangular loops. For example, suppose that we wish to strip-mine the outer loop of the example from Section 8.2.2 by a factor of K, where K divides the number of iterations in the outer loop evenly (once again this situation can be brought about by the use of a preloop).

```
DO I = 2, N
    DO J = 1, I - 1
        A(I,J) = A(I,I) + A(J,J)
    ENDDO
ENDDO
```

After strip mining, we get

```
DO I = 2, N, K
    DO ii = I, I + K - 1
        DO J = 1, ii - 1
            A(ii,J) = A(ii,ii) + A(J,J)
        ENDDO
    ENDDO
ENDDO
```

Now if we interchange the middle loop to the innermost position (using triangular loop interchange), we get

```
DO I = 2, N, K
   DO J = I, I + K - 1
      DO ii = MAX(J+1,I), I + K - 1
         A(ii,J) = A(ii,ii) + A(J,J)
      ENDDO
   ENDDO
ENDDO
```

which would have good cache performance, assuming that K was chosen carefully.

9.4.2   Special-Purpose Transformations

Many of the kinds of programs that arise in linear algebra are fairly unusual. Nevertheless, much can be learned from studying them. We begin with an analysis of LU decomposition, the most frequently used algorithm for the solution of linear systems of equations.

Most versions of LU decomposition use some form of pivoting to ensure stability. However, pivoting presents special problems, which will be discussed later. For the moment, we begin our discussion with a version of the algorithm without pivoting.

In LU decomposition without pivoting, the central loop nest is as follows:

```
       DO K = 1, N - 1
       ! the pivot is always A(K,K)
          DO I = K + 1, N
S₁           A(I,K) = A(I,K) / A(K,K)
          ENDDO
          DO J = K + 1, N
             DO I = K + 1, N
S₂              A(I,J) = A(I,J) - A(I,K) * A(K,J)
             ENDDO
          ENDDO
       ENDDO
```

The problem with this code is that the second part of the loop nest gets no reuse of either $A(I,K)$ or $A(K,J)$ on the right-hand side, assuming that N is large enough. To achieve reuse, you would like to strip-mine the outer loop on K and interchange the strip loop inside the loops on J and I in the second nest. Performing the strip mining, we get

```
DO K = 1, N - 1, S
   DO kk = K, K + S - 1
```

```
      !       the pivot is always A(kk,kk)
              DO I = kk + 1, N
S₁               A(I,kk) = A(I,kk) / A(kk,kk)
              ENDDO
              DO J = kk + 1, N
                 DO I = kk + 1, N
S₂                  A(I,J) = A(I,J) - A(I,kk) * A(kk,J)
                 ENDDO
              ENDDO
           ENDDO
         ENDDO
```

In order to interchange the kk-loop inward, we must first distribute it over the two loop nests. However, this is not permissible because there is a recurrence involving statements S_1 and S_2. The loop-independent dependence due to the two occurrences of A(I,kk) seems obvious. What is not so obvious is that, since J > kk, the store into A(I,J) in S_2 is to a location that is read in a later iteration of the kk-loop.

It seems as if the desired blocking is not possible. However, if we notice that on each iteration of the K-loop, statement S_2 produces

$$A(K+1:N,K+1:N)$$

while statement S_1 uses

$$A(K+1:N,K:K+S-1)$$

the implication is that, outside the range of iterations in which the output of S_2 is used, there is no recurrence. Thus we use index-set splitting to divide the inner loop nest around S_2 into two so that the second of these nests produces no values used in S_1:

```
      DO K = 1, N - 1, S
         DO kk = K, K + S - 1
      !       the pivot is always A(kk,kk)
              DO I = kk + 1, N
S₁               A(I,kk) = A(I,kk) / A(kk,kk)
              ENDDO
              DO J = kk + 1, K + S - 1
                 DO I = kk + 1, N
S₂                  A(I,J) = A(I,J) - A(I,kk) * A(kk,J)
                 ENDDO
              ENDDO
              DO J = K + S, N
                 DO I = kk + 1, N
```

S$_3$ A(I,J) = A(I,J) - A(I,kk) * A(kk,J)
                  ENDDO
               ENDDO
            ENDDO
         ENDDO

The kk-loop can now be distributed to produce a nest containing S$_1$ and S$_2$ and one containing S$_3$:

```
DO K = 1, N - 1, S
   DO kk = K, K + S - 1
!      the pivot is always A(kk,kk)
      DO I = kk + 1, N
```
S$_1$
```
         A(I,kk) = A(I,kk) / A(kk,kk)
      ENDDO
      DO J = kk + 1, K + S - 1
         DO I = kk + 1, N
```
S$_2$
```
            A(I,J) = A(I,J) - A(I,kk) * A(kk,J)
         ENDDO
      ENDDO
   ENDDO
   DO kk = K, K + S - 1
      DO J = K + S, N
         DO I = kk + 1, N
```
S$_3$
```
            A(I,J) = A(I,J) - A(I,kk) * A(kk,J)
         ENDDO
      ENDDO
   ENDDO
ENDDO
```

Finally, the kk-loop can be moved to the inside of the I- and J-loops in the final nest:

```
DO J = K + S, N
   DO I = K + 1, N
      DO kk = K, MIN(I-1,K+S-1)
```
S$_3$
```
         A(I,J) = A(I,J) - A(I,kk) * A(kk,J)
      ENDDO
   ENDDO
ENDDO
```

This inner loop greatly improves cache reuse.

In experiments conducted by Carr and Kennedy on a MIPS M120, the improved code achieved the timings shown in Table 9.3 on arrays of 100 elements.

Table 9.3 LU decomposition timing

Original code	8.36 sec
Transformed code	6.40 sec
Hand-coded by Sorensen	6.69 sec
After unroll-and-jam	3.55 sec
Speedup	2.35

We note that the automatic method produced a different and slightly better version than the hand code for this problem produced by Dan Sorensen as part of the LAPACK implementation effort. In addition, the application of triangular unroll-and-jam to the result, which in all fairness could also have been applied to the Sorensen version, produced a total speedup of 2.35.

9.5 **Software Prefetching**

Program reorganization, as effective as it is, cannot eliminate some kinds of cache misses:

1. Misses on data that is being used for the first time

2. Misses on data that is being reused in a way that cannot be predicted at compile time

The following loop contains an example of each kind of miss:

```
DO I = 1, N
    A(I) = B(LOC(I))
ENDDO
```

The store into A(I) will miss on each new cache line because this is the first use of A(I) in the nest. If duplicate values are stored in LOC(I), there may be a great deal of temporal reuse of B(LOC(I)). However, it is difficult to reorganize the loop nest to exploit it at compile time because the values of LOC(I) are unknown at that point.

In order to ameliorate these problems, machine designers in the late 1980s and early 1990s introduced *prefetch* instructions into modern processors. A prefetch instruction is typically implemented like a load, except that it does not cause a value to be put in a register. Instead, it causes the cache line that contains the target address in memory specified by the instruction to be preloaded into cache. A second difference is that prefetch operations do not typically cause processor stalls—if the desired data is not in cache, the containing block is loaded into cache in parallel with other operations.[1] Thus prefetch instructions provide one mechanism for overlapping memory accesses with other processor instructions.

To use prefetch instructions available on the processor, the programmer or compiler must generate them—the process of doing this is called *software prefetching*. If the compiler is able to insert a prefetch instruction for each line used in the loop far enough ahead, all miss latencies can be eliminated (assuming a large enough cache). The value of prefetching is clear here because program reorganization has no effect on this loop by itself.

In spite of its obvious advantages, however, prefetching has some significant disadvantages:

1. It increases the number of instructions that must be executed, requiring one instruction for the prefetch itself and possibly other instructions for the calculation of the prefetch address.

2. It can result in the premature eviction of useful cache lines.

3. It can bring lines to cache that are evicted before use or never used, needlessly increasing memory traffic.

To minimize the impact of these three disadvantages, we must carefully design the prefetching algorithm so that (a) the number of prefetches is close to what is needed, (b) the prefetches do not arrive too early, and (c) prefetches are rarely invoked for references that do not need them.

In the following sections we present a prefetching algorithm based on the work of Callahan, Kennedy, and Porterfield [61] and of Mowry [216]. The effectiveness of software prefetching will then be discussed in the light of experimental results presented by these research groups.

9.5.1   A Software Prefetching Algorithm

Generally, a prefetching algorithm will attempt to insert prefetch instructions for references in loops. References to subscripted variables are especially appealing targets because the same source references cause accesses to different memory locations. However, because cache blocks are typically longer than a single word, the prefetching algorithm must be careful to generate only prefetches for the first reference to a new cache block, lest it produce lots of useless prefetch operations. Thus, the critical steps in an effective prefetching algorithm are

1. accurate determination of the references requiring prefetching, so needless prefetching is minimized, and

2. insertion of the prefetching instructions far enough in advance so that the data arrives neither too late nor too soon.

---

1.   Ideally, prefetches do not cause exceptions on out-of-bounds fetches.

The first of these is referred to as *prefetch analysis,* while the second is *prefetch insertion.* These two phases will be discussed in detail later in this section.

The analysis phase must accurately determine which references are in need of prefetching and transform the program so that it distinguishes instances where a prefetch is required from those where it is not. For example, consider the following loop nest:

```
DO I = 1, N
   DO J = 2, M
      A(J,I) = A(J,I) + B(J) * A(J-1,I)
   ENDDO
ENDDO
```

The reference to A(J,I) will generate a miss once for each cache line since the accesses are sequential in memory. The reference to B(J) will also miss once every cache line multiplied by the number of times the J-loop is executed.

This means that, even though values of B(J) are reused in each iteration of the I-loop, none of that reuse is realized if the loop upper bound M is large enough. We can achieve that reuse if strip-mine-and-interchange is applied to the J-loop, but the size of the strip loop must be carefully chosen so as not to exceed cache as described in Section 9.3. Let us assume that this is done and the following code results:

```
DO J = 2, M, S
   JU = MIN(J+S-1,M)
   DO I = 1, N
      DO jj = J, JU
         A(jj,I) = A(jj,I) + B(jj) * A(jj-1,I)
      ENDDO
   ENDDO
ENDDO
```

Once this transformation is completed, we have removed latency for B(jj) except for the first iteration of each instantiation of the I-loop.

However, there are still a number of misses due to A(jj,I) and A(jj-1,I) that can be ameliorated by prefetching. The goal of analysis is to determine which iterations of the loop nest require a prefetch of A and which require a prefetch of B. The next section will discuss how the prefetches can be scheduled.

As we have previously indicated, there are two general types of locality in the program. *Temporal* locality occurs when there is reuse of the same memory location, and *spatial* locality occurs when two references are to the same cache line. In the example above, the references to A(jj-1,I) and A(jj,I) exhibit temporal locality because they reference the same location on subsequent iterations of the loop. However, there is spatial locality for the references to A(jj,I) on subsequent iterations of the jj-loop. If the cache line length is L words, then a cache miss would be incurred on the reference A(jj,I) every L iterations.

If we perform an analysis similar to the analysis for temporal locality to improve the performance of register allocation in Section 8.3, we would discover that references to A(jj,I), both the read and write, and A(jj-1,I) form a single *name partition* and hence represent a temporal reuse group. Furthermore, A(jj,I) would be identified as the generator of that group. As a result, the goal would be to determine the iterations on which to prefetch A(jj,I). Note that the reference to A(jj-1,I) would require a prefetch only on the first iteration of the jj-loop.

Assuming for the moment that A(1,I) is lined up on a cache line boundary for each value of I and that S is a multiple of the cache line size L, we can see that a prefetch of A(jj,I) is needed on iterations of the jj-loop where MOD(jj-J,L) = L - 1 or on iterations J + L - 1, J + 2 * L - 1, J + 3 * L - 1, and so on.

What about the reference to B(jj)? If we assume that B(1) is aligned on a cache boundary, then on the first iteration of the I-loop we will need a prefetch for B before the first iteration and on each iteration of the jj-loop where MOD(jj-J,L) = L - 1 or on iterations J + L - 1, J + 2 * L - 1, and so on. However, since S has been chosen so that all the values in B(J:JU) fit into cache, we can prefetch all of them prior to the jj-loop. The implementation of this observation is called *prefetch vectorization*.

To summarize the prefetch requirements:

1. Prefetch B(jj), for I = 1 and jj = J + k * L - 1, $0 \leq k \leq$ (JU-J)/L. In other words, on the first iteration of the I-loop, prefetch B(J-1:JU:L).
2. Prefetch A(jj-1,I) for all I and for jj = J.
3. Prefetch A(jj,I) for all I and for all jj = J + k * L - 1, $1 \leq k \leq$ (JU-J)/L.

Determining the iterations on which prefetching is required in this fashion is the goal of *prefetch analysis*.

Once the iterations requiring prefetches are determined, we can partition the iteration space of the loop to ensure that prefetches occur only for the references requiring them. The prefetches for B, all of which should happen on the first iteration of the I-loop, can be handled by peeling that iteration off and inserting the prefetch in the peeled iteration. In this case, however, the same effect can be achieved by simply hoisting the prefetches for B out of the I-loop.

To isolate the prefetches for A, we need to strip-mine the jj-loop into blocks of length L, after a preliminary block of length L - 1. Assuming for the moment that A(1,I) is lined up on a cache line boundary for each value of I, we can see that the following set of loops will achieve the desired result:

```
DO J = 2, M, S
   JU = MIN(J+S-1,M)
   ! prefetch here for B
   DO I = 1, N
      ! prefetch here for A(J,I)
```

```
        ! preloop to align prefetches
        DO jk = J, MIN(J+L-2,JU)
            A(jk,I) = A(jk,I) + B(jk) * A(jk-1,I)
        ENDDO
        DO jj = J, JU, L
            jju = MIN(jj+L-1,JU)
            ! prefetch here for A(j,I)
            DO jk = jj, jju
                A(jk,I) = A(jk,I) + B(jk) * A(jk-1,I)
            ENDDO
        ENDDO
    ENDDO
ENDDO
```

Assuming that each prefetch is to be placed immediately before the reference that it relates to, the following placement of prefetches would result:

```
DO J = 2, M, S
    JU = MIN(J+S-1,M)
    DO jj = J - 1, JU, L
        prefetch(B(jj))
    ENDDO
    DO I = 1, N
        prefetch(A(J,I))
        ! preloop to align prefetches
        DO jk = J, MIN(J+L-2,JU)
            A(jk,I) = A(jk,I) + B(jk) * A(jk-1,I)
        ENDDO
        DO jj = J, JU, L
            jju = MIN(jj+L-1,JU)
            prefetch(A(jj,I))
            DO jk = jj,jju
                A(jk,I) = A(jk,I) + B(jk) * A(jk-1,I)
            ENDDO
        ENDDO
    ENDDO
ENDDO
```

At this stage, we have identified the latest points at which the prefetch can be issued if it is to take place before the data being prefetched is actually accessed. However, a good placement algorithm will move the prefetches to points early enough in the program to ensure that they are complete before the data is used. This will require moving the prefetches across several iterations in many cases. Most prefetching systems leave this task to the instruction scheduler (see Chapter 10), so we will not discuss it further here.

Prefetch Analysis

The analysis phase of our prefetching algorithm consists of determining which iterations will suffer a prefetch miss. To do this, we will make use of the dependence analysis strategy described in Section 8.3. Recall that graph analysis routines were used to determine name partitions and generators. Unlike that case, stores will not kill a name partition when dealing with cache because a cache handles stores much like loads on most machines—if the cache block being stored into is not found in the cache, a cache miss is taken. Therefore, there will be no bad edges in the graph except those that correspond to inconsistent dependences.

On the other hand, for this approach to work we must ensure that every edge that is unlikely to correspond to reuse is eliminated from the graph so that the target of the edge is assumed to correspond to a miss, except when it is saved by temporal locality.

We assume that the analysis phase begins after the loop nest has been stripmined and interchanged to increase locality. This process will entail moving the loops with the best spatial locality to the innermost possible positions, as described in Section 9.2. The algorithm then traverses the loops from innermost to outermost to determine which dependences must be marked "ineffective" because reuse is not possible. Reuse is not possible whenever the amount of data accessed by the code between the source and sink exceeds the assumed cache size. (In this algorithm the cache is typically assumed to be substantially smaller than its actual size to compensate for mapping effects.)

To carry out this analysis, Porterfield [227] estimated the amount of data that was used by each iteration and then determined the *overflow iteration*, which is one more than the number of iterations whose data can be accommodated in cache at the same time. Any dependence with a threshold equal to or greater than the overflow iteration is then deemed to be ineffective for the purposes of reuse.

Once all ineffective edges have been identified and eliminated, we identify all points where misses might take place and hence prefetching is required. To accomplish this, we must account for two cases:

1. If the group generator is not contained in a dependence cycle, a miss is expected on each iteration unless references to the generator on subsequent iterations display spatial locality (in other words, if the accesses to the generating references are sequential locations in memory). In this case a miss is expected on every iteration that begins on a cache line.

2. If the group generator is contained in a dependence cycle carried by some loop, then a miss is expected only on the first few iterations of the carrying loop, depending on the distance of the carrying dependence. In this case, a prefetch to the reference can be placed before the loop carrying the dependence.

A simple example will clarify these two cases:

```
DO J = 1, M
   DO I = 1, 32
      A(I+1,J) = A(I,J) + C(J)
   ENDDO
ENDDO
```

The reference to A(I,J) is the generator for a group of references that also includes A(I+1,J). Since these references are not part of a dependence cycle carried by either loop, they fall into the first case and will generate a miss on every iteration of the inner loop that hits a new cache line. On the other hand, the reference to C(J) is involved in an input dependence carried by the inner loop, so its prefetch could be placed before the entrance to the inner loop.

Note that there is a special consideration in the second case. If the dependence edge is carried by an outer loop and the generator reference for the name partition is indexed by the inner loop, then the entire vector of references represented by that generator can be prefetched. If there were not room enough in the cache, the carrying edge would have been marked "ineffective" by the cache size analysis. As an example, consider the following loop nest:

```
DO J = 1, M
   DO I = 1, 32
      A(I,J) = A(I,J) + B(I) * C(I,J)
   ENDDO
ENDDO
```

There is an input dependence involving B(I) carried by the outer loop. If the cache size analysis determines that B(1:32) can fit entirely in cache, the edge involving B(I) will be marked "effective" and the prefetches for B(1:32) can be placed outside the J-loop. This corresponds to *prefetch vectorization*, as described in the introduction to Section 9.5.1.

Note that in this example the prefetches for A(I,J) and C(I,J) should be placed inside the I-loop, at least until instructions are scheduled.

Prefetch Insertion for Acyclic Name Partitions

We begin with a discussion of placement for name partitions that do not form a strongly connected region. Consider the case where there is a single name partition with a single generator that needs to be prefetched in the loop. There are two cases:

1. If the references to the generator do not iterate sequentially in cache within the loop (i.e., there is no spatial reuse of the reference in the loop), then simply insert a prefetch before each reference to the generator.

2. If the references to the generator have spatial locality within the loop, then determine the index i_0 of the first iteration after the initial iteration that causes a miss on the access to the generator and the iteration interval l between misses in the cache. Note that the interval l can be shorter than the length of a cache line if the stride is greater than one. Note also that $i_0 \leq l + 1$ because we have defined the initial index in such a way that it cannot be the first iteration.

a. Partition the loop into two parts: an initial subloop running from 1 to $i_0 - 1$ and the remainder running from i_0 to the end.

b. Strip-mine the second loop to have subloops of length l. Insert a prefetch of the generator prior to each subloop.

c. Insert all prefetches needed to avoid misses in the initial subloop prior to that loop. Note that a prefetch of the line containing the generator reference in the first iteration is not sufficient if there is a carried data dependence in the name partition and the reference of the sink of that dependence is in an earlier cache line than the generator reference.

d. Eliminate any very short loops by unrolling. Here "very short" may depend on machine-specific parameters, but clearly a loop with a single iteration is very short.

In both cases, the final positioning of the prefetches will be determined by the instruction scheduler.

As an example of this procedure, consider the following loop:

```
DO I = 1, M
   A(I,J) = A(I,J) + A(I-1,J)
ENDDO
```

The name partition involving references to A(I,J) and A(I-1,J) has the store into A(I,J) as its generator. If we assume that A(0,J) begins a new cache line and the lines are four words in length, then $i_0 = 4$ and $l = 4$.

Thus the initial subloop, or preloop, consists of three iterations, and the remaining iterations can be strip-mined to a size of 4.

```
DO I = 1, 3
   A(I,J) = A(I,J) + A(I-1,J)
ENDDO
DO I = 4, M, 4
   IU = MIN(M,I+3)
   DO ii = I, IU
      A(ii,J) = A(ii,J) + A(ii-1,J)
   ENDDO
ENDDO
```

Clearly, a prefetch of A(I,J) is needed before every iteration of the inner loop, but what needs to be prefetched before the preloop? A(0,J) must be prefetched, and this prefetch will also bring in A(1,J) on the same cache line. With this prefetch instruction, the code becomes

```
prefetch(A(0,J))
DO I = 1, 3
    A(I,J) = A(I,J) + A(I-1,J)
ENDDO
DO I = 4, M, 4
    IU = MIN(M,I+3)
    prefetch(A(I,J))
    DO ii = I, IU
        A(ii,J) = A(ii,J) + A(ii-1,J)
    ENDDO
ENDDO
```

Note that the set of lines that must be prefetched before the first loop is the set of lines containing all references in the first iteration of the preloop. This can typically be determined by inspection.

How can this procedure be extended to handle multiple name partitions with different generators? The extension is straightforward: simply determine the initial miss index for each of the name partitions, use the smallest one as the actual i_0, and insert prefetches for the other misses directly in the body of an unrolled version of the strip loop.

To illustrate this extension, we present another example, assuming that A(0,J) and B(0,J) start a cache line:

```
DO I = 1, M
    A(I,J) = A(I-1,J) + B(I+2,J)
ENDDO
```

The reference to B(I+2,J) will have an initial miss when I = 2, while the initial miss index for A(I,J) is 4. Using the smaller index 2, we get the following loop after unrolling and inserting prefetches:

```
prefetch(A(0,J))
prefetch(B(0,J))
A(1,J) = A(0,J) + B(3,J)
DO I = 2, M, 4
    prefetch(B(I+2,J))
    A(I,J) = A(I-1,J) + B(I+2,J)
    A(I+1,J) = A(I,J) + B(I+3,J)
    A(I+2,J) = A(I+1,J) + B(I+4,J)
    prefetch(A(I+3,J))
    A(I+3,J) = A(I+2,J) + B(I+5,J)
ENDDO
```

This code is correct under the assumption that MOD(M-1,4) = 0. If this is not so, the loop on I will require a postloop of up to three iterations, which is straightforward to generate.

Prefetch Insertion for Cyclic Name Partitions

For those name partitions that are cyclic, the prefetch instruction is inserted just prior to the loop carrying the cycle. In the case of an innermost loop, this is fairly straightforward, since the generator reference (in this case, the target of the carried dependence) is simply repeated in the prefetch instruction.

However, in the case where the loop carrying the dependence is an outer loop, the prefetch can be vectorized. The following procedure accomplishes this:

1. Begin by placing the prefetch loop nest outside the loop carrying the backward dependence of a cyclic name partition. The prefetch loop should include copies of the loop headers of the loops containing the generator reference, using the same iteration ranges.

2. Rearrange the loop nest so that the loop iterating sequentially over cache lines is innermost.

3. Split the innermost loop into two loops—a preloop up to the first iteration of the innermost loop that contains a generator reference that begins on a new cache line (the preloop may be empty) and a main loop that begins with the iteration containing the new cache reference. Replace the preloop by a prefetch of the first generator reference. Set the stride of the main loop to the interval between new cache references.

To illustrate this process, we present the following example loop:

```
DO J = 1, M
   DO I = 2, 33
      A(I,J) = A(I,J) * B(I)
   ENDDO
ENDDO
```

The prefetches for A(I,J) are straightforward and will simply be presented in the body of the example. Because the input dependence involving B(I) is carried by the J-loop, the prefetches for B will be placed outside that loop. Assuming that B(1) and A(1,J) are aligned with cache line boundaries and cache lines are of length 4, the first prefetch will be of B(2), with subsequent prefetches of B(5), B(9), and so on.

```
prefetch (B(2))
DO I = 5, 33, 4
   prefetch(B(I))
```

```
ENDDO
DO J = 1, M
   prefetch(A(2,J))
   DO I = 2, 4
      A(I,J) = A(I,J) * B(I)
   ENDDO
   DO I = 5, 33, 4
      prefetch(A(I,J))
      A(I,J) = A(I,J) * B(I)
      A(I+1,J) = A(I+1,J) * B(I+1)
      A(I+2,J) = A(I+2,J) * B(I+2)
      A(I+3,J) = A(I+3,J) * B(I+3)
   ENDDO
   prefetch(A(33,J))
   A(33,J) = A(33,J) * B(33)
ENDDO
```

Note that the prefetches of B before the outer loop are arranged so that no prefetch is issued for a reference that does not occur in the body of the computation loop, and all lines referenced in the body are prefetched. This is accomplished by the loop splitting strategy used in the algorithm.

Prefetching Irregular Accesses

Irregular accesses present special problems because they typically consist of an array access in which a subscripted variable appears in one of the subscript positions:

```
A(IX(I),J)
```

In these cases, we assume that no spatial locality exists for the outer array, so we prefetch each reference. Spatial locality can exist, however, for the index array, so it is treated as a normal prefetch. The standard prefetch algorithms can then be applied.

Consider an example:

```
DO J = 1, M
   DO I = 2, 33
      A(I,J) = A(I,J) * B(IX(I),J)
   ENDDO
ENDDO
```

Here the prefetching of A will be like previous examples, but B will be prefetched on each iteration. The prefetches of IX, which might normally appear right before the prefetch of B, can in this case be moved outside the J-loop to yield the following code:

```
prefetch (IX(2))
DO I = 5, 33, 4
   prefetch(IX(I))
ENDDO
DO J = 1, M
   prefetch(A(2,J))
   DO I = 2, 4
      prefetch(B(IX(I),J))
      A(I,J) = A(I,J) * B(IX(I),J)
   ENDDO
   DO I = 5, 32, 4
      prefetch(A(I,J))
      prefetch(B(IX(I),J))
      A(I,J) = A(I,J) * B(IX(I),J)
      prefetch(B(IX(I+1),J))
      A(I+1,J) = A(I+1,J) * B(IX(I+1),J)
      prefetch(B(IX(I+2),J))
      A(I+2,J) = A(I+2,J) * B(IX(I+2),J)
      prefetch(B(IX(I+3),J))
      A(I+3,J) = A(I+3,J) * B(IX(I+3),J)
   ENDDO
   prefetch(A(33,J))
   prefetch(B(IX(33),J))
   A(33,J) = A(33,J) * B(IX(33),J)
ENDDO
```

A problem with prefetching indirect references is that if the index array is modified in the loop, the prefetch address might be invalid at the time of the prefetch, which could result in a prefetch to an illegal address [216]. Since prefetches do not take memory exceptions on most machines, this does not generally result in unsafe code. However, if we attempt to prefetch through two levels of indirection, we may attempt to *load* from an illegal address. To avoid this problem, we limit prefetching to a single level of indirection.

9.5.2 Effectiveness of Software Prefetching

Mowry examined the effectiveness of a selective prefetching similar to the one described above for a variety of kernel programs and showed that the method achieves substantive speedups ranging from 1.05 to 2.08 over the same programs without prefetching [216]. These results are reproduced in Figure 9.8. These results were achieved simulating a 100 Mhz MIPS R4000 with a primary cache of 8K bytes and a secondary cache of 256K bytes. The penalty for a primary cache miss to secondary cache is 12 cycles, and the total penalty for a miss that goes all the way to memory is 75 cycles.

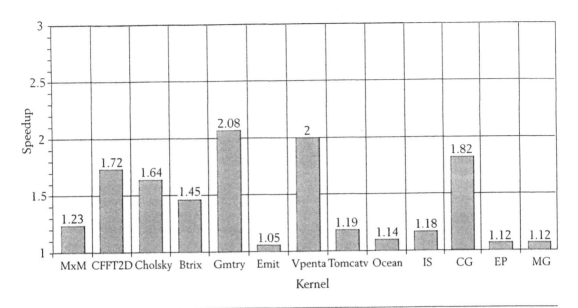

Figure 9.8 Speedups from software prefetching.

Mowry's speedups include the costs of executing the extra instructions required by prefetching. Sometimes these extra instructions may need to recompute prefetch addresses, so the instruction execution overhead can be as high as 15% in some cases. However, these overheads are far outweighed by the savings from reduced memory access stalls.

These results show that prefetching is an important optimization on machines with modern memory architectures.

9.6 Summary

In dealing with cache memories, two different types of reuse are important. *Temporal reuse* occurs when two different memory operations access the same data element. This kind of reuse was studied in Chapter 8. *Spatial reuse*, which is unique to cache, occurs when two different accesses are to memory locations close enough together to occupy the same cache block. In this chapter we have considered two strategies for increasing both temporal and spatial reuse:

- *Loop interchange*, to improve the utilization of long cache lines in inner loops both by achieving short-stride access (spatial reuse) in the inner loop and by reducing the distance between accesses to the same memory location (temporal reuse)

- *Cache blocking*, to transform programs to exploit reuse in outer loops in a manner similar to unroll-and-jam from Chapter 8

These techniques have been shown to be applicable to loops that include control flow and have trapezoidal iteration ranges. Their effectiveness can be enhanced by the application of previously studied transformations such as loop fusion with alignment.

In addition, this chapter introduced *software prefetching*, a transformation designed to hide the latency of accesses to main memory by asynchronously preloading cache blocks specified by special prefetch instructions.

9.7   Case Studies

In support of his dissertation research, Porterfield extended the PFC system at Rice to carry out strip-mine-and-interchange as described in this chapter. In addition, he implemented a rudimentary form of fusion. Rather than using alignment as described here, that implementation looked for opportunities to apply a second transformation called *peel-and-jam* whenever the alignments made direct fusion impractical. Peel-and-jam is similar to fusion with alignment in that it peels off iterations of one loop before carrying out fusion in order to effect an alignment. However, Porterfield did not drive the search process by a general fusion algorithm, so he was able to find only a few opportunities for using it. Nevertheless, peel-and-jam was critical to improving some important programs; it accounted for about a quarter of the improvement via transformation on WANAL1, reported in Section 9.3.8. On SIMPLE, a major hydrodynamics benchmark, peel-and-jam eliminated about half the misses in the loops to which it could be applied; however, these loops represented a small fraction of the computational load, so that the aggregate increase in hit ratio was only 1%—from 77% to 78%. Porterfield also described the combination of skewing with blocking but found no applications for it in his study.

Porterfield evaluated the performance of codes before and after transformation by integrating a cache model into PFC to yield an event-driven simulation facility called PFC-Sim, in which the simulation ran concurrently with the program execution, reducing the need for large data storage facilities to hold detailed trace information. This required that every statement that accessed cache memory be annotated with a call to the cache model. Because this work was done on a machine with limited computational power, most experiments only monitored accesses to subscripted array variables. The inaccuracies introduced by this simplification were fairly minor as the number of scalar variables in any given routine is quite small.

Porterfield also used PFC to conduct studies on the efficacy of software prefetching. For this study he assumed a cache in which each floating-point quantity occupied a single cache line. This permitted a simpler prefetching algorithm than the one presented in this chapter, which attempts to reduce the number of needless prefetches due to long cache lines. Nevertheless, it showed the promise of prefetching, particularly for indirect references of the sort found in irregular computations, for which the prefetching algorithm was basically the same as the one used by Mowry, Lam, and Gupta [217, 216]. Porterfield's study was the earliest known investigation of software prefetching.

The ParaScope system, a successor to PFC, included facilities for blocking cache and carrying out loop interchange to improve reuse. These facilities were used by Kennedy and McKinley [175] and by McKinley, Carr, and Tseng [210] for experiments on the effectiveness of loop interchange combined with blocking to improve cache utilization. The strategies described in this chapter are derived from that work.

More recently, Chen Ding extended the D system, a later version of ParaScope, to do aggressive multilevel loop fusion to reduce memory bandwidth consumption of applications [103]. This system incorporated loop alignment in a global algorithm similar to the one described in Chapter 8 and used in this chapter.

The Ardent Titan had a cache, but did not use it for floating-point quantities because all floating-point operations were carried out in the vector unit, which bypassed cache for loads and stores. For this reason, the Titan compiler implemented the register usage improvement operations described in Chapter 8 and included no cache management strategies.

9.8 Historical Comments and References

The techniques of blocking for cache have been known in practice for many years. Abu-Sufah, working with Kuck, produced one of the first published treatments of dependence-based program transformation [1]. Building on the work of Abu-Sufah, several researchers produced papers on management of cache by compilers including Gannon, Jalby, and Gallivan [117] and Callahan, Kennedy, and Porterfield [61, 227]. The treatment by Wolf and Lam [276] featured multidimensional tiling and showed that performance scaled much better with problem size after tiling. McKinley, Carr, and Tseng [210] integrated techniques of cache blocking and loop interchange.

Because cache blocking is so profitable on modern machines, it is worth expending significant effort to produce good tilings. Examples of more powerful and sophisticated techniques have been presented by Wolfe [282] and by Kodukula, Ahmed, and Pingali [186].

Recent work by Ding and Kennedy [103, 105] has demonstrated the effectiveness of multilevel fusion and alignment in improving cache reuse and hence reducing memory bandwidth requirements. The implementation fuses loops of different shapes and nesting levels, on the observation that the cost of a few extra conditionals is more than compensated for by increases in reuse and associated improvements in effective bandwidth to memory.

Software prefetching has been a subject of much speculation over the years as a way of improving cache performance. The term was coined by Callahan, Kennedy, and Porterfield [61, 227] in their original paper, which also presented a compiler algorithm for its implementation and simulation results demonstrating its promise. The technique of selective prefetching described in this chapter was developed by Mowry, Lam, and Gupta as part of Mowry's dissertation [217, 216].

Exercises

9.1 The algorithm for loop ordering in Figure 9.1 permutes loops in order to reduce the stride of access to memory. Will it work for imperfectly nested loops?

9.2 Determine the memory ordering of loops for the following code:

```
DO I = 1, N
   DO J = 2, M
      A(I,J) = A(I,J-1) + B(I,J) + C(J)
   ENDDO
ENDDO
```

9.3 When simulating a changing system, many programs use a time step loop as in the following example:

```
DO TIME = 1, N
   DO I = 1, N
      POSITION(I) = F(POSITION(I))
   ENDDO
ENDDO
```

Can you improve cache performance of this loop using any of the techniques discussed in this chapter?

9.4 Memory access is slow because of not only high latency but also low bandwidth. What is the effect of prefetching on the bandwidth constraint? Give at least two reasons why software prefetching may cause unnecessary memory transfer.

CHAPTER 10

Scheduling

10.1 Introduction

Much of this book has focused on finding parallelism in a program, using the theory of dependence as a fundamental tool. In this chapter we examine how the same theory can be used to support the *mapping* of parallelism to the available machine resources on a computer system with limited parallel resources. This problem is generally referred to as *scheduling* because the principal strategy used is to sacrifice some execution time in order to fit a given program within the available resources. The essence of the scheduling problem is to minimize the amount of time that must be sacrificed. As we shall see, good scheduling can have a dramatic effect on the performance of compiled programs on high-performance computers.

We examine two different variants of the scheduling problem: instruction scheduling and vector unit scheduling.

1. *Instruction scheduling* is the process of specifying the order in which instructions will be executed—an important optimization on all architectures. At the uniprocessor level, instruction scheduling requires a careful balance of the resources required by various instructions with the resources available within the architecture. The key goal is to minimize the length of the critical path through an instruction sequence.

2. The goal of *vector unit scheduling* is to make the most effective use of the instructions and capabilities of a vector unit. It requires both pattern recognition and synchronization minimization.

Multiprocessor scheduling, which distributes work to asynchronous parallel co-processors in an attempt to balance the load and minimize running time, was discussed in Section 6.6.

Although this chapter covers both scheduling problems, the bulk of the treatment focuses on simple instruction scheduling. As transistor sizes have shrunk, the amount of available functionality on chips has increased tremendously, and to date, most designers have focused that available functionality on fine-grained parallelism. As a result, instruction scheduling has grown from an optimization that was nice to do if the compiler writer had the time to one that is critical for a successful compiler hardware system.

10.2   Instruction Scheduling

All modern machine architectures have the capability of issuing several instructions on each cycle, and thereby have the theoretical capability of achieving a high degree of fine-grained parallelism. Effectively utilizing that capability requires that instructions be presented in an order that allows the processor to find and issue those instructions that can be executed in parallel. There are two principal impediments to achieving that goal: (1) dependences between instructions that force a sequential ordering, and (2) resource limitations that force serialization of instructions that need the same resource. The goal of instruction scheduling for uniprocessors is to generate instructions in an order that places dependent instructions far enough apart so that the dependence does not cause delays and to ensure that as many functional units as possible are busy on each cycle.

Most processors that support fine-grained parallelism fall into two categories: superscalar and VLIW (see Section 1.4). *Superscalar* processors—the most common—have multiple functional units controlled and scheduled by the hardware, which means that the instruction decode unit reads a group of instructions (usually a cache-word size and on cache-word boundaries) at the same time and determines the hazards (or dependences) between them. The unit then schedules the instructions across multiple functional units if there are free resources for doing the work and the instructions can be safely scheduled in parallel. Superscalar processors generally provide hazard protection by either stalling execution or using register renaming to avoid executing an instruction whose operands are not quite ready. It's fairly easy to see why superscalar execution has been popular—because the instruction unit reads existing binaries, a superscalar machine can provide some speedup without the need to recompile.

Less common, but enjoying a recent resurgence, are VLIW (Very Long Instruction Word) architectures. In contrast to superscalar architectures, where the bulk of the work is placed on the hardware designer, VLIW architectures place most of the burden of achieving high performance on the compiler. A VLIW architecture uses a long instruction word that contains a field controlling each available functional unit. As a result, one instruction can cause all functional units to execute. For a VLIW machine, the compiler must explicitly specify the parallelism and must be more observant of hazards, since VLIW architectures typically provide no protection against using results that are not yet available. One major drawback of VLIW machines is their lack of binary compatibility; since the instruction length is proportional to the number of functional units, newer machines with a different number of functional units cannot run existing binaries without invoking some form of translation. The practical result is that users and software vendors must recompile their source code for each different version of a VLIW machine.

With both superscalar and VLIW architectures, the key to effective parallelism is ordering the instruction stream so that as many functional units as possible are being used on every cycle. The standard approach taken by compilers to achieve that goal is to first issue a sequential stream of instructions, known to be correct, and then reorder that stream to more effectively utilize available parallelism. That reordering, of course, must not violate the dependences present in the original instruction stream. However, one of the key problems in instruction scheduling is that the very act of creating a sequential stream must consider the available resources and, by doing so, may create some artificial dependences that are not present in the higher-level computation.

Registers are the most common example. For example, one possible instruction stream for the code fragment

```
a = b + c + d + e;
```

is (assuming that all variables are in registers called by the same name)

```
add    a,b,c
add    a,a,d
add    a,a,e
```

This instruction stream as written cannot be reordered to take advantage of multiple adders because each instruction depends on the results of the previous one. These dependences are purely artificial, however, and arise because the intermediate results were all accumulated into the same register. If a different register allocation is used, such as

```
add    r1,b,c
add    r2,d,e
add    a,r1,r2
```

then the first two additions can be done in parallel. The original instruction stream was designed to minimize the number of registers used; by doing so, it also minimized the available parallelism. Antidependences at this level are all due to reuse of resources.

The previous example illustrates one of the fundamental conflicts in instruction scheduling: obtaining the original instruction stream. If the original instruction stream takes into account the resources available on the machine (registers, in particular), then it is probably going to introduce artificial dependences based on resource reuse. On the other hand, if the original stream does not consider available resources but instead treats them symbolically, then there may not be enough resources in the machine to execute the rescheduled stream correctly. For instance, the second version above could not be executed on an architecture with only five registers, since executing the two adds in parallel requires six registers (if we cannot destroy the contents of any input). This is an example of the general trade-off between parallelism and storage.

This section presents methods for scheduling instructions on single-processor machines that can issue several instructions on each cycle, whether superscalar or VLIW. The focus is on arranging the instructions of the object program in such a way as to take maximum advantage of the parallelism in the machine architecture—parallelism in instruction processing and function execution—without compromising the meaning of the program. The assumption is that some sets of resources, registers in particular, have already been allocated. Other resources, such as functional units, have not.

In order to provide a general treatment of scheduling, we will define an abstract machine model that will be used as the target for the strategies developed in this chapter. The machine will have an arbitrary number of functional units and the capability of issuing one or more instructions of each functional type on each machine cycle. This machine model should be reasonably close to the practical machine designs that will be found in new computers for some time.

10.2.1   Machine Model

The basic assumption is that a machine contains a number of *issue units* of various types. Each issue unit corresponds to a machine resource such as an integer or floating-point arithmetic unit. Each issue unit will be able to issue one operation per cycle on the functional unit it controls, assumed to be pipelined. Each issue unit will have an associated *type*, which specifies the kind of resource it controls, and a *delay*, which is the number of cycles required before the result of an operation, once issued, is available.

Issue units are indexed by two integers: the unit type and the index of the particular unit within that type. The notation

$$I_j^k$$

will be used to denote the jth unit of type k. The number of units of type k is m_k. Thus the total number M of issue units in the machine is

$$M = \sum_{i=1}^{l} m_i \qquad (10.1)$$

where l is the number of issue unit types available in the machine. Since each issue unit can issue one operation per cycle, the peak issue rate of the machine is M operations per cycle.

For the purpose of exposition, the model is assumed to be a VLIW architecture in which each wide instruction consists of M subinstructions (one for each issue unit). The job of the compiler is to select, for each cycle, a set of $\leq M$ operations to be included in the wide instruction, such that the number of operations of type k is $\leq m_k$. Assume that if the number of instructions of type k is strictly less than m_k, the operation for each unused instruction issue slot is a no-op. Code can be generated for an equivalent superscalar version by listing the instructions that can be scheduled together in a straight line.

A scheduling problem will be represented in this model as a graph in which the vertices represent instructions of a given type and the edges represent dependences with a given delay equal to the delay for the type of operation at the source vertex of the edge.

10.2.2 Straight-Line Graph Scheduling

The simplest scheduling problem is that of scheduling a basic block, or straight-line code. As might be expected, a fundamental requirement is a dependence graph, annotated with extra information required for scheduling. This graph, called a *scheduling graph*, has four components:

$$G = (N, E, type, delay) \tag{10.2}$$

where N is the set of instructions in the code. Each $n \in N$ has a type given by $type(n)$ and a delay given by $delay(n)$. An edge exists between two instructions if the second must await completion of the first due to a shared register—the concepts of true dependence (usually called a read after write, or RAW, hazard in this context), antidependence (write after read), and output dependence (write after write) are all important here.

A correct schedule is a mapping S from vertices in the graph to nonnegative integers, representing cycle numbers, such that

1. $S(n) \geq 0$ for all $n \in N$,
2. if $(n_1, n_2) \in E$, $S(n_1) + delay(n_1) \leq S(n_2)$, and
3. for any type t, no more than m_t vertices of type t are mapped to a given integer.

Intuitively, condition (1) guarantees that all instructions are executed at some point; condition (2) guarantees that no dependences are violated; and condition (3) guarantees that only the available resources are in use during any cycle.

The *length* of the schedule S, denoted $L(S)$, is defined as

$$L(S) = \max_{n \in N} (S(n) + delay(n)) \qquad (10.3)$$

The goal of straight-line scheduling is to find a shortest possible correct schedule, where a straight-line schedule S is said to be *optimal* if

$$L(S) \leq L(S_1)$$

for any other correct schedule S_1 for the same graph. Obviously, the shortest schedule is the one that takes the least time to execute.

10.2.3 List Scheduling

The simplest way to schedule a straight-line graph is to use a variant of topological sort that builds and maintains a list of instructions that have no predecessors in the graph. Any instruction in this list can be scheduled without violating any dependences, and scheduling an instruction will allow new instructions (successors of the scheduled instruction) to be entered into the list. This algorithm, known naturally enough as *list scheduling*, is given in Figure 10.1.

The basic idea is to schedule an instruction at the first opportunity after all its dependent operations have completed. The *count* array is used to determine when the final predecessor has been scheduled, and the *earliest* array is used to determine the earliest possible scheduling time for a given instruction. When an instruction's last predecessor has been scheduled, its *earliest* value is just late enough to ensure that all inputs to the instruction will be available. This value is then used to determine which of the worklists will hold the instruction. Enough worklists are necessary to ensure that no instruction will be scheduled ahead of an instruction upon which it depends. The number of worklists guaranteed to satisfy this condition is the largest delay plus one. Thus, if the earliest cycle on which an instruction could be scheduled is c, we will put it on worklist $W[\mathrm{mod}(c, MaxC)]$.

The algorithm in Figure 10.1 is a fairly standard topological sort-based algorithm. One of the typical characteristics of such algorithms is that they select randomly from the worklist. Random selection does not matter when all the instructions on the worklist for a cycle can be scheduled in that cycle, but it can matter when there are not enough resources to schedule all possible instructions. In this case, all nonscheduled instructions are placed on the worklist for the next cycle; if one of the delayed instructions is on the critical path, the schedule length is increased. To illustrate with a simple example:

```
mult    c,a,b
mult    f,d,e
add     f,f,g
add     f,f,h
add     f,f,c
```

procedure *list_schedule(G,instr)*

    // $G = (N,E,type,delay)$ is the scheduling graph
    // *instr[c]* is the output table that maps cycles to sets of instructions
    // $W[MaxC]$ is an array of worklists to hold ready instructions
    // *MaxC* is 1 greater than the largest delay of any instruction

    for each $n \in N$ **do begin** *count[n]* := 0; *earliest[n]* := 0; **end**
    for each $(n_1,n_2) \in E$ **do begin**
        $count[n_2]$:= $count[n_2]$ + 1;
        $successors[n_1]$:= $successors[n_1] \cup \{n_2\}$;
    end
    for i := 0 **to** $MaxC - 1$ **do** $W[i]$:= $\varnothing$;
    Wcount := 0;
    for each $n \in N$ **do**
        if *count[n]* = 0 **then**
            begin $W[0]$:= $W[0] \cup \{n\}$; *Wcount* := *Wcount* + 1; **end**
    c := 0; *instr[c]* := $\varnothing$; // c is the cycle number
    cW := 0; // cW will be the number of the worklist for cycle c
    while *Wcount* > 0 **do begin**
        while $W[cW] = \varnothing$ **do begin**
            c := c + 1; *instr[c]* := $\varnothing$; cW := $mod(cW+1,MaxC)$;
        end
        nextc := $mod(c+1,MaxC)$;
        while $W[cW] \neq \varnothing$ **do begin**
            select and remove an arbitrary instruction x from $W[cW]$;
            if there are free issue units of *type(x)* on cycle c **then begin**
                instr[c] := *instr[c]* $\cup \{x\}$; // schedule the instruction
                Wcount := *Wcount* – 1;
                for each $y \in successors[x]$ **do begin**
                    count[y] := *count[y]* – 1;
                    earliest[y] := $max(earliest[y],c+delay(x))$;
                    if *count[y]* = 0 **then begin**
                        loc := $mod(earliest[y],MaxC)$;
                        $W[loc]$:= $W[loc] \cup \{y\}$; *Wcount* := *Wcount* + 1;
                  end
                end
            else $W[nextc]$:= $W[nextc] \cup \{x\}$;
        end
    end
end *list_schedule*

Figure 10.1 Naive list scheduling algorithm.

If this sequence is scheduled on a machine with only one multiply unit, the scheduling algorithm must choose one of the two multiplies to execute in the first cycle. The second one is the correct choice; the first one will increase the length of the schedule by delaying evaluation of critical additions. The correct choice can be ensured by altering the algorithm to make a preliminary pass through the graph, determining minimum number of cycles that remain after each instruction (a standard algorithm from project scheduling). Such a backward sweep through the graph is shown in Figure 10.2.

Critical path information can be incorporated into list scheduling by selecting the instruction with the highest *remaining* value as opposed to a random instruction. Such a selection requires organizing the worklist as a priority queue, which can insert a logarithmic factor in the time complexity. This approach is referred to in the literature as the *highest levels first* (HLF) heuristic.

10.2.4 Trace Scheduling

List scheduling produces an excellent schedule within a basic block, but does not do so well at transition points between basic blocks. Because it does not look across block boundaries, a list scheduler must insert enough instructions at the end of a basic block to ensure that all results are available before scheduling the

---

procedure *find_remaining*(G,*remaining*)

    // $G = (N,E,type,delay)$ is the scheduling graph
    // *remaining*$[x]$ is an output variable containing the number of cycles
    //   remaining on a critical path from instruction x
    //   to the last instruction depending directly or indirectly on x

    for each $n \in N$ **do begin** *count*$[n] := 0$; *remaining*$[n] := delay(n)$; **end**
    for each $(n_1,n_2) \in E$ **do begin**
        count$[n_1] := count[n_1] + 1$;
        predecessors$[n_2] := predecessors[n_2] \cup \{n_1\}$;
    end
    $W := \emptyset$;
    for each $n \in N$ **do if** *count*$[n] = 0$ **then** $W := W \cup \{n\}$;
    while $W \neq \emptyset$ **do begin**
        select and remove an arbitrary instruction x from W;
        $r := remaining[x]$;
        for each $y \in predecessors[x]$ **do begin**
            count$[y] := count[y] - 1$;
            remaining$[y] := \max(remaining[y], r+delay(y))$;
            if *count*$[y] = 0$ **then** $W := W \cup \{y\}$;
        end
    end
end *find_remaining*

Figure 10.2 Determining critical instructions.

next block. Given the number of basic blocks within a typical program, these shutdown instructions can create a significant amount of overhead.

One way to eliminate this overhead is to create a very long basic block, called a *trace*, to which list scheduling can be applied. Simply stated, a trace is a collection of basic blocks that form a single path through all or part of a program. *Trace scheduling* schedules instructions for an entire trace at a time, assuming that control follows the basic blocks in the trace. Of course, this means that some fixup code must be inserted at points where control flow can enter or exit the trace. In the ideal, the first trace selected for scheduling represents the most frequently executed path through the program, so that the resulting schedule is optimal for the most common case. Because trace scheduling uses basic block scheduling techniques, it cannot schedule cyclic graphs. Either loops must be unrolled or the body must be scheduled as one basic block, with fixup code at the boundaries.

Given a directed acyclic scheduling graph, the first step in trace scheduling is to divide the graph into a collection of traces. The first trace chosen is what is hoped to be the most probable path through the graph. This trace is scheduled as one large basic block. Next, the most probable path through the remaining unscheduled blocks is chosen as a trace, and this is scheduled. At any point where this second trace may branch into the first, fixup code is inserted to satisfy the resource assumptions present in the first trace. Similarly, at any point where the first trace may branch into the second, fixup code is inserted between the jump and the start of the second trace to satisfy the resource assumptions present there. This process is repeated until all basic blocks in the program have been scheduled.

Summarizing, trace scheduling can be described as the repeated application of three distinct steps:

1. *Select a trace* through the program. Trace selection is not quite so easy as it might initially appear, even when profile information is available.

2. *Schedule* the trace.

3. *Insert fixup code*. Since this fixup code is new code outside of the scheduled trace, it creates new blocks that must be fed back into the trace schedule.

The third step is the most interesting aspect of trace scheduling. To illustrate the types of code fixups required, consider the simple example in Figure 10.3.

The trace is designated by the blocks down the left side of the figure. If this trace happens to get scheduled as

```
j = j + 1
if e1
i = i + 2
```

then the assignment to i has moved below the split, which will cause the assignment to k to receive the wrong results. This problem can be fixed by duplicating the assignment to i along the split edge in the control graph (Figure 10.4).

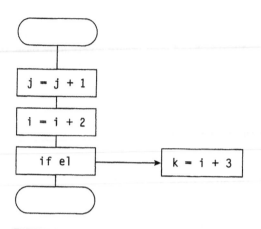

Figure 10.3 Trace requiring fixup code.

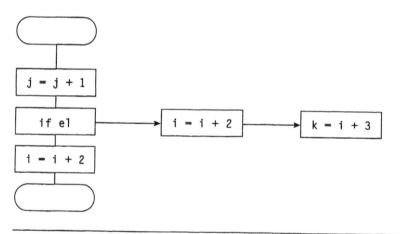

Figure 10.4 Scheduled trace with fixup code.

The newly inserted instruction will be scheduled either as its own trace or as part of a trace involving the block with the assignment to k. In general, moving operations below a split in a trace or above a join in a trace will require fixup code similar to that shown in the figure. Trace scheduling avoids moving operations above splits or below joins unless it can prove via dependence analysis that other instructions will not be adversely affected.

Given the fact that scheduling one trace can cause new traces to appear, a natural question to ask is, Will trace scheduling converge? That is, is it possible for trace scheduling to reach a state where it is continually inserting as many or more new traces as it is scheduling during a given step? Fortunately, the answer to the second question is no; trace scheduling is guaranteed to converge. However, in the worst case, that convergence may result in a very large amount of inserted fixup code. The example in Figure 10.5 from Ellis's dissertation [109] illustrates the worst case.

Trace scheduling can move branches above blocks as well as operations, so that one possible schedule that could result from this trace is the branches scheduled in inverse order:

$$C_n$$
$$A_n$$
$$C_{n-1}$$
$$A_{n-1}$$
$$\ldots$$
$$C_1$$
$$A_1$$

Such a scheduling would require the fixup code shown in Figure 10.6. Every offtrace edge requires a duplicate of all the other blocks except the one controlling the edge.

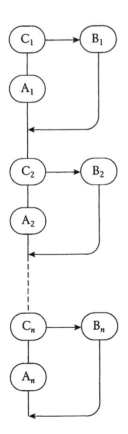

Figure 10.5 Example with worst-case code explosion.

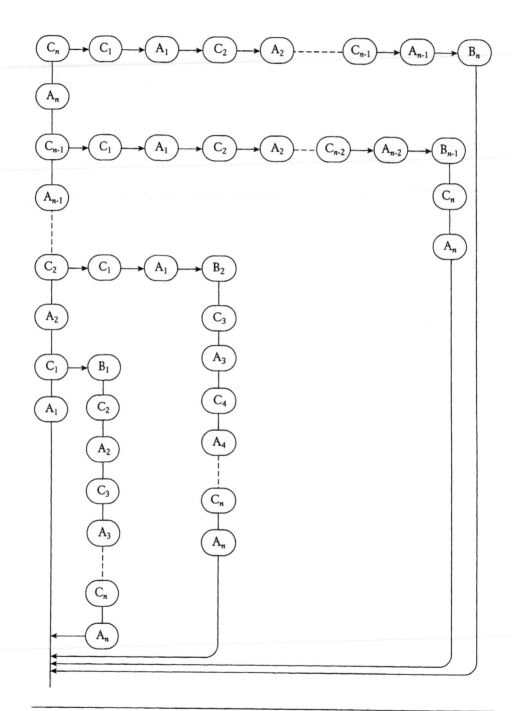

Figure 10.6 Code explosion from trace scheduling.

The total number of operations has increased to roughly $O(nn!)$, which is roughly $O(ne^n)$. While such extreme cases have not been seen in practical implementations of trace scheduling, it is certainly easy to construct reasonable test cases similar to the one above. Given that trace scheduling handles loops by unrolling them, a simple inner loop that contains only a conditional could meet the pattern shown above if the loop is unrolled enough times.

One of the key pieces of information conveyed by looping structures in programming languages is the indication that the body of the loop will be executed many times. Dependence analysis and vectorization both exploit that fact by focusing on the iterative nature of the body, and attempting to analyze and schedule the body in terms of loop iterations. One of the drawbacks of trace scheduling is that it is unable to treat loops in this manner; instead it converts them into straight-line code. Later sections will introduce scheduling methods that focus on the iterative nature of loops; however, before doing so, it is worthwhile to introduce the key issues associated with straight-line scheduling.

Issues in Straight-Line Scheduling

From the discussion presented so far, instruction scheduling has appeared no more complicated than project management—build a PERT chart and topologically sort. In fact, most of the sophisticated analysis required for instruction scheduling has been hidden as detail underneath the fundamental algorithms. This section exposes that detail in more depth.

One key machine resource that has been ignored so far in the discussion of instruction scheduling has been registers. To this point, each algorithm presented has assumed that registers had already been allocated before instruction scheduling had been invoked. While this simplifies instruction scheduling greatly by restricting one set of resources, it also restricts the amount of parallelism that results. Once a variable has been confined to a particular register, artificial dependences can easily arise due to other unrelated variables being allocated to the same register. These dependences, in turn, may prevent two instructions from being executed concurrently when in fact there is nothing in the program proper forcing sequentiality. The relative ordering of register allocation and instruction scheduling is a question debated among many computer scientists.

A second effect that results from register allocation is a disguising of the real dependence analysis necessary for effective scheduling. When variables are reduced to registers, it is easy to assume that dependence graphs are easy to construct, since registers are well-defined scalar quantities. For registers proper, this is true; however, one of the things that this overlooks is memory loads and stores. Loads from memory tend to be very slow if the load misses cache, and most computations must wait for loads of needed values to complete. As a result, scheduling memory loads as early as possible is critical for an effective instruction ordering. Dependence analysis is necessary in these cases, since loads cannot be moved above stores to the same location. Without fairly sophisticated analysis, almost no movement is possible among memory references, and the result will be a poor scheduling.

10.2.5 Scheduling in Loops

As mentioned earlier, one of the major drawbacks of straight-line scheduling and trace scheduling is the fact that their treatment of loops is inelegant at best. Their general approach is to unroll loops, making the body as large as possible, and then to try to schedule that body as effectively as possible. This approach ignores parallelism across loop iterations. This section presents an alternative approach, which is to try to maximize the parallelism across loop iterations, rather than focusing on straight-line techniques. Given that loops represent computations that are executed repeatedly, this approach focuses more attention on the areas that are likely to be the hot spots in execution time.

Kernel Scheduling

A direct scheduling strategy for loops will reorganize each loop into three components:

1. A *kernel*, which includes the code that must be executed on every cycle of the loop, once it has reached steady state
2. A *prolog*, which includes the code that must be performed before steady state can be reached
3. An *epilog*, which contains the code that must be executed to finish the loop once the kernel can no longer be executed

The goal in this case is to minimize the execution time required for the kernel, since it represents the repeated portion of the loop. The prolog and epilog portions merely set up execution of the kernel proper. Given the focus on the kernel leads to the following definition.

**DEFINITION
10.1**

The *kernel scheduling problem* seeks to find a minimal-length kernel for a given loop.

Does minimizing the kernel guarantee an optimal schedule for the loop? For loops with large iteration counts, the answer is obviously yes. For loops with small iteration counts (zero being the worst case because any prolog code represents a slowdown), the answer is not clear. However, since loops with small iteration counts probably do not represent a large fraction of execution time, their scheduling is usually not significant. As a result, the assumption throughout the rest of this chapter is that an optimal kernel schedule represents an optimal loop schedule.

**DEFINITION
10.2**

A *kernel scheduling problem* is a graph

$$G = (N, E, delay, type, cross)$$

where $cross(n_1, n_2)$, defined for each edge in E, is the number of iterations crossed by the dependence relating n_1 and n_2.

Again, an edge exists between two nodes if a dependence exists between the two, and *cross* simply represents the threshold (distance) of the dependence. Thresholds of loop-independent dependences are 0.

The goal of kernel scheduling is to focus on temporal movement of instructions through loop iterations rather than on spatial movement within a single-loop iteration. This means that critical instructions whose results are needed early are moved to earlier loop iterations, so that their results become available within the current iteration just as they are needed. Similarly, instructions at the tail end of the critical path are moved to future iterations so as to shorten completion of the current iteration. In other words, the body of one loop iteration is pipelined across multiple iterations in order to take fullest advantage of available resources within one iteration. This process, commonly known as *software pipelining*, is more formally defined as follows:

**DEFINITION
10.3**

A solution to the kernel scheduling problem is a pair of tables (S, I), where the *schedule* S maps each instruction n to a cycle within the kernel and the *iteration* I maps each instruction to an iteration offset from zero, such that

$$S[n_1] + delay(n_1) \leq S[n_2] + (I[n_2] - I[n_1] + cross(n_1, n_2))L_k(S) \qquad (10.4)$$

for each edge (n_1, n_2) in E, where $L_k(S)$ is the length of the kernel for S.

$$L_k(S) = \max_{n \in N}(S[n]) \qquad (10.5)$$

This concept should become clearer with a simple example. Assume that we are scheduling the following loop body:

```
        lw      r1,0
        lw      r2,400
        lf      fr1, c
10      lf      fr2,a(r1)
11      addf    fr2,fr2,fr1
12      sf      fr2,b(r1)
13      addi    r1,r1,8
14      comp    r1,r2
15      ble     10
```

Unit	Load-Store	Integer	Floating point
Cycle 1	lf a(r1)	addi r1,r1,8	
Cycle 2		comp r1,r2	
Cycle 3	sf fr2,b-16(r1)	ble	addf fr2

Figure 10.7 Example kernel schedule.

Similarly, assume that there are three units in the machine: a load-store unit, an integer unit, and a floating-point unit. All loads have a delay of two cycles; stores have a delay of one cycle; and floating-point addition has a delay of three cycles. The integer unit handles all branch instructions with a delay of one cycle on the branch taken side for blt. All other integer instructions have a delay of one cycle. For the instructions in the loop, the following is a legal schedule with three cycles in the kernel:

$$S[10] = 0; I[10] = 0;$$
$$S[11] = 2; I[11] = 0;$$
$$S[12] = 2; I[12] = 1;$$
$$S[13] = 0; I[13] = 0;$$
$$S[14] = 1; I[14] = 0;$$
$$S[15] = 2; I[15] = 0;$$

This schedule, depicted graphically in Figure 10.7, specifies that on the first cycle of a given iteration, the floating load and the increment are performed; the comparison is performed on the second; and the branch, floating add, and floating store are performed on the third.

Note that this schedule is illegal with the instructions as written in the original program; it is necessary to change the instructions somewhat to obtain correct results. For instance, the floating store is executed one iteration ahead, after r1 has been incremented twice and after the next iteration's floating load has already overwritten the results. This means that the store must be adjusted for r1, and that an extra floating-point register is needed to hold the result of the floating-point addition until the store is ready to execute. Assuming fr3 is available for this purpose, we are left with the following correct kernel:

```
k1   lf fr2,a(r1);      addi r1,r1,8
k2                      comp r1,r2
k3   sf fr3,b-16(r1);   ble  k1          addf fr3,fr2,fr1
```

Of course, this code is incorrect on the first iteration, since it assumes that fr3 and r1 have been set by previous iterations. This means that one execution of the loop (minus the code that depends on a previous iteration having completed) must be executed prior to entering the kernel, setting up the appropriate initialization.

```
    lw r1,0
    lw r2,400
    lf fr1,c
p1  lf fr2,a(r1);    addi r1,r1,8
p2                   comp r1,r2
p3                   beq  e1;        addf fr3,fr2,fr1
```

Finally, the results of the last iteration are never stored away. This requires another few instructions of epilog:

```
e1  nop
e2  nop
e3  sf  fr3,b-8(r1)
```

The schedule for the entire loop is given below. The length of the kernel is 3 cycles, and given that the integer unit is busy on every cycle, no shorter schedule is possible.

```
    lw r1,0
    lw r2,400
    lf fr1,c
p1  lf fr2,a(r1);      addi r1,r1,8
p2                     comp r1,r2
p3                     beq  e1;        addf fr3,fr2,fr1
k1  lf fr2,a(r1);      addi r1,r1,8
k2                     comp r1,r2
k3  sf fr3,b-16(r1);   ble  k1;        addf fr3,fr2,fr1
e1  nop
e2  nop
e3  sf fr3,b-8(r1);
```

Instructions p1–p3 form the prolog, k1–k3 the kernel, and e1–e3 the epilog.

DEFINITION 10.4

Let N be the loop upper bound. Then the *schedule length* $L(S)$ is given by

$$L(S) = NL_k(S) + \max_{n \in N}(S[n] + delay(n) + (I[n]-1)L_k(S)) \qquad (10.6)$$

This definition leads us to the observation that for very large N, minimizing the length of the kernel minimizes the length of the schedule. Since N will usually be unknown at compile time and since loops with small iteration counts usually have little effect on the overall execution time regardless of how they are scheduled, it seems reasonable to assume that N is large and thereby to try to construct the shortest possible kernel.

A Kernel Scheduling Algorithm

Is there an optimal kernel scheduling algorithm? In order to answer that question, it is necessary to establish a reasonable lower bound for how well scheduling can do. In fact, we can derive two different lower bounds based on different kinds of analysis.

Resource Usage Constraint. Assume that there is no recurrence inside the loop. Let #t denote the number of instructions in each iteration that must issue in a unit of type t. Then,

$$L_k(S) \geq \max_t \left\lceil \frac{\#t}{m_t} \right\rceil \tag{10.7}$$

In other words, if you can only issue m_t operations of type t on each cycle, then you need at least $\lceil n/m_t \rceil$ cycles to issue n instructions. Thus the kernel can be no shorter than the max over all operation types of these lower bounds.

We can show that, for a loop with no recurrence and no control flow changes, there exists a schedule S such that

$$L_k(S) = \max_t \left\lceil \frac{\#t}{m_t} \right\rceil \tag{10.8}$$

In other words, it is always possible in the absence of recurrences to find a kernel schedule of optimal length. To establish this result, we construct an algorithm, shown in Figure 10.8, that finds the kernel schedule for the given length L. Note that this algorithm expects L to satisfy the inequality in Equation 10.7.

The algorithm is essentially a list scheduler augmented with scoreboarding to track the use of resources across loop iterations. As the scheduler assigns each instruction an issue slot, it also marks the corresponding resource on the scoreboard for the time it is busy. The one modification to the scheduler occurs when it attempts to issue an instruction n at a time that would fall after the end of the kernel of length specified by Equation 10.8. Rather than doing that, the scheduler wraps to the beginning and increases the value of $I[n]$, thereby moving the instruction to a later iteration. Since the schedule length is set by the most tightly constrained resource, all other instruction types will fit into this schedule trivially. For the most tightly constrained resource, shifting instructions into future iterations (possible because there are no recurrences) ensures that we will eventually be able to find an empty slot in the kernel into which the instruction can be placed because there are exactly as many such slots as we need. There may well be

procedure *loop_schedule*(*G,L,S,I*)

    // G is the schedule graph for the loop body
    // S and I define the kernel in the resulting schedule
    // L is the number of instructions into which the loop is scheduled
    //   which is at least the minimum schedule length given by Equation 10.8;

    topologically sort G;
    for each instruction *x* in *G* in topological order **do begin**
        earlyS := 0; *earlyI* := 0;
        for each predecessor *y* of *x* in *G* **do begin**
            thisS := *S*[*y*] + *delay*(*y*); *thisI* := *I*[*y*];
            if *thisS* ≥ *L* **then begin**
                thisS := mod(*thisS,L*); *thisI* := *thisI* + ⌈*thisS/L*⌉;
            end
            if *thisI* > *earlyI* **or** *thisS* > *earlyS* **then begin**
                earlyI := *thisI*; *earlyS* := *thisS*;
            end
        end
        starting at cycle *earlyS*, find the first cycle c_0
            where the resource needed by *x* is available,
            wrapping to the beginning of the kernel if necessary;
        S[*x*] := c_0;
        if c_0 < *earlyS* **then** *I*[*x*] := *earlyI* + 1; **else** *I*[*x*] := *earlyI*;
    end
end *loop_schedule*

Figure 10.8 Find a minimum-length kernel in a loop with no dependence cycles.

an impact on registers, but the assumption is that there are enough, so the kernel is guaranteed to fit in the given length.

To illustrate this approach, consider scheduling the following somewhat nonsensical sequence on a machine with three integer units and two load-store units:

```
10   lw    a,x(i)
11   addi  a,a,1
12   addi  a,a,1
13   addi  a,a,1
14   sw    a,x(i)
```

The theorem states that there exists a kernel schedule of length one—three integer instructions divided by three integer units. A normal list scheduler could not find such a schedule, since each instruction in this sequence depends on the previous one, thereby requiring five cycles to complete.

Scheduling the first instruction is simple, leading to the following resource utilization:

Memory 1	Integer 1	Integer 2	Integer 3	Memory 2
10: $S = 0; I = 0$				

Normal scheduling of the second instruction would push it past the end of the schedule, so it instead gets wrapped around to the next iteration:

Memory 1	Integer 1	Integer 2	Integer 3	Memory 2
10: $S = 0; I = 0$	11: $S = 0; I = 1$			

The process will repeat similarly for each of the remaining instructions, leading to a final resource utilization of

Memory 1	Integer 1	Integer 2	Integer 3	Memory 2
10: $S = 0; I = 0$	11: $S = 0; I = 1$	12: $S = 0; I = 2$	13: $S = 0; I = 3$	14: $S = 0; I = 4$

This schedule is of length one; interestingly enough, on every cycle, each unit is working on a different iteration of the loop. This fact means that the sequence cannot be executed as originally written, since each unit now needs a different register for its iteration. The final code would have to be transformed into something similar to

```
10   lw    a, x(i)
11   addi  b, a, 1
12   addi  c, b, 1
13   addi  d, c, 1
14   sw    d, x(i)
```

This example illustrates the major problem with the result: it does not address the question of whether there are enough machine registers. This issue will be further discussed in a later subsection, "Register Resources."

The benefit of restricting recurrences from consideration in Equation 10.8 was the guarantee that an instruction could always be scheduled as soon as a resource was available. A recurrence can push that across more iterations, lengthening the size of the minimal schedule, as the following constraint demonstrates.

Cyclic Data Dependence Constraint. Given a cycle of dependences $(n_1, n_2, \ldots, n_k)$, then

$$L_k(S) \geq \frac{\sum\limits_{i=1}^{k} delay(n_i)}{\sum\limits_{i=1}^{k} cross(n_i, n_{i+1})} \qquad (10.9)$$

Hence,

$$L_k(S) \geq \max_c \left(\frac{\sum\limits_{i=1}^{k} delayn_i}{\sum\limits_{i=1}^{k} cross(n_i, n_{i+1})} \right) \qquad (10.10)$$

where c ranges over all dependence cycles in the loop.

The quantity in the numerator of Equation 10.9 is the number of machine cycles required to execute a single traversal of the recurrence, while the denominator counts the number of loop iterations crossed by the recurrence. Thus the right-hand side of Equation 10.9 measures the number of cycles per iteration required to compute the recurrence. Clearly, no correct kernel can have fewer cycles per iteration and compute a correct value for the recurrence.

**DEFINITION
10.5**
The quantity of the right-hand side of Equation 10.9 is called the *slope* of the recurrence.

These two constraints, specified by Equations 10.7 and 10.10, form the basis for a kernel scheduling algorithm for loops with recurrences, shown in Figure 10.9. The algorithm begins by computing the minimum size for the kernel schedule using Equations 10.7 and 10.10. It then attempts to find a schedule of that length, using the algorithm *loop_schedule* in Figure 10.8. Since this algorithm always finds a schedule in the kernel of length L so long as L satisfies the inequality in Equation 10.7, we must ask, What constitutes failure? In this case, we fail to get a satisfactory schedule if the length of any recurrence increases because this will increase the total number of times the kernel must be iterated to complete the computation. This is tested by seeing if any instruction in a recurrence slips an iteration or if a schedule slip causes the last instruction in a recurrence to produce an output too late for the first instruction in the next iteration of the recurrence.

If the algorithm fails to find a suitable schedule, it increments the minimum-length schedule for which it is searching and tries again, until it finally succeeds. Note that it must eventually succeed because the loop can always be scheduled into a kernel the length of the loop body. Even if the algorithm succeeds, it may require more registers than the machine has.

procedure *kernel_schedule(G,S,I)*

    // G is the schedule graph for the loop
    // *sched* is the output schedule

    use the all-pairs shortest-path algorithm to find the cycle in the schedule graph G
       with the greatest slope;
    designate all cycles with this slope as *critical cycles*;
    mark every instruction in G that is on a critical cycle as a *critical instruction*;

    compute the lower bound *LB* for the loop as the maximum of the slope of the
       critical recurrence given by Equation 10.10 and the hardware constraint
       as given in Equation 10.7;

    N := the number of instructions in the original loop body;
    let G_0 be G with all cycles broken by eliminating edges into the earliest instruction
     in the cycle within the loop body;
    failed := *true*;
    for L := LB **to** N **while** *failed* **do begin**

        // try to schedule the loop to length L
        loop_schedule(G₀,L,S,I);

        // test to see if the schedule succeeded
        allOK := *true*;
        for each dependence cycle C **while** *allOK* **do begin**
           for each instruction *v* that is a part of C **while** *allOK* **do begin**
             if $I[v] > 0$ **then** *allOK* := *false*;
             else if *v* is the last instruction in the cycle C **and**
               v_0 is the first instruction in the cycle **and**
               $mod(S[v]+delay(v),L) > S[v_0]$
               then *allOK* := *false*;
           end
        end
        if *allOK* **then** *failed* := *false*;
    end
end *kernel_schedule*

Figure 10.9 Algorithm for kernel scheduling.

    The effectiveness of the kernel scheduling algorithm in Figure 10.9 can be improved by a slight modification to *loop_schedule* from Figure 10.8 similar to the improvement in the list scheduling algorithm discussed earlier. When selecting the next instruction to be scheduled, if more than one instruction is ready, the algorithm should select one that is on a critical dependence cycle first or any recurrence second before scheduling an instruction that is not part of any dependence cycle. This modification is straightforward.

The algorithms in this section compute the kernel schedule for a loop, but the prolog and epilog generation still remains. The next section describes these details.

Prolog and Epilog Generation

In earlier, simple kernel scheduling examples, the key information required to generate prolog and epilog code was the number of iterations required to set up steady-state computation. That same information is necessary in these examples and is known as the *range* of an iteration of the schedule:

$$range(S) = \max_{n \in N}(I[n]) + 1 \qquad (10.11)$$

Thus defined, the *range* of a schedule is the number of iterations required for all the instructions corresponding to a single iteration of the original loop to issue.

Range provides the number of loop iterations that must be executed to gear up the loop into steady state (priming the pipeline) as well as the number of iterations required to wind down the loop after steady state (draining the pipeline). Getting a full kernel, with actual copies of each of the instructions in steady state, requires instructions from $range(S)$ different iterations, including the one currently starting. Thus if $r = range(S)$, the first complete iteration to execute is the rth, making the length of the prolog

$$(r-1)L_k(S)$$

With this information, the prolog can be created by laying out $r - 1$ copies of the kernel, with any instruction n such that $I[n] = i < r - 1$, replaced by a no-op in copies 1 through i. Without no-op insertion, the prolog cannot be rescheduled effectively (it is guaranteed optimal), but when no-ops are inserted, it may be possible to compress the prolog significantly. In those cases, rescheduling the prolog with a list scheduling algorithm is beneficial and may reduce the length of the prolog.

We can use a similar method to get a bound on the length of the epilog. Once the last full iteration of the kernel is complete (this is the iteration on which instructions on the last iteration of the original code begin to issue), it can be completed in $r - 1$ iterations. However, this is not enough. Unlike the prolog case, the epilog requires some extra time for the last instructions to complete, to ensure that all hazards with code outside the loop are accommodated. For instance, if the last instruction in a schedule is a store, and stores take five cycles to complete, the epilog code must contain an extra five no-ops to ensure the store has finished so that no following loads retrieve an invalid value. The additional time needed for epilog code is

$$\Delta(S) = \left(\max_{n \in N}(((I[n]-1)L_k(S)+S[n]+delay(n)) - rL_k(S) \right)^+ \qquad (10.12)$$

where the superscript "+" denotes the *positive part* of the expression, defined in Chapter 3 to be equal to the quantity to which it applies if that quantity is greater than zero, and zero otherwise.

Thus the length of the epilog has the following upper bound:

$$(r-1)L_k(S) + \Delta(S)$$

As in the case of the prolog, the length of the epilog can be reduced by list scheduling.

Thus, to generate code for the epilog, simply lay out $r - 1$ copies of the kernel, replacing any instruction n such that $I[n] = i < r - 1$ with a no-op in copies $i + 1$ to $r - 1$.

Register Resources

So far, the discussion of software pipelining has noted the problem of increased register requirements due to pipelining, but has deferred discussion of any solution to the problem. It would be nice to say that the discussion was deferred so as to present a general software pipelining algorithm that elegantly solves the problem. The truth is that there is no overarching, elegant solution. When a pipelined schedule requires more registers than a machine has available, either registers must be spilled or the code must be rescheduled. A number of heuristic techniques have been advanced for solving this problem, but no completely satisfactory solution has yet been developed. Assuming register overflow is relatively infrequent (which seems like a reasonable assumption), inserting memory spills and rescheduling when there are too few registers for an optimal schedule seems reasonable.

Lack of registers is not the only problem faced by software pipelining, however. Even when there are enough registers, there can be a name clash between existing registers. Such clashes are caused by trying to use the same register to hold two different values on different original iterations whose live ranges overlap. However, as we saw in Chapter 8, naming problems of this sort can often be resolved by loop unrolling.

Control Flow

So far, software pipelining has been discussed only in terms of loops that have no control flow. Such loops present regular, predictable execution that can be scheduled with relative certainty of improving results. Control flow complicates software pipelining in two ways:

1. Because there are different control flow paths of different schedule lengths, it is no longer possible to assume that the same number of cycles will be required on every iteration.

2. Instructions that execute conditionally under the guard of control flow must be issued before control flow joins back together. Instructions from different iterations cannot be allowed to freely intermix. If a conditional instruction is not issued before the join, some mechanism of saving control flow decisions must be implemented, and these are neither easy nor efficient.

The result is that control flow is difficult to handle in software pipelining because the loop is less predictable and there is less room for moving instructions. One alternative is to use trace scheduling on the loop body; doing so is basically betting on the more likely control flow path.

A second approach is frequently used on machines with hardware support for predicated execution. If we employ if-conversion, as described in Section 7.2, we can eliminate every forward branch by converting instructions under branches to predicated form. To be most effective, the algorithms from that section will need to be modified to minimize the number of conditional values to be evaluated. However, such modifications are straightforward.

An alternative strategy for predicated hardware is to construct control dependences as described in Section 7.3, schedule using the control dependences, and then use the code generation algorithm in Figures 7.25 and 7.26 to produce the final code, predicating every instruction by the Boolean variable produced through evaluation of the most immediate condition controlling it. This strategy is being pursued by at least one group generating code for the Intel IA-64 architecture [107].

A final approach for incorporating control flow into software pipelining, suggested by Lam [194], is to schedule control flow regions first, using a nonpipelining approach, then treat those regions as black boxes when pipelining. In other words, the control flow regions are assumed to be a single macroinstruction that requires all resources for some number of cycles. The instructions outside the control flow region can be scheduled before or after the region using software pipelining. This strategy is illustrated in Figure 10.10.

Each of the paths in the control flow region is scheduled independently, then the entire control flow region is reduced to a superinstruction, taking all resources for a number of cycles equal to the length of the longest path. Once this is completed, the preflow region, superinstruction, and postflow region are scheduled using standard software pipelining.

An improvement to this strategy is to refine the view of the superinstruction as having different delays for different outputs. That is, the superinstruction is still issued as one instruction in a single output, but its outputs become available at different times and it releases some resources prior to the superinstruction completion. Doing this could permit some instructions in the postflow region to be scheduled into all paths of the control flow region, shortening the length of the kernel.

A similar strategy can be used to shorten the preflow region. A dependence with delay d between an instruction i_1 in the preflow region and an instruction i_2

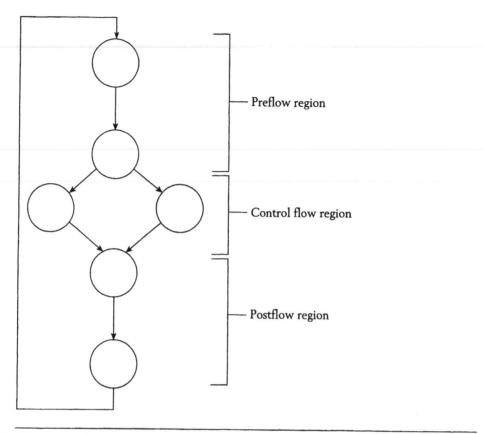

Figure 10.10 Software pipelining in the presence of control flow.

in the control flow region may not require that i_1 issue d cycles before the superinstruction. If i_2 has been scheduled on the kth cycle of the superinstruction, then i_1 can be issued as few as $d - k + 1$ cycles before the superinstruction. If $d - k + 1$ is negative, i_1 can be overlapped with the superinstruction if empty resources are available on both paths.

10.3 **Vector Unit Scheduling**

As a general rule, scheduling vector instructions is a much simpler task than scheduling an instruction unit. First, a vector instruction by definition involves the execution of many scalar instructions, all of which are pipelined as efficiently as possible through the hardware. As a result, just issuing a vector instruction already represents a significant speedup and efficient reordering. Second, a vector instruction generally takes so long to execute that it is impossible to keep all other execution units busy. The vector instruction is an umbrella whose cost hides all other instruction costs.

Nevertheless, there is some room for instruction scheduling on most vector processors. Vector processors commonly support *operation chaining* in hardware; on such processors a small amount of time spent reordering instructions can yield a tremendous improvement in the execution time of the program. Similarly, vector processors often operate as a memory-mapped coprocessor. Such coprocessors can often be sped up by careful scheduling of synchronization instructions. This section briefly discusses some important aspects of these scheduling opportunities.

10.3.1 Chaining

Given the length of time that a typical vector operation takes to complete plus the fact that vector units tend to have a number of separate execution units, a common optimization available on many vector units is *chaining*. Chaining is a hardware mechanism that recognizes when the output of one vector operation serves as the input to a different vector operation. In those cases, chaining hardware will cause the output of the first operation to feed directly to the execution unit for the second operation, essentially overlapping execution of the two instructions. To give a simple example:

```
vload  t1,a
vload  t2,b
vadd   t3,t1,t2
vstore t3,c
```

This fragment loads two vectors from memory, sums them, and stores the result to memory. The assumption is that there are two load pipes from memory, a and b (as indicated in the load instructions), and that each operates independently of the other. If each vector instruction is naively assumed to take 64 cycles and if the two loads are assumed to initiate simultaneously, a nonchained execution of this fragment will take 192 cycles: 64 to load the two vector registers, 64 to do the add, and 64 to do the store. A chained equivalent would take 66 cycles, almost three times as fast. Chained execution would have the vector add start on cycle 1 (assuming that the first elements from the vector load arrived in one cycle) and would start the vector store on cycle 2 (assuming the first add completed in one cycle). The loads, add, and store would all overlap execution in pipelined fashion.

Given that most vector units that implement chaining maintain a full scoreboard covering the vector registers and operation units, the burden of recognizing chaining opportunities generally falls upon the hardware (much as the burden of recognizing superscalar opportunities falls upon the hardware). However, some form of support is necessary from the compiler as well. In the worst case, the compiler must set special bits in instruction opcodes to notify the hardware that two operations are to be chained. Generally, however, it is only necessary to move the operations close enough together for the scoreboard to recognize the chaining opportunity.

When proximity is all that is required, generating chaining opportunities is simply a minor modification of instruction scheduling, upgraded with the capability of recalling and recognizing patterns that satisfy chaining constraints. Hazard detection at this point obviously requires full dependence analysis, since vectors rather than scalars are involved.

It might appear on first glance that obtaining an optimal use of chaining is trivial. In most practical cases, it is true that an optimal chaining tends to fall out from simple instruction scheduling. This is not guaranteed, however, as the following example illustrates:

```
i1   vload a,x(i)
i2   vload b,y(i)
i3   vadd  t1,a,b
i4   vload c,z(i)
i5   vmul  t2,c,t1
i6   vmul  t3,a,b
i7   vadd  t4,c,t3
```

Assume that this code is executed on a vector unit with two load pipes, one addition pipe and one multiplication pipe. As written, the first add will chain with the loads, the first multiply will chain with the third load, and the last add will chain with the last multiply. The overall computation will require three full vector operations. This is pretty good, but it is possible to do better by rearranging the code:

```
vload a,x(i)
vload b,y(i)
vadd  t1,a,b
vmul  t3,a,b
vload c,z(i)
vmul  t2,c,t1
vadd  t4,c,t3
```

In this version, the number of full vector operations has been reduced to two. The trick is to cluster any operations that rely on the same operation as input.

The chaining problem can be solved by using a variant of the weighted fusion algorithm introduced in Section 8.6.4. Ding and Kennedy [104] have introduced a version of this algorithm that takes resource constraints into account. This variant makes it possible to determine at every fusion step whether the fusion will create a group that requires too many resources. In the case of fusion, we want to group all the vector instructions that can be chained so long as we have enough resources to run the operations simultaneously in chained mode. For example, on a machine that has two load pipes, one store pipe, two addition units, and one multiplication unit, we would not want to try to chain more than two loads, two additions, one multiplication, and one store.

A useful property that is shared by the fusion algorithm in Section 8.6.3 and the constrained version is that, after fusion, weights are recomputed dynamically. This means that if an addition and multiplication are selected for chaining, a second load that is input to both the addition and multiplication will be given a higher weight after fusing those two instructions.

Using this strategy, the algorithm goes as follows:

1. Construct a dependence graph for the straight-line code to which chaining is to be applied.

2. Weight each edge with the length of the vector it represents. If this cannot be determined, use the full vector register length.

3. Apply the constrained weighted fusion algorithm to determine maximum fusion groups. At each step where the next fusion edge is selected, if several edges are tied for the heaviest weight, select one that is incident on the most recent fusion group, favoring the edge with the source and sink that are earliest in the original order.

If we apply this algorithm to the example at the beginning of this section, we begin by constructing the dependence graph shown in Figure 10.11, in which all edges have equal weight. Then fusion begins.

Initially, the algorithm chooses to group instruction 1 and instruction 3. It then groups instruction 2 with the first two to produce the graph in Figure 10.12.

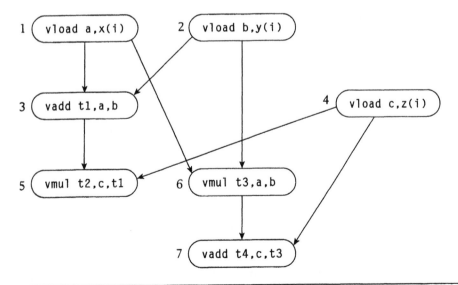

Figure 10.11 Dependence graph for chaining example.

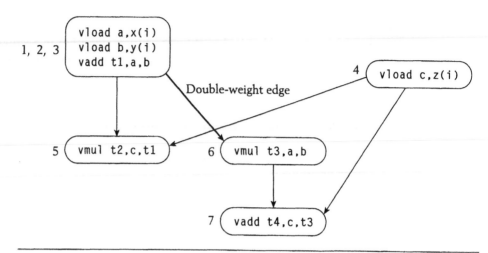

Figure 10.12 Dependence graph after partial chaining.

Note that reweighting after fusion has doubled the weight of the edge between the fusion group with instructions 1, 2, and 3 and instruction 6 because that instruction takes two inputs from the same group. Thus it will be chosen over instruction 5 to fuse next with the first group, which fills out all the resources for that group. The other three instructions will then be fused into a second group to produce the desired result.

10.3.2   Coprocessors

With many specialized applications, it is common to "attach" a processor tailored to accelerate specific parts of the application code. For instance, graphics coprocessors exist for many personal computers to off-load rendering and other basic graphic computations from the main processor, simultaneously accelerating its performance. Before floating-point and integer processors were integrated onto one chip, vector and floating-point coprocessors that were attached to standard machines were common. Currently, field programmable gate array (FPGA) technology makes it possible to dynamically create coprocessors specialized for key parts of any computation.

At one level, scheduling for coprocessors is similar to scheduling for VLIW or superscalar architectures. The coprocessor is just another functional unit that has a broader range of capabilities than the typical adder or multiplier unit used in fine-grained machines. As a general rule, the functions of the coprocessor are well defined, and it is easy to know which code should go onto the coprocessor and which should stay on the main processor; a graphics coprocessor, for instance, is generally expected to do graphics operations. However, there is one nuance that complicates the scheduling of coprocessors. Coprocessors are commonly attached to the system bus, and main processors generally invoke them via a "memory-mapped" interface. That is, the main processor signals the coprocessor of work to be done by storing magic values to magic memory locations; the coprocessor reads these values off the system bus to determine the work it is supposed to do. The coprocessor has access to main memory and values on the system bus, but the only internals it sees from the main processor are those the main processor sends it.

Because memory caches are attached to the central processor, the coprocessor cannot see into them, and similarly, the caches do not usually know of the existence of the coprocessor. As a result, when a coprocessor stores a computed value to memory, the updated value may not be immediately reflected into the caches on the central processor. Likewise, a store from the central processor may not immediately appear in main memory, which can cause the coprocessor to read an invalid value. One way of fixing this problem is to provide a special set of memory synchronization instructions that guarantee the memory is consistent with caches. One such instruction generally stalls the central processor until all writes it has issued have made it into main memory; another invalidates the caches so that new values are read from memory. Not so obviously, the scheme also requires an instruction to force a stall until reads are complete on each processor because a coprocessor may issue a read before the main processor issues a corresponding write, but the write gets through first. All of these instructions can be expensive, so using a minimal number of them is essential for fast execution.

Data dependence can be used to determine where wait instructions are required. When the source of a data dependence is executed on one processor and the sink is executed on the other, some form of memory synchronization is needed in between. If the dependence is a true dependence, then the main processor must ensure that all stores have completed on the source processor before the sink processor reads memory. If the dependence is an antidependence, the main processor must ensure that all reads have completed on the source processor before the write is issued on the sink processor. If the dependence is an output dependence, the central processor must ensure that the second store completes after the first. Since these waits are expensive, the compiler must minimize the number of them that appear in the instruction stream. The positioning of operations is also important, since many architectures guarantee that stores will make their way to memory within a given number of clocks. As a result, if the source and sink can be separated by enough other instructions, the correctness of the memory accesses can be guaranteed without an intervening wait.

Instruction position is important for a second reason: it can reduce the number of waits necessary. Consider the example in Figure 10.13. The first dependence can be covered with a wait in region 1 or in region 2; the second dependence can be covered with a wait in region 2 or in region 3. A naive placement would result in waits in both region 1 and region 3; an intelligent placement would result in a single wait in region 2, just before the load of A(I).

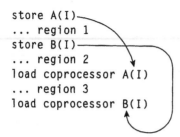

```
store A(I)
... region 1
store B(I)
... region 2
load coprocessor A(I)
... region 3
load coprocessor B(I)
```

Figure 10.13 Minimizing generated waits.

Within a basic block, minimizing waits is simple and can be done in a single pass. Starting at the beginning of the block, sources of edges are noted as instructions are examined. When the target of an uncovered edge is reached, a wait is inserted, and all edges whose sources have been seen so far are marked as covered, since the wait will protect all those edges. This algorithm is guaranteed to protect all edges within the basic block, since all sources and targets will be seen, thereby causing all edges to be covered.

It is not too difficult to see that this algorithm produces a minimal number of waits. The proof, only outlined here, involves attempting to remove one wait and rearrange the others to cover the exposed edges. Any motion that covers the exposed edge will uncover another edge. While the number of waits produced is minimal, the placement is not unique, and there are usually many solutions that produce the minimal number of waits. For instance, a symmetric solution is possible by starting at the end of the block and working upward, inserting waits at exposed sources as they are encountered. The advantage of moving downward is that it gives the greatest possible time between an offending memory access and its wait, thereby decreasing the possibility that the wait will be needed in architectures that guarantee a time limit on memory stores.

While a fairly simple algorithm will produce the minimal number of waits in the absence of control flow, minimizing waits in the presence of control flow is *NP*-complete. Thus a compiler must use a heuristic algorithm to produce a good solution.

The issue of synchronization between processors over memory accesses occurs in parallel processors as well as with coprocessors—symmetric, shared-memory multiprocessors are just a collection of equivalent coprocessors. Explicit scheduling for memory access is less of a concern to the compiler writer in those systems, however. Since hardware designers recognize that such systems will support multiple processors (they do not always know about coprocessors), they generally build support into the system bus to avoid many of these problems. Furthermore, barriers are always present on entering and exiting parallel regions, providing clear points where synchronization can be inserted. However, a number of strategies have been proposed for minimizing the amount of synchronization needed in parallel loops [62, 214].

10.4 **Summary**

In this chapter we have examined two problems associated with scheduling that can be attacked with the help of dependence.

1. *Instruction scheduling* on uniprocessors involves minimizing the number of cycles used by a VLIW or superscalar processor to perform a given set of operations. It is typically performed by constructing a dependence graph among the instructions and applying a scheduling algorithm to the resulting graph. Three different approaches were presented in the chapter. *List scheduling* attempts to find the best schedule for a single block of straight-line code. *Trace scheduling* extends list scheduling to code with control flow by scheduling single control flow paths, called *traces*, one at a time and inserting code to fix the resulting interface problems. *Kernel scheduling* or *software pipelining* attempts to minimize the running time of loops by minimizing the number of cycles in the computational kernel that executes the body of the loop once steady-state execution is achieved.

2. *Vector instruction scheduling* attempts to minimize the impact of delays due to vector start-up time by overlapping vector instructions with one another wherever possible. The chapter presents an algorithm for *vector chaining* that uses a variant of weighted fusion to accomplish the maximum overlap.

All of these problems are *NP*-complete under fairly simple assumptions, so the algorithms presented are heuristics.

10.5 **Case Studies**

Since it was primarily a source-to-source transformation system, PFC did not perform any kind of instruction scheduling. The Ardent Titan compiler, on the other hand, produced code for a RISC processor and an associated vector unit.

One of the major challenges for the original Titan architecture was floating-point execution, both scalar and vector. Because the floating-point unit on the Titan 2000 was an asynchronous, memory-mapped coprocessor, it faced exactly the challenges listed in Section 10.3.2. The compiler was responsible for inserting wait instructions to synchronize memory access between the floating-point unit and scalar unit for both vector and scalar floating-point instructions. The compiler also had to synchronize memory access between loads and stores within the floating-point unit proper. The algorithms used to insert the waits are basically the ones described in this chapter.

The original choice to do scalar floating-point operations inside the vector unit was not an easy decision and was dictated by a number of considerations, most of which involved the hardware design. At the time the design decision was made, the belief was that synchronization between the floating-point unit and the scalar unit would be an issue only with vector instructions, since (supposedly) data accessed as floating-point numbers would not be accessed as integers. Memory synchronization involving scalar floating-point loads and stores outside of loops were believed to be infrequent enough not to be an issue.

The decision to do all floating-point operations in the coprocessor turned out to be one that met with mixed success. Inside loops, where the control and data flow were clearly understood by the compiler, the decision was a clear win. Table 10.1 shows the results of the Titan compiler on the Livermore loops, which are a mixture of scalar and vector computations representative of the workload at Livermore National Laboratory. The vector kernels are identified in the next to last column; when vectorization was turned on, it achieved dramatic speedups on the Titan.

However, Table 10.1 is intended to show that even the scalar kernels show a significant speedup on the Titan system. The Titan compilers supported an option that invoked dependence analysis in the support of scalar optimization but suppressed vector code generation. The columns labeled "O1 Megaflops" and "O1 with Dependence" show the achieved megaflops on each kernel for scalar optimizations with and without dependence. With dependence off, the principal scalar optimizations were strength reduction and coprocessor instruction scheduling as described in Section 10.3.2. When dependence was not available, wait minimization was restricted to loads and stores of scalars. With dependence turned on, this optimization was extended to array variables. In addition, the compiler was able to use scalar replacement techniques from Section 8.3 to hike most memory references into registers, significantly reducing the number of waits required to synchronize the memory access. As a result, both the integer and the floating-point unit were able to run asynchronously at full speed, producing near vector speeds on nonvectorizable kernels.

For the kernels with significant improvements using dependence, the last column indicates which optimizations were critical to the improvement, where "SR" denotes scalar replacement, "IS" denotes instruction scheduling, "STR" denotes strength reduction, and "LI" denotes loop invariance recognition—an optimization that eliminates loops around statements that perform the same computation, storing into the same memory location, on each iteration (opportunities for use of this optimization occur with surprising frequency).

Despite these results, the synchronization issue was a big one in the Titan system. The belief that data was only accessed as either integer or floating point was wrong—particularly within mathematical libraries, where floating-point numbers are commonly dissected into exponent and mantissa. Also, synchronization between scalar floating-point accesses outside of loops was a significant issue in many codes. Without the dependence analysis available for loops, the code generator basically assumed that all floating-point accesses could be dependent, and the resulting wait insertion significantly degraded program performance. Another issue not fully appreciated at the beginning was the time and effort required to debug programs that were missing necessary waits. The behavior of such programs was highly dependent on the machine load and memory context, so typically they

Table 10.1 Scalar performance improvements on Titan due to dependence

Kernel	O1 megaflops	O1 with dependence	Percent improved	Vectorizable?	Key optimizations
11	0.4514	1.3558	200.1	No	SR, IS
12	0.4397	1.2560	185.6	Yes	IS
5	0.7301	1.9633	168.9	No	SR, IS
10	0.5136	1.3211	157.2	Yes	IS
21	0.6787	1.6991	150.3	Yes	STR, IS
6	0.6894	1.7203	149.5	Yes	SR, IS
1	1.2589	2.1979	74.5	Yes	IS
13	0.2954	0.4237	43.4	Yes	STR, IS
23	1.8059	2.4598	36.2	No	SR, IS
2	1.1035	1.4349	30.0	Yes	IS
9	1.5206	1.7720	16.5	Yes	IS
20	1.6663	1.8809	12.9	No	SR, 1S
7	2.3657	2.6227	10.9	Yes	IS
19	1.6792	1.9030	7.4	No	SR
14	0.4565	0.4775	4.6	Yes	IS
15	0.7601	0.7908	4.0	Yes	LI
18	1.8216	1.8262	0.3	Yes	
3	1.9713	1.9684	−0.1	Yes	
24	0.3825	0.3828	−0.1	Yes	
17	0.9663	0.9644	−0.1	No	
22	0.4924	0.4914	−0.2	Yes	
4	1.8936	1.8873	−0.3	Yes	
16	0.8522	0.8479	−0.5	No	
8	2.0733	1.9089	−7.9	Yes	
Mean	1.1195	1.4773	32.0		
Geometric	0.9346	1.2959	38.7		
Harmonic	0.7724	1.0786	39.6		
Median	0.9093	1.7097	88.0		

would run correctly nine times out of ten. Getting the correct wait insertion eventually involved the development of a number of tools to support the debugging effort of finding missing waits in compiled programs.

Because of these issues and because of changes in hardware design, the second-generation Titan architecture, the Titan 3000, did scalar floating point in the integer unit, thereby requiring waits only for synchronizing vector instructions. The result was an extremely efficient compiler hardware system, as indicated by the Livermore loop results in Table 10.1. Since waits were only necessary in vector loops where the compiler had full knowledge of the control and data flow, the resulting performance was good across the spectrum of loop kernels.

The Titan compiler implemented two other interesting optimizations for scheduling instructions. One was necessitated specifically by the memory banking structure inside the Titan. The Titan was heavily geared toward floating-point operations, and the load-store architecture was focused on 64-bit quantities, being banked at that size. Since integers were only 32 bits long, a contiguous vector integer load or store was a bad thing to do on the Titan because the memory bank was still busy with the first of a pair of integers at the time the load or store for the second was issued. As a result, the hardware would stall until the bank had completed its operation, causing a contiguous vector integer load or store to run three to five times slower than the equivalent double-precision load or store. The compiler addressed this issue by splitting vector loops involving contiguous integer operations into two loops involving stride-two operations, where this split was safe. The safety of this operation was easily determined based on the dependences in the loop and, when it was permissible, resulted in a factor of three speedup in vector integer code.

The second optimization, which has more general applicability, involved reduction operations. On the Titan, and on most other architectures that support vector reduction operations, the results of a reduction went into a set of accumulators. Before the reduction was initiated, it was necessary to initialize the accumulators to the proper values, and at the end of the reduction, it was necessary to move the results of the reduction out of the accumulators.

Experience with the Titan compilers establishes the value of dependence as a vehicle for summarizing execution constraints and as an indicator of the memory locations that will be most frequently referenced in the program. The value of this analysis has long been recognized for vector and parallel machines. In addition, the Titan showed that these concepts are also valuable for less radical machines—those with floating-point coprocessors, unsynchronized memory accesses, and deep memory hierarchies. Given the prevalence of new microprocessor designs with similar features—the Sony Playstation 2 and the PowerPC G4, to name just two—it is clear that dependence will continue to be a useful tool into the foreseeable future.

10.6 Historical Comments and References

List scheduling has a long history in the computer science literature. It has been studied in the context of microcode compaction, instruction scheduling, and task scheduling. This work is effectively summarized in Fisher's Ph.D. thesis [113], which also presents the *highest levels first* (HLF) heuristic described in Section 10.2.3. This heuristic was also discussed by Adam, Chandy, and Dickson [2]. Basic block schedulers that use list scheduling have been described by Touzeau [258], Gibbons and Muchnick [120], and Warren [268]. A proof that list scheduling is *NP*-complete appears in the book by Garey and Johnson [119]. An excellent overview of scheduling strategies can be found in the book by Muchnick [218].

Trace scheduling was developed by Fisher [113, 114]. It was first implemented commercially in the Multiflow compiler, which was based on a Ph.D. thesis by Ellis [109], carried out under the supervision of Fisher at Yale.

Kernel scheduling, also known as *software pipelining* [72] or *cyclic scheduling*, was originally developed by Rau and his colleagues [232, 233], drawing on earlier work by Davidson and others [98, 99, 100] on the design of hardware pipelines. This original formulation included the concepts of minimum iteration interval based on the lower bounds due to resource constraints and data dependence cycles. These ideas were later refined by Hsu [153, 154], Lam [193, 194], and Su and Wang [255]. Hsu and Lam independently proved that the problem of scheduling with resource constraints on loops with arbitrary recurrences is *NP*-complete [153, 193].

Rau and Fisher [231] provide an excellent overview of instruction-level parallelism and software approaches to scheduling.

Exercises

10.1 Construct an example where simple list scheduling, with the *highest levels first* heuristic improvement of always favoring a precomputed critical path, produces a suboptimal result.

10.2 Instruction scheduling is performed at the assembly code level after code generation. Why is it not a good idea to schedule at the source level and then generate code?

10.3 Dependence analysis for array accesses needs to know the shape of array references and their enclosing loop nests. Without such source-level information, how can you determine data dependences among memory loads and stores? What are the problems of inaccurate dependence analysis?

10.4 Kernel scheduling needs to find the largest slope of all dependence cycles of a loop. The algorithm in Figure 10.8 uses an all-pairs shortest-path algorithm. How does it find the largest slope? Can you think of another method to find the largest slope? Can you find an efficient way to find the dependence cycle that has the smallest slope? What is the complexity of these methods?

10.5 On modern processors with multiple levels of cache, the latency of a memory reference varies depending on whether the data is in cache and which level cache it is in. What are the problems if the varied memory latency is not taken into account in scheduling? How could a compiler determine the likely latency for a memory reference?

10.6 Instruction scheduling works well when the latency for memory operations is small. Will it still work well if the latency is large, for example, over 200 machine cycles for a memory load? What remedy do you suggest?

CHAPTER 11

Interprocedural Analysis and Optimization

11.1 Introduction

As machines and languages have become more complicated, compiler technology has necessarily become more sophisticated. With the advent of vector and parallel computers, single-procedure analysis is no longer enough to produce high-quality parallelized code. In this chapter we introduce some of the problems that can be solved with the help of an interprocedural analysis and optimization system. We also present methods for the solution of these problems, summarizing research on interprocedural compilation over the past 15 years.

We begin with a definition of the terms "interprocedural analysis" and "interprocedural optimization." *Interprocedural analysis* refers to gathering information about the entire program instead of a single procedure. This is usually comparable to the sort of information that a single-procedure data flow analysis system would collect. Examples of interprocedural analysis problems are determining the variables that are modified as side effects of a procedure call and finding whether a given pair of variables might be aliased to one another on entry to a given procedure.

An *interprocedural optimization* is a program transformation that involves more than one procedure in a program. The most familiar example is *inlining*, by which the body of a procedure is substituted at the point of invocation. Although interprocedural optimizations typically modify more than one subroutine, it is reasonable to view any optimization that is based on interprocedural knowledge—gathered by an interprocedural analysis phase—as an interprocedural optimization. However, for the purposes of this chapter we will adhere to the narrower view.

11.2 Interprocedural Analysis

The value of procedures for programming is that they hide unnecessary details from the programmer. A corollary is that they also hide details from the compiler. However, in this case, the details may not be so unnecessary, as they may provide opportunities for optimization. The goal of interprocedural analysis is to uncover enough of these details to support advanced optimization strategies.

11.2.1 Interprocedural Problems

To illustrate the need for interprocedural analysis methods we will introduce several important problems through a series of examples.

Modification and Reference Side Effects

We begin with a simple vectorization problem. Suppose we have the following code fragment:

```
      COMMON X, Y
      . . .
      DO 100 I = 1, N
S₀       CALL S
50       X(I) = X(I) + Y(I)
100 CONTINUE
```

Without some sort of interprocedural optimization, it is impossible to vectorize the call, but might it be possible to vectorize the assignment at statement 50? Since both X and Y are in COMMON, we must be concerned with side effects to these variables due to the call at S_0. A statement can be vectorized if it is legal to distribute the loop around the two statements S_0 and 50. In turn, this is possible if there is no cycle of dependences involving both statements. We can be sure that there is no such dependence cycle if the call meets both of the following criteria:

1. It neither uses nor modifies X.
2. It does not modify Y.

The first condition ensures that there can be no dependence cycle involving both the call and statement 50 due to variable X. The second condition rules out a dependence cycle due to Y.

To address this problem, we introduce the interprocedural MOD and REF problems.

DEFINITION
11.1

At a given call site *s*, the *modification side effect set* MOD(*s*) is the set of all variables that may be modified as a side effect of the call at *s*. The *reference side effect set* REF(*s*) is the set of all variables that may be referenced as a side effect of the call at *s*.

With these definitions, we can now formally restate the condition under which the assignment statement above can be vectorized, namely:

$$X \notin \text{REF}(S_0) \text{ and } X \notin \text{MOD}(S_0) \text{ and } Y \notin \text{MOD}(S_0).$$

Alias Analysis

Suppose we have the following subroutine:

```
        SUBROUTINE S(A,X,N)
          REAL A(*), X, Y
          COMMON Y
          DO 100 I = 1, N
S₀            X = X + Y * A(I)
100       CONTINUE
        END
```

In compiling this loop for any machine, it would be efficient to keep both variables X and Y in registers throughout the duration of the loop, without storing X until the loop is completed. This looks straightforward, but what if subroutine S is invoked by "CALL S(A,Y,N)"? In this case Y is *aliased* to X, so by not storing X on every iteration, we may be overlooking required updates to the variable Y within the loop.[1]

To avoid problems like this, the compiler must determine when two variables might be aliased to one another on entry to a given subroutine.

DEFINITION
11.2

For a procedure *p* and a formal parameter *x* passed to *p*, the *alias set* ALIAS(*p*,*x*) is the set of variables that may refer to the same location as *x* on entry to *p*.

In the example above, X and Y may be kept in registers without storing to memory if $Y \notin \text{ALIAS}(S,X)$.

---

1. Knowledgeable readers will comment that the Fortran standard defines this usage to be illegal, saying that if two variables are aliases on entry to a loop, then the program is not standard conforming if the subroutine stores into either. Although this is an easy escape from the specific problem presented, it only works for Fortran, as C has no such prohibition.

Call Graph Construction

The call graph of a program is a graph that models the calling relationships between procedures in a program.

**DEFINITION
11.3**

The *call graph* of a program is a graph $G = (N,E)$ where the vertices in N represent procedures in the program and the edges in E represent possible calls.

It is common for each distinct call site in a program to be represented by a distinct edge, in which case the call graph is actually a multigraph. We will adopt this convention in the remainder of the chapter.

The accuracy of the call graph directly affects the precision of the data flow information produced. However, construction of a precise call graph is in itself an interprocedural analysis problem. In a language in which each call must be to a named constant procedure, the call graph is easy to construct—you need only examine the body of each procedure p, entering for each call site s in p an edge (p,q) to the procedure q called at s.

However, a precise call graph is more difficult to construct in a language that permits procedure variables. Even in Fortran, where there are no assignable procedure variables, problems arise due to *procedure parameters*—formal parameters that may be bound to procedure names at the point of call. Consider the following example:

```
        SUBROUTINE S(X,P)
S₀          CALL P(X)
            RETURN
        END
```

The question is, What procedure or procedures may be called at statement S_0? In other words, what values can P have at this call site? We could attempt to answer this question by examining the actual parameters at all the call sites for subroutine S, but any actual parameter could itself be a procedure parameter. Thus we must propagate procedure constants through the call graph before we can finish building it.

**DEFINITION
11.4**

For a given procedure p and call site s within p, the *call set* CALL(s) is the set of all procedures that may be invoked at s.

Although it is stated as a property of call sites, CALL(s) is not a side effect problem. It is really asking what procedures can be passed to formal parameters on entry to the procedure containing s. Because it depends on the context in which the procedure containing s is invoked, it resembles alias analysis more closely than any side effect problem.

Live and Use Analysis

An important data flow problem that has been studied extensively in the literature is the analysis of *live variables*. A variable x is said to be *live* at a given point s in a program if there is a control flow path from s to a use of x that contains no definition of x prior to the use.

One important application of live analysis is in determining whether a private variable in a parallel loop needs to be assigned to a global variable at the end of the loop's execution. Consider the following code fragment:

```
DO I = 1, N
   T = X(I) * C
   A(I) = T + B(I)
   C(I) = T + D(I)
ENDDO
```

This loop can be parallelized by making T a local variable in the loop. However, if T is used later in the program before being redefined, the parallelized program must assign the last value of the local version of T to the global version of T. In other words, the code must be transformed as follows:

```
PARALLEL DO I = 1, N
   PRIVATE t
   t = X(I) * C
   A(I) = t + B(I)
   C(I) = t + D(I)
   IF (I.EQ.N) T = t
ENDDO
```

Here we are using the typographic convention that variables introduced in small letters are compiler generated.

This code could be simplified if we could determine that variable T is not live on exit from the original loop. In this case, the conditional at the end of the loop could be eliminated to produce

```
PARALLEL DO I = 1, N
   PRIVATE t
   t = X(I) * C
   A(I) = t + B(I)
   C(I) = t + D(I)
ENDDO
```

Although live analysis can itself be viewed as an interprocedural problem, it is conveniently dealt with in terms of another interprocedural problem. *Use analysis* is the problem of determining whether there is an *upwards-exposed use* of a variable on some path through a procedure invoked at a particular call site *s*. An upwards-exposed use is one that is not preceded by a definition of the variable on some path to the use from the point of invocation.

DEFINITION
11.5

For a given call site *s*, which invokes procedure *p*, the *use side effect set* USE(*s*) is the set of variables that have an upwards-exposed use in *p*.

Given this definition, we can give a more formal specification of when a variable is live. A variable x is *live* at a call site s if $x \in$ USE(s) or if there is a path through the procedure called at s that does not assign a new value to x and x is live at some control flow successor of s.

Kill Analysis

Problems like REF, MOD, and USE ask questions about what might happen on some path through a called subprocedure. It is often useful to ask about what *must* happen on every path through a procedure. The following example illustrates this:

```
L     DO I = 1, N
S₀       CALL INIT(T,I)
         T = T + B(I)
         A(I) = A(I) + T
      ENDDO
```

There are two problems that might keep this loop from being correctly parallelized. First, not knowing what the subroutine INIT does, we must assume that it assigns variables in a way that creates a cycle of dependences. One way to do this would be to use and then assign a variable that is global to the program. For example, if INIT were defined as in the following code, parallelization would be precluded:

```
SUBROUTINE INIT(T,I)
   REAL T
   INTEGER I
   COMMON X(100)
   T = X(I)
   X(I+1) = T + X(1)
END
```

Here INIT creates a cycle of dependences involving the COMMON array X, with respect to the loop in the calling program.

However, even if we can prove that the loop does not modify any global variables or even any static local (i.e., "SAVE") variables, the call presents a more subtle problem. If this loop is to be parallelized, it must be possible to recognize that variable T can be made private to each iteration. This is possible, for example, if subroutine INIT is simply there for the purpose of initializing T, as in

```
SUBROUTINE INIT(T,I)
   REAL T
   INTEGER I
   COMMON X(100)
   T = X(I)
END
```

Here T is initialized before being used on every iteration of the loop. Thus it is not involved in any kind of carried dependence within the loop and may be made private.

How can we discover this fact? Certainly, MOD can tell us that no global variables are modified within the subroutine, and we assume that a similar analysis could be used to preclude the possibility that any static local variable in INIT is used before being modified. Therefore, the key to determining that the loop can be parallelized is to establish that variable T is assigned before being used *on every path* through INIT.

The problem of discovering whether a variable is assigned on every path through a called procedure is known as KILL because an assignment is said to "kill" a previous value of the variable.

DEFINITION 11.6   For a given call site s, the *kill side effect set* KILL(p) is the set of variables that are assigned on every path through the procedure p invoked at s and procedures invoked from within p.

Assuming that there are no global variables in MOD(p) and that p does not use any static local variables before they are assigned, then the loop L can be parallelized if variable T is killed on every path through the procedure called at S_0 and there is no path into that procedure on which a use appears before any kill. This can be expressed formally as

$$T \in (\text{KILL}(S_0) \cap \neg\text{USE}(S_0)).$$

Assuming that call site s is in a block by itself, it is possible to define LIVE(s) within the procedure containing s as follows:

$$\text{LIVE}(s) = \text{USE}(s) \cup \left(\neg\text{KILL}(s) \cap \bigcup_{b \in succ(s)} \text{LIVE}(b)\right) \qquad (11.1)$$

This generalizes the live computation to the interprocedural case if we know, by some additional analysis, the set of variables that are live on exit from the procedure.

Constant Propagation

Constant propagation, one of the most important problems in single-procedure data flow analysis, is also an important interprocedural problem. Consider the following program, which is abstracted from code in LINPACK:

```
      SUBROUTINE S(A,B,N,IS,I1)
         REAL A(*), B(*)
L        DO I = 0, N - 1
S₀          A(IS*I+I1) = A(IS*I+I1) + B(I+1)
         ENDDO
      END
```

If we wish to vectorize loop L in this subroutine, a problem arises because the variable IS might take on the value 0. If that is so, there is an output dependence. In that case statement S_0 is actually a reduction and cannot be vectorized using the usual techniques. Although we could test for this situation at run time, we can avoid it entirely if we can determine that, on every invocation of subroutine S in the program containing it, the value of IS is always 1 (the most common case).[2]

DEFINITION 11.7	Given a program and a procedure p within that program, the *set of interprocedural constants* CONST(p) contains the variables that have known constant values on every invocation of p. For a variable $x \in$ CONST(p), *valin*(x,p) is a function returning the value of x on entry to p.

Although even the single-procedure constant propagation problem is intractable, approximate solutions in single procedures have been shown to be effective [273]. Similarly, approximate solutions of the interprocedural constant propagation problem have been shown to determine many facts that are useful for optimization and parallelization [127, 136].

11.2.2 Interprocedural Problem Classification

We will now explore various classifications of interprocedural data flow problems. These classifications are useful because problems in the same class can generally be solved by the same algorithmic approach.

---

2. Barring that, it would be vectorizable if it can be established that IS ≠ 0 every time the loop is entered. Analysis of predicates like this can also be handled by a variation of constant propagation.

May and Must Problems

We have already seen that there is a distinction between problems that ask whether some event "may" happen or "must" happen. MOD, REF, and USE are *may problems* because they compute sets of variables that may be modified, may be referenced, or may be used before being defined, respectively. On the other hand, KILL is a *must problem* because it computes a set of variables that must be killed.

Although this distinction has been extensively discussed in the literature, it is not a deep one because the converse of every may problem is a must problem and vice versa. For example, ¬MOD(s) is the set of all variables that are not in MOD(s). Therefore, the ¬MOD problem seeks to find those variables that must not be modified as a side effect of a given call site. Thus ¬MOD is a must problem. Similarly, ¬REF is also a must problem. On the other hand, ¬KILL seeks to find for each call site s in the program the set of variables that may pass unmodified through the procedure being invoked. Thus the converse of KILL, a must problem, is a may problem. Since the solution to any set problem may be converted to the solution of its converse by subtraction from the universal set (usually bit-vector complementation), which takes time linear in the number of answer sets, there is no difference in complexity of a must problem and its corresponding may problem.

Flow-Sensitive and Flow-Insensitive Problems

Banning [37] introduced a seemingly related notion of flow-sensitive and flow-insensitive problems. Intuitively, a *flow-sensitive* problem is one whose solution requires tracing individual control flow paths through the body of the subroutine being called. A *flow-insensitive* problem, on the other hand, can be solved by examination of the body of called subroutines without regard to control flow. Thus, MOD and REF are flow-insensitive problems because, assuming all code in a subroutine is reachable, any modification of a variable x in the body of a subroutine p means that $x \in$ MOD(s) for any call site s that invokes p. On the other hand, KILL is a flow-sensitive problem because, for a given variable x, its solution requires checking every path through the procedure body to ensure that it contains a definition of x.

Banning [37] presents a more formal definition of flow-sensitive and flow-insensitive problems based on how solutions on subregions of a call graph would be composed into solutions for a larger region. Consider the two call graph regions depicted in Figure 11.1.

Suppose we have MOD for each subregion A and B of regions R_1 and R_2. Then we can compose these into solutions for the whole regions as follows:

$$\text{MOD}(R_1) = \text{MOD}(A) \cup \text{MOD}(B)$$

$$\text{MOD}(R_2) = \text{MOD}(A) \cup \text{MOD}(B)$$

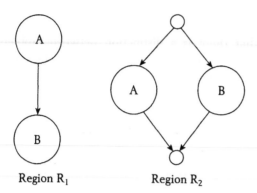

Region R_1 Region R_2

Figure 11.1 Call graph subregions.

This is because in either decomposition, a variable may be modified if it may be modified in either subregion. There is a similar pair of equations for REF:

$$\text{REF}(R_1) = \text{REF}(A) \cup \text{REF}(B)$$
$$\text{REF}(R_2) = \text{REF}(A) \cup \text{REF}(B)$$

Now let us carry out the same exercise for KILL. In the case of region R_1, a variable is killed if it is killed in the first region or if it is killed in the second region:

$$\text{KILL}(R_1) = \text{KILL}(A) \cup \text{KILL}(B)$$

In the case of region R_2, a variable must be killed in both regions to be in KILL(R_2):

$$\text{KILL}(R_2) = \text{KILL}(A) \cap \text{KILL}(B)$$

The equations for USE are equally easy to develop:

$$\text{USE}(R_1) = \text{USE}(A) \cup (\neg\text{KILL}(A) \cap \text{USE}(B))$$
$$\text{USE}(R_2) = \text{USE}(A) \cup \text{USE}(B)$$

Only this second equation is the same as the corresponding equation for MOD and REF.

In examining these equations, we notice that the equations for MOD and REF use only set union as a connector, while the equations for KILL and USE are more complicated, using other connectors and often other local sets. This leads us to the following definition.

DEFINITION **11.8**	An interprocedural data flow problem is *flow insensitive* if and only if, on the parameter-free version of the problem, the value of the solution on both sequentially and alternatively composed regions (R_1 and R_2 of Figure 11.1) is determined by taking the union of the solutions for the subregions.

The literature on optimization sometimes refers to *flow-insensitive analysis* of a flow-sensitive problem. Our interpretation of this term is that it refers to approximating a flow-sensitive problem with a flow-insensitive one. As an example, suppose you wished to approximate a solution to the USE problem with the solution to one or more flow-insensitive problems. Note that most optimizations will be performed when it is known that a variable is not in USE(p) for a particular procedure p called from within the procedure being optimized. Therefore, we wish any approximation APUSE to be conservative in the sense that it contain all of USE:

$$\text{USE}(p) \subseteq \text{APUSE}(p) \text{ or } \neg\text{APUSE}(p) \subseteq \neg\text{USE}(p)$$

If this is the case we will never depend on an untrue fact. One possible approximation is given by

$$\text{APUSE}(p) = \text{REF}(p)$$

which is clearly a superset of USE(p) and can be computed by solving a flow-insensitive problem. This might be useful because, as we shall see, flow-insensitive problems are easier to solve than flow-sensitive ones. However, we do not recommend the use of approximations like this one because more precise approximations can be computed in reasonable time using flow-sensitive analysis.

Side Effect Problems versus Propagation Problems

A final classification of interprocedural problems is by direction of data flow. Some interprocedural problems ask what may or must happen as a side effect of a procedure call that is about to be made. This class, which we refer to as *side effect problems*, includes MOD, REF, KILL, and USE. Problems of this sort are analogous to the backward data flow problems of single-procedure analysis.

A second class of problems asks what conditions may or must hold upon entry to the current procedure (which presumably we are interested in optimizing). We call these *propagation problems*. They include ALIAS, CALLS, and CONST. The method we developed for classifying side effect problems as flow sensitive or flow insensitive will not work for propagation problems because these problems look back up the call chain. However, it is generally agreed that the ALIAS problem for Fortran is flow insensitive since aliases can only be introduced through the use of reference formal parameters. Thus, flow through a subroutine to a call site is unimportant because aliases can only be introduced at procedure invocation.

On the other hand, the constant propagation problem for Fortran is flow sensitive because, for a constant to propagate to a called procedure, the variable must receive the same constant value on every path through every procedure in the call chain. By the same argument, alias analysis for languages like C with pointer assignment is also flow sensitive.

The breakdown of problems in the two dimensions is summarized in Table 11.1. The classification into flow sensitive and flow insensitive is an important one because Banning established, by providing an algorithm, that flow-insensitive problems can be solved in time that is polynomial in the size of the call graph [37], while Myers showed that flow-sensitive problems are intractable in the presence of aliasing and arbitrary nesting [220].

11.2.3 Flow-Insensitive Side Effect Analysis

We now turn to the solution of the flow-insensitive side effect analysis problems. Throughout this section, we use the modification side effect analysis (MOD) problem as our example. The reference side effect analysis (REF) problem can be solved using exactly the same approach.

Assumptions

We begin by establishing a set of assumptions that are representative characteristics of Fortran and, in some cases, C. First, we assume that there is no procedure nesting—that is, variables are subdivided into local and global sets. Local variables are known only within their home procedure, and global variables are known in every procedure. Although this might seem restrictive, the methods we will introduce here have easy extensions to the case of general nesting.

A second assumption, already hinted at, is that all parameters are passed by reference and that there are no pointer variables. The purpose of this restriction is to simplify the aliasing patterns that the algorithms must deal with. Under this restriction, aliases can only be introduced at call sites. Although both Fortran 90 and C have pointer variables, this assumption is valid for Fortran 77, which is the input language for most automatic parallelization systems.

Even though Fortran 77 does not support recursion, the algorithms presented here work correctly in the presence of recursive procedure calls. We do, however, make an assumption about the size of parameter lists to procedures, namely, that

Table 11.1 Interprocedural problem classification

Problem type	Propagation	Side effect
Flow insensitive	ALIAS, CALLS	MOD, REF
Flow sensitive	CONST	KILL, USE

the maximum number of formal parameters to a procedure does not grow with the size of the program. In other words, programmers do not typically deal with the increasing complexity of a large program by increasing the complexity of the procedure interfaces. Thus we will assume that there exists a constant μ, such that the number of formal parameters in any procedure p is less than or equal to μ.

MOD Problem Formulation

The goal is to compute, for each call site s in the program, the set MOD(s) that contains every variable that may be modified as a side effect of the procedure call at s. Our first step is to note that we can simplify the problem by disregarding potential aliases. Specifically, we will compute the set DMOD(s), the *direct modification side effect set*, which contains all variables visible at s that are directly modified as a side effect of the call. DMOD(s) may be smaller than MOD(s) because it does not take into account the fact that a variable x that is directly modified as a side effect may have several possible aliases at the point of call. Each of these aliases must be in the final MOD(s) if the solution is to be precise. However, once DMOD(s) has been computed, it can be updated to MOD(s) with the help of the ALIAS sets described in Section 11.2.1.

Recall that for a given procedure p, ALIAS(p,x) contains the set of all variables that may be aliased to x on entry to p. Given these sets, we can update DMOD(s) to MOD(s) according to the following formula:

$$\text{MOD}(s) = \text{DMOD}(s) \cup \bigcup_{x \in \text{DMOD}(s)} \text{ALIAS}(p, x) \qquad (11.2)$$

where p is the procedure containing call site s. Construction of ALIAS(p,x) will be discussed in Section 11.2.4.

We will compute DMOD(s) for each call site by first computing, for each procedure p in the program, the set GMOD(p), called the *general modification side effect*. GMOD(p) contains the set of global variables and formal parameters of p that are modified, either directly or indirectly, as a result of the invocation of p. Once these sets are available, we can compute DMOD(s) by the following formula:

$$\text{DMOD}(s) = \{v \,|\, s \text{ invokes } p, v \xrightarrow{s} w \text{ and } w \in \text{GMOD}(p)\} \qquad (11.3)$$

where $v \xrightarrow{s} w$ means that at call site s actual parameter v is bound to formal parameter w of the called procedure or v and w are references to the same global variable. (In other words, in this formulation, a global variable is viewed as a kind of parameter to a called procedure.)

We can illustrate the definitions of DMOD and GMOD by an example. If we have a call site

$$S_0 \quad \text{CALL P(A,B,C)}$$

where subroutine P is defined

```
SUBROUTINE P(X,Y,Z)
    INTEGER X, Y, Z

    X = X * Z
    Y = Y * Z
END
```

then $\mathrm{GMOD}(P) = \{X,Y\}$ and $\mathrm{DMOD}(S_0) = \{A,B\}$.

Equation 11.3 reduces the DMOD problem to computing, for every procedure p in the program, the set $\mathrm{GMOD}(p)$ of variables that may be changed as a side effect of invoking p. Generally, $\mathrm{GMOD}(p)$ will contain two types of variables:

1. Those that are explicitly modified in the body of procedure p
2. Those that are modified as a side effect of some procedure invoked in the body of p

Let $\mathrm{IMOD}(p)$, the *immediate modification side effect set*, denote the set of variables explicitly modified in p. Then the following formula holds:

$$\mathrm{GMOD}(p) = \mathrm{IMOD}(p) \cup \bigcup_{s=(p,q)} \{z \mid z \overset{s}{\to} w \text{ and } w \in \mathrm{GMOD}(q)\} \qquad (11.4)$$

Note that the union is over all call sites s within p.

Problem Decomposition

The system of data flow equations in Equation 11.4 can be solved by the iterative method of data flow analysis. However, the solution may take a long time because the system does not satisfy the conditions under which the iterative method can be guaranteed to converge rapidly [164]. Furthermore, it is not formulated in a way that permits the use of a fast elimination method [125]. Fast solution methods rely on being able to limit the number of times that the analysis must traverse a loop in the problem graph. For flow-insensitive interprocedural analysis, the problem graph is the call graph, so convergence problems are limited to recursive regions.

A closer examination of the problem with recursion reveals that it is related to reference formal parameters. Consider the following example:

```
SUBROUTINE P(F₀,F₁,F₂,....,Fₙ)
    INTEGER X, F₀, F₁, F₂,....,Fₙ
    . . .
S₀      F₀ = some expression
    . . .
```

S_1 CALL P(F$_1$,F$_2$,....,F$_n$,X)

           · · ·

        END

In this example it is possible to see why, in the general case, an analysis routine must iterate around the recursive cycle an unbounded number of times. The question being asked is, How many of the parameters of subroutine P may be modified as a side effect of invoking P? Clearly, F_0 can be modified at statement S_0, but we have to examine the recursive call at S_1 to discover that F_1 is passed to F_0, so it too can be modified. One more time around the recursive loop reveals that F_2 can also be modified. This procedure continues until it is discovered that F_n—the last parameter—may also be modified. If n is unbounded, the number of iterations over the recursive cycle is unbounded as well.

These observations make it clear why we wished to assume an upper bound on the number of parameters to any subroutine—it permits us to establish a constant upper bound on the number of iterations required for the process to converge. However, we can achieve a better time bound by decomposing the problem further, treating side effects to reference parameters separately from side effects to global variables. This is achieved by introducing an extended version of the immediate modification side effect set IMOD(p), called IMOD$^+$(p), which will contain all of IMOD(p) plus all those variables that may be modified as a result of side effects to reference formal parameters of procedures invoked from within p. In other words, a variable x is in IMOD$^+$(p) if

1. $x \in$ IMOD(p) or
2. $x \xrightarrow{s} z$ and $z \in$ GMOD(q), where $s = (p,q)$ and z is a formal parameter of p.

If we can compute IMOD$^+$(p) for every procedure p in the program, we can solve for GMOD(p) using the following simple system of equations:

$$\text{GMOD}(p) = \text{IMOD}^+(p) \cup \bigcup_{s=(p,q)} \text{GMOD}(q) \cap \neg \text{LOCAL} \qquad (11.5)$$

where LOCAL is the set of all local variables in the program, so its complement is the set of all global variables. Since all side effects to reference formal parameters of p are reflected in IMOD$^+$(p), we need only be sure that all side effects to global variables are added by the union of the GMOD sets for successors. If a global variable is modified as a side effect of invoking p, it must be modified directly in the text of the subroutine, in which case it is in IMOD(p) $\subseteq$ IMOD$^+$(p), or it is passed as an actual parameter to another subroutine where it is modified, in which case it is in IMOD$^+$(p) by definition, or it is modified as a global by some subroutine called directly or indirectly from p, in which case it must be in GMOD(q) for some successor q of p, which establishes Equation 11.5.

We have thus decomposed the problem into two parts:

1. The computation of $\text{IMOD}^+(p)$ for every procedure p in the program
2. The propagation of global modification according to Equation 11.5

We will cover these calculations in the next two subsections.

Solving for IMOD⁺

We construct a special data structure, called the *binding graph*, as follows:

1. Construct a vertex for each formal parameter f of every procedure in the program.
2. Construct a directed edge from formal parameter f_1 of procedure p to formal parameter f_2 of procedure q if f_1 is bound to f_2 at a call site $s = (p,q)$ in p.

A preliminary question we might ask is: How large is the binding graph? If N is the number of vertices in the call graph and E is the number of edges, then the number of vertices in the binding graph can be no more than μN, where μ is the upper bound on the number of parameters to any procedure in the program. This is true because there can be no more vertices than the number of formal parameters in the entire program, which is clearly bounded by μN. Similarly, each call graph edge can give rise to no more than μ edges, since no more than one formal reference parameter can appear in a single actual parameter position. Thus the total number of edges in the binding graph is no larger than μE, and the binding graph is no more than a constant factor greater in size than the call graph; that is, its size is $O(N+E)$.

Let $\text{RMOD}(p)$ be the set of formal parameters in procedure p that may be modified in p, either directly or by assignment to a reference formal parameter of q as a side effect of a call to q from within p. Clearly, the following formula, which is a direct analog of Equation 11.4, holds:

$$\text{IMOD}^+(p) = \text{IMOD}(p) \cup \bigcup_{s=(p,q)}\{z \mid z \xrightarrow{s} w \text{ and } w \in \text{RMOD}(q)\} \qquad (11.6)$$

Thus we need only construct $\text{RMOD}(p)$ for every procedure in the program, and then apply Equation 11.6, to construct $\text{IMOD}^+(p)$.

To construct $\text{RMOD}(p)$, we will use a simple marking algorithm on the binding graph, in which each vertex is annotated with a logical mark implementable with a single bit. Initially, all the marks are set false, then the marks for formals of any procedure p that are in $\text{IMOD}(p)$ are set true. True bits are propagated around the graph using the rule that any formal f_1 that is bound to formal f_2 with a true mark must also be marked true. When no more propagation is possible, $\text{RMOD}(p)$ is the set of formals of p that are marked true. The algorithm is given in Figure 11.2.

procedure *computeRmod*$(P, N_B, E_B, \text{IMOD}, proc, \text{RMOD})$

      // P is the collection of procedures in the program
      // N_B is the collection of formal parameters in the binding graph
      // E_B is the collection of edges in the binding graph
      // *mark*$[f]$ maps formal parameters to their mark values
      // *proc*$[f]$ maps a parameter to its procedure
      // IMOD$[p]$ maps a procedure to its immediate mod side effect set
      // RMOD$[p]$ is the collection of output sets
      // *worklist* is a working set of formal parameters

L_1:   **for each** $f \in N_B$ **do** *mark*$[f]$:= *false*;
      worklist := $\varnothing$;

L_2:   **for each** $f \in N_B$ such that $f \in$ IMOD$[proc[f]]$ **do begin**

S_1:   *mark*$[f]$:= *true*;
       worklist := *worklist* $\cup$ $\{f\}$;
      end

L_3:   **while** *worklist* $\neq \varnothing$ **do begin**
      f := an arbitrary element in *worklist*;
      worklist := *worklist* $-$ $\{f\}$;

L_4:   **for each** v such that $(v, f) \in E_B$ **do begin**

S_2:   **if** *mark*$[v]$ = *false* **then begin**

S_3:   *mark*$[v]$:= *true*;
          worklist := *worklist* $\cup$ $\{v\}$;
        end
       end
     end

L_5:   **for each** $p \in P$ **do** RMOD$[p]$:= $\varnothing$;

L_6:   **for each** $f \in N_B$ **do**
      if *mark*$[f]$ **then** RMOD$[proc[f]]$:= RMOD$[proc[f]]$ $\cup$ $\{f\}$;

end *computeRmod*

Figure 11.2 Algorithm for constructing RMOD sets.

Correctness. To show that algorithm *computeRmod* in Figure 11.2 correctly computes the RMOD sets, we must show that on exit we have $f \in$ RMOD$[proc[f]]$ if and only if f may be modified as a side effect of invoking the procedure $p = proc[f]$.

    If. Assume that f may be modified. Then either it is modified in the procedure to which it is a parameter, in which case it is marked true in statement S_1, or there is a path in the binding graph to a formal parameter f_0 that is in IMOD$[proc[f_0]]$. Thus f_0 is marked true and added to the worklist in loop L_1. Let $f = f_n, f_{n-1}, \dots, f_1,$

f_0 be the sequence of parameters in the binding graph that constitutes the path from f to f_0. Suppose $f = f_n$ is never marked true. Then there must be a minimum k such that f_k is never marked true by the algorithm but f_{k-1} is marked true. But since f_{k-1} is put on the worklist when it is marked true and it is taken off the worklist eventually and every incoming edge to f_{k-1} is examined at that time, f_k must be marked true, a contradiction. Thus every parameter that may be modified as a side effect of invoking $proc[f]$ is put into RMOD[$proc[f]$].

Only if. Suppose f is a parameter that is marked true but cannot be modified. The algorithm only marks formal parameters true if they are modified within the body of their procedure or if there is a path in the binding graph to another parameter that is modified in its procedure. Since the binding graph has an edge only if the corresponding procedure call is possible, it must be the case that the original parameter f may be modified.

Complexity. Algorithm *computeRmod* operates in the worst case $O(N+E)$ steps, where N and E are the number of vertices and edges, respectively, in the call graph. This is because its running time is proportional to the size of the binding graph. Let N_B and E_B be the number of vertices and edges, respectively, in the binding graph. From the preceding discussion, we know that $N_B \leq \mu N$ and $E_B \leq \mu E$.

All that remains is to show that the algorithm runs in time proportional to the size of the binding graph, and we will have established the result. Clearly, loop L_1 requires N_B steps. Assuming that IMOD is implemented so that membership testing can be done in constant time (i.e., via a bit vector), loop L_2 also runs in N_B steps. Loop L_5 takes time proportional to the number of procedures in the program times the time to initialize the RMOD sets. If these sets are implemented as bit vectors of length μ, then this takes $O(N_B)$ time. Loop L_6 takes $O(N_B)$ time, assuming that adding to RMOD takes constant time, as it would with a bit-vector implementation.

Thus, the key is the running time of loops L_3 and L_4. If we assume that the worklist is implemented as a linked list, so that taking an arbitrary element from the front takes constant time, the body of the loop will be executed no more than N_B times, since a vertex is put onto the worklist no more than once. Let us assume that, as in topological sort algorithms, the edges are arranged as predecessor lists, so that all predecessors of a particular vertex can be found in time proportional to the number of predecessors. Then the body of the loop is executed once for each predecessor of each vertex in the program, for a total of E_B times.

Thus, we have established that the algorithm takes $O(N_B+E_B) = O(N+E)$ steps in the worst case.

To expand RMOD to IMOD$^+$ requires that we visit each call site in the program and each parameter at that call site to determine if it is bound to a variable in RMOD(p) for the called procedure p. If the RMOD sets are represented as bit vectors, this determination takes constant time, so the conversion to IMOD$^+$ takes $O(N+E)$ time. This assumes that IMOD$^+$ can be initialized in $O(N+E)$ time. If IMOD$^+(p)$ is represented as a bit vector, it must have length proportional to the number V of global variables in the program plus the number of formal parameters to p. Since the number of such parameters is $\leq \mu$, the time to initialize the bit-vector set for each procedure is $O(V+\mu) = O(V)$. Since this is done once for each procedure, the initialization time is $O(NV)$. Thus the computation of IMOD$^+$ takes $O(NV+E)$ time if we include the initializations.

Solving for GMOD

Once we have constructed IMOD$^+(p)$ for each procedure p in the program, we must use it to compute GMOD(p) according to Equation 11.5, which we repeat here:

$$\text{GMOD}(p) = \text{IMOD}^+(p) \cup \bigcup_{s=(p,q)} \text{GMOD}(q) \cap \neg\text{LOCAL}$$

This equation implies that a variable x is in GMOD(p) if it is in IMOD$^+(p)$ or x is global and there is a nonempty path in the call graph from p to procedure q where $x \in \text{IMOD}^+(q)$. In other words, we have reduced the problem to a variant of the reachability problem in the call graph. It is well known that reachability can be solved in time linear in the size of the problem graph using a depth-first search algorithm based on Tarjan's algorithm for finding strongly connected components of a directed graph. Algorithm *findGmod* in Figure 11.3 accomplishes this.

Complexity. Since this is a direct adaptation of depth-first search, it runs in $O(N+E)$ steps, where each step may involve a bit-vector operation of length V, the number of variables in the program. Thus the algorithm takes $O((N+E)V)$ elementary steps in the worst case.

Correctness. We now show that algorithm *findGmod* in Figure 11.3 correctly computes the GMOD(p) for every procedure p in the program. The algorithm is a direct adaptation of Tarjan's algorithm for finding strongly connected components. However, as the algorithm backs up in reverse invocation order, instead of collecting a set of strongly connected regions, it updates the GMOD(p) computation at each node. When it reaches the head of a strongly connected component, it updates GMOD(u), for every u in the component, to include the nonlocal part of the GMOD set for the head. Thus, the global parts of GMOD(u) for every procedure u in the SCR are identical, as they should be. The GMOD sets for nodes that are not in loops are correct by virtue of the order of visit, and the GMOD sets for nodes that are in loops are correct because of the updates of all procedures in the cycle.

Taken together the results from this section and the previous one establish that the entire computation can be done in $O((N+E)V)$ steps. Since DMOD can be computed from GMOD in $O(NV+E)$ time, the complete computation of DMOD also takes $O((N+E)V)$ steps. This is the best possible time bound as you must evaluate Equation 11.5 at least once at every node in the call graph, which would require $O((N+E)V)$ time.

```
procedure findGmod(N,E,n,IMOD⁺,LOCAL)
    integer dfn[n], lowlink[n], nexdfn, p, q, d,
        IMOD⁺[n], GMOD[n], LOCAL;
    integer stack Stack;
    procedure search(p);
        dfn[p] := nexdfn; nexdfn:= nexdfn + 1;
        GMOD[p] := IMOD⁺[p]; lowlink[p] := dfn[p];
        push p onto Stack;
        for each q adjacent to p do begin
            if dfn[q] = 0 then begin // tree edge
                search(q);
                lowlink[p] := min(lowlink[p], lowlink[q]);
            end
            if dfn[q] < dfn[p] and q ∈ Stack then
                lowlink[p] := min(dfn[q], lowlink[q]);
            else // apply equation
                GMOD[p] := GMOD[p] ∪ (GMOD[q] ∩ ¬LOCAL);
        end
        // test for root of strong component
        if lowlink[p] = dfn[p] then begin
            // adjust GMOD sets for each member of the SCR
            repeat
                pop u from Stack;
                LOCAL[u] := LOCAL[u] ∪ (LOCAL[p] ∩ ¬LOCAL);
            until u = p
        end
    end search;
    // subroutine body
    nexdfn := 1; dfn[*] := 0; Stack := ∅;
    search(1); // by convention root = 1
end findGmod
```

Figure 11.3   Algorithm for propagation of global modification side effects.

11.2.4   Flow-Insensitive Alias Analysis

Having treated the problem of alias-free side effect analysis, we now turn our attention to the problem of alias analysis and how it can be integrated into a general side effect algorithm.

Update of DMOD to MOD

Once the direct modification side effect sets have been computed, there still remains the problem of factoring in aliasing. We can illustrate the issue by showing an example with three procedures:

```
          SUBROUTINE P
             INTEGER A
    S₀       CALL S(A,A)
          END
          SUBROUTINE S(X,Y)
             INTEGER X,Y
    S₁       CALL Q(X)
          END
          SUBROUTINE Q(Z)
             INTEGER Z
             Z = 0
          END
```

We are interested in computing the set $\text{MOD}(S_1)$. Our analysis to date gives us $\text{GMOD}(Q) = \{Z\}$, which yields, after back translation to the call site, $\text{DMOD}(S_1) = \{X\}$. But to truly determine which variables might be modified at S_1 we must be aware that X could be aliased to Y at the point of call because of call site S_0, which passes the same variable to both parameters—this aliasing information yields $\text{MOD}(S_1) = \{X,Y\}$.

Recall the formula from Equation 11.2, which we repeat here:

$$\text{MOD}(s) = \text{DMOD}(s) \cup \bigcup_{x \in \text{DMOD}(s)} \text{ALIAS}(p, x)$$

A naive algorithm for implementing this conversion is shown in Figure 11.4. Let us analyze the complexity of this loop nest. The loop L_1 is executed $O(E)$ times, where E is the number of edges in the call graph. The assignment in statement S_1 takes time proportional to the length of the bit-vector representation or $O(V)$ steps, where V is the number of variables in the program. Since this is done $O(E)$ times, the running time attributable to this statement is $O(EV)$. For each iteration of L_1, L_2 is executed once for each variable in $\text{DMOD}(s)$. Since this could be essen-

procedure *findMod*(N,E,DMOD,ALIAS,MOD)

L_1:   **for each** call site s **do begin**

S_1: $\text{MOD}[s] := \text{DMOD}[s]$;

L_2:   **for each** $x \in \text{DMOD}[s]$ **do**

L_3:   **for each** $v \in \text{ALIAS}[p,x]$ **do**

S_2: $\text{MOD}[s] := \text{MOD}[s] \cup \{v\}$;

        end
end *findMod*

Figure 11.4 Naive alias update of DMOD to produce MOD.

tially all the variables $O(V)$, this loop is entered an aggregate of $O(EV)$ times. Finally, L_3 is entered $O(EV)$ times, and each time, it executes one iteration for each element of ALIAS(p,x). If we assume that ALIAS(p,x) might contain every variable in the program, the loop body could be executed $O(EV^2)$ times. Finally, statement S_2 takes constant time if we use a bit-vector implementation. Thus the total running time for the update procedure is $O(EV^2)$.

If we cannot improve the running time of alias analysis, it may dominate the running time of the entire side effect analysis, making it impractical for use on programs with nontrivial aliasing patterns. However, we can achieve a significant improvement by carefully classifying aliasing patterns that may arise. First, we note that, in a two-level naming hierarchy, containing only global and local variables, two global variables can *never* be aliases of one another. They can only be aliased to reference formal parameters. Thus, for a global variable x, ALIAS(p,x) can only contain reference formal parameters of procedure p. This means that ALIAS(p,x) can be no larger than μ entries, where μ is the maximum number of formal parameters of any procedure in the program.

On the other hand, for a given formal parameter f of procedure p, ALIAS(p,f) may contain any global or any other formal parameter. Thus, it may be of size $O(V)$.

These observations suggest that we break down the update of DMOD to MOD into two cases: one for formal parameters and the other for global variables. When considering the aliases of a particular variable $x \in$ DMOD(s),

1. if x is a global variable, we will add a very small set ($\leq \mu$ elements) to MOD(s), but we may need to do this $O(V)$ times, and

2. if x is a formal parameter of the procedure p containing s, we will add up to $O(V)$ elements to MOD(s), but we will only do this a small number of times ($\leq \mu$).

In either case, the amount of work is $O(V)$, not $O(V^2)$. The entire algorithm is given in Figure 11.5.

It should be clear from the previous discussion that the overall running time of the combining strategy in Figure 11.5 is $O(V)$ per call site, for a total of $O(EV)$ time. This is promising because if we can compute the ALIAS in $O((N+E)V)$, the time bound for the entire MOD computation will be $O((N+E)V)$.

Computing Aliases

We now turn to the problem of computing the sets ALIAS(p,x) for each procedure p and each variable x that is either global or a parameter of some procedure. To do this as rapidly as possible, we will once again take advantage of the observation that globals can only be aliases of formal parameters. We first compute, for each formal parameter in the program, an intermediate quantity $A(f)$, which is defined to be the set of global variables that may be aliased to a formal parameter f through a sequence of parameter bindings in the binding graph:

procedure *updateMODwithAlias*

    for each call site s in the program **do**
        $t := \varnothing;$ // t is a temporary bit vector of length μ
        for each global variable $x \in$ DMOD(s) **do**   // $O(V)$ iterations
            $t := t \cup \{x\};$ // constant time
            $t := t \cup$ ALIAS$[p,x]$ // $O(\mu)$ time
        end
        MOD$[s] :=$ MOD$[s] \cup t;$ // $O(V)$ time
        for each formal parameter $f \in$ DMOD$[s]$ **do begin**   // $O(\mu)$ iterations
            MOD$[s] :=$ MOD$[s] \cup \{f\};$ // constant time
            MOD$[s] :=$ MOD$[s] \cup$ ALIAS$(p,f);$ // $O(V)$ time
        end
    end
end *updateMODwithAlias*

Figure 11.5 Fast combination of side effect and alias information.

$$g \rightarrow f_0 \rightarrow f_1 \rightarrow f_2 \rightarrow \ldots \rightarrow f_{n-1} \rightarrow f_n = f$$

To compute $A(f)$, we will use a forward propagation on a variation of the binding graph in which cycles have been reduced to single nodes. Note that $A(f)$ is an approximation to ALIAS(p,f), containing all the global variables in that set. The algorithm for computing $A(f)$ for each formal parameter in the program is given in Figure 11.6. In this algorithm, the set $A(f)$ will be represented by a bit vector of length $O(V)$.

It is easy to see that the forward propagation phase of this algorithm requires $O(NV)$ steps in the worst case, and updating the sets in a cycle can also be done in $O(NV)$ steps.

Once the sets $A(f)$ are available for every formal parameter in the program, the alias sets for every global variable can be computed by a simple inversion, as shown in Figure 11.7. This computation can be subdivided into two components: initializing the alias sets and computing the inversion. Recall that we can represent an alias set for a global variable within a given procedure as a bit vector of length μ. Therefore, the initializations in step S_0 of Figure 11.7 take no more than $O(NV\mu) = O(NV)$ time. However, since an update can be done in constant time, the total cost of the updates in statement S_1 is also $O(NV)$.

All that remains is the computation of aliases for formal parameters. Note that $A(f)$ is an approximation for ALIAS(p,f), containing all the global aliases of f. To expand $A(f)$ to ALIAS(p,f), we need only add the formal parameters that may be aliased to f. In the simple two-level language we are considering, the only formals that may be aliased to f are other parameters of the same procedure. Thus there can be no more than $\mu(\mu+1)/2$ formal pairs in any given procedure.

procedure *computeA*(N,E,N_B,E_B,A)

    for each formal parameter $f \in N_B$ **do** $A[f] := \varnothing$;

    for each call site $s \in N$ **do begin**

        for each global g mapped to formal parameter f at s **do**

            $A[f] := A[f] \cup \{g\}$;

    end

    replace every cycle in the binding graph with a single node,

        reducing the graph to a directed, acyclic form;

    for each f in the reduced graph in topological order **do**

$$A[f] := A[f] \cup \bigcup_{(f_0,\,f) \in E_B} A[f_0] \ ;$$

    for each cycle in the original binding graph **do begin**

        let C be the reduced binding graph node for the cycle;

        for each $f \in C$ **do** $A[f] := A[C]$;

    end

end *computeA*

Figure 11.6 Algorithm for computing approximate alias sets for formal parameters.

---

procedure *computeAlias*

    for each procedure p **do**

        for each global variable g **do**

S_0:   ALIAS$[p,g] := \varnothing$;

    for each formal parameter f in the program **do begin**

        let p be the procedure for parameter f;

        for each $g \in A[f]$ **do**

S_1:   ALIAS$[p,g] := $ ALIAS$[p,g] \cup \{f\}$;

    end

end *computeAlias*

Figure 11.7 Inversion to compute ALIAS(g) for each global variable g.

To compute the formals that may be aliased to one another, the algorithm *computePairs* in Figure 11.8 keeps track of the set FPAIRS(p) of pairs of formal parameters that may be aliased to one another in a given procedure p. After initializing all the FPAIRS sets to the empty set, we examine each call site for alias introductions, occurring when the same variable is passed to two different parameters. Whenever one is found, we add the formal parameter pair in the alias to a worklist. Then we iterate over the worklist looking for possible alias propagations, which occur when two parameters that may be aliased are both passed to another procedure. If the resulting pair of formals in the called procedure is not already in

procedure *computePairs*

$W := \emptyset$;

L_1: **for each** procedure p in the program **do** FPAIRS$[p] := \emptyset$;

L_2: **for each** alias introduction site (e.g., "CALL P(X,X)") **do**
    insert the resulting formal pair in FPAIRS$[p]$ and in the worklist W;

L_3: **while** $W \neq \emptyset$ **do begin**
    remove $\langle f_1, f_2 \rangle$ from W;

L_4:   **for each** call site s in procedure p passing both f_1 and f_2 **do begin**
        let q be the procedure invoked at s;
        if f_1 and f_2 are passed to f_3 and f_4 at s **and**
        $\langle f_3, f_4 \rangle \notin$ FPAIRS$[q]$ **then begin**
        FPAIRS$[q] :=$ FPAIRS$[q] \cup \{\langle f_3, f_4 \rangle\}$;
        $W := W \cup \{\langle f_3, f_4 \rangle\}$;
        end
        end
    end
end *computePairs*

Figure 11.8 Algorithm to compute formal parameter pairs that may be aliased.

the FPAIRS set, the pair is added to the worklist. This procedure continues until the worklist is empty.

Let us now analyze the running time of the algorithm *computePairs*. Note that there can be no more than $\mu(\mu+1)/2$ parameter pairs in any subroutine. The initialization loop L_1 takes O(N) time, since it is constant time for each procedure. Since it must look at each call site, the loop at L_2 takes O(E) time, but the operations are all constant time, assuming we use some sort of linked structure for both W and FPAIRS. Loop L_3 is entered once for each pair that is put on the worklist. Since there can be at most $\mu(\mu+1)/2$ pairs for each call site, the total number of times L_3 is entered is less than or equal to $\mu(\mu+1)N/2$, so L_3 is entered O(N) times. Similarly, each call site in the program is examined no more than $\mu(\mu+1)/2$ times, so loop L_4 is entered O(E) times. Since the body of L_4 takes constant time, the entire process takes O($N+E$) time.

Thus, we have established that alias analysis can be done in O($(N+E)V$) time, which means that the entire MOD solution can be completed in this time.

11.2.5 Constant Propagation

Constant propagation is an important data flow analysis problem that improves the performance of a variety of optimizations [127, 136]. Unfortunately, the problem is difficult even in a single procedure, as obtaining a precise solution has been shown unsolvable [165]. Even the usual single-procedure approximate problem is flow sensitive in the interprocedural setting, hence intractable [220].

One important reason for the difficulty is that constants propagated into a program region can make it possible to evaluate program expressions in that region, yielding new constants on exit. An example illustrating the interprocedural case is the following:

```
SUBROUTINE PHASE(N)
   INTEGER N,A,B
   CALL INIT(A,B,N)
   CALL PROCESS (A,B)
END
SUBROUTINE INIT(A,B,N)
   INTEGER A,B,N
   A = N + 1
   B = (N*A)/2
END
```

The purpose of subroutine INIT is to initialize the variables A and B. Thus if N is a constant 10 on entry to procedure PHASE, A will be a constant 11 and B will be a constant 55 on exit from INIT. Hence these constant values will be available on entry to PROCESS. This section will develop an approach to determine these facts.

A single-procedure constant propagation algorithm was presented in Section 4.4.3. This algorithm, which is shown in Figure 4.5, uses an iterative process on the definition-use graph or the static single-assignment (SSA) form [96]. The iterative method is guaranteed to converge because it is based on a constant propagation lattice shown in Figure 4.4. Furthermore, the algorithm is linear in the size of the base graph upon which it operates because an instruction can have its output value lowered in the lattice at most twice and, hence, it is put on the worklist at most twice.

Our strategy is to develop an interprocedural analog of the iterative single-procedure constant propagation. In fact, we hope to use the same algorithm, but on a different definition-use graph that we call the *interprocedural value propagation graph*. In this graph, the vertices represent "jump functions" that compute values out of a given procedure from known values into a procedure. Jump functions are analogous to "transfer functions" from intraprocedural and interprocedural interval analysis [131].

Let s be a call site within procedure p and x a formal parameter of the procedure q called at s. The *jump function* for x at s, denoted J_s^x, determines the value of x in terms of the values of inputs to the procedure p containing s. The *support* of J_s^x is the set of inputs actually used in the evaluation of J_s^x. Jump functions can be computed in a preliminary phase that examines the individual procedures of the program.

We now return to the construction of the *interprocedural value graph*. Here are the steps:

1. Construct a node for each forward jump function J_s^x.
2. If $x \in support(J_t^y)$, where t is a call site in the procedure called at s, then construct an edge from J_s^x to J_t^y.

The iterative constant propagation algorithm can be applied to the resulting graph.

We now present a simple example of this process. Consider the program shown in Figure 11.9. From this example we can easily derive the jump functions

$$J_\alpha^X = \{1\}; \ J_\alpha^Y = \{2\}$$

$$J_\beta^U = \{X+Y\}; \ J_\beta^V = \{X-Y\}$$

The call graph and the resulting interprocedural value propagation graph are shown in Figure 11.10.

It can easily be seen that the constant propagation algorithm applied to the interprocedural value propagation graph in Figure 11.10 will quickly converge to the constant assignments:

$$X = 1; \ Y = 2; \ U = 3; \ V = -1$$

To estimate the total cost of the algorithm, recall that the cost of the iterative constant propagation algorithm on which this is based is proportional to the number of vertices and the number of edges in the graph, assuming the jump function evaluations can be done in constant time. However, it is unrealistic to expect every jump function to be evaluated in constant time because, as we shall see, different strategies for constructing jump functions produce functions of varying execution costs.

Thus, we must argue about the number of times that a jump function is evaluated. A jump function J has $support(J)$ inputs, each of which can be lowered at most twice. Thus a jump function J can be evaluated no more than $O(|support(J)|)$ times. Let $cost(J)$ denote the cost of executing jump function J. For each jump function the total cost of execution will be $O(|support(J)|) \cdot cost(J))$. Therefore, the total cost of executing the interprocedural constant propagation algorithm is

$$O\left(\sum_s \sum_x |support(J_s^x)| \cdot cost(J_s^x)\right) \tag{11.7}$$

where s ranges over the call sites in the program and x ranges over the input parameters to the subroutine.

```
        PROGRAM MAIN
            INTEGER A,B
            A = 1
            B = 2
    α       CALL S(A,B)
        END
        SUBROUTINE S(X,Y)
            INTEGER X,Y,Z,W
            Z = X + Y
            W = X - Y
    β       CALL T(Z,W)
        END
        SUBROUTINE T(U,V)
            PRINT U,V
        END
```

Figure 11.9 Interprocedural constant propagation example.

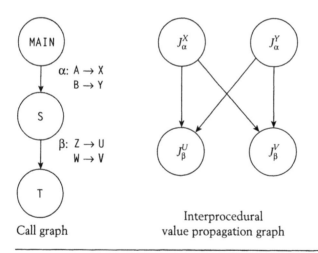

Call graph

Interprocedural
value propagation graph

Figure 11.10 Interprocedural value propagation graph example.

Construction of Jump Functions

Jump functions can vary widely in precision and cost of the approximation. A jump function could involve full symbolic interpretation of the procedure it represents. On the other end of the spectrum, it could evaluate only the assignments that are on every path through the subroutine and not contained in any loop. In this case, variables assigned on optional control paths or in loops would receive the value ⊥ (bottom) in the constant lattice.

One major problem is how to construct jump functions for procedures that have function calls within their bodies. Consider the example in Figure 11.11. To build a jump function for T at call site γ, we need to know what action will be taken by subroutine INIT invoked at call site β. We address this problem by defining "return jump functions," which summarize the constants propagated out of a subprogram when it is called with a particular set of inputs.

If x is an output of the procedure p, the *return jump function* R_p^x determines the value of x on return from an invocation of p in terms of the values of input parameters to p. The *support* of R_p^x is the same as the support of a forward jump function. In the simple case of the subroutine INIT shown in Figure 11.11, we have the following return jump function:

$$R_{\text{INIT}}^{X} = \{2 \ast Y\}$$

and in the case of SOLVE, we have

$$R_{\text{SOLVE}}^{C} = \{T \ast 10\}$$

We can use return jump functions in the normal jump functions for constant propagation. For example, the jump function for call site γ is as follows:

$$J_{\gamma}^{T} = \{\text{if } I \in \text{MOD}(\beta) \text{ then } R_{\text{INIT}}^{X}(N) \text{ else } \textit{undefined-const}\}$$

where *undefined-const* is used to signify a special value given to uninitialized variables. To round out the example, we present the remainder of the jump functions:

$$J_{\alpha}^{N} = \{15\} \text{ and } J_{\beta}^{Y} = \{N\}$$

One important jump function remains to be determined, namely, the return jump function for subroutine PROCESS, which is the key to determining whether a constant can be substituted for the variable A in the print statement in the main program. This return jump function must invoke the return jump function for both INIT and SOLVE, but the call to the return jump function for INIT will be automatic if we use the forward jump function to determine the value of the input formal parameter T of SOLVE. The resulting function is

$$R_{\text{PROCESS}}^{B} = \begin{cases} \text{if } B \in \text{MOD}(\gamma) \\ \quad \text{then } R_{\text{SOLVE}}^{C}(J_{\gamma}^{T}(N)) \\ \text{else } B \end{cases}$$

Using these jump functions we can see that the value of the variable A on exit from the procedure PROCESS is given by

```
        PROGRAM MAIN
          INTEGER A
    α     CALL PROCESS(15,A)
          PRINT A
        END
        SUBROUTINE PROCESS(N,B)
          INTEGER N, B, I
    β     CALL INIT(I,N)
    γ     CALL SOLVE(B,I)
          RETURN
        END
        SUBROUTINE INIT(X,Y)
          INTEGER X, Y
          X = 2 * Y
          RETURN
        END
        SUBROUTINE SOLVE(C,T)
          INTEGER C, T
          C = T * 10
          RETURN
        END
```

Figure 11.11 A complex interprocedural constant folding example.

$$R^B_{\text{PROCESS}} = (2*(15)) * 10 = 300$$

The study of scientific Fortran programs by Grove and Torczon [127] suggests that MOD should be computed prior to computing jump functions and prior to performing a global constant propagation to initialize the interprocedural propagation, because in any case where a variable is not in MOD for a given call site, the return jump function is simply the identity. In these cases, a return jump function is not needed, which simplifies the construction of other jump functions for the same variable whose scope includes the given call site. This is the single most useful type of return jump function. The same study also established that

1. simple jump functions get almost all the constants in scientific Fortran, and
2. return jump functions only infrequently deliver new constants, but when they do, the payoff is high.

11.2.6 Kill Analysis

We can adapt some of the ideas used to solve the MOD and constant propagation problems to deal with kill analysis as well. Recall that KILL(p) is the set of all variables that must be modified on every path through procedure p. For convenience in the algorithm formulation, we will compute $\text{NKILL}(p) = \neg\text{KILL}(p)$, the set of all variables that are not killed as a side effect of calling procedure p. A method similar to the one presented here can be used to compute $\text{USE}(p)$ for every procedure p in the program.

Let us begin by considering how we would solve the single-procedure NKILL problem. Suppose we have, for each extended basic block b and each successor c of b, the set $\text{THRU}(b,c)$ of all variables that are not killed on some path through b to c. Then the following set of data flow equations can be used to solve for $\text{NKILL}(b)$:

$$\text{NKILL}(b) = \bigcup_{c \in succ(b)} \text{THRU}(b,c) \cap \text{NKILL}(c) \qquad (11.8)$$

If e is the exit node for the procedure, then

$$\text{NKILL}(e) = \Omega \qquad (11.9)$$

where Ω denotes the set of all variables. This set of equations can be solved using the simple iterative method of data flow analysis.

An analogous process can compute $\text{NKILL}(p)$ for every procedure p in the program. First we need a formula for computing $\text{NKILL}(p)$ for a single procedure. This is more complicated than the case for single blocks because it depends on procedure-specific control flow. To carry out the computation, we will first construct the *reduced control flow graph* G_{THRU} for a procedure. G_{THRU} is a graph in which each vertex is a call site, the entry node or the exit node for the procedure. Every edge (x,y) in G_{THRU} is annotated by the set $\text{THRU}(x,y)$ of variables that are not killed on some path from x to y not containing a call site. G_{THRU} is constructed by the algorithm in Figure 11.12.

It is easy to see that the algorithm in Figure 11.12 can be implemented in time linear in the size of the control flow graph using a variant of topological sort.

Once we have the reduced control flow graph, the algorithm shown in Figure 11.13 can be used to compute $\text{NKILL}(p)$ for a procedure p given NKILL values for all procedures that can be called from within p.

A simple iterative data flow analysis algorithm, employing the procedure in Figure 11.13, can be used to compute NKILL, assuming that all variables in the program are global. Although this algorithm can take $O(N^2 V)$ time in the worst case, if the call graph is reducible, the algorithm will require only $O((N+E)d)$ bit-vector steps, where d is the maximum number of back edges in any noncircular path in the call graph [143]. The total time required in this case is $O((N+E)dV)$. In practice, iterative methods are very fast.

The algorithm described so far can compute $\text{NKILL}(p)$ rapidly only if there are no reference formal parameters in the program. If there are reference formal parameters, the algorithm can be adapted to produce the correct answers if the appropriate actual-to-formal mappings are observed. However, it may take significantly longer to converge because of the possibility of a "shift-register effect," in

procedure *ComputeReducedCFG*(G)

    remove all back edges from the control flow graph G;
    let b_0 denote the procedure entry node;
    mark b_0 processed;
    worklist := ∅;
    for each s ∈ *successors*(b_0) **do** *worklist* := *worklist* ∪ {(b_0,s)};
    while *worklist* ≠ ∅ **do begin**
        take an arbitrary element (b,s) from the worklist,
            such that all predecessors of s have already been processed
            or merged into b;
        if s is a call site **then begin**
            for each t ∈ *successors*(s) **do**
                worklist := *worklist* ∪ {(s,t)};
            mark s as processed;
        end
        else if s is the exit node **then** do nothing
        else begin // s is normal node
            merge s into b;
            for each t ∈ *successors*(s) **do**
                if THRU[b,t] is undefined **then**
                    THRU[b,t] := THRU[b,s] ∩ THRU[s,t];
                else
                    THRU[b,t] := THRU[b,t] ∪ (THRU[b,s] ∩ THRU[s,t]);
        end
    end
    end *ComputeReducedCFG*

Figure 11.12 Algorithm for constructing the reduced control flow graph.

which parameters are passed to other parameters in a recursive loop. This is the same problem we observed in dealing with the MOD problem in Section 11.2.3.

    Fortunately, we can use the same general technique—use of a formal parameter binding graph—to ameliorate this problem. We will construct a binding graph and mark it as shown in Figure 11.14.

    This algorithm is simply a variation on the iterative algorithm, except that we update NKILL(p) for a procedure only if we discover that the status of one of its parameters might have changed to "killed" because a parameter that it is passed at some call site has changed its status. Since each parameter can be added to the worklist only once and since the algorithm visits each predecessor of a parameter taken from the worklist, the total number of NKILL updates is limited to $O(E_B+N_B) = O(E+N)$, where E_B and N_B are the number of edges and vertices in the binding graph, respectively, and E and N are the number of edges and vertices in the call graph. The number of updates can be further reduced by carefully selecting the order of extraction of elements from the worklist.

procedure *ComputeNKILL(p)*

    for each b in $G_{THRU}(p)$ in reverse topological order **do begin**
        if b is the exit node **then** NKILL$[b] := \Omega$;
        else if b is a call site **then begin**
            NKILL$[b] := \varnothing$;
            for each successor s of b in $G_{THRU}(p)$ **do**
                NKILL$[b] :=$ NKILL$[b] \cup ($NKILL$[s] \cap$ THRU$[b,s])$;
            NKILL$[b] :=$ NKILL$[b] \cap$ NKILL$[q]$,
                where q is the procedure called at b;
        end
        else begin // b is the entry node for $G_{THRU}(p)$
            NKILL$[b] := \varnothing$;
            for each successor s of b in $G_{THRU}(p)$ **do**
                NKILL$[b] :=$ NKILL$[b] \cup ($NKILL$[s] \cap$ THRU$[b,s])$;
            NKILL$[p] :=$ NKILL$[b]$;
        end
    end
end *ComputeNKILL*

Figure 11.13 Computing NKILL(p).

We note that the kill sets computed by this process are not precise because they do not take aliasing into account. Suppose we know that on every visit to a procedure p the variables $x_1, x_2, \ldots, x_n$ must all refer to the same location, then a variable is in KILL(s) if one of the aliases is killed on every path through the procedure called at s and any procedures invoked from within it. In other words, we may be able to increase the size of the KILL sets by taking aliasing into account. However, this will be computationally expensive because it requires computing the set of all tuples of variables that refer to the same location on some invocation of the procedure, which could take time that is exponential in the number of variables used as parameters in the program.

11.2.7 Symbolic Analysis

In addition to the basic analysis problems discussed so far, successful program parallelization requires that some more sophisticated interprocedural problems be solved. Two that are especially important are symbolic analysis and array section analysis [142, 136].

Although constant propagation provides valuable information about variables on entry to a procedure, it is usually not possible to establish that a given variable is constant because, in most cases, it is not. However, it may not be necessary to prove a variable constant to improve global program analysis. It may be enough to

procedure *BindingComputeNKILL(P)*

    initially, let the binding graph consist of a vertex
       for each formal parameter in the program *P*;
    worklist := ∅;
    for each procedure *p* in the program **do begin**
      let $\text{NKILL}_0[p]$ be the result of applying the algorithm in
         Figure 11.13 with $\text{NKILL}[q] = \Omega(q)$
         for each successor *q* of *p*,
         where $\Omega(q)$ denotes the set of formal parameters of *q*;
      $\text{NKILL}[p] := \text{NKILL}_0(p)$;
      for each formal parameter *f* of *p* **do begin**
        if $f \in \text{NKILL}_0[p]$ **then**
          killed(f) := *false*;
          for each formal parameter *g* to which *f* is passed
            at a call site within *p* **do**
            add an edge *(f,g)* to the binding graph;
        end
        else begin
          killed(f) := *true*; *worklist* := *worklist* ∪ *{f}*;
        end
      end
    end
    while *worklist* ≠ ∅ **do begin**
      select an arbitrary element *f* ∈ *worklist*;
      worklist := *worklist* − *{f}*;
      for each *g* such that there is an edge *(g,f)* in the binding graph
        and *killed(g)* = *false* **do begin**
        let *q* be the procedure of which *g* is a formal;
        $\text{NKILL}[q] :=$ the result of applying the algorithm in
          Figure 11.13 with the current NKILL sets
          for its successors;
        if $g \notin \text{NKILL}[q]$ **then begin**
          killed(g) := *true*; *worklist* := *worklist* ∪ *{g}*;
        end
      end
    end
end *BindingComputeNKILL*

Figure 11.14 Construct and mark the binding graph for NKILL.

establish bounds on its values or to prove that its value can be expressed as a function of the values of other variables at the same point in the program. Such symbolic relationships can be used to prove facts, such as the absence of a dependence. For example, consider the following sample code:

```
SUBROUTINE S(A,N,M)
   REAL A(N+M)
   INTEGER N, M
   DO I = 1, N
      A(I+M) = A(I) + B
   ENDDO
END
```

If we could prove that $N = M$ on entry to S, we could show that the loop within the subroutine carries no dependence.

The goal of *interprocedural symbolic analysis* is to prove facts about the values of variables that may hold on entry to a given subroutine or on return from a given call site. There are three types of symbolic analyses that are often carried out:

1. *Symbolic expression analysis*, which seeks to determine a symbolic expression for the value of a variable in terms of the values of other variables at the same point in the program

2. *Predicate analysis*, which seeks to establish a relationship between values that a pair of variables may have at a given point in the program

3. *Range analysis*, which seeks to establish a range of values with known constant lower and upper bounds (and possibly strides) that a variable may take on at a given point in the program

Often, the results of these analyses can be substituted for one another. For example, the fact that $M = N$ in the previous example could be established by either symbolic expression analysis or predicate analysis. The distinction between the two is that expression analysis can produce values that involve many other values, while predicate analysis typically relates only to pairs of variables. On the other hand, the analysis that produces symbolic expressions can be more complicated than the analysis required for simple predicates.

Range analysis can be used effectively in program analysis to rule out certain possibilities. For example, consider the following subroutine:

```
SUBROUTINE S(A,N,K)
   REAL A(0:N)
   INTEGER N, K
   DO I = 2, N
      A(I) = A(I) + A(K)
   ENDDO
END
```

If we can prove that $K \in [0:1]$ on entry to the subroutine, we can establish that the loop carries no dependence.

Within a single procedure, symbolic expression analysis is typically performed using some form of *value numbering* [27, 236], which uniquely numbers each expression so that expressions with equal value numbers at a given point will have equal values at run time. Since global program value numbering is likely to be complex, it is typically used only within a procedure. Interprocedurally, a restricted set of relationships, such as those represented by predicates involving only two variables, are propagated across procedure boundaries [141].

It is easy to see that range analysis and symbolic expression analysis can be handled by variations on the constant propagation algorithm from Section 11.2.5. To use this algorithm, we will need to define three things:

1. The process by which new symbolic information is introduced in a program

2. *Jump functions* that produce information at a call site from information at the entry to a procedure containing that call site

3. *Return jump functions* that determine the relationships on output from a procedure, given the relationships that hold on entry

Let us consider how these three functions could be put together to compute range information. Range information is typically introduced at control flow points in the program. For example, in a loop headed by

```
DO I = 1, N
```

it is safe to assume that $I \in [1:N]$. Similarly, conditional statements introduce partial ranges that can be composed to produce full ranges.

In all the symbolic analysis methods, jump functions compute values in lattices that are significantly more complex than the simple constant propagation lattice. For example, in the case of range analysis, we might use a lattice in which the meet operation picks the larger upper and smaller lower bound of the pair of ranges on the two joining control flow branches. A fragment from such a lattice is depicted in Figure 11.15. If we bound the number of times that an upper bound can be increased before being taken as ∞ and we similarly bound the number of times a lower bound can be decreased, this lattice can be used anywhere a finite descending chain lattice is required, such as in an iterative algorithm.

Symbolic predicate analysis is more complicated than range analysis because it examines the relationship between a pair of variables. For example, it is useful to know whether two variables x and y are related by equality or are offset from one another by a constant. This might be represented as

$$x - y = c$$

where c is a compile-time constant. A more general linear relationship between variables can be characterized as

$$c_1 x + c_2 y = c_0$$

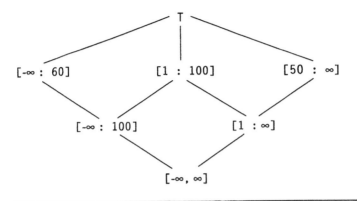

Figure 11.15 Simple value lattice for range analysis.

where c_0, c_1, and c_2 are all constants. Note that this relationship is transitive: if variables y and z are related by

$$d_1 y + d_2 z = d_0$$

then we can find constants e_0, e_1, and e_2 such that

$$e_1 x + e_2 z = e_0$$

In particular,

$$c_1 d_1 x - c_2 d_2 z = c_0 d_1 - c_2 d_0$$

Thus, at any point in the program, we can find groups of variables that are linearly related to one another. The goal of symbolic predicate analysis is to propagate these sets throughout the program. This can also be done by employing a variant of interprocedural constant propagation.

11.2.8 **Array Section Analysis**

The analysis presented so far does not help much with one of the most important problems we need to solve if we are to automatically parallelize programs—namely, how to analyze dependences in loops that contain procedure calls. Consider the following code:

```
      SUBROUTINE S
        DIMENSION A(100,100)
        ...
        DO I = 1, N
S₁        CALL SOURCE(A,I)        ! assigns to A
S₂        CALL SINK(A,I)          ! uses A
        ENDDO
        RETURN
      END
```

If we wish to parallelize the loop in this subroutine, we must determine whether any dependence is carried by the loop. Interprocedural information of the sort described in previous sections is of little use, telling us only that array A is modified by SOURCE and used by SINK. With no better information than that, we must assume that there is an assignment in SOURCE to a location that is used by SINK on a later iteration of the loop; in other words, we must assume that the loop carries a dependence and cannot be parallelized.

The situation would be different if we were able to show that the accesses to A in both routines are confined to the Ith column, which is suggested by the use of I as a parameter to both routines. Then we know that different iterations of the loop deal with distinct portions of the array, so no carried dependence is possible. We would like to refine interprocedural analysis methods to be able to establish conditions like this, which means that our analysis needs to be able to recognize subarrays of the whole array.

Suppose that we are able to compute the set $M_A(I)$ of locations within the array that may be modified within SOURCE on the Ith iteration of the loop and the set $U_A(I)$ of locations that may be used in SINK on iteration I. These quantities might be computed by array versions of MOD and USE, respectively. Then the loop carries true dependence if and only if there exist indices I_1 and I_2, $1 \le I_1 < I_2 \le N$, such that

$$M_A(I_1) \cap U_A(I_2) \neq \varnothing$$

In order to reason about subarrays, we need a method of representing them. The representation should be such that unions and intersections are reasonably easy to represent as well.

It is straightforward to extend the standard data flow algorithms, which work on vectors of bits in which each bit can represent only two states (e.g., may be modified or must be preserved), to vectors of more general lattice elements. If we can find a lattice that represents subarrays accurately enough, we can use this lattice in our interprocedural data flow analysis routines to determine side effects to subarrays.

Some important properties that a lattice representation should have are as follows:

1. The representation should be as accurate as possible.

2. The *meet* operation, which is invoked whenever two control flow paths merge, must be efficient.

3. The dependence test, which usually involves intersection of region representations, should also be efficient.

4. It should be possible to handle recursion in the analysis framework, which implies that the lattice should have the *finite descending chain property*—that is, every descending chain in the lattice must reach a lattice minimum after a finite number of steps.

5. It should be possible to deal with the parameter transformations that occur at call sites.

Let us consider one possible lattice for subarrays, depicted in Figure 11.16, that satisfies a number of these requirements. The elements of this lattice are referred to as *simple regular sections* because they can represent a very limited number of regular subarrays, namely, points, rows, columns, and the entire matrix. Note that this lattice may extend to an infinite size because we can use arbitrary variables and constants in the subscripts. However, it has the finite descending chain property because no element in the lattice can be "lowered" more than three times.

Evaluating this lattice representation, we find that meet, which represents union in a case like the MOD calculation, has the following properties:

1. The depth of the lattice is $k + 1$, where k is the number of subscript positions in the array represented.

2. The cost of a meet operation is $O(k)$, because each subscript position must be examined and compared for the two references to determine what the meet must be.

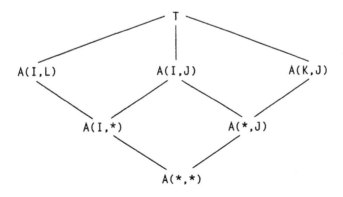

Figure 11.16 Simple regular section lattice.

3. Intersection, which is essential to the dependence test, is a limited form of unification, which can also be done in linear time in the number of subscripts.

To see the truth of this last claim, note that each subscript position in the lattice is either a symbolic expression or a constant or "*", which represents an entire row or column. Thus, if the two subscripts are symbolic expressions, then the result subscript should be the same expression if they are equal and "*" otherwise. If one is an expression and the other is "*", the result subscript should be "*".

One question remains: How accurate is this representation? It turns out that in practice this representation is too simple because it does not allow subarrays whose extents are bounded. Thus in an array A(100,100) the best approximation to subarray A(1:10,1:10) is A(*,*). A much better representation is *bounded regular sections*, in which upper and lower bounds for each dimension are permitted. These can be thought of as any section represented by Fortran 90 triplet notation in which the stride is one. Widely used extensions include arbitrary stride triplet notation and triangular subarrays.

Interprocedural algorithms like the MOD solution can be directly adapted to deal with vectors of lattice elements, so long as the lattice has the finite descending chain property. The component of the MOD algorithm on the binding graph will converge because no formal parameter can be put on the worklist more than k times, where k is the maximum depth of the lattice. The reachability portion of the algorithm converges because, when a strongly connected region is found, the element vector for each element of the region is set to the minimum lattice element in the region.

Note that in the four side effect problems described so far—MOD, REF, NKILL, and USE—we always want to overapproximate the array section involved because we will optimize only when we *know* a variable cannot be in one of those sets for the call site in question. Consider the privatization example in Section 11.2.1. We will be able to make a variable P private to a loop if we discover that, for the call site S_0 at the beginning of the loop,

$$P \in (\text{KILL}(S_0) \cap \neg\text{USE}(S_0))$$

In other words, we optimize when

$$P \notin (\text{NKILL}(S_0) \cup \text{USE}(S_0))$$

so we must overestimate rather than underestimate those sets to ensure that inaccuracy results only in missed opportunities, not in incorrect code.

11.2.9   Call Graph Construction

So far, we have assumed a precise call graph on which to solve interprocedural data flow analysis problems. At first blush, it seems easy to construct such a graph—simply examine each procedure in the program and, for each call site, construct an edge from the calling procedure to the called procedure. This simple approach works well, so long as there are no procedure parameters. On the other hand, if there are procedure parameters, we can have code like this:

```
      SUBROUTINE SUB1(X,Y,P)
          INTEGER X, Y
S₀        CALL P(X,Y)
          RETURN
      END
```

The problem here is determining what the called procedure might be at call site S_0. If there is only one invocation sequence for SUB1, it may be simple to follow the call chain back to determine the procedure passed to parameter P. However, we cannot assume that a single chain exists because procedure parameters were added to the language to ensure that many different procedures could be passed to P, even in the same program.

To solve this problem, we must be able to determine, for each procedure parameter P, the names of procedures that may be passed to P, directly or indirectly. However, we must be careful to avoid loss of precision in cases where more than one procedure parameter is passed. Consider the following example:

```
      SUBROUTINE SUB2(X,P,Q)
          INTEGER X
S₁        CALL P(X,Q)
          RETURN
      END
```

Suppose we have the following two calls:

```
CALL SUB2(X,P1,Q1)
CALL SUB2(X,P2,Q2)
```

where P1 and P2 simply invoke their procedure parameter on their integer parameter and return

```
      SUBROUTINE P1(X,Q)
          INTEGER X
S₂        CALL Q(X)
          RETURN
      END
```

Then at call site S_1 in subroutine SUB2, we can pass procedure Q1 to procedure P1 or we can pass procedure Q2 to procedure P2. We can *never* pass Q1 to P2 or Q2 to P1. In other words, P1 can only call Q1, and P2 can only call Q2 in this program.

However, a naive procedure-tracking scheme that simply maintains lists of procedures that could be passed to a given parameter might report edges from P1 to Q2 and from P2 to Q1 because the list for possible procedures passed to parameter Q in P1 includes both Q1 and Q2.

To overcome this problem, a precise call graph construction algorithm must keep track of which pairs of procedure parameters may be *simultaneously* passed to the procedure formal parameters in S_2. This suggests a general algorithm for call graph construction.

Suppose we collect, for every procedure p that accepts procedure parameters, a set PROCPARMS(p) of tuples of procedure names that may simultaneously be passed to p, where the order of the procedure names in the tuple corresponds to the order of the procedure parameters in the parameter list of p. Then the iterative algorithm in Figure 11.17 can be used to determine the correct set of procedure parameter tuples passed at each call site.

Correctness. To show that procedure *ComputeProcParms* in Figure 11.17 produces the correct result, we must show that the iteration terminates and, for every procedure p in the program, it computes PROCPARMS(p) such that $\langle N_1, N_2, \ldots, N_k \rangle \in$ PROCPARMS(p) if and only if there exists a call chain that passes parameter names $N_1, N_2, \ldots, N_k$, in that order, to the corresponding procedure parameter positions for p.

Termination. If, for each procedure p, v_p is the limit on the number of parameters and if N_P is the total number of procedure names passed as parameters in the program, then the total number of possible tuples in the program is

$$\sum_p N_P^{v_p} \tag{11.10}$$

which is clearly finite. Since no tuple is put on the worklist more than once and there can be only a finite number of tuples and one tuple is processed on each iteration of the while loop, the algorithm must terminate.

If. Suppose there exists a call chain $p_0, p_1, \ldots, p_l$ such that p_0 is the main program and $p_l = p$ that passes $N_1, N_2, \ldots, N_k$ to the procedure parameters of p, and suppose that $\langle N_1, N_2, \ldots, N_k \rangle \notin$ PROCPARMS(p). At each p_i in the chain, there must be a tuple t_i of procedure names. Assume without loss of generality that $p = p_l$ is the first procedure in the chain for which the input tuple is not in PROCPARMS. That is, $t_i \in$ PROCPARMS(p_i) for all i such that $0 \le i < l$. If $l = 1$, then the parameters $N_1, N_2, \ldots, N_k$ are names that are explicitly passed to p in the main program (which can have no procedure parameters). In this case, $\langle N_1, N_2, \ldots, N_k \rangle$ is added to PROCPARMS(p) by the initialization loop. As this would be a contradiction of our assumption, it must be the case that $l > 1$. Therefore $t_{l-1} = \langle M_1, M_2, \ldots, M_j \rangle$ must be taken from the worklist and put into PROCPARMS (p_{l-1}) at some point in the execution of the algorithm. At that point $\langle N_1, N_2, \ldots, N_k \rangle$ must be put on the worklist for the call site invoking p because each N_i passed to p must be either an explicit procedure name or M_n, where n is the index of the procedure parameter of p_{l-1} that is passed in the ith position to p.

procedure *ComputeProcParms*

    for each procedure p in the program **do** PROCPARMS(p) := $\emptyset$;
    $W := \emptyset$;
    for each call site s in the program **do begin**
        if the call site passes procedure names to all procedure
            parameters of the called procedure **do begin**
            let $t = \langle N_1, N_2, \ldots, N_k \rangle$ be the tuple of procedure names passed
                in order of the parameters to which they are passed;
            $W := W \cup \{\langle t,p \rangle\}$, where p is the procedure called;
        end
    end
    while $W \neq \emptyset$ **do begin**
        let $\langle t = \langle N_1, N_2, \ldots, N_k \rangle, p \rangle$ be an arbitrary element of W;
        $W := W - \{\langle t,p \rangle\}$;
        PROCPARMS[p] := PROCPARMS[p] $\cup \{t\}$;
        let $\langle P_1, P_2, \ldots, P_k \rangle$ be the set of procedure parameters to which
            the elements of the tuple $t = \langle N_1, N_2, \ldots, N_k \rangle$ are mapped;
        for each call site s within p where P_i for some i, $1 \leq i \leq k$,
            is passed as a procedure parameter **do begin**
            let $u = \langle M_1, M_2, \ldots, M_k \rangle$ be the set of procedure names
                passed to the procedure q called at s, where each M_i is
                either the procedure name in the ith position or
                N_j if P_j is passed in the ith position;
            if $u \notin$ PROCPARMS[q] **then** $W := W \cup \{\langle u,q \rangle\}$;
        end
    end
end *ComputeProcParms*

Figure 11.17 Algorithm for computing procedure parameter tuples.

Only if. Suppose $\langle N_1, N_2, \ldots, N_k \rangle \in$ PROCPARMS(p). Either N_1, N_2, $\ldots$, N_k are all explicit procedure names, in which case they are passed directly to p at some call site s (which would establish the result), or there is at least one procedure parameter name in the list. In the latter case, $\langle N_1, N_2, \ldots, N_k \rangle$ must have been added to PROCPARMS(p) when $\langle \langle N_1, N_2, \ldots, N_k \rangle, p \rangle$ was taken from the worklist W. This must have been put onto the worklist because there exists a procedure q that calls p with N_1, N_2, $\ldots$, N_k as parameters when q is invoked with M_1, M_2, $\ldots$, M_j and $\langle M_1, M_2, \ldots, M_j \rangle \in$ PROCPARMS(q). Since there can only be a finite number $\leq N^\mu$ of different tuples of procedure names and since each tuple may be put on the worklist at most once, we must eventually work back to a call with explicit procedure names. Then the sequence of procedures visited during this process, taken in reverse order, forms the call chain. This establishes the result.

Complexity. We saw above that the number of tuples is given by the summation in Equation 11.10. Let $v_{max} = \max_p(v_p)$, let N_C be the number of procedures with at least one procedure parameter, and let N_P be the number of procedure names that are passed to a procedure somewhere in the program. Then the running time can be approximated as

$$\sum_p N_P^{v_p} = O(N_C N_P^{v_{max}}) \leq O(NN^{v_{max}}) = O(N^{v_{max}+1}) \tag{11.11}$$

where N is the number of procedures in the program. In the special case where there is no more than one procedure parameter to any procedure in the program, the running time is $O(N^2)$. In typical Fortran usage, the running time will not be a significant factor because the use of procedure parameters is limited. However, for languages with more complex usage patterns, there exist approximate algorithms that run in linear or near linear time in the size of the call graph [133, 130].

11.3 Interprocedural Optimization

Having developed the theory underlying the analysis of whole programs, we now apply that analysis to interprocedural optimizations.

11.3.1 Inline Substitution

The most familiar interprocedural optimization is inline substitution, by which the text of a subroutine is substituted at the point of call, with formal parameters replaced by actual parameters in the substituted text.

An example of inline substitution is presented in the following:

```
PROGRAM MAIN
   REAL A(100)
   CALL INPUT(A,N)
   DO I = 1, N
      CALL PROCESS(A,I)
   ENDDO
   CALL REPORT(A,N)
END
SUBROUTINE PROCESS(X,K)
   REAL X(*)
   X(K) = X(K) + K
   RETURN
END
```

If we inline subroutine PROCESS, substituting A and I for X and K, respectively, we get the following code:

```
PROGRAM MAIN
   REAL A(100)
   CALL INPUT(A,N)
   DO I = 1, N
      A(I) = A(I) + I
   ENDDO
   CALL REPORT(A,N)
END
```

This code illustrates several well-known advantages of inline substitution:

1. Procedure call overhead can be eliminated.

2. Procedure body code can be tailored to the environment at the point of call. For example, the index variable I in the example can be kept in a register rather than in memory.

3. Optimizations that would not be possible before substitution can be carried out. In this case, the loop can be vectorized.

The advantages of inlining are so compelling that many have suggested it as a generalized alternative to interprocedural analysis methods. If all the procedures in a program are inlined, ordinary single-processor analysis methods can be used to optimize the result.

However, overuse of inlining can cause a number of problems:

1. The massive substitution required can overwhelm the compilation system, since procedures after substitution might grow to unmanageable size, straining the capabilities of single-module compilers. In one notable example, a program resulting from systematic inlining took 95 hours to compile [83].

2. The object code generated from an inlined program may run more slowly because optimizing compilers do not handle codes resulting from systematic inlining well [83].

3. Any code that is changed inside an inlined subroutine will force the recompilation of every procedure into which it has been substituted. In the limit, any change could require recompilation of the entire program.

4. Some subroutines are difficult to inline because of problems in substituting actual parameters for formals. This is illustrated by the following ugly, but legal, example:

```
PROGRAM MAIN
   REAL A(100,100)
   ...
   CALL S(A(26,2),N)
   ...
END
```

```
SUBROUTINE S(X,M)
   REAL X(*)
   DO I = 1, M
      X(I) = X(I) + M
   ENDDO
   RETURN
END
```

The difficulty in this example is caused by the treatment of the two-dimensional actual parameter A as a single-dimensional array in subroutine S. We could introduce an equivalence between array A in the main program and a single-dimensional array, to produce the following code:

```
PROGRAM MAIN
   REAL A(100,100), a$(10000)
   EQUIVALENCE (A(1,1),a$(1))
   . . .
   DO I = 1, N
      a$(I+125) = a$(I+125) + N
   ENDDO
   . . .
END
```

The main problem with this approach is that it loses the information about the independence of different rows and columns, which can be critical to dependence analysis. Furthermore, this fix would not be available to us if the call to S were in another procedure that was passed to A as a parameter.

Instead of systematic inlining, we recommend a selective, goal-directed inlining that uses global program analysis to determine when inlining would be profitable [44].

11.3.2 Procedure Cloning

Often the main benefit of inlining is the ability to take advantage of some specific optimizations that are possible at some but not every call site for that procedure. Consider the following example:

```
PROCEDURE UPDATE(A,N,IS)
   REAL A(N)
   INTEGER N, IS
   DO I = 1, N
      A(I*IS-IS+1) = A(I*IS-IS+1) + PI
   ENDDO
END
```

At first glance, this code looks vectorizable, and it would be were it not for the possibility that the step size IS = 0, in which case the computation would become a sum of N * PI into A(1).

The obvious solution to this problem is to tailor the code to different specific versions based on the value of IS. This could be done by a run-time test, but if we know the value of IS at compile time in every calling context, we can produce two versions of the program, one for the case IS ≠ 0 and another for the case IS = 0. The compiler would be able to replace the call to UPDATE at the point of call with a call to one of the cloned procedures whenever it could determine the value at compile time.

Cloning is a particularly useful way to enhance the impact of constant propagation by treating parameters that are called with different constant values as constants in different clones of the original version of the procedure. This is the goal of cloning in the Convex Applications Compiler, the only commercial compiler we know that performs this optimization [213].

11.3.3 Hybrid Optimizations

There are cases where transformations involving more than one procedure can be used to gain some of the benefits of inlining without suffering the disadvantages. One such *hybrid optimization* is *loop embedding*, in which a loop is moved from one procedure to another [134].

Consider the original example for inlining in Section 11.3.1. If we interchanged the loop into subroutine PROCESS, we would get the following code inside that routine, which would vectorize well:

```
SUBROUTINE PROCESS(X,N)
    REAL X(*)
    DO K = 1, N
        X(K) = X(K) + K
    ENDDO
    RETURN
END
```

Note that the subroutine interface has changed to include the loop upper bound as a parameter instead of the loop index.

Interprocedural optimizations like this have been found useful in a number of cases, although there is as yet limited evidence as to their generality.

11.4 Managing Whole-Program Compilation

One of the problems presented by interprocedural compilation is the difficulty it causes for compilation management. In a conventional compilation system, the object code for any single procedure is a function only of the source code for that procedure. In an interprocedural compilation system, the object code for a procedure may depend on the source code for the entire program. This is a problem because it means that a change in source code could force recompilation of every procedure. Users will be unhappy if a large program needs to be completely recompiled after every small change.

We might expect that the interprocedural effects of changes made during the maintenance phase of a program would be somewhat limited. Thus, global program analysis methods that can examine the effects of interprocedural information flow might be useful in reducing the amount of recompilation.

We begin by subdividing the procedural compilation into two distinct phases, one that depends on interprocedural information and one that does not. The first of these phases, which we shall call *local analysis*, includes many of the usual compilation tasks—lexical analysis, parsing, semantic analysis. At the same time, it examines the procedure for input to interprocedural analysis, determining the local sets used in each of the interprocedural analysis algorithms, such as the IMOD sets in MOD analysis. With this subdivision, the compilation process is structured as shown in Figure 11.18.

Although this organization permits interprocedural compilation, it still does not solve the recompilation problem. However, if intermediate representations are saved, the local analysis phase will not need to be reinvoked for any unchanged procedures.

To address the recompilation problems more directly, we could organize our compilation system as shown in Figure 11.19. In this scheme, the job of lexical analysis is performed by a separate system component, which could reside in the module editor or in an importing tool. Information about each source procedure is stored in an intermediate representation that includes the parsed source. Programs are defined in this system by specification of a *program composition* via a *composition editor*, which can be viewed as an editor for lists of procedure names. Note that a program composition could be as simple as an input file to the Unix utility *make*. The *program compiler* is the system component responsible for the compilation of the whole program. It reads all the local information for procedures in the

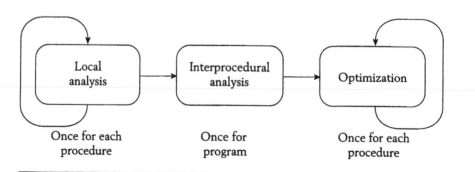

Figure 11.18 Monolithic interprocedural compilation process.

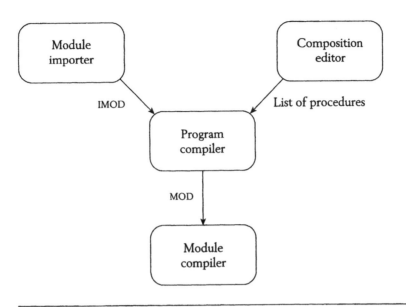

Figure 11.19 Interprocedural compilation system.

program and carries out the various interprocedural analyses and optimizations required by the user. Once all interprocedural information is available, the *module compiler*, which is just a sophisticated optimization system, carries out the optimizing transformations on each procedure. Note that by separating the local analysis from the optimization, we have eliminated compilation order dependencies between the various procedures in the program.

This system, by itself, does not solve the recompilation problem. It must be coupled with a feedback system from the individual module compilations that indicate which interprocedural analysis facts have been relied upon by the module compiler. To illustrate this process, consider the interprocedural recomputation of MOD sets, depicted in Figure 11.20.

We define the set MUSTNOTMOD(p,s) to contain all the variables that must not be modified as a side effect of the procedure call at site s within p if the code generated for procedure p is to remain correct. Thus if the source code of procedure q called at s is modified so that a variable in MUSTNOTMOD(p,s) is changed in q, then p must be recompiled. Think of MUSTNOTMOD(p,s) as a recording of the actions of the optimizing module compiler when it was last invoked on p. Whenever the optimizer used the fact that a variable was not modified at call site s to perform some optimization, it entered that variable into MUSTNOTMOD(p,s).

In focusing on MUSTNOTMOD, we are relying on the observation that an optimizer will make program transformations based upon information only when it is sure that an undesirable event that would invalidate the optimization is not possible. Thus optimizations are based upon the *absence* of variables from MOD(s)

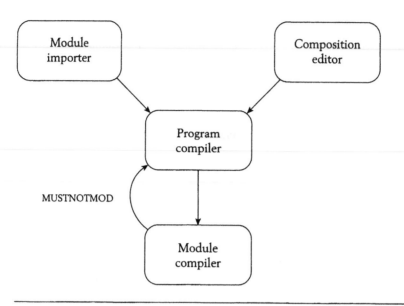

Figure 11.20   Recompilation analysis.

because that absence means that the variable cannot possibly be modified as a side effect of the call. Similarly, optimizations would be based on the absence of a variable from REF(s), so MUSTNOTREF(p,s) would be the corresponding recompilation set of interest. On the other hand, we will make optimizations like privatization based on the knowledge that a variable must be killed by a procedure call, so MUSTKILL(p,s) could be used to hold recompilation information.

In the case of MOD, let us consider what must be done by the program compiler to ensure correctness after a change to some procedure in the program.

1. First, the program compiler must recompute the MOD sets for every call site in the program.

2. For each call site $s \in p$ in the program, if

$$\text{MUSTNOTMOD}(p,s) \cap \text{MOD}(s) \neq \emptyset$$

then recompile procedure p.

The computation of MUSTNOTMOD sets is dependent on the optimizations used in the module compiler, which may be burdensome to collect accurately. However, simple approximation methods often work well in practice. Here are two such approximations for MUSTNOTMOD:

1. MUSTNOTMOD(p,s) = ¬MOD(s) on the most recent compilation of p. Certainly, the module compiler cannot have depended on anything that was not true at the last compile.

2. MUSTNOTMOD(p,s) = ¬MOD(s) ∩ REF(p). This approximation goes one step farther than the previous one in that it does not force recompilation as a result of changes in status to variables that are merely passed through p.

The second of these approximations was used by the designers of the $\mathbf{R}^n$ programming environment [63, 50].

11.5 Summary

Although interprocedural analysis has limited applicability in optimizing code for uniprocessors, it is important for automatic parallelization systems. To be totally effective, a variety of analysis problems must be addressed. These include two types of problems:

1. Forward propagation problems that determine the context in which a given procedure is called

2. Backward propagation problems that determine side effects of procedure calls

In addition, interprocedural analysis problems can be classified into the following:

1. Flow-insensitive problems, for which a precise solution does not require tracing control flow through the procedures down the call chain

2. Flow-sensitive problems, which require control flow tracing for a precise solution

It has been shown that flow-insensitive forward and backward problems can be solved in $O((N+E)V)$ time, where N is the number of procedures in the program, E is the number of call sites, and V is the number of global variables and parameters in the program.

In the most general case, flow-sensitive problems have been shown to be intractable. However, for typical programming languages, good approximations can be achieved in time that is polynomial in the size of the call graph. In practice, these algorithms perform in near linear time.

Interprocedural problems for single variables can be extended in a natural way to handle analysis of value ranges and symbolic values. In addition they can also be extended to analyze side effects to regular sections of array variables. In both cases, the running time will be expanded by a factor proportional to the maximum depth of the lattice of approximations used.

To be usable, an interprocedural analysis system needs to minimize the number of procedures that must be recompiled as a result of local program changes. Users will not tolerate a recompilation system that requires recompiling an entire program after a simple change to one procedure. The functions required to do this may be best embedded in a more general program management system.

11.6 Case Studies

The authors are familiar with several interprocedural compilation systems:

1. The vectorization and parallelization system PFC [20], developed at Rice University, used interprocedural constant propagation and array side effect analysis to improve its dependence analysis. The results of dependence analysis could be displayed in a special browser called PTOOL. PFC was also used as a dependence server by later systems, including ParaScope, described below.

2. The Ardent Titan compiler, which will be discussed further below.

3. The R^n programming environment [63, 89, 90], also developed at Rice, was the first one designed to support interprocedural analysis in a practical compilation system. Recompilation analysis, discussed in Section 11.4, was first tried in the R^n system, which implemented constant propagation, ALIAS, MOD, and REF.

4. ParaScope [79], a successor to R^n, was designed to use interprocedural information in program parallelization. The FIAT interprocedural analysis framework [135] was originally developed for ParaScope, before being adapted into the SUIF compiler (see below). Although it computed solutions to several interprocedural problems, ParaScope initially used PFC as a server for interprocedural array section analysis.

5. The D System [6], which was initially based on ParaScope, is intended to support programming in High Performance Fortran. It includes a framework that extends FIAT to perform interactive recompilation of interprocedural information when the user is editing in the context of a given program. In addition to classical analyses and optimizations, the D System propagates array distribution information interprocedurally to support compilation of Fortran D and High Performance Fortran [79].

6. The Stanford SUIF compiler was constructed with the aid of the interprocedural framework FIAT, a tool that facilitates rapid prototyping of interprocedural systems [135]. It performs a complete set of interprocedural analyses including constant propagation, kill analysis for arrays, and live analysis. In a recent experiment, programs from the NAS, Spec-92, and Perfect benchmark suites were run through the compiler without any modification to the original source code. For this total of 27 programs, 16 of them yielded more parallel loops as a result of interprocedural optimization. For 4 of these, significant speedups have been obtained only as a result of interprocedural optimization [131].

7. The Convex Application Compiler [213], which was modeled after the R^n and ParaScope systems, was the first commercial system to perform interprocedural analysis on whole programs represented by multiple files. The Application Compiler did a complete job of interprocedural analysis and optimization for parallelization, computing the solutions to flow-sensitive interprocedural problems, cloning based on interprocedural constants, and employing array section analysis.

In addition to these, a number of commercial and research systems employ interprocedural information.

The Ardent Titan compiler was designed for interprocedural analysis and optimization from the outset. Given that the primary target applications for the Titan I were scientific floating point and graphics, the compiler designers felt that some form of interprocedural analysis would be essential. Graphics code tends to use lots of small C kernels: 3×3 and 4×4 matrix multiplications are extremely common and very important. Because C does not provide the aliasing restrictions that Fortran does (see Chapter 12), the calling context had to be known by the optimizer in order to safely vectorize these kernels. Large scientific codes, particularly vectorizable ones, also tend to be built around a small set of vectorizable Fortran kernels; in early vector machines with weak compilers, these kernels were often replaced with assembly if the compiler was unable to vectorize them.

While there was no doubt that the Ardent compiler would be able to vectorize the kernels, there was a lot of doubt that it could effectively parallelize these codes. These kernels are typically single loop, which meant that without interprocedural analysis, the compiler would have to parallelize and vectorize the same loop. Given that one processor in vector mode could saturate the memory bus, the feeling (which turned out to be true) was that such parallel loops would run slower than the nonparallel version. However, it is also true that many of these kernels are called from within loops—loops that can be easily and effectively parallelized when interprocedural information is available.

Having decided that interprocedural analysis was a requirement, the next decision was what form of analysis to implement. The compiler designers decided on two forms:

1. *Procedure inlining:* As discussed earlier, the biggest bang for the buck is clearly inlining.

2. *User input:* For parallel subroutines where inlining was inappropriate, the compiler provided a set of directives for a user to declare parallel-safe routines with appropriate storage control. In those cases (and only those cases) the compiler would parallelize a loop containing a subroutine call.

The decision to do inlining had wide-ranging effects, some of which were anticipated and some of which were surprises. One of the main surprises was the large number of places in the optimizer that had to be tuned for inlining, particularly when inlining a C function into a Fortran function. One of the effects we correctly anticipated was the impact on the intermediate representation. When doing inlining and other forms of interprocedural analysis, the compiler must visit and revisit compilation units (or procedures). Scanning and parsing the source on each visit is obviously not desirable. A better solution is to allow the intermediate representation to "persist" in a nonintrusive form so that the compiler can quickly integrate it with other procedures at the level of intermediate code.

The Ardent compiler supported a facility that permitted the creation of libraries of procedures to be inlined. Procedures that the user might often wish to inline, such as the BLAS from LINPACK or short, frequently used graphics routines, could be stored into a library in a "precompiled" format that permitted easy inlining even when the original source was not available. The user could invoke these library procedures by naming the library file on the compiler command line. As an example, consider the simple routine for computing the hypotenuse of a triangle:

```
REAL FUNCTION HYPOT(X,Y)
   HYPOT = X**2 + Y**2
   RETURN
END
```

If this were compiled into a library and that library were to be named on the command line invoking a compilation containing the following loop, which processes an array of triangles

```
DO I = 1, N
   A(I) = HYPOT(B(I),C(I))
ENDDO
```

the Ardent compiler would generate the loop

```
DO I = 1, N
   A(I) = B(I)**2 + C(I)**2
ENDDO
```

which would be vectorized and parallelized on the Titan to achieve near optimal performance.

11.7 Historical Comments and References

Interprocedural analysis was introduced in a number of works published in the 1970s. Allen showed how interprocedural data flow analysis could be carried out on programs without recursion [13]. In an unpublished abstract, Allen and Schwartz later extended these techniques to programs with recursion. Spillman

[252] described the interprocedural analysis that was available in the IBM PL/I compiler for procedures in a single file. A principal goal of this implementation was analysis of pointer targets.

Barth [38] was the first published paper to discuss may and must problems. Banning [37] introduced the notion of flow-sensitive and flow-insensitive problems and presented a polynomial-time algorithm for solving such problems. Myers [220] presented a general algorithm for flow-insensitive problems, which he proved to be co-*NP*-complete in the presence of aliasing.

Algorithms for flow-sensitive analysis have been described by Myers [220]; Sharir and Pnueli [246]; Harrison [139]; Landi and Ryder [197]; Choi, Burke, and Carini [74]; and Hall, Murphy, and Amarasinghe [136]. The algorithm for flow-insensitive interprocedural analysis presented in Section 11.2.3 is due to Cooper and Kennedy [85, 86, 88, 87] as is the alias analysis algorithm in Section 11.2.4 [88]. The flow-sensitive constant propagation algorithm presented in Section 11.2.5 is based on the work of Callahan, Cooper, Kennedy, and Torczon [56]. The flow-sensitive kill analysis algorithm is modeled after an algorithm proposed by Callahan [53], although this particular formulation is new.

Interprocedural symbolic analysis has been discussed by a number of researchers, including Haghighat and Polychronopoulos [129]; Irigoin, Jouvelot, and Triolet [160]; and Hall, Murphy, and Amarasinghe [136]. The treatment in Section 11.2.7 follows Havlak [141].

Array section analysis, discussed in Section 11.2.8, has been the subject of work by a number of authors, including Triolet, Irigoin, and Feautrier [261]; Burke and Cytron [49]; Callahan and Kennedy [59, 52]; Li and Yew [200]; Havlak and Kennedy [142]; Irigoin, Jouvelot, and Triolet [160]; and Hind et al. [148]. Several researchers have developed algorithms for flow-sensitive array analysis, including Irigoin [159]; IItsuka [156]; Tu and Padua [263]; and Hall, Murphy, and Amarasinghe [136].

Call graph analysis has been studied by Walter [267]; Weihl [274]; Spillman [252]; Burke [48]; and Shivers [248, 249, 250]. The call graph construction algorithm in Section 11.2.9 is based on an algorithm due to Ryder [240]. The proof that the same algorithm converges in the recursive case is due to Callahan et al. [54]. An algorithm that is not precise but that generates its approximation in time linear in the size of the resulting call graph is given by Hall and Kennedy [133, 130].

Inline substitution has been widely studied [101, 234]. Cooper, Hall, and Torczon noted its disadvantages [83]. The inlining facility in the Ardent Titan compiler was described by Allen [24]. Cloning was studied by Cooper, Hall, and Kennedy [78, 80, 81]. Hybrid optimizations have been studied by Hall, Kennedy, and McKinley [134]. Techniques and algorithms closely related to cloning as described in this paper have been studied by Wegman [271] for intraprocedural analysis; Bulyonkov [47] and Ruf and Weise [239] for partial evaluation; Johnston [162] for dynamic compilation of APL; and Chambers and Ungar [70] for the language SELF.

The approach to program management described in Section 11.4 was pioneered in the $\mathbf{R}^n$ programming environment [63, 86, 87]. Recompilation analysis was developed by Burke, Cooper, Kennedy, and Torczon [91, 50].

The treatment in this chapter is derived from the tutorial survey by Cooper et al. [82].

11.8 **Exercises**

11.1 Compare call graphs with binding graphs. Give a formula for the size of both types of graphs for a given program.

11.2 Suppose you are implementing an optimization that changes the layout of data arrays. One problem of data transformation is illustrated in the following example:

```
SUBROUTINE DATA1()
    INTEGER A(M,N)
    CALL FOO(A)
END
SUBROUTINE DATA2()
    INTEGER B(M,N)
    CALL FOO(B)
END
SUBROUTINE FOO(T)
    INTEGER T(M,N)
    ...
END
```

If we decide to change the layout of A to be A(N,M) but keep the array B unchanged, then we will run into a problem in subroutine FOO because its formal parameter can be of two data formats. Can you design an interprocedural analysis to detect such problems?

11.3 In programming languages like Pascal, scopes are nested where functions can be defined inside another function, and the local data of the parent function is visible to children functions. Give an algorithm for MOD analysis for such languages.

11.4 Grove and Torczon [127] found that the construction of return jump functions is faster after MOD analysis. Give a plausible explanation for this result.

Dependence in C and Hardware Design

12.1 Introduction

The focus of this book so far has been on the use of dependence analysis to optimize programs written in Fortran. Although this focus is a natural byproduct of the historical development of the concepts, it implies that dependence is useful only for application to Fortran programs. This implication grossly understates the power of dependence, which applies to any language and any translation context where arrays and loops are useful. This chapter expands the range of applicability of dependence by extending it to handle languages more complex than Fortran and by applying it in contexts other than language compilation and optimization.

From its inception, Fortran was designed to be a language amenable to high degrees of optimization. The simple input and problem domain originally envisioned for Fortran, the strong requirement for optimization, and the early development of the language all result in an absence of many of the language features common to more modern languages, such as pointers and structures. The first section of this chapter presents some of the issues involved in extending dependence analysis to handle more modern languages such as C.

The second section introduces some of the applications of dependence analysis to hardware design. Modern hardware design is generally done using a language-based approach, where higher-level languages similar to general-purpose programming languages are used to describe the device being designed. That description is then translated by tools (essentially compilers) into a lower-level description that permits actual chip production. Dependence analysis is a potent technique for enhancing the tools used in that design flow.

12.2 **Optimizing C**

The designers of Fortran focused on run-time performance of scientific code, under the belief that the language would be accepted by users only if Fortran compilers generated code that performed within a factor of two of what an expert human could achieve with tuned assembly code (see Backus [30]). Because of this, Fortran is oriented more toward the constructs that are useful in scientific programming and can be automatically optimized; thus, support for data structures other than arrays was omitted.

Later languages expanded the domain of application of programming by including support for programming with advanced data structures, with the consequence of increasing the challenges for compilers. At the same time, by giving the user more control over performance, they made optimization less essential to the program preparation process. The C language is an excellent example of this. C was initially developed as a "typed assembly language" that permitted a sophisticated programmer to specify at a relatively high level pretty much the precise hardware operations desired. Preincrements and postincrements, for instance, have natural analogs in the instruction sets that were prominent during C's early development. The "register" variable declaration, now in relative disuse, really *meant* "use a hardware register" in the early days of C.

Given the correspondence between C constructs and native hardware, the philosophy of C in many contexts was not only that optimization was not required, it was in many cases not even desired. Consider, for instance, operating systems, an area where C is popular. Operating systems commonly access external devices (such as a keyboard) by reading and writing special memory addresses, leading to code similar to

```
while (!(t=*p));
```

Such a fragment might be used to continue polling a keyboard until a character is entered (p in this case would contain the address of the memory location that maps to the keyboard). An optimizer would move the read of the contents of p outside the loop since it appears loop invariant (at least in the absence of a "volatile" declaration). As a result, the keyboard would never be read, leading to a hung system. This type of construct was prevalent in the early uses of C.

Because of this early use and philosophy, C was initially targeted more toward usability than toward optimization. C++ continued this trend by adding in features that simplified program development, at the expense of optimizability. Despite this trend in language direction, however, optimization did become important for both languages. Machine architectures underwent a shift away from instruction sets that permit a direct mapping from C source constructs, and the use of C and C++ expanded into areas, such as technical computing, where optimization is both desired and required. As a result, even though C was not designed with optimization in mind, optimization is now an important part of any successful C compiler.

To illustrate some of the challenges that C poses for optimization on advanced architectures, consider the following simple routine:

```
void vadd(double *a, double *b, double *c, int n) {
    while(n--)
        *a++ = *b++ + *c++;
}
```

This routine is a simple vector add, which would be easily vectorized and optimized if written as equivalent Fortran. The C version, on the other hand, is difficult to vectorize or optimize. Some of the problems include the following:

1. *Pointers:* It is not immediately clear which memory locations are accessed by the C pointers, particularly since the pointers are passed as subroutine parameters. The equivalent code in Fortran would use easy-to-analyze arrays. Arrays could be used in the C version, but the use of pointers has become standard in the idiomatic style for writing such loops.

2. *Aliasing:* Closely related to the problem of pointers is that of aliasing. The Fortran standard guarantees that arrays passed into subroutines as pointers do not overlap in storage in any way that can create a hazard for vectorizing—that is, different parameters represent different storage locations. The C standard provides no such guarantee. As a result, a C optimizer cannot directly vectorize the previous loop, even if it can precisely determine the memory accessed by each distinct pointer.

3. *Side effect operators:* As noted in earlier chapters, induction-variable substitution is essentially the inverse of the classic strength reduction optimization. C's side effect operators, particularly its pre- and postincrement, encourage a style in which the programmer manually reduces the strength of calculations needed to access multidimensional arrays. Because of this, C optimizers must focus extra effort on transformations such as induction-variable substitution, in order to explicitly expose the index calculations for addressing arrays.

4. *Loops:* The Fortran DO-loop precisely specifies its iteration range in a way that is ideal for dependence analysis. Furthermore, it imposes a number of restrictions, such as not permitting jumps into loops, that simplify optimization. C has no similar restrictions on loops, and the iteration range specifics necessary for dependence analysis are not so explicitly available.

This section provides an overview of these and other problems that C poses for advanced optimization. In most cases, the theory developed in previous chapters for Fortran can be easily extended to handle the additional challenges introduced by C and similar languages.

12.2.1   **Pointers**

Without a doubt, the most difficult challenge that C presents to optimization is the use of unrestricted pointers. Pointers introduce two fundamental problems:

1. A pointer variable can point to different memory locations during its use. Determining which memory location is accessed by indirection through a pointer at any given time is a difficult problem.

2. A given memory location can be accessed by more than one pointer variable at any given time, creating aliases for the location. Not only does this mean that different pointer variables may point to the same location, but it also means that when testing an array reference in C, it is necessary to test that reference against all pointers that might alias the same memory.

In other words, pointers not only access different variables, they also allow the same variable to be accessed by different names. The result is that dependence testing becomes a much more difficult and expensive process.

Dependence Testing Strategy

How might a C compiler carry out dependence testing in the presence of pointers using dependence testing machinery from Chapter 3? As the introduction pointed out, idiomatic usage in C programs favors indirection through pointers rather than subscripted array expressions to access individual elements of an array. Because the dependence testing procedure from Chapter 3 examines pairs of subscripted array references, a compiler must have some way of translating each indirect access through a pointer, such as "*p", into an equivalent subscripted array reference. One strategy is to associate each indirect reference *p with a (compiler-generated) name n that is entered into the symbol table and that represents all pointer accesses that could reference the same storage as *p. More specifically, if "n" is the name associated with *p, then every indirect reference through p should be interpreted as something like "*(&n+e)," where e is an arbitrary expression that may be known or unknown at compile time. In other words, we would like to be able to write every such reference as the equivalent array expression:

$$n[e]$$

Note that the name n will be associated with every appearance of *p within the scope of the declaration of p, albeit with a different index expression at each appearance. If p is updated in a regular fashion within the visible program, say, through a postincrement operator in a loop, it may be possible to replace *p with something like "n[a*i+c]," where i is the index of the loop in which the reference appears, a is a compile-time constant, and c is some expression whose value does not vary in the loop. Once all instances of *p have been associated with a corresponding subscripted array reference, dependence testing can be carried out as described in Chapter 3, by testing every pair of references to the pseudoarray n.

The problem with this approach is that there may be indirections through other pointer variables, say, q, that the compiler cannot prove distinct from *p. That is, in the absence of other information, *q must be assumed to overlap with *p. Each such reference must be associated with the same name n that *p is associated with. Furthermore, the difference in offset relative to the start of storage for n between *p and *q is likely to be unknown unless one is set by an assignment involving the other that is visible to the compiler. In the worst case, if none of the pointer indirections can be distinguished from one another, dependence testing degenerates to marking every pair of references dependent, which will preclude all optimizations. The two strategies for avoiding this eventuality are the subjects of the next few paragraphs.

Safety Assertions

In a separate compilation system with no interprocedural analysis, the problem of pointers is unsolvable. Without knowing all possible addresses a pointer can reference (knowledge that is obtainable only when the entire program is analyzed), the compiler must conservatively assume that any two references through two different pointers, or through a pointer and a nonlocal array, are dependent. In practice, this assumption means that all reference pairs will be assumed dependent and no useful optimizations can be carried out.

While strictly automatic analysis in a separate compilation system is impractical, there are effective compromises. Although the compiler must assume that pointers are used in the most undisciplined way possible, in real programs, pointers are used in a well-behaved, regular fashion that is understood by the programmers (if the usage is too complex and not understood by the programmers, the program probably doesn't work anyway). As a general but not immutable rule, an array is usually pointed to by only one pointer at a time, and pointers passed as function arguments generally point to independent storage elements. This type of usage can be asserted by the programmer through the use of two pragmas or compiler options:

1. *Safe parameters:* All pointer parameters to a function are guaranteed to point to independent storage.

2. *Safe pointers:* All pointer variables (whether parameter, local, or global) are guaranteed to point to independent storage.

These assertions hold in most programs, and when they do not, programmers are generally aware of that fact. When explicitly asserted, these two simple pragmas permit the disambiguation of indirect references through different pointers passed as parameters, thus making it possible for the compiler to conduct meaningful dependence analysis and optimization.

Whole-Program Analysis

While the problem of pointers is not solvable in a separate compilation system, the problem is merely difficult when the entire program can be analyzed. If it can examine all calling procedures, a compiler may be able to determine the entire collection of variables that a pointer may reference. With this knowledge, two indirect accesses through pointers, *p and *q, cannot overlap if the intersection of the set of variables they can point to is empty. This brings the problem into the realm of the solvable, although the solutions to date are still less than satisfactory.

The simplest approach to this analysis uses techniques similar to interprocedural constant propagation to propagate addresses forward as far as possible and to build sets of variables that pointer variables may access in given routines. This provides a worst-case bound on the variables that may be accessed, but it is usually insufficient—once a pointer can reference more than one variable, the resulting dependences will usually block any rearrangement. A significant volume of research has been undertaken to improve the precision of pointer analysis in C [144, 206, 197, 274, 152], but the problem still does not have a completely satisfactory solution. As a result, the use of pragmas is still the most common approach in production compilers.

12.2.2   Naming and Structures

To use the framework described in the previous section, each indirect access through a pointer variable must be associated with a "name" or "bucket" that represents all the storage locations that might be accessed. In Fortran (or at least in all variants of Fortran that do not include a pointer statement), a block of storage can be uniquely identified by a single name—the array name—providing an easy basis for calculating dependences. Even when EQUIVALENCE and COMMON statements are involved, array references can be statically reduced to an offset from the base segment storage for the COMMON block or the variables equivalenced together. Such a reduction is not always possible in C, and that fact provides complications in the process of building a dependence graph.

Consider the problem of associating a name for storage referenced through a pointer in C. This process must ensure that any pair of references that might access the same memory location are annotated with the same name so that the dependence testing process will compare the references to one another. Consider the storage referenced by the following constructs in C:

```
p;
*p;
**p;
*(p+4);
*(&p+4);
```

In the first case, the memory location referred to by the pointer variable p is clear and easy to name—it refers to a cell in program memory that, if desired, can be precisely identified.

In the second case, the memory location referenced is not clear and is difficult to name. "*p" is actually an alias for some storage in the program that is "named" or created by another variable. Determining which variables p can be aliased to in this case is certainly one problem that must be solved, as discussed in Section 12.2.1. However, a second problem is what name to use for testing the storage using the algorithms for dependence testing. For efficiency, those algorithms are all based on partitioning references into buckets based on variable names—the assumption being that barring aliasing, things within a bucket can only depend on the other things within the bucket. "*p" cannot be placed within the p bucket, since p refers to storage that is totally different from that referred to by the address in that storage. The assumption is that p's value cannot be uniquely determined at the point of testing, since if that were true its value can be used and there is no need for the pointer. Given that lack of a unique value, the result is that a new name must be created for testing "*p", and since the testing process is driven from the symbol table, a symbol for that new name needs to be entered in the table, so that all pairs of references through that pointer are tested together.

This requirement tends to be overlooked the first time you implement testing for pointers because it is very easy to assume that the bucket for p can be used for both p and *p. The same concept applies again for the third example: a new name is needed for **p to distinguish storage that can be referenced there from storage referenced by *p and p.

Note that the creation of the name alone is not enough; in the fourth example, for testing to be successful, it is essential that the reference resolve to the *p bucket rather than any other; that reference should be tested against all things that *p can refer to and no others. This means that intelligence is needed to simplify expressions involving * operators and to partition them into the appropriate buckets.

The need for that intelligence is further reinforced by the fifth example: that should correctly simplify to

```
p[1];
```

and should be tested against the p bucket rather than any other.

Because of these complexities, the dependence testing framework for C requires some beefing up over that required for Fortran. A powerful expression simplifier that places expressions into a well-defined canonical form is essential, as is strong understanding of the contents of expressions underlying the * operator.

Another complication in C is the presence of structures. Each member of a structure is essentially its own little array, while unions allow aliases to exist for that array. These again create some naming problems (what is the name of "a.b"?), as well as some problems in testing. In particular, since unions can use different-sized objects to overlap the same storage, it is necessary to reduce references to the same common unit of the smallest storage possible—either bytes or, if bit fields are to be supported for dependence testing, bits. If a structure element can be referenced via a union as both a byte array and an integer array, then the fourth element of the byte array does conflict with the first element of the integer array, although a naive implementation would not detect that. The easiest way to manage that is to decompose the integer reference into four 1-byte references, testing each.

12.2.3   Loops

While C includes a `for`-loop, its use is far less restricted than a corresponding Fortran `DO`-loop. In C, a `for`-loop can have jumps into its body; the induction variable (if one exists) can be modified in the body of the loop; the loop increment value may be changed within the loop; and the conditions controlling the initiation, increment, and termination of the loop have essentially no constraints on their form. In other words, someone who expects to be able to look at an arbitrary C `for`-loop and immediately uncover a loop variable, a starting value, an ending value, and a concrete increment is going to be disappointed. Because of this, trying to vectorize C `for`-loops directly is generally not worthwhile. For that matter, supporting a separate representation in the intermediate language for `for`-loops is probably not worth the effort. Front ends can easily translate incoming `for`-loops into `while`-loops, and since analysis is required anyway to determine whether loops are viable as `DO`-loops, having a single `while`-loop format simplifies both analysis and transformation.

In order to be rewritten as a `DO`-loop, a `while`-loop must meet the following conditions:

1. It must have a single, clearly identifiable induction variable.
2. That variable must be initialized with the same value on all paths into the loop.
3. The variable must have one and only one increment within the loop.
4. That increment must be executed on every iteration through the loop; there can be no paths that bypass the increment.
5. The termination condition in the `while`-loop must match that expected by a `DO`-loop.
6. There can be no jumps from outside the body of the `while`-loop into the body.

Obviously, determining whether a loop meets these conditions is not something that can be done with simple pattern matching, but instead requires a combination of control and data analysis. Items 2 and 4 require both data flow analysis, in order to identify the increment locations, and control flow analysis, to ensure that assignments dominate the execution of the loop header. Item 6 requires a simple check of the control flow graph. The other items require some amount of data flow analysis for locating the appropriate assignments as well as pattern matching to ensure that the assignments meet the requirements. The quick summary is that for-loops cannot be converted into DO-loops prior to building up scalar data flow information on the program. While somewhat complicated, this conversion pass can be inserted relatively easily into the optimization flow described earlier.

12.2.4 Scoping and Statics

C's scoping rules and support of file-static variables in conjunction with the address operator also create extra aliasing problems that must be considered. The scoping rules generally get handled by the front end with the creation of unique symbols for variables that have the same name but lie within different scopes. If that approach is taken, then such variables are correctly handled by the remainder of the dependence testing framework with no modifications. However, it is worth noting that users frequently misuse such variables in a "use before def" fashion. In those cases, optimization may often change the values seen in undefined use, leading to perceived compiler bugs that are in fact user problems. Explaining those problems to the user is difficult and well worth avoiding.

Static variables can be modified by procedure calls, just as Fortran variables can. However, the rules are more complicated because a variable can only be modified by procedures that can see its declaration. Determining these can usually be done easily from the scope information that should be present in a C symbol table.

Static variables used in conjunction with the address operator create a nuance that is often overlooked by compilers. When the address of a variable is passed as a parameter into a procedure call, it is possible (and in areas such as graphics and windowing systems, it is likely) that the procedure stores the address inside a static or external variable. Once that happens, any number of procedures can modify the contents of the original variable by indirecting through the static variable. This case is easy to overlook in an optimizer.

12.2.5 Dialect

A particularly difficult challenge in optimizing C is dealing with the idiomatic dialect that has been developed over 20 years of C usage. It is possible in C to write loops and array references that are very Fortran-like in appearance, and with some allowances for the greater range of aliasing permitted by C, such references are easy to optimize and vectorize. However, the historical usage of C has been such that no one writes in that style. It is much more common to use pointers, side effect operators, and abbreviated code, as in the example at the beginning of Section 12.2. One of the major requirements for optimizing C is to separate the regular, predictable computations that could have been written in Fortran from the messy, junky applications that have limited potential for optimization.

Most of the difficulty introduced by C idiomatic usage results from three stylistic conventions:

1. *Use of pointers rather than arrays:* C programmers have historically strength-reduced their own array references, using pointers to sweep through arrays rather than subscripted references proper.

2. *Use of side effect operators:* Side effect operators save typing and, at the time of C's invention, mapped directly to instructions on machines in common use. By injecting changes in the middle of an expression, they complicate the work of optimizers; additionally, they are often used to strength-reduce array references into pointers.

3. *Use of address and dereference operators:* Use of these operators follows naturally from the first two conventions.

Of the three constructs, side effect operators are the major concern. If the intermediate representation is allowed to support a notation for side effect operators, the work of the optimizer is enormously complicated. Before an expression can be substituted forward, it has to be checked for side effects; before two statements can be reordered, they have to be checked for side effects; and so on. Remembering to do all these checks is difficult and leads to tedious, hard-to-find bugs. A much simpler, more reliable optimizer results if the intermediate representation does not support a notation for side effect operators, but instead forces their decomposition into more atomic elements.

This was the approach taken in the Titan C compiler [26]. The front end removed all side effect operators during the parsing process, converting operations such as

```
x++;
```

into

```
t = x;
x = t + 1;
```

with the temporary t introduced to avoid some of the problems that arise due to volatiles (Section 12.2.6). After the parser, the intermediate form included no way to change values other than through explicit assignments.

With the removal of side effect operators from the intermediate representation, C's standard dialect can be put into a canonical form, although it requires enhancements to a number of transformations, including the following:

1. *Constant propagation:* Because of the ambiguity that results from pointer references, it's essential to remove as many of these as possible. As a result, treating address operators as constants and propagating them where possible is essential; replacing a generic pointer inside a dereference with an actual address enhances optimization opportunities enormously.

2. *Expression simplification and recognition:* As noted in Section 12.2.2, C's dialect forces stronger recognition of which variable within an expression is actually the "base variable."

3. *Conversion into array references:* As part of the previous item, it is useful to directly convert pointer references into array references where possible. That requires not only good recognition but also strengthened induction-variable substitution.

4. *Induction-variable substitution:* In C's natural dialect, array references are reduced in strength to indirect accesses through pointers before the optimizer can see them—something that has already been shown to thwart dependence analysis. Induction-variable substitution must be enhanced to "unreduce" these. Note that expanding out side effect operators also requires changes to induction-variable substitution, since these forms, which don't fit "traditional" auxiliary induction variables, have to be recognized and removed.

These enhancements are all straightforward, although induction-variable removal requires some significant improvement in the methods for tracking and incrementally updating use-def information for side effect variables. A backtracking algorithm is also necessary in that context, as the form of C side effect operators causes some induction variables to be "uncovered" after others are removed.

12.2.6 Miscellaneous

In addition to the general hazards present in C, there are a number of specific hazards that arise from the history and general use of C in the past. Unfortunately, with most of these, little if any optimization is possible.

Volatile

One of the constructs introduced into C from its operating system heritage is the notion of "volatile" variables. Variables declared with the "volatile" description in C may not be optimized; the programmer has declared that such variables are special cases, such as the keyboard interface mentioned earlier in this chapter, and that the compiler should not optimize their use in any way. While such variables can be handled individually inside an advanced optimization system, it's probably not worth the effort to do so. Optimizing an entire function without affecting individual volatile variables is a process that can be prone to mistakes (for instance, the order of references of two different volatile variables must be kept the same, so that code rearrangement or scheduling may easily cause problems), and code that uses volatile variables is usually neither a good candidate for optimization nor a desired target of optimization. One prominent example from our past experience involved a code fragment that initialized the vector unit for a machine. That code had many loops that vectorized well when optimized. However, since the function of the code was to initialize the vector unit, using the vector unit to implement the code was a bad idea. Most code that uses volatile variables falls into this category, and it's usually better just to bypass these functions with the optimizer.

Setjmp and Longjmp

Setjmp and longjmp are two special C library calls, usually implemented directly in the compiler, that are primarily designed to facilitate error handling. When setjmp is called, it causes the current context to be saved in a buffer. Longjmp can then be called from deeper in the calling chain; when called with a context, it will immediately bypass the calling chain and act as though the corresponding setjmp had just returned (with a special return code indicating that the return is a longjmp return and not the setjmp return). The pair setjmp-longjmp can be used when error conditions are encountered deep in a call chain to avoid having to check return codes in each routine in the call chain.

Setjmp and longjmp not only create unusual control flow; they also require that the state of the computation be preserved at a setjmp call and restored when longjmp is executed. Preserving and restoring the state is difficult and complex when optimization is performed and variables are allocated to registers. It is relatively simple when no optimization is performed and variables are simply allocated to memory locations. As a result, not optimizing routines containing setjmp calls is a reasonable, simple, and effective strategy.

Varargs and Stdargs

One handy facility in C and C++ is the ability to declare functions such as "printf" that accept a variable number of arguments, depending on the circumstances at the call site. The interface for using this facility is a set of macros contained in the header files "varargs.h" (older version) and "stdargs.h" (newer, more portable version). In either case, the macros expand into directives that tell the compiler to save all register parameters to the stack in predetermined locations and that manipulate a pointer variable through the stack to access the variable argument list. The pointer variable is obviously an alias for many different parameters in the program and, as such, is a complication for optimization. Thus, not optimizing programs that contain a variable argument directive is generally a good strategy for compilers.

Unfortunately, this is not the end of the story. Machine architectures that were prevalent during the early days of C use tended to have a predictable stack layout and passed arguments only on the stack without using registers. Given this predictability, programmers often created their own variable argument lists by taking the address of a passed-in parameter and using it to access other parameters—essentially a home-brewed `varargs`. As with regular `varargs`, the aliasing created by this access makes optimization essentially useless, and turning off optimizations in such procedures is generally the most effective approach. If backward compatibility is important, then the compiler should also save all register parameters to stack in the prolog to such procedures.

Note that even though `varargs` procedures make use of implicit knowledge about the stack layout, correct handling of pointers during dependence construction will enable correct optimization of `varargs` functions. However, the resulting dependence graph will most likely be large and complex, inhibiting most optimization, and even in the best case such functions can usually be only slightly optimized. As a result, an optimizer is usually better off ignoring such procedures and focusing its time and effort on procedures that will yield more optimization with less effort.

12.3 Hardware Design

As is the case with many disciplines that have become automated, hardware design has evolved radically over the past two decades. In the early 1980s, hardware design was typically done at the gate or transistor level with designers explicitly specifying gates and connecting wires using graphical entry. Today, most hardware design is language based. Designers textually describe hardware in languages that are similar to those used to develop software. The abstraction level of the description can vary over a wide range—at the lowest levels, designers still specify gates and connections (usually by listing all connections in a netlist format), while at the highest levels, designers specify operations such as addition and multiplication, relying on tools to substitute in the appropriate gates. The level of abstraction that is suitable for a given design depends on a number of factors, including the criticality of time, area, and power constraints, the comfort level of the designer, time-to-market considerations, and the implementation process that will be used to fabricate the design. Regardless of all other factors, however, the level of design abstraction has been in general moving away from detailed implementation toward behavioral specification. A key factor in enabling and continuing that trend is the ability of compiler technology to support efficient implementations from high-level specifications.

Hardware design is commonly classified into four levels of design abstraction: (1) *circuit level* (or more commonly today, the *physical level*), (2) *logic level*, (3) *register transfer level* (RTL), and (4) *system level* [116]. At the circuit level, designs are usually expressed in terms of schematic diagrams and are composed of transistors, capacitors, and resistors. Physical layout information is also important at this level.

At the logic level, designs are specified in terms of Boolean equations; the level of implementation is gates and flip-flops. Even though logic-level designs are specified in terms of gates, the gates that are implemented in silicon are often different from those specified in the design. The difference arises because technology libraries do not implement a common set of functionality across different technologies. Thus, if a design specifies an AND gate but uses a technology library that does not provide AND gates, that gate will have to be converted into a NAND and a NOT gate (or some other logically equivalent set of gates). *Technology mapping* is the process of performing that translation, and technology mappers may also optimize the resulting gates for timing, area, or power.

RTL designs specify control state transitions and data transfers between registers in terms of arithmetic units, multiplexers (MUXs), registers,[1] and memories. These designs usually specify a state machine that controls execution of a number of functional units, registers to hold values across clock cycle, and a notion of timing in terms of clock cycles per state. *Synthesis* is the process of converting an RTL design into a functionally equivalent set of gates and flip-flops, and optimizing those gates for a specified technology.

Finally, at the system level, a design is specified more by its behavior than by its implementation. Variables are used, but they are not bound to either registers or memories; timing is specified only to the degree of the order in which variable assignments are executed. System-level designs are converted into implementable designs by *behavioral synthesis*. Behavioral synthesis chooses resources (arithmetic units—a half adder, a ripple-carry adder, a carry-save adder, etc.) for implementing the design, schedules operations onto the resources, and imposes a notion of timing onto the behavior.

As is probably evident from the discussion above, behavioral synthesis is really a compilation problem, and synthesis is close to compilation. Compilers translate a problem description from a representation that is at a human level down to a representation that is executable on a given architecture. The resources available for the compiler are the processors, registers, and memories of the given architecture; the compiler schedules those operations onto those resources using the instruction set of the machine. Behavioral synthesis does much the same process, except it is not given a target architecture or set of resources ahead of time; it must choose resources, balancing the area and power required by extra resources against the time saved. Once the resources are chosen, the problems of allocation and scheduling are similar in both domains.

Regardless of the level of abstraction of the design, hardware development always involves two fundamental tasks: verification and implementation, more typically called *simulation* and *synthesis*. *Verification* is the process of ensuring that the description of desired hardware behavior does in fact do what it is intended to do. Verification is most often accomplished by simulating the hardware description in software on a general-purpose computer. *Implementation* is the process of automatically converting the hardware description into a form that can be masked

---

1. The term "register" as used in this section does not refer to the high-speed access registers in a processor, but rather to a storage element that retains a value through a clock cycle, as opposed to a wire, which passes a value only when driven.

into silicon. Since RTL is the most commonly used level of abstraction today, implementation generally involves the process of synthesis.

Simulators and synthesizers (particularly higher-level synthesizers) are basically compilers at heart. And in both cases, optimization is a critical component of the process. Since simulation involves executing a description in software of a hardware device on a computer, it is inherently slower (by orders of magnitude) than the device proper. Unlike software, once it is manufactured, hardware is immutable; as a result, there are never enough simulation cycles available. Similarly, the cycle time, area, and power are critical aspects of hardware devices, and any transformation that reduces the time, area, or power of the final implementation increases the value of the resulting device. Thus, optimization is an essential function of tools supporting hardware design.

The remainder of this section describes some applications of dependence analysis and advanced optimization to hardware simulation and synthesis. Before describing any optimizations proper, we will briefly tour hardware description languages to provide a common basis for introducing optimizations. After that, we present the basic ideas behind simulation transformations, followed by transformations for higher-level synthesis.

12.3.1 Hardware Description Languages

There are two main hardware description languages (HDLs) in use today: Verilog [265] and VHDL [155]. Verilog first came into use in the early 1980s and, at the coarsest level, can be viewed as C extended with extra primitives necessary to describe hardware. While it was initially developed and marketed primarily by one company, the IEEE produced a standard for the language in 1994, and it is now supported by a number of vendors. VHDL, on the other hand, is extremely similar to Ada and can be viewed as Ada extended with extra primitives to describe hardware. As with Ada, VHDL was developed by committee and has been supported by a number of vendors since its inception in 1984.

Because Verilog is similar to C, Verilog will be used to express examples written later in this section. The primitives and extensions used for hardware description provide the same basic functionality in both languages. In Verilog, these extensions include the following:

1. *Multivalued logic:* Unlike C, where bits can only take the binary values 0 and 1, bits in Verilog can take on four values: 0, 1, x, and z. The extra values are used to represent unknown or conflicting hardware states: "x" indicates a value in an unknown state (either 0 or 1), while "z" typically indicates a conflict in driving a bus. For example, division by zero in Verilog produces x as a result. All higher-level data types (such as the Verilog "integer," which corresponds to a C "int") are vectors of these multivalued bits (also called "scalars"). As a result, simulation cannot always directly map arithmetic operations to existing machine instructions. An addition of

two integers in Verilog, for instance, will result in x's in the result if there are x's in the inputs, and thus cannot be directly executed as a straightforward add.

2. *Reactivity:* One of the characteristics of hardware is that changes in a signal's value are propagated automatically to the devices to which it is connected in a manner similar to data flow systems. This is in stark contrast to C, which relies on a strictly procedural execution model. Reactive behavior is described in Verilog primarily by a combination of the "always" statement and the "@" operators. The always statement is essentially a forever loop—it causes a block to be continually executed. The @ operator blocks execution until one of its operands makes a specified change in value. When combined, as in

```
always @(b or c)
    a = b + c;
```

the result is to cause a new result value to be computed whenever any of the inputs change. In the example, any change to b or c automatically causes a to be updated with the new sum. There are other ways of representing this type of behavior in Verilog, but they can all be canonically reduced to this form.

3. *Objects:* In C, functions are one of the main mechanisms for abstracting behavior, and parameters are the main methods of communicating information into and out of functions. Unfortunately, this functionality is not powerful enough to adequately describe hardware. The object of interest in hardware is a section of a chip; because it is a specific area of silicon, it has its own registers and state. These semantics are significantly different from those of a function call—function calls represent a single code location that may retain state from calls from different locations. Since each instance of the same hardware object is a completely separate area on the chip, no state can be (or at least should be) retained between different objects, and each object retains its own state between calls. Because of this difference, the primary object for data encapsulation in Verilog is the *module*, which is similar in many ways to a C++ class.

4. *Connectivity:* In addition to requiring modules to represent different instances on a chip, hardware also requires connections into objects. Parameters to C functions are transitory mechanisms for briefly passing information in and out of functions, while hardware modules are interconnected by physical wires that continuously pass information in and out. Verilog supports this functionality with *ports* to a module: an *input port* continually passes information in from an outside source, while an *output port* continually passes information out to an outside target. Thus, if we were to encapsulate the adder presented previously into a module, we would make the following declaration:

```
module add(a,b,c)
    output a;
    input b, c;
    integer a,b,c;

    always @(b or c)
        a = b + c;
endmodule
```

This module declares an object that performs 32-bit addition (integers are always 32 bits wide in Verilog). Any changes to the variables connected to the input ports would automatically update the variable connected to the output port with the new sum.

5. *Instantiation:* Declaring objects is of little use unless there is a way of creating instances of objects. In Verilog (as in C++) a new instance of an object is created by instantiation. Unlike C++, Verilog allows only static (and not dynamic) instantiation of modules. Modules are instantiated by declaring a new instance:

```
integer x,y,z;
add adder1(x,y,z);
```

This declaration creates a new adder called "adder1." The variables x, y, and z are connected to the ports a, b, and c in the module add, so that any time y or z change in value, x will be invisibly updated to be their new sum. Each instantiation of the module add corresponds to a different location in silicon, so that internal variables to the module (which in Verilog are always declared static as opposed to automatic) are unique to each instantiation. Thus, each instance of the module retains internal state between changes, but there is no preserved state to the module declaration.

6. *Vector operations:* Given its scalar orientation and its view of other data structures as being collections or vectors of scalars, it is very natural for Verilog to support simple vector operations. Single bits can be extracted using the bit select operator (e.g., A[1]); vectors can be extracted via part selects (e.g., A[3:4]—no stride other than one is permitted); and vectors can be concatenated together ({A[0], A[1:15]} yields the leftmost 16 bits of A).

Verilog contains a number of other primitives and extensions for describing timing of operations and the context in which modules should be generated, but the features described above provide enough context for this discussion. Verilog contains language support for all levels, from the very lowest (circuit) to the very highest level (system). Practically, however, it tends to be used most often for gates and RTL. The circuit level tends to be too detailed for most designers, and the system-level support in Verilog gets clouded by the lower-level support. For instance, the fact that all variables are four-state leads to slower simulation at the system level, where unknowns are typically unimportant.

From an optimization point of view, Verilog has a number of desirable properties. First, there is essentially no aliasing. Since compilers have to be able to figure out where wires go if they're going to generate hardware and connect it, the language definition has no way (outside of one fairly explicit construct) to alias a value. Second, vectors are extensively used in designs, and the language restricts the form of subscripts to a form that permits easy analysis. Finally, for historical reasons, Verilog requires that the entire hardware design be presented to the compiler at one time; separate compilation is not supported. As a result, effective interprocedural analysis is possible in Verilog compilers.

However, Verilog (and more generally, hardware design) also provides a number of twists for optimizers. The first is the nonprocedural continuation semantics introduced by always blocks and the introduction of time. Control no longer flows smoothly and predictably from basic block to basic block. Instead, a change in one variable will trigger the activation of another always block, which may in turn trigger other activations, and so on. A second oddity is the absence of loops. While Verilog does provide looping constructs as well as vectors, in practice loops are only used at the system level. Looping constructs are executed at lower levels, but the loops are implicitly represented through always blocks and the scheduler, rather than explicitly represented in the source. As a result, identifying repeated parts of the computation is much more difficult than in procedural languages. Finally, there is the matter of size. Hardware designs are *large*, and the requirement that the entire design be presented to the compiler at one time has bad as well as good implications. Memory utilization and compilation time are critical considerations for compilers and optimizers in this area. Even synthesizers that pay obsessive attention to memory utilization and compile time take days and gigabytes to compile a modest-size hardware design. A synthesizer that exhibits any sloppiness in these areas will be unusable.

Given this introduction to Verilog and hardware designs, the following sections will present some of the challenges faced in simulation and synthesis and how optimization techniques such as dependence analysis can be applied to help address them.

12.3.2   Optimizing Simulation

In simulation, the goal for the compiler (which is what a good simulator really is) is to map the hardware description to the instruction set of the processor on which the design is to be simulated. Described at this level of detail, the problem is a straightforward compiler problem, and simulation done only to this level of detail is not a difficult proposition. However, this completely misses the real problem in simulation as well as the real opportunity for optimization. To see this, consider the following behavioral level adder:

```
module adder(a,b,c)
    input b[0:3], c[0:3];
    output a[0:3];
    always @(b or c)
        a = b + c;
endmodule
```

Given this input, a reasonable compiler should recognize that, so long as no unknowns are involved, the addition can be performed as a single instruction on any machine that contains a 32-bit adder (as virtually all machines today do)—28 bits of the result are unused, but the fastest execution is achieved by mapping the operation to a native add, with a preceding check to ensure that there are no unknowns. Since unknowns generally do not appear in a hardware design once it has gotten past reset conditions, the operation will always be performed as the single addition in steady-state computation.

However, this behavioral form is not the only one the adder may take. It is also very likely that the simulator may be presented with

```
module adder(a,b,c)
    input b[0:3], c[0:3];
    output a[0:3];
    wire carry;

    add2 add_l(a[0:1],0,b[0:1],c[0:1],carry);
    add2 add_r(a[2:3],carry,b[2:3],c[2:3],0);

endmodule
module add2(sum,c_out,op1,op2,c_in)
    output sum[0:1], c_out;
    input op1[0:1], op2[0:1], c_in;
    wire carry;

    add1 add_r(sum[0],carry,op1[0],op2[0],c_in);
    add1 add_l(sum[1],c_out,op1[1],op2[1],carry);
endmodule
module add1(sum,c_out,op1,op2,c_in)
    input op1, op2, c_in;
    output sum c_out;
    always @(op1 or op2 or c_in) begin
        sum = op1 ^ op2 ^ c_in;
        c_out = (op1 & op2) | (op2 & c_in) |
                (c_in & op1);
    end
endmodule
```

This fragment performs exactly the same function as the behavioral-level adder. However, a direct mapping of this to typical instruction sets is going to simulate more slowly than the first example. The reason is the level of detail. The behavioral example maps directly to the single add instruction; the lower-level example explicitly states all the details going on in the add instruction (which is of course required in hardware). A straightforward simulation is going to execute all of the detail in different machine instructions rather than recognizing that the entire fragment can be pulled into one machine instruction.

These two fragments illustrate the real crux of optimizing hardware simulations. Outside of taking care of the details of good scheduling and use of two-state rather than four-state logic where possible, compiling behavioral-level code for simulation is pretty much a standard compiler problem; the level of the code is relatively close to the level of the target instruction set. As a result, simulation of behavioral designs is fast—typically close to the speed of compiled code. Lower-level designs, however, insert details that consume simulation time and obscure the behavioral-level functionality. As a result, simulation is very slow. The key to obtaining optimal simulation speeds is to recognize the intended functionality in lower-level designs and map it to the less detailed functionality available in machine instruction sets.

Another way of saying this is that simulation speed is related to the level of abstraction of the simulated design more than anything else—the higher the level, the faster the simulation. Since higher-level designs tend to simulate efficiently given reasonable optimization techniques, one of the prime optimization techniques for a good simulator is to rederive higher-level functionality from the lower-level design. Doing so enables good simulation performance at all design levels. Performance across all levels is important because, even though designers are using higher levels of abstraction, hardware engineers, being justifiably paranoid, quite often simulate synthesis results to ensure that the synthesis tools have not made a mistake. Also, the nature of hardware often forces some lower-level decisions. For instance, hardware is eventually implemented as single-bit gates, even though in conglomeration a group of gates may compose an adder. As a result, descriptions similar to the second example are not unusual; when expressed that way, it is easy to swap out the lowest-level modules for a new technology.

Fortunately, the techniques introduced in earlier chapters form a good basis for rederiving the higher-level functionality of lower-level designs, as well as improving the scheduling of designs at lower or higher levels. The next few sections illustrate how those techniques can be used to improve simulation.

Inlining Modules

As should be obvious from the previous examples, a fundamental optimization required for simulators is the ability to expand modules inline. While data encapsulation is a good programming technique for hiding unnecessary details from programmers, it has the side effect of hiding information necessary for optimization from the compiler. This is particularly true when the goal is to rederive basic functionality of an operation that has been divided into a number of modules.

Fortunately, HDLs have two properties that make module inlining a relatively simple process:

1. The entire design is presented to the simulator at one time. This means that the source to all modules can always be found.

2. Recursion is not permitted (recursive hardware is a somewhat frightening thought). As a result, a topological ordering can always be imposed on the instance graph (the "module" equivalent of a call graph), and inlining can be performed in linear time with no fear of infinite recursion.

Deciding when to stop inlining requires some careful thought, since it is usually fruitless to inline above the level of functional units.

Revisiting the second example again, here is the result after inlining all modules:

```
module adder(a,b,c)
     input b[0:3], c[0:3];
     output a[0:3];
     wire carry, temp, temp1;

     always @(b[1] or c[1] or carry) begin
         a[1] = b[1] ^ c[1] ^ carry;
         temp = (b[1] & c[1]) | (c[1] & carry) |
                 (carry & b[1]);
     end

     always @(b[0] or c[0] or temp) begin
         a[0] = b[0] ^ c[0] ^ temp;
         0 = (b[0] & c[0]) | (c[0] & temp) | (temp & b[0]);
     end

     always @(b[3] or c[3] or 0) begin
         a[3] = b[3] ^ c[3] ^ 0;
         temp1 = (b[3] & c[3]) | (c[3] & 0) | (0 & b[3]);
     end

     always @(b[2] or c[2] or temp1) begin
         a[2] = b[2] ^ c[2] ^ temp1;
         carry = (b[2] & c[2]) | (c[2] & temp1) |
             (temp1 & b[2]);
     end
endmodule
```

Note that one result above is mapped to the constant 0, which is one way to throw an output away in hardware design.

Execution Ordering

A familiar refrain in this book has been the statement that the order in which statements are executed can have a dramatic effect on the efficiency with which they are executed. This statement is as true in the world of hardware simulation as it is anywhere else. Consider, for instance, the inlined example in the previous section, and assume that the value of c changes from 0 to 1 and that b has the binary value 1111. All of the result bits are obviously going to ripple in a change from 1 to 0. Hardware for this simple adder will bring about the change efficiently: the change in c causes the third `always` block to activate. Its execution causes the value of `temp1` to change from 0 to 1. This change, in turn, activates the fourth block, which changes the value of `carry` from 0 to 1. This process continues, next activating the first block and finally the second. The triggering of current flows in real hardware efficiently follows the ideal activation model.

While resulting hardware will execute efficiently, a software simulation of the hardware may not execute so efficiently. The key to efficiency in the hardware comes from triggering on changes in individual bits, which occurs naturally given the wires connecting up the gates of the adder. Software cannot always afford the convenience of tracking individual bits, however, as doing so can require an inordinate amount of memory. Instead, a software simulator may be forced in some cases to associate one "change" bit with each entity. For instance, in the example above, rather than having individual change bits for a[0], a[1], a[2], and a[3], a simulator may well have just one bit that represents any change in the value of a, ignoring the specific bit that changes. The situation is equivalent to data flow analysis in compilers, where arrays are not "killed" and where a change in value of any element of the array is indicated as a change in all elements of the array.

When individual change bits are not possible, execution ordering becomes a major factor in the simulation efficiency of the adder above. Consider the execution for the same input changes as before with change bits only for the array entities, and not their individual elements. The change in c, even though only one bit, causes all the `always` blocks to be scheduled. Assuming they execute in lexical order, the first and second `always` blocks will execute, but cause no change in outputs. When the third block executes, it will cause a[3] to change from 1 to 0 and set the carry bit `temp1` to be 1, activating changes based on it. The only block dependent on `temp1` is block 4, which was already scheduled for execution from the original change. Block 4 then executes, causing a[2] and `carry` to change, which reactivates block 1. Block 1 will then ripple the carry through block 2, and the result will have stabilized. This ordering is clearly not as efficient as the underlying hardware and can be quadratic in the worst case (particularly if the carry bits are represented in a single array rather than as individual variables).

The solution is obvious: execute the blocks in a topological order based on the dependence graph of individual array elements. When the blocks are reordered topologically

```
module adder(a,b,c)
    input b[0:3], c[0:3];
    output a[0:3];
    wire carry, temp, temp1;

    always @(b[3] or c[3] or 0) begin
        a[3] = b[3] ^ c[3] ^ 0;
        temp1 = (b[3] & c[3]) | (c[3] & 0) | (0 & b[3]);
    end
    always @(b[2] or c[2] or temp1) begin
        a[2] = b[2] ^ c[2] ^ temp1;
        carry = (b[2] & c[2]) | (c[2] & temp1) |
                (temp1 & b[2]);
    end
    always @(b[1] or c[1] or carry) begin
        a[1] = b[1] ^ c[1] ^ carry;
        temp = (b[1] & c[1]) | (c[1] & carry) |
               (carry & b[1]);
    end
    always @(b[0] or c[0] or temp) begin
        a[0] = b[0] ^ c[0] ^ temp;
        0 = (b[0] & c[0]) | (c[0] & temp) | (temp & b[0]);
    end

endmodule
```

data changes flow through the block in the same direction as the lexical execution. The result is simulation that is as efficient as having individual change bits, but without the memory overhead.

Since explicit loops are nonexistent in simulations at this level and there is no aliasing, computing the dependence graph is a simple proposition based on the index values. However, the topological sort is not completely straightforward, as the dependence graph may contain cycles. Just as with Fortran call graphs, these cycles should only be static (a dynamic cycle implies very unsettled hardware). As a result, a procedure similar to the parallel *codegen* algorithm (Figure 2.2) is necessary for ordering the blocks. However, this procedure is somewhat more complicated. With *codegen*, the properties of loop-carried dependences ensure that recursive calls will break all cycles. There is no analogous concept with hardware. As a result, picking the appropriate edges to break cycles is a sophisticated process and represents the key component of the algorithm.

Dynamic versus Static Scheduling

As is evident in the previous section, one of the main issues in hardware simulation is scheduling. Emulating hardware's natural data flow execution efficiently in deterministic software involves difficult trade-offs that are hard to evaluate a priori. The most difficult trade-off is that of dynamic versus static scheduling.

The most natural way of simulating hardware's data flow execution is to dynamically track changes in values and propagate those changes along the connected wires to affected computation units. This approach is known as *dynamic scheduling*. If this model is adopted, every time the simulator computes a value for an object, it compares the new value to the existing value. If the object has changed in value, the simulator schedules all connected objects to be updated with the new value. If the object's value is unchanged, the simulator does nothing. As is evident in the previous example, the advantages of such an approach (so long as it computes changes at the bit level) are that it exactly mimics hardware execution and computes only changed values. The disadvantage is the overhead of the change checks. This overhead can dominate the computation time, particularly when the checks are performed on every bit.

An alternative that avoids the overhead of change checks is to statically schedule simulation (*static scheduling*), following the topological model, introduced in the previous section. Under this model, the simulator never checks whether objects change in value; instead, it blindly (or *obliviously*, the more common technical phrase) sweeps through the simulation computing values for all objects regardless of whether there are actually any changes to propagate. The advantage is that all change checks are avoided. Purely static scheduling can only be used with designs that introduce no evaluation cycles in the dependence graph. While this restriction eliminates some designs from consideration, the design style that it enforces is one that is generally supported by hardware designers.

The key determinant of whether dynamic or static scheduling is the more efficient approach is the level of circuit activity. If relatively few elements of a circuit change during each time step, then the change checks scheduled dynamically tend to quickly locate the changed elements and bring the circuit to quiescence without evaluating unchanged areas of the circuit. On the other hand, if the circuit is highly active, oblivious updating all portions of the circuit is more efficient than performing change checks that are almost always true. It is difficult to know in advance whether a circuit (or whether portions of a circuit) are highly active or dormant for a particular set of test vectors, making it difficult to predetermine whether static or dynamic scheduling will be the more efficient approach. However, using static analysis to improve the order in which things are dynamically scheduled always improves simulation performance, usually by factors of four to five times.

Our experience has shown that in hardware simulation (as well as in parallel execution) using dynamic scheduling guided by static analysis provides the best results. The remainder of this section assumes this scheduling strategy.

Fusing Always Blocks

Given that one of the major overheads in dynamic scheduling is evaluation and propagation of change checks, one of the simplest optimizations to perform is fusing always blocks that have the same triggering conditions. Fusing blocks increases the amount of computation performed per unit of overhead, resulting in more efficient simulation.

Fusing `always` blocks is particularly important in *synchronous* designs, where events are triggered by changes in a system clock. Most modules in a synchronous design take a form similar to

```
module add1(sum, c_out, op1, op2, c_in, clk)
    input op1, op2, c_in, clk;
    output sum c_out;
    always @(posedge(clk)) begin
        sum = op1 ^ op2 ^ c_in;
        c_out = (op1 & op2) | (op2 & c_in) |
                (c_in & op1);
    end
endmodule
```

The rising edge of the clock is used to update the sum, regardless of changes in input values. When this *synchronous* adder is used in place of the previously introduced *asynchronous* adder (which triggers only on input values, independent of any system clock) to create a 4-bit adder, the following results after module inlining:

```
module adder(a,b,c,clk)
    input b[0:3], c[0:3], clk;
    output a[0:3];
    wire carry, temp, temp1;

    always @(posedge(clk)) begin
        a[3] = b[3] ^ c[3] ^ 0;
        temp1 = (b[3] & c[3]) | (c[3] & 0) | (0 & b[3]);
    end
    always @(posedge(clk)) begin
        a[2] = b[2] ^ c[2] ^ temp1;
        carry = (b[2] & c[2]) | (c[2] & temp1) |
                (temp1 & b[2]);
    end
    always @(posedge(clk)) begin
        a[1] = b[1] ^ c[1] ^ carry;
        temp = (b[1] & c[1]) | (c[1] & carry) |
               (carry & b[1]);
    end
    always @(posedge(clk)) begin
        a[0] = b[0] ^ c[0] ^ temp;
        0 = (b[0] & c[0]) | (c[0] & temp) | (temp & b[0]);
    end

endmodule
```

Since the blocks all trigger off the same condition, this can be more efficiently executed as

```
module adder(a,b,c,clk)
    input b[0:3], c[0:3], clk;
    output a[0:3];
    wire carry, temp, temp1;
    always @(posedge(clk)) begin
        a[3] = b[3] ^ c[3] ^ 0;
        temp1 = (b[3] & c[3]) | (c[3] & 0) | (0 & b[3]);
        a[2] = b[2] ^ c[2] ^ temp1;
        carry = (b[2] & c[2]) | (c[2] & temp1) |
                (temp1 & b[2]);
        a[1] = b[1] ^ c[1] ^ carry;
        temp = (b[1] & c[1]) | (c[1] & carry) |
                (carry & b[1]);
        a[0] = b[0] ^ c[0] ^ temp;
        0 = (b[0] & c[0]) | (c[0] & temp) | (temp & b[0]);
    end
endmodule
```

invoking the overhead of scheduling a block once rather than four times. While the overhead of scheduling a block is not that high, avoiding it enough times can lead to a significant savings in simulation time.

In general, an always block can be fused into a prior block when the condition controlling the execution of the prior block implies that the condition of the fused block will be true. This assumes that the condition of the prior block is used to control execution of the fused block and permits fusion in such common cases as

```
always @(posedge(clk)) begin
    blk1
end
always @(posedge(reset) or posedge(clk)) begin
    blk2
end
```

Fusion in this case requires some code duplication, yielding the following as the fused result:

```
always @(posedge(clk)) begin
    blk1
    blk2
end
always @(posedge(reset)) begin
    blk2
end
```

While fusing always blocks with common or implied controlling conditions is a straightforward optimization, it is not quite so straightforward as it initially appears. The primary problem involves the nondeterminism inherent in parallel languages. Fusing always blocks can change the output of a design. Even though the change is valid given the semantics of the language, seeing program output change under optimization does not usually make a designer happy. While many output changes such as this indicate buggy designs that should be fixed, others are annoyances known by designers to be OK. Simulators cannot easily distinguish between the two cases, making the safest course the one that avoids any output changes.

To see how block fusion can change a design's output, consider again the original synchronous adder with all 1-bit adders inlined. Without fusion, the final result depends on the order in which the always blocks are triggered. If triggered in the order in which they are lexically listed in the program, the simulation will produce the expected results for an adder and fusion does not change the results. If they are triggered in reverse lexical order (the order in which blocks are triggered in this case is not guaranteed by Verilog, and the design is in this case incorrect), then the original design does not produce correct results for an adder until 3 clocks after inputs change, since it takes that long for the carry to ripple from the first bit to the last bit. However, fusion will change the results, by combining the individual blocks (where execution order is indeterminate) into one block (where execution order is determinate). This change can be avoided by not fusing blocks that are connected by true dependence edges and by not fusing blocks that will result in a block moving across a dependence edge into it.

Synchronous logic usually contains a reset condition as well as a clock edge controlling its always blocks. An extremely common template is

```
always @(posedge(clk) or reset) begin
   if reset then
      // Code to perform hardware reset
   else
      // True block functionality
end
```

Since reset code is rarely executed, the block is almost always taken on the posedge condition. In cases like this, it is always beneficial to split the block into two:

```
always @(posedge(clk)) begin
   if reset then
      // Code to perform hardware reset
   else
      // True block functionality
end
```

```
always @(reset) begin
   if reset then
      // Code to perform hardware reset
   else
      // True block functionality
end
```

and then, recognizing that the changed controls will always imply that only one branch is executed in each block,

```
always @(posedge(clk)) begin
   // True block functionality
end
always @(reset) begin
   // Code to perform hardware reset
end
```

Block fusion after this will pull all the reset code into one block that is rarely executed and all the typical code into a block that is commonly executed.

Vectorizing Always Blocks

In gate-level simulation, a major goal is to rederive the higher-level abstraction that was the original intent of the gates to be simulated. Given that one of the main transformations done by hardware design tools and hardware designers is breaking the abstract operations down into single-bit operations, an important transformation for a hardware simulator is to regroup those operations. This regrouping amounts to nothing more than vectorization.

While vectorization is an important optimization for hardware simulation, the way in which it is performed differs from the techniques used in compilers. The reason comes from the nature of hardware description and the input language. Consider again the inlined asynchronous adder presented earlier:

```
module adder(a,b,c)
     input b[0:3], c[0:3];
     output a[0:3];
     wire carry, temp, temp1;

     always @(b[3] or c[3] or 0) begin
        a[3] = b[3] ^ c[3] ^ 0;
        temp1 = (b[3] & c[3]) | (c[3] & 0) | (0 & b[3]);
     end
     always @(b[2] or c[2] or temp1) begin
        a[2] = b[2] ^ c[2] ^ temp1;
        carry = (b[2] & c[2]) | (c[2] & temp1) |
```

```
                (temp1 & b[2]);
   end
   always @(b[1] or c[1] or carry) begin
      a[1] = b[1] ^ c[1] ^ carry;
      temp = (b[1] & c[1]) | (c[1] & carry) |
                (carry & b[1]);
   end
   always @(b[0] or c[0] or temp) begin
      a[0] = b[0] ^ c[0] ^ temp;
      0 = (b[0] & c[0]) | (c[0] & temp) | (temp & b[0]);
   end

endmodule
```

This version has been slightly optimized by propagating in the carry-in value of 0 and noting that the carry-out bit is not used. If we remove those optimizations and do scalar expansion on the individual elements representing the carries:

```
module adder(a,b,c)
    input b[0:3], c[0:3];
    output a[0:3];
    wire carry[0:3]

    always @(b[3] or c[3] or carry[3]) begin
       a[3] = b[3] ^ c[3] ^ carry[3];
       carry[2] = (b[3] & c[3]) | (c[3] & carry[3]) |
                   (carry[3] & b[3]);
    end
    always @(b[2] or c[2] or carry[2]) begin
       a[2] = b[2] ^ c[2] ^ carry[2];
       carry[1] = (b[2] & c[2]) | (c[2] & carry[2]) |
                   (carry[2] & b[2]);
    end
    always @(b[1] or c[1] or carry[1]) begin
       a[1] = b[1] ^ c[1] ^ carry[1];
       carry[0] = (b[1] & c[1]) | (c[1] & carry[1]) |
                   (carry[1] & b[1]);
    end
    always @(b[0] or c[0] or carry[0]) begin
       a[0] = b[0] ^ c[0] ^ carry[0];
       cout = (b[0] & c[0]) | (c[0] & carry[0]) |
                   (carry[0] & b[0]);
    end

endmodule
```

Each block is now an exact replicate of the same thing, but with slightly different parameters. This is to be expected, since the blocks were created by inlining the same module into different contexts. While there are dependences between the blocks, the blocks can be merged into

```
always @(b[3] or c[3] or carry[3]
          or b[2] or c[2] or carry[2]
          or b[1] or c[1] or carry[1]
          or b[0] or c[0] or carry[0]) begin
    a[3] = b[3] ^ c[3] ^ carry[3];
    carry[2] = (b[3] & c[3]) | (c[3] & carry[3]) |
               (carry[3] & b[3]);
    a[2] = b[2] ^ c[2] ^ carry[2];
    carry[1] = (b[2] & c[2]) | (c[2] & carry[2]) |
               (carry[2] & b[2]);
    a[1] = b[1] ^ c[1] ^ carry[1];
    carry[0] = (b[1] & c[1]) | (c[1] & carry[1]) |
               (carry[1] & b[1]);
    a[0] = b[0] ^ c[0] ^ carry[0];
    cout = (b[0] & c[0]) | (c[0] & carry[0]) |
           (carry[0] & b[0]);
end
```

Following the dependences, these can be rearranged into

```
always @(b[3] or c[3] or carry[3]
          or b[2] or c[2] or carry[2]
          or b[1] or c[1] or carry[1]
          or b[0] or c[0] or carry[0]) begin
    carry[2] = (b[3] & c[3]) | (c[3] & carry[3]) |
               (carry[3] & b[3]);
    carry[1] = (b[2] & c[2]) | (c[2] & carry[2]) |
               (carry[2] & b[2]);
    carry[0] = (b[1] & c[1]) | (c[1] & carry[1]) |
               (carry[1] & b[1]);
    cout = (b[0] & c[0]) | (c[0] & carry[0]) |
           (carry[0] & b[0]);

    a[3] = b[3] ^ c[3] ^ carry[3];
    a[2] = b[2] ^ c[2] ^ carry[2];
    a[1] = b[1] ^ c[1] ^ carry[1];
    a[0] = b[0] ^ c[0] ^ carry[0];
end
```

and given that there are no dependences among the last four statements, this can be further reduced to

```
always @(b[3] or c[3] or carry[3]
        or b[2] or c[2] or carry[2]
        or b[1] or c[1] or carry[1]
        or b[0] or c[0] or carry[0]) begin
   carry[2] = (b[3] & c[3]) | (c[3] & carry[3]) |
              (carry[3] & b[3]);
   carry[1] = (b[2] & c[2]) | (c[2] & carry[2]) |
              (carry[2] & b[2]);
   carry[0] = (b[1] & c[1]) | (c[1] & carry[1]) |
              (carry[1] & b[1]);
   cout = (b[0] & c[0]) | (c[0] & carry[0]) |
          (carry[0] & b[0]);

   a = b ^ c ^ carry;
end
```

At this point, the original addition has not been fully recovered, but the exclusive-or producing the sum can be done as a single unmasked machine instruction, rather than as a series of masked individual instructions. This code will simulate fairly well because once it is entered, it will sweep through once to the end of the block; at the end of that sweep, all variables will have their correct updated values, and no other sweeps are necessary. However, the bitwise operations computing the carry array will be slow. For the average case execution, performance can probably be enhanced by vectorizing the carry operations:

```
always @(b or c or carry) begin
   carry[0:2] = (b[1:3] & c[1:3]) |
               (c[1:3] & carry[1:3]) |
               (carry[1:3] & b[1:3]);
   cout = (b[0] & c[0]) | (c[0] & carry[0]) |
          (carry[0] & b[0]);
   a = b ^ c ^ carry;
end
```

From a strict semantics point of view, this vectorization is incorrect. However, in this context it is correct because the change propagations for carry will cause the block to be reactivated until the fixed point value of carry is reached. With some static control over the scheduling, this could most efficiently be converted into

```
always @(b or c) begin
   carry[0:2] = (b[1:3] & c[1:3]) |
               (c[1:3] & carry[1:3]) |
               (carry[1:3] & b[1:3]);
   cout = (b[0] & c[0]) | (c[0] & carry[0]) |
          (carry[0] & b[0]);
end
```

```
always @(carry) begin
   carry[0:2] = (b[1:3] & c[1:3]) |
                (c[1:3] & carry[1:3]) |
                (carry[1:3] & b[1:3]);
   cout = (b[0] & c[0]) | (c[0] & carry[0]) |
          (carry[0] & b[0]);
end
always @(b or c or carry) begin
   a = b ^ c ^ carry;
end
```

Assuming the blocks are scheduled so that the first block is the initial one triggered after any changes, the second is then continually triggered until carry stabilizes, and only then the final block is executed, this schedule will require a minimal amount of computation. Alternatively, dependence analysis can be used to determine that the carry recurrence will converge in at most three iterations, and the recurrence block can be statically unrolled to avoid the necessity of change checks. Regardless of whether the block is statically or dynamically scheduled, the critical transformation is to distribute the recurrence into one block and the nonrecurrence into a different block.

As a final comment, once the blocks have been vectorized and the parameters from the instantiation substituted forward

```
always @(b or c or carry) begin
   carry[0:2] = (b[1:3] & c[1:3]) |
                (c[1:3] & {carry[1:2],0}) |
                ({carry[1:2],0} & b[1:3]);
   0 = (b[0] & c[0]) | (c[0] & carry[0]) |
       (carry[0] & b[0]);
   a = b ^ c ^ carry;
end
```

and then simplified into

```
always @(b or c or carry) begin
   carry[0:2] = (b[1:3] & c[1:3]) |
                (c[1:3] & {carry[1:2],0}) |
                ({carry[1:2],0} & b[1:3]);
   a = b ^ c ^ carry;
end
```

it becomes feasible to use pattern matching to recognize the sequence of operations as a simple addition with a carry-in of 0. Given that the carry-out bit and none of the carry intermediates are used again elsewhere, this can be rewritten simply as

```
always @(b or c) begin
   a = b + c;
end
```

regenerating the designer's original thought. The code will not quite simulate as a single add instruction, as some masking is necessary to reduce the 32-bit result down to 4 bits, but this will simulate within factors of the designed hardware rather than orders of magnitude slower, as will be the case with the gate-level representation.

Two-State versus Four-State Logic

Given that four-valued logic incurs extra overhead as compared to two-valued logic, plus the fact that few people want to buy hardware that enters unknown states, an obvious improvement to simulation performance is to utilize two-valued logic where possible. A four-valued logic operation is usually most quickly performed as a table lookup, requiring roughly five instructions with the possibility of a cache miss. The two-valued analog is usually only one instruction. That one instruction can perform 32 operations, however, when the two-valued analog is vectorized. As a result, simulation using two-valued logic can be between three and five times faster than the same simulation run in four-valued logic.

Unfortunately, utilizing two-state logic is not so simple. Even though unknowns should not be seen past power-up, except in rare cases of bus contention or possible cache initialization, isolating portions of a design that can only see two-state logic is difficult. The existence of all source and the use of interprocedural analysis provides a theoretical basis for uncovering regions with no unknowns, but the fact that unknowns can result from virtually all operations usually limits severely the regions that can be executed purely in two-state logic.

However, given the large efficiency of two-state execution over four-state, plus the fact that the test for detecting unknowns is usually only two or three instructions, a reasonable approach is to check for unknowns but default quickly to two-state execution. Such an approach provides a modest speedup in all cases, with no loss of generality.

Rewriting Block Conditions

The semantics of synchronous blocks are that changes are updated regularly on the change of a system clock. Verilog specifications that describe synchronous blocks make it look like results are recomputed every time the clock ticks. For instance, the previously described synchronous adder as written

```
always @(posedge(clk)) begin
   sum = op1 ^ op2 ^ c_in;
   c_out = (op1 & op2) | (op2 & c_in) |
           (c_in & op1);
end
```

has sum and c_out being recomputed on every rising edge of the clock. This recomputation is extra simulation that is not done in the actual hardware. Hardware computation units change results only when input values change; clocking is simply a matter of gating the results through a register where they are made available outside the module. If the input operands have not changed between two clock cycles, no recomputation will be done; the same results will simply continue flowing through the register.

This same behavior can be achieved in a simulator, thereby saving simulation overhead, by rewriting the block as

```
always @(op1 or op2 or c_in) begin
    t_sum = op1 ^ op2 ^ c_in;
    t_c_out = (op1 & op2) | (op2 & c_in) |
             (c_in & op1);
end
always @(posedge(clk)) begin
    sum = t_sum;
    c_out = t_c_out;
end
```

Computations are done whenever input values change (presumably less frequently than every clock tick), and the results are released to the output registers on the clock tick. Most hardware designers will design with this style, but when they do not, this transformation can improve simulation performance.

Basic Optimizations

While the most effective optimizations for simulators are those geared toward reconstructing high-level intent, thereby raising the level of abstraction, many compiler optimizations described in this book can also improve simulation performance. For example, optimizations geared toward recovering high-level intent provide little benefit for designs that are already expressed at a high level. Standard compiler optimizations improve the performance of high-level designs, regardless of how the level was achieved, although not nearly so dramatically as optimizations that reconstruct higher levels of abstraction.

Aside from module inlining, which is basically the equivalent of procedure inlining, global compiler optimizations are not effective for improving simulation performance. The reasons are easy to understand. Given the asynchronous, activate-on-change semantics of always blocks, the control flow graph for a design is a huge morass of edges that represents the potential of control flow from any block to any other block. As a result, focusing on optimizations within an always block is the most effective strategy. If blocks have been previously fused and vectorized, the resulting blocks are large sources of computation.

High-level designs do on occasion use loops, so vectorization is a valuable optimization for simulation. Given the restricted form of subscripts supported by hardware description languages, vectorizing loops is a straightforward process. Other useful optimizations include constant propagation and dead code elimination. Both of these derive their utility from the reusability of hardware: designers reuse modules and components where possible, thereby leading to general components being tailored specifically at instantiation sites. Things such as carry-in bits that are zero are picked up by constant propagation, and things such as carry-out bits that are not used are eliminated by dead code elimination.

Probably the most beneficial optimization, however, is common subexpression elimination. Even in highest-level designs, bits and parts of vectors are accessed and set. This leads to a large number of redundant masking and shifting operations in even simple code fragments. Common subexpression elimination detects and removes this redundancy.

12.3.3 Synthesis Optimization

In simulation, the goal is to "undo" much of the detail inserted by a designer in the process of creating hardware to perform certain functionality. The goal in high-level synthesis is just the opposite; it is to automatically insert that detail for the designer, allowing the human to focus on the functionality while the synthesizer focuses on the details. This goal is analogous to standard compilers, where the human describes the desired functionality and the compiler takes care of mapping that functionality to the underlying machine architecture. As a result, it is natural to expect that synthesis would rely heavily on compiler techniques.

While that expectation is true in many respects, synthesis has one complication that makes it a significantly harder problem than any faced by standard compilers. As a general rule (retargetable compilers are an exception), compilers are designed toward a fixed, well-understood architecture usually with the single goal of minimizing execution time. High-level synthesis, on the other hand, is not targeted toward a fixed, well-understood target—part of the goal of high-level synthesis is to determine the range of architectures that fit the problem and what the performance can be on those architectures. Similarly, there is not a single goal for synthesis. Most often, minimizing cycle time (that is, the speed at which the piece of hardware executes) is the key consideration for hardware design, but the area or size of the resulting implementation is also a key consideration (far more often than the memory footprint of a compiled executable) and power consumption is critical in some applications. In other words, a synthesizer is nothing more than a compiler with an undefined target architecture and with a set of goals that shift among cycle time, area, and power consumption. This lack of clarity with respect to target definition makes synthesis a complicated process. Imagine a compiler that must, while doing register allocation, decide on the number of registers it has based on getting the best performance but without going over limits on area and power. Register allocation for a fixed number of registers is difficult enough.

Despite this complexity introduced with synthesis, it is very much a compiler problem, and there are definite ways in which the techniques described in this book provide a strong basis for synthesis technology. These techniques will not completely automate high-level synthesis in the near future, as the ill-defined nature and wide range of optimization criteria will require human guidance. However, these techniques can certainly optimize a resulting implementation along any of the metrics of timing, area, or power, even if it is not yet to accurately gauge the interaction among the mixtures. Furthermore, many of the key algorithms that designers wish to synthesize are precisely those algorithms that are well suited to the analysis presented in this book: matrix multiplication, dot products, and other vector computations.

The current state of high-level synthesis mirrors in many ways the state of compilers for parallel architectures in the late 1970s. High-level synthesizers currently focus exclusively on maximizing the parallelism exploited within a basic block, ignoring the flow of data across loop iterations. The main techniques current synthesizers possess for increasing the amount of available parallelism are those that increase the size of basic blocks. Loop unrolling is the primary method and is currently the only method for handling loops. While such an approach generates good hardware for loops with small iteration counts, it does not work well for loops with large iteration counts. Effectively handling large loops requires (just as it does in standard compilation) scheduling the computation as a real loop, pipelining the computation based on analysis of the values that pass across loop iterations. And that, of course, requires data dependence.

As you might expect, the optimization techniques presented in this book are directly applicable to hardware synthesis of loop-oriented computations. The remainder of this section details ways in which compiler techniques and optimizations can be applied to hardware synthesis of loop-oriented algorithms. "Hardware synthesis" is a term that encompasses a wide range of technologies. At lower levels, designers specify computations in terms of gates, and the synthesizer remaps and optimizes those gates for the design technology. At intermediate levels, the designer specifies the computation in terms of clocks and cycle times and allows the synthesizer to optimize to those constraints. At the highest level, the design is specified purely in terms of its functional behavior, leaving all control of clock periods and cycle times to the synthesizer. This is the level considered through the rest of this section. Since designers specify only the behavior of the computation at this level, C will be used as the language of representation for most examples.

This section attempts only to present a number of ideas about how optimization techniques may be applied to high-level synthesis. It is not attempting to present a concise algorithm for performing high-level synthesis. High-level synthesis algorithms are themselves book-level topics.

Basic Framework

At the fundamental level, the problem of hardware synthesis is one of reducing a computation such as a simple dot product

```
for(i=0;i<100;i++)
    t = t + a[i] * b[i];
```

to a series of gates—ANDs, ORs, NOTs, and so on. The simplest approach to solving this problem is straightforward: convert the multiplication into gates, convert the addition into gates, and then try to optimize the result to reduce area, time, and possibly power. In an ideal world, this approach would probably work; in the practical world, it does not. The reason is that the process of reducing an operation such as multiplication or addition into gates introduces assumptions and constraints into the result—assumptions and constraints that are not easily removed afterwards by optimization.

One option for multipliers, for instance, is to pipeline them across cycle boundaries so that one multiplication takes multiple clocks to complete. If the multiplication is converted into a pipelined multiplier, the back-end process may, as part of its optimization, need to reduce or totally eliminate the pipelining—something that is difficult to do automatically. Similarly, if a nonpipelined multiplier is inserted, it may be necessary to pipeline it. Given the large number of gates in a multiplier, the number of possible pipelinings is huge and difficult to exploit automatically. As a result, this parameter is difficult to exploit automatically as well. Pipelining is only one aspect of one component that can be explored; there are many others. Adders, for instance, can be carry-lookahead, ripple-carry, carry-save, half, full, or other variations. Each differs slightly in functionality in ways that are optimal in different contexts. Converting from the gate-level representation of one form to another automatically is difficult precisely because each of these has slightly different semantics that happen to include addition as one aspect. The complexity increases exponentially when multiple components are considered: the combination of adders and multipliers into a highly efficient multiply-accumulate unit (MAC) provides just one example. While it would be great if one output mass of gates could be automatically optimized to the most appropriate of all of the possible variations, in practice the search space is too large—particularly given the fact that components are often comprised of hundreds or thousands of gates.

As a result, the strategy of optimizing a simple conversion to gates is not effective in high-level synthesis. That implies that one of the key aspects of getting good synthesis results is the selection of components. Getting a good selection requires two things: having a rich library of highly tuned components from which to select, and selecting the optimal component for each operator or set of operators in its context. Generating a good library of components is straightforward for an experienced designer in conjunction with a good low-level synthesis tool. Selecting the optimal set of components is not straightforward, however.

To illustrate some of the difficulties, consider the possibilities for the dot product sample at the beginning of this section. If pipelined components are temporarily ignored and it is assumed that both array references can be obtained from memory every iteration, then the simplest selection is to use a multiplier to do the multiplication chained into a full adder to complete the computation. Using function calls to represent the functional units, this would result in

```
t = ADD(t,MULTIPLY(LOAD(a[i],LOAD(b[i]))));
```

Assuming all the functional units make their results available 1 cycle after the inputs are present, this naive approach would take 3 cycles to add a new value to t (ignoring the obvious pipelining possibility). However, MACs were designed exactly to speed up this type of computation, by passing the values from the multiplier directly into the adder. Using a MAC would give

```
t = MAC(t,LOAD(a[i]),LOAD(b[i]));
```

which takes only 2 cycles per naively scheduled update. In other words, this very simplest of computations has at least two different viable selections. This simplest form is most likely not going to be the one used, primarily because it does not have obvious pipelining scheduled and it assumes the capability of loading two operands from memory. Memory bandwidth in particular is an issue that cannot be ignored.

More likely, component selection is going to be based on an unrolled version similar to

```
for(i=0;i<100;i=i+4)
   t = t + a[i] * b[i] + a[i+1] * b[i+1] +
           a[i+2] * b[i+2] + a[i+3] * b[i+3];
```

Here the large number of possibilities becomes immediately clearer. There are five additions and four multiplications for each loop iteration; one obvious selection is to use five adders and four multipliers. Four MACs will also work equally well. However, multi-input MACs are commonly used, so another alternative is to use either one 4-input MAC or two 2-input MACs connected with an adder. If the additions can be reassociated (which is true for fixed point), then the expression can be reformed to utilize half adders rather than full adders, saving time and area. MACs that are unused during given cycles can also be used to perform additions or multiplications. In other words, component selection in this example and in most cases is a complicated process.

While the process is complicated, it does have an exact well-studied analogy in compiler technology. That analogy is instruction selection for Complex Instruction Set Computers (CISC). CISC architectures were the dominant architectures in the 1960s and 1970s and had complex instructions that did memory-to-memory arithmetic operations as well as multiple arithmetic operations. On CISCs, instruction selection is far more critical to performance than instruction scheduling, and accordingly, instruction selection was thoroughly researched in the compiler community. The result of that research is a body of tree-matching algorithms that can generate optimal instruction selections under reasonable sets of constraints and optimization criteria. These algorithms are directly applicable to component selection [46, 11, 257].

The existence of fast, effective tree-matching algorithms provides the basis of a simple framework for high-level synthesis and optimization. At the coarsest level, high-level synthesis can be described as selecting components, allocating operations to components (resource allocation), then scheduling what operations occur when. Although described as distinct, the last two steps (as with regular compilers) are closely intertwined, since binding operations to components restricts when the operations can be executed. The analogous compiler framework presented in this book performs high-level optimization followed by a reduction to a lower-level representation, register allocation, and instruction scheduling. Ideally, high-level optimization can be placed in the same position in synthesis as in compilers: as a precursor to register allocation and scheduling that improves "performance" and provides useful information. This placement is not so obvious for synthesis, since (1) there are multiple optimization criteria in synthesis rather than the single one of execution time in compilers and (2) there is not a clearly defined target like a machine's instruction set and registers when synthesizing. Fortunately, fast tree-matching algorithms alleviate the second problem, since they allow quick adaptation to a currently "optimal" architecture. A few simplifying assumptions eliminate the other problem, permitting such a placement.

The simplifying assumptions required involve constraints. Lower-level synthesis accepts constraints on the maximum time allowed for signals to propagate along certain paths and how much area is allowed for certain components. Such constraints clearly do not fit the requirements of high-level synthesis, where only functionality is defined. Some form of constraint is necessary at the behavioral level, however, since otherwise solutions quickly gravitate to a fairly useless global minimum. For instance, if told to minimize time without any maximum bound on area, a high-level synthesis tool should legitimately generate a separate functional unit for each operation in the computation that can be done in parallel—maximal parallelism. The resulting mass of hardware will be fast, but it will also be wasteful and largely unused. Similarly, told to minimize area with no maximum bounds on time, a high-level synthesis should legitimately generate only one functional unit per unique operation, basically serializing the computation as much as possible. This, again, is a wasteful extreme. The most useful solutions are between these two, but without some form of constraint to force the optimizer into this central space, only the extremes will be returned.

The form of high-level constraint that does support a push into this space is a constraint on the number and types of functional units required—essentially an area constraint. Bounds on the numbers of functional units are well understood by high-level designers and—when combined with a directive to minimize overall time, given constraints on the units available—allow a reasonable exploration of the design space. Furthermore, it puts the high-level optimizer back in the design space with which it is familiar: minimizing execution time on a fixed set of functional resources, and minimizing resource use (such as registers and memory access) after that. In this space, the paradigm of high-level optimization, followed by component selection, allocation, and scheduling, makes sense. Loop-based transformations are predictable in terms of monotonically decreasing execution time, at the possible expense of creating the need for new functional units. These units, however, will only be of the same type as that currently used within the loop, so numbers constraints will in the worst case cause operations to simply be scheduled on top of existing units, with no decrease in execution time.

Moreover, the difference in compile-time requirements for synthesizers versus compilers permits a stronger approach. Ideally, a compiler would optimize and generate code, execute that code on a reasonable input, profile the results, and use the feedback from that to repeat the optimization and generation process. That ideal model is not followed in practice during development, primarily because of the turnaround time required. However, a similar model is possible in a synthesis framework. While it's not realistic to "execute" resulting gates, it is certainly feasible to optimize a computation, select components, allocate, and schedule, then given feedback on the expected execution time and area, repeat the optimization sequence. In essence, this approach allows investigation of how well the problem maps to different architectures. Such an approach is viable in high-level synthesis, where the fact that hardware is being generated alleviates the requirement for rapid compile times.

The rest of this section assumes a framework along the lines of that described so far, which performs high-level optimizations directed toward reducing execution time subject to a bound on functional units, followed by component selection, allocation, and scheduling. Moreover, the assumption is that tree matching is fast enough that the process can be repeated as necessary to reject or explore alternative solutions.

Loop Transformations

Just as changes in execution order can affect execution speed, such changes can also affect functional unit utilization, which in turn affects the amount of time required for a synthesized piece of hardware to complete a computation. In other words, loop-based transformations such as loop interchange and loop distribution can affect the efficiency of synthesized hardware.

As an illustration, consider the following fairly common example:

```
for (i=0;i<100;i++) {
    t[i] = 0;
    for(j=0;j<3;j++)
        t[i] = t[i] + (a[i-j] >> 2);
}
for(i=0;i<100;i++) {
    o[i] = 0;
    for(j=0;j<100;j++)
        o[i] = o[i] + m[i][j] * t[j];
}
```

This fragment takes a set of input data a, smooths it using a FIR filter into a temporary t, then remaps that data via a matrix m into an output vector o. This type of transformation is extremely common in the digital signal processing (DSP) world. Assuming enough memory and functional units to do the add, shift, and

MAC all at once (actually a pretty *unreasonable* assumption, as that would take a lot of area), this would take on the order of 10,300 cycles to complete.

If we distribute loops, we get

```
for (i=0;i<100;i++)
    t[i] = 0;
for (i=0;i<100;i++)
    for(j=0;j<3;j++)
        t[i] = t[i] + (a[i-j] >> 2);
for(i=0;i<100;i++)
    o[i] = 0;
for(i=0;i<100;i++)
    for(j=0;j<100;j++)
        o[i] = o[i] + m[i][j] * t[j];
```

Rearranging the order topologically, so that things with no dependences are first, brings the initialization to the top:

```
for (i=0;i<100;i++)
    t[i] = 0;
for(i=0;i<100;i++)
    o[i] = 0;
for (i=0;i<100;i++)
    for(j=0;j<3;j++)
        t[i] = t[i] + (a[i-j] >> 2);
for(i=0;i<100;i++)
    for(j=0;j<100;j++)
        o[i] = o[i] + m[i][j] * t[j];
```

So far, there's been no improvement in execution. There are several opportunities for loop fusion, which is generally a useful thing to do so long as no functional units are overloaded. That can be accomplished if the two major loops are fused. In the current configuration, fusion is precluded because the last loop might get wrong values for t[j]. However, if the last loop is interchanged

```
for (i=0;i<100;i++)
    t[i] = 0;
for(i=0;i<100;i++)
    o[i] = 0;
for (i=0;i<100;i++)
    for(j=0;j<3;j++)
        t[i] = t[i] + (a[i-j] >> 2);
for(j=0;j<100;j++)
    for(i=0;i<100;i++)
        o[i] = o[i] + m[i][j] * t[j];
```

then fusion can be applied to give

```
for(i=0;i<100;i++)
   o[i] = 0;
for (i=0;i<100;i++){
   t[i] = 0;
   for(j=0;j<3;j++)
      t[i] = t[i] + (a[i-j] >> 2);
   for(j=0;j<100;j++)
      o[j] = o[j] + m[j][i] * t[i];
}
```

Simple scalar replacement on t yields

```
for(i=0;i<100;i++)
   o[i] = 0;
for (i=0;i<100;i++){
   t = 0;
   for(j=0;j<3;j++)
      t = t + (a[i-j] >> 2);
   for(j=0;j<100;j++)
      o[j] = o[j] + m[j][i] * t;
}
```

Following this by exploiting the input dependence on a carried by the i-loop
gives

```
for(i=0;i<100;i++)
   o[i] = 0;
a0 = a[0];
a1 = a[-1];
a2 = a[-2];
a3 = a[-3];
for (i=0;i<100;i++) {
   t = 0;
   t = t + (a0 >> 2) + (a1 >> 2) + (a2 >> 2) +
           (a3 >> 2);
   a3 = a2;
   a2 = a1;
   a1 = a0;
   a0 = a[i+1];
   for(j=0;j<100;j++)
      o[j] = o[j] + m[j][i] * t;
}
```

This form will easily execute in 10,000 cycles, as the demands on memory and the operational units have been greatly reduced. With any reasonable pipelining across the loop iterations, the amount of time required will drop drastically.

Some of the loop-based transformations that make sense in terms of increasing execution efficiency include the following:

1. *Loop fusion:* When two loops perform different operations that do not use the same functional units, the loops can be pipelined together by fusing them so that the second does not have to wait for the first to complete.

2. *Loop distribution:* Loop distribution can be used to separate operations that are using the same functional units. Doing so may increase parallelism by allowing overlap of different, nonconflicting operations with each of those in the distributed loops.

3. *Vectorization:* When a given functional unit is known to be pipelined (something that can be figured out by actually doing component selection), one of the easiest ways to guarantee that the component is fully utilized is to vectorize the operation that uses it. The exploitation of the input dependence on the i-loop above was essentially vectorizing the j-loop.

4. *Loop interchange:* Loop interchange can be used directly to increase parallelism by creating new opportunities for pairings such as MACs. However, it is probably more effective by increasing the opportunities for other transformations, such as the use to enhance fusion in the previous example.

Table 12.1 illustrates more specifically the types of efficiency improvements that are possible using loop transformations. The table contains the execution time in nanoseconds as well as the number of transistors required for a pair of combined matrix multiplications. This pairing provides the core of a Discrete Cosine Transformation (DCT) module, which is one of the computationally intensive parts of MPEG and JPEG. The basic loop transformations used in this book,

Table 12.1 Effects of loop optimizations on DCT core

Design	Latency (ns)	Area (transistors)
Sequential	37,684	25K
Loop unrolling once	23,552	44K
Loop unrolling/chaining	18,842	41K
Loop unrolling/multicycle	14,131	42K
Pipelining processes	18,842	50K
Loop fusion/pipeline	9,476	26K
Loop and FU pipeline	4,040	30K

Source: "Exploring DCT Implementations" by G. Aggarwal and D. Gajski, Technical Report UCS-ICS 98-10, Department of Information and Computer Science, University of California, Irvine, CA, March 1998, page 23.

in combination with reasonable scheduling techniques, provided roughly a factor of 10 speed improvement with only a modest increase in area. The greatest improvement was obtained by pipelining the results across iterations—a transformation that will also be discussed in the section titled Pipelining and Scheduling.

Control and Data Flow

One element of component selection that requires more than just tree matching concerns the difference between control and data flow. In von Neumann architectures, data flow involves the movement of data between memory and registers, while control flow refers to changes in the program counter due to sequential execution and branches. In synthesized hardware, however, data flow involves the movement of data among the various functional units, while control flow involves specifying which units should be active on what data at any given time step. Control flow in this context is much more complicated: at each time step it must ensure that the right data is routed to the appropriate functional units and that units are active or inactive as needed. This extra control requires a state machine, where the states are the basic blocks of the original computation and the transitions are governed by the control flow among the basic blocks. Outside of this state machine derivation, control and data flow analysis is the same in compilers as it is in hardware.

However, there are a few other wrinkles in hardware involving commonly used components. Consider the following simple fragment:

```
if (a)
    o = b;
else
    o = c;
```

If a is nonzero, the output o is set to b; otherwise it is set to c. This could be treated correctly as multiple basic blocks and embedded as such into the state machine. However, such a selection is very common, and there is a standard component for this function—a *mux*, or selector. A mux is a three (or more) input function that uses the value of one input to determine which of the remaining input values to pass through. As such, it can be treated as a single basic block.

A mux bears a great deal of similarity to the SSA selector function φ for good reason: they have exactly the same effect. The φ function is used to represent selection when different values may join together along variant control paths; in hardware, a mux is required for the same function. As a result, using SSA as an internal representation has the added benefit of making it easy to detect and insert muxes.

There are several other special hardware constructs that need accommodation as well. Hardware is complicated by the presence of a clock, which introduces time into a computation. This creates four different classes of variables:

1. *Wires:* Wires represent actual hardware interconnections between units. Results gated onto wires are available immediately. Wires do not have to hold values across clock cycles; thus, they are the hardware equivalent of compiler temporaries.

2. *Latches:* Latches represent values that have to be held constant throughout one clock cycle, but not beyond. A latch can be thought of as a wire whose input may change in midcycle, but whose output must remain constant to the units it drives, at least until the end of the cycle. There is no direct C analog to latches.

3. *Registers:* Registers correspond to static variables in C; they hold values across one or more clock cycles. A register is needed when a value for a variable comes in from another state; it is easily detected by looking for upwards-exposed uses.

4. *Memories:* Memories are special cases of registers that are large (and thus cannot be accessed as a scalar) and have an indeterminately long lifetime. Memories correspond to arrays in C.

Wires and registers are easy to detect from live analysis; the algorithms are similar to those used to detect which scalars are live across loop iterations. Latches cannot occur in a strictly behavioral specification, and memories are easily detected as array references. Data flow analysis must detect and mark the class of each variable, as each class requires very different hardware treatment.

Except for the recognition of special hardware constructs and the conversion of the control graph into a state machine, control flow analysis and data flow analysis for hardware are exactly the same as for software. While it is common in hardware to combine the control graph and the data flow graph into a single Control Data Flow Graph (CDFG), there is no real advantage to doing so. In fact, state machine generation is usually simpler when the graphs are kept separate.

Pipelining and Scheduling

The next step after selecting components (including muxes) is to schedule the selection. As is the case in compilers with scheduling and register allocation, the right ordering of component selection and scheduling is not obvious. In fact, scheduling for hardware divides fairly cleanly into two distinct tasks: pipelining the loops using dependence information, which can easily happen before any component selection, and final scheduling using straightforward techniques like list scheduling, which must happen after component selection.

Pipelining hardware is identical to pipelining in software, and loop techniques such as software pipelining apply directly to scheduling hardware. With loop-based algorithms, the key idea is to schedule the computation across loop iterations to find parallelism among computations from different iterations, rather than scheduling the loop body as a basic block. This type of scheduling can be represented at a source level, using an approximation to components that are selected, to give a rough idea of the natural pipelining of the loop.

After components have been selected, scheduling can be applied again. If pipelining is available at the source level from an earlier schedule, then simple scheduling can be used to fit the components together. If the schedule does not fully utilize all the units that are available, rescheduling with a stricter limit on the allowed area (i.e., number of components) can be used to reduce the number of units used.

Memory Reduction

As is the case in compilation, one of the most critical factors in achieving optimal execution speed is to move operands to execution units at a rate that is fast enough to keep those units running at full speed. While this is important in compilers generating code for processors, it is essential for a synthesizer when feeding custom units from external memories. Memory access is typically very slow compared to execution unit speeds, so minimizing the frequency and volume of memory access is critical.

Fortunately, this problem maps exactly into the analogous compiler problem, which has been thoroughly analyzed in Chapters 8 and 9. All of the techniques described in those chapters apply to this problem, including

1. *Loop interchange:* Loop interchange can adjust the order of execution so that operands are reused, thereby allowing them to be kept in registers rather than in memories.

2. *Loop fusion:* Loop fusion can be used to increase the number of times an operand is reused within a single loop, thereby reducing the number of fetches required.

3. *Scalar replacement:* Scalar replacement, while more a source transformation than an actual technique, does permit the easy recognition of memory locations that are reused throughout a loop, so that they may be maintained in registers rather than memories.

4. *Strip mining:* Memory units can return more than one value at a time—typically a cache line is the minimum data unit that can be fetched from memory. This means that strip mining, blocking, and even simple vectorization can all be used to increase the reuse of operands that are obtained "for free."

5. *Unroll-and-jam:* Unroll-and-jam reduces memory traffic, which is good for both hardware or software.

6. *Prefetching:* To the extent that loads can be predicted, load times can be reduced by prefetching operands well ahead of their use.

These and other transformations are described in much more detail by Panda, Dutt, and Nicolau [223].

12.4 **Summary**

This chapter has explored the application of dependence in three very different contexts:

- *Compiling C:* C presents numerous challenges for advanced optimization, including the use of many small procedures, a standard idiomatic dialect, the lack of aliasing restrictions, and side effect operators. Fortunately, the analysis framework presented in this book can be successfully adapted to C, as has been demonstrated by several commercial compilers, including the Ardent Titan compiler [26].

- *Simulating hardware written in a hardware description language:* In simulation, the overriding goal is to minimize simulation time. The main strategy is to recover, where possible, the designer's original intent so the intent and not the detail can be simulated. Given that hardware design naturally decomposes things into bitwise operations, vectorization is a natural technique for recovering the original abstract intent. However, the implicit looping of always blocks imposes a different design structure for the optimization phases that depends strongly on a globally oriented dependence graph rather than a loop-oriented graph.

- *Synthesizing hardware from a high-level description:* Synthesis is the process of translating a hardware design written at a high level of abstraction into an implementation that can be realized as low-level hardware. Fundamentally, high-level synthesis is a compiler problem, although it is complicated because there is no fixed target architecture and the optimization criteria are variable. Component selection simplifies the problem considerably and can be carried out by an analog of the tree-matching techniques used in code selection for CISC processors. Scheduling across loop iterations rather than through single blocks is one of the key advantages achieved by the use of dependence analysis, but others include better cycle times, increased memory efficiency, and decreased need for temporaries. There are still many difficult problems to be solved in this area, but advanced optimizations have shown significant improvements in key loop-oriented benchmarks.

This is by no means a complete compendium of all domains of applicability for dependence, but it demonstrates that dependence is useful in contexts that go well beyond optimizing Fortran applications for parallel and vector machines.

12.5   **Case Studies**

The approach for optimizing C described in Section 12.2 was employed in the Ardent Titan compiler [26], which shared a common intermediate representation, optimizer, and code generator between Fortran and C front ends, allowing both languages full access to the parallel and vector hardware in the Titan. The optimizer was designed to be retargetable, and over time produced code for several different architectures. The compiler was successful in compiling both scientific and graphic applications as well as the base OS kernel and windowing applications. By developing a high-level intermediate representation and analyzing it for optimization opportunities, this compiler took a very different approach from most previous C compilers. However, despite that difference, it was relatively easy to port existing applications to the compiler. The one major area where code often had to be adjusted was in the use of side effect operators in situations where the result was undefined according to the language definition (e.g., a[i] = i++;). Regardless of the fact that the result was undefined, users had grown to accept the output of PCC (Portable C Compiler) [161] as correct and expected the same result from all compilers. Given that one of the authors of the Titan compiler, Steve Johnson, was also the author of PCC, this point at times was difficult to argue.

The area of language-based hardware development, particularly in the area of high-level synthesis, is still a research topic that does not yet possess any universally accepted methods. The techniques reviewed in this chapter certainly enhance the quality of hardware generated from a high-level description, but do not provide a complete solution. However, it appears virtually certain that the techniques that eventually prove successful will use a loop-oriented rather than a basic block-oriented approach.

12.6   **Historical Comments and References**

The first commercial vectorizing C compilers—the Convex vectorizing C compiler [212] and the Ardent Titan C compiler [24]—appeared in the 1980s. Prior to that time, a few research efforts had dabbled in vectorization and parallelization of C, but for the most part, research concentrated on Fortran. Since these first compilers, a substantive body of research has focused on the problems of pointers and aliasing in C [144, 206, 197, 274, 152], but no totally satisfactory solution has yet been found.

Exercises

12.1 Compute the dependence graph for the following loop:

```
for(i=0;i<100;i++)
    a[i] = *p++;
```

12.2 Can the following C loop be vectorized? Why or why not?

```
for(i=0;i<100;i++)
    a[i] = b[i++];
```

12.3 What is the correct value of a[0] and a[1] in the following fragment?

```
i = 0;
a[0] = 0;
a[1] = 0;
a[i] = i++;
```

12.4 Virtually all architectures support left and right shifts on a register. However, some do not support these operations directly, but instead support "extract" and "deposit" operations, which fetch a set of contiguous bits from a register and which store into a set of contiguous bits in a register. For example, extract(a,1,3) returns bits 1 through 3 inclusive from a (a[1:3]) shifted appropriately, while deposit(a,0,2,extract(a,1,3)) will set the zeroth through second bits of a to the specified values, essentially performing a left shift. How would you write the equivalent of deposit(a,0,2,extract(a,1,3)) in vector Verilog notation?

12.5 Given a positive value *s* that is guaranteed less than or equal to 4, write Verilog code that performs in place a left shift on a 4-bit variable. Can this code be sectioned to a size of 1?

12.6 Given a negative value *s* that is guaranteed greater than or equal to –4, write Verilog code that performs in place a right shift on a 4-bit variable. Can this code be sectioned to a size of 1?

12.7 Can you combine the results of Exercises 12.5 and 12.6 into a single shifter that performs both left and right shifts?

CHAPTER 13

Compiling
Array Assignments

13.1 Introduction

Array assignments and expressions have become an important language construct because of the emergence of Fortran 90. Although the Fortran 90 definition took over 13 years and the language was slow to gain widespread acceptance, it is now beginning to replace Fortran 77 as the language of choice for scientific programming.

One reason that the scientific computing community did not immediately embrace Fortran 90 was the slow emergence of mature compiler technology. The language added many new features that presented real problems for the implementer. As a result, Fortran 90 compilers must do much more work to achieve the same relative level of performance as compilers for Fortran 77.

This chapter is intended as a simple introduction to some of the complexities of compiling a single new feature of Fortran 90: the array assignment statement. Although this statement was originally intended to provide a direct mechanism for specifying parallel or vector execution, it must still be carefully implemented for the specific hardware available for execution. In particular, to implement the array assignment on a uniprocessor, the statement must be converted to a scalar loop. This conversion, which is referred to as *scalarization*, must be done in a way that makes efficient use of the memory hierarchy, no matter what the final target architecture is.

At first glance, scalarization seems simple—simply replace each array assignment by a D0-loop whose induction variable iterates over the range of the array triplet in one of the subscripts. However, the problem is complex for two reasons. First, we wish to avoid the excessive storage requirements and array copying operations that are needed if we must use a compiler-generated array temporary as large as the array value being assigned. Furthermore, the naive scalarization strategy above will produce a single-statement loop for each array assignment statement, so an important optimization is fusing as many of these loops as possible to increase reuse of quantities in registers. As we shall see, the theory of dependence plays a key role in implementing these strategies.

In summary, there are two principal goals for a good scalarization scheme, in addition to producing a correct translation:

1. Avoiding the necessity for generating array temporaries of unbounded size

2. Producing scalarized loops that can be optimized to exhibit a good memory hierarchy performance using the techniques described in Chapters 8 and 9

The next section introduces correct scalarization and the issues involved in minimizing the size of temporaries introduced by the process. Although the results are presented in terms of compiling Fortran 90 for a scalar machine, they can be easily adapted to vector register machines as shown in Section 13.5.

13.2   Simple Scalarization

The obvious strategy for scalarization is to replace any single vector statement by a loop iterating over the elements of the vectors. Consider the following example loop:

```
A(1:200) = 2.0 * A(1:200)
```

A scalar implementation would be as follows:

```
S₁   DO i = 1, 200
S₂      A(i) = 2.0 * A(i)
     ENDDO
```

Here S_1, the *loop*, iterates from 1 to the length of the complete operation. The *scalar statement*, S_2, can be implemented by single-element operations on any scalar machine. Note that there is a direct translation of the iteration space in the vector operations to the iteration space of the resulting loop.

Recall that the semantics of Fortran 90 require that the vector statement behave as if all inputs to the statement are fetched before any results are stored. This is not only natural, it also accurately reflects the vector hardware on vector register machines, where sections of arrays are loaded and stored in single operations. However, this differs from the semantics of sequential loops where loads and stores are interleaved on an iteration-by-iteration basis. This difference causes problems when scalarizing array statements like the following variant of our original example:

```
A(2:201) = 2.0 * A(1:200)
```

Here, the simple translation strategy yields

```
DO i = 1, 200
   A(i+1) = 2.0 * A(i)
ENDDO
```

This version produces different answers from the original because the value computed on each iteration is used on the next iteration, whereas the vector statement must be implemented so that the values used on the right-hand side are those that exist before any stores take place.

This example shows that the implementation of vector statements on scalar hardware is not straightforward. Problems arise because the registers can hold only a single value rather than all the values needed on the right-hand side. Errors of the sort illustrated in the example, where the meaning of statements is changed by the scalarization process, are called *scalarization faults*.

Figure 13.1 contains an informal specification of a procedure *SimpleScalarize* that carries out the naive translation from a one-dimensional array assignment statement to a simple scalar loop. In the input program, the range of a vector operation is specified by triplets or vector specifiers of the form (*lower bound* : *upper bound* : *increment*) found in subscripts within the statement. The scalarization is determined by examining the triplet on the left-hand side of the assignment.

It is easy to see how scalarization faults arise from the method presented in Figure 13.1. The sequence of scalar operations may not preserve the semantics of the original vector statement because the original statement requires that all results be stored after all values from the right-hand side have been fetched, while the sequence of scalar operations may interleave loads and stores. Thus, if one scalar operation stores a value that is fetched by a later operation, a scalarization fault will occur. Fortunately, this situation can be accurately detected using dependence analysis.

PRINCIPLE 13.1   A vector assignment generates a scalarization fault if and only if the scalarized loop carries a true dependence.

To see the truth of this principle, recall that the array assignment executes by loading all values on the right before performing any stores on the left-hand side of the assignment. The only possible fault, then, is for one iteration of the scalarized loop to store into a memory location that a later iteration fetches. This is precisely the definition of a loop-carried true dependence.

This principle provides a precise mechanism for distinguishing vector statements that create scalarization faults from those that do not. Since true dependences carried by the scalarization loop create such faults, these dependences are known as *scalarization dependences*.

procedure *SimpleScalarize(S)*

> // *S* is the statement to be scalarized;
>
> let $V_0 = (L_0:U_0:D_0)$ be the vector iteration specifier on the left side of *S*;
>
> // Generate the scalarizing loop
> let i be a new loop index variable;
> generate the statement DO i = L_0, U_0, D_0;
>
> > **for each** vector specifier $V = (L:U:D)$ in *S* **do**
> > replace *V* with ($i+L-L_0$);
> > generate an ENDDO statement;
> **end** *SimpleScalarize*

Figure 13.1 Scalarizing a single vector operation.

To preserve the correct execution of a program, the compiler must never generate a scalarization dependence. This objective can be accomplished in a simple-minded way by using temporary storage [279], as the following example illustrates.

```
A(2:201) = 2.0 * A(1:200)
```

This statement can be split into two vector statements

```
T(1:200) = 2.0 * A(1:200)
A(2:201) = T(1:200)
```

(where T is a compiler-generated temporary) and then scalarized using *Simple-Scalarize* from Figure 13.1 to produce the following code:

```
DO i = 1, 200
    T(i) = 2.0 * A(i)
ENDDO

DO i = 2, 201
    A(i) = T(i-1)
ENDDO
```

This method of scalarization is guaranteed to avoid a scalarization dependence because T is a new array that cannot overlap any storage for the program's data arrays. In other words, a scalarization fault is avoided because the entire result vector is stored into a temporary array and then copied to the result array only after all the operations on the right-hand side, including loads, are complete.

Unfortunately, the cost of this approach is high for two reasons:

- It requires a substantial increase in memory because T (which has length that may be hard to predict at compile time) must be in memory. Furthermore, the cost of dynamic allocation of the array T may be substantial.

- It requires that each element in the result vector be stored, then loaded, then stored again. This represents two more memory operations per vector element than would be required if the temporary array were not needed. It would be far more efficient if it were possible to keep the temporary array elements in registers.

Because of these drawbacks, the use of full-length temporary storage is best left as a last resort.

Note that the drawbacks of temporary storage can be avoided by "fusing" loops afterwards, where possible [279]. The conditions under which the two loops can be safely fused are precisely those under which a single statement scalarization is safe by the principle above—that is, if the two loops may be legally fused, then the original statement could have been safely scalarized. Hence, we prefer to use a direct test to avoid generating the temporary whenever possible. Note that loop fusion can still be effective as a scalarization optimization. This subject is discussed in Section 13.6.

Figure 13.2 shows an improved scalarization procedure, *SafeScalarize*, that avoids generating scalarization faults by using the test in Principle 13.1. Initially, a full dependence graph involving all loops (not just scalarization loops) is computed for each vector statement. If the statement has no scalarization dependence on itself, then it is scalarized using *SimpleScalarize*; otherwise, temporary storage is used to ensure safety. Although it is not evident from Figure 13.2 why the full dependence graph should be constructed (and not just the true dependences,

procedure *SafeScalarize(S)*

    if S has no scalarization dependence
    then *SimpleScalarize* (S);
    else begin
        let T be a new temporary array long enough to hold all
            elements computed by S;
        split S into S_1 and S_2 using temporary storage T so that
            in S_1, the right-hand side of S is assigned to T
            in S_2, T is assigned to the left-hand side of S;
        SimpleScalarize (S_1);
        SimpleScalarize (S_2);
    end
end *SafeScalarize*

Figure 13.2 Safe scalarization.

which are the only ones that can create scalarization faults), later sections will make this point clear.

SafeScalarize is guaranteed to generate a correct scalarization for every vector statement. However, given the performance penalties associated with large array temporaries, it is best to avoid executing the else clause whenever possible. The next section introduces transformations that can eliminate scalarization faults without using temporary storage.

13.3   Scalarization Transformations

Procedure *SafeScalarize* in Figure 13.2 resorts to an expensive solution whenever naive simple scalarization would result in a true dependence carried by the scalarization loop. The expense can often be avoided by transforming the code to eliminate such dependences. The next few sections present several transformations that can be used to eliminate scalarization dependences. Although it may seem counterintuitive that achieving correctness means eliminating true dependences from the program, keep in mind that the true dependences in question are ones that have been incorrectly introduced by the scalarization algorithm. In making these transformations, we are merely returning the program to its original meaning.

13.3.1   Loop Reversal

Consider the vector statement

```
A(2:256) = A(1:255) + 1.0
```

SimpleScalarize in Figure 13.1 will produce a scalarization fault for this example because each output is stored into the location of the input to the next iteration of the scalar loop. However, it is easy to see a simple but elegant solution in this case—we simply run the scalarization loop backward, eliminating the carried true dependence.

```
DO i = 256, 2, -1
   A(i) = A(i-1) + 1.0
ENDDO
```

In this case the array elements stored on the left-hand side overwrite array elements that have already been loaded—the desired result. This familiar transformation, known as *loop reversal* [270], was introduced in Chapter 6.

In order to apply loop reversal to scalarization, a vector statement is first scalarized, and then the scalarization loop is reversed. From the above discussion, it should be easy to see that loop reversal converts true dependences carried by a scalarization loop into antidependences. Thus, it appears ideal for scalarization.

Unfortunately, the transformation also maps antidependences into true dependences. As a result, loop reversal will not correct a scalarization fault when the scalarization loop also carries an antidependence, as in the following vector statement:

```
A(2:257) = (A(1:256)+A(3:258))/2.0
```

which yields the straightforward scalarization loop

```
DO i = 2, 257
   A(i) = (A(i-1)+A(i+1))/2.0
ENDDO
```

This loop carries both a true dependence (due the first operand on the right-hand side) and an antidependence (due to the second operand). If the scalarization loop is reversed,

```
DO i = 257, 2, -1
   A(i) = (A(i-1)+A(i+1))/2.0
ENDDO
```

the first operand now gives rise to a carried antidependence and the second operand yields a carried true dependence. The lesson of this example can be summarized in a simple observation: loop reversal will eliminate scalarization faults carried by a loop if and only if the loop carries no antidependences. The proof of this result is left as an exercise to the reader.

The implication of this observation is that more sophisticated techniques are required when the scalarization loop carries both a true dependence and an antidependence. Input prefetching is one such transformation.

13.3.2 Input Prefetching

Let us consider the example of the previous section in more detail.

```
A(2:257) = (A(1:256)+A(3:258))/2.0
```

The scalarization loop produced by *SimpleScalarize* carries both a true dependence and an antidependence, so there is a scalarization fault no matter which order is used for loop iteration. The problem is that the input vectors overlap with the output vector and with each other. This causes the naive scalarization loop

```
DO i = 2, 257
   A(i) = (A(i-1)+A(i+1))/2.0
ENDDO
```

to store into the first element of the left-hand input to the next iteration.

Since the scalarization dependence has a threshold of one iteration, we might seek to keep the result in temporary storage until the input for the next iteration is loaded. Let T1 be used to hold an element of the first input array and let T2 be used to hold an element of the output array. A naive use of T1 and T2 in this context would be as follows.

```
DO i = 2, 257
    T1 = A(i-1)
    T2 = (T1+A(i+1))/2.0
    A(i) = T2
ENDDO
```

Although this loop has the same scalarization problem, we can now correct it by migrating the assignment to T1 into the previous iteration, just before the store of T2. The overlap is thus eliminated.

```
T1 = A(1)
DO i = 2, 256
    T2 = (T1+A(i+1))/2.0
    T1 = A(i)
    A(i) = T2
ENDDO
T2 = (T1+A(258))/2.0
A(257) = T2
```

Notice that an initialization has been inserted before the loop and that the assignment to T1 has been rewritten to load the value for the next iteration. In addition, we have peeled the last iteration to avoid the extra access to A.

This approach, called *input prefetching*, is superior to the naive use of temporary storage because it only requires temporaries of length one. Because these temporaries will be assigned to registers by a good scalar register allocation scheme, the resulting code avoids all the disadvantages of full-length array temporaries.

Input prefetching is more generally applicable than loop reversal because it can be used in many situations where reversal fails to eliminate all scalarization dependences. The question now arises: How general is it? Input prefetching causes the inputs for the next iteration to be loaded before the outputs of the current iteration are stored to avoid having those outputs overwrite the inputs. But what if the outputs might overwrite inputs to the iteration after the next, as in the following example?

```
DO i = 2, 257
    A(i+2) = A(i) + 1.0
ENDDO
```

Here input prefetching becomes more complicated because we now must prefetch two iterations ahead. This means that we must always have two copies of the input in temporaries. Suppose we define the quantities T1, T2, and T3 as follows: at the point where the output of the current iteration is stored, T1 holds the input to the next iteration, T2 holds the input to the iteration after next, and T3 holds the output to be stored. Then the following code can be used to eliminate the scalarization dependences:

```
T1 = A(1)
T2 = A(2)
DO i = 2, 255
    T3 = T1 + 1.0          ! the operation
    T1 = T2                ! copy input to next iteration
    T2 = A(i+2)            ! load for iteration after next
    A(i+2) = T3            ! now it is safe to store
ENDDO
T3 = T1 + 1.0
T1 = T2
A(258) = T3
T3 = T1 + 1.0
A(259) = T3
```

Although this form has fewer accesses to main memory than the code generated by the procedure *SafeScalarize* in Figure 13.2, it has drawbacks—it involves a register-to-register copy and it requires a significant number of scalar registers. However, as we saw in Section 8.3, the copies can be eliminated by unrolling the scalarization loop, at no additional cost in scalar registers.

In general, input prefetching can be used to eliminate any scalarization dependence for which the threshold is known at compile time. It requires one register temporary and one extra copy operation for each iteration beyond the first. With this restriction, the condition for applying input prefetching can be simply stated.

PRINCIPLE   Any scalarization dependence with a threshold known at compile time can be
13.2   corrected by input prefetching.

This follows directly from the definition of threshold. Since a threshold of one means that the fetch occurs on the iteration immediately following the store, and since input prefetching inserts the load for the next iteration before the store for the current iteration, it necessarily corrects the fault.

The input prefetching algorithm in Figure 13.3 works for prefetch distances of length one. It can be generalized to greater thresholds by using methods similar to those in Section 8.2.

procedure *InputPrefetch(S_loop,D)*

// *S_loop* = DO i = L, U, INC; S; ENDDO is the scalarization loop.
// It is assumed that the need for prefetching has already been established and
//   that the statement has been scalarized using *SimpleScalarize*.
// *D* is the graph that represents the scalarization dependences of the
//   scalar statement.
// Every edge *e* in *D* maps a section reference *source(e)*
//   to another reference *target(e)*. The threshold is always one
// Input prefetching is only applied to true dependences,
//   so *source(e)* is always the left-hand side of *S*

for each edge *e* ∈ *D* **do begin**

create a new temporary called T_0; // Presumably a register

// Two assignments must be generated:
//   one initialization before the scalarization loop and a prefetch of the input
//   for the next iteration after the vector statement S

create the initialization statement T_0 = *init_reference* where
   init_reference can be generated by replacing all instances of the
   scalarization loop variable i in *target(e)* with L, the lower bound of
   the original scalarization loop;

insert the update statement T_0 = *update_reference* after S in the
   scalarization loop, where *update_reference* can be generated by
   replacing all instances of the scalarization loop variable I
   in *target(e)* by i + INC;

replace *target(e)* in S by T_0;
end

// Now we generate the temporary that holds the output of the current
// iteration, along with the appropriate assignments.

create a new temporary T_1;
insert the assignment *source(e)* = T_1 at the end of the scalarization loop;
replace *source(e)* in S, the left-hand side of S, with T_1;

end *InputPrefetch*

Figure 13.3 Input prefetching algorithm.

InputPrefetch is a procedure to eliminate scalarization dependences of threshold one. The algorithm, a straightforward adaptation of previous comments, takes time linear in the number of scalarization dependence edges.

Although the prefetching algorithm can be extended to cases with threshold greater than one, the implementation cost and the demands on registers grow quite rapidly. An alternative approach is to use *loop splitting* to reduce the complexity.

There are a number of situations in which a scalarization dependence does not have a constant threshold, but in which input prefetching can be beneficial. To illustrate this situation, consider the Fortran 90 statement

```
A(1:N) = A(1:N)/A(1)
```

This would be naively scalarized as

```
DO i = 1, N
    A(i) = A(i)/A(1)
ENDDO
```

This has an antidependence from the first iteration to itself and a carried dependence from the first iteration to every other iteration, all due to the use of the reference A(1). In the Fortran 90 semantics, the value of A(1) should be the value that existed before any iteration of the loop. Thus this case can be handled by prefetching the single value needed prior to entering the scalarization loop.

```
tA1 = A(1)
DO i = 1, N
    A(i) = A(i)/tA1
ENDDO
```

This strategy works correctly even if the single constant value is not used on the first iteration. A second example illustrates a more complex version of this situation.

```
A(1:N,1:M) = A(1:N,1:M)/SPREAD(X(1:M),1,N)
```

The SPREAD intrinsic replicates N copies of the vector X(1:M) to produce a matrix of the appropriate size. The naive scalarized version of this code would be

```
DO j = 1, M
    DO i = 1, N
        A(i,j) = A(i,j)/X(j)
    ENDDO
ENDDO
```

Here the input prefetching should be done just before the inner loop.

```
DO j = 1, M
    tX = X(j)
    DO i = 1, N
        A(i,j) = A(i,j)/tX
    ENDDO
ENDDO
```

13.3.3 Loop Splitting

The basic problem with applying *InputPrefetch* to scalarization dependences with thresholds greater than one is that temporary values must be saved for each iteration of the scalarization loop up to the threshold. If this can be avoided, prefetching becomes more practical. Loop splitting (Figure 13.4) is one way to do this. Consider the problem of scalarizing the following vector statement:

```
A(3:6) = (A(1:4)+A(5:8))/2.0
```

The scalarization loop carries both a true dependence and an antidependence, each with a threshold of two.

```
DO i = 3, 6
   A(i) = (A(i-2)+A(i+2))/2.0
ENDDO
```

procedure *SplitLoop(S_loop,D)*
    // *S_loop* = DO i = L, U, INC; S; ENDDO is the loop to be split.
    // the graph *D* contains all scalarization dependences for this loop

    let *e* be any true dependence edge in *D*;
    T := threshold(*e*);
    all_the_same := *true*;

    for each dependence edge *e* in *D* **while** *all_the_same* **do**
        if *e* represents a true dependence **and** threshold(*e*) ≠ *T*
            or *e* represents an antidependence
            and *T* does not divide threshold(*e*)
        then *all_the_same* := **false**;

    if *all_the_same* **then begin**
        replace the scalarization loop with a new loop nest:
        S_1 DO i1 = L, L + T * INC, INC
        S_2 DO i2 = i1, U, T * INC
            S
          ENDDO
        ENDDO;

        let D_2 be the scalarization dependences for loop S_2;
        InputPrefetch(S,D_2);

    end
  end *SplitLoop*

Figure 13.4 Loop splitting algorithm.

Extension of *InputPrefetch* to handle this example would require temporaries for two elements of A. However, since *both* the true dependence and the antidependence have a threshold of two, we could actually rewrite the scalarization loop as two independent loops that do not interact with one another.

```
DO i = 3, 5, 2
    A(i) = (A(i-2)+A(i+2))/2.0
ENDDO
DO i = 4, 6, 2
    A(i) = (A(i-2)+A(i+2))/2.0
ENDDO
```

The scalarization dependences for each of these loops cross only one iteration, so simple input prefetching can be used to eliminate them. Notice that the division would produce incorrect results if the antidependence had a threshold that was not divisible by 2 because then the first loop might store into a location loaded as A(I+2) by the second. As a stylistic convention, we will always write the splitting as a nested pair of loops.

```
DO i1 = 3, 4
    DO i2 = i1, 6, 2
        A(i2) = (A(i2-2)+A(i2+2))/2.0
    ENDDO
ENDDO
```

In split form, the inner loop carries a scalarization dependence with threshold 1, while the outer loop carries no dependences. Input prefetching can now be directly applied to the inner loop, yielding

```
DO i1 = 3, 4
    T1 = A(i1-2)
    DO i2 = i1, 6, 2
        T2 = (T1+A(i2+2))/2.0
        T1 = A(i2)
        A(i2) = T2
    ENDDO
ENDDO
```

By creating a loop with a unitary scalarization dependence, loop splitting reduces the number of registers required to carry out prefetching.

Although loop splitting can be applied to a loop carrying multiple dependences each with a different threshold [221, 16], it will not produce a loop in which all dependences have a threshold of one unless the thresholds are identical. Thus, vector operations such as

```
A(5:104) = A(1:100) + A(3:102) + &
   A(7:106) + A(9:108)
```

in which there are true dependences with constant thresholds of one and two after loop splitting regardless of the direction in which the loop is iterated, cannot easily be scalarized with this method. Also, dependences that do not have constant thresholds cannot be accommodated.

The value of input prefetching and loop splitting can be summarized as follows:

PRINCIPLE 13.3	Any scalarization loop in which all true dependences have the same constant threshold *T* and all antidependences have a threshold that is divisible by *T* can be transformed, using input prefetching and loop splitting, so that all scalarization dependences are eliminated.

A proof of this principle can be found in Allen's dissertation [16].

Loop reversal, loop alignment, and loop splitting provide relatively inexpensive alternatives to the large temporary arrays required by procedure *SafeScalarize* in Figure 13.2. Figure 13.5 presents a revised scalarization algorithm, called *FullScalarize*, that incorporates these transformations. Although *FullScalarize* cannot section all possible Fortran 90 statements without the use of temporary storage, it can successfully section most of the statements that should be encountered in practice.

FullScalarize will work well with all statements containing a single dimension of vectorization. Fortran 90, however, allows for multiple dimensions of vectorization. Multiple vector dimensions provide opportunities for new strategies, discussed in Section 13.4.

13.4 Multidimensional Scalarization

So far, all the methods presented have dealt with only one vector dimension. However, vector statements in Fortran 90 are not limited to single dimensions of vectorization. For instance, the following statement

```
A(1:100,1:100) = A(1:100,1:100) + 1.0
```

has vector iterators in more than one subscript on both the left- and right-hand side of a vector assignment. When this happens, the dimensions are assumed to correspond from left to right. For example, the statement

```
A(1:100,1:100) = B(1:100,1,1:100)
```

procedure *FullScalarize*

   for each vector statement *S* **do begin**

      compute the dependences of *S* on itself
        as though *S* had been scalarized;

      if *S* has no scalarization dependences upon itself
      then *SimpleScalarize(S)*;

      else if *S* has scalarization dependences,
          but no self-antidependences

      then begin
        SimpleScalarize(S);
        reverse the scalarization loop;
      end

      else if all scalarization dependences have a threshold of one
      then begin
        SimpleScalarize(S);
        InputPrefetch(S);
      end

      else if all scalarization dependences for *S*
        have the same constant threshold *T*
        and all antidependences have thresholds that are divisible by *T*
      then *SplitLoop(S)*;

      else if all antidependences for *S*
        have the same constant threshold *T* **and**
        all true dependences have thresholds that are divisible by *T*
      then begin
        reverse the loop;
        SplitLoop(S);
      end

      else *SafeScalarize(S)*;
   end
end *FullScalarize*

Figure 13.5 Revised scalarization algorithm.

should have the same effect as the loop

```
DO J = 1, 100
   A(1:100,J) = B(1:100,1,J)
ENDDO
```

The introduction of multiple dimensions of vectorization creates many new possibilities as well as many new problems in scalarization. In the simplest case, the multiple dimensions may be collapsed into a single vector operation. More complicated cases may require sophisticated transformations such as loop interchange in order to achieve a safe scalarization. The following sections discuss these transformations and their application to scalarization of multiple-dimension vector statements.

13.4.1   Simple Scalarization in Multiple Dimensions

Scalarization in multiple dimensions means simply converting each iterator to a corresponding loop. For example, in the following statement

```
A(1:100,1:100) = 2.0 * A(1:100,1:100)
```

this approach would yield

```
DO j = 1, 100
   DO i = 1, 100
      A(i,j) = 2.0 * A(i,j)
   ENDDO
ENDDO
```

When viewed in this manner, the central issue of safely scalarizing multiple vector dimensions is clear—as each scalarization loop corresponds to a different vector iterator, any scalarization loop that carries a true dependence changes the semantics of the original statement. Thus, the same transformations (loop reversal, loop alignment, etc.) for correcting single vector operations can be applied to each scalarization loop, although the expense may be significantly greater than in the single-dimension case.

An obvious question is: What should the order of the loops be after scalarization? In general, the answer to this question depends on the target machine. For example, on most machines, the most important goal is to get stride-one access in the innermost loop. However, on a vector machine like the Cray T90, the innermost loop is likely to be vectorized and, since vector loads of almost any stride can be performed efficiently because of interleaved memory,[1] the innermost loop should be one that can be vectorized to high efficiency.

While it is possible to accommodate machine dependencies by defining an objective function *score* that indicates the speed with which given vector operations will execute on particular hardware, a much simpler model will suffice for this chapter. We will assume that shorter strides are always better, so the optimal choice for the innermost position is the one that runs along a column with a stride

---

1.   Certain vector strides can cause memory bank conflicts, degrading performance.

of one. Thus, the leftmost vector iterator in a set of multiple iterators should correspond to the innermost loop.

With these assumptions, the extension of the results of Section 13.3 to multiple dimensions is straightforward. Each vector iterator can be scalarized individually. The scalarization loop for the leftmost vector iterator in any reference (which, by our assumptions, should be the most profitable) becomes the innermost loop; the rest, taken from left to right, correspond to scalarization loops beginning at the next innermost position and moving outward.

Once an initial loop order is available, for each scalarization loop starting from the outermost to the innermost, do the following:

1. Test to see if the loop carries a scalarization dependence. If not, then proceed to the next loop.

2. If the scalarization loop carries only true dependences, reverse the loop and proceed to the next loop.

3. Apply input prefetching, with loop splitting where appropriate, to eliminate dependences to which it applies. At first, this might seem undesirable outside the inner loop because registers would be quickly exhausted. Observe, however, that in outer loops, prefetching is done for a single submatrix (the remaining dimensions). This is always superior to generating a temporary for the whole matrix, as illustrated in the next section.

4. Otherwise, the loop carries a scalarization fault that requires temporary storage. Generate a scalarization that utilizes temporary storage and terminate the scalarization test for this loop, since temporary storage will eliminate all scalarization faults.

Although this simple strategy will work reasonably well in most cases, it does not take advantage of an important opportunity. When there are multiple scalarization loops, the *order* in which they are executed may affect not only the scalarization dependences, but also the cost of other transformations.

13.4.2 Outer Loop Prefetching

The effectiveness of input prefetching in an outer loop can be illustrated by the following example:

```
A(1:N,1:N) = (A(0:N-1,2:N+1)+A(2:N+1,0:N-1))/2.0
```

If we attempt to section the column accesses to vector register length, two scalarization dependences are generated. First, there is a true scalarization dependence with direction vector "(<,>)" involving the second input on the right-hand side. Second, there is an antidependence with direction vector "(>,<)" involving the first input on the right-hand side. Hence, we cannot use loop reversal on the outer loop.

However, it is possible to use input prefetching on the outer loop. If we do this, the temporaries will not be single variables, but temporary arrays as in the following output code:

```
T₀(1:N) = A(2:N+1,0)
DO j = 1, N - 1
    T₁(1:N) = (A(0:N-1,j+1)+T₀(1:N))/2.0
    T₀(1:N) = A(2:N+1,j)
    A(1:N,j) = T₁(1:N)
ENDDO
T₁(1:N) = (A(0:N-1,N+1)+T₀(1:N))/2.0
A(1:N,N) = T₁(1:N)
```

The total amount of temporary space required is equal to two rows of the original matrix, which is much smaller than the storage required for a complete copy of the result matrix. At first glance, however, it appears that the total number of loads and stores in this example is greater than that required by the naive approach. This is because each iteration of the j-loop copies one row of the input into T_0, one row of the output to T_1, and one row of T_1 to the output matrix—two loads and two stores more per element than if we could have scalarized it directly, and one load and one store more per element than required by the naive scalarization using temporaries.

However, this analysis is misleading. Consider what happens when we scalarize the inner loop.

```
DO i = 1,N
    T₀(i) = A(i+1,0)
ENDDO
DO j = 1, N - 1
    DO i = 1, N
        T₁(i) = (A(i-1,j+1)+T₀(i))/2.0
    ENDDO
    DO i = 1, N
        T₀(i) = A(i+1,j)
    ENDDO
    DO i = 1, N
        A(i,j) = T₁(i)
    ENDDO
ENDDO
DO i = 1, N
    T₁(i) = (A(i-1,N+1)+T₀(i))/2.0
ENDDO
DO i = 1, N
    A(i,N) = T₁(i)
ENDDO
```

There are no scalarization dependences in any of the inner loops and, as we shall see in Section 13.6, loop fusion can be used to merge all three loops into a single scalarization loop.

```
DO i = 1,N
    T0(i) = A(i+1,0)
ENDDO
DO j = 1, N - 1
    DO i = 1, N
        T1(i) = (A(i-1,j+1)+T0(i))/2.0
        T0(i) = A(i+1,j)
        A(i,j) = T1(i)
    ENDDO
ENDDO
DO i = 1, N
    T1(i) = (A(i-1,N+1)+T0(i))/2.0
    A(i,N) = T1(i)
ENDDO
```

Now it should be clear that the temporary T_1 does not carry useful values across loop boundaries and can be replaced by a register. Hence, the final code will look something like the following:

```
DO i = 1,N
    T0(i) = A(i+1,0)
ENDDO
DO j = 1, N - 1
    DO i = 1, N
        R1 = (A(i-1,j+1)+T0(i))/2.0
        T0(i) = A(i+1,j)
        A(i,j) = R1
    ENDDO
ENDDO
DO i = 1, N
    R1 = (A(i-1,N+1)+T0(i))/2.0
    A(i,N) = R1
ENDDO
```

This code uses the same number of loads and stores as the naive scalarization, with far less temporary storage (one row of A).

Once we have applied outer-loop prefetching to eliminate the two scalarization dependences, these dependences cannot appear in the inner loop. Hence, it can be scalarized trivially. In general, applying outer loop prefetching will eliminate from consideration only those dependences that are carried by the outer loop. Prefetching in the inner loop may still be required to eliminate dependences that are carried by that loop.

13.4.3   Loop Interchange for Scalarization

Although the chosen loop ordering may be optimal from an execution point of view, it may not always be optimal from a scalarization point of view. Consider, for instance,

```
A(2:100,3:101) = A(3:101,1:201:2)
```

Scalarization in the prescribed order would yield

```
DO i = 3, 101
   DO j = 2, 100
      A(j,i) = A(j+1,2*i-5)
   ENDDO
ENDDO
```

The outer loop carries a true dependence, and hence a scalarization fault. Neither loop input prefetching nor loop reversal will eliminate this fault because the loop also carries antidependences, and the thresholds of the dependences are irregular. Thus, the dependence of the statement upon itself is really two dependences with direction vectors "(<,>)" (when $i = 3$ the loop stores into $A(*,3)$ and it loads from the same column when $i = 4$) and "(>,>)" (when $i = 6$ the loop loads from $A(*,7)$ and subsequently stores into the same column when $i = 6$.

However, if we interchange the two loops, we get direction vectors "(>,<)" and "(>,>)". Now the outer loop carries two antidependences and can be trivially scalarized to a length of one. This eliminates the two dependences from consideration in the inner loop, and it, too, can be easily scalarized.

```
DO j = 2, 100
   DO i = 3, 101
      A(j,i) = A(j+1,2*i-5)
   ENDDO
ENDDO
```

While this ordering may not make optimal use of strided memory access, it is far more efficient than using temporary storage.

At first glance, it may appear that the interchange of scalarization loops should be illegal because one of the scalarization dependences is converted from a true dependence to an antidependence. However, keep in mind that we are looking for a scalarization that has no true scalarization dependences carried by the scalarization loop. Any scalarization that has such a dependence is incorrect. By that criterion, the original scalarization is incorrect but the final one is correct. In general, we are free to choose any order for the scalarization loops, and any direction for each loop, so long as none of the resulting loops carries a scalarization dependence. We will use this principle to derive a general algorithm for scalarization.

Even when loop interchange does not remove a scalarization fault, it can still be a useful transformation for reducing the size of temporaries. Suppose we wish to section the following statement, making the column iterators correspond to the inner loop.

```
A(1:128,1:128) = A(1:128,0:127)
```

In the straightforward scalarization of the outer loop

```
DO i = 1, 128
    A(1:128,i) = A(1:128,i-1)
ENDDO
```

the outer loop carries a true dependence, which could be eliminated by outer loop prefetching.

```
T₀(1:128) = A(1:128,0)
DO i = 1, 127
    T₁(1:128) = T₀(1:128)
    T₀(1:128) = A(1:128,i)
    A(1:128,i) = T₁(1:128)
ENDDO
T₁(1:128) = T₀(1:128)
A(1:128,128) = T₁(1:128)
```

After scalarization of the column iterators, and fusing the statements where possible (see Section 13.6), this becomes

```
DO j = 1, 128
    T₀(j) = A(j,0)
ENDDO
DO i = 1, 127
    DO j = 1, 128
        T₁(j) = T₀(j)
        T₀(j) = A(j,i)
        A(j,i) = T₁(j)
    ENDDO
ENDDO
DO j = 1, 128
    T₁(j) = T₀(j)
    A(j,128) = T₁(j)
ENDDO
```

Because the load of A in the loop is now from column i, the only dependence involving A has direction vector "(=,=)". Thus the loops can be interchanged to yield

```
DO j = 1, 128
    T₀(j) = A(j,0)
ENDDO
DO j = 1, 128
    DO i = 1, 127
        T₁(j) = T₀(j)
        T₀(j) = A(j,i)
        A(j,i) = T₁(j)
    ENDDO
ENDDO
DO j = 1, 128
    T₁(j) = T₀(j)
    A(j,128) = T₁(j)
ENDDO
```

The resulting outer loops can now be fused to yield

```
DO j = 1, 128
    T₀(j) = A(j,0)
    DO i = 1, 127
        T₁(j) = T₀(j)
        T₀(j) = A(j,i)
        A(j,i) = T₁(j)
    ENDDO
    T₁(j) = T₀(j)
    A(j,128) = T₁(j)
ENDDO
```

Because values of T_0 and T_1 are never reused across different iterations of the j-loop, and a good scalar replacement algorithm will reduce them to scalar variables.

```
DO j = 1, 128
    T₀ = A(j,0)
    DO i = 1, 127
        T₁ = T₀
        T₀ = A(j,i)
        A(j,i) = T₁
    ENDDO
    T₁ = T₀
    A(j,128) = T₁
ENDDO
```

By interchanging loops, we have eliminated all temporary storage and all superfluous loads and stores.

Notice that we could have made the decision to move the input prefetch operation to the inner loop when the order of scalarization was determined. In general, it is always better to interchange so input prefetching is applied to the innermost loop because it minimizes the temporary storage needed while improving performance by ensuring that the temporaries can be stored in registers rather than stored back to memory. Of course, these must be weighed against the cost of nonunit stride access to A in the i-loop.

General methods for improving register usage by loop interchange and loop fusion are the subject of Section 13.6.

13.4.4 General Multidimensional Scalarization

Our general approach to multidimensional scalarization will involve construction of a special data structure called the *scalarization direction matrix* for the scalarization loop nest. Assume we wish to section a single statement that has m vector dimensions. Suppose $(l_1, l_2, \ldots, l_m)$ represents the ideal order of scalarization loops from outermost to innermost, as determined by some cost-benefit analysis. Let $d_1, d_2, \ldots, d_n$ be the direction vectors for all true dependences and antidependences of the statement upon itself carried by some loop in the loop nest, in which the directions are reversed in a direction vector for each antidependence. The *scalarization direction matrix* for the statement is an $n \times m$ matrix of elements "<", ">", or "=" formed by making the kth row be d_k for all k, $1 \le k \le n$. For example, in the statement

```
A(1:N,1:N,1:N) = A(0:N-1,1:N,2:N+1) + &
     A(1:N,2:N+1,0:N-1)
```

if we choose the loop order that has the innermost loop iterating over a column, we get the following scalarization direction matrix:

$$\begin{bmatrix} > & = & < \\ < & > & = \end{bmatrix}$$

If we examine any column of the direction matrix, we can immediately see if the corresponding loop can be safely scalarized as the outermost loop of the nest:

- If all entries of the column are "=" or ">", it can be safely scalarized as the outermost loop without loop reversal.

- If all entries are "=" or "<", it can be safely scalarized with loop reversal.

- If it contains a mixture of "<" and ">", it cannot be scalarized by simple means.

In the previous example, the proposed outer loop cannot be scalarized by simple means, but each of the other two loops could be if they were moved to the outermost position.

Once a loop has been selected for scalarization, the dependences carried by that loop—any dependence whose direction vector does not contain an "=" in the position corresponding to the selected loop—may be eliminated from further consideration. The scalarization of the inner loops may then restrict consideration to a submatrix of the direction matrix from which the selected column, and any rows that had a symbol other than "=" in that column, have been eliminated. In our example, we could choose the second column for scalarization as the outer loop. If we move this column to the outside, the scalarization matrix becomes

$$\begin{bmatrix} = & > & < \\ > & < & = \end{bmatrix}$$

Scalarization in this way will eliminate the second row from further consideration, reducing the scalarization matrix to

$$\begin{bmatrix} > & < \end{bmatrix}$$

The leftmost column, corresponding to the previous outer dimension, can now be scalarized without reversal. Once this is done, all dependences are gone, and the inner dimension can be scalarized easily. On the example, this results in the following code:

```
DO j = 1, N
   DO k = 1, N
      DO i = 1, N
         A(i,j,k) = A(i-1,j,k+1) + A(i,j+1,k-1)
      ENDDO
   ENDDO
ENDDO
```

The algorithm in Figure 13.6 is a more formal presentation of this approach. It assumes that the vector operations have been initially ordered from outermost to innermost according to the optimal execution ordering in the list *loop_list*. It attempts to maintain this ordering if possible without the use of temporary storage.

Variations on *CompleteScalarize* can accommodate various machine types. For machines where temporary storage reduction is not worth moving the stride-1 dimension, the algorithm can be adjusted to preclude selecting the inner loop until all other loops are scalarized.

The time complexity of this algorithm is no worse than $O(m^2n)$, where m is the number of loops and n is the number of dependences. To see this, observe that a scan for the next column that can be scalarized takes no more than $O(mn)$ time

procedure *CompleteScalarize(S,loop_list)*

   // *Scalarize* attempts to section a vector operation
   //   without use of temporary storage.
   // *S* is the statement to be scalarized;
   // *loop_list* is a list of the loops ordered
   //   in "optimal" execution order.

   let *M* be the scalarization direction matrix
      resulting from scalarization *S* to *loop_list*;

   while there are more loops to be scalarized **do begin**

      let *l* be the first loop in loop list that can be simply scalarized
         with or without loop reversal (determine this by examining the
         columns of *M* from left to right);

      if there is no such *l* **then begin**
         let *l* be the first loop on *loop_list*;
         section *l* by input prefetching;
         if the previous step fails
         then section *S* using the naive temporary method and exit;
      end

      else // make *l* the outermost loop
         section *l* directly or with loop reversal, depending on the
            entries in the column of *M* corresponding to *l*;

      remove *l* from *loop_list*;
      let *M′* be *M* with the column corresponding to *l* and the
         rows corresponding to non-"=" entries
         in that column eliminated;
        $M := M′$;
   end
end *CompleteScalarize*

Figure 13.6 A complete scalarization algorithm.

because it must look at each element no more than once. Since there are *m* loops, we need to do this no more than *m* times.

    For a given statement *S* and loop list, *CompleteScalarize* produces a correct scalarization with the following properties:

1. *Input prefetching* is applied to the innermost loop possible.

2. The order of scalarization loops is the closest possible to the order specified on input among scalarizations with property (1).

Correctness follows from the definition of the direction matrix. Since we are free to choose, as the outermost scalarization loop, any loop that does not introduce a scalarization fault, we need only find some loop for which all carried dependences will be antidependences or true dependences. In the first case, the scalarization loop is iterated normally, and in the second, the scalarization loop is iterated in reverse.

Once the outermost scalarization loop is selected, the dependences carried by that loop cannot be scalarization dependences for an inner loop because the value of the outer loop index at the source and target of such a dependence must not be equal. For a scalarization fault to occur at an inner loop, it must be possible for two different values of the inner loop index to access the same memory location for the *same value* of the outer index. This is only possible if the dependence has an "=" symbol in the position for the outer loop. Hence, eliminating dependences that are carried by the outer loop is correct.

Once the matrix contains only columns with both "<" and ">", input prefetching is applied. Once applied, the dependences carried by the loop to which it applies can be eliminated (by the argument above) and the process continued.

To establish property (1), we must show that there cannot exist a sequence of loop selections different from the one selected by the algorithm that requires input prefetching only at a deeper nesting level than the sequence selected by *CompleteScalarize*. In other words, at some stage in constructing a nest of scalarization loops, there may be more than one choice for the next outer loop. Is it possible that the wrong selection will permit one additional loop selection before input prefetching? The answer is no if the process of loop selection has the *finite Church-Rosser* property [12, 245], which holds if any sequence of selections arrives at the same limit. In the loop selection system, finiteness follows from the fact that there are only a finite number of loops, and one is selected at each stage. Thus, every selection sequence terminates with the loop list exhausted or in a situation where input prefetching would be required.

To establish that the selections always arrive at the same limit, we must define what we mean by the "same." For our purposes, a problem configuration is defined by the direction matrix. Two configurations will be the same if they have the same number of columns (loops remaining) and the rows are the same, but possibly permuted. Sethi has proved that a replacement system has the finite Church-Rosser property if it satisfies two properties, named P1 and P3 [245]:

- *P1:* If any transformation (loop selection) step is made, then there is a sequence of steps that takes the original configuration to a limit and a sequence of steps that takes the new configuration to the same limit.

- *P3:* If two different transformation steps are made from an original configuration, then there exist sequences of transformations that take each of the resulting configurations to the same limit.

Property P1 is trivial in our system because we can take the new configuration as the limit and reach it in a single step from the original by selecting the same loop. Property P3 is almost as easy. Suppose we begin in configuration c_0 and select loop l_1 to arrive at c_1 in one case and select l_2 to arrive at c_2 in the other. Since l_2 is eligible for selection in c_1, we can now select it to arrive in c_3. Similarly, we can select l_1 in c_2 to arrive at c_4. Now the direction matrix for c_3 is different from c_0 in that it has exactly those rows that contained an "=" in column l_1 or l_2 and it is missing those columns. But the direction matrix for c_4 has exactly the same rows and columns. Thus, the configurations are the same, establishing P3 and the finite Church-Rosser property.

Thus, no matter how we select eligible columns, we always arrive at the same limit. Hence the selection order in *CompleteScalarize* cannot be improved upon, establishing property (1). But since the first (outermost) eligible loop is always selected, the order of scalarization loops that results is the closest possible to the desired one, establishing property (2).

Although *CompleteScalarize* provides scalarization for a loop nest that might be called optimal in a restricted sense, it is still possible to improve register reuse by interchanging the scalarization loops with loops that surround the original vector statement and by fusing the scalarization loops of adjacent vector statements. This is the subject of Section 13.6.

13.4.5 A Scalarization Example

The previous sections have described a number of dependence-based techniques for scalarizing vector code. In this section we illustrate the effectiveness of these transformations on a common example from scientific computing—finite-difference relaxation solutions for differential equations. A Fortran 90 version of this algorithm is

```
DO J = 2, N - 1
    A(2:N-1,J) = (A(1:N-2,J) + A(3:N,J) + &
        A(2:N-1,J-1) + A(2:N-1,J+1))/4
ENDDO
```

Roughly speaking, this fragment sets the value of every point to be the average of the four surrounding points. As a result, there are many conflicts between memory locations, leading to a concentrated dependence graph. Figure 13.7 illustrates the dependences for this fragment, assuming that the vector operation is done by a scalar loop on index variable i.

This example contains a scalarization dependence (the true dependence on the scalarization loop δ_i) as well as a dependence that prevents loop reversal (the antidependence on the scalarization loop δ_i^{-1}). As a result, a naive compiler would use temporary storage to correctly scalarize the statement, yielding the following:

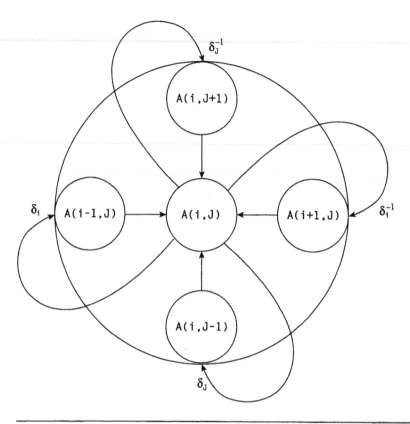

Figure 13.7 Dependence graph for finite-difference loop.

```
DO J = 2, N - 1
   DO i = 2, N - 1
      T(i-1) = (A(i-1,J) + A(i+1,J) + A(i,J-1) + A(i,J+1))/4
   ENDDO
   DO i = 2, N - 1
      A(i,J) = T(i-1)
   ENDDO
ENDDO
```

The references to T require $2(N-2)^2$ accesses to memory (half to store and the other half to fetch).

Because the dependences carried by the scalarization loop are regular dependences with a constant threshold of one, the analysis described in Section 13.3.2 would reveal this statement to be a candidate for input prefetching. Straightforward application of input prefetching would yield the following:

```
DO J = 2, N - 1
   tA0 = A(1,J)
   DO i = 2, N - 2
      tA1 = (tA0+A(i+1,J)+A(i,J-1)+A(i,J+1))/4
      tA0 = A(i,J)
      A(i,J) = tA1
   ENDDO
   tA1 = (tA0+A(N,J)+A(N-1,J-1)+A(N-1,J+1))/4
   A(N-1,J) = tA1
ENDDO
```

If the temporary variables are allocated to registers, this version requires no additional memory references above what the original Fortran 90 program required. The cost is the allocation of two registers during execution of the loop. Given the relative costs of register operations and memory accesses, the transformed code should perform much better on most machines.

13.5 **Considerations for Vector Machines**

When generating code for a vector machine, the compiler should use a variation of scalarization that generates vector operations in the inner loop that are matched to the size of the vector register on the target machine. Doing this is straightforward in general, but may require some extra code to ensure that vector lengths work out correctly. To illustrate the issues, we revisit a simple scalarization example, with unknown bounds:

```
A(1:N) = A(1:N) + 1.0
```

As we saw in Section 13.2, scalarization of this loop is straightforward. However, if we are to produce operations of length matched to the native vector length of the target machine, say, 64 elements, we must be careful to correctly handle cases where N is not an even multiple of 64. The strategy we recommend is to begin with a short vector operation of length mod(N, 64), which will ensure that all the remaining vector sections can be exactly length 64.

```
VL = MOD(N,64)
IF (VL.GT.0) A(1:VL) = A(1:VL) + 1.0
DO I = VL + 1, N, 64
   A(I:I+63) = A(I:I+63) + 1.0
ENDDO
```

With these modifications, all the scalarization strategies described in this section can be extended to vector machines.

13.6   **Postscalarization Interchange and Fusion**

The scalarization strategies described in this chapter do a good job of generating code for an individual statement. However, scalarization generally produces numerous individual loops. Furthermore, these loops carry no dependences, so reuse of quantities in registers is not common. To overcome these problems, it is essential that the techniques of loop interchange, loop fusion, unroll-and-jam, and scalar replacement, described in Chapter 8, be applied to the results of scalarization.

The following example, abstracted from a linear equation solver, illustrates some of these issues:

```
      DO K = 1, N
S₁      M(K,K:N+1) = M(K,K:N+1)/M(K,K)
S₂      M(K:N+1,K+1:N+1) = M(K:N+1,K+1:N+1) -
           SPREAD (M(K,K+1:N+1),1,N-K+2) * &
           SPREAD (M(K:N+1,K),2,N-K+1)
      ENDDO
```

We have seen the SPREAD intrinsic previously in Section 13.3.2. To correctly scalarize statement S_1, we note that even though there is a scalarization dependence involving M(K,K), it can be eliminated by a degenerate form of input prefetching. The scalarization loop becomes

```
      tM = M(K,K)
      DO j = K, N + 1
         M(K,j) = M(K,j)/tM
      ENDDO
```

The statement S_2 is complicated because it is a two-dimensional array statement that uses the SPREAD intrinsic, which simply replicates the array found in the first parameter by the number of copies specified by the third parameter, repeating them in the dimension specified by its second parameter. The effect of the usage in the example above is simply to take the outer product of the two vectors specified in the first parameters of the spread. The naive scalarization of this statement would be

```
      DO j = K + 1, N + 1
         DO i = K, N + 1
            M(i,j) = M(i,j) - M(K,j) * M(i,K)
         ENDDO
      ENDDO
```

However, the i-loop carries a scalarization dependence due to the use of M(K,j) on the right-hand side, which incorrectly uses the value of M computed on the first iteration. This, too, can be eliminated with input prefetching.

```
DO j = K + 1, N + 1
   tMKj = M(K,j)
   DO i = K, N + 1
      M(i,j) = M(i,j) - tMKj * M(i,K)
   ENDDO
ENDDO
```

Note that there is no problem with the reference to M(i,K) because j begins at iteration K + 1. Now we can present the entire scalarization.

```
DO K = 1, N

   tM = M(K,K)
   DO j = K, N + 1
      M(K,j) = M(K,j)/tM
   ENDDO

   DO j = K + 1, N + 1
      tMKj = M(K,j)
      DO i = K, N + 1
         M(i,j) = M(i,j) - tMKj * M(i,K)
      ENDDO
   ENDDO
ENDDO
```

Since interchange is precluded in this nest, loop fusion is tried first. After alignment, the two j-loops can be fused to produce

```
DO K = 1, N
   tM = M(K,K)
   M(K,K) = tM/tM
   DO j = K + 1, N + 1
      M(K,j) = M(K,j)/tM
      tMKj = M(K,j)
      DO i = K, N + 1
         M(i,j) = M(i,j) - tMKj * M(i,K)
      ENDDO
   ENDDO
ENDDO
```

Next, unroll-and-jam is applied to the j-loop to take advantage of the opportunity to reuse M(i,K). In this case, we use a factor of two, but much larger factors are possible. After rearranging and fusing the inner loops, this becomes

```
DO K = 1, N
    tM = M(K,K)
    M(K,K) = tM/tM
    DO j = K + 1, N + 1, 2
        M(K,j) = M(K,j)/tM
        tMKj = M(K,j)
        M(K,j+1) = M(K,j+1)/tM
        tMKj1 = M(K,j+1)
        DO i = K, N + 1
            M(i,j) = M(i,j) - tMKj * M(i,K)
            M(i,j+1) = M(i,j+1) - tMKj1 * M(i,K)
        ENDDO
    ENDDO
ENDDO
```

Finally, we apply scalar replacement along with some further rearrangement to get the result:

```
DO K = 1, N
    tM = M(K,K)
    M(K,K) = tM/tM
    DO j = K + 1, N + 1, 2
        tMKj = M(K,j)/tM
        M(K,j) = tMKj
        tMKj1 = M(K,j+1)/tM
        M(K,j+1) = tMKj1
        DO i = K, N + 1
            tMiK = M(i,K)
            M(i,j) = M(i,j) - tMKj * tMiK
            M(i,j+1) = M(i,j+1) - tMKj1 * tMiK
        ENDDO
    ENDDO
ENDDO
```

This form achieves four flops for every five memory operations. With additional use of unroll-and-jam, it can be made to approach one flop per memory operation.

13.7   **Summary**

This chapter has addressed the problem of generating good code for Fortran 90 array assignments. The principal strategy in this process is the conversion of array assignments to nests of sequential loops that correctly implement the semantics of the original statement. This process would be easy if it were not for the goal of avoiding the use of large compiler-generated temporary arrays.

The chapter presents a variety of strategies for reducing the amount of temporary storage required including *loop reversal*, *input prefetching*, and *loop splitting*. For multidimensional array statements, picking the correct loop order may also be used to avoid generation of temporaries.

It is important to note that these techniques are also required for efficient implementations of Fortran 90 on *vector machines*, for which the innermost loop should be strip-mined to the size of native vector operations.

A second problem addressed is how to improve the performance of scalarized code after it has been generated. It is shown that by judicious use of the techniques of scalar register allocation given in Chapter 8, it is possible to produce code that best approaches what can be done by hand optimization.

13.8 Case Studies

Neither PFC nor the Ardent Titan ever implemented Fortran 90, so the scalarization strategies described here were unnecessary. Recently, these strategies have been implemented in the context of the dHPF compiler at Rice by Yuan Zhao. In addition to the strategies that are described in this chapter, Zhao's implementation included a major improvement—it used alignment in conjunction with temporary array contraction to further reduce the amount of temporary array storage needed in loops generated by Fortran 90. Although this might seem like a minor advance, it had deep implications for the cache behavior of the resulting programs. In one case, SOR using a nine-point stencil written as a single HPF program, Zhao's alignment strategy led to an integer factor speedup in the performance of the code on a single processor SGI using the native Fortran 90 compiler. The technical report arising from this work also suggests that, in some cases, loop skewing can be used to reduce the temporary storage required for scalarization loops generated from Fortran 90 statements [287].

13.9 Historical Comments and References

Wolfe introduced the notion of scalarization and stated that the simple algorithm (Figure 13.2) can always be applied [279]. He observed that loop fusion, where it is legal, can be used to eliminate the temporary storage. He also observed the importance of keeping loop-invariant vectors, such as the result vector in matrix multiplication, in a register during a loop.

The scalarization algorithms in this chapter are taken from a paper by Allen and Kennedy [22] and from Allen's dissertation [16]. Recently, Zhao and Kennedy have improved on these strategies by using alignment and loop skewing [287].

Sarkar [241] observes that there is a trade-off between parallelization and minimizing the size of temporaries in scalarization. He presents an algorithm that combines scalarization and parallelization to obtain the benefits of both.

In his dissertation and associated papers, Roth [238, 179, 178, 180] proposed a compilation strategy that would analyze Fortran 90 at the whole-array level and perform preliminary transformations to reduce the cost of implementing it on specific parallel machines. Roth's strategy was particularly effective for reducing communication in stencils written for the Thinking Machines CM-5 in CM Fortran, which included many different shift operations for the same array.

Exercises

13.1 What is a scalarization fault? Can a scalarization fault always be eliminated?

13.2 Prove that loop reversal will eliminate scalarization faults carried by a loop if and only if the loop carries no antidependences. Why are output dependences not mentioned in this proposition? Will they be a problem in scalarization?

13.3 Prove the proposition that any scalarization loop in which all true dependences have the same constant threshold T and all antidependences have a threshold that is divisible by T can be transformed, using input prefetching and loop splitting, so that all scalarization dependences are eliminated.

13.4 Compare array syntax with PARALLEL DO loops of the sort introduced in Chapter 1. Do they have exactly the same meaning? That is, can a statement in array syntax always be translated into a PARALLEL DO loop, and can a single-statement PARALLEL DO loop always be translated into array syntax?

CHAPTER 14

Compiling
High Performance
Fortran

14.1 Introduction

At the end of the 1980s, high-end parallelism made the transition from bus-based shared-memory systems, which are today called *symmetric multiprocessors* (SMPs), to designs in which the system memory was broken up and packaged with individual processors to make a scalable computer. Typical of the early designs were the hypercubes, originated at Caltech and popularized by Intel and other companies. Later designs used different network architectures, while retaining the distributed-memory design. Such machines came to be called *distributed-memory multiprocessors*.

Because the individual processors in early distributed-memory systems used 32-bit addressing, they could not address every word in the aggregate memory of a large configuration. Therefore, most such machines used some form of "message passing" to communicate data between processors. Whenever one processor needed a block of data resident in the memory of another, the owner would have to explicitly *send* the data to the processor that needed it, which in turn executed a *receive* to extract the data block. These send and receive operations were typically programmed via calls to system libraries from Fortran or C. The drawback of such libraries was that each one was specific to a particular machine, making codes difficult to port between systems. This problem was solved by the release of *Message-Passing Interface* (MPI), a standard interface for message-passing calls from high-level languages. Today, MPI is used on the majority of programs written for scalable parallel machines.

However, MPI and its relatives have a serious drawback—they are not easy to master and use. To write an MPI program, the user must typically rewrite an application into *single-program, multiple-data* (SPMD) form. To illustrate this, we begin with a simple sum reduction calculation that would be written as follows in the Fortran 77 subdialect of Fortran 90:

```
PROGRAM SUM
    REAL A(10000)
    READ (9) A
    SUM = 0.0
    DO I = 1, 10000
        SUM = SUM + A(I)
    ENDDO
    PRINT SUM
END
```

To carry out this calculation on a parallel message-passing machine, we must convert it to the SPMD form, in which each processor executes exactly the same program operating on a different subset of the data space. A processor determines the data on which it is to operate by interrogating processor-specific environment variables. Here is a simple, but inefficient, SPMD program to read a collection of data items, send subsets of the collection to be stored on different processors, compute the sum, and print the result.

```
PROGRAM SUM
    REAL A(100), BUFF(100)
    IF (PID == 0) THEN
        DO IP = 0, 99
            READ (9) BUFF(1:100)
            IF (IP == 0) A(1:100) = BUFF(1:100)
            ELSE SEND(IP,BUFF,100) ! 100 words to Proc I
        ENDDO
    ELSE
        RECV(0,A,100) ! 100 words from proc 0 into A
    ENDIF
    SUM = 0.0
    DO I = 1, 100
        SUM = SUM + A(I)
    ENDDO
    IF (PID == 0) SEND(1,SUM,1)
    IF (PID > 0) RECV(PID-1,T,1)
        SUM = SUM + T
        IF (PID < 99) SEND(PID+1,SUM,1)
        ELSE SEND(0,SUM,1)
    ENDIF
    IF (PID == 0) THEN; RECV (99,SUM,1); PRINT SUM; ENDIF
END
```

Although this program overlaps the computation of 100-element local partial sums, it sequentializes the computation of the global sum from the partial sums. Thus it does not achieve the best overall parallelism. Nevertheless, it illustrates some of the difficulties of programming in SPMD form with message passing. The principal difference from the Fortran 90 version is that the programmer must manage all of the data placement, movement, and synchronization. To do that, he or she must strip-mine the code by hand to produce SPMD code.

The idea behind High Performance Fortran, an extended version of Fortran 90 produced by an informal standardization process in the early 1990s, is to automate most of the details of managing data. In HPF, the critical intellectual task for the programmer is to determine how data is to be laid out in the processor memories in the parallel machine configuration. HPF includes three directives, coded as comments, to accomplish this:

- The TEMPLATE directive provides a mechanism for the user to declare a fine-grained virtual processor array that represents the maximum amount of parallelism that might be useful in the problem. For the problem above, the following directive might suffice:

```
!HPF$ TEMPLATE T(10000)
```

- The ALIGN directive provides a way for arrays to be aligned with a template or with one another. For this problem we might use

```
!HPF$ ALIGN A(:) WITH T(:)
```

- The DISTRIBUTE directive is a machine-independent specification of how to distribute a virtual processor array or a data array onto the memories of a real parallel machine. For example, the example problem distributes all the data across 100 processors. This can be accomplished in HPF by

```
!HPF$ DISTRIBUTE T(BLOCK)
```

Alternatively, the effect of all three directives above can be achieved by

```
!HPF$ DISTRIBUTE A(BLOCK)
```

which is a direct distribution of a data array onto real processors.

With these directives the sum reduction program can be written as

```
PROGRAM SUM
   REAL A(10000)
   !HPF$ DISTRIBUTE A(BLOCK)
   READ (9) A
   SUM = 0.0
   DO I = 1, 10000
      SUM = SUM + A(I)
   ENDDO
   PRINT SUM
END
```

This is clearly much simpler than the message-passing program, but it has a down-side—the compiler must do a substantial amount of work to generate a program that displays reasonable efficiency. In particular, it must recognize that the main calculation is a sum reduction and replicate the values of SUM on each processor. Then it must generate the final parallel sum at the end.

In addition to the distribution directives, HPF has special directives that can be used to assist in the identification of parallelism. The directive

```
!HPF$ INDEPENDENT
```

specifies that the loop that follows can be parallelized without concern for com-munication or synchronization. Many compilers can detect this fact for them-selves, but the directive ensures that all compilers to which the program is presented will execute the loop in parallel.

In the example above, the directive would not be applicable because of the sum reduction. However, because reduction is so common in scientific programs, HPF permits a special qualifier to specify that a particular variable is the target of a sum reduction.

```
!HPF$ INDEPENDENT, REDUCTION(SUM)
```

With this directive, the example can be written in HPF as

```
PROGRAM SUM
   REAL A(10000)
   !HPF$ DISTRIBUTE A(BLOCK)

   READ (9) A
   SUM = 0.0

   !HPF$ INDEPENDENT, REDUCTION(SUM)
   DO I = 1, 10000
      SUM = SUM + A(I)
   ENDDO

   PRINT SUM
END
```

This version is much easier for the compiler to process into an efficient message-passing program.

As a final example, we present a simple HPF code fragment that is intended to model a multigrid method. Here a TEMPLATE is used to align the coarse grid APRIME with the fine grid A. Independent directives are used to ensure portability across compilers that would not recognize the parallelism in the computation loops.

```
      REAL A(1023,1023), B(1023,1023), APRIME(511,511)
!HPF$ TEMPLATE T(1024,1024)
!HPF$ ALIGN A(I,J) WITH T(I,J)
!HPF$ ALIGN B(I,J) WITH T(I,J)
!HPF$ ALIGN APRIME(I,J) WITH T(2*I-1,2*J-1)
!HPF$ DISTRIBUTE T(BLOCK,BLOCK)

!HPF$ INDEPENDENT, NEW(I)
      DO J = 2, 1022   ! Multigrid Smoothing (Red-Black)
   !HPF$    INDEPENDENT
         DO I = MOD(J,2), 1022, 2
            A(I,J) = 0.25 * (A(I-1,J) + A(I+1,J) + A(I,J-1) &
                     + A(I,J+1)) + B(I,J)
         ENDDO
      ENDDO

!HPF$ INDEPENDENT, NEW(I)
      DO J = 2, 510    ! Multigrid Restriction
   !HPF$    INDEPENDENT
         DO I = 2, 510
            APRIME(I,J) = 0.05 * (A(2*I-2,2*J-2) + &
                     4*A(2*I-2,2*J-1) + A(2*I-2,2*J) + &
                     4*A(2*I-1,2*J-2) + 4*A(2*I-1,2*J) + &
                     A(2*I,2*J-2) + 4*A(2*I,2*J-1) + &
                     A(2*I,2*J))
         ENDDO
      ENDDO

      ! Multigrid convergence test
      ERR = MAXVAL(ABS(A(:,:)-B(:,:)))
```

In the example, the qualifier NEW(I) is used in the INDEPENDENT directive for the outer loop to ensure that the inner loop induction variable I is replicated on each group of processors that execute different iterations of the outer loop. This is roughly equivalent to the PRIVATE directive in other parallel dialects.

In the remainder of this chapter we present some compiler strategies that build on the machinery developed earlier in this book to compile HPF programs into reasonably efficient message-passing programs. A goal of this work is to achieve performance that approaches the performance of the best hand-coded message-passing program.

14.2 HPF Compiler Overview

In this section we will discuss the typical structure of an HPF compiler and illustrate the various phases with a simple example. The usual target for HPF compilation is Fortran 77 or Fortran 90 with calls to MPI for communication. For the purposes of the treatment here, we will use as our target language the Fortran 77 subdialect of Fortran 90 plus some simple communication calls that will be explained as we go along. We will make the assumption that all the array assignments have been transformed into sequential loops (scalarized) as described in Chapter 13. For the purposes of this treatment, we will also assume that the number of processors used in the computation is fixed and known at compile time, although this assumption can easily be relaxed.

The principle used to partition computation in most implementations of HPF is the *owner-computes rule*, which says that the owner of the left-hand side of every assignment must compute expression on the right-hand side. Although this rule is implicit in the standard, it is not required. In fact the compiler is free to relax the owner-computes rule in any way that it sees fit. However, it should do this only when there is a clear performance advantage, as the user expects a distribution of computation according to the owner-computes rule, so he or she may have crafted the data distributions with this in mind. Later in the chapter we will explore optimizations that relax this rule.

The HPF compilation process proceeds in several stages:

1. *Dependence analysis:* A complete set of dependences will be needed to determine whether communication is needed and where it should be placed in the final program.

2. *Distribution analysis:* An analysis of the data distributions is performed to determine at each point in the program which distributions can hold for each data structure. Although it is possible for multiple distributions for the same data structure to reach a given point, it is not likely, so we will not deal with that case here.

3. *Partitioning:* Once the distributions are known everywhere in the program, a *computation partitioning* is determined. That is, we must identify with each statement instance in the program, where a statement instance is parameterized by the indices of the loops that control its execution, a processor that executes it. For the compilers we will discuss here, this corresponds to annotating each statement with an ON HOME directive as described in the modified version of our example below.

4. *Communication analysis and placement:* The locations where communication is required must be determined. This involves examining dependences in the program, both between statements and within statements.

5. *Program optimization:* Next, the compiler performs transformations to improve the performance of the program to be generated. For the most part, this means structuring communication and synchronization to minimize the cost and maximize parallelism.

6. *Code generation:* Generation of an SPMD program usually involves three tasks. First the actual SPMD code must be generated by a strip-mining and conditional masking procedure. Then the communication must be finalized. Finally, transformations must be made to manage the storage required on each processor.

We illustrate these steps on a simple HPF code fragment that models a relaxation computation. To keep focused on the issues of most importance, we have left out any input-output or subroutine calls in this code.

```
      REAL A(10000), B(10000)
      !HPF$ DISTRIBUTE A(BLOCK), B(BLOCK)
      DO J = 1, 10000
         DO I = 2, 10000
S₁          A(I) = B(I-1) + C
         ENDDO
         DO I = 1, 10000
S₂          B(I) = A(I)
         ENDDO
      ENDDO
```

Figure 14.1 shows the dependences for this example. Because different arrays are used in each of the inner loops, neither carries a dependence. There is a loop-independent true dependence from statement S_1 to statement S_2 because the output of S_1 is used as input on two different iterations of the loop around S_2. Similarly, there is a true dependence from S_2 to S_1 carried by the outer loop. There are

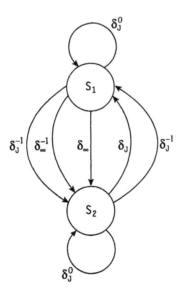

Figure 14.1 Example dependences.

output dependences from S_1 to itself and S_2 to itself carried by the outer loop, and there are antidependences carried by the outer loop from S_1 to S_2 and S_2 to S_1. We will see shortly how these dependences will contribute to the communication analysis. However, an important point is that the loop on I carries no dependence.

Distribution analysis for this example is simple—both array A and array B have block distributions everywhere in the fragment. This means that if the owner-computes rule is followed, any loop that iterates over an entire array is distributed evenly over all the processors. Based on these observations, it is clear that the desired partitioning is one that distributes the work of the I-loops.

Communication analysis should determine where the communications are to be placed. Initially, communication will be placed near the data accesses that need it. Later, communication will be moved based on dependence. Communication requirements are determined by examining the footprints of various references in the loop. For example, in the loop around S_1, each processor will compute results for A(L:L+99) where A(L:L+99), is the range of locations in A owned by that processor (on processor 0, the result for A(1) is not computed). On the other hand, the right-hand side will access B(L-1:L+98). Notice the reference to B(L-1), which is not owned by the processor executing the statement. Therefore, this is an *off-processor* reference. We will refer to the process that arrives at this conclusion as *footprint analysis*. By a similar footprint analysis, we can see that the loop around S_2 includes no off-processor references. Once this analysis is complete, we know that communication is required only on one iteration of the first I-loop. If we were to strip-mine now, the resulting code would be as follows:

```
          ! Shadow location B(0) receives data
          REAL A(1:100), B(0:100)
          !HPF$ DISTRIBUTE A(BLOCK), B(BLOCK)
          DO J = 1, 10000
I₁          IF (PID /= 99) SEND(PID+1,B(100),1)
I₂          IF (PID /= 0) THEN
                RECV(PID-1,B(0),1)
                A(1) = B(0) + C
            ENDIF
            DO I = 2, 100
S₁              A(I) = B(I-1) + C
            ENDDO
            DO I = 1, 100
S₂              B(I) = A(I)
            ENDDO
          ENDDO
```

Notice that the conditional for the receive in each loop has been merged with the use of the received value. This is a minor optimization but allows us to get double duty from the conditional, which avoids executing the first iteration on processor 0 in addition to avoiding a wait for data that will never be sent.

Another interesting feature of this example is the use of extra allocated storage on each processor—location B(0) in this case—to hold data communicated from neighboring processors. These additional allocated cells are often collectively referred to as *overlap areas* or *shadow regions*.

Next, the compiler must determine the correct placement of communication. Clearly, we need to receive the data just before using it, but how early can we send it? For example, could we send it outside the J-loop? The answer is no in this case because of the dependence involving values of A that are carried by the J-loop. Since values computed in the loop are used later in the same loop, we must keep the communication within the loop. We could attempt to move the send in I_1 to a point nearer to where the value B(100) is created at the end of the previous iteration of the J-loop. However, we cannot carry out this move without making a special case to ensure that the first iteration receives expected values. Since this complication would not buy much overall improvement, we leave the loop as it is.

The next step is optimization. There are three general strategies for optimization of communication:

1. *Aggregation* of data to be sent between the same pair of processors into a single message, to amortize the message start-up costs. This is not too useful in the example code because there is not much data to aggregate—basically, we are sending one word in each direction between pairs of processors on each step.

2. *Overlapping communication with computation.* This is quite profitable on the current example, as we will see in a moment.

3. Recognition of special communication patterns that can be replaced with a fast system call to perform *collective communication*. A primary example of this optimization is recognition of sum reductions, for which most machines have fast system routines. Another example is broadcast.

For our running example, the most profitable optimization is overlap of communication with computation. If we examine the code carefully, we can see that all but one of the iterations of the loop around S_1 are purely local—requiring no communication at all. If we can place this code between a send and a receive of data, we will get significant overlap. This can be accomplished by moving the code to receive and compute (the code within the conditional statement at I_2) to a position after the loop around S_1:

```
      ! Shadow location B(0) receives data
      REAL A(1:100), B(0:100)
      !HPF$ DISTRIBUTE A(BLOCK), B(BLOCK)
      DO J = 1, 10000
I₁        IF (PID /= 99) SEND(PID+1,B(100),1)
          DO I = 2, 100
S₁            A(I) = B(I-1) + C
          ENDDO
```

```
I₂        IF (PID /= 0) THEN
              RECV(PID-1,B(0),1)
              A(1) = B(0) + C
          ENDIF
          DO I = 1, 100
S₂            B(I) = A(I)
          ENDDO
      ENDDO
```

At this point the loop is in pretty good shape and the final version of SPMD code would be generated to look like the code above. When generating SPMD code, the compiler must strip-mine the distributed data regions down to the size for one processor plus some overlap or shadow region storage (such as B(0) above).

In the next few sections we will present algorithms to accomplish some of these optimizations and others that cannot be demonstrated on this example. This is not intended to be a thorough discussion of HPF compilation, which would require a book all by itself. Instead, the treatment attempts to give the reader a sense of how the ideas and principles developed in this book can be applied to HPF language processing.

14.3 Basic Loop Compilation

In this section, we present a detailed discussion of methods for implementing loop nests in HPF. As a general overview, the compilation strategy can be seen as preliminary analysis followed by a process that examines a whole loop nest and transforms it to an equivalent loop nest in SPMD format with communication inserted at the appropriate places.

14.3.1 Distribution Propagation and Analysis

The first step is to determine which distributions for a given array may hold at a particular point in the program so that code may be generated for accesses to that array. This is a nontrivial problem for two reasons:

1. HPF supports dynamic redistribution as an approved extension to the language. That is, the user may insert REALIGN and REDISTRIBUTE statements, both of which are executable, on different control flow paths leading to the point of interest.

2. HPF provides a mechanism by which distributions for formal parameters of a subroutine can be inherited from the calling program. If different calling points then pass arrays with different distributions to the same formal parameter, more than one distribution might apply in the subroutine.

Clearly, ambiguity of this sort is best avoided because the only way to structure code in which it cannot be eliminated is by interrogating the run-time system for the precise distribution during execution, which could add substantial overhead in code, space, or both. First, however, it must be determined whether any ambiguity exists.

Locally, distribution analysis can be performed by solving a data flow analysis problem called *reaching decompositions*, which is a direct analog of the reaching definitions problem discussed in Section 4.4. In fact, the reaching decompositions problem is exactly the reaching definitions problem with any REALIGN or REDIS-TRIBUTE statement (or pair) serving as a definition. The analysis must also assume an initial decomposition at the beginning of the program start vertex. Across procedures, an interprocedural version of the reaching decompositions problem must be solved. This is a flow-sensitive problem similar to a simple form of constant propagation. It will be discussed in Section 14.4.7. In those cases where more than one distribution reaches a program point, the distribution can be disambiguated by code duplication at run time based on a run-time test of the distribution. Ambiguities caused by different call chains can usually be eliminated by procedure cloning, also discussed in Section 14.4.7.

For the rest of this chapter, we assume that at each point in the program there is a single applicable distribution for each array. In fact, we will assume for simplicity that the same distribution governs all references to the same array in a single subprogram. We can therefore construct a mapping from the global index space for the array to a processor and the local index space for that processor:

$$\mu_A(i) = (\rho_A(i), \delta_A(i)) = (p, j) \tag{14.1}$$

where ρ_A maps a multidimensional global index i for the array into a processor that owns the array element indexed by i, and δ_A maps the global index to a local index j on the owning processor. As an example, suppose a one-dimensional array A is declared to be distributed BLOCK over the entire processor collection numbered 0 to $p - 1$. If A is declared to have N elements indexed from element 1, then the block size for the array is given by

$$B_A = \lceil N/p \rceil \tag{14.2}$$

which ensures that all block sizes are the same except for the incompletely filled block on the last processor. Given the definition, we can compute the values of the mapping functions:

$$\rho_A(i) = \lceil i/B_A \rceil - 1 \tag{14.3}$$

$$\delta_A(i) = (i-1) \bmod B_A + 1 = i - \rho_A(i)B_A \tag{14.4}$$

These mapping functions will be an essential component of the loop analysis described in the next section.

Once we know the distributions that can hold for the various arrays used in a loop nest, we are ready to determine the computation partition and communication placement for the loop. We begin with a computation partitioning.

14.3.2   Iteration Partitioning

Most HPF compilers use the (left-hand side) owner-computes rule to drive computation partitioning. This rule specifies that, on a single-statement loop, each iteration will be executed on the owner of the data item on the left-hand side of the assignment for that iteration. Thus, in the loop

```
REAL A(10000), B(10000)
!HPF$ DISTRIBUTE A(BLOCK), B(BLOCK)
DO I = 1, 10000
    A(I) = B(I) + C
ENDDO
```

iteration I is executed on the owner of A(I). If there are 100 processors, then the first 100 iterations are executed on processor 0, the next 100 on processor 1, and so on.

Given the left-hand side owner-computes rule, how should we handle multiple-statement loops? A simple strategy would be to use loop distribution to make them into collections of single-statement loops. Later these loops could be fused back together using typed fusion as described in Chapter 6. This would take care of all but the case of recurrences that could not be further distributed.

For recurrences, the compiler must choose to perform all computations on the owner of the left-hand side of one of the statements in the recurrence. We will refer to this reference as the *partitioning reference*. The choice of a partitioning reference in a recurrence loop should be made by a heuristic strategy that has as its goal minimizing the number of carried dependences in the collection of statements. As we will see in Section 14.4.3, the overall number of carried dependences can be reduced by an alignment optimization similar to the one developed in Section 6.2.3.

Once a partitioning reference is chosen, the partitioning must be carried out. The main result of this is to determine the mapping from global iterations of the given loop to the processors that will execute them. For a given loop with induction variable I in loop header

$$DO\ I = 1,\ N$$

suppose the partitioning reference is

$$A(\alpha(I))$$

where α is a function that may also include indices of other loops nested outside and within the loop under consideration. We assume for the moment that α is a linear function or some other one-to-one mapping on the index. Then the processor that *owns* iteration I in a given loop L with partitioning reference $A(\alpha(I))$ (i.e., the one responsible for performing the computation for iteration I) is given by the expression

$$\theta_L(I) = \rho_A(\alpha(I)) \tag{14.5}$$

The set of indices that are to be executed on a given processor p is specified by the expression

$$\{I \text{ such that } 1 \leq I \leq N \text{ and } \theta_L(I) = \rho_A(\alpha(I)) == p\} \tag{14.6}$$

This set can be more concisely defined:

$$\alpha^{-1}(\rho_A^{-1}(\{p\})) \cap [1{:}N] \tag{14.7}$$

The problem with this set of iterations is that it is a subset of the global iteration set. For efficiency, we would like to convert this to local iteration sets. To do this, we need to compute the mapping from global to local iterations. For a given loop L, we will call this mapping Δ_L.

It will be convenient for local iteration sets to run from 1 to some upper bound, so we will make the smallest value in

$$\alpha^{-1}(\rho_A^{-1}(\{p\}))$$

map to the index 1. The cases of the processor owning the partitioning references on iterations 1 and N must be handled as special cases, which we shall deal with momentarily.

As an example, consider the following loop:

```
DO I = 1, N
    A(I+1) = B(I) + C
ENDDO
```

The reference A(I+1) is the partitioning reference. If A is declared as in the previous example,

```
REAL A(10000)
!HPF$ DISTRIBUTE A(BLOCK)
```

and there are 100 processors, the block size is 100 and

$$\rho_A^{-1}(\{p\}) = \left[100p + 1 : 100p + 100\right]$$

Since $\alpha(i) = i + 1$, the inverse subtracts 1:

$$\alpha^{-1}(\rho_A^{-1}(\{p\})) = \left[100p : 100p + 99\right]$$

Since $100p$ is the smallest value in the iteration range of the global index, we will use the mapping to create a new iteration variable $\hat{\imath}$ for each processor, which will begin at 1 and iterate to 100. Specifically,

$$\hat{\imath} = I - 100 \star PID + 1 \tag{14.8}$$

where $\hat{\imath}$ is a local variable on each processor. This can be rewritten to provide a value for I:

$$I = \hat{\imath} + 100 \star PID - 1 \tag{14.9}$$

Given this example, we can define the abstract mapping $\Delta_L(I, p)$ from the global iteration space to the local iteration space for processor p as

$$\Delta_L(I, p) = I - \min(\alpha^{-1}(\rho_A^{-1}(\{p\}))) + 1 \tag{14.10}$$

In our example, the mapping is

$$\Delta_L(I, PID) = I - 100 \star PID + 1 \tag{14.11}$$

Our next step is to adjust the subscripts of the arrays to match the mapping to local index sets. Consider a reference to array B as follows:

$$B(\beta(I))$$

Our goal is to map this reference to a reference

$$B(\gamma(\hat{\imath}))$$

for the local B, where $\gamma(\hat{\imath})$ maps the local index $\hat{\imath}$ to the correct location in local B. In other words, to generate the correct code, we must compute a local index function γ that will replace β in the subscript of the array referenced. The desired relationship is determined by Figure 14.2. In this diagram, GL stands for the global loop iteration, GI for the global array index, LL for the local loop index, and LI for the local array index. The mapping β is the function in the global array subscript. The function Δ is as described earlier, and the function δ, described in the previous section, maps global to local array indices.

From Figure 14.2, it is clear that for a given processor p, the desired function for the local subscript is given by

$$\gamma(\hat{\imath}) = \delta(\beta(\Delta^{-1}(\hat{\imath}))) \tag{14.12}$$

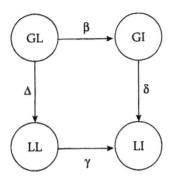

Figure 14.2 Mapping between index and iteration sets.

In our example, the function δ is given by

$$\delta_B(K) = K - 100 * PID \qquad (14.13)$$

and the inverse of Δ_L (from Equation 14.11) is given by

$$\Delta_L^{-1}(i, PID) = i + 100 * PID - 1 \qquad (14.14)$$

Since β is the identity, we can simply apply Δ_L as given in Equation 14.11 to yield

$$\gamma(i) = i + 100 * PID - 1 - 100 * PID = i - 1 \qquad (14.15)$$

The mapping for array A is a slightly different mapping because the subscript function α adds 1 to its parameter. Therefore, the reference A(I+1) is rewritten as A(i) for the local loop.

After all these considerations, for interior processors, the loop becomes

```
DO i = 1, 100
    A(i) = B(i-1) + C
ENDDO
```

However, there remains the detail of how to handle the global loop upper and lower bounds. These are important only on the processors that own iterations L (the lower bound) and N. On the processor that owns iteration L, we must ensure that the loop begins no earlier than iteration

$$\Delta_L(L,p) = L + 1 - \min(\alpha^{-1}(\rho_A^{-1}(\{p\}))) \qquad (14.16)$$

Similarly, on the processor that owns iteration N, we must ensure that the iteration does not proceed beyond

$$\Delta_L(N,p) = N + 1 - \min(\alpha^{-1}(\rho_A^{-1}(\{p\}))) \tag{14.17}$$

Note that the owner of a given iteration K is given by $\theta_L(K) = \rho_A(\alpha(K))$. Therefore, we can identify the processors by testing for equality. These points can be illustrated in the example calculation. Applying Equation 14.16, we find that processor 0 owns global iteration 1, so on that processor the corresponding lower bound is 2. For the upper bound N, it is owned by processor

$$p_N = \lceil(N+1)/100\rceil - 1 = \lfloor N/100 \rfloor$$

By Equation 14.17, the corresponding local iteration is given by

$$N + 1 - PID * 100 = N + 1 - 100 * (\lfloor N/100 \rfloor) = N \text{ mod } 100 + 1$$

Thus, the final form of the example loop is given by

```
lo = 1
IF (PID==0) lo = 2
hi = 100
IF (PID==CEIL(N+1/100)-1) hi = MOD(N,100) + 1
DO i = lo, hi
    A(i) = B(i-1) + C
ENDDO
```

At this point, we have been able to address the problem of translating to local indices and local subscript expressions. We still have the problem of what to do when the processor computing an expression does not own it. This is the goal of communication generation, treated in the next section.

14.3.3 Communication Generation

The final step in the loop compilation process is to generate the communication required by the loop. As we indicated earlier, this can be done by analyzing the *footprint* of each reference—the set of iterations that the reference processes on the local iteration space.

Suppose we have a reference on the right-hand side of the assignment in a distributed loop on index I with a subscript expression $\beta(I)$:

$$B(\beta(I))$$

The set of index values on which this reference refers to an element of B that is local to processor p is given by

$$\beta^{-1}(\rho_B^{-1}(\{p\})) \tag{14.18}$$

If the reference is the only one on the right-hand side, then the set of iterations on which no communication is required is given by

$$\alpha^{-1}(\rho_A^{-1}(\{p\})) \cap \beta^{-1}(\rho_B^{-1}(\{p\})) \cap [1:N] \qquad (14.19)$$

Any other iteration will require receiving data from some other processor. That is, if

$$I \in (\alpha^{-1}(\rho_A^{-1}(\{p\})) - \beta^{-1}(\rho_B^{-1}(\{p\}))) \cap [1:N] \qquad (14.20)$$

then on iteration I we must receive the data for the reference on the right-hand side from the processor that owns it.

On some iterations, we will be required to send data to another processor. This happens on any iteration in which processor p owns the data but does not execute the statement that does the calculations. In our set notation, this arises whenever

$$I \in (\beta^{-1}(\rho_B^{-1}(\{p\})) - \alpha^{-1}(\rho_A^{-1}(\{p\}))) \cap [1:N] \qquad (14.21)$$

Let us now return to our example to explore the implications of these formulas.

```
REAL A(10000), B(10000)
!HPF$ DISTRIBUTE A(BLOCK), B(BLOCK)
    . . .
DO I = 1, N
    A(I+1) = B(I) + C
ENDDO
```

We have already seen that

$$\alpha^{-1}(\rho_A^{-1}(\{p\})) = \left[100p : 100p + 99\right]$$

The set of iterations on the right-hand side in which the data is local is given by

$$\beta^{-1}(\rho_B^{-1}(\{p\})) = \left[100p + 1 : 100p + 100\right]$$

By Equation 14.19, the set of iterations on which no communication is required on processor p is

$$\left[100p : 100p + 99\right] \cap \left[100p + 1 : 100p + 100\right]$$
$$= \left[100p + 1 : 100p + 99\right]$$

Following Equation 14.20, the set of iterations on which data must be received from another processor is given by

$$\left[100p : 100p + 99\right] - \left[100p + 1 : 100p + 100\right] = \left[100p : 100p\right]$$

and, following Equation 14.21, the set of iterations on which data must be sent to an adjacent processor before computing begins is

$$\left[100p + 1 : 100p + 100\right] - \left[100p : 100p + 99\right]$$
$$= \left[100p + 100 : 100p + 100\right]$$

Before we generate the code for the local iterations, we must determine what local storage allocation must be. In this case, we need on each processor storage to hold 100 elements of A. In addition, we need enough storage to hold 100 values of B plus an additional location to be used to hold the value of B that is passed from the processor immediately to the left. Let us therefore assume that we have storage for local values of A(1:100) and B(0:100).

Before we explore the code to be generated, we need a way to map the iterations on which communication is required to the local iteration set. Let us begin with the "receive," as it is clear that we must receive data on an iteration on which a computation is performed. The local iteration for the loop is

$$\Delta_L(100*PID,PID) = 100 * PID - 100 * PID + 1 = 1 \tag{14.22}$$

Thus we must receive on iteration 1. The loop code, adjusted to include receiving data, would then look like this:

```
lo = 1
IF (PID==0) lo = 2
hi = 100
IF (PID==CEIL((N+1)/100)-1) hi = MOD(N,100) + 1
DO i = lo, hi
   IF (i==1 .AND. PID /= 0) RECV (PID-1,B(0),1)
   A(i) = B(i-1) + C
ENDDO
```

The receive operation above does not actually need the condition to ensure that PID ≠ 0 because lo will never be equal to 1 on that processor, but we leave it in for completeness.

The send must happen on local iteration

$$\Delta_L(100*PID+100,PID) = 100 * PID - 100 * PID + 101 = 101 \tag{14.23}$$

Note, however, that this is not in the normal iteration range of the computation. Therefore, we must either extend the iteration range to include this iteration for sending or have special code outside the loop to perform the send. Furthermore, we must ensure that we do not send on the last iteration of the loop, since no receive will occur. If we choose the first of these alternatives, we will need another conditional statement in the loop, controlling the execution of every iteration:

```
lo = 1
IF (PID==0) lo = 2
hi = 100
lastP = CEIL((N+1)/100) - 1
IF (PID==lastP) hi = MOD(N,100) + 1
DO i = lo, hi + 1
    IF (i==1 .AND. PID /= 0) RECV(PID-1,B(0),1)
    IF (i<=hi) THEN
        A(i) = B(i-1) + C
    ENDIF
    IF (i == hi+1 .AND. PID /= lastP) &
        SEND(PID+1,B(100),1)
ENDDO
```

This code can be significantly simplified by moving the send to a position outside the loop:

```
lo = 1
IF (PID==0) lo = 2
hi = 100
lastP = CEIL((N+1)/100) - 1
IF (PID==lastP) hi = MOD(N,100) + 1
IF (PID<=lastP) THEN
    DO i = lo, hi
        IF (i==1 .AND. PID /= 0) RECV(PID-1,B(0),1)
        A(i) = B(i-1) + C
    ENDDO
    IF (PID /= lastP) SEND(PID+1,B(100),1)
ENDIF
```

We note that we could further simplify the code by moving the receive outside the loop as well. For reasons that will become clear later, we will choose to do this by peeling the receive iteration out of the main computation loop:

```
lo = 1
IF (PID==0) lo = 2
hi = 100
lastP = CEIL((N+1)/100) - 1
IF (PID==lastP) hi = MOD(N,100) + 1
IF (PID<=lastP) THEN
    IF (lo == 1) THEN
        RECV (PID-1,B(0),1)
        A(1) = B(0) + C
    ENDIF
    ! lo = MAX(lo,1+1) == 2
    DO i = 2, hi
        A(i) = B(i-1) + C
    ENDDO
    IF (PID /= lastP) SEND(PID+1,B(100),1)
ENDIF
```

This is the sort of code that you would hope a compiler could generate. However, there remains one problem with this code. As written, the loop is serialized on processors in the processor array. That is, processor 0 will execute the loop to completion before processor 1 begins because the send is placed at the end of the loop and the receive is placed at the beginning. If the code can be safely rearranged to do all the sends first, then parallelism can be significantly enhanced. The code is

```
lo = 1
IF (PID==0) lo = 2
hi = 100
lastP = CEIL((N+1)/100) - 1
IF (PID==lastP) hi = MOD(N,100) + 1
IF (PID<=lastP) THEN
    IF (PID /= lastP) &
        SEND(PID+1,B(100),1) ! Moved from end
    IF (lo == 1) THEN
        RECV (PID-1,B(0),1)
        A(1) = B(0) + C
    ENDIF
    DO i = 2, hi
        A(i) = B(i-1) + C
    ENDDO
ENDIF
```

This leads to the question, When is such a rearrangement legal? To answer, we must have some mechanism for computing dependence in loops involving communication, such as given above. The trick will be to make communication operations look like memory accesses, so that the machinery for dependence that we have already developed can be directly applied. The solution is to adopt the convention that a receive is simply a copy from a global memory location for A to a local location. Similarly, a send is a copy from a local to a global location for A. In these terms the original loop above looks like the following:

```
        IF (PID<=lastP) THEN
S₁          IF (lo == 1) THEN
                B(0) = B_g(0) ! RECV
                A(1) = B(0) + C
            ENDIF
            DO i = 2, hi
                A(i) = B(i-1) + C
            ENDDO
S₂          IF (PID /= lastP) B_g(100) = B(100) ! SEND
        ENDIF
```

If we were now to perform dependence analysis on this code, we would discover that there is no chain of dependences leading from S_1 to S_2. Therefore, these statements can be rearranged within the containing IF statement.

On the other hand, if the original code were

```
REAL A(10000)
!HPF$ DISTRIBUTE A(BLOCK)
    ...
DO I = 1, N
    A(I+1) = A(I) + C
ENDDO
```

the loop would be rewritten as

```
        IF (PID<=lastP) THEN
S₁          IF (lo == 1) THEN
                A(0) = A_g(0) ! RECV
                A(1) = A(0) + C
            ENDIF
            DO i = 2, hi
                A(i) = A(i-1) + C
            ENDDO
S₂          IF (PID /= lastP) A_g(100) = A(100) ! SEND
        ENDIF
```

Here there is a dependence that necessarily serializes the computation. Therefore, the rearrangement would not be correct.

14.4 **Optimization**

Once the basic framework for loop code generation is in place, we can see a number of optimizations that might be undertaken. The goal of these optimizations is to improve the performance of communication or hide it by overlapping communication and computation. In addition, some calculations that may not be completely parallel can achieve partial parallelization through pipelining. Finally, we will consider the problems associated with storage management and how they might complicate the communications optimization problems.

14.4.1 **Communication Vectorization**

On most message-passing machines, the cost of sending a message has two components: a start-up cost and a cost per unit transferred. Typically, the start-up costs are large, so it is profitable to combine multiple messages between the same pair of processors into a single message. This is a goal of communication vectorization. The transformation can be illustrated by a generalization of the example we have been considering into two loops:

```
REAL A(10000,100), B(10000,100)
!HPF$ DISTRIBUTE A(BLOCK,*), B(BLOCK,*)
DO J = 1, M
   DO I = 1, N
      A(I+1,J) = B(I,J) + C
   ENDDO
ENDDO
```

If we apply the code generation procedure from the previous section, we will get a loop that looks like the following:

```
DO J = 1, M
   lo = 1
   IF (PID==0) lo = 2
   hi = 100
   lastP = CEIL((N+1)/100) - 1
   IF (PID==lastP) hi = MOD(N,100) + 1
   IF (PID <= lastP) THEN
      IF (PID /= lastP) &
         SEND(PID+1,B(100,J),1)
      IF (lo==1) THEN
         RECV (PID-1,B(0,J),1)
         A(1,J) = B(0,J) + C
      ENDIF
      DO i = 2, hi
```

```
          A(i,J) = B(i-1,J) + C
      ENDDO
    ENDIF
ENDDO
```

If we can determine that the J-loop can be distributed around the three components in the code as follows

```
lo = 1
IF (PID==0) lo = 2
hi = 100
lastP = CEIL((N+1)/100) - 1
IF (PID==lastP) hi = MOD(N,100) + 1
IF (PID<=lastP) THEN
    DO J = 1, M
        IF (PID /= lastP) &
            SEND(PID+1,B(100,J),1)
    ENDDO
    DO J = 1, M
        IF (lo==1) THEN
            RECV (PID-1,B(0,J),1)
            A(1,J) = B(0,J) + C
        ENDIF
    ENDDO
    DO J = 1, M
        DO i = 2, hi
            A(i,J) = B(i-1,J) + C
        ENDDO
    ENDDO
ENDIF
```

we can then vectorize all the receive operations in the code to produce much longer messages:

```
lo = 1
IF (PID==0) lo = 2
hi = 100
lastP = CEIL((N+1)/100) - 1
IF (PID==lastP) hi = MOD(N,100) + 1
IF (PID<=lastP) THEN
    IF (lo==1) THEN
        RECV (PID-1,B(0,1:M),M)
        DO J = 1, M
            A(1,J) = B(0,J) + C
        ENDDO
```

```
        ENDIF
        DO J = 1, M
            DO i = 2, hi
                A(i,J) = B(i-1,J) + C
            ENDDO
        ENDDO
        IF (PID /= lastP) &
            SEND(PID+1,B(100,1:M),M)
    ENDIF
```

So what are the conditions for performing such a distribution? In other words, when can we move the send and receive statements outside of a containing loop like the J-loop? To understand this issue, we use the dependence computation strategy used in the previous section—we treat a communication statement as a copy between local and global values. After the first code generation step, the loop becomes

```
        DO J = 1, M
            lo = 1
            IF (PID==0) lo = 2
            hi = 100
            lastP = CEIL((N+1)/100) - 1
            IF (PID==lastP) hi = MOD(N,100) + 1
            IF (PID<=lastP) THEN
S₁              IF (PID /= lastP) B_g(100,J) = B(100,J)
                ! SEND(PID+1,B(100,J),1)
                IF (lo==1) THEN
S₂                  B(0,J) = B_g(0,J) ! RECV (PID-1,B(0,J),1)
S₃                  A(1,J) = B(0,J) + C
                ENDIF
                DO i = 2, hi
S₄                  A(i,J) = B(i-1,J) + C
                ENDDO
            ENDIF
        ENDDO
```

Assuming the J-loop can be interchanged with the IF statements, the issue is whether the outer loop can be distributed around the statements under the IF statements. This is possible if the J-loop does not carry a recurrence involving the communication statements. In the previous example, the only dependence among the marked statements is the one between S_2 and S_3. Hence, there is no recurrence involving the J-loop and all communication can be vectorized.

We are now ready to generalize these ideas into a rule for communication vectorization.

Communication statements resulting from an inner loop can be vectorized with respect to an outer loop if the communication statements are not involved in a recurrence carried by the outer loop.

To see the validity of this principle, recall that we know loop distribution is possible so long as the statements over which distribution is to be performed do not form a recurrence carried by the loop being distributed (see Section 2.4.2). If such a recurrence exists, then the distribution cannot be performed and communication vectorization is prohibited.

Here is another example that is a slight variation of our original:

```
REAL A(10000,100), B(10000,100)
!HPF$ DISTRIBUTE A(BLOCK,*), B(BLOCK,*)
DO J = 1, M
    DO I = 1, N
        A(I+1,J+1) = A(I+1,J) + B(I,J)
    ENDDO
ENDDO
```

Like the previous example, we need communication for array B because of the distribution over the I-loop. On the other hand, no communication is required for the reference to A because the references are aligned on the same iteration of the I-loop. Thus this loop will have a communication dependence pattern identical to the previous example, so communication can once again be vectorized.

On the other hand, suppose we create a situation where communication is required for A, the variable that is being computed.

```
REAL A(10000,100) B(10000,100)
!HPF$ DISTRIBUTE A(BLOCK,*), B(BLOCK,*)
DO J = 1, M
    DO I = 1, N
        A(I+1,J) = A(I,J) + B(I,J)
    ENDDO
ENDDO
```

After the first code generation steps, the code looks like this, where communication has been replaced by copies as before:

```
DO J = 1, M
    lo = 1
    IF (PID==0) lo = 2
    hi = 100
    lastP = CEIL((N+1)/100) - 1
    IF (PID==lastP) hi = MOD(N,100) + 1
```

```
            IF (PID<=lastP) THEN
                IF (lo==1) THEN
                    B(0,J) = Bg(0,J) ! RECV (PID-1,B(0,J),1)
      S1          A(0,J) = Ag(0,J) ! RECV (PID-1,A(0,J),1)
      S2          A(1,J) = A(0,J) + B(0,J)
                ENDIF
                DO i = 2, hi
      S3            A(i,J) = A(i-1,J) + B(i-1,J)
                ENDDO
      S4      IF (PID /= lastP) THEN
                    Bg(100,J) = B(100,J) !SEND(PID+1,B(100,J),1)
                    Ag(100,J) = A(100,J) !SEND(PID+1,A(100,J+1),1)
                ENDIF
            ENDIF
        ENDDO
```

Here the dependences carried by the I-loop have prevented us from rearranging the send and receive statements, although sending the values of B could be moved to the beginning. However, the J-loop carries no dependence, so communication can still be vectorized:

```
        lo = 1
        IF (PID==0) lo = 2
        hi = 100
        lastP = CEIL((N+1)/100) - 1
        IF (PID==lastP) hi = MOD(N,100) + 1
        IF (PID<=lastP) THEN
            IF (lo==1) THEN
                RECV (PID-1,B(0,1:M),M)
      S1          RECV (PID-1,A(0,1:M),M)
                DO J = 1, M
      S2              A(1,J) = A(0,J) + B(0,J)
                ENDDO
            ENDIF
            DO J = 1, M
                DO i = 2, hi
      S3              A(i,J) = A(i-1,J) + B(i-1,J)
                ENDDO
            ENDDO
      S4      IF (PID /= lastP) THEN
                SEND(PID+1,B(100,1:M),M)
                SEND(PID+1,A(100,1:M),M)
            ENDIF
        ENDIF
```

Finally, we show an example where vectorization is not possible.

```
REAL A(10000,1000)
!HPF$ DISTRIBUTE A(BLOCK,*)
DO J = 1, M
   DO I = 1, N
      A(I+1,J+1) = A(I,J) + C
   ENDDO
ENDDO
```

After partitioning the I-loop and inserting communication we get

```
      DO J = 1, M
         lo = 1
         IF (PID==0) lo = 2
         hi = 100
         lastP = CEIL((N+1)/100) - 1
         IF (PID==lastP) hi = MOD(N,100) + 1
         IF (PID<=lastP) THEN
            IF (lo==1) THEN
S₀             A(0,J) = A_g(0,J) ! RECV(PID-1,A(0,J),1)
S₁             A(1,J+1) = A(0,J) + C
            ENDIF
            DO i = 2, hi
S₂             A(i,J+1) = A(i-1,J) + C
            ENDDO
            IF (PID /= lastP) THEN ! SEND(PID+1,A(100,J),1)
S₃             A_g(100,J+1) = A(100,J+1)
            ENDIF
         ENDIF
      ENDDO
```

Here the communication statements cannot be vectorized because there is a recurrence carried by the J-loop. Note that the distance of the recurrence is equal to the block size for array A. Therefore, we can get a partial message vectorization by strip mining, as in the following code:

```
      DO J = 1, M, 100
         lo = 1
         IF (PID==0) lo = 2
         hi = 100
         lastP = CEIL((N+1)/100) - 1
         IF (PID==lastP) hi = MOD(N,100) + 1
         IF (PID<=lastP) THEN
            IF (lo==1) THEN
```

```
S₀              RECV(PID-1,A(0,J:J+99),100)
                DO j = J, J + 99
S₁                  A(1,j+1) = A(0,j) + C
                ENDDO
            ENDIF
            DO j = J, J + 99
                DO i = 2, hi
S₂                  A(i,j+1) = A(i-1,j) + C
                ENDDO
            ENDDO
            IF (PID /= lastP) THEN
S₃              SEND(PID+1,A(100,J:J+99),100)
            ENDIF
        ENDIF
    ENDDO
```

14.4.2 Overlapping Communication and Computation

The cost of communication can often be hidden by overlapping it with computation. To see how this might take place, let us return to the example we used in the previous section.

```
REAL A(10000), B(10000)
!HPF$ DISTRIBUTE A(BLOCK), B(BLOCK)
    ...
DO I = 1, N
    A(I+1) = B(I) + C
ENDDO
```

We have already seen that this example leads to the following local code:

```
    lo = 1
    IF (PID==0) lo = 2
    hi = 100
    lastP = CEIL((N+1)/100) - 1
    IF (PID==lastP) hi = MOD(N,100) + 1
    IF (PID<=lastP) THEN
S₀      IF (PID /= lastP) SEND(PID+1,B(100),1)
S₁      IF (lo==1) THEN
            RECV (PID-1,B(0),1)
            A(1) = B(0) + C
        ENDIF
```

```
L₁      DO i = 2, hi
            A(i) = B(i-1) + C
        ENDDO
    ENDIF
```

Notice that none of the code in the loop L_1 depends on values communicated from other processors. Therefore, we can rearrange so that this computation takes place between the sends and the receives:

```
        lo = 1
        IF (PID==0) lo = 2
        hi = 100
        lastP = CEIL((N+1)/100) - 1
        IF (PID==lastP) hi = MOD(N,100) + 1
        IF (PID<=lastP) THEN
S₀          IF (PID /= lastP) SEND(PID+1,B(100),1)
L₁          DO i = 2, hi
                A(i) = B(i-1) + C
            ENDDO
S₁          IF (lo == 1) THEN
                RECV (PID-1,B(0),1)
                A(1) = B(0) + C
            ENDIF
        ENDIF
```

This transformation, known as *iteration reordering*, hides as much of the communication delay as possible between the send and receive. If all the processors send simultaneously, then the time for computation can be subtracted from the effective communication time, significantly reducing communication costs.

Iteration reordering can be used whenever there is no dependence carried by the original loop—that is, whenever there is no dependence in the generated code that would force the receive to precede the computation in the loop body.

Another approach to communication optimization is to move the communication within the control flow graph to the earliest possible point in the program. It is possible to determine the correct insertion point by establishing a set of data flow equations and solving them using a calculation similar to partial redundancy determination [137].

14.4.3 Alignment and Replication

Given the scheme for distributing the iterations of a loop described in Section 14.3, we do not need to use loop distribution to make every loop as small as possible. Instead, we can pick a partitioning reference within a large loop and partition the entire loop together. The drawback of this scheme is that the loop may have many carried dependences, each requiring communication. In this section we describe how to ameliorate this problem.

Suppose we are generating code for a loop that iterates over a distributed dimension—that is, the iterations of the loop will execute on different processors. Then every true dependence carried by that loop requires communication. Thus the total amount of communication is reduced if we can eliminate carried dependences.

Suppose for the moment that there is no recurrence in the loop. Then we know from Section 6.2 that all carried dependences can be eliminated by a combination of loop alignment and code replication. Consider for a moment the following code:

```
DO I = 1, N
   A(I+1) = B(I) + C(I)
   D(I) = A(I+1) + A(I)
ENDDO
```

This loop has a carried dependence involving A with threshold 1 and a loop-independent dependence involving A that prevents alignment alone from solving the problem. Using alignment and replication, this loop would be converted to

```
DO I = 1, N
   TO = B(I) + C(I)
   A(I+1) = TO
   IF (I==1)THEN
       T1 = A(I)
   ELSE
       T1 = B(I-1) + C(I-1)
   ENDIF
   D(I) = TO + T1
ENDDO
```

The code generation process can then be applied to the result to produce a perfectly parallel loop, albeit with a bit of extra computation in each iteration.

In the case where there is a recurrence, this strategy can be used to minimize the total amount of communication required during execution of the recurrence. The basic idea would be to arrange the code so that the minimal number of backward dependences exist and then to align the body so that forward carried dependences are eliminated.

This strategy will permit the focus of the pipelining process to shift to be exclusively on the backward-carried dependences.

14.4.4 **Pipelining**

Whenever the inner loop of a loop nest must be serialized, some parallelism can be achieved if the outer loops contain no processor-crossing dependences. Here is a simple example:

```
REAL A(10000,100)
!HPF$ DISTRIBUTE A(BLOCK,*)
DO J = 1, M
   DO I = 1, N
      A(I+1,J) = A(I,J) + C
   ENDDO
ENDDO
```

The initial code generation for loop I yields

```
lo = 1
IF (PID==0) lo = 2
hi = 100
lastP = CEIL((N+1)/100) - 1
IF (PID==lastP) hi = MOD(N,100) + 1
IF (PID<=lastP) THEN
   DO J = 1, M
      IF (lo==1) THEN
         RECV (PID-1,A(0,J),1)
         A(1,J) = A(0,J) + C
      ENDIF
      DO i = 2, hi
         A(i,J) = A(i-1,J) + C
      ENDDO
      IF (PID /= lastP) &
         SEND(PID+1,A(100,J),1)
   ENDDO
ENDIF
```

Although the communication operations can be completely vectorized in this case, it is unwise to do so because it gives up parallelism. In fact, the loop as written has more parallelism than a vectorized loop because processor 1 can begin work on computing its local A(1:100,1) as soon as processor 0 finishes the first iteration of the J-loop. In other words, the iterations of the J-loop can be overlapped. This is illustrated by Figure 14.3.

The problem with this scheme is that the overhead of communicating one word at a time will outweigh the value of parallelism gains. Figure 14.3 is misleading because it does not show any overhead for initiating or carrying out communication. A more realistic diagram is given in Figure 14.4, which shows both the overhead on the processor and the communication delay for carrying out a send.

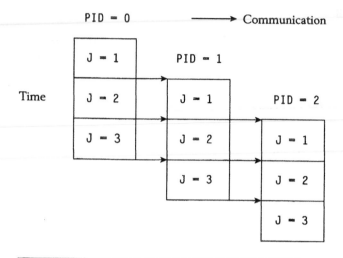

Figure 14.3 Pipelined parallelism with communication.

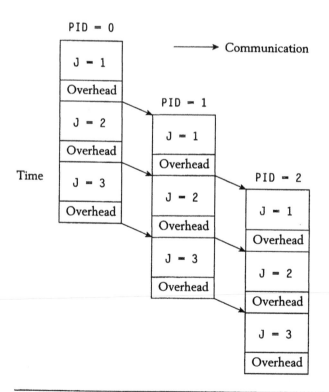

Figure 14.4 Pipelined parallelism with communication overhead.

Because most of the overhead cost is the same no matter how many words are sent, it is usually profitable to increase the granularity of pipelining by computing several iterations of the J-loop before communicating the values, as in

```
lo = 1
IF (PID==0) lo = 2
hi = 100
lastP = CEIL((N+1)/100) - 1
IF (PID==lastP) hi = MOD(N,100) + 1
IF (PID<=lastP) THEN
    DO J = 1, M, K UB = min(J+K-1,M)
        IF (lo==1) THEN
            RECV (PID-1,A(0,J:UB),UB-J+1)
            DO j = J, UB
                A(1,j) = A(0,j) + C
            ENDDO
        ENDIF
        DO j = J, UB
            DO i = 2, hi
                A(i,j) = A(i-1,j) + C
            ENDDO
        ENDDO
        IF (PID /= lastP) &
            SEND(PID+1,A(100,J:UB),UB-J+1)
    ENDDO
ENDIF
```

Here the blocking factor K is a tuning parameter that depends on both the machine and the amount of computation in the loop. A variety of strategies for determining the parameter could be used. For example, a test run on each machine could determine the optimal blocking for short loops. This same blocking could then be used for larger loops as well.

14.4.5 Identification of Common Recurrences

Many calculations carried out on parallel machines involve recurrences that take, as input, values from arrays that are distributed across multiple memories. Most such recurrences are standard patterns such as sum reduction. These patterns usually have a fast library implementation on each machine. A good HPF compiler should be able to identify and replace raw calculations with the use of such library routines. As an example, suppose that we are given the following program:

```
REAL A(10000), B(10000)
!HPF$ DISTRIBUTE A(BLOCK), B(BLOCK)
    ...
S = 0.0
DO I = 1, N
    S = S + A(I) * B(I)
ENDDO
```

The variable S here is assumed to be replicated on each processor, so the result should be a value for S on each processor that is equal to the sum of products of A and B. The compiler must first separate this calculation into local and global components. Assume that there are 100 processors, so the block size is 100.

```
lo = 1
hi = 100
lastP = CEIL(N/100) - 1
IF (PID==lastP) hi = MOD(N-1,100) + 1
Slocal = 0.0
IF (PID<=lastP) THEN
   DO i = lo, hi
      Slocal = Slocal + A(i) * B(i)
   ENDDO
ENDIF
```

Once this is done, the final values can be computed by calling the library routine

```
S = GLOBAL_SUM(Slocal)
```

Other standard recurrences can be handled in a similar manner.

14.4.6 Storage Management

A good HPF compiler must take steps to ensure that the code it generates does not require temporary storage in excess of what is possible. Usually, a computation should require no more temporary storage than the arrays owned by each processor. In other words, we should assume that no more than half of the memory on each processor is held for communicated values.

To keep within these bounds, the compiler may be required to reorganize the computation significantly. To see this, we should consider the example of matrix multiplication, as shown in the following:

```
!HPF$ ALIGN A(I,J), B(I,J), C(I,J) WITH T(I,J)
!HPF$ DISTRIBUTE T(BLOCK,BLOCK) ONTO P(4,4)
DO K = 1, N
   DO J = 1, N
      DO I = 1, N
         C(I,J) = C(I,J) + A(I,K) * B(K,J)
      ENDDO
   ENDDO
ENDDO
```

It should be pointed out that, in this loop, the communication can be moved out of all loops, a fact that the compiler easily determines. But should it make that move? What are the storage requirements of various code positions? As we shall see, placing the communication inside the outermost loop achieves a significant reduction in storage requirements.

Let us begin with an examination of what happens if we attempt to move the code entirely out of the outermost loop. If this is done, the generated code might look like this, where we assume that local storage holds n-by-n blocks of A, B, and C:

```
! Resource-independent placement
  DO pR = 0, nRows - 1
     IF (pR /= myR) &
        SEND ((pR,myC),B(n*myR+1:n*myR+n,1:n),n*n)
  ENDDO
  DO pC = 0, nCols - 1
     IF (pC /= myC) &
        SEND ((myR,pC),A(1:n,myC*n+1:myC*n+n),n*n)
  ENDDO
  DO pR = 0, nRows - 1
     IF (pR /= myR) &
        RECV ((pR,myC),B(n*pR+1:n*pR+n,1:n),n*n)
  ENDDO
  DO pC = 0, nCols - 1
     IF (pC /= myC) &
        RECV ((myR,pC),A(1:n,n*pC+1:n*pC+n),n*n)
  ENDDO
  DO K = 1, n * 4 ! = N
     DO J = 1, n
        DO I = 1, n
           C(I,J) = C(I,J) + A(I,K) * B(K,J)
        ENDDO
     ENDDO
  ENDDO
```

Note that the special variables myR and myC refer to the column and row of the executing processor, so that the pair (myR,myC) is equivalent to the current PID.

The problem with this code is that it requires storage for four blocks of array A, each of size n^2, four similarly sized blocks of array B, and a single block of storage for array C. The total storage required is thus nine blocks of size n^2. Of these, only three are local. Thus, in this communication pattern, each processor requires $6n^2$ locations for data communicated from other processors—twice the storage required for local variables. The problem is illustrated in Figure 14.5.

Here storage is needed on each processor for every block of A and every block of B needed to compute block C_{ij}.

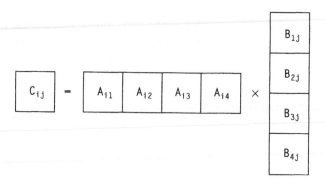

Figure 14.5 Storage for matrix multiplication.

If we leave the communication inside the outermost loop, we get a much more modest storage requirement, as illustrated in the following code:

```
! Resource-based placement
  DO K = 1, n * 4 ! = N
    kP = CEIL(K/n) - 1
    kloc = MOD(K-1,n) + 1
    sR = MOD(myR+kP,4); sC = MOD(myC+kP,4)
    rR = MOD(myR-kP,4); rC = MOD(myC-kP,4)
    IF (sR /= myR) SEND ((sR,myC),B(kloc,1:n),n)
    IF (sC /= myC) SEND ((myR,sC),A(1:n,kloc),n)
    IF (rR /= myR) THEN
       kR = n + 1
       RECV ((rR,myC),B(kR,1:n),n)
    ElSE
       kR = kloc
    ENDIF
    IF (rC /= myC) THEN
       kC = n + 1
       RECV ((myR,rC),A(1:n,kC),n)
    ElSE
       kC = kloc
    ENDIF
    DO J = 1, n
       DO I = 1, n
          C(I,J) = C(I,J) + A(I,kC) * B(kR,J)
       ENDDO
    ENDDO
  ENDDO
```

The storage required by this strategy is much smaller—just 2*n* extra locations on each processor. These are allocated in the column *n* + 1 of array A and row *n* + 1 of array B. This is much less than the $3n^2$ storage locations required for local arrays. Thus this is the best place for insertion of communication. However, somewhat better performance can be achieved if we block the K-loop as follows:

```
! Resource-based placement with strip mining
DO kP = 0, 3
   sR = MOD(myR+kP,4); sC = MOD(myC+kP,4)
   rR = MOD(myR-kP,4); rC = MOD(myC-kP,4)
   IF (sR /= myR) SEND ((sR,myC),B(1:n,1:n),n*n)
   IF (sC /= myC) SEND ((myR,sC),A(1:n,1:n),n*n)
   IF (rR /= myR) THEN
      kR = n
      RECV ((rR,myC),B(n+1;n+n,1:n),n*n)
   ElSE
      kR = 0
   ENDIF
   IF (rC /= myC) THEN
      kC = n
      RECV ((myR,rC),A(1:n,n+1:n+n),n*n)
   ElSE
      kC = 0
   ENDIF
   DO K = 1, n
      DO J = 1, n
         DO I = 1, n
            C(I,J) = C(I,J) + A(I,K+kC) * B(K+kR,J)
         ENDDO
      ENDDO
   ENDDO
ENDDO
```

In addition to local storage, this example requires two additional blocks of storage, each of size n^2. As a result the storage for communication is roughly 2/3 the local storage. We should note that this formulation is the optimal way to do matrix multiplication on many parallel systems.

To summarize, an HPF compiler must analyze buffer resources required for each placement of communications within a loop nest. It should then choose the placement that requires no more storage than required for local variables. In some cases, strip mining can be used to achieve less frequent communication at the expense of some storage without exceeding the storage guidelines, as the previous example shows.

14.4.7   **Handling Multiple Dimensions**

We conclude this section with a discussion of communication in two dimensions. Suppose we are given the loop

```
REAL A(1000,1000) B(1000,1000)
!HPF$ DISTRIBUTE A(BLOCK,BLOCK), B(BLOCK,BLOCK)
    ...
DO J = 1, M
   DO I = 1, N
      A(I+1,J+1) = B(I,J+1) + B(I+1,J)
   ENDDO
ENDDO
```

Assume that we have 100 processors arranged in a 10-by-10 grid. Then by analogy with the previous example, the code generated for the inner loop might look like the following:

```
ilo = 1
IF (myR==0) ilo = 2
ihi = 100
ilastP = CEIL((N+1)/100) - 1
IF (myR==ilastP) ihi = MOD(N,100) + 1
IF (ilo==1) THEN
   RECV ((myR-1,myC),B(0,J+1),1)
ENDIF
DO i = ilo, ihi
   A(i,J+1) = B(i-1,J+1) + B(i,J)
ENDDO
IF (myR /= ilastP) &
   SEND((myR+1,myC),B(100,J+1),1)
```

If we then apply the same process to the outer loop, distributing where appropriate, we get

```
! Compute local upper and lower bounds
jlo = 1
IF (myC==0) jlo = 2
jhi = 100
jlastP = CEIL((M+1)/100) - 1
IF (myC==jlastP) jhi = MOD(M,100) + 1
ilo = 1
IF (myR==0) ilo = 2
```

```
ihi = 100
ilastP = CEIL((N+1)/100) - 1
IF (myR==ilastP) ihi = MOD(N,100) + 1
! Receive data
IF (jlo==1) THEN
   DO i = ilo, ihi
      RECV ((myR,myC-1),B(i,0),1)
   ENDDO
ENDIF
IF (ilo==1) THEN
   DO j = jlo, jhi
      RECV ((myR-1,myC),B(0,j),1)
   ENDDO
ENDIF
! Compute
DO j = jlo, jhi
   DO i = ilo, ihi
      A(i,j) = B(i-1,j) + B(i,j-1)
   ENDDO
ENDDO
! Send data
IF (myR /= ilastP) THEN
   DO j = jlo, jhi
      SEND((myR+1,myC),B(100,j),1)
   ENDDO
ENDIF
IF (myC /= jlastP) THEN
   DO i = ilo, ihi
      SEND((myR,myC+1),B(i,100),1)
   ENDDO
ENDIF
```

We note that the communication is vectorizable and that the computation and communication can be overlapped, so after optimization the code becomes

```
! Compute local upper and lower bounds
jlo = 1
IF (myC==0) jlo = 2
jhi = 100
jlastP = CEIL((M+1)/100) - 1
IF (myC==jlastP) jhi = MOD(M,100) + 1
nJ = jhi - jlo + 1
ilo = 1
```

```
         IF (myR==0) ilo = 2
         ihi = 100
         ilastP = CEIL((N+1)/100) - 1
         IF (myR==ilastP) ihi = MOD(N,100) + 1
         nI = ihi - ilo + 1
         ! Send data
         IF (myR /= ilastP) THEN
               SEND((myR+1,myC),B(100,jlo:jhi),nJ)
         ENDIF
         IF (myC /= jlastP) THEN
               SEND((myR,myC+1),B(ilo:ihi,100),nI)
         ENDIF
         ! Compute
         DO j = MAX(2,jlo), jhi
            DO i = MAX(2,ilo), ihi
               A(i,j) = B(i-1,j) + B(i,j-1)
            ENDDO
         ENDDO
         ! Receive and compute
         IF (jlo==1) THEN
            RECV ((myR,myC-1),B(ilo:ihi,0),nI)
            DO i = MAX(2,ilo), ihi
               A(i,1) = B(i-1,1) + B(i,0)
            ENDDO
         ENDIF
         IF (ilo==1) THEN
            RECV ((myR-1,myC),B(0,jlo:jhi),nJ)
            DO j = jlo, jhi
               A(1,j) = B(0,j) + B(1,j-1)
            ENDDO
         ENDIF
```

Note that in this last version we have peeled off the executions of computations that depend on data received from another processor, thus permitting the overlap of communication with the compute-only loop.

14.5 Interprocedural Optimization for HPF

Although HPF compilers can benefit from many interprocedural analyses and optimizations, two processes are especially important. First, as we mentioned earlier, it is important to track decompositions interprocedurally in an effort to ensure that only one data decomposition reaches every point in the program. At those places where the decomposition is known at compile time, much more efficient code can be generated because there is no need for a run-time test.

Reaching decompositions can be formulated as a direct analog of interprocedural constant propagation. In this formulation, specific decompositions become the constant values, and the variables are the unknown decompositions associated with distributed arrays. Just as in constant propagation, cloning can be used to reduce the number of different decompositions that reach a given subroutine. If two different call chains can pass different decompositions to the same procedure, then cloning two copies, one for each call chain, eliminates the ambiguity.

A second important interprocedural transformation is communication generation. Consider the following loop:

```
!HPF$ ALIGN A(I,J), B(I,J) WITH T(I,J)
!HPF$ DISTRIBUTE T(BLOCK,*) ONTO P(16)
   ...
   DO J = 1, N
      CALL SUB(A(*,J), B(*,J)
   ENDDO
   ...
SUBROUTINE SUB(X,Y)
   !HPF$ INHERIT X,Y
   DIMENSION X(*), Y(*)
   DO I = LBOUND(X), UBOUND(X)
      X(I) = Y(I+1) + C
   ENDDO
END
```

In this code, interprocedural decomposition analysis determines that X and Y are distributed using BLOCK across the iterations of the loop within the subroutine. However, the distributed array contains a requirement for communication associated with the I-loop. This communication can be moved outside the loop. However, for most efficient operation, we should move the communication outside of the subroutine call where it can be vectorized. This kind of transformation is referred to as *interprocedural communication optimization.*

14.6 **Summary**

We have shown that principles developed earlier in the book are useful in compiling and optimizing High Performance Fortran (HPF). The basic compilation algorithm consists of the following:

1. Distribution analysis and propagation

2. Iteration partitioning

3. Communication generation

A variety of optimizations can improve the performance of communications generated by the compiler while ensuring the resource constraints are not yet violated. These include message vectorization, overlap of communication with computation, alignment and replication, pipelining, reduction recognition, and storage analysis and management.

14.7 **Case Studies**

The authors have been affiliated with two implementations of HPF features. The initial Fortran D compiler project, led by Hiranandani, Kennedy, and Tseng [149, 150, 151], implemented most of the distribution features described in this chapter, including computation partitioning according to the owner-computes rule, communication placement, and recognition of special cases such as reductions. The principal optimizations were focused on improving communication. It employed message vectorization, overlap of computation and communication, and coarse-grained pipelining. Experiments on several kernels and small applications, including linear algebra and relaxation codes, demonstrated the promise of this approach. Table 14.1 summarizes the kernels and applications that were used for the experiment. The first three rows are well-known kernels, including a sum reduction and two stencil kernels. The next two are kernels where pipelining is required to get any meaningful parallelism. Finally, there are four applications, including a Gaussian elimination benchmark and a simple shallow water weather model.

Table 14.1 HPF kernels and applications

Name	Type	Data size
Livermore 3: Inner Product	Reduction kernel	1024K
Jacobi Iteration	Kernel	2K × 2K
Livermore 18: Explicit Hydrodynamics	Kernel	512 × 512
Successive Over Relaxation	Pipeline kernel	2K × 2K
Livermore 23: Implicit Hydrodynamics	Pipelined kernel	1K × 1K
Shallow	Application	1K × 1K
Disper	Application	256 × 8 × 8 × 4
DGEFA	Linear algebra benchmark	2K × 2K
Erlebacher	Application	128 × 128 × 128

The performance measurements were all taken on a 32-processor Intel iPSC 860. The HPF version was passed through the Fortran D compiler, and the running time of the resulting program was compared against a hand-coded message-passing version implemented using the Intel communication library (Figure 14.6). Speedups are over the sequential running time. In some cases superlinear speedups were achieved because the parallel version fit into the cache of a single processor. On the pipelined kernels, the Fortran D compiler outperformed the hand-coded version, probably due to anomalous behavior of the i860 node compiler. Details of the experiments conducted in this study are reported in Tseng's dissertation [262].

Although the experiments were restricted to relatively small programs, these results established that a good compiler could produce code from HPF programs that was competitive with hand coding using a message-passing library. As a result the Fortran D effort was extremely influential on the early commercial compiler projects.

In the mid-1990s, a second HPF implementation project, called dHPF, was initiated at Rice under the leadership of John Mellor-Crummey and Vikram Adve. This project attempted to overcome the limitations of Fortran D and commercial

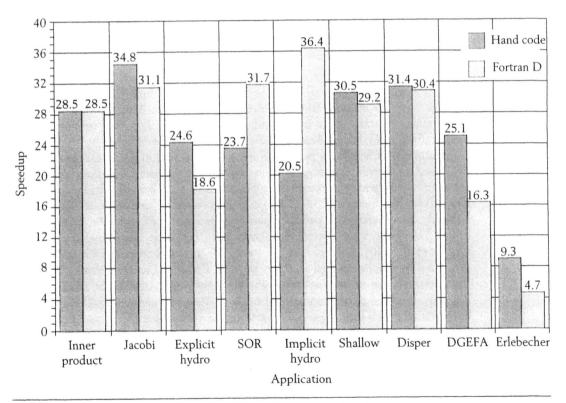

Figure 14.6 Performance of HPF kernels and applications versus hand code.

HPF compilers by using much more aggressive strategies for optimization of computation partitioning and communication. Two important improvements were made over the original Fortran D work. First, the owner-computes rule was relaxed to permit computation partitionings that minimized communication. This approach resembles the alignment strategy discussed in Section 14.4.3. Second, the project implemented the set operations discussed throughout this chapter using the Omega system, developed at the University of Maryland [166, 228]. This system provided a convenient method for experimenting with the index-set splitting operations that are required for HPF. When combined with alignment, this permitted the use of partial replication of computation to reduce communication costs. Omega was also used for code generation because it could generate sets of loops that handle all the special cases required by the set analysis. Experiments have shown that these improvements have high payoff when dealing with real codes. In particular, the performance of HPF versions of the NAS Parallel Benchmarks SP and BT, coded in a style that made no concessions to the strengths and weaknesses of the compiler, has been shown to achieve over 90% of the performance of the versions hand-coded by NAS [73].

14.8   Historical Comments and References

The HPF language had its roots in the Fortran D project at Rice University [115] and the Vienna Fortran project at the University of Vienna [71, 289]. These two projects were the most visible proponents of distribution-based compilation. High Performance Fortran itself was standardized by the High Performance Fortran Forum [146, 147], led by Kennedy, over a period of several years.

Many researchers have produced articles on compilation for distributed memory based on distribution specification. Two of the earliest articles on compilation for distributed-memory strategy were produced by Callahan and Kennedy [60] and Zima, Bast, and Gerndt [288]. This chapter is based on the work of Hiranandani, Kennedy, and Tseng, who produced an experimental HPF compiler at Rice [149, 150, 151]. Important compilation strategies were also developed by Hatcher, Quinn, et al. [140]; Koelbel and Mehrotra [187]; and Rogers and Pingali [235]. A group led by Fox developed an alternative HPF implementation strategy based on the extensive use of packaged communications and computation libraries [42]. Recently, the Rice dHPF project, led by John Mellor-Crummey and Vikram Adve, has pursued much more aggressive optimization strategies [8, 7] based on the use of powerful integer set manipulation software from Pugh and colleagues at the University of Maryland [166, 228]. Kennedy and Sethi developed the methods presented here for resource-based communication placement [181].

Exercises

14.1 Compared to the compilation of a sequential Fortran program, what are the extra steps needed for a compiler to generate code for an HPF program?

14.2 Compute total bytes of communication by each processor in executing the following program on a four-processor machine. Can you change the data distribution to make the program communication free?

```
REAL A(N), B(N)
!HPF$ TEMPLATE T(N)
!HPF$ ALIGN A(I) WITH T(I)
!HPF$ ALIGN B(I) WITH T(I)
!HPF$ DISTRIBUTE T(BLOCK)
DO I = 1, N - 1
   A(I) = B(I+1)
ENDDO
```

14.3 Compute total bytes of communication by each processor in executing the following program on a four-processor machine. Assuming a fixed data distribution, can you find another way to evenly partition the iterations and to reduce the amount of communication by half?

```
REAL A(N), B(N)
!HPF$ TEMPLATE T(N)
!HPF$ ALIGN A(I) WITH T(I)
!HPF$ ALIGN B(I) WITH T(I)
!HPF$ DISTRIBUTE T(BLOCK)
DO I = 1, N - 1
   A(I) = A(I+1) + B(I+1)
ENDDO
```

14.4 How many communication messages are there when executing the following loop nest on four processors? Can you modify the program and reduce the number of messages to half of the original? Can you reduce the total number of messages to three? Does your optimization cause any negative effect?

```
REAL A(N,N)
!HPF$ TEMPLATE T(N,N)
!HPF$ ALIGN A(I,J) WITH T(I,J)
!HPF$ DISTRIBUTE T(*,BLOCK)
DO I = 2, N
   DO J = 1, N - 1
      A(I,J) = A(I-1,J) + 1.0
   ENDDO
ENDDO
```

14.5 (Continued from the previous question) The method for reducing the number of messages is to unroll the I-loop by a factor of k and interchange with the J-loop as the following program shows. This transformation is known as coarse-grained pipelining. Is this transformation always legal? (*Hint:* It obeys the same legality condition as unroll-and-jam.)

```
REAL A(N,N)
!HPF$ TEMPLATE T(N,N)
!HPF$ ALIGN A(I,J) WITH T(I,J)
!HPF$ DISTRIBUTE T(*,BLOCK)
DO II = 2, N, K
   DO J = 1, N - 1
      DO I = II, min(II+K-1,N)
         A(I,J) = A(I-1,J) + 1.0
      ENDDO
   ENDDO
ENDDO
```

14.6 *Programming exercise.* Generate the parallel code for the example program in Exercises 14.4 and 14.5 using PVM or MPI. Measure the performance gain of coarse-grained pipelining. How can you find the optimal unroll factor? Test your methods.

Fundamentals of Fortran 90

Introduction

In this appendix we provide a brief introduction to the features of Fortran 90 (and one from the newer standard, Fortran 95) that are relevant to understanding the material in this book. This represents only a small subset of the properties of the language. Interested readers may wish to consult one of the references described in the "Further Reading" at the end of this appendix to read more about the language.

Lexical Properties

Fortran 90 introduced a new lexical input format called *free source form*, in which the old column-oriented form is replaced by a line-oriented form that permits multiple statements on a line. Since this book uses free source form exclusively, we concentrate on those features that are most relevant to understanding the text.

As in the old format, statements are assumed to be ended by the end of a line. However, if the line contains an ampersand (&) not in a comment, the statement continues on the next line. If a keyword or character string is split across lines, an ampersand must begin the continuing line as well.

Multiple statements can appear on a line, separated by semicolons (;). The last statement before the end of a line need not be terminated by a semicolon.

The exclamation point (!) is used to begin a comment if it appears outside a quoted string or another comment.

Blanks are significant and may not appear inside a keyword, name, or number. The exception is a keyword that is really a multiword phrase, such as "END DO".

Labels are numeric, as in previous versions of Fortran, but they may appear anywhere before the statement, even after column 6. In addition, it is possible to have a *construct name* to label a construct such as a DO-loop. A construct name is a variable followed by a colon. A construct name may not be used as a variable name in the same program. Construct names can be used in EXIT and CYCLE statements to exit a particular construct or, in the case of a loop, to go to the next iteration of the construct.

Fortran 90 introduces new comparison operators (==, /=, <, >, <=, >=) to be used in place of the old dotted equivalents.

The following example illustrates some of these concepts:

```
      PROGRAM MAIN
          REAL A(10000), B(10000) &
              C(1000,1000) ! this is the big data array
          CALL GETDATA(A,B,C); CALL CHECKDATA(A,B,C)
OUTER:    DO I = 1, 10000
INNER:        DO J = 1, 1000
                  IF (A(J) == 0.0) EXIT OUTER
50                C(I,J) = C(I,J) + A(I) * B(J)
              END DO INNER
          END DO OUTER
          CALL WRITEDATA(C)
      END PROGRAM
```

Array Assignment

Since one of the main purposes of Fortran 90 is providing support for vector and parallel hardware, it is quite natural to assume that Fortran 90 contains vector and parallel operations. One way in which this is accomplished is the treatment of vectors and arrays as aggregates in the assignment statement. If X and Y are two arrays of the same dimension, then

```
    X = Y
```

copies Y into X element by element. In other words, this assignment is equivalent to the sequence

```
    X(1) = Y(1)
    X(2) = Y(2)
    ...
    X(N) = Y(N)
```

Scalar quantities may be mixed with vector quantities using the convention that a scalar is expanded to a vector of the appropriate dimensions before operations are performed. Thus,

```
X = X + 5.0
```

adds the constant 5.0 to every element of array X.

Array assignments in Fortran 90 are viewed as being executed *simultaneously;* that is, the assignment must be treated so that all input operands are fetched before any output values are stored. For instance, consider

```
X = X/X(2)
```

Even though the value of X(2) is changed by this statement, the original value of X(2) is used throughout, so that the result is the same as

```
T = X(2)
X(1) = X(1)/T
X(2) = X(2)/T
...
X(N) = X(N)/T
```

These semantics match the semantics of vector hardware presented in Section 1.3, except that the vectors are of unbounded length.

Triplet Notation

Sections of arrays, including individual rows and columns, may be assigned using *triplet notation.* In Fortran 90, a triplet of three integer expressions separated by colons can be used in a subscript of an array assignment. The components of the triplet are

$$(\text{ initial} : \text{final} : \text{stride})$$

where the integer expression *initial* specifies the first index in the vector iteration; *final* specifies the last index in the vector iteration; and the expression *stride* specifies the index increment. In the most common usage, the final colon and the stride are omitted, in which case the increment defaults to 1.

The triplet notation can best be illustrated by examples. For instance, if A and B are 100-by-100 matrices, then

```
A(1:100,I) = B(J,1:100)
```

assigns the Jth row of B to the Ith column of A. Since we are assigning a whole row or column in this case, we can omit the expressions for initial and final index, as these default to the declared bounds. Thus,

```
A(:,I) = B(J,:)
```

has the same effect as the previous example. The real value of triplet notation is realized when the range of iteration in a vector operation is smaller than a whole row or column. The following assignment could be used to assign the first M elements of the Jth row of B to the first M elements of the Ith column of A.

```
A(1:M,I) = B(J,1:M)
```

This statement has the effect of the assignments:

```
A(1,I) = B(J,1)
A(2,I) = B(J,2)
...
A(M,I) = B(J,M)
```

where M might contain a value much smaller than the actual upper bound of these arrays in the dimensions in which it appears.

The third component, when it appears, specifies a "stride" for the index vector in that subscript position. For example, the first M elements of the Jth row of B may be assigned to the first M elements of the Ith column of A *in odd subscript positions* with the following:

```
A(1:M*2-1:2,I) = B(J,1:M)
```

Triplet notation is also useful in dealing with operations involving shifted sections. The assignment

```
A(I,1:M) = B(1:M,J) + C(I,3:M+2)
```

has the effect

```
A(I,1) = B(1,J) + C(I,3)
A(I,2) = B(2,J) + C(I,4)
...
A(I,M) = B(M,J) + C(I,M+2)
```

Conditional Assignment

The Fortran WHERE statement will permit an array assignment to be controlled by a conditional masking array. For example,

```
WHERE (A < 0.0) A = A + B
```

specifies that the vector sum of A and B be formed, but that stores back to A take place only in positions where A was originally less than zero. The semantics of this statement require that it behave as if only components corresponding to the locations where the controlling condition is true are involved in the computation.

In the special case of statements such as

```
WHERE (A /= 0.0) B = B/A
```

the semantics require that divide checks arising as a result of evaluating the right-hand side not affect the behavior of the program; the code must hide the error from the user. In other words, any error side effects that might occur as a result of evaluating the right-hand side in positions where the controlling vector is false are ignored.

Multidimensional Array Assignment

Fortran 90 permits whole matrices and arrays of even larger dimensionality to be assigned in a single statement. For example,

```
A(1:N,1:M) = A(1:N,1:M)/X(1:N,1:M)
```

divides every element of A in rows 1 to N and columns 1 to M by the corresponding element of X and stores the result back into A. According to the Fortran 90 standard, for array assignments like this to be legal, every array subexpression must match the left-hand side in rank (number of dimensions) and extent (size) in each dimension. The dimensions are always matched from left to right, so

```
A(1:N,1:M) = A(1:N,1:M)/X(1:M,1:N)
```

is illegal even though the dimensions could be matched by transposing X. It that is what is desired, then the transpose operation must be made explicit:

```
A(1:N,1:M) = A(1:N,1:M)/TRANSPOSE(X(1:M,1:N))
```

Scalars may be freely used in array assignments because the intent is always clear. In effect, every scalar is automatically expanded into an array of the right rank and extents, with each element equal to the original scalar. Thus

```
A(1:N,1:M) = A(1:N,1:M)/X(1,1)
```

divides every element of A by X(1,1).

There are some instances in which it is desirable to write expressions in which the different component arrays have different ranks. For example, suppose we wish to divide every row of matrix A by a vector X. Then we must use the SPREAD intrinsic to extend the vector into two dimensions:

```
A(1:N,1:M) = A(1:N,1:M)/SPREAD(X(1:M),1,N)
```

The SPREAD intrinsic replicates N copies of the vector X(1;M) to produce a matrix of the appropriate size in which each row is a copy of the original X. If replication into columns were desired, the second parameter to SPREAD would be 2.

Scatter and Gather Operations

Fortran 90 permits the use of index arrays in subscript positions. For example,

```
A(1:N) = A(1:N) + B(IX(1:N))
```

fetches the vector IX and uses its elements to select elements of B for use in the vector expression.

FORALL Statement

Although it was deleted from the Fortran 90 standard at the last moment, the Fortran 95 standard provides a special kind of vector operation called the FORALL. Since this is a useful construct for representing unusual vector concepts, we include it in the treatment here. The FORALL statement can be found in two forms. The first includes a single statement on a line:

```
FORALL (I=1,N) A(I) = B(I) + C(I)
```

The second form looks like a loop that contains one or more Fortran 90 statements. For example,

```
FORALL (I=1,N)
   A(I) = B(I) + C(I)
END FORALL
```

The FORALL statement is interpreted as a vector assignment statement in which the index in the FORALL statement indicates the dimension of vector iteration. Thus, the example FORALL above has the same meaning as the simple array assignment:

```
A(1:N) = B(1;N) + C(1:N)
```

Since the FORALL statement has the same meaning, it means that it must behave as if all quantities used on the right-hand side are fetched from memory before any value is stored. So

```
FORALL (I=1,N) A(I) = B(I)/A(2)
```

uses the old value of A(2) for every iteration of the loop.

The examples so far have provided no functionality that is not available using array assignment with triplet notation. However, the FORALL statement makes it possible to write vector statements that cannot be expressed using simple triplet notation. For example, suppose we wish to assign the vector B to the diagonal of matrix A. The following FORALL accomplishes this:

```
FORALL (I=1,N) A(I,I) = B(I)
```

Although it is possible to get the same effect by writing a complex conditional assignment statement, the performance of that statement would not be very good. Thus the FORALL statement is a useful way to write tricky vector assignments, making it useful for the output of a vectorizing compiler.

One final example will show how FORALL makes it possible to write another construct that is awkward to express without it. The following loop multiplies rows of matrix A by columns of matrix B:

```
FORALL (I=1,N) A(I,1:N) = A(I,1:N) * B(1:N,I)
```

To express this without using FORALL, you would need to write

```
A(1:N,1:N) = A(1:N,1:N) * TRANSPOSE(B(1:N,1:N))
```

which is clear enough but might generate unnecessary data movement if the Fortran 90 compiler does not recognize that the transpose can be replaced by an index swap.

Library Functions

Mathematical library functions, such as SQRT and SIN, are extended on an elementwise basis to vectors and arrays. In addition, new intrinsic functions are provided, such as inner matrix product (DOTPRODUCT) and transpose (TRANSPOSE).

The special function SEQ(1,N) returns an index vector from 1 to N. Reduction functions, much like those in APL, are also provided. For example, SUM applied to a vector returns the sum of all elements in that vector, while PRODUCT returns the product over those values.

Fortran 90 also includes some useful array operations. The circular shift CSHIFT can be used to perform a circular shift of the array in any dimension, while the end-off shift EOSHIFT shifts the array off, filling empty locations with a specified boundary value. Finally MAXLOC and MINLOC return the location of the maximum and minimum value of an array, respectively, in the form of a one-dimensional array of size equal to the rank of the argument array.

A complete listing of Fortran 90 and 95 library functions can be found in the ISO Fortran Standard documents [157, 158].

Further Reading

For further reading on Fortran 90 and Fortran 95, we recommend the following:

1. The official standard, *ISO 1539: 1991, Fortran Standard* [157], is the best source for precise definitions of Fortran 90 features.

2. The official Fortran 95 standard, *ISO/IEC 1539-1: 1997, Information Technology–Programming Languages–Fortran* [158], plays a similar role for Fortran 95.

3. *Fortran Top 90* [3] by Adams et al. is a collection of discussions of specific new features of the language. As such, it is a good tutorial introduction to the changes from Fortran 77.

4. *Fortran 90 Handbook* [4] and *Fortran 95 Handbook* [5] by Adams et al. provide a detailed overview of the entire language.

References

[1] W. Abu-Sufah. Improving the performance of virtual memory computers. Ph.D. thesis, Department of Computer Science, University of Illinois at Urbana-Champaign, 1979.

[2] T. L. Adam, K. M. Chandy, and J. R. Dickson. A comparison of list schedules for parallel processing systems. *Communications of the ACM*, 17(12): 685–690, December 1974.

[3] J. C. Adams, W. S. Brainerd, J. T. Martin, and B. T. Smith. *Fortran Top 90*. Unicomp, San Bernadino, CA, 1994.

[4] J. C. Adams, W. S. Brainerd, J. T. Martin, B. T. Smith, and J. L. Wagener. *Fortran 90 Handbook*. McGraw-Hill, New York, 1992.

[5] J. C. Adams, W. S. Brainerd, J. T. Martin, B. T. Smith, and J. L. Wagener. *Fortran 95 Handbook*. The MIT Press, Cambridge, MA, 1997.

[6] V. Adve, A. Carle, E. Granston, S. Hiranandani, C. Koelbel, J. Mellor-Crummey, C. Tseng, and S. K. Warren. The D System: Support for data-parallel programming. Technical Report CRPC-TR94-378, Rice University, Center for Research on Parallel Computation, January 1994.

[7] V. Adve and J. Mellor-Crummey. Using integer sets for data-parallel program analysis and optimization. In *Proceedings of the SIGPLAN '98 Conference on Programming Lanaguage Design and Implementation*, June 1998.

[8] V. Adve and J. Mellor-Crummey. Advanced code generation for High Performance Fortran. In *Languages, Compilation Techniques, and Run-Time Systems for Scalable Parallel Systems*, Springer-Verlag, New York (to appear).

[9] G. Aggarwal and D. Gajski. Exploring DCT Implementations. Technical Report ICS-TR-98-10, University of California, Irvine, March 1988.

743

[10] A. V. Aho, J. E. Hopcroft, and J. D. Ullman. *Design and Analysis of Computer Algorithms*. Exercise 2.12. Addison-Wesley, Reading, MA, 1974.

[11] A. V. Aho and S. C. Johnson. Optimal code generation for expression trees. In *Seventh Annual ACM Symposium on Theory of Computing*, pages 207–217, May 1975.

[12] A.V. Aho, R. Sethi, and J. D. Ullman. Code optimization and finite Church-Rosser systems. In R. Rustin, editor, *Design and Optimization of Compilers*, Prentice Hall, Upper Saddle River, NJ, 1972.

[13] F. E. Allen. Interprocedural data flow analysis. In *Proceedings of the IFIP Congress 1974*, pages 398–402, North Holland, Amsterdam, 1974.

[14] F. Allen, M. Burke, R. Cytron, J. Ferrante, W. Hsieh, and V. Sarkar. A framework for determining useful parallelism. In *Proceedings of the 1968 ACM International Conference on Supercomputing*, pages 207–215, July 1988.

[15] F. E. Allen and J. Cocke. A program data flow analysis procedure. *Communications of the ACM*, 19(3):137–147, March 1976.

[16] J. R. Allen. Dependence analysis for subscripted variables and its application to program transformations. Ph.D. thesis, Department of Mathematical Sciences, Rice University, May, 1983.

[18] J. R. Allen, D. Bäumgartner, K. Kennedy, and A. Porterfield. PTOOL: A semi-automatic parallel programming assistant. In *Proceedings of the 1986 International Conference on Parallel Processing*, IEEE Computer Society Press, Silver Spring, MD, August 1986.

[19] J. R. Allen and K. Kennedy. Automatic loop interchange. In *Proceedings of the SIGPLAN '84 Symposium on Compiler Construction*, June 1984.

[20] J. R. Allen and K. Kennedy. PFC: A program to convert Fortran to parallel form. In K. Hwang, editor, *Supercomputers: Design and Applications*, pages 186–203. IEEE Computer Society Press, Silver Spring, MD, 1984.

[21] J. R. Allen and K. Kennedy. Automatic translation of Fortran programs to vector form. *ACM Transactions on Programming Languages and Systems*, 9(4):491–542, October 1987.

[22] J. R. Allen and K. Kennedy. Vector register allocation. *IEEE Transactions on Computers*, 41(10):1290–1317, October 1992.

[23] J. R. Allen, K. Kennedy, C. Porterfield, and J. Warren. Conversion of control dependence to data dependence. In *Conference Record of the Tenth Annual ACM Symposium on the Principles of Programming Languages*, January 1983.

[24] R. Allen. Unifying vectorization, parallelization, and optimization: The Ardent compiler. In *Third International Conference on Supercomputing*, 2:176–185, 1988.

[25] R. Allen, D. Callahan, and K. Kennedy. Automatic decomposition of scientific programs for parallel execution. In *Conference Record of the Fourteenth ACM Symposium on Principles of Programming Languages*, January 1987.

[26] R. Allen and S. Johnson. Compiling C for vectorization, parallelization, and inline expansion. In *ACM SIGPLAN '88 Conference on Programming Language Design and Implementation*, pages 241–249, June 1988.

[27] B. Alpern, M. N. Wegman, and F. K. Zadeck. Detecting equality of variables in programs. In *Conference Record of the Fifteenth ACM Symposium on the Principles of Programming Languages*, 1988.

[28] S. Amarasinghe, J. Anderson, M. Lam, and C.-W. Tseng. An overview of the SUIF compiler for scalable parallel machines. In *Proceedings of the Seventh SIAM Conference on Parallel Processing for Scientific Computing*, February 1995.

[29] E. Anderson, Z. Bai, C. Bischof, J. Demmel, J. Dongarra, J. Du Croz, A. Greenbaum, S. Hammarling, A. McKenney, S. Ostrouchov, and D. Sorensen. *LAPACK Users' Guide*, second edition. SIAM Publications, Philadelphia, 1995.

[30] J. Backus. The history of FORTRAN I, II, and III. *ACM SIGPLAN Notices* 13(8):165–180, August 1978.

[31] V. Balasundaram, K. Kennedy, U. Kremer, K. S. McKinley, and J. Subhlok. The ParaScope Editor: An interactive parallel programming tool. In *Proceedings of Supercomputing '89*, November 1989.

[32] U. Banerjee. Data dependence in ordinary programs. Master's thesis, Department of Computer Science, University of Illinois at Urbana-Champaign, November 1976. Report No. 76-837.

[33] U. Banerjee. Speedup of ordinary programs. Ph.D. thesis, Department of Computer Science, University of Illinois at Urbana-Champaign, October 1979. Report No. 79-989.

[34] U. Banerjee. *Dependence Analysis for Supercomputing*. Kluwer Academic Publishers, Boston, 1988.

[35] U. Banerjee. A theory of loop permutations. In D. Gelernter, A. Nicolau, and D. Padua, editors, *Languages and Compilers for Parallel Computing*. The MIT Press, Cambridge, MA, 1990.

[36] U. Banerjee. Unimodular transformations of double loops. In A. Nicolau, D. Gelernter, T. Gross, and D. Padua, editors, *Advances in Languages and Compilers for Parallel Computing*. The MIT Press, Cambridge, MA, August 1990.

[37] J. P. Banning. An efficient way to find the side effects of procedure calls and the aliases of variables. In *Proceedings of the Sixth Annual Symposium on Principles of Programming Languages*, January 1979.

[38] J. M. Barth. A practical interprocedural data flow analysis algorithm. *Communications of the ACM*, 21(9):724–736, September 1978.

[39] W. Baxter and H. R. Bauer III. The program dependence graph and vectorization. In *Proceedings of the Sixteenth Annual ACM Symposium on Principles of Programming Languages*, January 1989.

[40] A. J. Bernstein. Analysis of programs for parallel processing. *IEEE Transactions on Electronic Computers*, 15(5):757–763, October 1966.

[41] K. V. Besaw. Advanced techniques for vectorizing dusty decks. In *Proceedings of the Second International Conference on Supercomputing*, May 1987.

[42] Z. Bozkus, A. Choudhary, G. Fox, T. Haupt, and S. Ranka. Fortran 90D/HPF compiler for distributed memory MIMD computers: Design, implementation, and performance results. In *Proceedings of Supercomputing '93*, pages 351–360, November 1993.

[43] T. Brandes. The importance of direct dependences for automatic parallelization. In *Proceedings of the Second International Conference on Supercomputing*, July 1988.

[44] P. Briggs, K. D. Cooper, M. Hall, and L. Torczon. Goal-directed interprocedural optimization. Technical Report TR90-148, Department of Computer Science, Rice University, November 1990.

[45] P. Briggs, K. D. Cooper, K. Kennedy, and L. Torczon. Coloring heuristics for register allocation. In *Proceedings of the SIGPLAN '89 Conference on Programming Language Design and Implementation, SIGPLAN Notices*, 24(7):275–284, July 1989.

[46] J. Bruno and R. Sethi. Code generation for a one-register machine. In *Journal of the Association for Computing Machinery*, 23(3):502–510, July 1976.

[47] M. A. Bulyonkov. Polyvariant mixed computation for analyzer programs. *Acta Informatica*, 21:473–484, 1984.

[48] M. Burke. An interval-based approach to exhaustive and incremental interprocedural analysis. Research Report RC 12702, IBM, Yorktown Heights, NY, September 1987.

[49] M. Burke and R. Cytron. Interprocedural dependence analysis and parallelization. In *Proceedings of the SIGPLAN '86 Symposium on Compiler Construction*, June 1986.

[50] M. Burke and L. Torczon. Interprocedural optimization: Eliminating unnecessary recompilation. *ACM Transactions on Programming Languages and Systems*, 15(3):367–399, July 1993.

[51] D. Callahan. Dependence testing in PFC: Weak separability. *Supercomputer Software Newsletter 2*, Department of Computer Science, Rice University, August 1986.

[52] D. Callahan. A global approach to the detection of parallelism, Ph.D. thesis, Department of Computer Science, Rice University, March 1987.

[53] D. Callahan. The program summary graph and flow-sensitive interprocedural data flow analysis. In *Proceedings of the SIGPLAN '88 Conference on Programming Language Design and Implementation, SIGPLAN Notices*, 23(7):47–56, July 1988.

[54] D. Callahan, A. Carle, M.W. Hall, and K. Kennedy. Constructing the procedure call multigraph. *IEEE Transactions on Software Engineering*, SE-16(4): 483–487, April 1990.

[55] D. Callahan, J. Cocke, and K. Kennedy. Estimating interlock and improving balance for pipelined machines. *Journal of Parallel and Distributed Computing*, 5(4):334–358, August 1988.

[56] D. Callahan, K. D. Cooper, K. Kennedy, and L. Torczon. Interprocedural constant propagation. In *Proceedings of the SIGPLAN '86 Symposium on Compiler Construction, SIGPLAN Notices*, 21(7):152–161, July 1986.

[57] D. Callahan, J. Dongarra, and D. Levine. Vectorizing compilers: A test suite and results. In *Proceedings of Supercomputing '88*, November 1988.

[58] D. Callahan and M. Kalem. Control dependences. *Supercomputer Software Newsletter 15*, Department of Computer Science, Rice University, October 1987.

[59] D. Callahan and K. Kennedy. Analysis of interprocedural side effects in a parallel programming environment. In *Proceedings of the First International Conference on Supercomputing*, Springer-Verlag, New York, June 1987.

[60] D. Callahan and K. Kennedy. Compiling programs for distributed-memory multiprocessors. *Journal of Supercomputing*, 3:151–169, October 1988.

[61] D. Callahan, K. Kennedy, and A. Porterfield. Software prefetching. In *Proceedings of the Fourth International Conference on Architectural Support for Programming Languages and Operating Systems, SIGPLAN Notices*, 26(4): 40–52, April 1991.

[62] D. Callahan, K. Kennedy, and J. Subhlok. Analysis of event synchronization in a parallel programming tool. In *Proceedings of the Second ACM SIGPLAN Symposium on Principles and Practice of Parallel Programming*, March 1990.

[63] A. Carle, K. D. Cooper, R.T. Hood, K. Kennedy, L. Torczon, and S. K. Warren. A practical environment for Fortran programming. *IEEE Computer*, 20(11): 75–89, November 1987.

[64] S. Carr. Memory hierarchy management. Ph.D. thesis, Department of Computer Science, Rice University, September 1992.

[65] S. Carr, D. Callahan, and K. Kennedy. Improving register allocation for subscripted variables. In *Proceedings of the ACM SIGPLAN 1990 Conference on Programming Language Design and Implementation*, June 1990.

[66] S. Carr and K. Kennedy. Compiler Blockability of Numerical Algorithms. In *Proceedings of Supercomputing '92*, November 1992.

[67] S. Carr and K. Kennedy. Scalar replacement in the presence of conditional control flow. *Software—Practice & Experience*, 24(1), January 1994.

[68] G. J. Chaitin. Register allocation and spilling via graph coloring. In *Proceedings of SIGPLAN 82 Symposium on Compiler Construction, SIGPLAN Notices*, 17(6):98–105, June 1982.

[69] G. J. Chaitin, M. A. Auslander, A. K. Chandra, J. Cocke, M. E. Hopkins, and P. W. Markstein. Register allocation via coloring. *Computer Languages*, 6:47–57, 1981.

[70] C. Chambers and D. Ungar. Customization: Optimizing compiler technology for SELF, a dynamically-typed object-oriented programming language. In *Proceedings of the SIGPLAN '89 Conference on Programming Language Design and Implementation, SIGPLAN Notices*, 24(7):146–160, July 1989.

[71] B. Chapman, P. Mehrotra, and H. Zima. Vienna Fortran—a Fortran language extension for distributed memory multiprocessors. In J. Saltz and P. Mehrotra, editors, *Languages, Compilers, and Run-Time Environments for Distributed-Memory Machines*, North-Holland, Amsterdam, 1992.

[72] A. E. Charlesworth. An approach to scientific array processing: The architectural design of the AP-120B/FPS-164 family. *Computer*, 14(9):18–27, 1981.

[73] D. Chavarria-Miranda, J. Mellor-Crummey, and T. Sarang. Data-parallel compiler support for multipartitioning. In *Proceedings of the European Conference on Parallel Computing* (Euro-Par), August 2001.

[74] J. Choi, M. Burke, and P. Carini. Efficient flow-sensitive interprocedural computation of pointer-induced aliases and side effects. In *Conference Record of the Twentieth Annual Symposium on Principles of Programming Languages*, January 1993.

[75] F. Chow. A portable machine-independent global optimizer—design and measurements. TR 83-254, Department of Electrical Engineering and Computer Science, Stanford University, December 1983.

[76] F. Chow and J. Hennessy. Register allocation by priority-based coloring. In *Proceedings of SIGPLAN 84 Symposium on Compiler Construction, SIGPLAN Notices*, 19(6):222–232, June 1984.

[77] W. Cohagan. Vector optimization for the ASC. In *Proceedings of the Seventh Annual Princeton Conference on Information Sciences and Systems*, March 1973.

[78] K. D. Cooper. Interprocedural data flow analysis in a programming environment. Ph.D. thesis, Computer Science Department, Rice University, April 1983.

[79] K. Cooper, M. W. Hall, R. T. Hood, K. Kennedy, K. S. McKinley, J. M. Mellor-Crummey, L. Torczon, and S. K. Warren. The ParaScope parallel programming environment. *Proceedings of the IEEE*, 81(2):244–263, February 1993.

[80] K. D. Cooper, M. W. Hall, and K. Kennedy. Procedure cloning. In *Proceedings of the IEEE International Conference on Computer Languages*, pages 96–105, April 1992.

[81] K. D. Cooper, M. W. Hall, and K. Kennedy. A methodology for procedure cloning. *Computer Languages*, 19(2), 1993.

[82] K. D. Cooper, M. W. Hall, K. Kennedy, and L. Torczon. Interprocedural analysis and optimization. To appear in *Communications in Pure and Applied Mathematics*.

[83] K. D. Cooper, M. W. Hall, and L. Torczon. An experiment with inline substitution. *Software—Practice and Experience*, 21(6):581–601, June 1991.

[84] K. Cooper, T. Harvey, and K. Kennedy. A simple, fast dominance algorithm. Draft, Computer Science Department, Rice University, November 2000.

[85] K. D. Cooper and K. Kennedy. Efficient computation of flow-insensitive interprocedural summary information. In *Proceedings of the SIGPLAN '84 Symposium on Compiler Construction, SIGPLAN Notices*, 19(6):247–258, June 1984.

[86] K. D. Cooper and K. Kennedy. Efficient computation of flow-insensitive interprocedural summary information—a correction. *SIGPLAN Notices*, 23(4):35–42, April 1988.

[87] K. D. Cooper and K. Kennedy. Interprocedural side-effect analysis in linear time. In *Proceedings of the SIGPLAN '88 Conference on Programming Language Design and Implementation, SIGPLAN Notices*, 23(7):57–66, July 1988.

[88] K. D. Cooper and K. Kennedy. Fast interprocedural alias analysis. In *Conference Record of the Sixteenth Annual ACM SIGACT/SIGPLAN Symposium on Principles of Programming Languages*, pages 49–59, January 1989.

[89] K. Cooper, K. Kennedy, and L. Torczon. The impact of interprocedural analysis and optimization on the design of a software development environment. In *Proceedings of the SIGPLAN '85 Symposium on Compiler Construction*, June 1985.

[90] K. Cooper, K. Kennedy, and L. Torczon. The impact of interprocedural analysis and optimization in the R^n environment. *ACM Transactions on Programming Languages and Systems*, 8(4):491–523, October 1986.

[91] K. D. Cooper, K. Kennedy, and L. Torczon. Interprocedural optimization: Eliminating unnecessary recompilation. In *Proceedings of the SIGPLAN '86 Symposium on Compiler Construction, SIGPLAN Notices,* 21(7):58–67, July 1986.

[92] G. Cybenko, L. Kipp, L. Pointer, and D. Kuck. Supercomputer performance evaluation and the Perfect benchmarks. In *Proceedings of the 1990 ACM International Conference on Supercomputing,* June 1990.

[93] R. Cytron. Compile-Time Scheduling and Optimization for Asynchronous Machines. Ph.D. thesis, Department of Computer Science, University of Illinois at Urbana-Champaign, October 1984.

[94] R. Cytron. Doacross: Beyond vectorization for multiprocessors. In *Proceedings of the 1986 International Conference on Parallel Processing,* August 1986.

[95] R. Cytron and J. Ferrante. What's in a name? or the value of renaming for parallelism detection and storage allocation. In *Proceedings of the 1987 International Conference of Parallel Processing,* August 1987.

[96] R. Cytron, J. Ferrante, B. Rosen, M. Wegman, and F. K. Zadeck. An efficient method of computing static single assignment form. In *Conference Record of the Sixteenth Annual Symposium on Principles of Programming Languages,* June 1989.

[97] R. Cytron, J. Ferrante, B. K. Rosen, M. N. Wegman, and F. K. Zadeck. Efficiently computing static single assignment form and control dependence graph. *ACM Transactions on Programming Languages and Systems,* 13(4): 452–490, October 1991.

[98] E. S. Davidson. Design and control of pipelined function generators. In *Proceedings of the 1971 International IEEE Conference on Systems, Networks, and Computers,* pages 19–21, January 1971.

[99] E. S. Davidson. Scheduling for pipelined processors. In *Proceedings of the 7th Hawaii Conference on Systems Sciences,* pages 58–60, 1974.

[100] E. S. Davidson, D. Landskov, B. D. Schriver, and P. W. Mallett. Some experiments in local microcode compaction for horizontal machines. *IEEE Transactions on Computers,* C-30(7):460–477, 1981.

[101] J. Davidson and A. Hollar. A study of a C function inliner. *Software—Practice and Experience,* 18(8):775–790, August 1988.

[102] H. Dietz. Finding large-grain parallelism in loops with serial control dependences. In *Proceedings of the 1988 International Conference on Parallel Processing,* August 1988.

[103] C. Ding. Improving effective bandwidth through compiler enhancement of global and dynamic cache reuse. Ph.D. thesis, Department of Computer Science, Rice University, January 2000.

[104] C. Ding and K. Kennedy. Resource-constrained loop fusion. Technical report, Computer Science Department, Rice University, November 2000.

[105] C. Ding and K. Kennedy. Improving effective bandwidth through compiler enhancement of global cache reuse. In *Proceedings of the 2001 International Parallel and Distributed Processing Symposium*, April 2001.

[106] J. Dongarra, J. Bunch, C. Moler, and G. Stewart. *LINPACK User's Guide.* SIAM Publications, Philadelphia, 1979.

[107] C. Dulong, R. Krishnayer, D. Kulkarni, D. Lavery, W. Li, J. Ng, and D. Sehr. An overview of the Intel IA-64 compiler. *Intel Technology Journal*, Q4, 1999.

[108] R. Eigenmann, J. Hoeflinger, Z. Li, and D. Padua. Experience in the automatic parallelization of four Perfect benchmark programs. In U. Banerjee, D. Gelernter, A. Nicolau, and D. Padua, editors, *Languages and Compilers for Parallel Computing*, Fourth International Workshop, Springer-Verlag, Berlin, August 1991.

[109] J. R. Ellis. *Bulldog: A Compiler for VLIW Architectures.* Ph.D. thesis, Department of Computer Science, Yale University, 1985.

[110] J. Ferrante and M. Mace. On linearizing parallel code. In *Conference Record of the Twelfth Annual ACM Symposium on the Principles of Programming Languages*, January 1985.

[111] J. Ferrante, M. Mace, and B. Simons. Generating sequential code from parallel code. In *Proceedings of the Second International Conference on Supercomputing*, July 1988.

[112] J. Ferrante, K. Ottenstein, and J. Warren. The program dependence graph and its use in optimization. *ACM Transactions on Programming Languages and Systems*, 9(3):319–349, July 1987.

[113] J. A. Fisher. The optimization of horizontal microcode within and beyond basic blocks: An application of processor scheduling with resources. Ph.D. thesis, Department of Computer Science, New York University, 1979.

[114] J. A. Fisher. Trace scheduling: A technique for global microcode compaction. *IEEE Transactions on Computers*, C-30(7):478–490, July 1981.

[115] G. Fox, S. Hiranandani, K. Kennedy, C. Koelbel, U. Kremer, C.-W. Tseng, and M. Wu. Fortran D language specification. Technical Report TR90-141, Department of Computer Science, Rice University, December 1990.

[116] D. Gajski, N. Dutt, A. Wu, and S. Lin. *High-Level Synthesis, Introduction to Chip and System Design.* Kluwer Academic Publishers, Norwell, MA, 1992.

[117] D. Gannon, W. Jalby, and K. Gallivan. Strategies for cache and local memory management by global program transformation. *Journal of Parallel and Distributed Computation*, 5(5):587–616, October 1998.

[118] G. Gao, R. Olsen, V. Sarkar, and R. Thekkath. Collective loop fusion for array contraction. In *Proceedings of the Fifth Workshop on Languages and Compilers for Parallel Computing*, August 1992.

[119] M. R. Garey and D. S. Johnson. *Computers and Intractability: A Guide to the Theory of NP-Completeness*. W. H. Freeman and Co., San Francisco, 1979.

[120] P. A. Gibbons and S. S. Muchnick. Efficient instruction scheduling for a pipelined processor. In *Proceedings of the SIGPLAN '86 Symposium on Compiler Construction*, July 1986.

[121] M. Girkar and C. Polychronopoulos. Compiling issues for supercomputers. In *Proceedings of Supercomputing '88*, November 1988.

[122] G. Goff. Practical techniques to augment dependence analysis in the presence of symbolic terms. Technical Report TR92-194, Department of Computer Science, Rice University, October 1992.

[123] G. Goff, K. Kennedy, and C.-W. Tseng. Practical dependence testing. In *Proceedings of the SIGPLAN '91 Conference on Programming Language Design and Implementation*, June 1991.

[124] A. Goldberg and R. Paige. Stream processing. In *Conference Record of the 1984 ACM Symposium on Lisp and Functional Programming*, pages 228–234, August 1984.

[125] S. L. Graham and M. Wegman. A fast and usually linear algorithm for global flow analysis. *Journal of the ACM*, 32(1):172–202, January 1976.

[126] T. Gross and P. Steenkiste. Structured dataflow analysis for arrays and its use in an optimizing compiler. *Software—Practice and Experience*, 20(2): 133–155, February 1990.

[127] D. Grove and L. Torczon. Interprocedural constant propagation: A study of jump function implementations. In *Proceedings of the SIGPLAN '93 Conference on Programming Language Design and Implementation*, June 1993.

[128] M. Haghighat and C. Polychronopoulos. Symbolic dependence analysis for high-performance parallelizing compilers. In *Advances in Languages and Compilers for Parallel Computing*, The MIT Press, Cambridge, MA, August 1990.

[129] M. Haghighat and C. Polychronopoulos. Symbolic analysis: A basis for parallelization, optimization, and scheduling of programs. In *Proceedings of the Sixth Workshop on Languages and Compilers for Parallel Computing*, August 1993.

[130] M. W. Hall. Managing interprocedural optimization. Ph.D. thesis, Department of Computer Science, Rice University, April 1991.

[131] M. W. Hall, S. P. Amarasinghe, B. R. Murphy, and M. S. Lam. Interprocedural analysis for parallelization: Preliminary results. Stanford Computer Systems Laboratory Technical Report, CSL-TR-95-665, March 1995.

[132] M. W. Hall, T. Harvey, K. Kennedy, N. McIntosh, K. S. McKinley, J. D. Oldham, M. Paleczny, and G. Roth. Experiences using the ParaScope Editor: An interactive parallel programming tool. In *Proceedings of the Fourth ACM SIGPLAN Symposium on Principles and Practice of Parallel Programming,* May 1993.

[133] M. W. Hall and K. Kennedy. Efficient call graph analysis. *ACM Letters on Programming Languages and Systems,* 1(3), September 1992.

[134] M. W. Hall, K. Kennedy, and K. S. McKinley. Interprocedural transformations for parallel code generation. In *Proceedings of Supercomputing '91,* November 1991.

[135] M. W. Hall, J. Mellor-Crummey, A. Carle, and R. Rodriguez. FIAT: A framework for interprocedural analysis and transformation. In *Proceedings of the Sixth Workshop on Languages and Compilers for Parallel Computing,* August 1993.

[136] M. W. Hall, B. R. Murphy, and S. P. Amarasinghe. Interprocedural analysis for parallelization: A case study. In *Proceedings of the Seventh SIAM Conference on Parallel Processing for Scientific Computing,* February 1995.

[137] R. V. Hanxleden and K. Kennedy. Give-N-Take—a balanced code placement framework. In *Proceedings of the SIGPLAN '94 Conference on Programming Language Design and Implementation,* June 1994.

[138] D. Harel. A linear-time algorithm for finding dominators in flow graphs and related problems. In *Proceedings of the Seventeenth Annual ACM Symposium on Theory of Computing,* pages 185–194, May 1985.

[139] W. L. Harrison. The interprocedural analysis and automatic parallelization of Scheme programs. *Lisp and Symbolic Computation,* 2(3/4):179–396, October 1989.

[140] P. Hatcher, M. Quinn, A. Lapadula, B. Seevers, R. Anderson, and R. Jones. Data-parallel programming on MIMD computers. *IEEE Transactions on Parallel and Distributed Systems,* 2(3):377–383, July 1991.

[141] P. Havlak. Interprocedural symbolic analysis. Ph.D. thesis, Department of Computer Science, Rice University, May 1994.

[142] P. Havlak and K. Kennedy. An implementation of interprocedural bounded regular section analysis. *IEEE Transactions on Parallel and Distributed Systems,* 2(3):350–360, July 1991.

[143] M. Hecht and J. D. Ullman. A simple algorithm for global data flow analysis of programs. *SIAM Journal of Computing,* 4: 519–532.

[144] L. J. Hendren, J. Hummel, and A. Nicolau. Abstractions for recursive pointer data structures: Improving the analysis and transformation of imperative programs. In *ACM SIGPLAN '92 Conference on Programming Language Design and Implementation,* pages 249–260, 1992.

[145] J. L. Hennessy and D. A. Patterson. *Computer Architecture: A Quantitative Approach*, second edition. Morgan Kaufmann, San Francisco, 1996.

[146] High Performance Fortran Forum. High Performance Fortran language specification. *Scientific Programming*, 2(1–2):1–170, 1993.

[147] High Performance Fortran Forum. High Performance Fortran language specification, version 2.0. CRPC-TR92225, Center for Research on Parallel Computation, Rice University, January 1997.

[148] M. Hind, M. Burke, P. Carini, and S. Midkiff. An empirical study of precise interprocedural array analysis. *Scientific Programming*, 3(3):255–271, 1994.

[149] S. Hiranandani, K. Kennedy, and C.-W. Tseng. Compiler optimizations for Fortran D on MIMD distributed-memory machines. In *Proceedings of Supercomputing '91*, November 1991.

[150] S. Hiranandani, K. Kennedy, and C.-W. Tseng. Compiler support for machine-independent parallel programming in Fortran D. In J. Saltz and P. Mehrotra, editors, *Languages, Compilers, and Run-Time Environments for Distributed-Memory Machines*, North-Holland, Amsterdam, 1992.

[151] S. Hiranandani, K. Kennedy, and C.-W. Tseng. Preliminary experiences with the Fortran D compiler. In *Proceedings of Supercomputing '93*, November 1993.

[152] S. Horowitz, P. Pfeiffer, and T. Reps. Dependence analysis for pointer variables. In *ACM SIGPLAN '89 Conference on Programming Language Design and Implementation*, pages 28–40, June 1989.

[153] P. Y. T. Hsu. Highly concurrent scalar processing. Ph.D. thesis, University of Illinois at Urbana-Champaign, 1986.

[154] P. Y. T. Hsu and E. S. Davidson. Highly concurrent scalar processing. In *Proceedings of the Thirteenth Annual International Symposium on Computer Architecture*, pages 386–395, 1986.

[155] IEEE. *Standard VHDL Language Reference Manual*. 1988.

[156] T. Iitsuka. Flow-sensitive interprocedural analysis method for parallelization. In *IFIP TC10/WG10.3 Working Conference on Architectures and Compilation Techniques for Fine and Medium Grain Parallelism*, January 1993.

[157] International Standards Organization. *ISO 1539: 1991, Fortran Standard*. 1991.

[158] International Standards Organization. *ISO/IEC 1539-1: 1997, Information Technology–Programming Languages–Fortran*. 1997.

[159] F. Irigoin. Interprocedural analyses for programming environments. In *NSF-CNRS Workshop on Environments and Tools for Parallel Scientific Programming*, September 1992.

[160] F. Irigoin, P. Jouvelot, and R. Triolet. Semantical interprocedural parallelization: An overview of the PIPS project. In *Proceedings of the 1991 ACM International Conference on Supercomputing*, June 1991.

[161] S. C. Johnson. A portable compiler: Theory and practice. In *SIGPLAN '78 Symposium on Principles of Programming Languages*, pages 97–104, 1978.

[162] R. L. Johnston. The dynamic incremental compiler of APL\3000. In *Proceedings of the APL '79 Conference*, pages 82–87, June 1979.

[163] D.-C. Ju, C.-L. Wu, and P. Carini. The classification, fusion, and parallelization of array language primitives. *IEEE Transactions on Parallel and Distributed Systems*, 5(10):1113–1120, October 1994.

[164] J. B. Kam and J. D. Ullman. Global data flow analysis and iterative algorithms. *Journal of the ACM*, 32(1):158–171, January 1976.

[165] J. Kam and J. D. Ullman. Monotone data flow analysis frameworks. *Acta Informatica*, 7(3): 305–318, 1977.

[166] W. Kelly, V. Maslov, W. Pugh, E. Rosser, T. Shpeisman, and D. Wonnacott. The Omega Library interface guide. Technical report, Department of Computer Science, University of Maryland, College Park, April 1996.

[167] K. Kennedy. Safety of code motion. *International Journal of Computer Mathematics*, Gordon and Breach, Section A, 3:117–130, 1972.

[168] K. Kennedy. Automatic translation of Fortran programs to vector form. Technical Report 476-029-4, Department of Mathematical Sciences, Rice University, October 1980.

[169] K. Kennedy. A survey of data-flow analysis techniques. In S. S. Muchnick and N. D. Jones, editors, *Program Flow Analysis: Theory and Applications*, pages 1–51. Prentice Hall, Upper Saddle River, NJ, 1981.

[170] K. Kennedy. Triangular Banerjee inequality. *Supercomputer Software Newsletter 8*, Department of Computer Science, Rice University, October 1986.

[171] K. Kennedy. Fast greedy weighted fusion. In *Proceedings of the 2000 ACM International Conference on Supercomputing*, May 2000.

[172] K. Kennedy. Fast greedy weighted fusion. *International Journal of Parallel Processing*, 29:5, October 2001.

[173] K. Kennedy, C. Koelbel, and M. Paleczny. Compiler support for out-of-core arrays on parallel machines. In *Proceedings of the Fifth Symposium of the Frontiers of Massively Parallel Computation*, February 1995.

[174] K. Kennedy and K. McKinley. Loop distribution with arbitrary control flow. *Proceedings: Supercomputing '90*, pages 407–416, November 1990.

[175] K. Kennedy and K. McKinley. Optimizing for parallelism and data locality. In *Proceedings of the 1992 ACM International Conference on Supercomputing*, pages 323–334, July 1992.

[176] K. Kennedy and K. McKinley. Maximizing loop parallelism and improving data locality via loop fusion and distribution. In U. Banerjee, D. Gelernter, A. Nicolau, and D. Padua, editors, *Languages and Compilers for Parallel Computing*, Lecture Notes in Computer Science, Number 768, pages 301–320, Springer-Verlag, Berlin, 1993.

[177] K. Kennedy and K. McKinley. Typed fusion with applications to parallel and sequential code generation. Technical Report CRPC-TR94646, Center for Research on Parallel Computation, Rice University, 1994.

[178] K. Kennedy, J. Mellor-Crummey, and G. Roth. Optimizing Fortran 90 shift operations on distributed-memory multicomputers. In *Proceedings of the 8th International Workshop on Languages and Compilers for Parallel Computing (LCPC '95)*, August 1995.

[179] K. Kennedy and G. Roth. Context optimization for SIMD execution. In *Proceedings of the Scalable High Performance Computing Conference*, May 1994.

[180] K. Kennedy and G. Roth. Dependence analysis of Fortran 90 array syntax. In *Proceedings of the International Conference on Parallel and Distributed Processing Techniques and Applications (PDPTA '96)*, August 1996.

[181] K. Kennedy and A. Sethi. Resource-based communication placement analysis. In *Proceedings of the Ninth Workshop on Languages and Compilers for Parallel Computing*, Springer-Verlag, New York, August 1996.

[182] G. A. Kildall. A unified approach to global program optimization. In *Conference Record of the First ACM Symposium on the Principles of Programming Languages*, pages 194–206, October 1973.

[183] D. Klappholz and X. Kong. Extending the Banerjee-Wolfe test to handle execution conditions. Technical Report 9101, Department of EE/CS, Stevens Institute of Technology, 1991.

[184] D. Klappholz, K. Psarris, and X. Kong. On the perfect accuracy of an approximate subscript analysis test. In *Proceedings of the 1990 ACM International Conference on Supercomputing*, June 1990.

[185] D. E. Knuth. *Fundamental Algorithms*. Addison-Wesley, Reading, MA, 1968.

[186] I. Kodukula, N. Ahmed, and K. Pingali. Data-centric multilevel blocking. In *Proceedings of the SIGPLAN '97 Conference on Programming Language Design and Implementation*, June 1997.

[187] C. Koelbel and P. Mehrotra. Compiling global name-space parallel loops for distributed execution. *IEEE Transactions on Parallel and Distributed Systems*, 2(4):440–451, October 1991.

[188] X. Kong, D. Klappholz, and K. Psarris. The I test: A new test for subscript data dependence. In *Proceedings of the 1990 International Conference on Parallel Processing*, August 1990.

[189] D. Kuck. *The Structure of Computers and Computations*, Volume 1. John Wiley and Sons, New York, 1978.

[190] D. Kuck, R. Kuhn, D. Padua, B. Leasure, and M. J. Wolfe. Dependence graphs and compiler optimizations. In *Conference Record of the Eighth Annual ACM Symposium on the Principles of Programming Languages*, January 1981.

[191] D. Kuck, Y. Muraoka, and S. Chen. On the number of operations simultaneously executable in Fortran-like programs and their resulting speedup. *IEEE Transactions on Computers*, C-21(12):1293–1310, December 1972.

[192] R. Kuhn. Optimization and interconnection complexity for parallel processors, single-stage networks, and decision trees. Ph.D. thesis, Department of Computer Science, University of Illinois at Urbana-Champaign, February 1980.

[193] M. Lam. A systolic array optimizing compiler. Ph.D. thesis, Carnegie Mellon University, 1987.

[194] M. Lam. Software pipelining: An effective scheduling technique for VLIW machines. In *Proceedings of the SIGPLAN '88 Conference on Programming Language Design and Implementation*, June 1988.

[195] L. Lamport. The parallel execution of DO loops. *Communications of the ACM*, 17(2):83–93, February 1974.

[196] L. Lamport. The coordinate method for the parallel execution of iterative DO loops. Technical Report CA-7608-0221, SRI, Menlo Park, CA, August 1976, revised October 1981.

[197] W. Landi and B. G. Ryder. A safe approximate algorithm for interprocedural pointer aliasing. In *SIGPLAN '92 Conference on Programming Language Design and Implementation, SIGPLAN Notices*, 27(7):235–248, July 1992.

[198] T. Lengauer and R. E. Tarjan. A fast algorithm for finding dominators in a flowgraph. *ACM Transactions on Programming Languages and Systems*, 1(1):121–141, July 1979.

[199] Z. Li. Array privatization for parallel execution of loops. In *Proceedings of the 1992 ACM International Conference on Supercomputing*, July 1992.

[200] Z. Li and P. Yew. Efficient interprocedural analysis for program restructuring for parallel programs. In *Proceedings of the ACM SIGPLAN Symposium on Parallel Programming: Experience with Applications, Languages, and Systems (PPEALS)*, July 1988.

[201] Z. Li and P. Yew. Some results on exact data dependence analysis. In D. Gelernter, A. Nicolau, and D. Padua, editors, *Languages and Compilers for Parallel Computing*. The MIT Press, Cambridge, MA, 1990.

[202] Z. Li, P. Yew, and C. Zhu. Data dependence analysis on multi-dimensional array references. In *Proceedings of the 1989 ACM International Conference on Supercomputing*, June 1989.

[203] A. Lichnewsky and F. Thomasset. Introducing symbolic problem solving techniques in the dependence testing phases of a vectorizer. In *Proceedings of the Second International Conference on Supercomputing*, July 1988.

[204] D. Loveman. Program improvement by source-to-source transformations. *Journal of the ACM*, 17(2):121–145, January 1977.

[205] L. Lu and M. Chen. Subdomain dependence test for massive parallelism. In *Proceedings of Supercomputing '90*, November 1990.

[206] T. J. Marlowe, W. A. Landi, B. G. Ryder, J. Choi, M. Burke, and P. Carini. Pointer-induced aliasing: A clarification. *SIGPLAN Notices*, 28(9):67–70, September 1993.

[207] D. Maydan, J. Hennessy, and M. Lam. Efficient and exact data dependence analysis. In *Proceedings of the SIGPLAN '91 Conference on Programming Language Design and Implementation*, June 1991.

[208] E. J. McCluskey. Minimization of Boolean functions. *Bell System Technical Journal* 35(5):1417–1444, November 1956.

[209] K. S. McKinley. Automatic and interactive parallelization. Ph.D. thesis, Department of Computer Science, Rice University, April 1992.

[210] K. McKinley, S. Carr, and C.-W. Tseng. Improving data locality with loop transformations. *ACM Transactions on Programming Languages and Systems*, 18(4), July 1996.

[211] N. Megiddo and V. Sarkar. Optimal weighted loop fusion for parallel programs. In *Proceedings of the Ninth Annual ACM Symposium on Parallel Algorithms and Architectures*, June 1997.

[212] R. Mercer. The Convex Fortran 5.0 compiler. In *Third International Conference on Supercomputing*, 2:164–175, 1988.

[213] R. Metzger and S. Stroud. Interprocedural constant propagation: An empirical study. *ACM Letters on Programming Languages and Systems*, 1(3), December 1992.

[214] S. Midkiff and D. Padua. Compiler algorithms for synchronization. *IEEE Transactions on Computer Systems*, C-36(12):1485–1495, December 1987.

[215] E. Morel and C. Renvoise. Global optimization by suppression of partial redundancies. *Communications of the ACM*, 22(2):96–103, February 1979.

[216] T. C. Mowry. Tolerating latency through software-controlled data prefetching. Ph.D. thesis, Department of Electrical Engineering, Stanford University, March 1994.

[217] T. C. Mowry, M. S. Lam, and A. Gupta. Design and evaluation of a compiler algorithm for prefetching. In *Proceedings of the Fourth International Conference on Architectural Support for Programming Languages and Operating Systems*, April 1991.

[218] S. S. Muchnick. *Compiler Design and Implementation*. Morgan Kaufmann, San Francisco, 1997.

[219] Y. Muraoka. Parallelism exposure and exploitation in programs. Ph.D. thesis, Department of Computer Science, University of Illinois at Urbana-Champaign, February 1971. Report No. 71-424.

[220] E. Myers. A precise inter-procedural data flow algorithm. In *Conference Record of the Eighth Annual Symposium on Principles of Programming Languages*, January 1981.

[221] D. A. Padua. Multiprocessors: Discussion of some theoretical and practical problems. Ph.D. thesis, Department of Computer Science, University of Illinois at Urbana-Champaign, November 1979. Report 79-990.

[222] D. A. Padua and M. J. Wolfe. Advanced compiler optimizations for supercomputers. *Communications of the ACM*, 29(12):1184–1201, December 1986.

[223] P. R. Panda, N. Dutt, and A. Nicolau. *Memory Issues in Embedded Systems—On-Chip: Optimizations and Exploration*. Kluwer Academic Publishers, Norwell, MA, 1999.

[224] K. Pieper. Parallelizing compilers: Implementation and effectiveness. Ph.D. thesis, Stanford Computer Systems Laboratory, June 1993.

[225] C. D. Polychronopoulos. *Parallel Programming and Compilers*. Kluwer Academic Publishers, Norwell, MA, 1988.

[226] C. D. Polychronopoulos and D. J. Kuck. Guided self-scheduling: A practical scheduling scheme for parallel supercomputers. *IEEE Transactions on Computers*, 36(12):1425–1439, 1987.

[227] A. Porterfield. Software methods for improving cache performance on supercomputer applications. Ph.D. thesis, Department of Computer Science, Rice University, 1989.

[228] W. Pugh. A practical algorithm for exact array dependence analysis. *Communications of the ACM*, 35(8):102–114, August 1992.

[229] W. Pugh and D. Wonnacott. Eliminating false data dependences using the Omega test. In *Proceedings of the SIGPLAN '92 Conference on Programming Language Design and Implementation*, June 1992.

[230] W. V. Quine. The problem of simplifying truth functions. *American Mathematical Monthly*, 59(8):521–531, October 1952.

[231] B. R. Rau and J. A. Fisher. Instruction-level parallel processing: History, overview and perspective. *The Journal of Supercomputing*, 7: 9–50, 1993.

[232] B. R. Rau and C. D. Glaeser. Some scheduling techniques and an easily schedulable horizontal architecture for high performance scientific computing. In *Proceedings of the Fourteenth Annual Workshop on Microprogramming*, pages 183–198, October 1981.

[233] B. R. Rau, C. D. Glaeser, and R. L. Picard. Efficient code generation for horizontal architectures. In *Proceedings of the Ninth Annual International Symposium on Computer Architecture*, pages 131–139, April 1982.

[234] S. Richardson and M. Ganapathi. Interprocedural analysis versus procedure integration. *Information Processing Letters*, 321(3), August 1989.

[235] A. Rogers and K. Pingali. Process decomposition through locality of reference. In *SIGPLAN '89 Conference on Programming Language Design and Implementation*, June 1989.

[236] B. K. Rosen, M. Wegman, and F. K. Zadeck. Global value numbers and redundant computations. In *Conference Record of the Fifteenth ACM Symposium on the Principles of Programming*, 1988.

[237] C. Rosene. Incremental dependence analysis. Ph.D. thesis, Department of Computer Science, Rice University, May 1990.

[238] G. Roth. Optimizing Fortran 90D/HPF for distributed-memory computers. Ph.D. thesis, Department of Computer Science, Rice University, 1997.

[239] E. Ruf and D. Weise. Using types to avoid redundant specialization. In *Proceedings of the PEPM '91 Symposium on Partial Evaluation and Semantics-Based Program Manipulation*, *SIGPLAN Notices*, 26(9):321–333, September 1991.

[240] B. Ryder. Constructing the call graph of a program. *IEEE Transactions on Software Engineering*, SE-5(3):216–225, 1979.

[241] V. Sarkar. Optimized execution of Fortran 90 array language on symmetric shared-memory multiprocessors. In *Proceedings of LCPC '98*, pages 131–147, Springer-Verlag, Heidelberg, 1999.

[242] V. Sarkar and G. Gao. Optimization of array accesses by collective loop transformations. In *Proceedings of the 1991 ACM International Conference on Supercomputing*, June 1991.

[243] R. G. Scarborough and H. G. Kolsky. A vectorizing FORTRAN compiler. *IBM Journal of Research and Development*, March 1986.

[244] A. Schrijver. *Theory of Linear and Integer Programming*. John Wiley and Sons, Chichester, Great Britain, 1986.

[245] R. Sethi. Testing for the Church-Rosser property. *Journal of the ACM,* 21(4), October 1974.

[246] M. Sharir and A. Pnueli. Two approaches to interprocedural data flow analysis. In S. Muchnick and N. D. Jones, editors, *Program Flow Analysis: Theory and Applications,* Prentice Hall, Upper Saddle River, NJ, 1981.

[247] Z. Shen, Z. Li, and P. Yew. An empirical study on array subscripts and data dependences. In *Proceedings of the 1989 International Conference on Parallel Processing,* August 1989.

[248] O. Shivers. Control flow analysis in Scheme. In *Proceedings of the SIGPLAN '88 Conference on Programming Language Design and Implementation, SIGPLAN Notices,* 23(7):164–174, July 1988.

[249] O. Shivers. Control-flow analysis of higher-order languages. Ph.D. thesis, School of Computer Science, Carnegie Mellon University, May 1991.

[250] O. Shivers. The semantics of scheme control flow analysis. In *Proceedings of the Symposium on Partial Evaluation and Semantics-Based Program Manipulation, SIGPLAN Notices,* 26(9):190–198, September 1991.

[251] Silicon Graphics, Inc. Performance tuning optimization for Origin2000 and Onyx. Technical report. *techpubs.sgi.com/library/manuals/3000/007-3511-001/html.*

[252] T. C. Spillman. Exposing side-effects in a PL/I optimizing compiler. In *Proceedings of the IFIP Congress 1971,* pages 376–381, North Holland, Amsterdam, 1971.

[253] V. C. Sreedhar and G. R. Gao. A linear time algorithm for placing ϕ-nodes. In *Conference Record of the 22nd Annual ACM Symposium on the Principles of Programming Languages,* pages 62–73, January 1995.

[254] Standards Performance Evaluation Corporation, SPEC release 1.2, September 1990.

[255] B. Su and J. Wang. GUPR*: A new global software pipelining algorithm. In *Proceedings of the 24th Annual International Symposium on Microarchitecture,* pages 212–216, November 1991.

[256] R. E. Tarjan. Depth first search and linear graph algorithms. *SIAM Journal of Computing* 1(2):146–160, 1972.

[257] S. Tjiang. *Automatic Generation of Data-Flow Analyzers: A Tool for Building Optimizers.* Stanford University, 1993.

[258] R. F. Touzeau. A Fortran compiler for the FPS-164 scientific computer. In *Proceedings of the SIGPLAN '84 Symposium on Compiler Construction,* June 1984.

[259] R. A. Towle. Control and data dependence for program transformation. Ph.D. thesis, Department of Computer Science, University of Illinois at Urbana-Champaign, March 1976.

[260] R. Triolet. Interprocedural analysis for program restructuring with Parafrase. CSRD Report No. 538, Department of Computer Science, University of Illinois at Urbana-Champaign, December 1985.

[261] R. Triolet, F. Irigoin, and P. Feautrier. Direct parallelization of call statements. In *Proceedings of the SIGPLAN '86 Symposium on Compiler Construction, SIGPLAN Notices*, 21(7):176–185, July 1986.

[262] C.-W. Tseng. An optimizing Fortran D compiler for MIMD distributed-memory machines. Ph.D. thesis, Department of Computer Science, Rice University, January 1993.

[263] P. Tu and D. Padua. Automatic array privatization. In *Proceedings of the Sixth Workshop on Languages and Compilers for Parallel Computing*, August 1993.

[264] J. D. Ullman. Fast algorithms for the elimination of common subexpressions. *Acta Informatica*, 2(3):191–213, July 1973.

[265] *Verilog Hardware Description Language Reference Manual (LRM)*. Open Verilog International, Los Gatos, CA, 1995.

[266] D. Wallace. Dependence of multi-dimensional array references. In *Proceedings of the Second International Conference on Supercomputing*, July 1988.

[267] K. Walter. Recursion analysis for compiler optimization. *Communications of the ACM*, 19(9):514–516, 1976.

[268] H. S. Warren. Instruction scheduling for the IBM RISC System/6000. *IBM Journal of Research and Development*, 34(1):85–92, January 1990.

[269] J. Warren. A hierarchical basis for program transformations. In *Conference Record of the Eleventh ACM Symposium on Principles of Programming Languages*, January 1984.

[270] D. Wedel. FORTRAN for the Texas Instruments ASC system. *SIGPLAN Notices*, 10(3):119–132, March 1975.

[271] M. Wegman. General and efficient methods for global code improvement. Ph.D. thesis, University of California, Berkeley, December 1981.

[272] M. Wegman and K. Zadeck. Constant propagation with conditional branches. In *Conference Record of the Twelfth Annual ACM Symposium on the Principles of Programming Languages*, pages 291–299, January 1985.

[273] M. Wegman and K. Zadeck. Constant propagation with conditional branches. Technical Report CS-89-36, Department of Computer Science, Brown University, May 1989.

[274] W. E. Weihl. Interprocedural data flow analysis in the presence of pointers, procedure variables, and label variables. In *Conference Record of the Seventh Symposium on Principles of Programming Languages*, January 1980.

[275] M. E. Wolf. Improving locality and parallelism in nested loops. Ph.D. thesis, Department of Computer Science, Stanford University, August 1992.

[276] M. E. Wolf and M. S. Lam. A data locality optimizing algorithm. In *Proceedings of the ACM SIGPLAN '91 Conference on Programming Language Design and Implementation*, June 1991.

[277] M. E. Wolf and M. Lam. A loop transformation theory and an algorithm to maximize parallelism. *IEEE Transactions on Parallel and Distributed Systems*, 2(4):452–471, October 1991.

[278] M. J. Wolfe. Techniques for improving the inherent parallelism in programs. Master's thesis, Department of Computer Science, University of Illinois at Urbana-Champaign, July 1978.

[279] M. Wolfe. Optimizing supercompilers for supercomputers. Ph.D. thesis, Department of Computer Science, University of Illinois at Urbana-Champaign, November 1982.

[280] M. J. Wolfe. Advanced loop interchanging. In *Proceedings of the 1986 International Conference on Parallel Processing*, August 1986.

[281] M. J. Wolfe. Loop skewing: The wavefront method revisited. *International Journal of Parallel Programming* 15(4):279–293, August 1986.

[282] M. Wolfe. Iteration space tiling for memory hierarchies. In *Proceedings of the Third SIAM Conference on Parallel Processing for Scientific Computing*, December 1987.

[283] M. J. Wolfe. *Optimizing Supercompilers for Supercomputers*. The MIT Press, Cambridge, MA, 1989.

[284] M. Wolfe. Beyond induction variables. In *Proceedings of the ACM SIGPLAN '91 Conference on Programming Language Design and Implementation*, pages 162–174, San Francisco, June 1992.

[285] M. J. Wolfe. *High Performance Compilers for Parallel Computing*. Addison-Wesley, Redwood City, CA, 1996.

[286] M. J. Wolfe and C.-W. Tseng. The Power test for data dependence. *IEEE Transactions on Parallel and Distributed Systems*, 3(5):591–601, September 1992.

[287] Y. Zhao and K. Kennedy. Scalarizing Fortran 90 array syntax. Technical Report TR01-373, Department of Computer Science, Rice University, March 2001.

[288] H. Zima, H.-J. Bast, and M. Gerndt. SUPERB: A tool for semi-automatic MIMD/SIMD parallelization. *Parallel Computing*, 6:1–18, 1988.

[289] H. Zima, P. Brezany, B. Chapman, P. Mehrotra, and A. Schwald. *Vienna Fortran—A Language Specification, Version 1.1*. Interim Report 21, ICASE, Hampton, VA, March 1992.

Index

Printed and bound by CPI Group (UK) Ltd, Croydon, CR0 4YY

03/10/2024

01040339-0017